# GEORGE HERBERT

*An Annotated Bibliography of Modern Criticism,*
*Revised Edition, 1905–1984*

# GEORGE
# HERBERT

## An Annotated Bibliography of Modern Criticism

*Revised Edition*

1905 - 1984

John R. Roberts

University of Missouri Press
*Columbia, 1988*

Library of Congress Cataloging-in-Publication Data

Roberts, John Richard.
George Herbert : an annotated bibliography of
modern criticism, revised edition, 1905–1984.

Includes indexes.
1. Herbert, George, 1593–1633—Bibliography.
I. Title.
Z8398.3.R6 1988 [PR3508] 016.821'3 87–19095
ISBN 0–8262–0487–2 (alk. paper)

To the Memory
of
Milissa Jane Roberts
(1960–1973)

Yet ev'n the greatest griefs
May be reliefs,
Could he but take them right, and in their wayes.
Happie is he, whose heart
Hath found the art
To turn his double pains to double praise.

From "Mans medley"

# Contents

# Preface

The primary purpose of this study is to provide students, critics, and scholars of seventeenth-century English poetry with a fully annotated, comprehensive enumerative bibliography of criticism on George Herbert. In addition to modern editions of Herbert's poetry and prose, the bibliography contains all books; parts of book-length studies; monographs; and critical, biographical, and bibliographical essays on the poet, written in English as well as in languages other than English, from 1905 through 1984. The present work is a revision, expansion, and continuation of my *George Herbert: An Annotated Bibliography, 1905–1974* (Columbia and London: University of Missouri Press, 1978), which is now out of print. Rather than simply reprint the earlier edition at great cost and then publish a second volume for the ten-year period from 1975 through 1984 that would contain numerous cross-references to the first volume, the University of Missouri Press agreed with me that it would be more practical and helpful for users to have the entire bibliography in one, fully revised and updated volume.

This study, then, is the first to collect and fully annotate the vast amount of criticism written on Herbert from 1905 through 1984. My own work has been greatly facilitated, however, by a number of previously published bibliographical essays and checklists and is, in one sense, an extension of and an elaboration on these earlier studies, especially *George Herbert: A Concise Bibliography* by S. A. and D. R. Tannenbaum (New York: S. A. Tannenbaum, 1946); *Studies in Metaphysical Poetry: Two Essays and a Bibliography* by Theodore Spencer and Mark Van Doren (New York: Columbia University Press, 1939); *A Bibliography of Studies in Metaphysical Poetry, 1939–1960* by Lloyd E. Berry (Madison: University of Wisconsin Press, 1964); "George Herbert: A Recent Bibliography, 1960–67" by Harry B. Caldwell, Edward E. Samaha, Jr., and Donna G. Fricke in *Seventeenth-Century News* 26, no. 3 (1968): 54–56, which was supplemented by "A Bibliography of George Herbert, 1960–1967: Addenda" by Humphrey Tonkin in *Seventeenth-Century News* 27, no. 2 (1969); "Herbert" by Margaret Bottrall in *English Poetry: Selected Bibliographical Guides*, edited by A. E. Dyson (London and New York: Oxford University Press, 1971), pp. 60–75; "Recent Studies in Herbert" by Jerry Leath Mills in *English Literary Renaissance* 6, no. 1 (1976): 105–18; the extensive bibliography by C. A. Patrides in *The English Poems of George Herbert* (London: J. M. Dent & Sons, 1974; Totowa, N.J.: Rowman and Littlefield, 1975); and "Nihon ni okeru Keijijo-shi Kenkyu Shoshi" [A Bibliography of Writings about Metaphysical Poetry in Japan] in *Keijijoshi Kenkyu* [Studies in Metaphysical Poets] (Tokyo, 1976) by Yoshihisa Aizawa. Although I gratefully acknowledge my debt to each of these earlier studies and, to varying degrees, have found each of them useful in preparing the present volume, my bibliography is more comprehensive and more fully annotated than any previous work.

The present study begins in 1905, the date of the publication of George Herbert Palmer's three-volume edition of *The English Poems of George Herbert* (Boston and New York: Houghton Mifflin and Co.). Although Palmer's edition has long been superseded by the work of F. E. Hutchinson and others, it represents, in one sense, the first major study of Herbert in the twentieth century and, therefore, seemed like a reasonable starting point. For information on Herbert's critical reception before 1905, we are all indebted to *George Herbert: The Critical Heritage*, edited by C. A. Patrides (London, Boston, Melbourne and Henly: Routledge & Kegan Paul, 1983); "The Herbert Allusion Book: Allusions to George Herbert in the Seventeenth Century" in *Studies in Philology: Texts and Studies* (Chapel Hill: University of North Carolina Press, 1986) by Robert H. Ray; "Herbert's Seventeenth-Century Reputation: A Summary and New Considerations" also by Robert H. Ray in the *George Herbert Journal* 9, no. 2 (1986): 1–15; an Oxford University D. Phil. dissertation by Helen Wilcox, "'Something Understood': The Reputation and Influence of George Herbert to 1715" (1984); as well as parts of books and/or essays published before 1985 by Arthur H. Nethercot, F. E. Hutchinson, Joseph E. Duncan, Joseph H. Summers, William Sloane, Karina Williamson, Elsie Leach, and Sebastian Köppel. The present study ends in 1984 because more recent studies were not always available and because bibliographical aids after this year were very incomplete. Since 1984 a number of important studies of Herbert have appeared, of course, such as the *The Herbert Allusion Book* mentioned above, Chana Bloch's *Spelling the Word: George Herbert and the Bible* (Berkeley: University of California Press, 1985), Gene Edward Veith, Jr.'s *Reformation Spirituality: The Religion of George Herbert* (Cranbury, N.J.: Bucknell/Associated University Presses, 1985), and Richard Todd's *The Opacity of Signs: Acts of Interpretation in George Herbert's* The Temple (Columbia: University of Missouri Press, 1986), to name but a few. I shall want to include these works, and the many others that continue to appear, when the present bibliography is again revised and updated. During the past two and one-half decades, more than one thousand books and/or essays on Herbert have appeared, more than twice the number published during the preceding fifty-five years; and there are no signs that interest in his poetry and prose is waning.

Although many items listed in this bibliography are quite obviously minor efforts, often inspired by religious zeal and enthusiasm rather than by serious critical thought and objective scholarship, others clearly represent important contributions to our understanding and appreciation of Herbert's poetry and prose, of the art and sensibility of the early seventeenth century, of metaphysical poetry and poets as a whole, and, in some cases, even of the very nature of poetry itself and the poetic process. Herbert's art has attracted and engaged some of the best minds of the scholarly world, especially during the past four decades. In part through their efforts, he has been fully established and recognized as one of the major poets in the English language. Today almost all serious critics and students of English literature would agree with Joseph H. Summers, who, in his 1967 edition of the selected poems, called Herbert "the author of the best extended collection of religious lyrics in English, a man whose art is as unquestionable as is his spiritual authenticity" (p. ix). No longer seen as merely one of the many followers of John Donne or as a simple, pious Anglican versifier, Herbert now occupies a permanent and central position in our understanding of the development of English poetry.

The present bibliography follows, for the most part, the principles and guidelines established for my earlier Herbert volume. The annotations are essentially descriptive, not evaluative, because I find that what is significant and/or useful to one scholar may not be equally so to another. Since I have made the annotations quite detailed and often have quoted extensively from an item so that the reader will have some notion of its critical approach and the level of its sophistication, users should be able to judge for themselves whether or not a particular work will be helpful to their purposes. I have listed items chronologically so that by glancing through the bibliography the reader will be able to obtain a sense of the various shifts and developments that have occurred in Herbert criticism during this century. Such an arrangement also allows the reader to observe that Herbert and his poetry and prose have been run through most of the critical sieves (linguistic, stylistic, biographical, psychoanalytical, bibliographic, textual, formalistic, affective, deconstructive, and so on) and that, in a sense, the work published on him represents a kind of microcosm of what has taken place in literary criticism over the past eighty years. By means of the three detailed indexes (author, subject, and poems and prose works of Herbert cited in the annotations), users can quickly locate individual studies that interest them.

As in my earlier volume, I have tried to make the bibliography as comprehensive as possible. Yet, even from the beginning, I had to impose certain limitations. The basic guiding principle has been to include every book, monograph, and essay specifically on Herbert published from 1905 through 1984; I have also included extended discussions of Herbert that appear in books and essays not centrally concerned with him or his art. Nearly all books and many essays on metaphysical poetry in general and on individual metaphysical poets contain at least some comment on or reference to Herbert, but to have included all items that simply mention Herbert in relation to Donne, Crashaw, Vaughan, Marvell, Traherne, and others would have extended the present study far beyond manageable bounds. Likewise, I have not included all anthologies that contain only selections from Herbert's poetry or prose, although I have included many that have brief critical discussions or contain notes or that, for one reason or another, seemed to have special significance, such as the *Norton Anthology*, which, for many years, has provided an introduction to Herbert's poetry for numerous American undergraduate students. I have included, however, all scholarly editions of both Herbert's poetry and prose, as well as those that have some historical interest, such as W. H. Auden's edition of the selected poems. Reprints of editions published before 1905 have been excluded, except for facsimiles of seventeenth-century editions. I have also included translations of Herbert's poetry and prose into foreign languages, which indicate their popularity and availability to those who do not read English. Except for a number of early reviews that, rather than focusing on the book supposedly under discussion, are essays that simply take the occasion to comment on Herbert's poetry, I have not annotated book reviews. I have, however, annotated review articles (usually discussions of two or more books); and, following the annotations for books that deal exclusively with Herbert, I have listed as many as I could find of the reviews of those books. Brief mentions of Herbert in books and articles, as well as references in literary histories, encyclopedias, anthologies, and textbooks, have been omitted. Doctoral dissertations have not been included because many of them are unavailable, especially those in languages others than English, and because a number of them have been published, partly or wholly, in later essays and books. The reader is encouraged, however, to consult *Dissertation Abstracts* and *Dissertation Abstracts International* for summaries, prepared by their authors, of many, but not all, American dissertations.

Many items in languages other than English (French, German, Dutch, Italian, Spanish, Japanese, Polish, Russian, and so on) have been included, but I have no assurance that I have located all items in these languages or in lesser-known ones. In referring to Herbert's poems, I have followed F. E. Hutchinson's edition (rev. ed., 1945). By doing so, I do not intend to indicate a preference for Hutchinson's text, but simply hope to avoid confusion and to establish consistency. Items in this bibliography are entered under the date of their first publication; reprints, revisions, and later editions, when known, have been recorded in the original entry.

It gives me great pleasure to acknowledge and to thank all those who have generously assisted me in this project. Above all, I wish to thank Melissa Poole, my research assistant, who gathered materials, checked numerous details, edited and proofread all the entries, checked cross-references, prepared the author index and the index of poems mentioned in the annotations, solved many bibliographical problems, and helped me in so many ways. Her dedication to this bibliography was second only to my own. I wish also to thank my former research assistant, Douglas Collins, who was immensely helpful to me when I was preparing the first edition of this bibliography by gathering materials and assisting me in translating German, French, and Italian items. I should also like to thank Mark Bassett and Michael Walker, two of my former graduate students, who, at different times during my work on the first edition, checked numerous bibliographies for me and helped me in sundry ways. I am also indebted to Yoshihisa Aizawa, Alla Barabtarlo, Paul Casey, James Curtis, John Foley, Gunilla Jansson, M. Bonner Mitchell, Edward Mullen, Dennis Mueller, Maika Takeda, Hugh Walter, and Russell Zguta, who assisted me with items in foreign languages; and to Jeaneice Brewer and Marilyn Voegele, librarians, who were most helpful in locating books and essays unavailable at the University of Missouri Ellis Library. Many scholars and friends called my attention to lesser-known items, supplied me with offprints and photocopies of difficult-to-locate items, and offered me professional advice and assistance, especially Lloyd E. Berry, Werner Bies, Wayne T. Caldwell, Amy Charles, Ira Clark, Peggy Curet, Jose Edmundo Clemente, Philip Dust, Sidney

Gottlieb, Robert W. Halli, Jr., James Harner, Dayton Haskin, Thomas Healy, John L. Idol, Jr., Edward C. Jacobs, Dorothy Keller, Hilton Kelliher, Harold Kollmeir, Vincent Leitch, Anthony Low, Bruno von Lutz, Michael McCanles, Edmund Miller, Hermine J. van Nuis, Witold Ostrowski, William H. Pahkla, C. A. Patrides, Ted-Larry Pebworth, Robert H. Ray, William J. Scheick, Michael Schoenfeldt, Giuseppe Soldano, Joseph H. Summers, Mark Taylor, Mother Thekla of the Greek Orthodox Monastery of the Assumption (North Yorkshire), Alastair Thomson, Richard Todd, Humphrey Tonkin, Jehanne Williamson, and Sachiko Yoshida. I wish also to thank Mrs. Valerie Eliot for permission to examine the unpublished manuscript of eight lectures (now at the Houghton Library, Harvard University) by T. S. Eliot.

I should also like to thank the Faculty Research Council of the Graduate School of the University of Missouri for a small grant that made it possible for me to spend a profitable week at the Widener Library, Harvard University, where I was most cordially received and allowed to search for Herbert materials. I wish also to thank the Development Fund Board of the University of Missouri for grants that supported my research assistant during much of the time this volume was in preparation, and I especially wish to thank Ronald Bunn, former provost of the University of Missouri–Columbia, for his generous support of my research activities over the years. I am also much indebted to Robert Kraft of the Religious Studies Department at the University of Pennsylvania, who optically scanned the items in the first edition and put them on computer disks for me, and to his students who ran a series of checks for accuracy on the disks. I am also grateful to Michael Smith, former chief bibliographer of the Modern Humanities Research Association (Cambridge), for making his files available to me on several occasions, and I wish to thank the members of the staff of numerous libraries, all of whom were generous with their time and advice, especially those of the University of Missouri Ellis Library, the Cambridge University Library, the University of Illinois Library, the New York Public Library, the British Library, Northwestern University Library, and the Boston Public Library. And to my wife, Lorraine, I owe a special note of thanks for having very generously supported me with her love and helped me with her scholarly advice and assistance throughout the years this bibliography was in preparation.

J. R. R.
Columbia, Missouri
8 December 1987

# Abbreviations of Titles of Journals

ABR * *American Benedictine Review*

AEB * *Analytical & Enumerative Bibliography*

AI * *American Imago: A Psychoanalytic Journal for Culture, Science, and the Arts*

AL * *American Literature*

AN&Q * *American Notes and Queries*

Anglia * *Anglia: Zeitschrift für Englische Philologie*

AQ * *American Quarterly*

ArAA * *Arbeiten aus Anglistik und Amerikanistik*

Arbor * *Arbor: Ciencia Pensamiento y Cultura*

Archiv * *Archiv: für das Studium der Neueren Sprachen und Literaturen*

ArielE * *Ariel: A Review of International English Literature*

AWR * *The Anglo-Welsh Review*

BSE * *Brno Studies in English*

BSEAA * *Bulletin de la Société d'Etudes Anglo-Américaines des XVIIe et XVIIIe Siècles*

BuR * *Bucknell Review: A Scholarly Journal of Letters, Arts and Science*

CahiersE * *Cahiers Elisabéthains: Etudes sur la Pré- Renaissance et la Renaissance Anglaises*

C&L * *Christianity and Literature*

CCrit * *Comparative Criticism: A Yearbook*

CE * *College English*

CEA * *CEA Critic: An Official Journal of the College English Association*

CHum * *Computers and the Humanities*

Cithara * *Cithara: Essays in the Judaeo-Christian Tradition*

CJ * *The Classical Journal*

CL * *Comparative Literature* (Eugene, OR)

CLAJ * *College Language Association Journal*

ClioI * *CLIO: A Journal of Literature, History, and Philosophy of History*

CLS * *Comparative Literature Studies*

CollL * *College Literature*

ContempR * *Contemporary Review* (London, England)

Costerus * *Costerus: Essays in English and American Language and Literature*

CP * *Concerning Poetry* (Bellingham, WA)

CritI * *Criticial Inquiry*

Criticism * *Criticism: A Quarterly for Literature and the Arts* (Detroit, MI)

Critique * *Critique: Revue Générale des Publications Françaises et Etrangères* (Paris, France)

CritQ * *Critical Quarterly*

CSR  *  Christian Scholar's Review
Diacritics  *  Diacritics: A Review of Contemporary Criticism
DUJ  *  Durham University Journal
EA  *  Etudes Anglaises: Grande-Bretagne, Etats-Unis
E&S  *  Essays and Studies (London, England)
EIC  *  Essays in Criticism: A Quarterly Journal of Literary Criticism (Oxford, England)
EigoS  *  Eigo Seinen (Tokyo, Japan)
EIRC  *  Explorations in Renaissance Culture
ELH  *  Journal of English Literary History
ELLS  *  English Literature and Language (Tokyo, Japan)
ELN  *  English Language Notes (Boulder, CO)
ELR  *  English Literary Renaissance
ELWIU  *  Essays in Literature (Macomb, IL)
EM  *  English Miscellany: A Symposium of History, Literature, and the Arts
English  *  English: The Journal of the English Association (London, England)
ES  *  English Studies: A Journal of English Language and Literature
ESA  *  English Studies in Africa: A Journal of the Humanities (Johannesburg, South
     Africa)
ESC  *  English Studies in Canada
Expl  *  Explicator
GHJ  *  George Herbert Journal
GR  *  Germanic Review
HLB  *  Harvard Library Bulletin
HLQ  *  Huntington Quarterly: A Journal for the History and Interpretation of English
     and American Civilization
HQ  *  Hopkins Quarterly
HSL  *  University of Hartford Studies in Literature: A Journal of Interdisciplinary Crit-
     icism
HudR  *  The Hudson Review
HumLov  *  Humanistica Lovaniensia: Journal of Neo-Latin Studies (Louvain, Belgium)
HUSL  *  Hebrew University Studies in Literature and the Arts
IR  *  The Iliff Review
JAAC  *  Journal of Aesthetics and Art Criticism
JDJ  *  John Donne Journal: Studies in the Age of Donne
JEGP  *  Journal of English and Germanic Philology
JEn  *  Journal of English (Sana'a Univ.)
JHI  *  Journal of the History of Ideas
JMRS  *  Journal of Medieval and Renaissance Studies
JWCI  *  Journal of the Warburg and Courtauld Institutes
KPAB  *  Kentucky Philological Association Bulletin

*KR* * *Kenyon Review*

*Lang&S* * *Language and Style: An International Journal*

*LangQ* * *The USF Language Quarterly* (Tampa, FL)

*Library* * *The Library: A Quarterly Journal of Bibliography*

*LRN* * *Literary Research News*

*M&H* * *Medievalia et Humanistica: Studies in Medieval and Renaissance Culture*

*McNR* * *McNeese Review*

*MichA* * *Michigan Academician: Papers of the Michigan Academy of Science, Arts and Letters*

*MiltonQ* * *Milton Quarterly*

*MissQ* * *Mississippi Quarterly: The Journal of Southern Culture*

*ML* * *Modern Languages: Journal of the Modern Language Association* (London, England)

*MLN* * *Modern Language Notes*

*MLQ* * *Modern Language Quarterly*

*MLR* * *Modern Language Review*

*Mosaic* * *Mosaic: Journal for the Interdisciplinary Study of Literature*

*MP* * *Modern Philology*

*N&Q* * *Notes and Queries*

*Neophil* * *Neophilologus* (Groningen, Netherlands)

*NEQ* * *The New England Quarterly: A Historical Review of New England Life and Letters*

*NigM* * *Nigeria Magazine*

*NM* * *Neuphilologische Mitteilungen: Bulletin de la Société Néophilologique / Bulletin of the Modern Language Society*

*NOR* * *New Orleans Review*

*NR* * *The Nassau Review: The Journal of Nassau Community College Devoted to Arts, Letters, and Sciences*

*NRF* * *Nouvelle Revue Française*

*PAAS* * *Proceedings of the American Antiquarian Society*

*PBA* * *Proceedings of the British Academy*

*PCP* * *Pacific Coast Philology*

*PHum* * *Przegląd Humanistyczny*

*PLL* * *Papers on Language and Literature: A Journal for Scholars and Critics of Language and Literature*

*PMLA* * *Publications of the Modern Language Association of America*

*PoetryR* * *Poetry Review* (London, England)

*PQ* * *Philological Quarterly*

*PR* * *Partisan Review*

*PULC* * *Princeton University Library Chronicle*

*QJS* * *The Quarterly Journal of Speech*

*QQ* * *Queen's Quarterly*

*Quadrant* * *Quadrant* (Sydney, Australia)

*RCEI* * *Revista Canaria de Estudios Ingleses*

*Ren&R* * *Renaissance and Reformation / Renaissance et Réforme*

*Renascence* * *Renascence: Essays on Value in Literature*

*RenB* * *The Renaissance Bulletin*

*RenP* * *Renaissance Papers*

*RenQ* * *Renaissance Quarterly*

*RES* * *Review of English Studies: A Quarterly Journal of English Literature and the English Language*

*RL* * *Revista de Literatura*

*RSH* * *Revue des Sciences Humaines*

*RUO* * *Revue de l'Université d'Ottawa / University of Ottawa Quarterly*

*SAQ* * *South Atlantic Quarterly*

*SCN* * *Seventeenth-Century News*

*SCR* * *South Carolina Review*

*SCRev* * *South Central Review: The Journal of the South Central Modern Language Association* [formerly *South Central Bulletin* (SCB)]

*SEL* * *Studies in English Literature, 1500–1900*

*SELit* * *Studies in English Literature* (Tokyo, Japan)

*ShakS* * *Shakespeare Studies* (Knoxville, TN)

*SHR* * *Southern Humanities Review*

*ShStud* * *Shakespeare Studies* (Tokyo, Japan)

*SLitI* * *Studies in the Literary Imagination* (Atlanta, GA)

*SMy* * *Studia Mystica*

*SN* * *Studia Neophilologica: A Journal of Germanic and Romance Languages and Literature*

*SoAR* * *South Atlantic Review*

*SoR* * *The Southern Review* (Baton Rouge, LA)

*SP* * *Studies in Philology*

*Sprachkunst* * *Sprachkunst: Beiträge zur Literaturwissenschaft*

*SR* * *Sewanee Review*

*SSEng* * *Sydney Studies in English*

*Style* * *Style* (DeKalb, IL)

*TCBS* * *Transactions of the Cambridge Bibliographical Society*

*Thought* * *Thought: A Review of Culture and Idea*

*TLS* * *Times Literary Supplement* (London, England)

*Trivium* * *Trivium* (Dyfed, Wales)

*TSLL* * *Texas Studies in Literature and Language: A Journal of the Humanities*

UCTSE * *University of Cape Town Studies in English*
UTQ * *University of Toronto Quarterly: A Canadian Journal of the Humanities*
VP * *Victorian Poetry* (Morgantown, WV)
VQR * *Virginia Quarterly Review: A National Journal of Literature and Discussion*
WascanaR * *Wascana Review*
WCR * *West Coast Review*
XUS * *Xavier Review* (New Orleans)
YES * *Yearbook of English Studies*
YR * *The Yale Review*

**1. Anon.** "George Herbert." *TLS*, 22 December, p. 456.

Favorable review of Palmer's edition (entry 2). Finds the editor's chronological arrangement of the poems "thoroughly sound." Praises Palmer's annotations, claiming that "hitherto no poet has been more grievously under-annotated" than Herbert. Maintains that, unlike Crashaw and Vaughan, Herbert is not a mystic. Calls Herbert "a careful and reverent artist" and cites the last two lines of "Prayer (I)" as "an end-couplet unrivalled for pregnancy and fire."

**2. Herbert, George.** *The English Works of George Herbert.* Newly Arranged and Annotated and Considered in Relation to His Life, by George Herbert Palmer. Vol. 1, *Essays and Prose*; vol. 2, *Cambridge Poems;* vol. 3, *Bemerton Poems.* Boston and New York: Houghton Mifflin and Co. xx, 429p.; xiv, 443p.; 455p.

Reprinted, London: Hodder, 1920.

Large-paper edition, in six volumes, limited to 150 copies, 1905.

2d ed., 1907: A few changes and several errors corrected, two additional title pages, two indexes changed in position, and two new indexes.

Reprinted, 1915, 1979.

One-volume edition of the poems with general preface, 1916. xii, 427p.

Vol. 1: Preface (pp. xi–xx); Chronology (pp. 3–13); Outlines of the Life (pp. 17–46); Traits of the Man (pp. 49–83); The Type of Religious Poetry (pp. 87–120); The Style and Technique (pp. 123–67); The Text and Order of Poems (pp. 171–91); The Country Parson, with preface (pp. 195–328); A Treatise of Temperance and Sobriety, written by Lud. Cornarus, translated into English by Mr. George Herbert, with preface (pp. 331–57); Prefatory Letter and Notes by George Herbert, To the Divine Considerations, Treating of Those Things Which Are Most Profitable, Most Necessary and Most Perfect in Our Christian Profession, by John Valdesso, with preface (pp. 363–86); Letters of George Herbert, with preface (pp. 389–412); Herbert's Will (pp. 413–16); Notes (pp. 419–29). Includes eleven illustrations. Vol. 2: The Printers to the Reader, by Nicholas Ferrar (pp. xi–xiv); The Church-Porch, with preface (pp. 3–67); The Resolve, with preface (pp. 71–107); The Church, with preface (pp. 111–203); Meditation, with preface (pp. 207–73); The Inner Life, with preface (pp. 277–319); The Crisis, with preface (pp. 323–401); Textual Variations of the Manuscripts (pp. 405–25); Indexes: Titles Alphabetically Arranged (pp. 429–31), Titles Arranged in the Traditional Order (433–34), Titles Arranged in the Order of This Edition (pp. 435–37), Index of First Lines (pp. 439–43). Includes nine illustrations. Vol. 3: The Happy Priest, with preface (pp. 3–63); Bemerton Study, with preface (pp. 67–167); Restlessness, with preface (pp. 171–239); Suffering, with preface (pp. 243–307); Death, with preface (pp. 311–43); Additional and Doubtful Poems, with preface (pp. 347–431); Textual Variations of the Manuscripts (pp. 435–38); Indexes: Titles Alphabetically Arranged (pp. 441–43), Titles Arranged in the Traditional Order (pp. 445–46), Titles Arranged in the Order of This Edition (pp. 447–49), Index of First Lines (pp. 451–55). Includes nine illustrations. In the 1907 edition, the indexes of "Titles Arranged in the Traditional Order" and "Titles Arranged in the Order of This Edition" are moved from vols. 2 and 3 to vol. 1, and two new indexes have been added: "Biblical Allusions" (1:439–43) and "Notes, Essays, and Prefaces," compiled by Grace R. Walden (3:451–85).

Reviews:

Anon. *TLS*, 22 December 1905, p. 456
A. V. G. Allen, *Atlantic Monthly* 97 (1906): 90–100
Frances Duncan, *The Critic* 49 (1906): 180–87

Francis Thompson, *Athenaeum*, 7 April 1906, p. 415
A. Clutton-Brock, *TLS*, 1 April 1920, pp. 205–6

**3. Palmer, George H.** "George Herbert As a Religious Poet." *Atlantic Monthly* 95:194–205.
Maintains that Herbert contributed to the four main varieties of sacred poetry prevalent before his time: the vision, the meditation, the paraphrase of psalms, and the hymn. Argues that his most significant and original contribution was to the development of the religious love lyric. Sees Southwell, Campion, and, to some extent, Donne, as precursors. Evaluates the piety, intellectual play, and artistic construction of Herbert's religious love lyrics.

# *1906*

**4. Anon.** "George Herbert." *TLS*, 5 October, pp. 333–34.
Lead article occasioned by the publication of Hyde's *George Herbert and His Times* (entry 11). Points out a number of errors in Hyde's biographical study but finds it suitable for popular reading. Maintains that Herbert led a very dedicated life and that "this fact is the secret of its psychological interest, as it is the key to the interpretation of his poetry" (p. 333). Presents a summary of the poet's life and singles out "Dialogue" as "the most perfect of all of the poems of surrender" to God (p. 333). Contends that what most attracts modern readers to Herbert is the personal note in his poems. Briefly compares *The Temple* to John Keble's *The Christian Year*, noting great differences between the works of the two men "who in point of sensibility, scholarship, high breeding, and devoutness of mind were closely akin" (p. 333).

**5. Anon.** "Holy Mr. Herbert." *Saturday Review* (London) 102:583–84.
Review of Hyde's *George Herbert and His Times* (entry 11). Comments on Herbert's life and his "elegant sanctity," which "helped to give Anglicanism that peculiar stamp of cultivation and refinement which, united to the sedate charm and quaintness, the old-world fragrance of the seventeenth century, fascinated the author of 'John Inglesant'" (p. 584).

**6. Allen, A. V. G.** "Palmer's Herbert." *Atlantic Monthly* 97:90–100.
Favorable review of Palmer's edition (entry 2) with a critical estimation of Herbert's life and poetry and remarks on Palmer's commentary. Discusses the development of the religious lyrical element in Christian literature and contends that "what Augustine did for the old world of the Graeco-Roman Empire, Herbert has done in his measure for the modern day" (p. 99), that is, reclaim the lyric for the expression of divine love.

**7. Clutton-Brock, A.** "The Fantastic School of English Poetry," in *The Cambridge Modern History*, edited by A. W. Ward, G. W. Prothero, and Stanley Leathes, 4:760–75. New York: Macmillan Co.
Contrasts metaphysical poetry (called "fantastic poetry") rather unfavorably with Elizabethan poetry, pointing out such major features as its private mode, roughness, argumentative rationality, wit, and ingenuity. Briefly discusses Herbert (pp. 765–69), commenting on his wedding of the homely and the sublime, his obscurity, his realism, and his wit. Compares Herbert to Donne: "He wrote, like Donne, to express his own

individual experiences; to explain himself to himself" (p. 768). Also compares Herbert with Vaughan, Traherne, and Crashaw.

**8. Corbett, Frederick St. John.** *The Poet of the Church of England: A Tribute to George Herbert.* Second impression. Illustrated by William Brown. London: A. R. Mowbray. 19p.

Biographical sketch of Herbert (pp. 5–9), followed by a 106–line original poem extolling Herbert's life and sanctity, with photographs of Bemerton and illustrations by William Brown. Asserts that "all that lives, and will live of his poetical works has a direct bearing upon ecclesiastical matters" (p. 5).

**9. Duncan, Frances.** "Life of George Herbert," in "Three Notable Biographies: Paul's Froude, Palmer's Herbert, and Traubel's Whitman." *The Critic* 49:180–87.

Favorably reviews Palmer's edition (entry 2). Calls Herbert a "comparatively unimportant poet" (p. 183) who may not always appeal to Americans, "with our scant supply of artistic instinct, our journalistic despatch, our matter-of-fact literalness" (p. 185). Maintains that Herbert is enjoying a revival but is more often bought than read. Finds Palmer's rearrangement of the poems effective and innovative.

**10. Grierson, Herbert J. C.** "English Poetry," in *The First Half of the Seventeenth Century,* 135–201. (Periods of European Literature, edited by George Saintsbury, vol. 7.) Edinburgh and London: William Blackwood and Sons.

Brief critical evaluation of Herbert's poetry (pp. 165–66). Characterizes Herbert's verse as didactic and rhetorically quaint.

**11. Hyde, A. G.** *George Herbert and His Times.* New York: G. P. Putnam's Sons; London: Methuen & Co. xiv, 327p.

Reprinted, Folcroft, Pa.: Folcroft Press, 1976; Norwood, Pa.: Norwood Press, 1976 (limited to 100 copies), reissued 1977; Philadelphia: R. West, 1978.

Biography of Herbert, which the author admits is "little more than a commentary on Walton's narrative, except when . . . an effort has been made to show the relation of its subject and his writings to his own and later times" (pp. vii-viii). Contains seventeen chapters: (1) The Poet and the Age (pp. 1–11); (2) Birthplace, Family and Childhood (pp. 12–28); (3) School and University (pp. 29–46); (4) Early Life and Writings at Cambridge (pp. 47–61); (5) Orator and Theologian (pp. 62–84); (6) Herbert As a Courtier (pp. 85–108); (7) The Lady Magdalen Herbert (pp. 109–28); (8) Friends and Contemporaries (pp. 129–50); (9) The Reordering of the Church (pp. 151–72); (10) Transitional (pp. 173–96); (11) Nicholas Ferrar and Little Gidding (pp. 197–222); (12) Bemerton: The Parson and His Cure (pp. 223–40); (13) Last Days (pp. 241–56); (14) *The Temple.* The Church-Porch (pp. 257–68); (15) *The Temple.* The Shorter Poems (pp. 269–88); (16) *The Country Parson* and Other Writings (pp. 289–308); (17) Conclusion (pp. 309–15). Index (pp. 317–27). Thirty-two illustrations.

Reviews:
Anon. *Saturday Review* 102 (1906): 583–84
Francis Thompson, *Athenaeum,* 16 March 1907, pp. 313–14

**12. More, Paul Elmer.** "George Herbert," in *Shelburne Essays,* 4th ser., 66–98. New York and London: G. P. Putnam's Sons.

Biographical sketch that, in part, challenges certain of Palmer's remarks that play down Herbert's saintliness and piety. Maintains that we bring to Herbert a defective religious sensibility that does not allow us to understand his intimacy with things divine. Sees a strong influence of Donne on Herbert.

13. [**Thompson, Francis**]. Review of *The English Works of George Herbert*, edited by George Herbert Palmer. *Athenaeum*, 7 April, p. 415.

Praises Palmer's edition (entry 2), for the most part, but dislikes Palmer's comments on Herbert's alleged artificiality: "This artificiality is spontaneous and glowing; as with many other poets, it is natural to him, though unnatural to the average modern man." Also questions Palmer's concern about the alleged "uncouthness of the poet's metre": "Herbert is too true a poet not to let the emotion mould his metre." Acknowledges that the reader may find "some arbitrariness" in the way in which Palmer divided the poems to show "the stages of the poet's psychical evolution" but maintains that "the grouping of the poems written in the Cambridge and Bemerton periods respectively is unimpeachable." Disagrees with Palmer's interpretation of the last two stanzas of "Easter." Praises Herbert's poetry for its superb diction and homely, felicitous imagery and calls the poet "the source and father of our religious lyric poets."

# *1907*

14. **Anon.** "News for Bibliophiles." *The Nation* 84:586.

Gives bibliographical data on two copies of *The Temple* with undated title pages, one in the Huth library and one in the Robert Hoe library. Notes that William Thomas Lowndes (1859) maintained that these copies were rare first editions issued by Nicholas Ferrar for presentation to Herbert's friends in 1631. Argues that this claim is invalid, that the copies were most likely printed between the first dated edition (1633) and the second dated edition (1633). See also L. S. Livingston (entry 17), Marion Cox (entry 60), F. E. Hutchinson (entry 249), William A. Jackson (entry 250), and F. S. Ferguson (entry 325).

15. **Crawshaw, William H[enry]**. "The Age of Milton (1625–1660)," in *The Making of English Literature*, 153–78. Boston, New York, Chicago: D. C. Heath & Co.

Revised, 1924.

General, appreciative evaluation of Herbert's poetry, calling him "a true poet, very even in quality, but seldom inspired" (p. 163), and maintaining that the chief value of his verse "lies in its reflection of the deep religious earnestness of the man and of the spiritual and poetic aspiration of a consecrated nature" (p. 164).

16. **Herbert, George.** *The Poems of George Herbert.* With an introduction by Arthur Waugh. (Oxford edition.) London, New York, Toronto: Henry Frowde, Oxford University Press. xxiii, 327p.

Reprinted, 1913; New York: AMS Press, 1976; London, New York, Toronto: Oxford University Press (The World's Classics, no. 109), 1907, 1912, 1914, 1934, 1952, 1955, 1958.

Introduction reprinted in *Reticence in Literature and Other Papers* (London: J. G. Wilson, 1915), 130–43.

"Second edition," with introduction by Helen Gardner and text based on Hutchinson's edition, The World's Classics, no. 109 (London, New York, Toronto: Oxford University Press, 1961), entry 551.

Text based on Grosart. Introduction (pp. iii-xv); contents (pp. xvii-xxiii); The Temple (pp. 1–196); The Church Militant (pp. 197–208); Additional Sacred Poems (pp. 229–37); Parentalia (pp. 239–52); Anti-Tami-Cami-Categoria et Georgii Herberti, Angli Musae Responsoriae, ad Andreae Melvini, Scoti, Anti-Tami-Cami-Categoriam (pp. 253–62); Pro Disciplina Ecclesiae Nostrae Epigrammata Apologetica (pp. 263–84); Alia Poemata Latina (pp. 285–94); Passio Discerpta. Lucus (pp. 295–318); index of first lines (pp. 319–27).

**17.** [Livingston, L. S.] "The Bibliophile." *The Evening Post (New York). Saturday Supplement*, 29 June, p. 7.

Agrees with William Thomas Lowndes (1859) that the undated copies of the first edition of *The Temple* were probably issued for presentation to Herbert's friends but challenges his assumption that they were printed before the dated copies. Argues that the undated copies were probably issued between the first dated edition and the second edition. See also Anon. (entry 14), Marion Cox (entry 60), F. E. Hutchinson (entry 249), William A. Jackson (entry 250), and F. S. Ferguson (entry 325).

**18. Nicoll, W. Robertson, and Thomas Seccombe.** "Religious Poetry," in *A History of English Literature*, vol. 1, *Caxton (1422) to Walton (1593)*, 377–85. New York: Dodd, Mead, & Co.

Biographical sketch of Herbert and general evaluation of his poetry. Maintains that Herbert was "deeply imbued by the intellectuality and ingenuity of Donne" and thus "the result is often an obscurity akin to the obscurity of Browning, an elusiveness resembling that of Emerson, a turn of phrase as far removed from the obvious and also from the superficial as a phrase of George Meredith" (p. 379). Maintains that Herbert's "sense of sin is more intimate than that of any other religious poet" (p. 379). Rejects the notion that Herbert's religious spirit is fundamentally Laudian and finds the comparison of Herbert to Keble misleading.

**19. Skipton, H. P. K.** "Some Friendships of Nicholas Ferrar," in *The Life and Times of Nicholas Ferrar*, 110–23. London, Oxford, New York: A. R. Mowbray & Co.; New York: T. Whittaker.

Reviews the scant information known about the friendship of Ferrar and Herbert. Points out that no record exists to prove that they ever met, but that it is known that they were both involved in the rebuilding of the church at Leighton Bromswold and that Herbert's good friend Arthur Woodnoth was first cousin of Ferrar.

**20. Stebbing, William.** "George Herbert," in *The Poets: Geoffrey Chaucer to Alfred Tennyson, 1340–1892*, vol. 1, *Chaucer to Burns*, 79–88. London, New York, Toronto: Henry Frowde, Oxford University Press.

Reprinted in *Five Centuries of English Verse* (London, New York, Toronto, and Melbourne: Henry Frowde and Oxford University Press, 1910), 1:79–88.

Revised, 1913.

Calls Herbert "the model, the exemplar, the prince, of sacred poets" (p. 79) and compares him favorably with Sidney. Finds his "artifices" and "fireworks of wit," to be "fashion's rather than his" (p. 80). Praises the musical quality of Herbert's lyrics and, by quoting extensively from individual poems, surveys some of his major themes and characteristics.

**21.** [Thompson, Francis]. Review of *George Herbert and His Times* by A. G. Hyde. *Athenaeum*, 16 March, pp. 313–14.

Reprinted in *Literary Criticisms by Francis Thompson, Newly Discovered and Collected*, edited by Terence L. Connolly (New York: E. P. Dutton, 1948), 79–82.

Praises Herbert's poetry for its "remarkable fusion of poetic fantasy and mystic imagination with strong, homely, practical sense, loving an aphoristic terseness" (p. 313). Finds Hyde's biography (entry 11) a competent, though dull, work. Notes that "so little new material has been recovered, as Mr. Hyde says, that a modern biography of George Herbert can be scarcely more than a commentary on Walton" but applauds Hyde's attempt to correlate Herbert's life and writings with the history and life of his time. Comments on Herbert's Welsh ancestry, his physical appearance, and his fundamentally ambitious nature and maintains that Herbert was much more human than his biographers have admitted. Argues that Herbert's conflict between worldly desires and the spiritual life" is what "gives his poetry the human and sympathetic element" (p. 314) and rejects the idea that Herbert became a saint "completed at a stroke, by one first act of self-abnegation" (p. 314).

# *1908*

**22. Herbert, George.** *A Priest to the Temple or, The Country Parson*. His Character and Rule of Holy Life by George Herbert. With an introduction and brief notes by the bishop of North Carolina [Joseph Blount Cheshire]. New York: Thomas Whittaker. 154p.

New edition, Milwaukee: The Young Churchman; London: A. R. Mowbray, 1915.

Introduction (pp. 5–13); The Author to the Reader (p. 15); contents (pp. 17–18); text of *The Country Parson* (pp. 19–149); Author's Prayer Before Sermon (pp. 150–53); Prayer After Sermon (p. 154). Notes that this is the first edition of *The Country Parson* "published in America separate from his Poems" (p. 5). Maintains that Herbert's prose "is wholly free from the faults which mar his verses" (p. 5). Praises both the style and the sound Christian advice contained in the book: "Its simplicity and unaffectedness, its directness of purpose, the practical good sense of its rules and suggestions, its genuine humility and sympathy, its condescension to human weakness yet with loyalty to divine righteousness, its absolute fidelity to truth and duty, its heavenly wisdom, and clear vision, are embodied in that quality of English prose which we love and admire but can no longer write or speak" (p. 6). Brief notes are primarily from Palmer's edition. One illustration.

**23. ———.** *The Temple & A Priest to the Temple*. Edited by Edward Thomas. (Everyman's Library, no. 309.) London and Toronto: J. M. Dent & Sons; New York: E. P. Dutton & Co. xvii, 304p.

Reprinted, 1927.

Introduction (pp. vii–xii); bibliography (pp. xiii–xiv); The Printers to the Reader (pp. xv–xviii); dedication (p. xix); *The Temple* (pp. 1–209); index of titles of poems (pp. 210–12); *A Priest to the Temple, or, The Country Parson* (pp. 213–93); "index of words" (a glossary) (pp. 295–301); and list of dates (pp. 302–5). Introduction is primarily a biographical sketch with general comments on the themes, tone, and techniques of Herbert's poetry. Praises in particular his ability to capture the spirit of the Anglican Church of his day: "I can believe that a century or so hence, when some of these things have grown a little dim with their own age and the dust of the velocity of progress, men poised in flying machines over continents resembling one vast Anerley and Tooting will be moved by George Herbert's verse to a passing melancholy at the thought of the poet's Church, his epoch, and his country, all irrecoverable and beautiful" (p. xii).

**24. Saintsbury, George.** "Caroline Lyric, Pindaric, and Stanza," in *A History of English Prosody from the Twelfth Century to the Present Day*, 2:321–43. London: Macmillan and Co.

Briefly comments on Herbert's prosody. Maintains that, although he does not censure Herbert for using shaped verse forms, he finds "more of the mechanical in Herbert's prosody than is shown merely by the adoption of these mechanical forms; and it is only when the fire of his poetry burns hottest that inspiration takes the place of mechanism" (p. 332). Maintains that Herbert is "scarcely ever bad" but "he has not the rarest touch of his fellow-disciples, Crashaw and Vaughan" (p. 332).

# *1909*

**25. Cook, Albert S.** "Notes On Milton's 'Ode on the Morning of Christ's Nativity.'" *Transactions of the Connecticut Academy of Arts and Sciences* 15:307–68.

Comments on the possibility of Herbert's influence on Milton, especially as reflected in certain parallels between "Christmas" and "Whitsunday" and Milton's "On the Morning of Christ's Nativity" (pp. 309–10, 334).

**26. Hinchman, Walter S.** "George Herbert: An Interpretation," in *Haverford Essays: Studies in Modern Literature*, 69–89. Haverford, Pa.: privately printed.

Divided into three sections. (1) "The Place," a rhapsodic tourist's impressions of Salisbury and Bemerton. (2) "The Man," a biographical sketch with some general comments on Herbert's poetry. Finds that "much of Herbert's verse . . . is of a not very high order" (p. 82); not only is it dwarfed by the accomplishments of his contemporaries (especially Chapman and Jonson), but "the quaintness often renders it dull to anyone who is not particularly interested in seventeenth century lyrics" (p. 82). (3) "The Medlar-Tree," a summary, in which the author poses the question that informs the whole essay: "We find it hard, under these old trees, to answer the searching question: which is it that you really like—Bemerton, or Herbert, or his verse?" (p. 86).

**27. Long, William J.** "The Puritan Age," in *English Literature: Its History and Significance for the Life of the English-Speaking World. A Text-Book for Schools*, 186–235. Boston: Ginn & Co.

Biographical sketch of Herbert and a general evaluation of his poetry. Maintains that the poems, in particular "The Collar," show that "the Puritan in him had struggled desperately before it subdued the pride and idleness of the Cavalier" and predicts that his poems "will probably be read and appreciated, if only by the few, just so long as men are strong enough to understand the Puritan's spiritual convictions" (pp. 196–97). Notes that Herbert's poetry has "strained imagery and fantastic verse forms" but urges the reader "to look for the deep thought and feeling that are hidden in these wonderful religious lyrics, even in those that appear most artificial" (p. 197).

**28. Rudler, M[iriam] N[ina].** *George Herbert: Courtier, Priest, Poet, 1593–1633.* With prefatory note by J. Lewis Paton. Wilmslow, Eng.: M. Jones. 60p.

Biographical sketch that relates Herbert's poetry to his life. Maintains that he belongs to no specific school of poetry but that he "may be regarded as the Laureate of Religious poetry" (p. 47). Praises Herbert's metrical inventiveness and his "power to charge a few common words full to over-flowing with meaning" (p. 52).

# 1910

**29. Buchanan, E. S.** *George Herbert Melodist.* London: Elliot Stock. x, 76p.

Hagiographic presentation of Herbert in which his poetry is valued only for being "the true expression of his own soul and its conflicts" (p. 9). Praises Herbert's poems for their conciseness of expression, great precision, and melody but does not rank them with hymns, since "they are too full of deep thought, too full of fancy, too delicately wrought, too intimate and personal" (p. 39). Maintains that "only to a sensitive and suffering soul will they yield their inner meaning" (p. 39).

**30. Griffinhoofe, C. G.** *Celebrated Cambridge Men.* Cambridge: A. P. Dixon; London: James Nisbet & Co. 215p.

Biographical sketches of famous men who were students at Cambridge from 1390 to 1908. Comments on Herbert's association with the university under the mastership of Henry Nevile and on his life after he left the university (pp. 69–70). Lists several of Herbert's associates and friends during his Cambridge days.

**31. Harland, Marion [Mary Virginia (Hawes) Teyhune].** "Gentle George Herbert at Bemerton," in *Where Ghosts Walk: The Haunts of Familiar Characters in History and Literature,* 2d ed., 237–62. New York and London: G. P. Putnam's Sons.

Personal account of the author's visit to Bemerton. Includes a hagiographic account of Herbert's life and personality. Notes that "his sacred lyrics have been for long, long years songs in the house of my pilgrimage, coming readily to my lips in moments of sudden joy or sorrow, staying my soul under the stress of homely toils and carking, belittling cares such as are known, in all their meanness and weariness, to women only" (p. 251). (The first edition of 1898 does not include the Herbert sketch.)

**32. Holliday, Carl.** "George Herbert." *SR* 18:268–82.

Reprinted in *The Cavalier Poets: Their Lives, Their Day, and Their Poetry* (New York: Neale Publishing Co., 1911; rpt. New York: Books for Libraries Press, 1974), 61–78.

Appreciative biographical sketch that focuses on Herbert's saintly personality. Comments only briefly on *The Temple,* calling it eccentric, odd, curious, quaint, and excessively ingenious: "Even the very forms of his most heartfelt poems are fantastic" (p. 277). Concludes, however, that "soul-earnestness goes a long way in art and will cover a multitude of technical sins" (p. 278).

**33. John, Francis, ed.** "Baxter and the Herbert Family," in *An Excerpt from Reliquiae Baxterianae or Mr. Richard Baxter's Narrative of The Most Memorable Passages of His Life and Times . . . ,* 155–60. London: Longmans, Green, and Co.

Comments briefly on Richard Baxter's dealings with the Herbert family. Indicates Baxter's great esteem for George Herbert.

**34. Thomas, Edward.** *Feminine Influence on the Poets.* London: Martin Secker; New York: John Lane Co. 351p.

Biographical sketch of Magdalene Herbert and a survey of her relationship with her two sons, Edward and George (pp. 124–28). Brief comments on Jane Danvers (pp. 151–54).

# *1911*

**35. Herbert, George.** *Gathered Rosemary from the Poems of George Herbert, for the Sundays and Some Holy Days of the Church's Year.* Edited by Mary Burn. With an introduction by the bishop of Hull. (Heart and Life Booklets, no. 32.) London: H. R. Allenson. 72p.

Herbert's poems arranged for each Sunday of the year and for various feast days of the Church calendar.

**36. Hutchinson, F. E.** "The Sacred Poets," in *The Cambridge History of English Literature*, edited by A. W. Ward and A. R. Waller, vol. 7, *Cavalier and Puritan*, 30–54. New York: G. P. Putnam's Sons; Cambridge: University Press.

Biographical sketch of Herbert, claiming that the fascination of Herbert "is due as much to his character as to his writings" and that his "personal history, therefore, is of more than ordinary moment for an understanding of his poems" (p. 30). Maintains that Palmer's reordering of the poems is at times arbitrary and unconvincing but that "no greater service has been done towards understanding Herbert than by this attempt to arrange his poems chronologically" (p. 34). Outlines some of the major characteristics of Herbert's poetry. Praises his skillful craftsmanship, his experimentation with form, his concentration, and his good humor. Laments that Herbert sometimes employs the "fantastic" conceit, a "serious defect of taste he shares with the poets whom Johnson styled 'metaphysical'" (p. 35). Maintains that Herbert's ingenuity "misleads him into what can only be called tricks" (p. 35) and frowns on Herbert's tendency "to draw from the sense of smell and taste images which make a modern reader, rightly or wrongly, ill at ease" (p. 36).

**37. Palmer, George Herbert.** *A Herbert bibliography being a catalogue of a collection of books relating to George Herbert, gathered by George Herbert Palmer.* (Bibliographical Contributions of the Library of Harvard University, edited by William Coolidge Lane, no. 59.) Cambridge, Mass.: Library of Harvard University. iv, 19p.

70 copies printed.

Reprinted, Folcroft, Pa.: Folcroft Library Editions, 1973; Norwood, Pa.: Norwood Editions, 1978.

Lists 142 titles and 159 volumes of books relating to Herbert: (1) biographies; (2) manuscripts; (3) writings other than *The Temple*; (4) editions of *The Temple* published during the first century after 1633; (5) modern editions of *The Temple*; (6) writings of the brothers of Herbert; (7) books relating to Nicholas Ferrar and Little Gidding; (8) books relating to other men associated with Herbert; and (9) desiderata.

**38. Tipple, Ezra.** "Bemerton," in *Some Famous Country Parishes*, 40–78. New York: Eaton & Mains; Cincinnati: Jennings & Graham.

Discusses Wilton, Bemerton, and Salisbury and describes a visit to various Herbert shrines. Appreciative biographical sketch. Scattered comments on the poems and prose works: "The poems of 'The Temple' are as didactic and hortatory as much of Longfellow" (p. 65). Praises *The Country Parson*: "No modern book of pastoral theology is richer in the wisdom of good sense or more prolific in helpful suggestions" (p. 69). Fourteen photographs.

**39. Vaughan Williams, R[alph].** *Five Mystical Songs.* Words by George Herbert set to music for baritone solo, chorus (ad lib.) and orchestra by R. Vaughan Williams. London: Stainer & Bell; New York: Galaxy.

Reprinted, New York: Galaxy, 1976, 1983.

Musical settings for "Easter" (two separate settings), "Love (III)," "The Call," and "Antiphon (I)."

# *1912*

**40. Lang, Andrew.** "Caroline Poets," in *History of English Literature from "Beowulf" to Swinburne*, 328–57. London: Longmans, Green and Co.

Biographical sketch of Herbert. Maintains that Herbert is not a truly great poet: "He never storms the cloudcapt towers, and 'flaming walls of the world,' like Crashaw" (p. 331). Considers "Easter-wings" and "The Altar" to be "examples of extreme decadence" (p. 331). Laments that Herbert's poetry is filled with conceits but concedes that he does not have "the extravagances that mar the work of Donne and Crashaw" (p. 331).

**41. Reed, Edward Bliss.** "The Jacobean and Caroline Lyric," in *English Lyrical Poetry from Its Origins to the Present Time*, 233–301. New Haven: Yale University Press; London: Humphrey Milford, Oxford University Press.

Reprinted, 1914.

Surveys briefly the works of twenty seventeenth-century poets. Maintains that Herbert created a new school of verse, the religious love lyric. Compares and contrasts Herbert and Donne and laments that many of Herbert's conceits are overly ingenious. Asserts that "his lyrics are rarely metrically perfect throughout" (p. 280) and that, "with exceptions, the musical appeal is not an immediate one" (p. 280). Claims that the real value of Herbert's poetry is that it reveals the inner character of the man.

**42. Tallentyre, S. G.** "The Parson-Poets." *North American Review* 195:84–93.

Biographical sketches of Herrick, Herbert, and Richard Barham. Praises Herbert for his exquisite feeling for lyric style, his serenity, his word play, and his delicate humor. "As for the quips, cranks, and oddities which were the poetical characteristics of the age, one can hardly dream of his poetry without them, and one loves him for them" (p. 89).

# *1913*

**43. Bett, Henry.** "The Hymns and the Poets," in *The Hymns of Methodism in Their Literary Relations*, 124–69. London: Charles H. Kelly.

New and enlarged ed., 1920.

3d ed., revised and enlarged, 1945; reprinted, 1946, 1956.

Comments on several adaptations of Herbert's poems made by John Wesley. Notes that Herbert was a favorite of Susanna Wesley, mother of John and Charles, and points out that Wesley used Herbert's lines in translating German hymns into English.

**44. Fleming, W[illiam] K[aye].** "Post-Reformation Mysticism in England—The Caroline Poets and the Cambridge Platonists," in *Mysticism in Christianity*, 194–212. (Library of Historic Theology, ed. W. C. Piercy.) New York and Chicago: Fleming H. Revell Co.; London: R. Scott.

Comments briefly on Herbert's religious sensibilities and contends that, although a good man, Herbert was not a mystic. Maintains that *The Temple* will always serve "to indicate and recall to men's minds the peculiar ideals and attractiveness of the English Church, its gravity, its mild rule, its sober beauty, its temperate delight in Nature and in Reason as intermediaries for communion with God" (p. 203). Mentions Herbert's "high gifts as a religious poet—imagination, and a curious felicity of diction set off by a touching homeliness—an especially persuasive one" (pp. 203–4). Comments briefly on Vaughan's indebtedness to Herbert and sees John Keble as the poet who carries on the Herbert tradition.

**45. Rhys, Ernest.** "The Later Amorists—Fashionable Lyric—The Herbert Group," in *Lyric Poetry*, 210–21. London and Toronto: J. M. Dent & Sons; New York: E. P. Dutton & Co.

Brief commentary on Herbert (pp. 215–18) that praises his "unusual adaptation of the personal narrative-note to the lyric" and his "melodic forms" (p. 216). Admits that Herbert "had a sense of lyric form which is rather wanting in some of his nearer associates in poetry" but wishes that "he had never been tempted by Donne and the metaphysical verse-men to be so over-ingenious" (p. 217). Compares Herbert to Vaughan (who took "every advantage of Herbert's bad example in the way of oddities and tricks of style" [p. 218]) and to Crashaw.

**46. Schelling, Felix E.** "The Lyric in the Reign of the First Two Stuart Monarchs," in *The English Lyric*, 73–111. Boston and New York: Houghton Mifflin Co.

Brief comment on Herbert (pp. 95–96) calls him "a concettist" who "delights not only in ingenious imagery but even in the puerilities of acrostics, anagrams, and shaped verses" (pp. 95–96) and maintains that, in spite of "surface foam and bubbles" (p. 96), Herbert is a major devotional poet because of his deep, irresistible fervor and sincerity of feeling.

**47. Spurgeon, Caroline F. E.** "Devotional and Religious Mystics," in *Mysticism in English Literature*, 111–58. Cambridge: University Press.

Brief discussion of Richard Rolle, Julian of Norwich, Crashaw, Herbert, Christopher Harvey, Blake, and Francis Thompson as mystics. Comments on the personal tone and homely intimacy of Herbert's religious lyrics.

**48. Vaughan Williams, Ralph.** "Sweet Day," in *Three Elizabethan Part Songs*, 1–4. London: J. B. Williams.

Adapted for three-part women's voices (SSA) (entry 272).
Musical setting for stanzas 1, 3, and 4 of "Vertue" for mixed voices (SATB).

# 1914

**49. Kashiwai, En.** "George Herbert to Inaka Bokushi no Seikatsu" [George Herbert and the Life of a Country Parson], in *Kirisuto to Jinsei* [Christ and Life], 276–87. Tokyo: Hokubunkan.
   Brief evaluation of Herbert's poetry. Quotes part of "Vertue" and translates the first stanza into Japanese.

# 1915

**50. Benson, Louis F.** *The English Hymn: Its Development and Use in Worship.* Richmond, Va.: John Knox Press. xvii, 624p.
   Reprinted, 1962.
   Survey of the development of the English hymn with several comments about the uses made of Herbert's poetry, particularly during the late seventeenth and the eighteenth centuries, by such hymnologists as Henry Playford, Joseph Boyse, Samuel Bury, Simon Browne, Isaac Watts, and especially John Wesley, whose *Hymns and Sacred Poems* (1739) included forty-two adaptations from Herbert.

**51. Currier, Albert H.** "George Herbert," in *Biographical and Literary Studies*, 183–207. Boston, New York, Chicago: Pilgrim Press.
   Appreciative biographical sketch of Herbert. Calls him the St. Francis of the English Church. Quotes extensively from *The Country Parson* and calls it a classic of religious literature.

**52. Heide, Anna von der.** "Die religiösen Lyriker," in *Das Naturgefühl in der englischen Dichtung im Zeitalter Miltons*, 61–89. (Anglistische Forschungen, 45.) Heidelberg: Carl Winters Universitätsbuchhandlung.
   Discusses the uses of nature in seventeenth-century English poetry and argues (pp. 65–69) that Herbert had a deeper understanding of the essence of nature than had most of his contemporaries. Points out, however, that Herbert always viewed nature from a theological perspective, as an expression of God's wisdom and power. Mentions several specific poems, especially "Providence."

**53. Inge, William Ralph.** "English Religious Poetry." *Transactions of the Royal Society of Literature* 2d ser. 33:177–203.
   Reprinted in *More Lay Thoughts of a Dean* (New York and London: Putnam, 1932), 225–54.
   Surveys English religious poetry and compares and contrasts poets influenced by different religious traditions and beliefs. Calls Herbert "a typically Anglican poet" (p. 192) who might have been a greater poet had he not imitated Donne, "but this influence affects only the form of his writing" (p. 192). Praises Herbert's piety and compares him with Vaughan.

# 1916

**54. Jackson, George.** "The Bookshelf by the Fire: I. George Herbert's 'Country Parson.'" *Expository Times*, March, pp. 248–52.

Calls Herbert a saint and comments on *The Country Parson* as "intimate self-revelation" (p. 249). Considers the work a collection of "simple pieties and sweet charities" (p. 251) but notes two minor defects: (1) the book is "a little too suggestive of a visitant from some other sphere who comes to right the wrongs of our poor world" (p. 252) and (2) there is "an undue emphasis on asceticism" (p. 252).

# 1917

**55. Hodgkin, John.** "Luigi Cornaro and Nicholas Ferrar." *TLS*, 28 June, pp. 309–10.

Reply to Francis Hutchinson (entry 56). Maintains that Ferrar had no part in editing or translating Lessius of Louvain's *Hygiasticon*, that Herbert translated only Cornaro's first treatise and had nothing to do with the translation of either Lessius or the anonymous Italian piece contained in the volume. Maintains that the real translator and editor of Lessius and the Italian piece is Thomas Sheppard, a friend of the Ferrars.

**56. Hutchinson, Francis.** "Luigi Cornaro." *TLS*, 7 June, p. 273.

Asserts that "the first of Cornaro's 'Discorsi della Vita Sobria' was introduced to English readers in a little volume of 1634 which had Nicholas Ferrar for editor, George Herbert for translator, and Richard Crashaw to commend the theme with his prefatory verses" (p. 273). Maintains that Ferrar consulted Herbert about printing a treatise by Lessius of Louvain ("The Right Course of Preserving Health of Extream Old Age"), that Herbert approved and suggested Cornaro's tract be added, and that a third treatise by an anonymous Italian on dieting was added, thus making up the volume *Hygiasticon*. For a reply, see John Hodgkin (entry 55).

# 1918

**57. Anon.** "George Herbert." *The Saturday Review* (London) 125: 47–48.
Reprinted in *The Living Age* 296 (1918): 813–15.

Appreciative sketch of Herbert's life and temperament, praising him as "the most sincere poet" of "religious moderation" (p. 47). Calls his poetry "sweet roses of undying fragrance from the garden of his soul" (p. 48).

**58. Palmer, George Herbert.** "George Herbert," in *Formative Types in English Poetry*, 101–31. Boston and New York: Houghton Mifflin Co. (The Earl Lectures of 1917.)

Reprinted, Freeport, N.Y.: Books for Libraries Press, 1968.

Discusses Herbert as a poet of the inner life, veracious, intellectual, individualistic, energetic" (p. 112). Includes a biographical sketch that stresses the various conflicts in Herbert's temperament and the introspective nature of his poetry. Maintains that Herbert is "a conscious artist" and has "a strong sense of orderly poetic form" (p. 114).

**59. Quiller-Couch, Arthur.** "Some Seventeenth Century Poets," in *Studies in Literature*, 96–167. New York: G. P. Putnam's Sons; Cambridge: University Press.

Reprinted, 1922, 1926.

Biographical sketch, maintaining that Donne "infected" Herbert and that few of Herbert's poems are flawless. Compares Herbert with Vaughan and argues that Vaughan is "actually more original and certainly of deeper insight as well as of ampler, more celestial range than the man he copied" (p. 141).

## *1919*

**60. Cox, E. Marion.** "Notes on Rare Books." *The Library* (London) 3d ser. 10:18–25.

"The First Edition of Herbert's 'Temple'" (pp. 23–25) challenges the assumption that the undated copies of the first edition of *The Temple* represent presentation copies printed a year or so earlier than the dated copies. Maintains, using evidence obtained from the Huth copy, that the undated copies were printed after the dated ones, shortly before the second edition of 1633; that the printer objected that the dated title page gave no information as to where the book could be purchased; and that the addition of "Francis Green Stationer" crowded the type, and the date, coming last, was omitted to avoid destroying the symmetry of the page. See also Anon. (entry 14), L. S. Livingston (entry 17), F. E. Hutchinson (entry 249), William A. Jackson (entry 250), and F. S. Ferguson (entry 325).

**61. Massingham, H[arold] J., ed.** *A Treasury of Seventeenth-Century English Verse from the Death of Shakespeare to the Restoration (1616–1660).* (Golden Treasury Series.) London: Macmillan. xxiii, 399p.

Reprinted, with slight revisions, 1920.

In the introduction surveys English poetry from 1616 to 1660, a period said to contain "the largest collection of mystical verse in the language" (p. xiii). Anthologizes nine poems by Herbert (pp. 136–42), with endnotes (pp. 347–48). In the notes maintains that Herbert literally carried out Wordsworth's theory of poetic language and that, in some respects, is not unlike Cowper. Claims that his "lasting virtues are poetic gravity and piety" and maintains that, in Herbert's poetry, "one seems to find a distinction between commonplace and truism" (p. 348).

**62. Osmond, Percy H.** "George Herbert, Harvey, and Quarles," in *The Mystical Poets of the English Church*, 67–111. London: SPCK; New York: Macmillan Co.

Anthology of mystical poets of the English Church, with a few extracts from those outside that communion. Calls Herbert "the foremost of the distinctively sacred poets of England" (p. 67), places him among the mystics, and reviews some of the major spiritual themes of his poetry. Criticizes Herbert's use of the conceit: "This failure is the result, not always of the use of obsolete phraseology, but sometimes of the abuse of analogy and the strained ingenuity of wit, into which he was led by his admiration of Donne" (p. 75). Laments Herbert's uses of "artificial tricks of rhyme and metre, which give a suggestion of insincerity" (p. 88).

63. W., E. W. "Donne's Puns." *TLS*, 11 December, p. 750.
Points out Herbert's use of the *sun-son* pun not only in "The Sonne" but also possibly in the last line of "Mattens" ("Then by a sunne-beam I will climb to thee").

## 1920

64. Clough, Benjamin C. "Notes on the Metaphysical Poets." *MLN* 35:115–17.
Points out that Dryden's lines in *Upon the Death of Lord Hastings* ("Each little pimple had a tear in it / To wail the fault its rising did commit") are reminiscent of stanza 70 in *The Church-Porch*.

65. [Clutton-Brock, A.] "George Herbert." *TLS*, 1 April, pp. 205–6.
Reprinted (in part) in *More Essays on Books* (London: Methuen; New York: Dutton, 1921), 14–23.
Complimentary review of Palmer's edition (entry 2). Comments on Herbert's poetry and method and laments that often he is dismissed as "quaint old Herbert." Briefly discusses some of Herbert's major themes, his distrust of external beauty and of love poetry, his uses of music, his mastery of form, and so on. Maintains that "it is never safe to reject a poem of Herbert as a failure; the failure may be in you, and with another attempt you may discover a secret beauty which seems all the more beautiful for having lain hid so long" (p. 206).

66. Colby, Elbridge. *The Echo-Device in Literature*. New York: New York Public Library. 61p.
Discusses various forms and techniques of the echo-device in poetry and drama and briefly traces the development and history of the device, starting with *The Greek Anthology*. Notes that the echo-device, frequently associated with the pastoral tradition, enjoyed a revival in England from 1575 (Gascoigne) to the middle of the seventeenth century. Discusses "Heaven" as representative of one technique, that of using a conversation between a speaker and an echo. Notes that Lord Herbert of Cherbury also used the device.

67. Herbert, George. *The Works of George Herbert. In Prose and Verse*. Edited from the latest editions, with Memoir, Explanatory Notes, &c. (Chandos Classics.) London and New York: Frederick Warne and Co. xiv, 488p.
Contains a preface (pp. v-vi), "The Printers to the Reader" (pp. vii-ix), table of contents (pp. xi-xiv), "The Life of Mr. George Herbert" by Izaak Walton (pp. 1–49), *The Temple* (pp. 53–255), *The Church Militant* (pp. 256–265), Miscellaneous Poems (pp. 266–69), *A Priest to the Temple; or, The Country Parson* (pp. 271–334), "Preface and Notes by George Herbert to 'Divine Considerations' by John Valdesso" (p. 335–45), "A Treatise of Temperance and Sobriety" (pp. 346–57), *Jacula Prudentum* (pp. 358–92), Letters by George Herbert (pp. 393–415), Orations by George

Herbert (pp. 416–28), Latin and Greek poems (pp. 429–88). In the preface, maintains that "in spite of the quaintness and conceits" Herbert's poems "still retain a high place in our literature" and praises the "depth and reality of their religious feeling" and the "excellence of their language" (p. v). Claims that of Donne, Herbert, and Cowley, Herbert is "the best" and "remains the only one of them popularly read in the present day" (p. v). Acknowledges that many of the notes of this edition were taken from the manuscripts of the late Rev. Richard Valentine.

**68. Rayson, Robert Spencer.** "The Poetry of George Herbert." *American Church Monthly* 8:132–46.

Appreciative essay and biographical sketch. Calls *The Temple* a "pleasant by-way of English poetry" (p. 146). Compares Herbert and Cowper. Comments on Herbert's High Church theology (such as his views on the Eucharist and on saints) as reflected in his poetry and praises his religious sensibility. Comments on the universal appeal of such a poem as "Vertue" but rejects *The Church-Porch* as lacking "the indefinable something . . . that is essential to great poetry" (p. 145). Finds Herbert least effective as a practical moralist.

**69. Wright, Thomas Goddard.** *Literary Culture in Early New England, 1620–1730.* New Haven: Yale University Press; London: Humphrey Milford, Oxford University Press. 322p.

Comments on education, libraries, and literary life in colonial New England. Notes that Increase Mather, in a list composed in 1664, indicated that he owned a copy of Herbert's poems and that his fragmentary diary for 1675–1676 shows that he was familiar with *A Priest to the Temple*. Points out that Ezekiel Rogers, in an epitaph on Thomas Hooker (1647), refers to *The Church Militant*, as does Daniel Gookin in his *Historical Collections of the Indians in New England* (1792). Notes that Samuel Sewall, in a letter dated 1711, asked John Love, his London agent, for a copy of Herbert's poems and that the Harvard Library catalog of 1723 lists Herbert's poems among the library's holdings.

# 1921

**70. Eliot, T. S.** "The Metaphysical Poets." *TLS*, 20 October, pp. 669–70.

Reprinted in *Selected Essays, 1917–1932* (London: Faber & Faber; New York: Harcourt, Brace, and Co., 1932) and several other collections.

Claims that "the poets of the seventeenth century, the successors of the dramatists of the sixteenth century, possessed a mechanism of sensibility which could devour any kind of experience" and that "in the seventeenth century a dissociation of sensibility set in, from which we have never recovered; and this dissociation, as is natural, was due to the influence of the two most powerful poets of the century, Milton and Dryden" (p. 669). Argues that, in contrast, the metaphysical poets were "engaged in the task of trying to find the verbal equivalent for states of mind and feeling" (p. 670). Illustrates the point by saying: "The difference is not a simple difference of degree between poets. It is something which happened to the mind of England between the time of Donne or Lord Herbert of Cherbury and the time of Tennyson and Browning; it is the difference between the intellectual poet and the reflective poet. Tennyson and Browning are poets, and they think; but they do not feel their thought as immediately as the odour of a rose." Maintains that "a thought to Donne was an experience; it modified his sensibility" (p. 669). Comments briefly on the simplicity of language in Herbert's poetry, "a simplicity emulated without success by numerous modern poets" (p. 669), yet finds in Herbert a complexity of structure that reflects "a fidelity to thought and feeling" (p. 669).

71. ———. "The Metaphysical Poets." *TLS*, 3 November, p. 716.
Reply to George Saintsbury (entry 75). Suggests that Saintsbury "appears to believe that these poets represent not merely a generation, but almost a particular theory of poetry." Maintains that "the 'second thoughts' to which he alludes are, I think, and as I tried to point out, frequent in the work of many other poets besides, of other times and other languages" and mentions in particular Chapman and the contemporaries of Dante. Concludes that he does not believe "that the author of *Hamlet* and *Measure for Measure* was invariably satisfied with 'the first simple, obvious, natural thought and expression of thought.'" For a reply, see George Saintsbury (entry 76).

72. **Gosse, Edmund.** "Metaphysical Poetry." *Sunday Times* (London), 4 December, p. 8.
Reprinted in *More Books on the Table* (London: William Heinemann, 1923), 307–13.
Review of Grierson's *Metaphysical Lyrics & Poems* (entry 73). Maintains that the common purpose of poets from Donne to Cowley "was an application of the psychological method to the passions." Maintains that Donne's greatest gift to his followers (Herbert is included as a disciple) was that "he taught the poets to regard mellifluousness with suspicion, if it concealed poverty of thought, and to be more anxious to find words, even stumbling and harsh words, for their personal emotions, than to slip over the surface of language in a conventional sweetness." Mentions Herbert only in passing.

73. **Grierson, Herbert J. C., ed.** *Metaphysical Lyrics & Poems of the Seventeenth Century: Donne to Butler.* Selected and edited, with an essay by Herbert J. C. Grierson. Oxford: Clarendon Press. lviii, 244p.
Reprinted several times.
Introduction reprinted in *The Background of English Literature* (London: Chatto and Windus, 1925), 115–66; translated into Japanese by Kin-ichiro Honda in *Keijijo-shijin Ron* (entry 792).
Pages xiii-xxxviii reprinted in *Seventeenth Century English Poetry: Modern Essays in Criticism*, edited by William Keast (entry 584), 3–21; rev. ed. (entry 879), 3–22.
Critical introduction (pp. xiii-lviii); selections from twenty-six poets divided into three major categories: love poems, divine poems, and miscellanies (pp. 1–215); notes (pp. 217–40); index of first lines (pp. 241–44). By the introduction and selection of poems, Grierson, in effect, defines the metaphysical school, although he is cautious with the term itself. Maintains, however, that the term *metaphysical* "lays stress on the right things—the survival, one might say the reaccentuation, of the metaphysical strain, the *concetti metafisici ed ideali* as Testi calls them in contrast to the imagery of classical poetry, of mediaeval Italian poetry; the more intellectual, less verbal, character of their wit compared with the conceits of the Elizabethans; the finer psychology of which their conceits are often the expression; their learned imagery; the argumentative, subtle evolution of their lyrics; above all the peculiar blend of passion and thought, feeling and ratiocination which is their greatest achievement" (pp. xv-xvi). Considers Donne "the great master of English poetry in the seventeenth century" (p.

xvi) and focuses the critical discussion on his poetry, considering the other poets primarily in contrast with or in comparison to Donne. Yet warns that "to call these poets the 'school of Donne' or 'metaphysical' poets may easily mislead if one takes either phrase in too full a sense" (p. xxx). Calls Herbert "the poet in whom the English Church of Hooker found a voice of its own" (p. xl). Comments on "the note of conflict, of personal experience, which troubles and gives life to poetry" (p. xli) and is found in Herbert's poetry, but concludes that, unlike Donne, Herbert reflects a feeling of reconciliation, joy, and peace. Maintains that Herbert learned the metaphysical manner from Donne but that, unlike his master, Herbert's interest in theology is always practical and devotional, not metaphysical. Maintains that "Herbert's central theme is the psychology of his religious experiences" (p. xlii), and thus he does for religious poetry what Donne did for love poetry. Compares Herbert also with Vaughan, Crashaw, and Quarles.

**74. Merrill, L. R.** "George Herbert's *Church Porch*." *MLN* 36:249–50.

Maintains that the closing sentiments in *The Church-Porch* are possibly derived from Nicholas Grimald's "Musonius, the Philosopher's saiying," in *Tottel's Miscellany*. Points out that Grimald was born at Bromswold and that Herbert was later a lay prebendary in that parish.

**75. Saintsbury, George.** "The Metaphysical Poets." *TLS*, 27 October, p. 698.

Reply to T. S. Eliot (entry 70). Maintains that when Dryden used the term *metaphysics* in connection with Donne's poetry, he did not equate it with philosophy but rather opposed it to nature. Points out that in Greek the word means "second thoughts, things that come *after* the natural first." Maintains that "this definition would . . . fit all the poetry commonly called 'metaphysical,' whether it be amatory, religious, satirical, panegyric, or merely trifling; while 'philosophical,' though of course not seldom suitable enough, sometimes has no relevance whatever" for "these poets always 'go behind' the first, simple, obvious, natural thought and expression of thought." For a reply, see T. S. Eliot (entry 71).

**76. ———.** "The Metaphysical Poets." *TLS*, 10 November, p. 734.

Brief reply to T. S. Eliot (entry 71). Says that he fully agrees with Eliot that, "in the great examples he quotes, and perhaps in all similar things, there *is* 'second thought.'" Maintains that "all true poetry must be in a way second thought, though much second thought is not in any way poetry." Concludes that his intention was to point out that, "*in this period* [the seventeenth century], the quest of the second thought became direct, deliberate, a business, almost itself a *first* thought."

**77. Thompson, Elbert N. S.** "Mysticism in Seventeenth-Century English Literature." *SP* 18:170–231.

Mentions Herbert only in passing. Comments on the enormous popularity of sacred poetry during the seventeenth century and discusses the element of mysticism in a number of poets of the period as well as in a number of their predecessors. Maintains that Herbert "had little if any mysticism in his temperament" even though "his poems show an unfaltering sense of the nearness of God" (p. 182). Maintains Plato's influence on Herbert's poetry, especially "Love (I)."

**78. Woodberry, George Edward.** "Notes on the Seventeenth Century Poets: A College Syllabus," in *Studies of a Litterateur*, 137–48. New York: Harcourt, Brace and Co.

Briefly comments on Herbert's life, personality, and poetry. Maintains that the poetry reflects the faults of his age: "The conceits, the tastelessness in diction, the intellectual, fantastic and uneven traits are all there" (p. 142), but, at the same time, "all these things are fused, and find their artistic wholeness in his spirituality" (p. 143).

# 1922

**79. Ault, Norman, ed.** *The Poets' Life of Christ.* Compiled, arranged and decorated by Norman Ault. London: Humphrey Milford, Oxford University Press. xxviii, 275p.

Reprinted, 1923; Freeport, N.Y.: Books for Libraries Press, 1972.

Introduction (pp. v-x); scheme and contents (pp. xi-xxvii); selection of poems on the life of Christ by various authors (pp. xxviii, 1–272); index of authors (pp. 273–75). Declares that the purpose of this anthology is "to reveal the extent to which the life and teaching of Christ have inspired the poets of the English-speaking race . . . as well as to illustrate that wonderful life itself by the poems thus inspired" (p. v). Nearly four hundred poems arranged in twelve main sections to illustrate chronologically Christ's life and teaching. Includes eleven of Herbert's poems. No notes and no commentary. Illustrations.

**80. Nethercot, Arthur H.** "The Term 'Metaphysical Poets' before Johnson." *MLN* 37:11–17.

Notes that "the use of the term metaphysical in connection with certain poets or with certain types of poetry was far from uncommon in the seventeenth and eighteenth centuries, and that therefore there were various sources from which Johnson might have got the suggestion for his phrase, altho probably the responsibility was mainly Dryden's" (pp. 12–13).

**81. Thompson, A. Hamilton.** "The Mystic Element in English Poetry." *E&S* 8:90–108.

Defines mystical poetry and surveys the work of English mystical poets. Sees Herbert as grounded in "safe Anglicanism" and as an ascetic, not a mystic: "His serene gladness falls short of mystical rapture" (p. 95). Calls "Easter" the "most beautiful and natural of his lyrics" and points out that its success "depends upon its perfect application of the joy and brightness of a spring morning to the hallowed associations of the queen of feasts" (p. 95) and contrasts the poem with Crashaw's Nativity hymn.

# 1923

**82. Butterworth, S.** "Wordsworth and George Herbert." *N&Q* 12th ser. 12:113.

Partly a reply to G. C. Moore Smith (entry 85). Maintains that Wordsworth's indebtedness to Herbert's "Constancie" in "Character of a Happy Warrior" is apparent, but that the resemblances between Herbert's "Mans medley" and Wordsworth's "Ode on Immortality" are less apparent. Points out Alice Meynell's borrowing from Herbert's "Christmas" for several of her lines in "Shepherdess."

**83. Fausset, Hugh l'Anson.** "Idealism and Puritanism," in *Studies in Idealism*, 87–116. London and Toronto: J. M. Dent & Sons; New York: E. P. Dutton & Co.

Reprinted, Port Washington, N.Y.: Kennikat Press, 1965.

Calls Herbert a mystical poet and considers him one of the first to attempt reconciling "a natural ecstasy with Christian devotion" (p. 87). Compares Herbert's view of the world with that of Vaughan: "In Herbert the sense of eternity, of infinite existence, is translated into a principle, that of Love. The translation is direct and logical. He who loves the Infinite loves every embodiment of it which he presupposes in the Finite. He does not criticise the Finite, or venture the opinion that in this creature the Infinite is less apparent than in that. He sees the Infinite in all things, and loves accordingly" (pp. 105–6). Comments on Herbert's vision of reality, his religious sensibilities, and his view of sin.

**84. Herbert, George.** *Poems by George Herbert.* Selected by Sir H. Walford Davies, with a woodcut of Montgomery Castle. Gregynog: Gregynog Press. xv, 26p.

Limited to 300 copies.

Reprints, in addition to "The Dedication," "The Printers to the Reader," and a selection from Walton's *Life of Mr. George Herbert*, twenty-three poems from *The Temple*, without notes or commentary. Davies observes in his foreword that he chose poems that "reveal George Herbert's love of building in words as in living stone" and that all the selections "show that our Author's love of fine form was part of his devout love of God" (p. vii).

**85. Moore Smith, G. C.** "Wordsworth and George Herbert." *N&Q* 12th ser. 12:30.

Maintains that Wordsworth was familiar with Herbert's poetry, as evidenced in his sonnet "Seathwaite Chapel" ("Such as the heaven-taught skill of Herbert drew"). Agrees with F. Haverfield (*N&Q* 6th ser. 8 [1883]:206) that Herbert's "Mans medley" suggested some lines near the beginning of "Ode on Immortality" and sees Herbert's "Constancie" as a possible source for Wordsworth's "Character of a Happy Warrior." For a reply, see S. Butterworth (entry 82).

**86. Read, Herbert.** "The Nature of Metaphysical Poetry." *Criterion* (London) 1:246–66.

Reprinted in *Reason and Romanticism: Essays in Literary Criticism* (London: Faber and Gwyer, 1926), 31–58; *Collected Essays in Literary Criticism* (London: Faber & Faber, 1938), 69–88. The latter book was reprinted as *The Nature of Literature* (New York: Horizon Press, 1956, 1970).

Defines the essential nature of metaphysical poetry "as the emotional apprehension of thought—or, to use words suggested by Dante, as thought transmuted into vision" (p. 249). Singles out Milton as having done more than any other poet to destroy the metaphysical tradition. No specific references to Herbert. Donne and Chapman are used to illustrate the general concepts.

# 1924

**87. Beresford, John.** "Holy Mr. Herbert," in *Gossip of the Seventeenth and Eighteenth Centuries*, 195–208. London: Richard Cobden-Sanderson.

Reprinted, Freeport, N.Y.: Books for Libraries Press, 1968.
Praises Walton's biography and chides Grierson for being "a little patronizing to George Herbert" (p. 197) in his 1921 anthology. Appreciative biographical sketch with numerous quotations from Walton and from the poems to illustrate Herbert's inner life and spirit. Maintains that Herbert's real genius can be appreciated only by reading the whole of *The Temple*, not by simply reading selected poems.

**88. Davidson, M. B.** "George Herbert and His Poetry." *Canadian Journal of Religious Thought*, July, pp. 290–99.
Appreciative biographical sketch. Contends that "it is not difficult to recount Herbert's sins as a poet" (p. 299): the poems are "overloaded with fantastic figures of speech, with strange conceits, with a love of complicated ornament, with a play on words" (p. 292) and strive for "prettiness rather than beauty" (pp. 292–93). Forgives Herbert for his lack of taste and praises his poems for their "uniformly religious character" (p. 294).

**89. Fausset, Hugh I'Anson.** "The Preacher," in *John Donne: A Study in Discord*, 233–312. London: Jonathan Cape.
Reprinted, New York: Russell and Russell, 1967.
Briefly compares the personalities and religious sensibilities of Herbert and Donne. Maintains that Herbert "was essentially a cultivated, a fastidious spirit, alike in his worldliness and his mysticism, and thus incapable of the barbarism to which Donne descended in search of reality, or of the obscene and violent depths over which he hung" (p. 269). Suggests that in Herbert "the artist predominated, in Donne the scientist; in the one the saint, in the other the seer" (p. 269). Comments briefly on the relationship between the two poets.

**90. Hulley, Lincoln.** "George Herbert," in *Sonnets on the Immortal Bards*, 13. n.p.
Original poem on Herbert.

**91. Legouis, E[mile] and L[ouis] Cazamian.** "La fin de la renaissance (1625– 1660)," in *Histoire de la littérature anglaise*, 511–78. Paris: Librairie Hachette.
Translated into English by Helen Douglas Irvine (New York: Macmillan, 1926). Revised and reprinted many times.
Praises *The Country Parson* for its simple, smooth prose and finds it characteristic of the prose writing of the time. Briefly discusses *The Temple*, "le plus populaire des poèmes anglican" (p. 540), praising Herbert's fervor, sincerity, and subtlety while criticizing his obscurity, fantastic uses of imagery, and lack of taste: "Le goût est sans cesse choqué par lui mais souvent il donne l'impression d'une sorte de sublimité" (p. 540). Claims that of all Donne's disciples, Herbert is most like him.

**92. Nethercot, Arthur H.** "The Reputation of the 'Metaphysical Poets' During the Seventeenth Century." *JEGP* 23:173–98.
Considers separately the reputations of Donne, Cowley, Cleveland, Carew, Herbert, Crashaw, Vaughan, and Quarles during the seventeenth century. Maintains that, although throughout the century "Herbert's admirers and imitators were almost legion" (p. 186), the critics emphasized his piety rather than his poetry. Reproduces the comments of such men as Lord Herbert of Cherbury, Barnabas Oley, Anthony à Wood, the anonymous writer of the preface to Crashaw's *Steps to the Temple*, Vaughan, Thomas Pestil, Fuller, Walton, James Duport (Dean of Peterborough),

Samuel Woodford, Charles Cotton, Edward Phillips, William Winstanley, and Richard Baxter. Lists several imitators, such as Dr. John Bryan, Archbishop Robert Leighton, John Dunton, and others. Discusses Dryden's critical comments on the metaphysicals and gives a brief account of the shifting literary tastes of the Restoration, which account, in part, for the decline of interest in the metaphysical poets.

**93. Whiting, Bartlett J., comp.** "George Herbert," in *Poems of Carew, Suckling, Lovelace and Herbert*, with biographical introductions by Bartlett J. Whiting, 58–64. (Little Blue Book, edited by E. Haldeman-Julius, no. 501.) Girard, Kans.: Haldeman-Julius Co. [ca. 1924].

Includes a general introduction to Herbert's poetry, a biographical sketch, and ten poems from *The Temple*. Praises Herbert for his piety but claims that "all the faults of the metaphysical school are to be found upon his pages; and there as well, we may discover their sturdy and whimsical virtues" (p. 59).

# 1925

**94. Graves, Robert.** "Jekyll and Hyde," in *Poetic Unreason and Other Studies*, 57–77. [London]: Cecil Palmer.

Reprinted, New York: Biblo and Tannen, 1968.

Calls "The Bag" an example of "poetry of the Jekyll and Hyde variety, that is poetry where the manifest content and the latent content represent opposite sides of a conflict" (p. 57). Maintains that the first stanza of the poem and the next two lines come from "the Jekyll life of Herbert the saint" while the remainder of the poem "is a chapter of the Hyde life of Herbert the sinner" (p. 59). Presents an imaginary conversation between Herbert and Donne that supposedly served as the background for Herbert's poem.

**95. Lea, Kathleen M.** "Conceits." *MLR* 20:389–406.

Discusses the nature and development of the conceit and contrasts the Elizabethans and the metaphysicals: "For the most part we may say that the besetting sin of the Elizabethans was the over-emphasis of the simile, the tendency to digress upon the comparison," a fault "corrected by the next generation" (p. 398). Suggests that "the 'metaphysical' poet regarded the simile as useful, not as an ornamental device" and thus "the conceits of their poetry were due to under-emphasis" (p. 398). Contrasts Herbert and Donne: "Herbert was arguing from the physical to the spiritual: Donne, certain of the spiritual experience, was searching for the clearest illustration by which he could communicate it," that "where Donne found poetry too difficult, Herbert found it too easy" (p. 401). Contrasts also Herbert and Vaughan: "Herbert is a moralist, weaving parables: Vaughan is a mystic" (p. 402). Briefly comments on Herbert's simplicity and uses of allegory.

**96. Legouis, Emile.** "George Herbert," in *Dans les sentiers de la renaissance anglaise*, 86–91. Paris: Société anonyme d'édition «Les Belles-Lettres».

Comments on the "alliance singulière de sincerité et de bizarrerie" (p. 86) in Herbert's poetry. Translates into French "The Quip," "The Elixir," and "Death."

**97. Nethercot, Arthur H.** "The Reputation of the 'Metaphysical Poets' During the Age of Johnson and the 'Romantic Revival.'" *SP* 22:81–132.

Surveys critical attitudes toward the metaphysical poets (especially Donne, Carew, Cowley, Cleveland, Crashaw, Herbert, Vaughan, and Quarles) during the later eighteenth century (1744–1800) and the early nineteenth century. Points out that in the eighteenth century the center of discussion was Cowley, rather than Donne or Herbert, and that the notion of a "school of metaphysical poets" was not generally recognized before Johnson. Notes that Johnson does not classify Herbert and Crashaw as metaphysical poets. Surveys Johnson's comments and discusses his importance in shaping critical opinion during the remainder of the eighteenth century. Treats very briefly the interest of the early Romantics in the metaphysical poets.

98. ———. "The Reputation of the 'Metaphysical Poets' During the Age of Pope." *PQ* 4:161–79.
Brief summary of early eighteenth-century attitudes toward the metaphysical poets. Maintains that, "in spite of the wide and continued diffusion of the Metaphysical taste through the early decades of the eighteenth century, readers and critics soon developed the reaction which had been indicated by the later seventeenth century, so that before many years scarcely any one dared admit himself an unswerving admirer of the Metaphysical writers" and notes that many of these were becoming neglected or else forgotten, although the more important ones still retained a reputation for certain qualities or types of work" (p. 176). Points out that three editions of Herbert appeared during the period (1703, 1709, 1711) and that Herbert still was admired by many, primarily for his piety. Refers to the comments of Giles Jacobs, John Dunton, Joseph Warton, Pope, and Addison. Points out that Cowley was the best known of the metaphysical poets, "thus showing that the populace does not always follow the verdict of the professional critics" (p. 177).

99. Praz, Mario. "Richard Crashaw," in *Secentismo e Marinismo in Inghilterra: John Donne—Richard Crashaw*, 143–283. Florence: La Voce. xii, 294p.
Includes a brief contrast between Herbert's rendition of Psalm 23 and Crashaw's paraphrase (pp. 252–53).

100. Stenberg, Theodore T. "Wordsworth's *Happy Warrior* and Herbert's 'Constancy.'" *MLN* 40:252–53.
Points out that both Emerson, in his *Journals*, and E. K. Chambers, in his edition of *Poems of Henry Vaughan*, note that Wordsworth's "Character of a Happy Warrior" is possibly indebted to Herbert's "Constancie," but argues that Wordsworth borrowed only the form, not the subject matter, from Herbert. Disagrees with Chambers's suggestion that Wordsworth also had Vaughan's "Righteousness" in mind.

# 1926

101. Eliot, T. S. "Lectures on the Metaphysical Poetry of the Seventeenth Century with Special Reference to Donne, Crashaw and Cowley delivered at Trinity College, Cambridge." 188p.
Unpublished manuscripts of eight lectures (now at Houghton Library, Harvard University), part of a projected book on the school of Donne. Intended as the first volume of a trilogy on the English Renaissance, detailing (through studies of metaphysical poetry, Elizabethan drama, and the poetical tradition descending from Jon-

son) a disintegration of the English mind. Mentions Herbert throughout, but there is no sustained treatment of him. In Lecture 1 proposes that Dr. Johnson would likely not have included Herbert among the poets that he called "metaphysical." In Lecture 4, primarily on Crashaw, asserts that seventeenth-century devotional poets, including Herbert, generally failed to distinguish between divine and human passion. Claims that Herbert's poetry is less intense than that of Crashaw and St. Teresa of Avila but in its phrasing is generally superior to most of the other devotional poetry of the time. In Lecture 7, primarily focused on Cowley, praises Herbert's ability to mix metaphysical effects into his poems. Quotes line 12 of "Redemption" to illustrate Herbert's ability to compress meaning and compares Herbert favorably with Shakespeare in this matter. Cites lines from "Prayer (I)" to illustrate Herbert's ability to assemble images that do not create a single effect but rather transport readers beyond the borders of thinking.

102. **Newbolt, Henry.** "Some Devotional Poets of the Seventeenth Century," in *Studies in Green and Gray*, 277–88. London, Edinburgh, New York: Thomas Nelson and Sons.

General essay on devotional poetry of the seventeenth century. Contrasts Herbert and Donne and comments on Herbert's influence on Crashaw and Vaughan. Argues that, unlike Donne, Herbert's "aim is not so much to discover, as to exhibit in new ways what he had long known. He had no need to invent a new kind of verse: and his concepts are above all designed to be intelligible—they are examples chosen from familiar life but used with a dexterous twist which makes them attractive and memorable" (p. 280).

# 1927

103. **Gillman, Frederick John.** *The Evolution of the English Hymn: An Historical Survey of the Origins and Development of the Hymns of the Christian Church.* Foreword by Sir H. Walford Davies. London: George Allen & Unwin. 312p.

Briefly discusses the "Herbert group, a family party, linked together by ties of blood or friendship or literary tastes, and presided over by the genial and kindly fisherman, Izaak Walton" (p. 164). Includes Donne, Wotton, Crashaw, Henry King, Nicholas Ferrar, Thomas Ken, Vaughan, and Richard Baxter. Calls Herbert the typical poet of the Anglican Church and refers to his version of Psalm 23 as "a perfect gem" (p. 152). Briefly compares Adam of Brito, a twelfth-century hymnist, to Herbert. Maintains that "Antiphon" is the best hymn among Herbert's lyrics. Comments also on Henry Playford's *Divine Companion* (1701) and John Wesley's *Charlestown Hymn Book* (1737), both of which include adaptations from Herbert.

104. **Herbert, George.** *George Herbert.* Edited by Humbert Wolfe. (The Augustan Books of English Poetry, 2d ser., no. 2.) London: Ernest Benn. 31p.

Anthology containing thirty-three poems with no notes or commentary. Brief introduction stresses Herbert's concept of God as a friend. Calls Herbert's poetry "cool," "silver," "the hautbois in that celestial orchestra" (p. iii).

105. ———. *The Temple. Sacred Poems & Private Ejaculations.* Edited by Francis Meynell. London: Nonesuch Press. x, 213p.

Limited to 1,500 copies.

Prefatory note on the text, the portrait, etc. (pp. v-viii); contents (pp. viii-x); text of the poems (pp. 1–194); bibliographical note by Geoffrey Keynes (pp. 197–202); textual notes with variant readings (pp. 203–13). Prints "for the first time the text of the Bodleian MS., on the ground that it is without doubt the nearest to Herbert's own, if it is not indeed Herbert's own" (p. v). Describes the manuscript and comments on the portrait of Herbert (reproduced) originally in the possession of George Young of Salisbury.

**106. Judson, Alexander Coffin, ed.** *Seventeenth-Century Lyrics.* Edited with short biographies, bibliographies, and notes. Chicago: University of Chicago Press. xix, 412p.

Anthology of fourteen seventeenth-century lyric poets containing 275 poems with modernized spellings. Herbert is represented by 17 poems (pp. 90–102). Biographical sketch provides a setting for each of the poems represented (pp. 302–3), selected bibliography (pp. 303–4), and notes on individual poems (pp. 305–10).

**107. Mann, Cameron.** *A Concordance to the English Poems of George Herbert.* Boston and New York: Houghton Mifflin. xii, 277p.

Reprinted, Folcroft, Pa.: Folcroft Press, 1970, 1977; St. Clair Shores, Mich.: Scholarly Press, 1972, 1979; Norwood, Pa.: Norwood Editions, 1976, 1977, 1978.

Based on Palmer's edition. Covers all the English poems and some of doubtful authorship. Modern spellings. Includes abbreviations for the titles of the poems and a list of words that occur only in titles. In cases of words that can have various grammatical functions, no distinctions are made, but the use of the words is obvious. Does not include all references to articles, prepositions, conjunctions, interjections, and auxiliary verbs, but select passages are given to illustrate each, and the number of times each appears is indicated in parentheses. Example: *bubble*

| | |
|---|---|
| earthly job is but a b. | Van. I, 18 |
| do end in b. s | E. S., I, 14 |
| my soul will turn to b. s | Nat. 9 |

**108. Schelling, Felix E.** "Devotional Poetry in the Reign of Charles I," in *Shakespeare and "Demi-Science": Papers on Elizabethan Topics*, 138–57. Philadelphia: University of Pennsylvania Press.

Briefly contrasts the moral poetry of the Elizabethans with the devotional poetry of the Caroline period and surveys the religious verse of Quarles, Wither, Herbert, Sandys, Crashaw, Herrick, Marvell, and Vaughan. Praises Herbert for "his sincerity, his piety, his rhetorical if somewhat artificial and 'conceited' style and his originality of figure" (p. 146). Contrasts Herbert with Crashaw: "Crashaw turns the passion of earth to worship and identifies the spiritual and material in his devotion; Herbert with all his love of ritual, has somewhat of the Puritan spirit in him, which is troubled in the contemplation of earthly vanities and struggles to rise above and beyond them" (p. 149). Maintains that Herbert is more restrained than Crashaw, more of the craftsman: "But if Herbert has never fallen into Crashaw's extravagances, he is equally incapable of his inspired, rhapsodic flights" (p. 149).

**109. Welby, T. Earle.** "George Herbert at Bemerton." *The Saturday Review* 144:538–39.

Recalls a visit to Salisbury and Bemerton. Comments briefly on Herbert's religious sensibilities and art: "He is very unequal, and in part of his work he forgets that if poetry is to witness to God it can be only through success in an ambition proper to it; but from time to time he writes, perhaps no more than a stanza, never more than a short poem, in which the passion for unity with God is a poetic no less than a religious passion" (p. 539).

# *1928*

110. **Emperor, John Bernard.** "George Herbert," in *The Catullian Influence in English Lyric Poetry, Circa 1600–1650*, 42. (University of Missouri Studies, vol. 3, no. 3.) Columbia: University of Missouri.

Points out that, in contrast to Donne and many others, "no trace of a Catullian influence appears in the poems of George Herbert," and attributes this phenomenon to the "almost wholly religious" nature of Herbert's poetry.

111. **Fehr, Bernhard.** "Die englische Literatur des 17. und 18. Jahrhunderts vom Bürgerkrieg bis zur Vorromantik (mit Einschluss des Bürgerlichen Romans und des Dramas)," in *Die englische Literatur von der Renaissance bis zur Aufklärung*, by Wolfgang Keller and Bernhard Fehr, 117–272. Wildpark-Potsdam: Akademische Verlagsgesellschaft Athenaion.

Biographical sketch of Herbert with some generally negative comments on *The Temple*: "Der Verse sind nur selten schlackenrein. Donnes 'metaphysischer Witz' und leidige Concetti trüben allzu oft den Ausdruck" (p. 136).

112. **Greg, W[alter] W[ilson], ed.** "Edward, Lord Herbert of Cherbury, & George Herbert," in *English Literary Autographs, 1550–1650*. Selected for reproduction and edited by W. W. Greg, in collaboration with J. P. Gibson, Hilary Jenkinson, R. B. McKerrow, A. W. Pollard, pt. 2, *Poets*, XLIX. Oxford: Oxford University Press.

Reprinted, Nendeln: Kraus Reprint, 1968.

Biographical sketches of Edward Herbert and of his brother, George. Briefly describes and comments on an undated letter in Latin from George Herbert to the Bishop of Winchester (British Library MS. Sloane 118, fols. 34–35) and reproduces the signature and postscript (fol. 35a) and the English address (fol. 35b). Maintains that the letter was written in 1626 and that the addressee is Lancelot Andrewes.

113. **Kemp, Violet I.** "Mystic Utterance in Certain English Poets." *Hibbert Journal* 26:474–83.

Discusses the nature of mysticism and the methods of the poet mystics. Argues that "poetry can only be mystical to a certain degree," for "pure mysticism, when the state of union is reached, is mute" (p. 475). Comments briefly on "The Collar" as reflecting the "anguished conflict and discouragement as well as the unavoidable obligation to follow on, in one who has once seen the way" (p. 476). Sees Vaughan and Traherne, among the seventeenth-century poets, as true mystics. Excludes Herbert because "he was too orthodox and good a churchman to be one of the mystics" (p. 481).

114. **Lee, A. H. E.** "English Mystical Poetry." *PoetryR* 19 (October): 321–34.

Discusses the nature of mysticism and its relation to mystical poetry and surveys the work of English mystical poets, including Herbert. Calls the seventeenth century "the golden age of English mystical poetry" (p. 323) and maintains that "very few people are aware that George Herbert was practically the first man to write an English hymn, as compared with the old Church hymns which were all in Latin" (p. 324). Asserts that, together with Crashaw, Herbert should be regarded as "the father of English devotional poetry" (p. 326) and maintains that Herbert is a "moral example to all politically minded parsons" because he "gave up the Court and dreams of a diplomatic career for the greater, though at first lowlier, fame of writing love-lyrics from the soul to God" (p. 325).

**115. Lucas, F. L.** "George Herbert." *Life and Letters* 1:548–61.
Reprinted as "The Poet of Anglicanism," in *Studies French and English* (London: Cassell and Co., 1934), 138–50.
Discusses Herbert as a poet of the Church of England. Biographical sketch and character study, based primarily on Herbert's works and on Walton's biography. Agrees with Coleridge's statement concerning *The Temple*: "To appreciate this volume, it is not enough that the reader possess a cultivated judgement, classical taste, or even poetic sensibility, unless he be likewise a *Christian*, and both a zealous and orthodox, both a devout and *devotional*, Christian. But even this will not suffice. He must be an affectionate and dutiful child of the Church" (p. 549).

**116. Naylor, E. W.** "Three Seventeenth Century Poet-Parsons and Music." *Proceedings of the Musical Association* (London) 54:93–113.
Reprinted in *The Poets and Music* (New York: E. P. Dutton & Co., 1928), 71–83.
Discusses Herbert, Herrick, and Traherne. Comments on Herbert's musical abilities and briefly explicates possible musical allusions and references in "The Pearl," "Easter," and "Prayer (I)." Wonders if Herbert knew the sequences of Notker Balbulus of St. Gall (ninth century), which closely echo Herbert's famous line, "Let all the world in every corner sing, My God and King."

**117. Read, Herbert.** "Poetry and Religion," in *Phases of English Poetry*, 57–82. (Hogarth Lectures on Literature.) London: Hogarth Press.
Reprinted, London: Faber and Faber, 1950.
Maintains that Herbert more than any other of the metaphysical poets "shows how the poetry of metaphysical wit can be transmuted into the poetry of religious experience" (p. 68). Comments on Herbert's uses of domestic imagery and praises his masculine strength. Contrasts him with Crashaw and Vaughan.

**118. Robbie, H. J. L.** "George Herbert." *Church Quarterly Review* 105:359–64.
Biographical account of Herbert, stressing his piety and dedication to the Anglican communion. Sees the poetry as spiritual autobiography. Comments on Herbert's complex uses of form, his "making the form of his verse fit a symbol of his thought" (p. 363). Praises Herbert for ridding his poetry of "fine phrases, glittering metaphors and the classical decorative allusion of his predecessors" (p. 363) and points out his simple diction, love for common things, and successful musical metaphors.

**119. Roberts, R[ichard] Ellis.** "George Herbert," in *Reading for Pleasure and Other Essays*, 170–74. London: Methuen & Co.
2d ed., 1931.
Comments on Herbert's intellectual affinities with Donne: "It is no exaggeration to say that it is to Donne's startling personality that we owe the poetry of Herbert, of Vaughan, of Traherne, of Crashaw, and of Marvell; and while none of them can fetch

so dangerous a course as Donne, nor bring to earth with quite a certain power the very glow and sunshine of eternity, Herbert, in some ways, remains nearest to his master's mind" (pp. 170–71). Calls Herbert "the one poet whose work has done most to make something passionate and extreme out of the religion of the middle way" (p. 172).

**120. Young, Stuart.** *The Shepherds Sing.* Song for Low or Middle Voice, with Obligato Parts for Violin and Harp. New York: H. W. Gray. [7p.]
   Musical setting for lines 15–22 of "Christmas" for voice and piano or organ, with obligato parts for violin and harp.

# *1929*

**121. Coffin, Robert P. Tristram, and Alexander M. Witherspoon, eds.** "George Herbert," in *A Book of Seventeenth-Century Prose,* 251–56. New York: Harcourt, Brace, and Co.
   Revised and expanded into *Seventeenth-Century Prose and Poetry* (entry 313).
   Biographical sketch that praises Herbert's great sanctity and his extraordinary virtues as a model country parson, suggesting that "episodes in his short life remind one of the Gospels" (p. 251). Presents extracts from *A Priest to the Temple* (pp. 252–56) and calls it "a compendium of practical observation that does not depend upon its author's sincerity alone for its power but has an eloquence and wings of its own" (p. 252). Calls Herbert "the Ben Franklin among preachers," "who could discuss the economy of a heavenly city" and "who could sing" and "whose kite brought more than a spark from the sky" (p. 252).

**122. Draper, John W.** *The Funeral Elegy and the Rise of English Romanticism.* New York: New York University Press. xv, 358p.
   Reprinted, New York: Phaeton Press, 1967.
   Refers in several instances to Herbert. Maintains that Herbert "was so utterly imbued with the Catholic tradition of the early seventeenth century English Church that his concept of the grave, like Donne's, is associated, not with bodily dissolution, but with the glory of the beatific vision" and argues that the "strange religious symbolism" of "The Pulley" is "clearly the effect of the pious allegorizing of the *Bible* that had gone on since the time of the Maccabees and that gave authority, *mutatis mutandis*, to a poetry of homely, sometimes perhaps incongruous, symbolism" (p. 35). Contends that Herbert's contemporary influence "was probably far greater than that of Milton" (p. 69).

**123. Fletcher, James M. J.** *George Herbert, A. D. 1593–1633. A Sermon.* Salisbury: Bennett Brothers. [8]p.
   Sermon preached in St. John's Church, Bemerton, on 3 March 1929, that portrays Herbert as a saint and comments on his life as a priest at Bemerton.

**124. Grierson, H. J. C.** "Humanism and the Churches," in *Cross Currents in English Literature of the XVIIth Century; or The World, the Flesh, & the Spirit, Their Actions & Reactions,* 166–231. (The Messenger Lectures on the evolution of civilization, Cornell University, 1926–27.) London: Chatto & Windus.
   Reprinted, 1948, 1951, 1958, 1965; New York: Harper Torchbooks, 1958; Gloucester, Mass.: Peter Smith, 1965; Baltimore: Penguin, 1966.

Comments briefly on the note of Christian humanism struck in Herbert's poetry (pp. 214–18). Calls Herbert the "most characteristic Anglican" of the period, "not in virtue of his doctrine . . . but of his feeling" (p. 215). Argues that Herbert's theme is "Christ's sacrifice, not as a doctrine of substitution and imputed righteousness, but as a history of human goodness and suffering, of how a man who was also God gave his life for erring, ungrateful humanity" (p. 215). Maintains that love in Herbert's poetry is "the centre and circumference of his Christianity . . . the tempered, disciplined, pure and deep yet gentle passion which the spirit in and behind nature awoke in Wordsworth" (p. 215). Argues that Herbert is more like Petrarch and Shakespeare than has been usually noticed, seeing *The Temple* as "the record of God's wooing of the soul of Herbert recorded in the Christian story and the seasons and symbols of the Church, and Herbert's wooing of God, a record of conflict and fluctuating moods" (p. 216). Compares and contrasts Herbert briefly with Vaughan, Donne, Crashaw, Milton, and Bunyan.

**125. Hebel, John William, and Hoyt H. Hudson, eds.** "George Herbert," in *Poetry of the English Renaissance, 1509–1660*, 724–48, 1020–22. New York: F. S. Crofts & Co.
Reprinted several times.
Anthologizes thirty-two poems (pp. 724–48) and presents a biographical sketch of Herbert and notes on the poems (pp. 1020–22). Maintains that Herbert, like Donne, "introduced into his religious poetry an intimate personal note that was scarcely heard among the Elizabethans" (p. 1020). Rejects the notion that Herbert was a mystic and calls him a "poet of the church," who gave "poetic expression to Archbishop Laud's conception of the Church, as exemplifying the 'beauty of holiness'" (p. 1020). Claims that Herbert had a "gift of metrical facility" that sometimes led him "into the over-exercise of ingenuity" but admits that "even in the extreme instances of this one marvels at the excellent fitting of the form to the matter" (p. 1021).

**126. Newbolt, Henry, ed.** *Devotional Poets of the XVIIth Century*. London & Edinburgh: Thomas Nelson. xxi, 293p.
Compares the aims, temperament, and methods of Herbert with those of Donne. Maintains that Donne tried "to find that which seems to him beyond discovery, to express that which was never yet expressed" (p. xiv), whereas Herbert's aim was not so much to discover as it was to exhibit in a new way what he had long known. Contrasts Herbert's simplicity with Donne's more violent temperament: "Herbert, with a less chaotic experience, and less strength of every kind, came nearer to success within his own chosen limits" (p. xiv). Includes thirty-eight of Herbert's poems.

**127. Taggard, Genevieve, ed.** *Circumference: Varieties of Metaphysical Verse, 1456–1928*. New York: Covici Friede. xiii, 236p.
Limited to 1,050 copies.
Anthology of metaphysical poems that includes six poems by Herbert. In part 1 (pp. 3–13) the editor broadly defines metaphysical poetry as primarily reflecting a state of mind. No specific comments on Herbert. Maintains that Donne and Emily Dickinson are the most genuine metaphysical poets in English and that Keats is "the clearest example of what a metaphysical poet is not" (p. 7).

# 1930

**128. Coffin, Robert P. Tristram.** *Laud: Storm Center of Stuart England.* New York: Brentano's. 331p.

Biographical study of William Laud and his times. Mentions Herbert throughout, primarily in contrast to Laud. Views both men as champions of the Anglican cause, each in his own way.

**129. Eliot, T. S.** "Thinking in Verse: A Survey of Early Seventeenth Century Poetry." *The Listener* 3:441–43.

No specific mention of Herbert. Maintains that the "profoundest thought and feeling" of the Elizabethan age "went into its dramatic blank verse" (p. 441) and that "the Elizabethans in their drama are forerunners of the Jacobean and Caroline poets in their lyrical verses" (p. 442). Argues that playwrights, like Chapman, "*think* in verse, rather than *sing* in verse" (p. 441). Calls the seventeenth century "the third most interesting period in the history of Christianity; the others being the early period which saw the development of dogma in the Greek and Latin churches, and the thirteenth century" (p. 442). Comments on the influence of the Counter-Reformation on the arts and literature, especially the importance of St. Ignatius Loyola and the Jesuits, as well as of St. Teresa of Avila and St. John of the Cross.

**130. ————.** "The Devotional Poets of the Seventeenth Century: Donne, Herbert, Crashaw." *The Listener* 3:552–53.

Distinguishes between religious poetry and devotional poetry: "I call 'religious' what is inspired by religious feeling of some kind; and 'devotional' that which is directly about some subject connected with revealed religion" (p. 552). Calls Herbert and Crashaw "devotional" poets and Vaughan "religious." Comments briefly on the wit and the uses of the conceit in "Prayer (I)." Compares and contrasts Herbert with Donne and Crashaw. Remarks about Donne and Herbert: "And if I set myself to imitate either, I think that Herbert might be the more difficult model of the two. There remains his personal quality, and the necessity for saturating oneself in his verse to get it" (p. 553).

**131. Empson, William.** *Seven Types of Ambiguity.* London: Chatto & Windus. 325p.

Reprinted, New York: Harcourt Brace and Co., 1931; Meridian Paperback, 1936.

2d ed., London: Chatto & Windus, 1947; New York: New Directions, 1947.

3d ed., London: Chatto & Windus, 1953; Norfolk, Conn.: New Directions, 1953; New York: Noonday Press (Meridian Books), 1957; New York: New Directions, 1966; Harmondsworth: Penguin Books, 1961; London: Chatto & Windus, 1963; Cleveland: World Publishing Co. (Meridian Books), 1964; New York: New Directions, 1974.

Italian edition: *Sette tipi di ambiguità.* Edizione italiana a cura de Giorgio Melchiori (Turin: Einaudi, 1965).

Defines ambiguity as that which "adds some nuance to the direct statement of prose" (p. 1). Later revises the definition and maintains that ambiguity is "any verbal nuance, however slight, which gives room for alternative reactions to the same piece of language" (p. 1, 2d ed.). In his discussion of the "third type of ambiguity" (when two apparently unconnected meanings are given at the same time), Empson comments on Herbert's use of symbols in "Hope" (pp. 150–58) and discusses "The Pilgrimage" (pp. 163–65), suggesting that it anticipates Bunyan's *Pilgrim's Progress* and "contains both special and general ambiguity of the third type, both pun, allegory, and variety of feeling" (p. 163). In his discussion of the "sixth type of ambiguity" ("when a statement says nothing, by tautology, by contradiction, or by irrelevant statements, if any; so that the reader is forced to invent statements of his own and they are liable to conflict with one another" [p. 223]), briefly comments on the last stanza of "Affliction (I)" (pp. 232–33) and calls the last line of the poem an example of an ambiguity of tautology. Comments rather extensively on the double meanings and apparent contradictions in "The Sacrifice" (pp. 286–95) as an example of the "seventh type of ambiguity" (when one finds complete contradiction, suggesting a division in the author's mind). In his preface to the third edition, Empson somewhat qualifies some of his earlier comments and notes that he regrets his "rather distracting leap into Depth Psychology" (p. xvi), but maintains his original point that in "The Sacrifice" Herbert "felt the paradox of the vengeful God of Love to be an extremely severe strain" and that "in treating a traditional theme, he had to heighten the paradoxes till a reader is forced to wonder whether they will manage to balance" (p. xvi). Firmly maintains, in spite of adverse criticism, that lines 202–3 of "The Sacrifice" ("Man stole the fruit, but I must climb the tree; / The tree of life to all, but onely me") "carry the usual homely quality of Herbert, but present Christ in torment, with ghastly pathos, as an adventurous boy" (p. xvi). See also Rosemond Tuve (entry 369) and William Empson (entry 362).

**132. Hamer, Enid.** "Trochaic Verse," in *The Metres of English Poetry*, 229–58. New York: Macmillan Co.

Brief comments on Herbert's experimentation with trochaic verse in "Discipline" (pp. 238–39).

**133. Jones, Richard Foster, ed.** "George Herbert," in *Seventeenth Century Literature*, 96–101, 396. (Nelson's English Readings, vol. 3.) New York: Thomas Nelson and Sons.

Reprinted, 1930, 1935; New York: Ronald Press, 1936.

Presents a biographical sketch of Herbert and anthologizes "Vertue," "Jordan (II)," "The Quip," "The Collar," and "The Pulley" (pp. 96–101), with notes (p. 396). Maintains that Herbert derived his habit of using "extravagant conceits" from Donne and that he was, in fact, "the channel through which Donne influenced Crashaw" (p. 97). Contends that, although Herbert's "literary qualities are not very great and his range is narrow, he was a careful artist, and his poetry reveals devotional fervour, sincere piety, and intense spiritual conflicts" (p. 97).

**134. Nethercot, Arthur H.** "The Reputation of Native Versus Foreign 'Metaphysical Poets' in England." *MLR* 25:152–64.

Discusses the reputation of Marino, Du Bartas, and Góngora in England: "In the early seventeenth century all three continental poets had considerable weight and authority. They were read, translated, and imitated. By the Restoration all were being severely attacked for excesses of style—whereas the English metaphysicals were yet fairly well entrenched in popular regard. During the age of Pope the foreigners were held in even more contempt than the English, for whom some readers and critics still had a good word to say. During the age of Johnson that dictator's criticisms of the English would seem fulsome encomiums compared to what was being generally said about the foreigners. There was a revival of interest in the English Metaphysicals as a minor aspect of the Romantic Revival. But there was not such a revival for Marino, Du Bartas, and Góngora" (p. 164). Herbert is not specifically mentioned.

**135. Williamson, George.** *The Donne Tradition: A Study in English Poetry from Donne to the Death of Cowley.* Cambridge, Mass.: Harvard University Press; Oxford: University Press. x, 264p.

Reprinted, New York: Noonday Press, 1958 (paperback), 1961; New York: Noonday Press, ed. bound by Peter Smith, 1958; New York: Octagon Books, 1973, 1980.

Maintains that, while the metaphysical poets did not regard themselves as belonging to a particular school of poetry, there was a Donne tradition, although perhaps not sharply defined: "There was no sealed tribe of Donne," but "his influence was the most profound and pervasive of any in the first half of his century" (p. 229). Traces the influence of Donne to the death of Cowley. Chapter 5 traces the sacred line of the tradition in the poetry of Herbert, Crashaw, and Vaughan. Maintains that, "of all the Metaphysicals, Herbert is in some ways most like Donne" (p. 99). Recognizes the individual talent of Herbert and outlines some of the major features of the Donne tradition that shaped Herbert's sensibility and manner. Challenges Palmer's assertion that Herbert "devised the religious love-lyric" and "introduced structure into the short poem" (p. 103): "Rather than give Herbert the emphasis of a pioneer, it is more exact to say that Herbert simply carried on the sacred side of the Donne tradition and developed it in certain ways" (p. 110). Suggests, therefore, that it is "through *The Temple* that the religious side of Donne passed to other poets who reflected his manner of praise even when they forgot his name" (p. 110).

# *1931*

**136. Beachcroft, T. O.** "Mysticism as Criticism." *The Symposium: A Critical Review* 2:208–25.

Dialogue between two fictitious disputants, "Sophister" and "Senior," about the nature of mystical poetry. Briefly mentions Herbert's use of emblems (p. 219). Contrasts the emblematic with the romantic imaginative symbol.

**137. ———.** "Quarles—and the Emblem Habit." *Dublin Review* 188:80–96.

Discusses the nature and function of the emblem and the symbolic habit of mind that it produced and reflected. Maintains that Quarles "was perhaps the first writer of the Theological School to introduce those multiplied images in illustration of a single thought that are so freely used in Crashaw, Herbert, and Donne" (p. 94). Comments briefly on Herbert's various uses of the emblem and maintains that "his basing a whole poem on the chequered floor of his church is as perfect a bodying forth of the emblem habit as could be found, while only the presence of emblems in an acute form could account for the attack of typographical topiary fever even in such a poem of Herbert's as 'Easter Wings'" (pp. 95–96). Mentions also "The Collar," "The Pulley," and "Clasping of hands."

**138. Kitchin, George.** "Jacobean and Later Seventeenth Century Parody and Burlesque," in *A Survey of Burlesque and Parody in English*, 68–98. Edinburgh and London: Oliver and Boyd.

Comments on Herbert's "A Parodie" (pp. 76–77). Maintains inaccurately that the poem is a Christian parody of Donne; it is actually a parody of "Song" ("Soules joy, now I am gone"), which is now attributed to William Herbert, third earl of Pembroke (see Rosemond Tuve, entry 566). Also reproduces a "genuine parody of Herbert's eccentric manner" (p. 77), a poem entitled "Confusion."

**139. Macaulay, Rose.** "Anglican and Puritan," in *Some Religious Elements in English Literature*, 84–126. (Hogarth Lectures on Literature Series, no. 14.) London: Leonard and Virginia Woolf at The Hogarth Press.

Contrasts the Anglican spirit of reserve, dignity, and restraint exemplified by Herbert with the voluptuousness of Catholic devotional poetry of the period. Calls Herbert "the first of the Anglican poets; coloured by and confined within the walls of his Church" (p. 96). Maintains that "The H. Communion" "breathes the very spirit of the Anglican catechism" (p. 98).

**140. White, Helen C.** *English Devotional Literature (Prose), 1600–1640.* (University of Wisconsin Studies in Language and Literature, no. 29.) Madison: University of Wisconsin Press. 307p.

Reprinted, New York: Haskell House, 1966.

Critically surveys Catholic and Protestant books of devotion published between 1600 and 1640 and discusses the historical circumstances from which they arose. Points out that Nicholas Ferrar was the first to translate into English one of the works of Juan de Valdés, his *Cento y diez consideraciones devinas*, "which the enthusiastic approval of George Herbert made popular" (p. 96).

**141. Wolfe, Humbert.** "George Herbert," in *Snow: Poems by Humbert Wolfe*, 49. London: Victor Gollancz.

Original poem on Herbert.

# 1932

**142. Bald, R. C.** *Donne's Influence in English Literature.* Morpeth, Eng.: St. John's College Press. 62p.

Reprinted, Gloucester, Mass.: Peter Smith, 1965.

Discusses Donne's influence on Herbert (pp. 24–28). Calls Herbert "the religious poet whose work was most directly influenced by Donne and whose life presents a certain parallel to his" (p. 24), yet recognizes certain differences as well: "Herbert's wit plays quaintly with the homeliest images, and expresses emotions originally complex in terms that are essentially simple, instead of refining them with Donne's subtle reasonings" (p. 26). Comments on Herbert's serenity, simplicity, subtlety, and especially on his uses of "images more homely even than that of the parables" (p. 25).

**143. Beachcroft, T. O.** "Nicholas Ferrar and George Herbert." *Criterion* 12:24–42.

Discusses Herbert's friendship with Nicholas Ferrar. Calls Herbert a mystical poet and contrasts him with Wordsworth. In Herbert's poetry "the images are not chosen for their emotional so much as for their reasonable equivalence" (p. 38). Contrasts Herbert's sense of a personal God with the more vague position of Wordsworth: "The mind accustomed to speak of religious issues in vague and pretentious generalities will find itself on unfamiliar ground with Herbert: ground where God is not collective unseen forces, spiritual principle, or the power that makes for good" (p. 39). Defends Herbert's style and witty use of words and devices. Maintains that Herbert's simplicity "is the *outcome*, not the lack of a critical and cultured mind, and of a poet's sensibility" (p. 40).

**144. Browne-Wilkinson, Arthur Rupert.** "The Catechism and Children's Worship," in *Liturgy and Worship: A Companion to the Prayer Books of the Anglican Communion*, edited by W. K. Lowther Clarke, with the assistance of Charles Harris, 429–42. New York: Macmillan Co.

Comments on the insistence of Anglican bishops and divines in the seventeenth century on the necessity of catechizing children in preparation for confirmation, a practice in fact very often neglected. Notes that the Puritans, who opposed confirmation, "had the effect, no doubt quite unintentionally, of weakening this system of instruction simply because it was, by the rubrics, devised as a preparation for that rite" (pp. 433–34). Comments briefly on Herbert's endorsement of the practice in *The Country Parson*.

**145. Eliot, T. S.** "Studies in Sanctity: VIII—George Herbert." *Spectator* 148:360–61.

Reprinted in *Spectator's Gallery: Essays, Sketches, Short Stories & Poems from The Spectator 1932*, edited by Peter Fleming and Derek Verschoyle (London: Jonathan Cape, 1933), 286–90.

Laments that Herbert has been generally neglected and often misunderstood: "Whatever Herbert was, he was not the prototype of the clergyman of Dickens' Christmas at Dingley Dell" (p. 361). Maintains that "of all the 'metaphysical' poets Herbert has suffered the most from being read only in anthologies" (p. 361). Comments on the spiritual stamina of *The Temple*: "Throughout there is brain work, and a very high level of intensity; his poetry is definitely an *oeuvre*, to be studied entire" (p. 361). Maintains that only religion could have evoked Herbert's full genius: "It is very rare to find a poet of whom one may say, that his poetic gift would have remained dormant or unfulfilled but for his religious vocation" (p. 361). Compares Herbert to Christina Rossetti and to Donne.

**146. Elton, Oliver.** "Poetry, 1600–1660," in *The English Muse: A Sketch*, 202–31. London: G. Bell and Sons.

Reprinted, 1937, 1950.

Brief survey of Herbert's poetry (pp. 217–19). Calls him "an inveterate quibbler, a too hard driver of his metaphors" (p. 218), but a poet who "has refreshed generations of devout Anglicans" (p. 218).

**147. Friederich, Werner P.** *Spiritualismus und Sensualismus in der englischen Barocklyrik.* (Weiner Beiträge zur englischen Philologie, vol. 57.) Vienna and Leipzig: Wilhelm Braumüller. 303p.

Shows that the term *baroque* is applicable to the English lyrics of the seventeenth century. Views the age as one of polarization, disharmony, and contrasts. Comments on the sensuality and spirituality of the period and on the effects of the conflicts between the two. Comments on specific baroque themes and features of Herbert's poetry, especially the intensity of religious feeling, the theme of the conflict of the soul suspended between hope and despair, the theme of death, the theme of renunciation of the world and of worldly goods, and the theme of the discrepancy between man and God. Considers certain baroque stylistic traits in Herbert's poetry, especially his use of exotic vocabulary in "The Odour" and his playful uses of rhymes in "Paradise."

**148. Hall, Bernard G.** "The 'Jacula Prudentum.'" *TLS*, 21 April, p. 291.

Argues that there is no solid evidence for attributing *Jacula Prudentum* to Herbert, finds the work incompatible with Herbert's wit, and suggests that it be dropped from the canon of his works.

**149. Huxley, Aldous.** *Texts and Pretexts: An Anthology with Commentaries.* New York and London: Harper & Brothers. vii, 322p.

Reprinted frequently.

A portion (p. 13) reprinted in *George Herbert and the Seventeenth-Century Religious Poets: Authoritative Texts/Criticism*, edited by Mario Di Cesare (entry 1140), 233.

References to Herbert throughout. Calls Herbert "the poet of inner weather": "Accurately, in a score of lyrics unexcelled for flawless purity of diction and appositeness of imagery, he has described its changes and interpreted, in terms of a mystical philosophy, their significance" and suggests that "within his limits he achieves a real perfection" (p. 13). Calls "The Collar" "one of the finest [poems] he ever wrote and among the most moving, to my mind, in all our literature" (p. 90). Argues that the real power of the poem is that Herbert's reply, "My Lord," is from "an intimate conviction . . . that the Being who had summoned him was a projection of his most real, his essential self" (p. 90). For a reply, see Mary Butts (entry 210).

**150. Mitchell, W. Fraser.** *English Pulpit Oratory from Andrewes to Tillotson: A Study of Its Literary Aspects.* London: SPCK; New York and Toronto: Macmillan Co. xii, 516p.

Reprinted, New York: Russell & Russell, 1962.

Comments on Herbert's objections to the then-fashionable "metaphysical" style of preaching, to "the total break up of anything approaching a connected prose style and the multiplying of endless divisions, due not to the careful working out of a sound rhetorical plan, but to the caprice and ingenuity of the preachers" (p. 362) as well as to a delight in Latin words and rhetorical ostentation. Points out that in the seventh chapter of *The Country Parson*, Herbert rejects what he calls this "crumbling a text into small parts" (p. 362). Briefly comments on Herbert's popularity among Anglican churchmen, noting that his works, like those of Jeremy Taylor, "have always ranked high among Anglican works of devotion" (p. 242).

**151. Palmer, G[eorge] H[erbert].** "E. C. Lowe's Edition of George Herbert's *Church Porch*." *N&Q* 162:442.

Asks for assistance in obtaining a copy of E. C. Lowe's edition of Herbert's *The Church-Porch*. Points out that Lowe, headmaster at Hurstpierpoint School, reportedly required all boys who entered St. John's School to memorize *The Church-Porch*. Notes that this edition is the only Herbert item that he has been unable to locate. Comments on the Herbert collection at Harvard, which he amassed: "No collection of Herbert equals it in size."

**152. Sharp, Thomas.** "The George Herbert Medlar." *The Gardener's Chronicle* 91:117, 119.

. Describes a medlar tree planted by Herbert in 1632 in the garden at Bemerton rectory. Two photographs. Comments that "a good many pieces of the dead trunk have been taken to America by literary pilgrims" (p. 119).

**153. Smith, Chard Powers.** "Quantitative Rhythms of Sound," in *Pattern and Variation in Poetry*, 112–229. New York: Charles Scribner's Sons.

Brief comparison of "The Collar" with Coventry Patmore's "Farewell" (pp. 192–94). Praises Herbert's poem for its "flashes of greatness" but finds it "irritating for its lack of technical control" (p. 192). Claims that Herbert "never ordered his life, and he never disciplined his talent" and that, "when he blunders into art, he writes greatly," observing, however, that "he seldom does" (p. 193).

**154. Young, G. M.** "Cock-sure." *TLS*, 29 December, p. 989.

Discusses the possible meanings of the term *cocksure* and suggests that it may mean "(objectively) the state of the hay, (subjectively) the state of the mind of the farmer when there is no sign of any break of weather before the hay is cocked." Illustrates this usage with a passage from *The Country Parson*, chap. 30.

# *1933*

**155. Anon.** "George Herbert, 1593–1633." *Cambridge Review* 54:291–93.

Defends Herbert's simplicity, sincerity, unpoetic plainness, uses of puns, and, in particular, his ability to make proverbs, allegories, and myths: "This ability to make myths, even little ones, is the gift which is most lacking in the metaphysicals; and the danger of a too exclusive admiration of their kind of poetry is that it leads to a neglect of this essential part of poetic creation—narrative on a mythological level is the primary, oldest, and most profound poetry" (p. 293). Challenges Dr. Johnson's negative comments about religious poetry and briefly contrasts Herbert with Vaughan and Crashaw. Maintains that Herbert's poems contain "an artlessness which make them more fit for the study of the religious than for the more objective student of poetry" (p. 291).

**156. Anon.** "George Herbert." *TLS*, 2 March, pp. 133–34.

Asks for a reassessment of Herbert as a poet and maintains that he is much less conventional than is popularly thought: "There is not one of our poets whose style is less easy-going, whose sweetness is less mild" (p. 133). Appreciative critical essay that comments briefly on Herbert's major themes, his obscurity and originality, his uses of music and diction, and so forth. Concludes, however, that "we do not read 'The Temple' to-day because it explains the world to us and justifies Providence," but rather "we read it because, in spite of Herbert's belief that he possessed an explanation, he passed through the strenuous and ultimate internal struggle which is imposed on every man, whether religion comes to him as a singular or as a universal mystery" (p. 134). For a reply, see H. Ince Anderton (entry 158).

**157. Anon.** "Parson Herbert: The Saint of Bemerton." *Times* (London), 3 March, pp. 15–16.

Praises Herbert's genuine saintliness: "To follow him through his short life is to discern a character much less simple than the conventional saint, much less melodramatic than the disappointed courtier, and much more worthy than either to be honoured by his Church and his country" (p. 15). Biographical sketch with only general comments on the poetry. Maintains that "it is in the parsonage at Bemerton rather than in 'The Temple' that we must look for George Herbert the Churchman" (p. 16).

**158. Anderton, H. Ince.** "George Herbert." *TLS*, 9 March, p. 167.

In part, a reply to an anonymous article in *TLS* (entry 156). Disagrees with Walton's statement (repeated in the article) that the king gave Herbert a sinecure that fell into his disposal by the death of Richard Parry, Bishop of St. Asaph, noting that "it was the same that Queen Elizabeth had formerly given to her favourite, Sir Philip Sidney." Traces various ecclesiastical benefices and appointments held by Herbert.

**159. Barratt, Kathleen I.** "George Herbert." *TLS*, 2 March, p. 147.

Asks for information on Herbert manuscripts, private letters, early musical settings, and so forth.

**160. Dearmer, Percy, comp.** *Songs of Praise Discussed: A Handbook to the Best-Known Hymns and to Others Recently Introduced.* Compiled by Percy Dearmer with notes on the music by Archibald Jacob. London: Humphrey Milford, Oxford University Press. xxxii, 559p.

Reprinted, London and New York: Oxford University Press, 1952.

Comments briefly on the following hymns adapted from Herbert's poems: (1) "Enrich, Lord, heart, mouth, hands in me" from "Trinitie Sunday" (pp. 219–20); (2) "Come, my way, my truth, my life" from "The Call" (p. 253); (3) "King of glory, King of Peace" from "L'Envoy" (p. 294); (4) "Let all the world in every corner sing" from "Antiphon (I)" (pp. 296–97); (5) "Sweet day, so cool, so calm, so bright" from "Vertue" (p. 345); (6) "Teach me, my God and King" from "The Elixir," giving John Wesley's adaptation (p. 346); (7) "The God of love my shepherd is" from "The 23d Psalme" (p. 347). Comments on music for each hymn, mostly eighteenth-, nineteenth-, and early twentieth-century versions. Includes biographical and historical notes on authors, composers, sources (pp. 376–532).

**161. Fletcher, J. M. J.** *Herbert of Bemerton: Poet and Saint.* n.p. 14p.

Notes from a lecture given on 23 February 1933 at the opening of the George Herbert Exhibition held in Salisbury. First published in the *Salisbury and Winchester Journal* on Friday, 24 February 1933. Primarily an appreciative biographical sketch of Herbert with very brief comments on his poetry. Mentions Wesley's adaptations of Herbert's verse and quotes Phillip Brooks on New England knowledge of Herbert's poems: "I think his lesson is one that we in America need greatly."

**162. Hall, Bernard G.** "The Text of George Herbert." *TLS*, 26 October, p. 731.

Describes and compares the Bodleian and Williams manuscripts. Maintains that the former is the work of the ladies of Little Gidding and that the printers never had Herbert's own manuscript to work from. Argues that the 1633 text is faulty in many respects, shows the difficulties of reconstructing the true text, and suggests several major emendations, based primarily on calligraphy. For a reply, see John Sparrow (entry 170).

**163. Hutchinson, F. E.** "George Herbert: A Tercentenary." *The Nineteenth Century and After* 113:358–68.

Succinct but comprehensive biographical sketch of Herbert. Describes in some detail Herbert's death (1 March 1633) and his burial on Quinquagesima Sunday, 3

March. Maintains that "Holy Mr. Herbert" was not an invention of Walton but can be authenticated by contemporary accounts. Sees Herbert's prolonged struggle toward saintliness as the main clue to understanding *The Temple*.

**164. Masefield, John.** *Words and Verses Spoken in the Garden of Bemerton Rectory, near Salisbury in the Afternoon of Tuesday, June 6th, 1933*. n.p. 38p.

Biographical sketch of Herbert and a general evaluation of his poetry. Praises the sincerity, devotion, and sanctity of Herbert's feelings but sees him as "infested with the thing called Gongorism" (p. 26) and, in comparison with the Elizabethans, as belonging to a "lesser school" (p. 25). Excuses Herbert's excesses and faults, however, by pointing out that they were those of his period. Cites the qualities of Herbert's poetry as (1) "a power of well-felt exhortation based upon personal goodness, temperance, and devotion," (2) "a power of speculation upon divine things, and of drawing to us through it a divine solace," and (3) "a holy man's account of certain cruel spiritual conflicts very deeply felt and therefore moving" (p. 27). Calls *The Church-Porch* "perhaps the best known of his poems" (p. 28). Reproduces selections from Herbert's verse that Judith Masefield, the author's daughter, and Chrystabel Dale Roberts read to the assembled audience after the talk.

**165. Orange, U. M. D.** "The Poetry of George Herbert." *PoetryR* 24:118–27.

Maintains that Herbert, unlike Donne and Marvell, has been generally neglected by modern readers and critics because he is "very much out of temper with the twentieth century" (p. 118). Comments rather unfavorably on some of the general characteristics of metaphysical poetry, especially its uses of conceits, its introspective nature, and its strong individuality. Maintains that Herbert, in spite of some lapses, "is really out of place in this group" (p. 125). Argues that Herbert is most successful when he is less ambitious and less under the influence of Donne. Concludes that Herbert is a great poet in small things: "Repose, commonsense, sanity, a delicate if not profound perception, an instinct both for the fitting and for the dramatic—these are not characteristics which make for great poetry perhaps, but they are associated in the minds of Herbert's readers with comfort and wisdom" (pp. 126–27).

**166. Philip, Adam.** *George Herbert: A Tercentenary Appreciation*. (Lutterworth Papers, no. 18.) London: Lutterworth Press. 16p.

Biographical sketch of Herbert that stresses his piety and his pastoral virtues. Calls *The Temple* "a devotional manual" and maintains that Herbert's poems have a "power" and "evangelical passion that is wanting in Milton" (p. 9). Praises Herbert's tenderness, wit, and humor as reflected in the poems but also finds "a certain stiffness and whimsicality in his work" (p. 13). Maintains that with Herbert "a new era begins" (p. 10).

**167. Pinto, Vivian De Sola.** "George Herbert After Three Hundred Years." *Wessex: An Annual Record of the Movement for a University of Wessex* 2:33–39.

General appreciative account of Herbert's life and works. Calls him "one of the most original, one of the most intensely personal, and one of the most passionate of English poets" (p. 37). Maintains that *The Temple* and *The Country Parson*, taken together, "may be said to contain the finest expression of seventeenth century Anglicanism" (p. 37). Announces a memorial service to be held in Herbert's honor at Bemerton in February 1933 and notes that in June of the same year the poet laureate will visit Bemerton to deliver an address.

**168. Slade, Hilda M.** "The George Herbert Tercentenary." *PoetryR* 24:115–17.
Biographical sketch with general comments on the poetry. Calls *The Temple* a collection of "simple verses."

**169. Smith, James.** "On Metaphysical Poetry." *Scrutiny* 2:222–39.
Reprinted in *Determinations*, edited by F. R. Leavis (London: Chatto & Windus, 1934; rpt. 1970), pp. 10–45; *Shakespearian and Other Essays* (Cambridge: University Press, 1974), 262–78.
Extended definition of metaphysical poetry that attempts to show precisely how it differs from other kinds of poetry that are sometimes closely associated with it. Maintains that the "verse properly called metaphysical is that to which the impulse is given by an overwhelming concern with metaphysical problems; with problems either deriving from, or closely resembling in the nature of their difficulty, the problem of the Many and the One" (p. 228). Discusses the nature of metaphysical poetry primarily in terms of Donne's poetry and contrasts Donne with Dante, Lucretius, Chapman, and others, poets who "wrote metaphysics in poetry, rather than metaphysical poetry" (p. 237). Argues that a distinguishing feature of metaphysical poetry is its particular use of the conceit, noting that in the metaphysical conceit "tension between the elements continues" (p. 234), yet the two elements "can enter into a solid union and, at the same time maintain their separate and warring identity" (p. 234), thereby effecting a union "of things that, though hostile, in reality cry out for association with each other" (p. 235). Mentions Herbert only in passing, but, in the light of his definition, calls Herbert a true metaphysical poet. Maintains that Herbert has much in common with Calderón.

**170. Sparrow, John.** "The Text of George Herbert." *TLS*, 14 December, p. 896.
Reply to Bernard G. Hall (entry 162). Questions Hall's method of correcting the 1633 text and disagrees with six of his suggested emendations.

**171. Squarey, Newell P., and Peter Offer.** "George Herbert at Bemerton." *Times* (London), 3 March, p. 10.
On the occasion of the tercentenary of Herbert's death the churchwardens at Bemerton ask for financial assistance for the parish.

**172. Thomas, Gilbert.** "George Herbert." *ContempR* 143:706–13.
Reprinted (in revised form) in *Builders and Makers: Occasional Studies* (London: Epworth Press, 1944), 17–24.
Appreciative essay on Herbert the man praising his religious sensibility and piety. Maintains that Herbert's hard-won piety is more worthy of remembrance than his art: "His work is not only narrow in artistic range, but is marred by unconscious awkwardness as well as by the deliberate mannerisms" that he "borrowed from the conventions of the hour." Finds that "he has his small, assured place in the best anthologies; but his main appeal is not, in the strict sense, literary" (p. 707).

# 1934

**173. Anon.** "Seventeenth-Century Verse." *TLS*, 1 November, pp. 741–42.
Lead article that is ostensibly a review of *The Oxford Book of Seventeenth Century Verse*, edited by H. J. C. Grierson and G. Bullough (Oxford: Clarendon Press, 1934),

Joan Bennett's *Four Metaphysical Poets* (entry 174), and J. B. Leishman's *The Metaphysical Poets* (entry 178). These books, however, serve primarily as a basis for the reviewer's own comments on the metaphysical poets. Maintains that the seventeenth century was fortunate to be a period between "fashionable" and "professional" poetry: "Poetry had stepped down from Court and out into a wider world" (p. 741), yet it had not become a profession as it would after the Restoration. No detailed discussion of Herbert. Observes, however, that the reader of the *Oxford Book of Seventeenth Century Verse* "will be surprised to find not how much, but how little, of the best verse of the seventeenth century recalls Donne to their minds" (p. 742).

**174. Bennett, Joan.** *Four Metaphysical Poets: Donne, Herbert, Vaughan, Crashaw.* Cambridge: University Press. 135p.

2d ed., 1953; rpt. with corrections, 1957.

Reprinted, "with an anthology of their poetry especially selected for the Vintage edition" (entry 525).

3d ed., with a new chapter on Marvell and title changed to *Five Metaphysical Poets*, 1963; rpt., 1966.

First edition contains seven chapters: (1) Introduction, (2) John Donne, 1573–1631, (3) Donne's Technical Originality, (4) George Herbert, 1593–1633, (5) Henry Vaughan, 1622–1695, (6) Richard Crashaw, 1613?-1649, and (7) Religious Poetry, a Postscript. Short bibliography. In the introduction summarizes the major characteristics of metaphysical poetry and maintains that "the word 'metaphysical' refers to style, not to subject matter; but style reflects an attitude to experience" (p. 3). Argues that "the peculiarity of the metaphysical poets is not that they relate, but that the relations they perceive are more often logical than sensuous or emotional, and that they constantly connect the abstract with the concrete, the remote with the near, and the sublime with the commonplace" (p. 4). Presents a biographical sketch of Herbert and comments that "all his poetry is spiritual autobiography" (p. 58). Surveys the major characteristics of Herbert's individual talent: his uses of dialectic structure, concrete imagery, familiar diction, sound patterns that imitate the rhythms of speech, and his metrical ingenuity and experimentation. Comments on his precision, intellectuality, simplicity, restraint, and playfulness. Maintains that "Herbert, like Donne, was capable of clear thought in conjunction with vehement feeling" (p. 61).

**175. Blunden, Edmund.** "George Herbert's Latin Poems." *E&S* (for 1933) 19:29–39.

Comments on the general neglect of the Latin poetry by English poets and singles out Herbert's Latin poems as worthy of critical attention. Translates several into English, commenting briefly on their interesting features. Expresses particular interest in Herbert's "In Honorem Illustr. D. D. Verulamij, S^ti: Albani." For a reply, see A. Brulé (entry 176).

**176. Brulé, A.** "Un Poème latin de George Herbert." *Revue Anglo-Americaine* 12:49–51.

Reply to Edmund Blunden (entry 175). Disagrees with Blunden's translation of a Latin poem from *Parentalia* ("Ah Mater, quo te deplorem fonte?"). Notes that Blunden claims the poem contains "the oddest figure of a man being mixed with a river to produce *ink* that ever was contrived" (p. 49). Brulé paraphrases the controversial lines and argues that they make perfect sense. Challenges the notion that Herbert's imagery is bizarre, maintaining that its spirit is simply different from the modern: "Mais il était aristocratiquement intelligent, son esprit suit toujours une marche parfaitement ordonnée; il n'aurait jamais condescendu à présenter, comme on le fait de nos jours, une image uniquement pour son étrangeté" (p. 51).

**177. Butt, John.** "Izaak Walton's Methods in Biography." *E&S* (for 1933) 19:67–84.

Surveys Walton's methods and varying aims in *The Lives*. Points out that Walton obtained information on Herbert from Arthur Woodnoth, a friend of both Herbert and Nicholas Ferrar. Calls *The Life of Herbert* Walton's "nearest approach to hagiography" (p. 71) and sees the influence of Barnabas Oley. Maintains that Walton's intention was "to recall the country clergy to a sense of their duty" (p. 71), and thus he keeps his eye always on Herbert's life of holiness at Bemerton. Maintains that Walton points out some of Herbert's weaknesses "because they are part of the truth, but he does not think them important" (p. 84). Comments on Walton's use of *The Temple* and *The Country Parson* as source books, explaining Walton's method of constructing conversations and commenting on episodes of Herbert's life by paraphrasing Herbert's work.

**178. Leishman, J. B.** "George Herbert," in *The Metaphysical Poets: Donne, Herbert, Vaughan, Traherne*, 99–144. Oxford: Clarendon Press.

Reprinted, New York: Russell and Russell, 1963.

Discusses Herbert's poetry within a biographical framework, quoting generously from Walton, *The Country Parson*, and the letters. Praises Herbert's faith ("the extraordinarily intimate and personal nature of his attitude to God" [p. 136]), his general common sense and humor, his technical excellence and originality, his control of form and rhythms ("He is a poet of poems and not, like so many of his contemporaries and predecessors, of passages" [p. 120]), and his impassioned conversational tone. Contrasts Herbert and Donne: "He has not Donne's curious detached interest in ideas for their own sakes, and although there are exceptions, his similes are on the whole less ingenious and remote than Donne's" (p. 120). Sees Herbert as the poet of religious faith and submission and Donne as the poet of religious tension.

**179. Praz, Mario.** *Studi sul concettismo.* Milan: Soc. Ed. La Cultura. viii, 168p.

English version (with revisions and new appendix): *Studies in Seventeenth-Century Imagery*, vol. 1 (entry 239).

2d Italian ed., Florence: G. S. Sansoni, 1946. vi, 321p.

Discusses the importance of emblem books and devices in seventeenth-century literature. See also "The English Emblem Literature" (entry 180).

**180. ———.** "The English Emblem Literature." *ES* 16:129–40.

Discusses English emblem books and compares Herbert's and Quarles's uses of the emblem: "Quarles's wit is all on the surface, gaudy and provincial, without a breath of that devotional spirit which animates the mute emblems of Herbert's *Temple*, or even the *Partheneia Sacra* . . . of the Jesuit Henry Hawkins" (p. 139). This discussion of the emblem is reprinted in *Studi sul concettismo* (entry 179) and in the English version, *Studies in Seventeenth-Century Imagery*, vol. 1 (entry 239).

**181. Sharp, Robert Lathrop.** "The Pejorative Use of *Metaphysical.*" *MLN* 49:503–5.

Traces the changing connotation of the word *metaphysical* from its simple meaning of "above the material world, supersensible, and hence above nature" (p. 504) to its pejorative meaning of "non-sensical." Maintains that both Dryden and Johnson chose the term because they were aware of its pejorative possibilities, "thereby suggesting to their readers not only that Donne, Cowley, and the rest were thoughtful, speculative, and abstract, but that they dealt in notions which, to a neo-classical mind, were incomprehensible, vague, and repugnant to common sense" (p. 505). No specific references to Herbert.

**182. Smith, W. Bradford.** "What Is Metaphysical Poetry?" *SR* 42:261–72.

Maintains that "Metaphysical Poetry is a paradoxical inquiry, imaginative and intellectual, which exhausts, by its use of antithesis and contradiction and unusual imagery, all the possibilities of a given idea." Further explains that "this idea will predominantly be a psychological probing of love, death, or religion as the more important matters of experience in the life of the poet, and will be embodied in striking metaphorical utterance or in the use of the common (familiar) or scientific word" (p. 263). Primarily uses Donne as an example of the definition and only briefly mentions Herbert. Maintains that Marvell's "To his Coy Mistress" is the perfect example of metaphysical poetry. Mentions Emily Dickinson several times as one who, "more than any other except Donne, has faithfully followed the metaphysical muse" (p. 267).

# *1935*

**183. Brooks, Cleanth.** "Three Revolutions in Poetry: I. Metaphor and the Tradition." *SoR* 1 (1935–1936): 151–63.

First in a series of three articles on modern poetry (see also entries 184, 185). Challenges certain modern conservative critics who maintain "the division of the world into poetic and nonpoetic, and the segregation of the intellect from the emotions" (p. 152). Views the modern conceit in a historical perspective. Argues that modern poets are "the restorers of orthodoxy, attempting to bring back into poetry some of the virtues of the School of Donne" (p. 162): "The relation of our moderns to the School of Donne is of the same type as the relation of Wordsworth and Coleridge to the folk ballad" and, "just as an appreciation of the folk ballad went hand in hand with appreciation of Romantic poetry, so an appreciation of our own radicals demands an ability to enjoy the metaphysicals, and involves a revision of our whole conception of poetry, a revision certainly no less radical than that sponsored by the *Lyrical Ballads* in 1798" (pp. 162–63). Stresses the importance of the so-called radical metaphor and argues that Donne's images (such as the compass) are functional, whereas Milton's metaphors and similes are primarily decorative. No specific mention of Herbert.

**184. ———.** "Three Revolutions in Poetry: II. Wit and High Seriousness." *SoR* 1 (1935–1936): 328–38.

Second in a series of three essays on modern poetry (see also entries 183, 185). Argues that "the play of the intellect and the play of wit are not intrinsically incompatible with the poet's seriousness, or with his sincerity in implying to the reader that he means to be taken seriously" (p. 329). Maintains that Herbert and Crashaw, "even when they fail, always impress the reader as being serious," and "they succeed often enough to make their poetry, with that of Donne and Vaughan, the greatest religious poetry which England can claim" (p. 331). Contends that much metaphysical poetry "occupies this shadowy borderline between frankly playful *vers de société* and deeply serious lyric poetry," and points out that it is "most important to notice that the deepening seriousness, when it occurs, is not accompanied by a correspondent lessening of the play of wit" (p. 330). Draws illustrations primarily from Donne, but briefly mentions Herbert.

**185.** ———. "Three Revolutions in Poetry: III. Metaphysical Poetry and the Ivory Tower." *SoR* 1 (1935–1936): 568–83.

Third in a series of three essays on modern poetry (see also entries 183, 184). Defines metaphysical poetry as "a poetry in which the heterogeneity of the materials and the opposition of the impulses united are extreme," or, "if one prefers to base himself directly on Coleridge: it is a poetry in which the poet attempts the reconciliation of opposite or discordant qualities" (p. 570). Challenges those who insist on the didactic function of poetry or on the scientific validity of the poetic statement, especially the Marxists. Agrees with I. A. Richards that "it is never what a poem says that matters, but what it is" (p. 573). Sees a number of modern poets returning to the orthodoxy of the past, especially to the seventeenth century, in an attempt to repair the damage caused by the Age of Reason and the Romantic Movement. Considers Eliot, Tate, Ransom, Crane, Warren, and even Hardy and Yeats in this light. No specific mention of Herbert.

**186. Eliot, T. S.** "Religion and Literature," in *Faith That Illuminates*, edited by V[igo] A[uguste] Demant, 29–54. London: The Centenary Press.

Reprinted in *Essays Ancient and Modern* (London: Faber and Faber, 1936), 93–112.

Public lecture delivered in the Parish Hall of St. John-the-Divine, Richmond, Surrey. Argues for the broad application of ethical and theological standards to all literature, not simply literature with religious subject matter. Discusses briefly the response of most modern readers to "devotional" poetry. Maintains that, for the great majority of people who love poetry, "'*religious* poetry' is a variety of *minor* poetry: the religious poet is not a poet who is treating the whole subject matter of poetry in a religious spirit, but a poet who is dealing with a confined part of this subject matter: who is leaving out what men consider their major passions, and thereby confessing his ignorance of them" (p. 35), adding that "this is the real attitude of most poetry lovers towards such poets as Vaughan, or Southwell, or Crashaw, or George Herbert, or Gerard Hopkins" (p. 36). Explains that "devotional" poetry is, in fact, often the product of limited or special religious awareness and maintains that none of the above-mentioned poets "are great religious poets in the sense in which Dante, or Corneille, or Racine, even in those of their plays which do not touch upon Christian themes, are great Christian religious poets" (p. 36) or "in the sense in which Villon and Baudelaire, with all their imperfections and delinquencies are Christian poets" (pp. 36–37). Concludes that, "since the time of Chaucer, Christian poetry (in the sense in which I shall mean it) has been limited in England almost exclusively to minor poetry" (p. 37).

**187. Herbert, George, trans.** *How to Live for a Hundred Years and Avoid Disease*, by Luigi Cornaro, with an introduction by George Cook. Oxford: The Alden Press. 63p.

In the introduction (pp. 7–31) compares Cornaro's system with modern theories of diet, followed by *A Treatise of Temperance and Sobrietie*, by Luigi Cornaro, translated by Herbert (modern spellings) (pp. 32–51); a letter from a nun of Padua, the granddaughter of Luigi Cornaro (pp. 52–55); *Maxims to Be Observed for the Prolonging of Life* by an unknown seventeenth-century writer (p. 56); and *The Spectator*, no. 195 (Saturday, 13 October 1711), by Addison (pp. 57–63).

**188. Praz, Mario.** Review of *The Oxford Book of Seventeenth Century Verse*, edited by H. J. C. Grierson and G. Bullough (Oxford: Clarendon Press, 1934); *The Metaphysical Poets*, by J. B. Leishman (entry 178); and *Four Metaphysical Poets: Donne, Herbert, Vaughan, Crashaw*, by Joan Bennett (entry 174). *ES* 17:101–5.

Maintains that, once neglected, the metaphysical poets "now risk becoming too popular," notes that the market for additional critical studies of them "has now reached the point of saturation," and asks if, in fact, the metaphysicals "lend themselves to endless investigation like geniuses of the first magnitude" (p. 101). Finds the studies of Leishman and Bennett highly derivative and excessively repetitive of the criticism of Eliot and of Praz himself. Approves of Leishman's rejection of the notion that Herbert was a mild, retiring gentleman and claims that his remarks on Herbert's use of symbols drawn from ordinary life and homely objects are interesting.

**189. Seaton, Ethel.** "Visits and Letters of Scandinavian Scholars," in *Literary Relations of England and Scandinavia in the 17th Century*, 149–201. Oxford: Clarendon Press.

Points out that Olaus Borrichius (Oluf Borch), a Danish medical scholar who visited England in the late seventeenth century, delivered a series of lectures on poets in Copenhagen that were later published as *Dissertationes Academicae de Poetis, Publicis Disputationibus in Regio Hafniensi Lyceo asserte, 1676–81* (1681), and that he lists Herbert in a short survey of recent English poets, including also Sidney, Spenser, Carew, Drayton, Donne, Cowley, and Denham. Notes that the list is "an extraordinary revelation, both in its inclusions and its omissions, of the English poetry known, or known by repute, to a well-informed foreign scholar" (pp. 168–69). Observes that the critical work of Borrichius very quickly found its way to England and influenced critical opinion.

**190. Sharp, Robert Lathrop.** "Observations on Metaphysical Imagery." *SR* 43:464–78.

Stresses the "organic growth of figurative language and the capacity of poets to adjust their imaginations to the resultant new levels of the poetic idiom" (p. 464) and cautions that "the delights of poetry for Donne and the metaphysicals were not wholly what they are for us" (p. 465). Maintains that "no other metaphysical possessed Donne's genius, but they all agreed with Donne that a faster, more efficient rhetoric should be used and that the rhetoric merely of periphrasis and adornment was exhausted" (p. 478). Argues that "because the poetic idiom of the Elizabethans was already a welter of metaphors, with countless variations of the same notion, the poetic necessity of being new and different led the metaphysicals to sensitize their perceptions" and points out that "whereas the Elizabethans began with an idiom on a lower figurative level, the metaphysicals began with the figures of Shakespeare" (p. 470). No specific mention of Herbert.

**191. Smith, Chard Powers.** *Annals Of the Poets: Their Origins, Backgrounds, Private Lives, Habits of Composition, Characters, and Personal Peculiarities.* New York and London: Charles Scribner's Sons. xxv, 523p.

Catalogs miscellaneous information about English poets—their hobbies, pets, friendships, formal education, early domestic attachments, looks and manners, and so forth. Mentions Herbert in sixteen instances. For example, under hobbies, Herbert is listed as enjoying music. He also appears in a list of poets who died between the ages of thirty-one and sixty-one.

**192. Thompson, W. Meredith.** *Der Tod in der englischen Lyrik des siebzehnten Jahrhunderts.* (Sprache und kultur der germanischen und romanischen völker . . . A Anglistische reihe . . . , vol. 20.) Breslau: Priebatsch. viii, 97p.

Discusses various attitudes toward death reflected in seventeenth-century poetry. Contrasts and compares Herbert's orthodox Christian position on death with the positions of Herrick, Donne, and Vaughan. Maintains that the only element of fear in Herbert's view is the possibility of the soul's exclusion from God as a result of sin.

**193. Wild, Friedrich.** "Zum Problem des Barocks in der englischen Dichtung." *Anglia* 59:414–22.

Defines the concept of the baroque for English literature and gives examples of poets and aspects of poetry that might be called baroque. Comments on Herbert's use of the "fantastic conceit" (for example, in "The Pulley") and calls this a baroque feature. Also remarks on Herbert's interior tension ("innere zerrissenheit") as seen in "The Pearl," "The Collar," and "Aaron."

**194. Wright, Herbert G.** "Was George Herbert the Author of *Jacula Prudentum*?" *RES* 11:139–44.

Reviews various arguments in the debate surrounding the authorship of *Jacula Prudentum* and maintains that the collection is the authentic work of Herbert. Presents an account of MS. 5301 E at the National Library of Wales as part of the proof.

# 1936

**195. Blackstone, Bernard.** "A Paper by George Herbert." *TLS*, 15 August, p. 664.

Reproduces a heretofore unpublished paper by Herbert found among the manuscripts in Magdalene College Library and bearing the inscription, written in a Ferrar hand: "Mr Herberts reasons for Arth. Woodenoths Liuing wth Sr Jhon Da[n]uers." Notes that the paper itself is in Herbert's hand and bears no date, and that Arthur Woodnoth, cousin of Nicholas Ferrar and close friend of Herbert, was apparently at the time in the service of Sir John Danvers, Herbert's stepfather. For a reply, see F. E. Hutchinson (entry 202).

**196. Brinkley, Roberta Florence.** "George Herbert," in *English Poetry of the Seventeenth Century*, selected and edited by Roberta Florence Brinkley, 209–33. New York: W. W. Norton & Co.

Expanded ed., 1942.

Brief introduction to Herbert's life and poetry (pp. 209–13), followed by twenty-one selections from *The Temple*, with brief explanatory notes (pp. 213–33). Maintains that "Herbert's character and his inspiration worked together to develop a new literary type, the religious lyric" (p. 209). Finds the main struggle in Herbert's life, fully recorded in his poetry, was that "between the lure of a brilliant public life to which all his natural tastes fitted him and the call of a quiet life of religious service" (p.

211). Briefly contrasts Herbert's religious sensibility with that of Donne and Crashaw: his relationship with God was "very simple and direct and unquestioning," unlike Donne's "fervor" or Crashaw's "ecstasy" (p. 212). Praises Herbert's poems for their superb craftsmanship, their structural unity, their experimentation with verse form, and their simplicity and clarity, but maintains that, for the modern reader, "the spell of the poems lies in their utter sincerity, appealing tenderness, and elevation of common things" (p. 213).

**197. Brittin, Norman A.** "Emerson and the Metaphysical Poets." *AL* 8:1–21.
Discusses the possibility of the influence of the metaphysicals on Emerson and Emerson's appreciation of these poets. Points out Emerson's particular admiration for Herbert. Notes that Emerson mentions Herbert in the *Journals* many times, lists him among his favorite poets (ahead of Shakespeare), mentions him frequently in speeches, and quotes him in *Nature*. Concludes that Emerson's poetry, "not in general, but in numerous individual passages, resembles slightly that of Donne and Cowley, and strongly, that of Herbert and Marvell" (pp. 20–21). See also John C. Broderick (entry 491).

**198. Coleridge, Samuel Taylor.** "Herbert's 'Temple' and Harvey's 'Synagogue,' " in *Coleridge's Miscellaneous Criticism*, edited by Thomas Middleton Raysor, 244–51. Cambridge, Mass.: Harvard University Press.
Reproduces Coleridge's comments on Herbert and Harvey. Calls Herbert a "true poet," but argues that unless the reader "be likewise a *Christian*, and both a zealous and an orthodox, both a devout and a *devotional* Christian" (p. 244), he cannot fully appreciate Herbert's poetry. Maintains that the reader "must be an affectionate and dutiful child of the Church, and from habit, conviction, and a constitutional predisposition to ceremoniousness, in piety as in manners, find her forms and ordinances aids to religion, not sources of formality; for religion is the element in which he [Herbert] lives, and the region in which he moves" (p. 244). Reproduces a letter of December 1818 to Collins in which Coleridge recommends most highly *The Temple*: "I find more substantial comfort now in pious George Herbert's Temple, which I used to read to amuse myself with his quaintness, in short, only to laugh at, than in all poetry since the poems of Milton" (p. 250). Singles out "The Flower" as particularly impressive.

**199. Harper, George McLean.** "George Herbert's Poems." *QR* 267:58–73.
Reprinted in *Literary Appreciations* (New York and Indianapolis: Bobbs-Merrill Co., 1937), 19–45.
Rejects the term *metaphysical poets*, disagrees with the notion of a school of Donne, and suggests that Donne is perhaps overrated in the twentieth century. Praises the excellences of Herbert's verses and sensibility—"the music, the pictorial power, the play of imagination that makes us sharers of his thought and feeling" (p. 62). Calls "The Flower" "the loveliest of Herbert's poems" (p. 67).

**200. Howard, Leon.** Introduction to *Daily Meditations* by Philip Pain, 5–12. (Huntington Library Publications.) San Marino, Calif.: Henry E. Huntington Library and Art Gallery.
Argues that Herbert's influence on Philip Pain's *Daily Meditations* was "direct and pervasive" (p. 8). Observes that more than a half-dozen stanzas in Pain's poem "suggest or echo Herbert more or less definitely" and "yet there is no greater resemblance between Pain's and Herbert's poems in form and phrase than there is in

spirit" (p. 9). Maintains that Herbert was "one of the best known English poets in seventeenth-century America" and that "no other poem published in this country at the time shows any sign of Herbert's poetic influence comparable to that found in Pain's work" (p. 9).

**201. Hutchinson, F. E.** "John Wesley and George Herbert." *London Quarterly and Holborn Review* 161:439–55.
Surveys the extent and nature of John Wesley's attraction to Herbert and, in particular, his adaptations of Herbert's poems for use as hymns. Maintains that during the eighteenth century Wesley "did more than any man to keep alive the knowledge of Herbert's poems" (p. 439). Contends that in adapting Herbert, Wesley not only revised Herbert's intricate metrical schemes to suit existing tunes but also eliminated obscurities, conceits, certain phraseology, remote allusions, and much of the humor: "The thought is Herbert's thought, but the voice is Wesley's voice; . . . sometimes we are surprised to find how completely the language and tone of the eighteenth century have imposed themselves on Herbert's verse" (p. 453).

**202.** ———. "A Paper by George Herbert." *TLS*, 22 August, p. 680.
Reply to Bernard Blackstone (entry 195), who announced the discovery of an unpublished paper in Herbert's hand addressed to Arthur Woodnoth. Points out that the paper clarifies a reference in Walton that Woodnoth "was a useful Friend of Mr. Herberts Father." Argues that the reference is to Herbert's stepfather, Sir John Danvers, not to his natural father. Marshals support for Blackstone's suggestion that the paper was written after 1628 and points out characteristics that are typical of Herbert.

**203. Olivero, Federico.** "Scuola metafisica," in *Lirica religiosa inglese*, 230–78. Turin: S. Lattes & Co.
Expanded version, Turin: Società Editrice Internazionale, 1941, 2:111–207.
Biographical sketch followed by general critical evaluation of Herbert's poetry. Calls *The Temple* "la descrizione simbolica di una chiesa" (p. 242) and comments on its emblematic imagery: "Questo emblematismo ci ricorda poeti medievali; supremo in Dante" (p. 242). Argues that Herbert "ricerca e scruta i più profondi recessi della coscienza, percorre le vie sotterranee del cuore; ne risulta una poesia analitica, concentrata in immagini che sono sintesi di stati d'animo e di sentimenti. Tuttavia le sue figure hanno una certa freddezza, un intellettualismo che le irrigidisce; mancano dell'ardore di quelle del Crashaw, sono pensate con sottigliezza, non *viste* come apparizioni eterne nell'esaltazione mistica del poeta cattolico. In lui, come nel Donne, impreviste associazioni di idee sono la base della sua arte. È curioso il contrasto, in tutta la sua opera, fra un linguaggio semplice e bizzarri tropi,—una dizione sottile e cavilosa ed una limpida grazia,—una strana ingegnosità di fantasia ed una semplicità spontanea del sentire" (p. 242).

**204. Pickel, Margaret Barnard.** "Other Royal Poets," in *Charles I as Patron of Poetry and Drama*, 69–94. London: Frederick Muller.
Surveys Charles I's patronage of various poets and dramatists and mentions Herbert briefly (pp. 74–75). Points out that Herbert's poems were part of the well-used library that consoled the king at Carisbrooke.

**205. Pulsford, Daniel B.** "The Passion and the Poets: Devotional Poets of [the] Seventeenth Century." *Sign* 15:505–7.

General introduction to Herbert, Vaughan, and Crashaw as devotional poets stressing that, although their religious poems are "quaintly pretty" and "have a fascinating exotic quality" (p. 505), they never achieve the grandeur and genius of Milton's poems. Maintains that all three poets were reacting against Puritanism and calls Herbert the best example of the "Cavalier pietists" (p. 505). Quotes lines from "The Sacrifice" to illustrate Herbert's style, especially his use of comparisons, "which are often felicitous and strike an unexpected note" (p. 505) but should be seen as an example of wit rather than of great poetry.

**206. Warren, Austin.** "George Herbert." *American Review* 7:249–71.
Reprinted in revised form in *Rage for Order: Essays in Criticism* (Chicago: University of Chicago Press, 1948; rpt. London and Ann Arbor: University of Michigan Press, 1959), 19–36.
Critical evaluation of Herbert's poetry with a biographical sketch. Explores Herbert's Anglican spirit, his sensibility, and his themes. Comments on his use of shaped verse and stanzaic experimentation: "Herbert's ingenuities proceed from a principle which is analogous to onomatopoeia and as readily apprehended: that adaptation of form to sense, or structure to theme" (p. 263). Finds that "in Herbert's stanzaic invention and precision of craftsmanship he shows the survival of his temperamental fastidiousness; he also, wittingly or not, creates that tension between inner struggle and outer neatness which gives living distinction to his poetry" (p. 264). Discusses the revival of metaphysical poetry and maintains that Donne's influence on Herbert was more personal than literary: "Herbert's nature had neither the complexity nor the intensity of Donne's, and these temperamental differences, together with Herbert's artistic sincerity, make difficult any attempt to trace palpable derivations" (p. 271).

**207. Watkins, W. B. C.** "Spenser to the Restoration (1579–1660)," in *Johnson and English Poetry Before 1660,* 58–84. (Princeton Studies in English, no. 13.) Princeton: Princeton University Press; London: Oxford University Press.
Comments on Dr. Johnson's slight acquaintance with Herbert's poetry. Points out that Johnson quotes Herbert only five times in the *Dictionary*.

**208. White, Helen C.** *The Metaphysical Poets: A Study in Religious Experience.* New York: Macmillan Co. ix, 444p.
Reprinted, 1956, 1962 (Collier Books), 1966.
Studies Donne, Herbert, Crashaw, Vaughan, and Traherne. In the introduction discusses how mysticism and poetry are alike and how they differ. Concludes that, although none of the poets discussed are genuine mystics in the strict sense of the word, all, to varying degrees, evidence elements of mysticism in their poetry. Chapter 1, "The Intellectual Climate"; chapter 2, "The Religious Climate"; and chapter 3, "Metaphysical Poetry," set up the necessary background and generalities as a framework for the discussion of the individual poets (two chapters to each poet). Chapter 6, "George Herbert and the Road to Bemerton" (pp. 150–75), presents a sketch of Herbert's life and a discussion of his religious temperament and intellectual sensibilities. Maintains that Herbert's essentially mystical aspiration gave to his ministry "its distinctive character and accounts for the peculiar effect it has exercised upon all who have come in contact with it, whether by actual experience or by report" (p. 165). Sees Herbert's poems as primarily reflections of his inner life, as "intensely and fully self-revelatory verse" (p. 166). Challenges Palmer's arrangement of the poems and concludes that the organization of the 1633 edition is metaphysical and that the symbol of the temple is capable of several references. Chapter 7, "George Herbert and

*The Temple"* (pp. 176–210), discusses the particulars of Herbert's religious sensibilities and attitudes as reflected in his poetry, such as the nature of his faith, his conception of God, the note of intimacy of feeling in his poetry, and his quiet confidence. Finds this last quality to be "the most persistent and central thing in Herbert's religious consciousness and the source of the peculiar power of his verse" (p. 189). Contrasts Herbert with Donne. In the conclusion presents a series of contrasts and comparisons among the five poets.

**209. Williamson, George.** "Senecan Style in the Seventeenth Century." *PQ* 15:321–51.

Traces the development of Senecan prose style during the seventeenth century and reproduces two brief comments on preaching style from *The Country Parson.* Argues that Herbert disliked the method of "crumbling the text into small parts" and therefore he "anticipates the method of Tillotson and condemns that of Andrewes, in which Donne was a lesser offender" (p. 335). Maintains that, although Herbert criticized witty preaching, he "reveals the profit to be derived from Senecan brevity" (p. 335).

# *1937*

**210. Butts, Mary.** "The Heresy Game." *The Spectator* 158:466–67.

Reply to Aldous Huxley, who, in *Texts and Pretexts: An Anthology with Commentaries* (entry 149), argued that "The Collar" has great appeal to the modern reader primarily because "the tragedy of the poem lay in Herbert's self-deception: that he was calling out when there was none to hear; that the tragedy meets out tragedy" (p. 466). Calls Huxley's interpretation "as pure a specimen of wish-fulfillment as one could hope to find" (p. 467).

**211. Harrison, Archibald W.** "Arminianism in England," in *Arminianism*, 122–56. London: Duckworth.

Outlines the Arminian controversy that began in England after the visit of Grotius to London in 1613. Comments briefly on Herbert's allegiance in the controversy. Maintains that both Herbert and Nicholas Ferrar "would be classed as Arminians in the phraseology of the period" (p. 142). Comments also on Herbert's loyalty to the Church of England and maintains that "the breadth of his charity could not be confined to the formulas of Geneva" (p. 143).

**212. Johnson, Thomas H.** "Edward Taylor: A Puritan 'Sacred Poet.'" *NEQ* 10:290–322.

Comments on the influence of Herbert on the poetry of Edward Taylor and maintains that Herbert's example and influence were "paramount" (p. 319). Points out that several of Taylor's poems reproduce exact stanzaic patterns from *The Temple.* Finds especially noteworthy Taylor's use of the six-line iambic pentameter rhyming *a b a b c c*, the form of Herbert's *The Church-Porch.* Maintains that the example of Herbert is also seen in Taylor's "holy aspiration, his devotional rather than mystical qualities, his homely comparisons, his intimate appeal to the person of Christ" (p. 318). Notes that both Taylor and Herbert employ many of "the same rhetorical devices of question, refrain, apostrophe, and direct address; there is especially an observable correspondence in the length of their songs" (p. 318).

**213. Jones, Thomas S., Jr.** "George Herbert," in *Shadow of the Perfect Rose: Collected Poems of Thomas S. Jones, Jr.*, with a memoir and notes by John L. Foley, 147. New York: Farrar & Rinehart.

Original sonnet on Herbert.

**214. Luke, Stanley.** "An Old Handbook on the Pastoral Office." *The London Quarterly and Holborn Review* 162:198–206.

Appreciative essay on various themes in *The Country Parson*, consisting primarily of many quotations from the work with an approving commentary. Presents the book as a manual of devotion appropriate for modern clergymen: "It has not a little which is of practical positive value for the conduct of a ministry in this day and a minister who absorbs its spirit and captures its mood will work not only with better heart but to better purpose" (p. 206).

**215. Marks, Harvey B.** "English Psalmody and Early English Hymnody," in *The Rise and Growth of English Hymnody*, 77–92. New York: Fleming H. Revell Co.

Brief comments on Herbert's life and his contribution to the development of the sacred lyric. Points out that *The Canadian Presbyterian Book of Praise* includes "Throw away Thy rod," a musical adaptation of "Discipline." Praises in particular "The Pilgrimage," "having but six stanzas, with its lines so full of thought that it contains the whole substance of Bunyan's 'Pilgrim's Progress'" (p. 88).

**216. N., C. L.** "Mr. Woodnot." *N&Q* 172:32.

Asks if the Mr. Woodnot who Walton says attended Herbert on his deathbed was Theophilius Woodnote (d. 1662). For a reply, see Wasey Sterry (entry 220).

**217. Phillips, C. S.** *Hymnody Past and Present.* London: SPCK; New York: Macmillan Co. x, 300p.

Laments that most of Herbert's poems were not written to be sung in church: "Most of them are unsuited to the purpose by reason of the elaborate and fantastic imagery which Herbert shared with the other poets of his time, and also on account of their peculiar metres" (p. 156). Maintains that Herbert "perfectly expresses the characteristic Anglican mentality at its best" (p. 156) and lists several of his poems that have come into use as hymns. Comments briefly on Henry Playford's *The Divine Companion* (1701), which included hymns by Herbert, and on John Wesley's *Collection of Psalms and Hymns* (1737), which also included adaptations from *The Temple*.

**218. Roberts, Michael.** "The Seventeenth Century—Metaphysical Poets and the Cambridge Platonists," in *The Modern Mind*, 88–117. New York: Macmillan Co.

General treatment of Herbert's attitude toward science. Notes that Herbert's poetry includes a number of images drawn from contemporary scientific discoveries and from the new astronomy and new mechanics but finds that in Herbert's poetry there is no real conflict with science. Maintains that Herbert's process in his poetry is exactly the opposite of that of science. For example, sees "Prayer (I)" as "a simile in which the feelings, not the measurements, are asserted to be congruent, and it deliberately uses a method which is not the method of science" (pp. 91–92).

**219. Schirmer, Walter F[ranz].** "Donne und die religiose metaphysische Dichtung," in *Geschichte der englischen Literatur von den Anfängen bis zur Gegenwart*, 297–308. Halle (Saale): Max Niemeyer Verlag.

2d ed., 1954.

Discusses the nature of metaphysical style and sensibility and maintains that they reflect the tension created by the breakdown of the old world view. Presents a general survey and critical evaluation of Herbert's poetry (pp. 299–301). Comments on the religious attitudes and sensibility expressed in Herbert's poetry and praises in particular his simplicity and his ability to address God with the familiarity of a lover. Notes the musical quality of Herbert's verse, his restraint, his use of natural diction and homely imagery, and his development of complex stanzaic patterns. Regards *The Temple* as a spiritual autobiography and suggests that Herbert wrote poems because he was unable to express his deepest thoughts and spiritual conflicts in his sermons. Maintains that the main charm of Herbert's poetry is its ability to present convincingly the struggle for human freedom. Compares and contrasts Herbert and Donne, emphasizing the differences in their spiritual temperaments.

**220. Sterry, Wasey.** "Mr. Woodnot." *N&Q* 172:105.

Reply to C. L. N. (entry 216). Argues that the Mr. Woodnot who Walton says attended Herbert on his deathbed is Theophilius Woodnote (d. 1662), first cousin of Nicholas Ferrar.

# *1938*

**221. Anon.** "Devotional Poetry: Donne to Wesley: The Search for an Unknown Eden." *TLS*, 24 December, pp. 814, 816.

Maintains that "religious verse is seldom the statement of assured belief but more often the passionate protestation of a mind that wishes to believe and believes and doubts again" (p. 814). Concludes that the periods most prolific of devotional masterpieces are those in which a certain body of religious faith is counterbalanced by a definite strain of inquietude" (p. 814). Contrasts Donne's "turbulent mysticism" with Herbert's "calm and collected piety" and maintains that Herbert is "a more accomplished technician though a lesser poet" (p. 814): "For Donne, God is the stern taskmaster, the supreme enigma; for Herbert, the welcome guest and familiar friend, a projection of the subtlety and charm of his own intelligence" (p. 814).

**222. Anon.** "Mr. T. S. Eliot on 'George Herbert.' " *The Salisbury and Winchester Journal*, 27 May.

Report of a lecture on Herbert and his poetry delivered by Eliot at the Chapter House of Salisbury Cathedral on Wednesday, 25 May 1938. Reports that Eliot said: "I have been reading the poetry of Herbert's period, over a long enough span of years to be able to observe a considerable development in my own appreciation and judgment. It is not only greater familiarity, but, I hope, greater maturity of mind and sensibility—for sensibility as well as intelligence should mature—which has brought me to concede to Herbert as a religious poet a pre-eminence among his contemporaries and followers. I am, therefore, at the stage of asking for a revision of his reputation; feeling, as I do, that he has not been so much critically as implicitly underrated." Notes Coleridge's appreciation of Herbert, calls Herbert "*the* poet of

Anglicanism," and finds Herbert as a religious poet superior to Donne. Maintains that Herbert "is the most intellectual of all our religious poets" and that he uses "the language of ordinary speech" but with "a classical purity and directness." Rejects the notion that Herbert was a "kindly silver-haired but rather mild and feeble country parson who might figure in one of the more sentimental tales of Dickens" and argues that Herbert "was a tough man in a tough age." Maintains that the only other poet in the same class with Herbert is St. John of the Cross, although the two men are different. Observes that we know Herbert "in his poetry and not through his poetry" and that Herbert achieved "the greatest universality in his art; he remains as the human soul contemplating the divine."

**223. Black, Matthew W., ed.** "The Devotional Lyricists," in *Elizabethan and Seventeenth-Century Lyrics*, 479–530. Chicago: J. B. Lippincott Co.

General introduction to the devotional lyric of the seventeenth century. Sees Herbert as Donne's disciple and maintains that "like Donne he can unite strong feeling with clarity of thought; but his mind is far less complex and his conceits are neither extended nor subtle" (p. 482). Calls Herbert's use of acrostics, anagrams, and shaped verse naive and puerile. Briefly compares Herbert to Crashaw, Vaughan, and Traherne and anthologizes fourteen of Herbert's poems (pp. 494–503).

**224. Blackstone, Bernard, ed.** *The Ferrar Papers; containing a life of Nicholas Ferrar; the Winding-sheet, an ascetic dialogue; a collection of short moral histories; a selection of family letters.* Cambridge: University Press. xxii, 323p.

Many references throughout to Herbert. The *Life of Nicholas Ferrar* here presented is "a composite of the surviving manuscript accounts, each of which derives ultimately from the original *Life* by John Ferrar" (p. xvii). The *Life* includes many references to Herbert: notes Herbert's approval of the night watches established at Little Gidding (p. 55); recounts the friendship of Ferrar and Herbert (pp. 58–60); and reproduces two letters from Herbert to Ferrar (pp. 77–79). Also reproduces two letters about Herbert from Arthur Woodnoth to Ferrar (pp. 266–69, 276– 77) and prints a newly discovered Herbert document (pp. 269–70), including a facsimile in Herbert's own hand of the first page (reduced) of the paper. This document is entitled "Mr Herberts reasons for Arth. Woodenoths Liuing wth Sr Jhon Da[n]uers" and was first published by Blackstone in *TLS* (entry 195).

**225. Bohannon, Mary Elizabeth.** "A London Bookseller's Bill: 1635–1639." *Library* ser. 4, 18:417–46.

Reproduces and comments on a nineteenth-century transcription of a book bill (extending from 16 December 1635 to 19 December 1639) sent by Richard Whitaker, a London bookseller, to Sir Thomas Barrington of Hatfield Broad Oaks, Essex, a well-known and influential Puritan. Lists the 4th edition of *The Temple* (1635) under the date 20 December 1637.

**226. Flower, Desmond, and A. N. L. Munby.** *English Poetical Autographs: A Collection of Facsimiles of Autograph Poems from Sir Thomas Wyat [sic] to Rupert Brooke.* London, Toronto, Melbourne, and Sydney: Cassell and Co. [62], 25p.

Limited to 1,500 copies.

Includes a facsimile of "The Elixir" (originally entitled "Perfection") from the Williams Library manuscript, with a transcription (p. 3). In the notes (pp. 16–17), points out that the English poems in the manuscript are by an unidentified hand but corrected by Herbert whereas the Latin poems are wholly in Herbert's hand. Notes that the substituted last verse of "The Elixir" is Herbert's autograph. Briefly comments on the transmission of the manuscript.

**227. Ford, Ford Madox.** *The March of Literature: From Confucius' Day to Our Own.* New York: Dial Press. vii, 878p.

Scattered references to Herbert throughout. Calls Herbert, Donne, Crashaw, Marvell, Vaughan, and Dryden "the most English of all writers" and maintains that "if there is any sustained beauty in the Anglo-Saxon soul it was they who proved its existence" (p. 477). Maintains that the last two lines of "Love (III)" "enshrine the very essence . . . of that so-called metaphysical poetic age" (p. 482). Contends that Herbert strikes a "Petrarchist-Christist" note not sounded again until Christina Rossetti.

**228. Hayes, Albert McHarg.** "Counterpoint in Herbert." *SP* 35:43–60.

Reprinted in *Essential Articles for the Study of George Herbert's Poetry*, edited by John R. Roberts (entry 1216), 283–97.

Comments in detail on Herbert's technical excellence and stanzaic experimentation: "The cause of this great variety in stanzas lies partly in Herbert's desire to make the outward form of each poem representative of its inner meaning" (p. 44). Discusses Herbert's theory and practice of versification: "Clearness and exactness were his aims; simplicity, his art" (p. 46). Discusses "counterpoint," his term for Herbert's major device for focusing attention on the sense of a poem rather than on its sound by constructing the pattern of line lengths independently of the pattern of rhymes and thus defeating "the excessive expectation of rime by making its position unpredictable" (p. 48). Suggests that Herbert may have gotten the idea of counterpoint from Donne and/or Puttenham's *Arte of English Poesie*. Divides Herbert's 127 stanzaic poems into seven major types: (1) harmonic stanzas, (2) approximately harmonic stanzas, (3) isometrical stanzas, (4) approximately contrapuntal stanzas, (5) contrapuntal stanzas, (6) off-balance stanzas, and (7) irregular stanzas. Points out that "half the poems (63) fall into the first three classifications, which are the normal pattern of English lyrics, and half (64) into the last four, the experimental types" (pp. 53–54). Comments on Herbert's love of and knowledge of music. Includes two tables of stanzaic types in order to compare Herbert with other major poets.

**229. Hutchinson, F. E.** "George Herbert," in *Seventeenth Century Studies Presented to Sir Herbert Grierson*, 148–60. Oxford: Clarendon Press.

Reprinted, New York: Octagon Books, 1967.

Comments on Herbert's fluctuating reputation during the past three centuries. Surveys the manuscript tradition of the poems and seriously questions the assumptions of Palmer, especially his attempt to arrange the poems in a chronological order based on his biographical interpretations. Presents a brief character sketch of Herbert, based partly on early biographical accounts and partly on themes and attitudes found in the poetry. Maintains that Herbert's principal temptation was ambition but that out of his many spiritual conflicts "he made music" (p. 155). Sees the tension and conflict in Herbert's soul "as exceptionally good material for a religious poet" and maintains that they are "the staple elements of the larger part of *The Temple*" (p. 156). Comments on Herbert's art and maintains that his imagery "grows naturally out of the idea of a poem and can therefore be developed without giving a sense of artificiality" (p. 156). Discusses Herbert's skill in choosing verse forms that match his subject, his ability to use plain words found in ordinary speech with natural dignity, his love for homely and proverbial material, and his complex simplicity of diction.

Discusses in particular "The Agonie" as an example of Herbert's artistry, to show how "out of familiar material, as old as the Christian religion, Herbert builds up a closely knit poem and makes his points with surprising freshness and force" (p. 159). Argues that, although Herbert did not invent the English religious lyric, "in his hands the religious lyric has travelled far beyond the dreary Scriptural paraphrases and obvious moralizings of the Elizabethan versifiers" (p. 160).

**230. May, G. L.** *George Herbert.* (Little Books on Religion, no. 141.) London: SPCK. 32p.

Biographical sketch that stresses Herbert's sanctity. Comments on the poems as autobiographical statements. Maintains that "it is a pity that much of Herbert's poetry loses its charm for us through the artificiality so loved by his age" (p. 15) but concedes that the piety of his poetry more than atones for his faults as a poet.

**231. Maycock, A. L.** *Nicholas Ferrar of Little Gidding.* London: SPCK. xiii, 322p.

Reprinted, 1963 (paperback); Grand Rapids, Mich.: Eerdmans, 1980.

Many references to Herbert throughout. Briefly surveys the friendship of Herbert and Ferrar (pp. 233–35): "It was a friendship springing from complete spiritual harmony" (p. 233) that "set its mark upon English spirituality for a hundred years or more" (p. 234). Notes that Herbert was consulted in the planning of the night watches at Little Gidding and that his opinion was sought in drawing up the famous inscription that was hung in the parlor at Little Gidding. Points out that, although the two met as undergraduates at Cambridge, they apparently never met thereafter, but sustained their friendship through correspondence and mutual friends, especially Arthur Woodnoth and Edmund Duncon.

**232. Meyer, Gerard Previn.** "The Blackamoor and Her Love." *PQ* 17:371–76.

Argues that Henry Rainolds's famous poem, "A Black-moor Maid wooing a fair Boy," is a capricious translation of Herbert's Latin poem, "Aethiopissa ambit Cestum Diuersi Coloris Virum," which the author calls Herbert's "only poem of human love" (p. 371). Notes that Rainolds's poem first appeared in an edition of Bishop Henry King's poems (1647) and occasioned a reply by King entitled "The Boys Answer to the Blackmoor." Maintains that Herbert's poem also inspired a poem by John Cleveland entitled "A Fair Nymph Scorning a Black Boy courting Her." For a reply, see Cornelia C. Coulter (entry 236).

**233. Rohr-Sauer, Philipp von.** "Poetry of the Baroque Tradition," in *English Metrical Psalms from 1600 to 1660,* 80–103. Freiburg: Universitätsdruckerei Poppen & Ortmann.

Calls Herbert's metrical translations of the twenty-third psalm and of Psalms 1–7 "somewhat of a disappointment" (p. 89) and maintains that Vaughan's renderings are clearly superior. Blames Herbert's mediocrity primarily on his choice of verse form and describes his translations as "thoroughly literal" (p. 101). Notes that Herbert's source was obviously the King James version and that he was influenced by the Sternhold and Hopkins tradition. Maintains that Herbert is "the only baroque poet who translates psalms in the light of the New Testament" (p. 91), noting, for instance, his use of references to the Trinity. Stresses that Herbert, as a psalmist, stands outside the early seventeenth-century tradition. Briefly contrasts Herbert to Vaughan and Crashaw and compares him to Carew.

**234. Untermeyer, Louis.** "The Religious Conceit: Play for God's Sake," in *Play in Poetry,* 27–51. New York: Harcourt, Brace & Co.

Comments on the variety and seriousness of play in Herbert's poetry: "It is not an irresponsible playfulness, but a mixture of play and passion which allows Herbert to embody his most profound thoughts in anagrams and acrostics, shaped whimsies and puns" (p. 28). Comments specifically on the wit of "Jesu," "Anagram of the Virgin Marie," "The Altar," "Coloss.iii.3," "Paradise," "Heaven," "Man," "Aaron," "Artillerie," "Discipline," "The Collar," and "The Pulley." Contrasts Herbert's playfulness with Crashaw's: "Crashaw pushed his comparisons further than they could bear to go, and thus made his metaphors not only incongruous, but unpleasantly comic" (p. 38). Maintains that the poetry of Emily Dickinson represents "the continuation, possibly the culmination, of the strain begun by Donne and Herbert: the mingling of rapture and irreverence which makes death a playmate and God a playfellow" (p. 51).

# *1939*

**235. Brown, B. Goulding.** "Place." *TLS*, 8 July, p. 406.
Response to R. F. Rattray's query in *TLS* (entry 240) on Herbert's use of the phrase *great places* in *The Church-Porch* (line 327). See also J. Middleton Murry (entry 238).

**236. Coulter, Cornelia C.** "A Possible Classical Source for The Blackamoor Maid." *PQ* 18:409–10.
In part a reply to Gerard Previn Meyer (entry 232). Maintains that the theme of the blackamoor maid in Herbert's "Aethiopissa ambit Cestum Diuersi Coloris Virum" may have been anticipated in two passages in Vergil's *Eclogues* (2, vv. 14–18 and 100, vv. 33–41), where the Latin poet carries on the motif of the despised lovers developed by Theocritus. Concludes that "it is quite conceivable that these two Vergilian passages, coupled with a hint from the Song of Songs, may have suggested to George Herbert the idea of featuring an Ethiopian maid in the rôle of the despised lover" (p. 410).

**237. Hutchinson, F. E.** "Missing Herbert Manuscripts." *TLS*, 15 July, p. 421.
Announces that while preparing his edition of Herbert's poems he has been unsuccessful in locating five Herbert manuscripts and asks for information about these items.

**238. Murry, J. Middleton.** "A Herbert Query." *TLS*, 1 July, p. 390.
Reply to R. F. Rattray (entry 240). Maintains that *great places* in *The Church-Porch* (line 327) means "positions of consequence in society, whether high offices under the Crown (which is the primary meaning of the phrase) or influential stations in the social order." Also argues that the whole poem is "a treatise on the practical Christian education of an aristocrat." See also B. Goulding Brown (entry 235).

**239. Praz, Mario.** *Studies in Seventeenth-Century Imagery.* 2 vols. (Studies of the Warburg Institute, edited by Fritz Saxl, 3.) London: Warburg Institute, 1939–1947. 233p.; xi, 209p.
2d ed. (considerably enlarged), Rome: Edizione di storia e letteratura, pt. 1, 1964; pt. 2, 1974.
Vol. 1 (1939) is an English version (with revisions and a new appendix) of *Studi sul concettismo* (entry 179). Comments on the extensive use of emblem books and

devices in seventeenth-century literature. Contrasts Herbert and Quarles: "Quarles' wit is all on the surface, gaudy and provincial, without a single breath of that devotional spirit which animates the mute emblems of Herbert's *Temple*, or even the *Partheneia Sacra*" (p. 150). Calls *The Temple* "a conspicuous case of a mute emblembook (i.e. wanting only the plates)" (p. 205). Vol. 2 (1947) is a bibliography of emblem books.

**240. Rattray, R. F.** "A Herbert Query." *TLS*, 24 June, p. 374.
Asks the meaning of *places* in *The Church-Porch* (line 327): "Kindnesse, good parts, great places are the way / To compasse this." For a reply, see J. Middleton Murry (entry 238) and B. Goulding Brown (entry 235).

**241. Saito, Takeshi.** "Eikoku no Sanbika (4)." [English Hymns] *EigoS* 82, no.4:106–7.
Briefly mentions Herbert in this survey of English hymns.

**242. Spencer, Theodore, and Mark Van Doren.** *Studies in Metaphysical Poetry: Two Essays and a Bibliography*. New York: Columbia University Press. 88p.
Reprinted, Port Washington, N.Y.: Kennikat Press, 1964.
Part 1 consists of two essays. (1) "Recent Scholarship in Metaphysical Poetry" (pp. 3–18), by Spencer, briefly outlines some of the major developments in metaphysical criticism and scholarship. Focuses primarily on Donne scholarship, but finds it to be "a kind of microcosm of scholarship relating to metaphysical poetry in general" (p. 14). (2) "Seventeenth-Century Poets and Twentieth-Century Critics" (pp. 21–29), by Van Doren, reviews various notions of metaphysical poetry, especially T. S. Eliot's concept of "unified sensibility." Maintains, however, that the outstanding feature of metaphysical poetry is its humor: "Humor is the life of their poetry; wit is its language" (p. 28). Part 2 presents an unannotated bibliography of studies in metaphysical poetry from 1912 to 1938 (pp. 33–83) compiled by Theodore Spencer, with the assistance of Evelyn Orr. "General Studies" (pp. 33–40), followed by studies of individual poets, arranged chronologically (pp. 40–83). There are 44 items listed under Herbert, compared to 199 for Donne. Index (pp. 85–88).

**243. Taketomo, Sofu.** "George Herbert no Keijijo-shi." [Metaphysical Poetry of George Herbert.] *SELit* 19:155–72.
General introduction to Herbert's life and art for a Japanese audience. Finds two opposing traits that account for much of the tension in the poetry—Herbert's saintly character and his aristocratic sensibility. Argues that the former emerged gradually through a life of asceticism and is evidenced in such works as "The Collar" and the "Affliction" poems. Outlines Herbert's major religious themes and comments on his devotion to Anglicanism. Compares Herbert with Donne and maintains that the differences in their poetry are primarily reflections of differences in their personalities. Sees a number of similarities between Herbert and Spenser, especially in their uses of allegory.

**244. Thompson, Elbert N. S.** "*The Temple* and *The Christian Year*." *PMLA* 54:1018–25.
Compares and contrasts *The Temple* with John Keble's *The Christian Year*. Sees Herbert as introspective, self-analytic, individualistic, personal—a Renaissance man, "caring less than Keble for the Church as a divine institution" (p. 1021). Argues that *The Christian Year* more fully and more adequately represents Anglican theology: "Its

author's main purpose was to present the 'sound rule of faith' and the 'sober standard of feeling in matters of practical religion' that are offered in the Book of Prayer" (p. 1022). Comments on Herbert's great condensation, his uses of conceit, his vigor of expression, his intellectual energy, and "his close fusion of mind and heart" (p. 1025). Maintains that the modern reader will find in Herbert's poetry "a touch of freshness not found in *The Christian Year*" (p. 1025).

# *1940*

**245. Bradner, Leicester.** *Musae Anglicanae: A History of Anglo-Latin Poetry, 1500–1925*. New York: Modern Language Association of America; London: Oxford University Press. xii, 383p.

Reprinted, New York: Kraus Reprint, 1966.

Comments favorably on Herbert's Latin poems, mentioning in particular the series of poems defending the Anglican Church against Andrew Melville's attacks in *Anti-Tami-Cami-Categoria*, and especially "De Musicâ Sacrâ"; the short poems on Christ's passion in *Passio Discerpta*; the poems on moral and religious themes in *Lucus*; and the short meditations on the death of his mother, the latter being called early examples of sacred epigram. Suggests that Herbert's poems, combining genuine religious sentiment and a high degree of polish, may be favorably compared to Crashaw's Latin epigrams. Maintains that the seventeenth-century movement toward experimental forms in Latin poetry may have influenced Herbert's experimentations in English. Notes in particular the similarity between the mixed ode in English (exemplified in such poems as "The Collar," "The Church-floore," "An Offering," and "Vanitie (II)") and the Latin mixed ode (exemplified by Herbert's "In Sacram Anchoram Piscatoris"). Contrasts Herbert also with Peter Du Moulin. Includes a chronological list of Anglo-Latin poetry (pp. 346–73).

**246. Cecil, David, ed.** *The Oxford Book of Christian Verse*. Oxford: Clarendon Press. xxxiii, 560p.

Reprinted, 1951, 1965.

Introduction (pp. xi-xxxiii) comments on the nature and limitations of religious poetry and briefly traces the history of English religious verse from Richard Rolle to T. S. Eliot. Compares Herbert favorably with Donne, Crashaw, and Vaughan and calls him "the most complete exponent in our poetry of the peculiar genius of the English Church" (p. xx). Selections from Herbert (pp. 136–55). No notes or commentary on individual poems.

**247. Daniels, R. Balfour.** "George Herbert's Literary Executor," in *Some Seventeenth-Century Worthies in a Twentieth-Century Mirror*, 80–90. Chapel Hill: University of North Carolina Press.

Reprinted, 1971.

Brief sketch of the life of Nicholas Ferrar and of the friendship between Ferrar and Herbert.

**248. Herbert, Thomas Walter.** *John Wesley as Editor and Author.* (Princeton Studies In English, no. 17.) Princeton: Princeton University Press; London: Humphrey Milford, Oxford University Press. vii, 146p.

Comments on John Wesley's attempts to adapt Herbert's verse for congregational singing. Maintains that these paraphrases were less successful as hymns than were Wesley's translations from German hymns: "They were not written as songs; their thought required too many lines to come to a comprehensible point" (p. 57). Concludes that the adaptations from Herbert were "relegated to the single function of providing poetry for Methodists" (p. 58). Comments also on Wesley's admiration of Herbert as reflected in his publication of a pamphlet in 1773 containing twenty-three poems from *The Temple* and in his frequent quotations from Herbert in his journals and letters.

**249. Hutchinson, F. E.** "The First Edition of Herbert's *Temple*." *Oxford Bibliographical Society: Proceedings and Papers* (for 1939) 5:187–97.

Presents evidence to challenge the assumption (made as early as 1859 by William Thomas Lowndes) that the few copies of the first edition of *The Temple* that are undated were printed before the dated copies of 1633. Argues that a fair copy of Herbert's original manuscript (such as MS. Tanner 307 in the Bodleian) was used by the printer and notes that the Bodleian manuscript bears strong resemblances to many examples of Gidding writing. Discusses possible reasons for the first edition having alternative title pages and for there being some slight variations in different copies. Accounts for the numerous, but mostly unimportant, differences between the Bodleian manuscript and the printed text of the first edition. Comments also on the date of Herbert's death: Friday, 1 March 1632/1633. See also Anon. (entry 14), L. S. Livingston (entry 17), Marion Cox (entry 60), William A. Jackson (entry 250), and F. S. Ferguson (entry 325).

**250. [Jackson, William A.]** *Carl H. Pforzheimer Library. English Literature, 1475–1700. A Catalogue of English Books and Manuscripts 1475–1700.* Vol. 2. New York: Privately Printed. 379–791p.

Limited to 150 copies.

Includes three Herbert entries, with full bibliographical descriptions: (1) No. 464—the first edition of *Herbert's Remains*. (2) No. 465—the dated first edition of *The Temple*. Discusses the dated and undated issues of the first edition. See also Anon. (entry 14), L. S. Livingston (entry 17), Marion Cox (entry 60), F. E. Hutchinson (entry 249), and F. S. Ferguson (entry 325). (3) No. 466—the second edition of *The Temple*.

**251. Jonas, Leah.** "George Herbert, Richard Crashaw, and Henry Vaughan," in *The Divine Science: The Aesthetic of Some Representative Seventeenth-Century English Poets*, 211–27. (Columbia University Studies in English and Comparative Literature, no. 151.) New York: Columbia University Press.

Reprinted, 1973.

Comments on the principles informing Herbert's poetic creed and on how, under the influence of Donne, he converted the techniques of the secular lyricists to the service of religion, "using them as a model for his own greater design" (p. 219). Discusses Herbert's resolution of the tension between his desire to express his spiritual temper in the simplest and most direct manner and his equally genuine delight in the perfection and mastery of complex artistic forms, always striving for "an eloquence proper to divine poetry" (p. 222). Comments on Herbert's influence on Crashaw and Vaughan and compares the three poets: "It was their aim to divert some of the beauty of poetry to the praise of its great Creator" (p. 227). Views such a theory and practice as ultimately constrictive and limiting: "The divine poet assumes more the role of a priest" (p. 227).

**252. Purishev, Boris Ivanovich.** "Herbert," in *Khrestomatiia po zapadno-evro-peiskoi literature semnadtsatogo veka* [An Anthology of Western European Literature of the Seventeenth Century], 343. Moscow: Uchebno-Pedagogicheskoe izdatel'stvo.

General biographical introduction to Herbert and his poetry, followed by very loose translations into Russian of stanzas 1, 8, 12, and 13 of "Miserie" and stanzas 1, 2, 5, and 6 of "Employment (II)."

**253. Reese, Harold.** "A Borrower from Quarles and Herbert." *MLN* 55:50–52.

Comments on *Miscellanea; or, a mixture of choyce observations and institutions, moral and divine, composed for private use. Being the product of spare hours, and the meditations of J. H. . . .* London, printed for Thomas Helder, at the Sign of the Angel in Little-Brittain, 1669. Notes that sixty four of its ninety-two chapters are taken wholly or partially from Quarles's *Enchiridion*. Points out that the compiler also made unacknowledged use of Herbert's "Providence," which appears, without title, in a prose chapter, and that the compiler rearranged stanzas and omitted a number of stanzas.

**254. Sharp, Robert Lathrop.** *From Donne to Dryden: The Revolt Against Metaphysical Poetry.* Chapel Hill: University of North Carolina Press. xiii, 221p.

Reprinted, Hamden, Conn.: Archon Books, 1965; St. Clair Shores, Mich.: Scholarly Press, 1965; New York: Octagon Books, 1973.

Traces the revolution in taste in the seventeenth century from poetry that the author calls extravagant, obscure, and harsh to poetry that exalts the standards and practice of propriety, clarity, and harmony. Examines both literary and nonliterary forces that set up a reaction to metaphysical poetry. Notes that "the revolt was not a silent one; it was articulate in criticism as well as in poetry" (p. xii). Maintains that "it reached to the root of poetry and affected the experience underlying literary creation" and that, "by following it, the reader should get a clearer notion of what happened to English poetry between 1600 and 1700" (p. xii). Several references to Herbert.

**255. Shuster, George N.** "Milton and the Metaphysical Poets," in *The English Ode from Milton to Keats*, 64–92. (Columbia University Studies in English and Comparative Literature, no. 150.) New York: Columbia University Press.

Several references to Herbert. Calls him "a mystic and a humanist" but points out that "his was a classicism not of Pindar and Horace but of Ambrose and Prudentius" (p. 86). Notes also Herbert's use of Horatian meters in his Latin verses but observes that "the waters of Arethusa are not in them" (p. 86). Compares Herbert briefly to Donne, Vaughan, Joseph Beaumont, and Crashaw.

**256. Wells, Henry W.** *New Poets from Old: A Study of Literary Genetics.* New York: Columbia University Press. x, 356p.

Studies the indebtedness of certain modern poets to earlier ones. Refers to Herbert in several instances and in particular suggests his influence on Genevieve Taggard, Elinor Wylie, and W. H. Davies.

# *1941*

**257. Anon.** "From Court to Sanctuary: George Herbert's Songs, An Emancipated Spirit." *TLS*, 12 July, pp. 334, 337.

Primarily a review of Hutchinson's edition (entry 266). Comments on the religious sensibility of Herbert's poems while warning against a too-literal autobiographical reading. Remarks on Herbert's analogies and metaphors: "Scripture, gardens, trees, herbs, stars, fencing, bowl, card games, medicine, anatomy, everything serves his purpose" (p. 334). Discusses briefly Herbert's "disciplined intellectual energy and conviction" (p. 334) and particularly the implications of music in his poetry: "The word 'music,' indeed, supplies the key to his dominant thought as the word 'light' supplies the key to Vaughan" (p. 337). Defends Herbert's uses of shaped verse and suggests that there are Herbertian echoes in Coleridge. For a reply, see H. S. Curr (entry 259).

**258. Bennett, Joan.** Review of *The Works of George Herbert*, edited by F. E. Hutchinson. *RES* 17:348–52.
Essentially a review of F. E. Hutchinson's edition (entry 266). Notes that "biography, critical apparatus, text and commentary are alike excellent" (p. 348). Agrees strongly with Hutchinson's decision to retain the traditional ordering of the poems in *The Temple*. Finds Herbert's obscurity, though different, no less challenging than Donne's, especially those difficulties that arise from Herbert's simple diction.

**259. Curr, H. S.** "George Herbert." *TLS*, 2 August, p. 371.
Response to an anonymous article in *TLS*, 12 July (entry 257). Argues that lines 239–40 of *The Church-Porch* "furnish an interesting and helpful commentary" on the exhortation from the metrical version of Psalm 100: "Himselve with mirth, His praise forth tell."

**260. Daniels, Earl.** *The Art of Reading Poetry*. New York: Farrar & Rinehart. vii, 519p.
Brief explication of "Prayer (I)" (pp. 202–5). Comments primarily on the uses of paradox in the poem. Also discusses "The Pulley" (pp. 206–10) and contrasts it with a hymn by Isaac Watts. Presents a series of critical questions, designed for students, on "Vertue" (p. 381) and "The Collar" (pp. 472–73).

**261. De Selincourt, Ernest.** "George Herbert." *Hibbert Journal* 39:389–97.
Praises Hutchinson's edition (entry 266). Presents a sketch of Herbert's life. Calls *The Temple* "Herbert's intimate autobiography, a kind of diary in which he set down from day to day the fluctuations of his inner experience" (p. 392), but agrees with Hutchinson that the order of the poems is not chronological. Maintains that Herbert's prevalent mood, "his besetting sin . . . was deep dejection, in which he doubted not merely his fitness for the priesthood, but even his right to be numbered among the children of God" (p. 392). Praises "Love (III)" as an "exquisite lyric" (p. 395) but expresses dislike for many features of Herbert's "metaphysical" style, such as his delight in anagrams, acrostics, and puns and his use of the farfetched conceit: "Such extravagances are little to our taste; yet they express clearly enough the ideas he wishes to convey, and expresses them in a manner which his age approved" (p. 396). Maintains that Herbert is consistently the artist but that he is not "the greatest of our sacred lyricists" (p. 396): "He lacks the passion and majesty of Donne; he never rises to the ecstasy of Crashaw; Vaughan surpasses him both in flashes of imaginative vision, and in delicate response to the beauty and wonder of the natural world" (p. 396).

**262. F., R.** "George Herbert's 'A Parodie.'" *N&Q* 180:334.

Asks the meaning of the word *parody* in Herbert's title.

**263. Freeman, Rosemary.** "George Herbert and the Emblem Books." *RES* 17:150–65.

Reprinted in revised and expanded form in *English Emblem Books* (entry 337), 148–72.

Reprinted in *Essential Articles for the Study of George Herbert's Poetry*, edited by John R. Roberts (entry 1216), 215–30.

Maintains that, although emblem books exercised considerable influence on scores of minor and major writers of the sixteenth and seventeenth centuries, Herbert's poetry "comes nearest to that of the emblem writers, while at the same time being infinitely more distinguished" (p. 150). Shows "how a convention which in itself produced only mediocre writing was modified to suit the purposes of a great poet" (p. 150). Briefly outlines the history of the emblem convention and comments on the chief characteristics of emblem books. Shows how Herbert transformed the convention and its methods into poetry. Discusses the visual aspects of Herbert's imagery ("Herbert's images remain emblems and nowhere encroach on the province of symbol" [p. 159]), his uses of patterned forms, the emblematic function of many of his titles, the liturgical roots of his poetry, and his use of personification. Maintains that Herbert's poetry is characterized "by a simplicity of image, an extreme unobtrusiveness, and a concentration of meaning in which the complexity becomes only gradually apparent" (p. 157).

**264. Fuller, Margaret [Sarah Margaret (Fuller), Marchesa D'Ossoli].** "The Two Herberts," in *The Writings of Margaret Fuller*, edited by Mason Wade, 273–89. New York: Viking Press.

Reproduces an essay originally published in *Papers on Literature and Art* (New York: Wiley and Putnam, 1846) that presents an imaginary dialogue between George Herbert and Edward, Baron, Herbert of Cherbury in which the two brothers contrast their philosophical and religious ideas. Poems (or parts of poems) by each are "recited" in this fanciful context to stress certain points made in the discussion.

**265. H., C. E.** "A Query from Herbert." *N&Q* 181:246.

Asks the meaning of the figure in line 30 of "The H. Communion" ("And all our lump to leaven"). Wonders if this is a reference to the "leaven of malice and wickedness."

**266. Herbert, George.** *The Works of George Herbert.* Edited with a commentary by F. E. Hutchinson. Oxford: Clarendon Press. lxxvii, 619p.

Revised, 1945.

Reprinted 1953, 1959, 1964, 1967, 1970.

Preface (pp. iv-viii) in which the editor states that his main object is to establish the text for *The Temple*. Contents (pp. ix-xvii); list of illustrations (p. xix). Introduction includes: (1) biography of Herbert (pp. xxi-xxxix), (2) contemporary and later reputation (pp. xxxix-l), (3) manuscripts of *The Temple* poems (pp. l-lvi), (4) early editions of *The Temple* (pp. lvi-lxii), (5) editions of *A Priest to the Temple* and other writings (pp. lxiii-lxv), (6) modern editions of Herbert's works (pp. lxv-lxx), (7) the text of *The Temple* (pp. lxx-lxxvii). *The Temple* (pp. 1–199). English poems in the Williams manuscript not included in *The Temple* (pp. 200–205). Poems from Walton's *Lives* (pp. 206–7). Doubtful poems (pp. 208–22). *A Priest to the Temple* (pp. 223–90). Herbert's translation of Cornaro, *A Treatise of Temperance and Sobrietie* (pp. 291–303). *Briefe Notes on Valdesso's "Considerations"* (pp. 304–20). *Outlandish Prov-*

erbs (pp. 321–55). Proverbs in *Jacula Prudentum* not included in *Outlandish Proverbs* (pp. 356–62). Letters (pp. 363–81). Herbert's will (pp. 382–83). *Musae Responsoriae* (pp. 383–403). *Passio Discerpta* (pp. 404–9). *Lucus* (pp. 410–21). *Memoriae Matris Sacrum* (pp. 422–31). Alia Poemata Latina (pp. 432–39). Orationes (pp. 440–55). Epistolae (pp. 456–73). Commentary (pp. 475–608). Appendix: *Pro Svpplici Evangelicorum Ministrorum in Anglia* (pp. 609–14). Index of first lines (pp. 615–19). Reviews:

Anon., *DUJ* n.s. 2 (1941): 223–24
Anon., *N&Q* 180 (1941): 288
Anon., *TLS*, 12 July 1941, pp. 334, 337
Joan Bennett, *RES* 17 (1941): 348–52
D. A. Roberts, *Nation* 153 (1941): 586
Walter Shewring, *DubR* 20 (1941): 213–14.
H. J. C. Grierson, *MLR* 37 (1942): 207–14
Frederick M. Padelford, *MLQ* 3 (1942): 127–28
Austin Warren, *MLN* 58 (1943): 402–3
Pierre Legouis, *SN* 18 (1946): 290–93

**267. Matthiessen, F. O.** *American Renaissance: Art and Expression in the Age of Emerson and Whitman.* London, Toronto, New York: Oxford University Press. xxiv, 678p.

Reprinted, 1949, 1968, 1979.

Mentions Herbert in several instances. Comments on Emerson's and Thoreau's admiration of Herbert and the seventeenth century: "The seventeenth-century frame is of greatest relevance for the practice of their art. In reading Herbert or Browne they were affected not only by ideas, or by form as an abstract pattern, but also by qualities of their own language which the eighteenth century had allowed to decay, and which they were determined to renew" (p. 102). Specifically mentions Emerson's delight in Herbert's "Man" and that Emerson's poem "Grace" was mistaken for one by Herbert. Concludes that "Herbert's face was turned upward; Emerson's and Thoreau's faces inward" and that, while "Herbert pleads with God for vision," Emerson and Thoreau "only pricked themselves perpetually on to further spiritual discoveries" (p. 113).

**268. Mortimer, Raymond.** "Books in General." *New Statesman and Nation* 21:534.

Essay on Herbert's poetry occasioned as a review of Hutchinson's edition. Praises Herbert's variety of feeling, experimentation with prosodic forms, and musicality. Evidences much distrust of the modern enthusiasm for metaphysical poetry and maintains that it is not in the mainstream of English verse. Calls it "a backwater exuberant with rare flowers, and not unconnected with certain little-visited Continental creeks named Gongora and Marini."

**269. Potter, George Reuben.** "A Protest Against the Term *Conceit*," in *Renaissance Studies in Honor of Hardin Craig*, edited by Baldwin Maxwell et al. (a special issue of *PQ*) 20, no. 3:474–83.

Reprinted as a separate monograph (Stanford: Stanford University Press, 1941), 282–91.

Surveys the various denotative and connotative meanings of the word *conceit* from the medieval period to modern times and urges that it be discontinued as a critical term. Comments specifically on the confusion that the term has caused when applied to the metaphysical poets. No specific mention of Herbert.

**270. Sampson, George.** "Cavalier and Puritan," in *Cambridge History of English Literature*, 344–400. Cambridge: Cambridge University Press.

Reprinted frequently.

Biographical sketch of Herbert and a brief critical evaluation of his poetry. Maintains that Herbert is a "most conscientious artist" but that, at times, "ingenuity misleads him into what can only be called tricks" (p. 347). Stresses, however, that Herbert "is never thin or facile" and that "his intensity, attained by daring omission and abrupt suggestion, is wonderful" (p. 347). Calls "Love (III)" "one of the most deeply moving religious lyrics in the language" (p. 347). Briefly contrasts Herbert with Crashaw. Maintains that Herbert's prose has "verbal reminiscences" of his poetry but that "the prose is good prose, not poetry spoilt" (p. 372).

**271. Shewring, Walter.** Review of *The Works of George Herbert*, edited by F. E. Hutchinson. *Dublin Review* 20:213–14.

Uses the review of Hutchinson's edition (entry 266) as a way of commenting on Herbert. Rejoices that, unlike Donne, Herbert has not become fashionable in the modern age: "His spirit has proved too tranquil, his real conflicts of soul are resolved too well, to make him in any sense an idol of our times; he is one who saw too clearly the differing values of motion and rest" (p. 213). Comments on Herbert's traditional moral theology, which "Catholics have a particular interest in observing" (p. 213). Praises the Latin poetry, especially "In Angelos," "which is in the true Scholastic tradition" (p. 214).

**272. Vaughan Williams, Ralph.** *Sweet Day.* New York: Galaxy Music. 5p.

Musical adaptation of "Vertue" for three-part women's voices (SSA). First published in a version for four-part harmony (SATB) in 1913 (entry 48).

# *1942*

**273. Bradbrook, M. C.** "The Liturgical Tradition in English Verse: Herbert and Eliot." *Theology* (London) 45:13–23.

Compares and contrasts Herbert and Eliot to "show how in Mr. Eliot a symbolic technique has been adapted to a less congenial age" and how "Herbert's successes throw light on Eliot's difficulties and help to an understanding of what he has achieved" (p. 13). Maintains that Eliot's essay on Lancelot Andrewes is also applicable to Herbert: "Herbert analysed and split up the Church building or the service, as Andrewes divided and subdivided his text, and upon this fixed and literal basis each will play those variations suggested by his learned and intellectual interests, his natural and simple tastes, and his deep devotional fervour" (p. 13). Sees Herbert as "one of those few English poets who relies upon liturgy not for its emotional effects, but for its power to concentrate dogma" (p. 14). Recognizes some flaws in Herbert's verse, especially excessive intellectuality and idiosyncrasy, but concludes: "In Herbert may be seen a mind sensitive and controlled presenting the *vie intérieure* in terms of liturgy and ritual, recording the widest emotional reverberations in terms of perpetual struggle and self-conquest with a flawless precision, honesty, and grace of statement" (p. 17).

**274. Brandenburg, Alice Stayert.** "The Dynamic Image in Metaphysical Poetry." *PMLA* 57:1039–45.

Maintains that the underlying quality that connects many of the seemingly unrelated features of metaphysical poetry might be called "the dynamic image." Distinguishes between two types of images: the static image, which "describes the appearance, taste, smell, feel, or sound of an object—the qualities in short, which mediaeval philosophers called accidents" (p. 1039), and the dynamic image, which "describes the way in which objects act or interact" (p. 1039). Comments primarily on the nature and function of Donne's dynamic images. Observes that Donne's followers, including Herbert, continued the use of dynamic images but "did not turn so frequently to science for their material or neutralize their images so thoroughly" (p. 1044). Mentions Herbert's "Artillerie."

**275. Grierson, H. J. C.** Review of *The Works of George Herbert*, edited by F. E. Hutchinson. *MLR* 37:207–14.

Essentially a detailed review of Hutchinson's edition (entry 266), but also includes Grierson's critical comments on Herbert. Finds Herbert, on the whole, more difficult than Donne and feels that as religious poets "they are poles asunder" (p. 208). Contrasts Herbert and Donne and concludes that there is "a closer link between Herbert and the Emblem writers, Quarles and his sources, than between the tormented Dean and the pastor of Bemerton" (p. 208). Laments that Hutchinson does not devote more space to commentary and critical analysis.

**276. Rowse, A. L.** "The Caroline Country Parson: George Herbert's Ideal." *Country Life*, 6 February, pp. 252–55.

Reprinted in *The English Spirit* (New York: Macmillan Co., 1945; rev. ed., 1966), 148–53.

General and popular account of Herbert's life and works with several photographs of places associated with him. Calls Herbert's poetry "the most perfect, the ideal, expression of it [the Caroline world], if not the most complete, because of its unworldliness" (p. 252). Finds that what is most remarkable about Herbert is "his combination of great common-sense, his feeling for the plain country people, with the rigorous standards of a saint" (p. 254), which is manifested, for example, in *The Country Parson*. Contrasts Herbert and Herrick: "Almost all of Herbert's poetry is concerned with this inner world of experience, as against his contemporary Herrick's frank acceptance of the good things of this world" (p. 255). Yet notes that "they had so much in common: their love of music, so true to Caroline England, of flowers and birds and church-bells, of the old country customs and the country people, their devotion to the English church they served and by which they are remembered" (p. 255).

**277. Tuve, Rosemond.** "Imagery and Logic: Ramus and Metaphysical Poetics." *JHI* 3:365–400.

Discusses Renaissance imagery in the light of rhetorical training, especially Ramist logic. Maintains that much confusion and uncertainty about the nature and function of Renaissance images results from "an insufficient understanding of the relation of the origin and function of images in sixteenth- and seventeenth-century practice to the poetic theory of their creators" (p. 369). No specific references to Herbert. See also A. J. Smith (entry 472) and George Watson (entry 505).

**278. Weil, Simone.** Letter to the Reverend R. P. Perrin.

First published in *Attente de Dieu* (Paris: La Colombe, 1950), pp. 31–51.

Translated into English by Emma Craufurd as *Waiting for God* (New York: G. P. Putnam's Sons, 1951); reprinted, New York, Evanston, San Francisco, London: Harper & Row Publishers, 1973.

In a letter to the Reverend R. P. Perrin, probably written on 15 May 1942 from Marseilles, relates that she was introduced to the seventeenth-century English metaphysical poets by a young English Catholic who was, like herself, staying at Solesmes during Holy Week of 1938. Points out that she had committed "Love (III)" to memory and often recited it when she experienced violent headaches. Adds that "je croyais le réciter seulement comme un beau poème, mais à mon insu cette récitation avait la vertu d'une prière" (p. 38). Notes that "c'est au cours d'une de ces récitations que, comme vous l'ai écrit, le Christ lui-même est descendu et m'a prise" (p. 38).

# *1943*

**279. L., E. W.** "Herbert's 'The Collar.'" *Expl* 2:question 16.
Asks for an explanation of the interrelation of the images in "The Collar," specifically "cordial fruit," "cage," "good cable," and "death's-head." For a reply, see Dan S. Norton (entry 296).

**280. McLuhan, Herbert Marshall.** "Herbert's 'Virtue.'" *Expl* 2:item 4.
Reprinted in *Readings for Liberal Education,* edited by Louis G. Locke, William M. Gibson, and George Arms (New York: Rinehart, 1948), 2:534–35.
Points out that each stanza of "Vertue" is a paradox and that the last stanza "is a paradox of religious faith which is intended to exalt over the melancholy contradictions of the other three." Maintains that the Church Fathers (as well as their baroque imitators) used the paradox not only to excite wonder and enthusiasm but also as a means of exegesis.

**281. Miles, Josephine.** "Some Major Poetic Words," in *Essays and Studies by Members of the Department of English, University of California,* 233–39. (University of California Publications in English, 14.) Berkeley and Los Angeles: University of California Press.
Presents various comparisons and generalizations based on lists of the ten words (excluding prepositions, conjunctions, and so forth) most frequently used by each of twenty-one poets from Chaucer to Housman (based on concordance data existing at the time of writing). For Herbert the list includes *make* (200), *God* (150), *man* (150), *heart* (130), *love* (130), *death* (120), *good* (120), *know* (120), *give* (120), *sin* (110), *life* (100), *thing* (100).

**282. Purcell, Henry.** *With Sick & Famished Eyes.* A song by Henry Purcell, the words by George Herbert. For voice, with piano (or harpsichord) and violoncello. Edited by Ina Boyle. 2 parts. London: Oxford University Press. 3p.; 8p.
First published in Henry Playford's *Harmonia Sacra* (1688).
Musical setting for Herbert's "Longing" (with some verses and words omitted).

**283. Wilson, F. P.** "A Note on George Herbert's 'Quidditie.'" *RES* 19:398–99.
Explains that the last line of "The Quidditie" ("I am with thee, and *most take all*") is based on a rare proverb. Argues that "most" is used in the sense of "the most

powerful." Maintains that the poem is called "The Quidditie" "because in it the poet distinguishes the essence or quiddity of the spiritual life from the accidents of the world" (p. 399). Maintains that as Herbert writes his verses, "dedicated not to the mundane activities, pleasures, and accomplishments enumerated in the poem but to the service of God, the poet is with God, and God the all-powerful takes complete possession of him ('Most take all')" (p. 399).

# *1944*

**284. Agatha, Mother.** "George Herbert: Poet of Right Intention." *Ave Maria* 59:327–30.
Hagiographic sketch of Herbert's life. Maintains that the poems "are not in any sense great," that "there is much that is artificial, cold and in spots ugly," and that "their technical and literary faults are largely atoned for by their spiritual content" (p. 329). Claims that the predominant theme in Herbert's poetry is death.

**285. Allen, Don Cameron.** "George Herbert's *Sycomore*." *MLN* 59:493–95.
Explains Herbert's use of *sycomore* in "The World" ("Then enter'd *Sinne*, and with that Sycomore, / Whose leaves first sheltred man from drought & dew / . . . The inward walls and sommers cleft and tore"). Maintains that Herbert is referring to the fig tree of Genesis. Explains the origin and extent of the confusion caused by various early translations of the Bible.

**286. Clokey, Joseph Waddell.** *The Temple, a Cycle of Poems by George Herbert (1593–1633).* Set for soli, chorus and orchestra with optional parts for singing by members of audience or congregation. With a foreword by Howard D. McKinney. New York: J. Fischer & Bro. 58p.
An oratorio based on Herbert's poems.

**287. D., G. H.** "George Herbert and Dante." *N&Q* 187:81.
Remarks that no. 553 of Herbert's *Outlandish Proverbs* ("We cannot come in honour under a Couerlet") reminds the author of Vergil's words to Dante in the *Inferno* (24:47–48). Wonders if the proverb comes from Dante or if Dante was quoting the proverb.

**288. Douds, J. B.** "George Herbert's Use of the Transferred Verb: A Study in the Structure of Poetic Imagery." *MLQ* 5:163–74.
Defines the "transferred verb" as a verb that "is transferred from its ordinary, literal, concrete meaning to an abstract and figurative one" (as in "See how spite *cankers* things" from "The Sacrifice") (p. 163). Calls this "one of the numerous grammatical devices used for fusing the terms of a metaphor" (p. 163). Discusses many poems to illustrate the wide range of effects that Herbert achieves through this device. Maintains that "because it is the most dynamic part of speech and because it offers one of the most compact ways of expressing a metaphor, the transferred verb is capable of great poetic force; and Herbert's extensive use of it is probably responsible in part for the impression of energy which his style produces" (p. 174).

**289. Eliot, T. S.** "What Is Minor Poetry?" *Welsh Review* 3:256–67.

Reprinted in *On Poetry and Poets* (New York: Farrar, Straus, and Cudahy, 1957), 34–51.

Discusses the nature and kinds of so-called minor poetry. Points out that "we mean different things at different times" by the term, and attempts to dispel "any derogatory association connected with the term" (p. 256). Comments on the various uses of different kinds of anthologies of poetry. Uses Herbert to illustrate that a poet who writes "a work which consists of a number of short poems, even of poems which, taken individually, may appear rather slight, may, if it has a unity of underlying pattern, be the equivalent of a first-rate long poem in establishing an author's claim to be a 'major' poet" (p. 263). Points out that if we read through the whole of *The Temple* we are "surprised to find how many of the poems strike us as just as good as those we have met with in anthologies" (p. 261). Maintains that *The Temple* is not simply "a number of religious poems by one author" but rather "a book constructed according to a plan; and as we get to know Herbert's poems better, we come to find that there is something we get from the whole book, which is more than a sum of its parts" (p. 261). Sees *The Temple* as "a continued religious meditation with an intellectual framework," as a book that "as a whole discloses to us the Anglican devotional spirit of the first half of the seventeenth century" (p. 261). Concludes that Herbert cannot be called a minor poet "for it is not of a few favorite poems that I am reminded when I think of him, but of the whole work" (p. 262). Briefly contrasts Herbert with Herrick and Thomas Campion.

**290. Gardner, W. H.** *Gerard Manley Hopkins (1844–1889): A Study of Poetic Idiosyncrasy in Relation to Poetic Tradition.* London: Martin Secker & Warburg, 1944–1949. 2 vols. Vol. 1: 1944; 2d rev. ed., 1948; reissued by Oxford University Press, 1958. xvi, 304p. Vol. 2: 1949; reissued by Oxford University Press, 1958. xiv, 415p.

2d ed. reprinted, 1961, 1966, 1969.

Numerous references to Herbert and a number of specific comparisons between Hopkins and Herbert. Notes Hopkins's admiration of Herbert: "Herbert's frank avowal of Christ; his passionate yet restrained colloquies with God; his vigorous and subtle exposition of doctrine; his significant quaintness and happy conceits—all of these elements are found, in duly modified form, in the later Hopkins" (2:73–74). Argues that "in the delicacy, ingenuity, and almost fantastic wit of many of his images, Hopkins continues the tradition of Donne, Herbert, Crashaw, Vaughan, and Marvell" (1:189). Suggests several direct borrowings from Herbert as well as less obvious echoes. For example, points out that in "The Storm" one finds "a concise statement of the central ethical theme of Hopkins's two poems of shipwreck" (1:171), that the image of the soul hunted by God in *The Deutschland* is anticipated by Herbert's "Affliction (IV)" (stanza 1), that the image of the sloes in *The Deutschland* may have been suggested by either "Bitter-sweet" or "Paradise," and that there are echoes of Herbert's "The Flower" in "Carrion Comfort" and similarities between *The Church-Porch* and Hopkins's "The Starlight Night." Maintains that "the most patently Herbertian of all his verse is a poem of 1864 with the characteristic title *New Readings*" (2:74).

**291. Grierson, H. J. C., and J. C. Smith.** "The Carolines," in *A Critical History of English Poetry*, 158–71. London: Chatto and Windus.

1st American ed., 1946.

2d rev. ed., 1947.

Reprinted, 1950, 1956, 1962, 1965, 1970; Atlantic Heights, N.J.: Humanities; London: Athlone, 1983.

Comments briefly on Donne's influence on Herbert. Praises Herbert's loving and reasonable temper in *The Temple*, thus "making us excuse, even find pleasure in, his metrical flourishes . . . and his innumerable conceits" (p. 164). Maintains that Herbert's conceits "are sometimes penetrating by their homely quaintness, never electrifying like those of Donne; they are the products of Fancy not Passion and Imagination, 'emblems' in the manner of Quarles" (p. 164).

**292. Howarth, R. G. "George Herbert." *N&Q* 187:122.**

Sees possible echoes of Kyd's *Spanish Tragedy* (act 4, scene 4, lines 90–92) in the third and fourth stanzas of "The Pilgrimage."

**293. Knights, L. C. "George Herbert." *Scrutiny* 12:171–86.**

Reprinted in *Explorations: Essays in Criticism Mainly on the Literature of the Seventeenth Century* (London: Chatto and Windus, 1946; 1st American ed., New York: George W. Stewart, 1947; rpt. 1966), 112–30; *Explorations 3* (Pittsburgh: University of Pittsburgh Press; London: Chatto and Windus, 1976), 64–80; *Selected Essays in Criticism* (Cambridge: Cambridge University Press, 1981), 25–43.

A portion was reprinted in *George Herbert and the Seventeenth-Century Religious Poets: Authoritative Texts/Criticism*, edited by Mario Di Cesare (entry 1140), 242–49.

Proposes to discuss the human value, as opposed to the specifically Christian, in Herbert's poetry and to show how the poetry "is an integral part of the great English tradition" (p. 171). Comments on Herbert's craftsmanship and sees it as "one with the moral effort to know himself, to bring his conflicts into the daylight and, as far as possible, to resolve them" (p. 172). Notes that, although Herbert's poetry clearly reflects his refined and cultivated background, it is, at the same time, generally informed by the homely manner of the popular preacher and contains much humor, mimicry, sarcasm, and common Elizabethan speech and homely illustration: "It is the artist's feeling for *all* the resources of 'our language' that gives to the greater poems of spiritual conflict their disturbing immediacy" (p. 175). Comments also on Herbert's use of allegory and symbol to tie together the natural and supernatural order of things. Sees the conflicts presented in Herbert's poetry as only partially caused by the temptation of ambition and maintains that his dejection of spirit, caused by his tendency to regard his life as worthless and unprofitable, likewise shaped his poetry. Argues that this despondency, in part, accounts for Herbert's preoccupation with time and death and reflects his feeling that "life, real life, is going on elsewhere, where he happens not to be himself" (p. 180). Illustrates through a discussion of several poems, especially "Affliction (I)," "The Collar," "Love (III)," and "The Flower," the mature and complex process of Herbert's "acceptance." Maintains that the poems "are important human documents because they handle with honesty and insight questions that, in one form or another, we all have to meet if we wish to come to terms with life" (p. 186).

**294. Mabbott, T. O. "Herbert's 'The Collar.'" *Expl* 3:item 12.**

Comments briefly on Herbert's use of *rope of sands* in "The Collar": "'What is impossible with man is possible with God' is the implication; and He can redeem the otherwise helpful human soul, as He can make sand serve to make a rope if He will." See also Dan Norton (entry 306).

295. **Moloney, Michael Francis.** "In the Wake of Donne," in *John Donne: His Flight from Mediaevalism*, 196–209. (Illinois Studies in Language and Literature, vol. 29, nos. 2–3.) Urbana: University of Illinois Press.

Comments on the rationalizing strain in Herbert's poetry and maintains that the poetry reflects some elements of the "dissociation of sensibility": "Too often in Herbert, the sensuous imagery disappears before a plodding rationalism" (p. 205). Notes the "over-logicality" in *The Church-Porch*, "The Thanksgiving," and "Discipline." Comments on Herbert's general suspicion of the flesh and of women. Compares and contrasts Herbert with both Donne and Crashaw.

296. **Norton, Dan S.** "Herbert's 'The Collar.'" *Expl* 2:item 41.

In part, a reply to E. W. L. (entry 279). Notes that the images in "The Collar," especially "cordial fruit," "cage," "good cable," and "death's-head," "contrast the fertility and freedom of worldly life with the sterility and constrictions of the Christian discipline, and the reality of things of the senses with the illusion of religious faith and scruple." Paraphrases the main argument of the poem and sees the conclusion as a complete reversal that "creates a powerful irony by which all the values of the images are changed, as if a positive print were instantly made from a photographic negative." Maintains that this reversal compels the reader "to review the imagery and to see it reinterpreted in Christian terms."

297. **Sypher, Wylie.** "The Metaphysicals and the Baroque." *PR* 11:3–17.

Argues that our modern admiration for Donne "is in a sense hollow and affected, and our depreciation of Milton wilful" (p. 4). Argues that Milton "is more characteristic of his century than Donne" and that, "if we understand the baroque, it is a questionable tactic to elevate Donne at the expense of Milton" (p. 4). Surveys baroque "manners" in sculpture, painting, architecture, and poetry. Refers to "the amazing profusion of freakish imagery in George Herbert" (p. 9).

# 1945

298. **Bush, Douglas.** *English Literature in the Earlier Seventeenth Century, 1600–1660.* (Oxford History of English Literature, edited by F. P. Wilson and Bonamy Dobrée, vol. 5.) Oxford: Clarendon Press. vi, 621p.

Reprinted, 1946, 1948, 1952, 1956.

Rev. ed., 1962; reprinted with corrections, 1966.

Issued as Oxford University Press paperback, 1973 (with omission of chronological tables and bibliography).

General critical and historical survey in which Herbert is mentioned throughout. Discusses Herbert's poetry primarily in chapter 4 (pp. 104–69, esp. pp. 136–39). Comments on the inner tensions of Herbert's poetry, his principal themes of sin and love, his exquisite sense of metaphor, his peculiar intimacy and honesty, his uses of everyday images or of images drawn from nature, the liturgy, and the Bible (in contrast to the scholastic and scientific imagery of Donne). Sees many of Herbert's poems as "allegorical anecdotes and transfigured emblems" (p. 139). Praises Herbert's technical mastery and metrical experimentation, his "functional sense of metre and rhythm" (p. 138). Maintains that Herbert avoided the surface classicism of his age but "had muscular density, precision, deceptive simplicity, and a dynamic sense of form" (p. 139). Maintains that one can distinguish essentially two poets in Herbert: (1) the affectionate son of the Church of England to whom "we owe much of our picture of the order, strength, and beauty of seventeenth-century Anglicanism at its best" (p. 138) and (2) "the very human saint who gives fresh and moving utterance to the aspirations and failures of the spiritual life" (p. 138). Presents a biographical sketch. Compares and contrasts Herbert with Donne, Quarles, Crashaw, Traherne, Marvell, and (in the revised edition) Sidney. Comments on Walton's life of Herbert (pp. 222–24). Bibliography (pp. 548–49).

**299. Feist, Hans.** "George Herbert," in *Ewiges England: Dichtung aus sieben Jahrhunderten von Chaucer bis Eliot*, 225–35, 577. Zurich: Verlag Amstutz, Herdeg & Co.
   Anthologizes "Vertue," "Life," "The Pulley," "The Collar," "The Elixir," and "Bitter-sweet" with German translations on facing pages. In a biographical note, calls Herbert one of the greatest religious poets of England (p. 577).

**300. Garrod, H. W.** "Donne and Mrs. Herbert." *RES* 21:161–73.
   Examines the relationship between Donne and Magdalene Herbert and other members of the Herbert family, especially Edward, Lord Herbert of Cherbury. Attempts to date several of Donne's poems that have been often associated with Mrs. Herbert and questions the evidence of some of those believed by Grierson and others to have been written to her. Mentions George Herbert only briefly.

**301. Knights, L. C.** "On the Social Background of Metaphysical Poetry." *Scrutiny* 13:37–52.
   Reprinted in *Further Explorations* (Stanford: Stanford University Press, 1965), 99–120.
   Examines "only a very few of the ways in which it is possible to work out *from* literature—from Metaphysical poetry—to 'the life of the time' in the early seventeenth century" (p. 39). Maintains that it is "much more likely that the distinctive note of Metaphysical poetry—the implicit recognition of the many-sidedness of man's nature—is in some ways socially supported; that—to borrow some phrases from a suggestive passage in Yeats' criticism—'unity of being' has some relation to a certain 'unity of culture'" (p. 42). Refers to Herbert to illustrate the social and cultural milieu of his time. For example, states that Herbert's "homely imagery is not simply a form of expression; it is an index of habitual modes of thought and feeling in which the different aspects and different levels of his personal experience are brought into intimate relation to each other" (p. 40). Calls Herbert "courtly" and "metaphysical" and maintains that he possessed "a mechanism of sensibility that could devour any kind of experience" (p. 41). Comments on the vital, enriching religious tradition that informs Herbert's poetry and contrasts it with the tradition expressed by Dryden.

**302. McCutchan, Robert Guy.** "England's Development of the Hymn," in *Hymns in the Lives of Men*, 138–54. New York and Nashville: Abingdon-Cokesbury Press.
   Comments on Herbert's contribution to the development of the English hymn, pointing out that Susanna Wesley was devoted to Herbert's poetry and that "The Elixir" and "Antiphon (I)" were adapted for use as hymns (pp. 142–43).

**303. Mead, D. S.** "Herbert's 'The Pulley.'" *Expl* 4:item 17.
   Explains the visual conceit of a pulley that informs the whole poem: "To make use of the pulley in the poem, God must be thought of as threading the rope through the

wheel. On one side he lets down man and from his 'glass of blessings' he gives man strength, beauty, wisdom, honor, pleasure—all the rest. Rest He withholds in his glass so that man without it will experience restlessness. Man can climb up the rope to God by virtue of his goodness, but in case he does not, and, spurning his earthly riches yearns in his weariness for peace, God need but release His rest on the other side of the pulley and its weight, greater than man's unburdened soul, will hoist or 'toss' man to His level."

**304. Miles, Josephine.** "From *Good* to *Bright*: A Note in Poetic History." *PMLA* 60:766–74.

Traces the "developing relation of the standard epithets *good* and *bad* to the qualities epithets *bright* and *dark* through the work and the concordance listing of four or five poets on either side of 1740" (p. 766). Although Herbert is mentioned, Donne is discussed as a pre-1740 representative.

**305. Nelson, Lawrence E.** "Altar and Angel Wings," in *Our Roving Bible: Tracking Its Influence Through English and American Literature*, 64–72. New York and Nashville: Abingdon-Cokesbury Press.

Brief comments on "The Altar" and on "Easter-wings." Quotes (with comment) W. S. Walsh, who in his *Hand-book of Literary Curiosities* (1925) says: "Heading the list of English word-torturers stands so good and great a man as George Herbert. We quote two specimens and then pass on with our eyes veiled, to avoid gazing too intently on a good man's shame" (p. 65). Calls emblem poems and metaphysical poems "rather harmless eccentricities which sometimes served as the channels for deep piety" (p. 72).

**306. Norton, Dan.** "Herbert's 'The Collar.'" *Expl* 3:item 46.

Points out the play on the words *collar* and *choler* in the title of the poem: "Until God speaks to him, Herbert is in a choler because he wears the collar of religious discipline; and galling restraint has caused his rage." Supports T. O. Mabbott's reading (entry 294) of *rope of sands*: "To make a rope of sands . . . is a symbol of futile or impossible industry." See also Dan S. Norton (entry 296) and Jack M. Bickham (entry 376).

**307. Oliver, Peter.** "George Herbert (1593–1633)." *Action*, 5 December, pp. 9–12.

Biographical sketch emphasizing Herbert's piety and dedication to the Church of England. Calls the seventeenth-century religious poets "missionaries of civilization" who "regarded the arts, not as pleasant pursuits, but as allies in the battle for a nobler future" (p. 9).

**308. Scott, Walter Sidney.** *The Fantasticks: Donne, Herbert, Crashaw, Vaughan.* London: John Westhouse. 170p.

General introduction to the four poets. The introduction to Herbert (pp. 55–60) presents a biographical sketch and comments very generally on Herbert's use of conceits, his "loveliness," and his "near approach to integration" (p. 58) in life. Selections from Herbert's poems (pp. 61–93).

**309. Todd, Mabel Loomis, and Millicent Todd Bingham, eds.** *Bolts of Melody: New Poems by Emily Dickinson.* New York and London: Harper & Brothers. xxix, 352p.

Reproduces stanzas 1 and 2 of Herbert's "Mattens" and attributes them to Dickinson (p. 125). In the third printing the error is corrected. See also William White, "Dickinson and Dover Publications," *AN&Q* 11 (1972): 7.

310. **Wilson, F. P.** *Elizabethan and Jacobean*. Oxford: Clarendon Press. vi, 144p. Reprinted, 1946.

Points out some of the major differences between Elizabethan and Jacobean literature. Mentions Herbert in several instances and compares him briefly with Donne. Comments on Herbert's use of close-knit, dialectical argumentation: "It is this 'sequaciousness,' this following through of logic and passion, which make it possible to say that George Herbert and Marvell (with all their many differences from Donne) belong to the same school of poetry as Donne, and that Southwell and Crashaw do not" (p. 58).

# *1946*

311. **Bethell, S. L.** "Two Streams from Helicon," in *New English Weekly*, 7, 28 February, 21 March, and 4 April, pp. 162–64, 193–94, 223–24, 243–44.

Expanded version reprinted in *Essays on Literary Criticism and the English Tradition* (London: Dennis Dobson, 1948), 53–87.

Contrasts two principal traditions in English poetry, one represented by Shakespeare and Donne and the other by Spenser, Milton, and Tennyson. Contrasts the uses of language, rhythms, imagery, and subject matter in each tradition and challenges F. R. Leavis and the *Scrutiny* critics for their assumptions about the superiority of the first group. Notes Herbert's use of proverbial phrases and folk idioms. Claims that Herbert "owes nothing directly to mediaeval writers and little to the contemporary ballad, but as a conscientious parson he was familiar with the way his parishioners thought and spoke; from his prose treatise, *A Priest to the Temple*, we know how he studied the rural mind in order to be 'understanded of the people' and it is this which is reflected in his verse" (p. 194). Maintains that there is no trace of folk tradition in Donne, Crashaw, Vaughan, or Marvell.

312. **Church, Margaret.** "The First English Pattern Poems." *PMLA* 61:636–50.

Discusses the origins and history of the pattern poem and comments on the earliest English poets who wrote shaped verse, among them Herbert. Suggests that the idea of pattern poems probably originated in Asia Minor and was transmitted to the Western World through *The Greek Anthology*. Points out that the first English pattern poem was written by Stephen Hawes in *The Convercyon of Swerers* (1509). Comments briefly on the tradition out of which such poems as "The Altar" and "Easter-wings" arose.

313. **Coffin, Robert P. Tristram, and Alexander M. Witherspoon, eds.** "George Herbert," in *Seventeenth-Century Prose and Poetry*, pt. 1:250–56; pt. 2:102–22. New York: Harcourt, Brace, and Co.

Two volumes bound as one with separate introductions and pagination; prose selection on Herbert (pt. 1:250–56) reprinted from *Seventeenth-Century Prose* (entry 121); rpt. (with continuous pagination), 1957.

2d ed., with new introduction to Herbert, ed. Alexander Witherspoon and Frank Warnke (entry 620); enlarged edition, 1982.

General introduction to Herbert's life, character, and poetry (2:102–3). Anthologizes twenty-nine poems (or selections from poems) with brief explanatory notes (2:104–22). Calls Herbert a saint and mystic and maintains that "probably no man's life is so thoroughly his poems as George Herbert's is" (2:102). Comments on general features of Herbert's poetry, especially his use of music, his plain style, his use of complex verse forms, the richness of his conceits, and his "sweet personifications and crystal-clear allegories" (2:103). Maintains, however, that Herbert is an uneven poet: "Only a small handful of his briefest lyrics are flawless enough to stand with the language's best," for "most of his short poems and all his longer ones, are full of flaws," such as "rhetoric running without rein, hypothetical hyperboles, shifted patterns of wit, cracked and crazed glazings of the pictorial, forced analogies and half-metaphors, [and] unnatural notes on nature" (2:103). Maintains Donne's influence but recognizes that Herbert greatly differs from Donne. Briefly compares Herbert to Bunyan.

**314. Daniells, Roy.** "English Baroque and Deliberate Obscurity." *JAAC* 5:115–21.

Attempts to define the baroque as it is applied to English literature: "Baroque may be regarded as the logical continuation and extension of High Renaissance art, with conscious accentuation and 'deformation' of the regular stock of techniques. These become more dynamic and (in both good and bad senses of the word) theatrical. Baroque is developed as a complete art form of wide influence and application, the expression of a specific artistic sensibility of which some of the marks are well known: a sense of triumph and splendour, a strenuous effort to unify opposite terms of paradoxes, a high regard for technical virtuosity" (p. 117). Maintains that the English baroque appears as early as 1590. Brief mention of Herbert as evidencing a baroque sensibility that "has lost the fragile unity and tentative balance of the best Elizabethans" (p. 117). Specifically comments on poetical uses of obscurity as "a cult of significant darkness" (p. 119).

**315. Milch, Werner J.** "Metaphysical Poetry and the German 'Barocklyrik.'" *CLS* (Cardiff) 23–24:16–22.

Comments on possible areas for comparative studies between the German *barock* poets and the English metaphysicals as well as between the larger aspects of each movement. Sees the *barock* poets and the metaphysicals as "the last great European attempt to bring about a unified world of thought since the rift between contemplative and active life, between unquestioned faith and scientific urge had become the central feature of all philosophy" (p. 20). Maintains that Herbert "should be considered in connection with Fleming and Gryphius, in order to study the motive of resignation and self-denial in seventeenth century religious poetry" (p. 21).

**316. Miles, Josephine.** *Major Adjectives in English Poetry from Wyatt to Auden.* (University of California Publications in English, vol. 12. no. 3, 305–426.) Berkeley and Los Angeles: University of California Press.

Incorporated into *The Vocabulary of Poetry: Three Studies*, along with nos. 1 and 2 of University of California Publications in English, vol. 12 (Berkeley and Los Angeles: University of California Press, 1946.)

Presents various statistical tabulations of the number of major adjectives used by twenty-five representative poets, including Herbert. Based on concordance data. Table 1 (pp. 314–15) lists the following adjectives most used by Herbert: *good* (120), *great* (70), *poor* (55), *dear* (40), *full* (35), *old* (30), *sweet* (30). Table 2 (pp. 316–18) lists major words most used by Herbert: *make* (200), *God* (150), *man* (150), *heart* (130), *love* (130), *death* (120), *give* (120), *good* (120), *know* (120), *sin* (110), *life* (100), *thing* (100). Presents an extended critical and comparative discourse on the language of selected major poets (excluding Herbert) based on the statistical data collected.

**317. Praz, Mario.** "Poesia metafisica inglese del Seicento." *Poesia* 3–4:232–41, 283–89.

Brief summary of modern critical reaction to metaphysical poetry. In a sketch of Herbert (pp. 236–37), relates Herbert to Donne: "Con lui la maniera metafisica si fa parrocchiale, discende all'emblematica spicciola, rasenta in modo pericoloso il concetto predicabile" (p. 237). Points out the sources of Herbert's inspiration and concludes that "ogni sia pur umile occasione vien trasportata al morale, ma la spontanea freschezza, il candore del poeta, e il suo fermo fervore devoto riescono ad avvivare la materia spesso artificiosa e didattica" (p. 237). Translates into Italian "Church-monuments," "The Windows," "Vertue," "The Collar," and "Easter-wings."

**318. Tannenbaum, Samuel A., and Dorothy R. Tannebaum.** *George Herbert: A Concise Bibliography.* (Elizabethan Bibliographies, no. 35.) New York: Samuel A. Tannenbaum. 52p.

Reprinted, 1967.

Unannotated listing of Herbertiana, divided into nine major sections: (1) poetical works (54 entries), (2) prose works (37 entries), (3) collected editions (41 entries), (4) selections (172 entries), (5) songs and hymns with music (53 entries), (6) biography and criticism (382 entries), (7) bibliography (7 entries), (8) addenda (21 entries), and (9) index of names and subjects.

**319. Wellek, René.** "The Concept of Baroque in Literary Scholarship." *JAAC* 5:77–109.

Reprinted in *Concepts of Criticism* (New Haven: Yale University Press, 1963), 69–127.

Surveys the various uses of the term *baroque*, particularly as it is applied to the literature of several countries. Although Herbert is not cited, the metaphysical poets, especially Donne and Crashaw, are mentioned throughout. Bibliography of writings on the baroque in literary scholarship (pp. 97–109).

**320. Wilson, F. P.** "English Proverbs and Dictionaries of Proverbs." *The Library* (London) 4th ser. 26:51–71.

Discusses "the value of an interest in proverbs for the student of literature, and especially to a student in the literature of the sixteenth and seventeenth centuries" (pp. 51–52). Several comments on *Outlandish Proverbs*. Calls Herbert "the only poet of the seventeenth century who made a collection of proverbs" (p. 56). Explicates the last line of "The Quidditie" ("I am with thee, and *most take all*") by referring to a proverb. Presents a short-title list of books containing collections of proverbs from 1640 to 1670. See also F. P. Wilson (entry 283).

**321. Zanco, Aurelio.** "L'Èta di Milton," in *Storia della letteratura inglese*, vol. 1, *Dalle origini alla restaurazione, 650–1660*, 520–55. Turin: Chiantore.

2d ed., Turin: Roescher Editore, 1964.

Finds Herbert's poetry, for the most part, overly conceited, too ingenious, and often bizarre and maintains that at times it reflects bad taste: "Il suo fu uno spirito ingegnoso e che si piccava di apparir tale" and claims that at times Herbert seems motivated "di mettere in evidenza la propria bravura" (p. 532). Maintains that the formal complexity of Herbert poetry does not necessarily reflect a deep psychological complexity and that "è appunto qui che si manifesta l'incrinatura per cui comincia a sfaldarsi la costruzione artificiosa di quel mondo immaginario" (p. 532). Praises Herbert, however, for the sincerity of his religious fervor and notes his skillful use of musical language and musical metaphors in his poetry.

# 1947

**322. Addison, William.** *The English Country Parson.* London: J. M. Dent & Sons. ix, 246p.

Reprinted, 1948.

Brief comments throughout on Herbert as the ideal parson: "In the long record of faithful ministry in the Church of England there is no name the passage of time has tarnished less than his" (p. 39). Number of references to *The Country Parson.* Calls John Keble a latter-day Herbert but claims that "as a poet he fell short of Herbert" (p. 152).

**323. Day-Lewis, Cecil.** *The Poetic Image.* New York: Oxford University Press. 157p.

Reprinted (pp. 80–81) in *Reading for Liberal Education* (New York: Rinehart & Co., rev. ed., 1952), 39–40.

Defines the nature and limits of the image and surveys various types of imagery as well as differing views of imagery from English poetry and literary criticism during the past four hundred years. Mentions Herbert and the metaphysical poets in several instances. Calls "The Collar" "an example of the strictly functional use of images; their use, that is, to point a theme already defined" (p. 80). Maintains that the central image of the poem is "the spiritual rope by which the Christian is tied to his God" (p. 80) and sees the poem as a dialogue between Christ and the devil.

**324. Delattre, Floris.** "De la chanson élizabéthaine au poème métaphysique." *ML* 28:91–96.

Points out that, in contrast to the Elizabethan lyricists, who stressed musicality, generalized emotional experience, and exquisite form, the metaphysical poets, especially Donne, rejected traditional views of beauty and classical allusion, stressed muscular tone, revolted against rhythmical regularity in their search for individual consciousness, and retained music in a privileged position. No specific comments on Herbert.

**325. Ferguson, F. S.** "The Temple." *TLS*, 3 May, p. 211.

Comments on the undated title page of some copies of the first edition of *The Temple.* Argues that the title page was not entirely reset (as suggested by Marion Cox [entry 60] and F. E. Hutchinson [entry 249]) but is rather a variant altered from the standing type of the dated title page (as suggested by William A. Jackson [entry 250]). Insists that "there is no doubt that when it was decided to make the change in the dated title-page all the type of the first signature, with the exception of that title, had already been distributed." See also Anon. (entry 14) and L. S. Livingston (entry 17).

**326. Hayward, John, comp.** *English Poetry: A Catalogue of First & Early Editions of the Works of the English Poets from Chaucer to the Present Day Ex-*

hibited by the National Book League at 7 Albemarle Street, London. Cambridge: Published for the National Book League by Cambridge University Press. x, 140p.

Illustrated ed. (with 7 additional pages), 1950.

Calls the exhibit "the most comprehensive and valuable loan collection of first and early editions of English poetry ever shown in public" (p. v). Item 66 is a copy of the first edition of *The Temple*, "with the first state of the title-page (i.e. dated 1633)" (p. 36). Observes that "the style and the amateur finish of the binding suggest it was executed by a member of the Community of Little Gidding" and speculates that "it is reasonable to infer that this copy was received by [Nicholas] Ferrar from the printer and handed to one of the inmates of Little Gidding for binding" (p. 36). Notes that Thomas Buck's binder instructed the Community in his craft. Lent by Sir Louis Sterling and by the Lady Annabel Crewe.

**327. Milch, Werner.** "Deutsche Barocklyrik und 'Metaphysical Poetry.'" *Trivium* 5:65–73.

Comments on the contemporaneity of the metaphysical poets and certain German baroque poets, noting that German baroque poetry was without a real leader whereas the English had Donne. Comments on religious, political, and philosophical conditions in both Germany and England that were favorable to the development of baroque poetry. Maintains that a comparison of Herbert with Fleming and Gryphius would show the place of the idea of renunciation in the two parallel movements.

**328. Ross, Malcolm MacKenzie.** "George Herbert and the Humanist Tradition." *UTQ* 16:169–82.

Reprinted in *Poetry and Dogma* (entry 434), 135–53.

Maintains that Herbert occupies a "unique place in a moment of cultural metamorphosis" (p. 170) and that, inheriting the tradition of the Elizabethan humanists (especially Hooker), Herbert "alters the tradition and imparts to it a new direction" (p. 170). Maintains that Herbert's work "reveals a significant interaction between the intellectual tradition as such and the disturbing pressures of Caroline society" (p. 181). Sees in Herbert a crucial conflict between worldly and otherworldly values that is not dominant in his immediate predecessors: "A very un-Elizabethan world comes through in the texture of Herbert's poetry" (p. 173). Discusses Herbert's attitude toward the court, as revealed in his poetry, as an example of "one aspect of the breakdown of the Elizabethan synthesis" (p. 173). Argues that, although never anti-royalist, Herbert's references to the court are fundamentally negative, as are his references to commerce, wealth, and trade: "Only once is Christ expressed in the metaphor of gold" (p. 177). Maintains that Herbert kept an inner balance between various and sometimes conflicting demands: "In this inner synthesis of awareness and withdrawal, crisis is never fully resolved nor is synthesis ever quite destroyed" (p. 182). Concludes that this synthesis "is almost mystical, almost Romanist, almost free of social conscience or concern—but never entirely any one of these. A quality and habit of mind steeped in a great tradition turns from an outer tangible world upon which it can make no impress and in which it can no longer 'its own resemblance find,' to the construction of an inner world where conflicts can be at least tentatively resolved" (p. 182).

**329. Rossi, Mario M.** *La Vita, Le Opere, I Tempi di Edoardo Herbert di Chirbury.* 3 vols. (Biblioteca Storica Sansoni, n.s. 14.) Florence: G. C. Sansoni. ix, 599p.; 544p.; 598p.

Numerous references to George Herbert. Compares him with his brother, Lord Herbert of Cherbury, and comments on their relationship with their mother, Magdalene Herbert. Portrays George as the dutiful son. Briefly discusses George's influence on his brother's poetry and the influence of Donne on both. Stresses George's Christian mysticism and Protestant piety. Detailed discussion of the Herbert family.

**330. Tuve, Rosemond.** *Elizabethan and Metaphysical Imagery: Renaissance Poetic and Twentieth-Century Critics.* Chicago: University of Chicago Press. xiv, 442p.

Reprinted, Chicago: University of Chicago Press (Phoenix Books), 1961.

Extracts appear in *Discussions of John Donne*, edited by Frank Kermode (Boston: D. C. Heath & Co., 1962), 106–17.

Reconsiders Elizabethan and metaphysical modes of expression in terms of the contemporary habits of thought, principally in terms of Renaissance theories of rhetoric and logic. Discusses the nature and function of imagery and provides a corrective evaluation of twentieth-century critical approaches to Renaissance poetry. Argues that many of the so-called unorthodox and new qualities of metaphysical poetry are much less novel than many contemporary critics suggest and are part of a large and consistent tradition. Mentions Herbert throughout, primarily as a vehicle for explaining generic critical points. See especially pp. 217–20, 225, 303, and apps. L, O.

**331. Wasserman, Earl R.** "The Elizabethan Lyric," in *Elizabethan Poetry in the Eighteenth Century*, 153–91. (Illinois Studies in Language and Literature, vol. 32, no. 3.) Urbana: University of Illinois Press.

Comments on various eighteenth-century revisions of Herbert's "Vertue," especially one found in *Universal Harmony* (1745), in which the poem is so "thoroughly refashioned to Augustan taste that it becomes a praise, not of the virtuous soul, but of wedded love" (p. 180), and one in the *Universal Magazine* (83 [1788]:159) by W. H. Reid who "removes the metaphysical wit, and turning Herbert's theme upside down, concludes with a *carpe diem*" (p. 180). Calls these adaptations "the most astonishing revisions of a pre-Restoration poem" (p. 179).

# 1948

**332. Addleshaw, G. W. O., and Frederick Etchells.** *The Architectural Setting of Anglican Worship: An Inquiry into the arrangements for Public Worship in the Church of England from the Reformation to the present day.* London: Faber and Faber. 288p.

Brief comments on various architectural features of the church at Leighton Bromswold, Huntingdonshire, which Herbert helped restore. Maintains that Herbert "set the fashion of making both reading pew and pulpit the same height and size" (p. 76), thus emphasizing the equal importance of preaching and prayer. Comments also on the positioning of the reading pew in the church (facing the congregation). Plan of the church at Leighton Bromswold (p. 79).

**333. Britting, Georg, ed.** "George Herbert," in *Lyrik des Abendlands*, gemeinsam mit Hans Hennecke, Curt Hohoff und Karl Vossler, ausgewählt von Georg Britting, 228–29, 634. Munich: Carl Hanser Verlag.

Several reprints.

Translation of "Vertue" into German by Richard Flatter (pp. 228–29), with biographical note (p. 634).

**334. Brooke, Tucker.** "Seventeenth-Century Poetry: II. The Moral Tradition," in *A Literary History of England*, edited by Albert C. Baugh, 637–50. New York and London: Appleton-Century-Crofts.

Reprinted, London: Routledge & Kegan Paul, 1950.

2d ed. (4 vols.), 1967.

General appreciative introduction to Herbert's life and poetry (pp. 642–46). Maintains that, although Herbert probably knew Donne's poetry, "he is not a follower of any one" and suggests that to find "a proper parallel to his glowing art, infinitely varied in decoration and uniquely personal in theme, one must go back to the art of the Old French troubadours" (pp. 642–43). Maintains that Herbert's poems are "intensely individual, addressed to a personal and patrician God, who is capable of appreciating the special sacrifices his high-born servant makes, and of understanding the most exquisite delicacies of technique" (p. 643). Calls Herbert "the sublest lyrist of his generation" (p. 644) and comments on his experimentation with stanzaic patterns, the structural balance and unity of the poems, and his emotional intensity and use of homely, simple language. Calls "Vertue" an "insurpassable ode" (p. 643), claims that "Bitter-sweet" is "as superb a piece of poetry as was ever compressed into eight short lines" (p. 644), and finds "The British Church" to be "one of the loveliest things that has been written since Horace on the *via media*" (p. 645).

**335. Cammell, Charles Richard.** "Sonnet: On the Divine Poets, Herbert and Crashaw." *New English Review* 1 (November): 187.

Original sonnet praising the religious poems of Herbert and Crashaw: "These poets took the way that Angels went, / And more than wisdom found—in Paradise" (lines 13–14).

**336. Clarke, George Herbert.** "Christ and the English Poets." *QQ* 55:292–307.

Comments on Herbert's deep, personal feelings for Christ as expressed in his poetry and praises his excellences as a writer of hymns.

**337. Freeman, Rosemary.** *English Emblem Books*. London: Chatto and Windus. xiv, 256p.

Reprinted, New York: Octagon Books, 1966.

Broad study of the emblem book in the sixteenth and seventeenth centuries. Chapter 6, "George Herbert" (pp. 148–72), is a revised and expanded form of "George Herbert and the Emblem Books" (entry 263). Discusses "the relation of the poetry of George Herbert to the fashion, since, apart from some poems in which even the material of the emblem books is used, there is much in his writing that is generally emblematic, and the conventions seem to provide an approach by which his real merits can be estimated and in which his peculiarities appear natural" (p. 7). Argues that Herbert transformed the emblem into poetry of the first order: "It is only in the ordered and controlled treatment of George Herbert that the potentialities of the convention for the expression of devotional and psychological themes were fully realised" (p. 147). Maintains that "to apply the same method to the work of other metaphysical poets would be lacking in a sense of perspective: for, although the emblem books were at hand for any writer to draw upon, Herbert's poetry is primarily and consistently emblematic where theirs is only spasmodically so" (p. 7). Compares Herbert briefly with Spenser, Christopher Harvey, and Bunyan.

**338. Fuson, Benjamin Willis.** "Monologs in English Poetry, 750–1750," in *Browning and His English Predecessors in the Dramatic Monolog*, 48–66. (State

University of Iowa Humanistic Studies, edited by Franklin H. Potter, vol. 8.) Iowa City: State University of Iowa.

Argues that the metaphysical poets' handling of emotional shifts in their subjective religious monologues was in effect an adaptation of Donne. Maintains that Herbert's "only overt objective monolog is the formalized but moving plaint of Jesus in the *quia amore langueo* tradition, 'The Sacrifice'" (p. 59, n. 131). Notes also certain dramatic shifts in mood and tone to be found in "Affliction," "Dialogue," "Assurance," "A Parodie," and "Conscience."

**339. Husain, Itrat.** *The Mystical Element in the Metaphysical Poets of the Seventeenth Century.* With a Foreword by Evelyn Underhill. Edinburgh and London: Oliver and Boyd. 351p.

Reprinted, New York: Biblio and Tannen, 1966.

Contains an introduction on the general characteristics of mysticism, followed by individual studies of Donne, Herbert, Crashaw, Henry and Thomas Vaughan, and Traherne. Announces an intent "to establish the amount of personal spiritual experience which lies behind the work of these poets" (foreword). Estimates "the content of the religious thought of these poets in order to determine the nature and significance of the mystical element in their poetry" (p. 13). Chapter 3, "The Mystical Element in the Poetry of George Herbert" (pp. 120–58), surveys Herbert's religious attitudes and personal sensibilities. Points out the main concerns of Herbert's verse—personal sin and the problems of sin, salvation, and grace. Comments on Herbert's love of Christ, the Church, the Bible, and music. Stresses the specifically Anglican dimension of his theology and piety. Divides Herbert's religious life into two main divisions: (1) awakening of the self and purgation, and (2) illumination. Maintains that the higher levels of the mystical life (the dark night of the soul and the unitive experience) are not found in Herbert's poetry. Concludes that, "though he has not the intensity and passion of a great mystic, his poetry is rich in mystical content" and that "he is the poet who has known God and has felt the peace and joy of His presence and also the pain and agony of His absence in a manner peculiar to the mystics," communicating his experience to us "with the complexity and richness characteristic of a sensitive and sincere artist" (p. 158).

**340. Miles, Josephine.** *The Primary Language of Poetry in the 1640's.* (University of California Publications in English, vol. 19, no. 1, pp. 1–160.) Berkeley and Los Angeles: University of California Press; London: Cambridge University Press.

Incorporated into *The Continuing of Poetic Language: Studies in English Poetry from the 1540's to the 1940's,* along with nos. 2 and 3 of University of California Publications in English, vol. 19 (Berkeley and Los Angeles: University of California Press; London: Cambridge University Press, 1951).

Distinguishes the major poetic vocabulary of the 1640s from the language that preceded and followed it. Mentions Herbert in several instances. Descriptive evaluations of the vocabulary of Donne and other metaphysical poets and a discussion of Donne's influence on the vocabulary of his followers.

**341. Mims, Edwin.** "George Herbert: Holy Shepherd," in *The Christ of the Poets,* 65–75. New York and Nashville: Abingdon-Cokesbury Press.

Discusses various attitudes toward Christ expressed by poets from Spenser to certain modern American Negro poets. Biographical sketch of Herbert. Comments on Herbert's devotional life and piety as reflected in *The Temple,* noting that "of the 169 poems that make up the volume, fully one half suggest some aspect of the Saviour's life or some evidence of his actual presence" (p. 70). Compares Herbert briefly with Donne.

**342. O'Connor, William van.** "The Influence of the Metaphysicals on Modern Poetry." *CE* 9:180–87.

In revised form, this essay appears in *Sense and Sensibility in Modern Poetry* (Chicago: University of Chicago Press, 1948), 81–92.

Surveys the importance and the extent of the modern revival of interest in seventeenth-century metaphysical poetry, especially the poetry of Donne, and comments on the influence of this renewed interest on the poetry of certain modern poets, especially Eliot, Stevens, Yeats, Aiken, Edith Sitwell, the Fugitive Poets, Robert Lowell, and Elinor Wylie. No specific mention of Herbert but a number of references by implication.

# *1949*

**343. Boase, Alan M.** "Poètes anglais et français de l'époque baroque." *RSH* 55–56:155–84.

Maintains that there was a poetry comparable to English metaphysical poetry in France during the late sixteenth and early seventeenth centuries. Uses Donne primarily as the touchstone of the comparison. Briefly comments on similarities in tone between Herbert's "Even-song" and Agrippa d'Aubigné's "Prière du Soir."

**344. Cropper, Margaret.** "George Herbert," in *Flame Touches Flame*, 1–28. London, New York, Toronto: Longmans, Green and Co.

An idealized biographical sketch that presents Herbert as an Anglican saint and uses the poems as autobiographical records of Herbert's religious experience and sensibility. Calls *The Country Parson* "one of the foundation books of the life of the parish priest in our communion, and when it was published after Herbert's death it became one of the formative books of the next period" (p. 14).

**345. Gibbs, J.** "An Unknown Poem of George Herbert." *TLS*, 30 December, p. 857.

Reproduces a heretofore unknown Latin poem ("Perigrinis Almam Matrem invisentibus") written in Herbert's script and found in a copy of the 1620 edition of the works of James I. Notes that the first two lines of the poem (with minor revisions) are found on page 459 of Hutchinson's edition (entry 266).

**346. Green, Julien.** *Journal: 1943-1945.* Paris: Librairie Plon. 234p.

Comments briefly on Herbert in two journal entries: (1) 25 May 1943, reflects on his reactions to rereading Herbert's poetry; calls it "la poésie en sourdine" (p. 38); (2) 16 October 1945, comments on "The Collar": "Je retrouve dans un poème de George Herbert tout l'essentiel de ma conversion, et même plusieurs détails très précis" (p. 241). Notes that Gide and he looked for the poem in the Oxford anthology and were unable to locate it.

**347. Gros, Léon-Gabriel.** "Métaphysiques anglais, du raisonnement en poésie." *Cahiers du Sud* 293:3–30.

Critical preface to a group of translations into French of several seventeenth-century poems, including Herbert's "Vertue." Evaluates metaphysical poetry in terms of Eliot's criticism. Praises Herbert as "le meilleur des poètes religieux de l'Eglise Anglicane" and calls him "le plus fidèle des disciples de Donne" (p. 18). Notes that "ses vers sont aussi durs que ceux de son maître, il abuse des images, mais c'est dans un langage simple et direct qu'il exprime les pensées les plus bizarres" (p. 18).

**348. Herbert, George.** *George Herbert's Country Parson: Selected Passages*, edited by G. M. Forbes. London: Faith Press; New York: Morehouse-Gorham Co. xiii, 56p.

Introduction (pp. vii-xii) is a general appreciative essay that stresses that *The Country Parson* is "an idealized seventeenth century portrait" (p. viii) that may have, nonetheless, a lesson for modern men who "have drifted away from the country to the more artificial 'civilization' of our towns" (p. xii). Herbert's "The Author to the Reader" (p. xiii); selected passages (pp. 1–54); index (pp. 55–56). No notes and no commentary.

**349. Knox, R[onald] A[rbuthnot].** "Richard Crashaw (Died 1649)." *Clergy Review* n.s. 32:373–88.

Reprinted in *Literary Distractions* (New York: Sheed and Ward, 1958), 59–77.

Contrasts Herbert and Crashaw as religious poets. Argues that Herbert was no more than a "moderate poet" and that what most appeals to modern readers is his "quaintness, rather than grandeur" (p. 373). Maintains that Herbert's piety was genuine and that "sometimes he rings the bell by achieving a happy phrase, polished and quotable," but insists that one does not "come across things in his works which make you say to yourself aloud, 'By Gad, that's good!'" (p. 374).

**350. McAdoo, H. R.** *The Structure of Caroline Moral Theology.* London, New York, Toronto: Longmans, Green and Co. xii, 179p.

Attempts "to assemble and to analyse Caroline writing on moral theology with a view to producing a picture of the science as a whole during the period" (p. ix) and "to show that Anglicanism had a well-defined plan of approach to moral theology, clear-cut principles and a positive concept of the science as it should be" (p. x). Several references to Herbert, especially to the country parson's use of moral theology in *A Priest to the Temple* and Herbert's devotion to the liturgy and to the practice of catechizing. Chapter 6, "The Spiritual Life in the English Church" (pp. 138–72), presents an overall view of Anglican piety during the period. Bibliography.

**351. Murdock, Kenneth B.** *Literature and Theology in Colonial New England.* Cambridge, Mass.: Harvard University Press. xi, 235p.

Reprinted, New York and Evanston: Harper & Row (Harper Torchbook), 1963.

References to Herbert throughout. Points out that, unlike most other Anglican writers of the seventeenth century, Herbert was read by the Puritans in America "because he concentrated his work on what was for the Puritan the core of religious life—the direct relation of the individual to God" (p. 149). Maintains that he appealed also because his imagery, compared with Donne's, was restrained and because "there are few of his lines that even a Puritan could consider dangerous in their appeal to man's vagrant passions" (p. 154). Contrasts Herbert's attitude toward wit, music, art, etc. with those of the Puritans: for Herbert "a poem or a piece of music, a witty sermon or an embroidered Communion cloth, might serve as a proper offering" (p. 24).

**352. Roberts, J. Russell.** "Emerson's Debt to the Seventeenth Century." *AL* 21:298–310.

Surveys the influence of the seventeenth century on Emerson. Points out that Herbert was Emerson's favorite metaphysical poet and suggests that reading Herbert influenced his own poetry. Notes that William Ellery Channing on one occasion mistook one of Emerson's poems for one by Herbert.

**353. Shapiro, I. A.** "The Date of Donne's Poem 'To Mr. George Herbert.'" *N&Q* 194:473–74.

Dates Donne's Latin and English verses entitled "To Mr. George Herbert, with one of my Seales, of the Anchor and Christ" as probably composed about January 1615, not just before Donne's death, as Walton implies.

**354. Symes, Gordon.** "Hopkins, Herbert, and Contemporary Modes." *Hibbert Journal* 47:389–94.

Discusses the influence of Gerard Manley Hopkins and seventeenth-century metaphysical poets on contemporary poets. Rejects the notion that Hopkins is a "unique and independent phenomenon" (p. 390) in the history of English poetry and sees him rather as a latter-day metaphysical poet. Maintains that in poetic technique and intention as well as in personality Hopkins is most like Herbert. Notes a number of possible echoes of Herbert in Hopkins's poetry, comments on their mutual interests in music and etymology, and maintains that the greatest similarity is their attempts to reconcile the contrarieties of existence in their poetry and to resolve life's conflicts. Recognizes also differences between the two poets, such as Herbert's simpler and more straightforward manner and his more extensive use of the past tense.

**355. Tate, Allen.** "Johnson on the Metaphysicals." *KR* 11:112–30.

Reprinted in *The Forlorn Demon: Didactic and Critical Essays* (Chicago: Henry Regnery Co., 1953), 112–30; *Collected Essays* (Denver: Alan Swallow, 1959), 488–506.

Reconsiders Dr. Johnson's estimate of the metaphysical poets. In particular, develops a contrast in the use of figurative language, with Dr. Johnson and his critical assumptions on one side and the metaphysical poets on the other. No direct mention of Herbert.

# 1950

**356. Arms, George, and Joseph M. Kuntz.** *Poetry Explication: A Checklist of Interpretations since 1925 of British and American Poems Past and Present.* New York: Swallow Press and William Morrow & Co. 187p.

2d ed., by Joseph M. Kuntz (Denver: Swallow Press, 1962).

3d ed., edited by Joseph M. Kuntz and Nancy Martinez (Boston: G. K. Hall, 1980).

Lists 17 items—notes, essays, and selections from books—discussing nine of Herbert's poems. The second edition lists 49 items, covering thirty poems. The third edition lists 175 items on eighty of the poems.

**357. Bailey, Albert Edward.** "The Fight for Freedom," in *The Gospel in Hymns: Backgrounds and Interpretations*, 19–42. New York: Charles Scribner's Sons.

Pious account of Herbert's life and poetry (pp. 25–29), maintaining that his life was "a mystic sainthood, revealed to us in his poems" (p. 27). Discusses briefly "Antiphon (I)" and "The Elixir" and comments on John Wesley's adaptations of Herbert's poems for the Methodist hymnal.

**358. Benjamin, Edwin B.** "Herbert's 'Vertue.'" *Expl* 9:item 12.

Comments on the structure of "Vertue," especially on the contrast built up between the first three stanzas of the poem and the last.

**359. Bullett, G. W.** "Some Seventeenth-Century Poets," in *The English Mystics*, 94–112. London: Michael Joseph.

Biographical sketch and discussion of Herbert's poetry. Maintains that, although the poems of *The Temple* are expressions of sincerity and saintliness, they are not mystical. Finds Herbert's poems "very unequal in merit, pious conceits and trivialities mingling or alternating with things of a freshness and beauty that silence criticism" (p. 102).

**360. Bush, Douglas.** "The New Science and the Seventeenth-Century Poets," in *Science and English Poetry: A Historical Sketch, 1590–1950*, 27–50. New York: Oxford University Press.

Reprinted, Oxford University Paperback, 1967.

Brief comment on Herbert to show that he, like most writers of his time, was convinced of the "priority of religious and moral insight over knowledge of the external world" (p. 38). Notes that, although Herbert praised Bacon, he shows little interest in science per se.

**361. Daiches, David, and William Charvat, eds.** "The Seventeenth Century," in *Poems in English, 1530–1940*, edited with critical and historical notes and essays, 53–121. New York: Ronald Press Co.

General introduction to seventeenth-century poetry. Comments on Herbert's principal themes and major characteristics. Maintains that Herbert's metaphysical qualities "consist largely in the way he pushes his imagery to its logical conclusion, however far-fetched the 'conceit' that might result, and in his ability to take images from everyday life and play with them intellectually until they became impressive symbols of spiritual reality" (p. 55). Compares Herbert briefly to Crashaw, Donne, and Vaughan. Anthologizes four of Herbert's poems (pp. 73–76) with notes (pp. 660–61).

**362. Empson, William.** "George Herbert and Miss Tuve." *KR* 12:735–38.

A reply to Rosemond Tuve's disagreement (entry 369) with the author's interpretation of "The Sacrifice" in *Seven Types of Ambiguity* (entry 131). While agreeing with some of Tuve's objections, Empson concludes that he "cannot feel that the mass of erudition she brings down like a steam hammer really cracks any nuts" (p. 735). Agrees with Tuve that a critic should not create an entirely new poem by his reinterpretation and that he "should entirely concentrate on how the poem was meant to take effect by its author and did take effect on its first readers" (p. 738). Adds that "this formula includes the way in which it took effect on them without their knowing it, and that opens an Aladdin's Cave of a positively limestone extent and complexity" (p. 738).

**363. Howarth, R. G.** "Hopkins and Sir Thomas More." *N&Q* 195:438.
Argues that the last line of "The Size" originates in Psalm 107 and suggests that Gerard Manley Hopkins may have taken the title for his poem "Heaven-Haven" from Herbert's line.

**364. Keast, William R.** "Johnson's Criticism of the Metaphysical Poets." *ELH* 17:59–70.
Reprinted in *Essential Articles for the Study of John Donne's Poetry*, edited by John R. Roberts (Hamden, Conn.: Archon Books, 1975), 11–19.
Reevaluates Johnson's criticism of the metaphysical poets in an attempt to determine "how far our disappointment with Johnson's treatment of the metaphysical poets reflects genuine deficiencies in Johnson and how far it reflects merely our own present conviction that Donne is a greater poet than, say Gray or even Milton" (pp. 59–60) and to determine how much of our disagreement with Johnson simply reflects "our preferences for a critical theory that specializes in detailed accounts of metaphorical structure to one that emphasizes the general condition of literary pleasure" (p. 60). Argues that, given Johnson's assumptions and premises about the nature and function of poetry, his censure of metaphysical poetry is understandable and just. Points out that Johnson developed no comprehensive literary theory but applied his taste and judgment to individual writers. Maintains that Johnson's comments on the metaphysicals can be more readily put into a proper perspective if one reads his *Life of Cowley* "in relation to the *Rambler*, the *Preface to Shakespeare*, and the other *Lives*" (p. 61). No specific mention of Herbert.

**365. Lloyd, J. D. K.** "The Herbert Tomb in Montgomery Church." *The Montgomeryshire Collections* 50:99–115.
Detailed account and description (with three photographs) of the tomb of Sir Richard Herbert, father of George Herbert, in the south transept of Montgomery Church. Notes that, although only Sir Richard Herbert's body lies beneath the monument, the tomb contains an effigy both of the deceased and of his wife, Magdalene Herbert, as well as a relief at the back that depicts the eight children, six boys and two girls, of Sir Richard and Magdalene Herbert. See also J. D. K. Lloyd, "The Architect of the Herbert Monument at Montgomery" (entry 766).

**366. Mahood, M. M.** *Poetry and Humanism.* New Haven: Yale University Press. 335p.
Reprinted, Port Washington, N.Y.: Kennikat Press, 1967; New York: W. W. Norton, 1970.
Mentions Herbert frequently in this study of Christian humanism and the arts. In "Two Anglican Poets" (pp. 22–53), compares and contrasts Herbert with Christina Rossetti. Shows Herbert's influence and comments on her imitation of him, especially in "Sweet Death." Comments on Herbert's "theocentric assurance of faith," the bravado and audacity in his poetry, his ability to invent parable and to convey a sense of play, and his uses of the emblem and Petrarchan traditions. Discusses Herbert's "acceptance of the human condition as one of tension" (p. 31) and illustrates the point by discussing "The Temper (I)," "The Flower," and "The Pulley." Mentions the importance of certain philosophical notions in Herbert's verse, such as the Great Chain of Being, the idea of correspondences, and cosmic harmony. Throughout compares Herbert with Vaughan, Donne, and Milton.

367. **Nicolson, Marjorie Hope.** *The Breaking of the Circle: Studies in the Effect of the "New Science" upon Seventeenth Century Poetry.* Evanston: Northwestern University Press. xxii, 193p.

Rev. ed., New York: Columbia University Press, 1960, 1962, 1965, 1970.

Many references to Herbert in this study of the impact of the New Science on the literary imagination of the seventeenth century. Observes that, with the encroachment of a mechanistic view of the world, the cosmological metaphors (especially the circle) that grew out of an earlier world view ceased to have the force of actuality and became mere similes. Uses Herbert's verse primarily to illustrate the world view commonly held before the introduction of the New Science. Maintains that Herbert, perhaps more than any other religious poet of the period, "taught the happiness of limitation and restraint" (p. 156) and that thus his works "might be called that word reiterated in so many of them—'Content'" (p. 156). Notes that, unlike many of his time, Herbert "put aside the restlessness of the too-inquiring mind" and "discovered the truly 'vast' things with which man need concern himself" (p. 157). Observes, for example, that Herbert, although he knew both the old and new astronomy, was not particularly stirred by it and that, for him, "the world and the universe might be threatened by scientists and philosophers, the circles broken, but man was all symmetry" (p. 159). Argues that Herbert "found shelter from the incomprehensible universe in faith" (p. 160).

368. **Symes, Gordon.** "The Paradoxes of Poetry." *English* (London) 8:69–73.

Discusses "The Collar" as an example of the complex uses of Christian paradox. Maintains that the basic paradox of the poem is "the all-embracing fatherhood of God which extends as well to the rebellious as to the devout" (p. 72). A further paradox proceeds from this one: "There can be no freedom except in submission to God" (p. 72). Contrasts the poem with Francis Thompson's "The Hound of Heaven": "Thompson's effects are not those of paradox at all. The paradox stands outside the poem, to be accepted by the reader as a condition of his enjoying the poem. It does not grow *out* of the poem, as Herbert's does" (p. 73).

369. **Tuve, Rosemond.** "On Herbert's 'Sacrifice.'" *KR* 12:51–75.

Expanded in *A Reading of George Herbert* (entry 409), 19–99.

Reprinted in *Essential Articles for the Study of George Herbert's Poetry*, edited by John R. Roberts (entry 1216), 434–52.

Challenges William Empson's treatment of "The Sacrifice" in *Seven Types of Ambiguity* (entry 131) and warns against the excesses and limitations of the "New Critics." Shows that Herbert's poem is not "original" (in Empson's sense of the word), "for its basic invention or structural situation, the sequence of ironies upon which it is built, the occurrence, setting and application of the refrain which binds it together, the very collocation of antitheses which make up the poem, are none of them Herbert's" (p. 52). Maintains that the poem "belongs with two interlinked groups, both well-known, of medieval lyrics; both groups belong as does his poem to a larger group, the Complaints of Christ to his People, and all apparently have their spring in the liturgical office of Holy Week, most obviously (for one group) in the *Improperia* or Reproaches of Good Friday" (p. 52). Comments on various typological, legendary, and liturgical elements that inform the poem to show that when one reads it in the light of the tradition in which it was written "it takes on a richness, a depth, complexity and moving power" (p. 57) that cannot be had otherwise. For a reply, see William Empson (entry 362).

370. **Wallerstein, Ruth.** *Studies in Seventeenth-Century Poetic.* Madison: Univer-

sity of Wisconsin Press. x, 421p.

Reprinted, 1961, 1965.

Several references to Herbert but no extended treatment. Comments briefly on Herbert's use of the emblem tradition and compares him with Marvell: "*On a Drop of Dew* and *The Coronet* remind us of the work of George Herbert, whose poems like *The Collar* they closely resemble in their religious motif, in their treatment of image, and in metrical structure" (p. 162). Argues that Herbert helps in understanding the religious feeling of Marvell's *Appleton House* (pp. 303–5) and maintains that Herbert's "Constancie" was "surely one germ of Wordsworth's *Character of a Happy Warrior*" (p. 261).

**371. Wedgwood, C. V.** "John Donne and Caroline Poetry," in *Seventeenth-Century English Literature*, 66–89. (Home University Library of Modern Knowledge, 218.) London: Geoffrey Cumberlege and Oxford University Press.

Reprinted, 1956, 1961, 1970; Folcroft, Pa.: Folcroft Library Editions, 1977; Norwood, Pa.: Norwood Editions, 1978.

Maintains that Herbert's poetry "has a serenity which is already beyond passion" (p. 83) and that "for that reason he can never stir the emotions as Crashaw or Donne can stir them; but he can convey the still wonder of unperturbed devotion more truly than any other poet" (p. 83).

**372. Wimsatt, W. K., Jr.** "Verbal Style: Logical and Counterlogical." *PMLA* 65:5–20.

Reprinted in *The Verbal Icon: Studies in the Meaning of Poetry* (Lexington: University of Kentucky Press, 1954), 201–17.

Studies verbal style in order "to correlate certain areas which have been noticed separately by earlier criticism: certain prose figures or merits defined in classical rhetoric, certain logical faults of prose, especially as defined by H. W. Fowler in his *Modern English Usage*, and certain poetic figures defined both by classical rhetoric and by recent semantic criticism" (p. 5). Discusses the pun as a "fully developed counterlogical figure" (p. 11) and comments specifically on Herbert's use of the pun *son-sun* in "The Sonne" and the pun on *rest* in "The Pulley."

**373. Zitner, Sheldon P.** "Herbert's 'Jordan' Poems." *Expl* 9:item 11.

Comments on the symbolic possibilities of Herbert's title for his two Jordan poems. Finds in a book of emblems, *Emblemata et Epigrammata Miscellanea Selecta ex Stromatis Peripateticis*, gathered by Fayi and published in 1610 at Geneva, some Latin verses that contrast the purity of the Jordan with the vile landscape through which it flows. Sees a possible parallel between this symbol and Herbert's contrast between moral and secular poetry in the two poems.


# *1951*


**374. Bateson, F. W.** "Contributions to a Dictionary of Critical Terms. II. Dissociation of Sensibility." *EIC* 1:302–12.

Reprinted in *Essays in Critical Dissent* (Totowa, N.J.: Rowman and Littlefield, 1972), 142–52; *Essential Articles for the Study of John Donne's Poetry*, edited by John R. Roberts (Hamden, Conn.: Archon Books, 1975), 58–65.

Traces the development of Eliot's notion of "dissociation of sensibility" to the critical writings of Rémy de Gourmont, particularly his *Probléme du Style* (1902), which provided Eliot "with a *framework* to which his own critical ideas and intuitions—even then incomparably profounder and more original than Gourmont's—were able to attach themselves" (p. 308): "What he has done . . . has been to transfer to the nation Gourmont's analysis of the mental processes of the individual. The unified sensibility that Gourmont found in Laforgue, Mr. Eliot finds in the England of the early seventeenth century" (p. 307). Notes inconsistencies in Eliot's uses of the term *dissociation of sensibility* and traces the evolution of Eliot's thinking. Concludes that "its use today as a loose, honorific synonym for 'taste' and 'personality' can only be deprecated" (p. 312). For a reply, see Eric Thompson (entry 408); for Bateson's reply to Thompson, see entry 394.

**375. Bethell, S. L.** *The Cultural Revolution of the Seventeenth Century*. London: Dennis Dobson. 161p.

Reprinted, 1963.

Divided into two parts: (1) a discussion of the concept of dissociation of sensibility, especially as it relates to certain theological questions, and (2) a study of Vaughan. Mentions Herbert throughout. Comments briefly on such matters as Herbert's possible assistance in translating Bacon's *Advancement* into Latin, his uses of the conceit, his influence on Vaughan, his hymns, and his Welsh background. Compares Herbert with Crashaw, Donne, and Vaughan.

**376. Bickham, Jack M.** "Herbert's 'The Collar.'" *Expl* 10:item 17.

In part a reply to Dan Norton (entry 306). Notes the triple verbal pun in the title of the poem: collar, choler, caller. Maintains that Herbert is choleric about the collar "only until he hears the voice of the *caller*, God"; thus, "the *caller* is more important in end effect than is the symbolic 'collar' or the mood of 'choler.'"

**377. Blackburn, William.** "Lady Magdalen Herbert and Her Son George." *SAQ* 50:378–88.

Biographical sketch of Herbert and his mother and outline of their relationship. Maintains that, as a result of his mother's constant supervision, Herbert's personal life and his poetry reflect a feeling of dependence. Argues that a constant theme in Herbert's poetry is "the dependence of the soul on God, though some of his most poignant poems, such for example as 'The Collar,' show him in rebellion against God's discipline—just as indeed the child is often in rebellion against the discipline of the parent. The figure is eloquent of Herbert's concept of religion: religion is a state of being tied to God—even as a child is tied to its mother's apron string" (p. 388).

**378. Brower, Reuben Arthur.** *The Fields of Light: An Experiment in Critical Reading*. New York: Oxford University Press. xii, 218p.

Reprinted as a Galaxy Book, 1962, 1968; Westport, Conn.: Greenwood Press, 1980.

A portion reprinted in *Perspectives on Poetry*, edited by James L. Calderwood and Harold E. Toliver (New York: Oxford University Press, 1968), 98–108.

In the introduction, announces his intent "to demonstrate some methods of reading analysis and to use them in discovering designs of imaginative organization in particular poems, plays, and novels" (p. xi). In discussing tonal patterns, comments on Herbert's "Love (III)" (pp. 27–31), noting primarily its "trio of tones—the reserved decently colloquial manner of the narrator and within the story the intimate deprecatory voice of the guest and the exquisite politeness and assurance of the host" (p. 29). Shows that in the poem "the gentle resolution of a deep conflict is expressed through a contrast between tones and the implied inner action of the drama" (p. 31). In discussing basic methods for interpreting metaphor, comments on "The Windows" (pp. 44–48) and presents a detailed diagram of the poem's metaphorical design. In a section on sound, uses the third stanza of "The Windows" to illustrate his point (pp. 59–61).

**379. Empson, William.** "Honest Man," in *The Structure of Complex Words,* 185–201. London: Chatto & Windus.
      Includes an explication of stanza 3 of "Jordan (I)" (p. 188). Shows how the stanza "gets its play from pastoral sentiment and patronage" (p. 188).

**380. Herbert, George.** "Four Poems of Herbert." Translated by Joseph H. Summers. *Quarterly Review of Literature* 6:211–12.
      Translation of four of Herbert's Latin poems into English: (1) "In Angelos" from *Lucus* ("The Angels"), (2) "Horti, deliciae *Dominae*" from *Memoriae Matris Sacrum* ("The Gardens: to the Memory of Magdalen Herbert"), (3) "Homo, Statua" from *Lucus* ("Man, the Statue"), and (4) "Patria" from *Lucus* ("Homeland").

**381. Naruse, Masaiku.** "George Herbert no Kenkyu" [A Study of George Herbert]. *Shodai Ronshu* [The Review of the Kobe University of Commerce] no. 5 (March): 1–24.
      Traces Herbert's spiritual development through *The Temple.* Maintains that Herbert is not merely a follower of Donne but is a forerunner in the exploration of a new kind of religious poetry in the seventeenth century.

**382. • Pinto, Vivian De Sola, ed.** *English Biography in the Seventeenth Century: Selected Short Lives.* (Life, Literature, and Thought Library, gen. ed. Vivian De Sola Pinto.) London: Harrap; New York: Barnes & Noble. 237p.
      Surveys the development of early English biography and comments on the *Life of Herbert,* calling it Walton's "artistic masterpiece" (p. 37), "possibly the most perfect embodiment of the spirit of Anglicanism" (p. 37), and "the most lyrical of all English biographies" (p. 38). Observes that, although Walton focuses on Herbert's saintliness, "there is a very delicate ironic humour in his portrayal of George Herbert, the aristocratic and academic dandy" (p. 38). Reprints Walton's *Life of Herbert* (pp. 47–97) with explanatory notes (pp. 203–10), omitting Walton's short introduction.

**383. Praz, Mario.** "The Critical Importance of the Revived Interest in Seventeenth-Century Metaphysical Poetry," in *English Studies Today,* edited by C. L. Wrenn and G. Bullough, 158–66. London: Oxford University Press.
      Reprinted in *Essential Articles for the Study of John Donne's Poetry,* edited by John R. Roberts (Hamden, Conn.: Archon Books, 1975), 3–10.
      Maintains that the revival of interest in the metaphysical poets, especially Donne, in the twentieth century "has not only resulted in a change of perspective in literary criticism, but has also furthered the reaction against the critical standards and poetic theory of romanticism: Donne, we may say without fear of exaggeration, has had in the last thirty years a catalytic function" (p. 166). Argues that the revaluation of the metaphysical poets "has been more than a literary fashion, has resulted not only in the adoption of certain images, in the cult of certain conceits and imaginative processes: it has rather amounted to the awareness of a similar disposition of spirit, of the same complexity in facing life, of the same ironical reaction" (p. 163). Outlines Eliot's key role in this process. No specific mention of Herbert.

384. ———. "George Herbert," in *Il libro della poesia inglese*, 179–84. Messina, Florence: Casa Editrice G. D'Anna.

General introduction to Herbert's life and poetry in Italian (p. 179) followed by "Church-monuments," "The Windows," "Vertue," "The Collar," and "Easter-wings" in English with Italian explanatory notes (pp. 180–84). Maintains that in Herbert's poetry "la maniera metafisica si fa parrocchiale, discende all'emblematica spicciola, rasenta in maniera pericolosa il concetto predicabile" (p. 179). Notes that for Herbert "ogni sia pur umile occasione vien trasportata al morale, ma la spontanea freschezza, il candore del poeta, e il suo fermo fervore devoto riescono ad avvivare la materia spesso artificiosa e didattica" (p. 179).

385. **Silver, Louis H.** "The First Edition of Walton's *Life of Herbert*." HLB 5:371–72.

Presents a collation of the complete first edition of Walton's *Life of Herbert* (1670) as it left the printer. Accounts for the two title pages involved.

386. **Smith, Harold Wendall.** "'The Dissociation of Sensibility.'" *Scrutiny* 18:175–88.

Reexamines Eliot's theory and maintains that the split between thought and feeling can be traced to its social and religious roots. Argues that Eliot's evaluation of Donne and the metaphysicals was in effect an effort to canonize his own tastes and reflects the tensions of his own sensibility. Notes that, by the time of the metaphysicals, "the two realms of abstract and sensible had already been divided; it was in the distance which separated them that the 'metaphysician' worked between them, and Eliot's very term 'unification' implies both elements must have been clearly distinguishable and in need of being utterly fused into one" (p. 178). No specific discussion of Herbert.

387. **Summers, Joseph H.** "Herbert's Form." *PMLA* 66:1055–72.

Reprinted in *George Herbert: His Religion and Art* (entry 435), 73–94; *Essential Articles for the Study of George Herbert's Poetry*, edited by John R. Roberts (entry 1216), 87–104.

Discusses Herbert's attitude toward form and order in religion and art. Maintains that Herbert saw the ritual of the Church as a means of achieving a state of grace: "If every aspect of it was understood, it could teach the way of salvation and the beautiful pattern of God's creation. Proper worship resulted in an ethical and spiritual ordering of the worshipper's life" (p. 1057). Maintains that from this notion follows Herbert's concept (perhaps derived in part from St. Augustine) that a work of art should reflect the divine pattern of creation and that "an unethical life or poem by definition represented that lack of order called 'ugly' or 'evil'—not a positive quality, but an absence of the good and beautiful" (p. 1058). Discusses Herbert's hieroglyphic view of the world and experience and comments on his uses of typology and emblems in his poetry. Maintains that, for Herbert, poetry was an act of worship and/or of edification, not direct autobiographical revelation or mere self-expression. Maintains that the title, *The Temple*, is a symbol "for all the types of order in the universe, both God's and man's" (p. 1065). Maintains that *The Temple* is "the symbolic record, written by a poet, of a 'typical' Christian life within the Church" (p. 1066). Discusses in particular "The Collar" as "one of Herbert's most deliberate ventures in 'hieroglyphic form'" (p. 1069). Sees the poem as a formalized picture of chaos, reflecting in its form the disordered life of self-will. Concludes that for Herbert, the composition of poems "was the act of the craftsman who shapes the imperfect materials of his own suffering as well as joy into a pattern symbolic of the divine order" (p. 1072).

**388. Van Doren, Mark.** *Introduction to Poetry: Commentaries on Thirty Poems.* New York: William Sloane Associates. xxviii, 568p.

Reprinted, 1962, 1966; New York: Hill and Wang, 1968.

Explication of "The Flower" (pp. 69–73). Discusses theme, stanzaic intricacies, uses of sound and metaphor, and tone.

**389. White, Helen C., Ruth C. Wallerstein, and Ricardo Quintana, eds.** "George Herbert," in *Seventeenth-Century Verse and Prose,* vol. 1, *1600–1660,* 259–78. New York: Macmillan Co.

2d. ed., 1971 (entry 889).

General introduction to Herbert's life and poetry, followed by a selected bibliography (pp. 259–60). Maintains that it is the element of individual spiritual struggle in Herbert's poems that primarily attracts readers to *The Temple.* Argues that in Herbert's best poems there is "an exquisite perfection of statement seldom surpassed" (p. 260). Cites as Herbert's strengths "the firmness of intellectual structure in the poem as a whole, the precision of phrasing, and the sharp vigor of the astonishing but revealing contrast in image and implication" and praises his ability to convey "tenderness of feeling quite his own," his "fine ear for verse music," and his "passion for craftsmanship" (p. 260). Anthologizes thirty-two poems with brief explanatory notes (pp. 261–78).

# 1952

**390. Arnold, Matthew.** *The Note-Books of Matthew Arnold,* edited by Howard Foster Lowry, Karl Young, and Waldo Hilary Dunn. London, New York, Toronto: Geoffrey Cumberlege for Oxford University Press. xv, 656p.

Includes two quotations from Herbert: lines 115–17 of *The Church-Porch* (thrice) and lines 17–20 of "The Elixir."

**391. Baker, Herschel.** *The Wars of Truth: Studies in the Decay of Christian Humanism in the Earlier Seventeenth Century.* Cambridge, Mass.: Harvard University Press. xi, 390p.

Reprinted, Gloucester, Mass.: Peter Smith, 1969.

Examines "the traditional and the emerging concepts of 'truth'—theological, scientific, political, and other—whose collision generated such heat and even light in the age of Milton" (p. vii). Adds that "in attempting to seek out the origin of this transformation in the early Renaissance and to sketch the progress through the earlier seventeenth century I have sought to indicate the intellectual and emotional pressures which shaped men's conception of 'truth' and of their capacity to attain it, and to suggest some of the consequences for literature" (p. vii). Several references to Herbert that place him within the intellectual framework of his time. Comments on Herbert's conception of Providence and on his love for tradition and for the Anglican establishment. Shows that both Donne and Herbert stayed closely within the ecclesiastical tradition.

**392. Baker, Robert.** *Let All the Worlds. Anthem S.A.T.B. with Organ Accompaniment and Solos for Baritone, Soprano and Mezzo-Soprano.* Melville, N.Y.: H. W. Gray Publications. 10p.

Musical setting for "Antiphon (I)."

**393. Baruch, Franklin R.** "Donne and Herbert." *TLS*, 30 May, p. 361.

Points out that in *The Church-Porch* (stanza 14) Herbert appropriates line 30 from Donne's "To Mr Tilman after he had taken orders." For a reply, see J. B. Leishman (entry 403).

**394. Bateson, F. W.** "The Critical Forum: 'Dissociation of Sensibility.'" *EIC* 2:213–14.

Reply to Eric Thompson (entry 408), who challenges Bateson's attack on the notion of "dissociation of sensibility" (entry 374). Insists that "however much we dress it up, the Dissociation of Sensibility cannot be made respectable," for it is simply "a lovely mouthful, full of sound and fury," that unfortunately "doesn't signify anything" (p. 214).

**395. Bottrall, Margaret.** "George Herbert and 'The Country Parson.'" *Listener* 47:558–59.

General appreciative comments about *The Country Parson*. Places the work within a seventeenth-century context and maintains that, although the book is not auto-biographical and is instead Herbert's conception of the life of the ideal parson (somewhat like a seventeenth-century character essay), Herbert indirectly reveals much about himself in it: "Only a man who loved pastoral work could have written of it so understandingly" (p. 559). Sees *The Country Parson* as an important document of social history and as an important commentary on Herbert's poetry.

**396. Bush, Douglas.** "The Renaissance," in *English Poetry: The Main Currents from Chaucer to the Present*, 21–79. London: Methuen; New York: Oxford University Press.

Reprinted, with minor revisions, 1961, 1963, 1965, 1966, 1971.

First published as a Galaxy Book, 1963.

General critical commentary on Herbert's poetry. Maintains that "the poetry of Herbert is a record of religious experience more central and comprehensive, and more humble, than Donne's" (p. 60). Comments on Herbert's use of the emblematic technique: "Whatever their themes and manner and length, Herbert's best poems are organized wholes. Usually his battles are fought under our eyes, and the issue may be in doubt, yet every image, line, and phrase contributes to the developing pattern; there is no fumbling or rambling" (p. 62).

**397. Cazamian, Louis.** *The Development of English Humor.* 2 parts. Durham: Duke University Press. viii, 421p.

Studies the development of English humor from the Old English period through the Renaissance. Suggests that Herbert, as well as such religious poets as Crashaw, Vaughan, Lord Herbert, and Traherne, are humorless poets: "The devout seriousness of their purpose precludes the possibility of a half-conscious element of intentional grotesqueness in their manner" (p. 356, n. 1). Maintains that "their conceits do not lend themselves to any suspicion of double meaning" (p. 388).

**398. D[avenport], A[rnold].** "Five Notes on George Herbert." *N&Q* 197:420–22.

Corrections or supplements to Hutchinson's commentary on five difficult passages in his edition of Herbert. (1) *The Church-Porch* (stanza 33). Points out that the word *cracked* in the seventeenth century had the special meaning of *bankrupt* and argues that Herbert is saying: "If you play for higher stakes than you can afford you will go bankrupt; your wife and children will be impoverished; your servants will be turned off; and at length your ancestral name will survive only in the armorial window of the family chapel in the parish church, of interest to antiquarians, but no longer important as a name of a prominent family" (p. 421). (2) "Superliminare." Argues that the two quatrains should be regarded as two parts of one poem and that Herbert's quatrains correspond to the two parts of the Sybil's speech in the *Aeneid* (6.258 ff.). (3) "The Sacrifice" (lines 121–23). Maintains that Herbert is referring to Exodus 17 and that Herbert has Christ saying: "I am accused of calling myself king of the Jews, but the people rejected me and say that Caesar is their sole King: it was Caesar, forsooth! who cleft the rock in Horeb, when, as now, the people denied my Lordship and my presence. I cleft the rock for them then, and I pour out my blood for them now, but neither then nor now have I touched their hearts" (p. 421). (4) "The Quidditie" (line 12): "I am with thee, and *most take all.*" Notes that the phrase is a gambling phrase and argues that Herbert is saying "that worldly people value this or that for the pleasure, honour, profit, etc. it provides, and scorn poetry as deficient in these ways; but he himself when writing his religious poetry is 'with God' and in that communion finds that he far surpasses the worldly in his possession of the very things they value, in pleasure, honour, profit, etc. In any competition with them he 'scoops the pool'" (p. 422). Sees three possible interpretations of the title of the poem. (5) "The Jews" (lines 5–6): "Who by not keeping once, became a debter; / And now by keeping lose the letter." Maintains that Herbert is saying: "The Jews, who, in the person of Adam, by not keeping the one commandment, became sinners . . . and had to be reinstated and controlled by Mosaic Law . . . , and now, by keeping to the Mosaic Law, losing Christ who lets us lose both from the sin of Adam and from subservience to the letter of the old law" (p. 422).

**399. Deutsch, Babette.** "Wars and Rumors of Wars," in *Poetry in Our Time*, 348–77. New York: Henry Holt and Co.

Comments briefly on Herbert's influence on Louis MacNeice, especially the echoes from Herbert's "Sighs and Grones" in "Prayer Before Birth" (pp. 364–67).

**400. Eldredge, Frances.** "Herbert's 'Jordan.'" *Expl* 11:item 3.

Maintains that Herbert's title "Jordan" refers primarily to the sacrament of baptism: "The Christian sacrament of baptism, with its significance of spiritual cleansing, regeneration, and consecration to the Christian vision, was the essential connotation . . . in the concept 'Jordan.'" In the two poems Herbert is "seeking regeneration and consecrating his talents to the highest service he knew."

**401. Gardner, Helen.** "Appendix G: Donne's Latin Poem to Herbert and Herbert's Reply," in *John Donne: The Divine Poems*, edited with introduction and commentary by Helen Gardner, 138–47. Oxford: Clarendon Press.

Discusses the date of Donne's Latin poem to Herbert (probably January 1615), its title and setting in both the 1650 edition of Donne's poems and Walton's *Life* (1658), and the nature of Herbert's Latin and English verses printed with it. Argues that Herbert's verses do not form one poem but are separate verses written at different times.

**402. Howell, A. C.** "Christopher Harvey's *The Synagogue* (1640)." *SP* 49:229–47.

Points out that the title page of the first edition of Harvey's *The Synagogue* closely resembles that of *The Temple* and that it was also frequently bound with *The Temple*. Notes that Philemon Stephens, "the enterprising seller of theological and devotional books, saw the possibility of bringing together these two volumes of verse as a good money-making proposition," and thus "his shop, the Gilded Lion, became the headquarters for Herbert's and Harvey's poems, inseparable for 200 years after 1650" (p. 232). Shows that "not until the appearance of a volume edited by R[ichard] Edwards . . . in 1806 did Herbert's *The Temple* appear in an edition separate from *The Synagogue*" (p. 233). Comments on how *The Synagogue* was both an imitation of *The Temple* and also intended to supplement it.

**403. Leishman, J. B.** "Donne and Herbert." *TLS*, 13 June, p. 391.
Reply to Franklin Baruch (entry 393). Points out that not only did F. E. Hutchinson in his edition of Herbert (entry 266) note that line 30 of Donne's "To Mr Tilman after he had taken orders" appear in stanza 14 of Herbert's *The Church-Porch*, but also that it appears, slightly revised, in *The Country Parson*.

**404. Mazzeo, Joseph Anthony.** "A Critique of Some Modern Theories of Metaphysical Poetry." *MP* 50:88–96.
Reprinted in *Seventeenth Century English Poetry: Modern Essays in Criticism*, edited by William Keast (entry 584), 63–74, rev. ed. (entry 879), 77–88; *Discussions of John Donne*, edited by Frank Kermode (Boston: D. C. Heath & Co., 1962), 118–25; *John Donne's Poetry: Authoritative Texts, Criticism*, edited by A. L. Clements (New York: W. W. Norton & Co., 1966), 134–43.
Comments on several modern theories about the nature of metaphysical poetry, such as the idea that metaphysical poetry is a decadent, exaggerated use of the Petrarchan and troubadour tradition; is best accounted for by the influence of Ramist logic; is closely allied to the baroque; or is closely related to the emblem tradition. Approaching the problem from the perspective of sixteenth- and seventeenth-century theorists, especially Giordano Bruno, Baltasar Gracián, and Emmanuele Tesauro, the author finds all modern theories wanting and at times inconsistent. Argues that "the principle of universal analogy as a poetic, or the poetic of correspondences," offers "a theory of metaphysical poetry which is simpler, in great harmony with the evidence, and freer from internal contradictions than the major modern theories that have yet been formulated" (p. 89). Points out that, according to contemporary critics, "the conceit itself is the expression of a correspondence which actually obtains between objects and that, since the universe is a network of universal correspondences or analogies which unite all the apparently heterogeneous elements of experience, the most heterogeneous metaphors are justifiable," and thus "the theorists of the conceit justify the predilection of the 'school of wit' for recondite and apparently strained analogies by maintaining that even the more violent couplings of dissimilars were simply expressions of the underlying unity of all things" (pp. 88–89). No specific references to Herbert.

**405. Raiziss, Sona.** *The Metaphysical Passion: Seven Modern American Poets and the Seventeenth-Century Tradition.* Philadelphia: University of Pennsylvania Press. xv, 327p.
Reprinted, Westport, Conn.: Greenwood Press, 1970.
Discusses the influence of, and the similarities between, the metaphysical poets of the seventeenth century and the work of certain modern poets, especially T. S. Eliot, John Crowe Ransom, Allen Tate, Robert Penn Warren, Hart Crane, Elinor Wylie,

and Archibald MacLeish. Argues that "if, from many of Donne's poems, we remove a seventeenth-century construction here and there and revert an inversion, we discover the experience and language of contemporary writing" (p. xiii). Part 1 (pp. 3–56) examines the temper of metaphysical poetry, its subject matter, methods, moods, and wit. Part 2 (pp. 59–164) discusses the sources of the metaphysical impulse, those tensions and conflicts that are parallel between the seventeenth and the twentieth centuries. Part 3 (pp. 167–241) discusses seven modern poets in the light of the preceding comments. Refers throughout to Herbert, primarily by way of illustration, and comments briefly on some of his major themes and images, his uses of ambiguity and wit, and so on. Sees the psychology of Herbert's poetry, as compared with Donne's, as "an apparently simpler and more direct kind" (p. 100). Briefly compares Herbert with Donne, Hopkins, Wylie, Eliot, Ransom, Anna Branch, Emily Dickinson, Emerson, MacLeish, and Samuel Greenberg.

**406. Ross, Malcolm MacKenzie.** "Analogy and Metaphor: A Note on the Decline of the Metaphysical Style." *SCN* 10:13.

Summary of the argument that is more fully presented in *Poetry and Dogma: The Transformation of Eucharistic Symbols in Seventeenth Century English Poetry* (entry 434). Sees a direct relationship between the decline of metaphysical style and the ascendancy of certain radical revisions of dogma, especially the dogma of the Eucharist. Maintains that "in the Eucharistic poetry of the Catholic Anglicans the world of flesh is clearly cut off from the world of spirit." Observes that in Herbert's "The H. Communion" "all sense of the analogical *participation* of the natural order in the divine disappears" and thus "in Herbert there is to be had the spectacle of analogical language dissolving into metaphor."

**407. Summers, Joseph H.** "Herbert's 'Trinitie Sunday.'" *Expl* 10:item 23.

Considers the poem, a prayer for Trinity Sunday, as one of Herbert's "most artful formal hieroglyphs." Notes the functional uses of the number *three* in the poem: "The poem is not merely a witty exercise in divine numerology: the ingenuity clarifies the central meaning." Close reading of each line of the poem.

**408. Thompson, Eric.** "The Critical Forum: 'Dissociation of Sensibility.'" *EIC* 2:207–13.

Challenges F. W. Bateson (entry 374). Maintains that Eliot's study of F. H. Bradley is central to understanding his concept of "dissociation of sensibility." For a reply, see Bateson (entry 394).

**409. Tuve, Rosemond.** *A Reading of George Herbert.* Chicago: University of Chicago Press; London: Faber and Faber; Toronto: W. J. Gage & Co. 215p. Reprinted, 1965, 1969, 1982.

Prefatory notes (pp. 9–10) explain that, in references to modern positions on Herbert, these "sets of ideas cannot be equated with 'The New Criticism,' although most all of the 'New Critics' take some or all of the positions discussed" (p. 9). Announces her intent "to show that criticism can be richer and truer if it will remain willing to bring all methods to bear, including those which scholarship can provide" (p. 10). Table of plates (pp. 13–16). Part 1, " 'The Sacrifice' and Modern Criticism" (pp. 19–99), portions of which were published previously (entry 369), challenges the critical presuppositions and attempts to repair the ignorance of many modern critics. Maintains that the poem should "speak so far as possible in its own voice" and that "a poem is most beautiful and most meaningful to us when it is read in terms of the tradition which gave it birth" (p. 22). Not only presents a detailed reading of "The Sacrifice" but specifically points out the inadequacies of Empson's reading of the poem in *Seven Types of Ambiguity* (entry 131). Shows that, although "The Sacrifice" is a great and original poem, its "basic invention or structural situation, the sequences of ironies upon which it is built, the occurrence, setting, and application of the refrain which bind it together, the very collocation of the antitheses which make it up, are none of them Herbert's" (p. 24). Comments on the poetical, typological, iconographical, and liturgical conventions of the poem in order to show that "much that is 'outside' a poem to us was well inside it to our forefathers, and still is to some readers" (p. 27). Uses the poem as a vehicle for criticizing the excesses of modern critics who fail to combine scholarship with their criticism. Shows that Herbert's originality must be seen in relation to the tradition and that thereby one is able "to perceive with greater pleasure those leaps and those masterful ordering actions of the single human mind by which new relationships are made and new unities created" (p. 79). Part 2 (pp. 103–203) contains several subsections. In the introduction, the author announces her intention to explain and illustrate a number of traditional symbols in Herbert's verse and thereby to demonstrate "what characterizes writing in the symbolic mode" (p. 103). Maintains that, as a Christian poet, Herbert "sees the world, both outside and inside himself; he sees it as a web of significances not as a collection of phenomena which we may either endow with significance or leave unendowed. He writes not of events and facts, but of meanings" (pp. 103–4). (1) "Images as Language" (pp. 112–37) discusses the problem of figures and language by considering a group of Herbert's poems that "use the set of conceits clustered around the ancient symbol of Christ as the miraculous grape-bunch which figured forth the inheritance of the Chosen People, crossing over Jordan to the promised Land" (p. 112). Comments also on the tradition of this Old Testament figure in the graphic arts. Discusses such poems as "The Bunch of Grapes," "The Agonie," "Sion," "The Bag," and "Good Friday" to show their typological and iconographical antecedents. Proposes to show "that symbols are a language which enables poems to be permanently valid, and that if we will learn the language, which is in some cases an archaic and difficult one, we shall not mistake the poet's tone of voice but accurately take his meanings even across intervening centuries" (p. 134). (2) "Wit" (pp. 137–58) argues that many of the details that to modern readers of Herbert seem most novel and witty are "either outright conventions in traditional allegorical materials, or take their spring from such inherited symbols" (p. 138). Comments on such images as the gilded *tabernaculum* or box, the image of man as God's music, the crucified Christ as a lyre, and the devotional uses of red and white in order to show that, if "we approach them innocent of their long use, traditional overtones, and serious fitness deriving from long-familiar connexions, we not only outright lose shades of meaning but we destroy the delicacy and decorous justness of the tone" (p. 158). (3) "Explanation" (pp. 158–82) comments on the iconographical conventions used in "Sunday," "Peace," "Church-rents and schismes," "Justice (II)," and "Whitsunday," which include figures that are apparently bizarre to certain modern readers but were clear and uneccentric to readers in Herbert's time. Discusses other poems that would have demanded a great deal from Herbert's contemporaries, such as the reference to "Josephs coat" in "Church-musick." (4) "Jordan" (pp. 182–203) discusses the two Jordan poems and maintains that "a better understanding of these two poems will illuminate some seven or eight others whose interrelations are revealing, and the process will serve to uncover basic elements in Herbert's poetic theory, which in turn are inextricable from his conceptions of the significance of human life" (p. 182). Three notes: (1) a note on the accessibility of

materials used, to the sixteenth- and seventeenth-century English reader (pp. 204–11); (2) a note on conventions of quoting used in this book (pp. 211–13); and (3) a note for students interested in certain types of texts (pp. 214–15). Concludes by pointing out that the book does not have an index because the author did not want it to be used as a "dictionary of symbols or as a repertory of specific sources."
Reviews:
Anon. *Listener* 48 (1952): 389, 391
Anon. *SCN* 10 (1952): 54
Anon. *TLS*, 22 August 1952, p. 551
Edwin Muir, *Observer*, 24 August 1952, p. 7
Robert Halsband, *Saturday Review*, 9 May 1953, p. 48
Ruth Wallerstein, *JEGP* 52 (1953): 419–21
George Whalley, *QQ* 60 (1954): 265–7
Millar MacLure, *UTQ* 23 (1954): 200–203
Patrick Anderson, *Cambridge Review* 6 (1954): 504–8
Joan Bennett, *MP* 51 (1953): 135–37
William Blackburn, *SAQ* 53 (1954): 592
Pierre Legouis, *EA* 7 (1954): 328–29
Arnold Stein, *MLN* 69 (1954): 610–13

**410. Wiley, Margaret L.** "Postscript: The Despair of God," in *The Subtle Knot: Creative Skepticism in Seventeenth-Century England*, 277–81. London: George Allen & Unwin.
    Comments briefly on Herbert's "The Sacrifice" as a poem that attempts to reveal God's frustration in his efforts to break through man's rejection of his love and truth. Presents a hypothetical soliloquy by God, who examines his own despair at reaching man.

# 1953

**411. Bethell, S. L.** "Gracián, Tesauro, and the Nature of Metaphysical Wit." *Northern Miscellany of Literary Criticism* 1:19–40.
    Reprinted in *Discussions of John Donne*, edited by Frank Kermode (Boston: D. C. Heath & Co., 1962), 136–49; *The Metaphysical Poets: A Selection of Critical Essays*, edited by Gerald Hammond (entry 985), 129–56.
    Agrees with Rosemond Tuve's position in *Elizabethan and Metaphysical Imagery: Renaissance Poetic and Twentieth-Century Critics* (entry 330) but attempts "to supplement and somewhat rectify her account of metaphysical poetry by means similar to her own, that is by going to contemporary theorists" (p. 20). Argues that early seventeenth-century England produced almost no theorists on the nature of wit and presents an account of metaphysical wit and of the nature of the conceit based primarily on a reading of Baltasar Gracián's *Agudeza y Arte de Ingenio* (1642) and Emmanuele Tesauro's *Il Cannocchiale Aristotelico* (1654). Maintains that both Gracián and Tesauro "are engaged with the wider functions of literary criticism, so what they have to say applies almost as much to English as to Spanish or Italian poetry" (p. 22). Concedes that "there is, of course, no suggestion that they are 'sources' of anything or 'influences' on anybody. But, coming as they do after Europe had been soaked for a half a century in metaphysical wit, we might expect them to articulate the

methods by which poets and other writers had been perhaps only half-consciously working" (p. 22). No specific references to Herbert.

**412. Borgerhoff, E. B. O.** " 'Mannerism' and 'Baroque': A Simple Plea." *CL* 5:323–31.

Explores the difficulty of using the terms *baroque* and *mannerism* in literary discussions, especially about French literature, yet maintains that, in spite of the controversial nature of the terms, both have a literary usefulness. No specific mention of Herbert, but Donne is cited as a Mannerist poet.

**413. Boulton, Marjorie.** *The Anatomy of Poetry.* With an introduction by L. A. G. Strong. London: Routledge & Kegan Paul. xiii, 189p.

Brief comments on several individual poems of Herbert by way of illustrating the nature and function of poetry: "Redemption" (pp. 107–8), "Discipline" (pp. 109–10), "Love (III)" (pp. 130–31). Notes Herbert's uses of pattern poems (p. 12).

**414. Burke, Kenneth.** "On Covery, Re- and Dis-." *Accent* 13:218–26.

An assessment of Rosemond Tuve's position in *A Reading of George Herbert* (entry 409) that, in order to understand and appreciate Herbert, the reader must study and understand the cultural, linguistic, and religious traditions that the poems reflect, especially the liturgical and iconographical contexts. Contrasts this emphasis on "recovery" of the past with the tendency of many modern critics to engage in "discovery," to find "new things about the workings of Herbert's mind by applying modern terms quite alien to his thinking" (p. 218). Argues that Tuve's conception of art is perhaps too narrow and that if one accepts her position too rigidly there are still left many "quandaries that concern both 'psychological' and 'sociological' motives" (p. 226) but considers "these quandaries as problems of 'knowledge' that works of art do not resolve for us, though they give us invaluable material for use in our search, a search over and above the delight that we can have if we read and ponder texts with the help of such able investigators as Miss Tuve" (p. 226).

**415. Duncan, Joseph E.** "The Revival of Metaphysical Poetry, 1872–1912." *PMLA* 68:658–71.

Reprinted in *Discussions of John Donne,* edited by Frank Kermode (Boston: D. C. Heath & Co., 1962), 126–35.

Reprinted in revised form as chapter 4 of *The Revival of Metaphysical Poetry: The History of a Style, 1800 to the Present* (entry 514), 113–29.

Examines the nineteenth-century fascination with Donne the man and surveys the background of Eliot's criticism of the metaphysicals. Maintains that Grierson's edition of Donne (1912) "marked the end of the first stage of the metaphysical revival" (p. 658) and that Eliot's essays "were not so much a new note as a sensitive formulation of ideas that had become familiar by 1912" (p. 658). Traces the ever-growing acceptance of metaphysical poetry from 1872 (Grosart's edition of Donne) to 1912. Mentions Herbert in several instances.

**416. Knieger, Bernard.** "Herbert's 'Redemption.' " *Expl* 11:item 24.

Paraphrases "Redemption" and argues that in order to understand the sonnet fully one must understand "the significance of the act narrated in the last line." Maintains that the meaning of the poem is further complicated by Herbert's "dual use of chronological sequence": "It is as if in a moment of spiritual depression Herbert visualizes, in contemporary terms, the overwhelming sacrifice which permits his spiritual well-being, and which makes his own suffering seem petty indeed." Comments in detail on the phrase *dearly bought*.

**417. Leach, Elsie A.** "John Wesley's Use of George Herbert." *HLQ* 16:183–202.

Comments on the forty-nine adaptations of Herbert's poems made by John Wesley for inclusion in various editions of his hymnal. Proposes "to suggest some reasons why Wesley's fondness for Herbert in spite of neo-classical hostility to the metaphysical poets and, in addition, to analyze in more detail than did Hutchinson [entry 266] the nature of the changes Wesley made in the *Temple* poems" (p. 184). Maintains that Wesley was particularly attracted to those poems of Herbert that celebrate the struggle of the inner life of the religious man and to those that emphasize eschatological or soteriological themes, especially those embued with a spirit of Arminianism: "Both the personal revelation and the Arminian themes would particularly appeal to Wesley, for they suited the evangelical fervor and the theology of Methodism" (p. 192). Shows how Wesley regularized the meter and the line and stanza lengths of Herbert's poems, how he simplified the thought and imagery, and how he often changed the tone and diction in order to reconcile eighteenth-century critical theory and taste with the emotional fervor of enthusiasm.

**418. Malloch, A. E.** "The Unified Sensibility and Metaphysical Poetry." *CE* 15:95–101.

Attempts to limit more precisely the terms *unified sensibility* ("an epitome of all that is most cryptic and pretentious in modern criticism" [p. 95]) and *metaphysical poetry* and to indicate the relationship between the two. Concludes that "the relation of the unified sensibility to metaphysical poetry is the relation of poetic process to poetic technique" (p. 100). Maintains that "certain techniques can validly be said to distinguish Donne, Herbert, Crashaw, and Marvell as a school (and there are significant differences within that school)" but finds that "the unification of sensibility, on the other hand, is a judgment on a poet's mode of creation, whatever the nature of his techniques" (pp. 100–101).

**419. Mazzeo, Joseph Anthony.** "Metaphysical Poetry and the Poetic of Correspondence." *JHI* 14:221–34.

Discusses the revival of interest in the nature and function of metaphor among certain European critics and rhetoricians in the seventeenth century, especially Baltasar Gracián, Emmanuele Tesauro, Cardinal Sforza-Pallavicino, Pierfrancesco Minozzi, and Matteo Pellegrini, and concludes that these theorists "envisaged a poet's universe as a complex system of universal analogical relationships which the poet expressed and revealed" (p. 234). Maintains that such a universe "contained relationships which no longer exist for us; they have been eliminated from our perception by Baconianism and Cartesianism" (p. 234). Suggests that "what may seem to us strange and far-fetched similitudes were often truths, even commonplaces, in their world of insight" (p. 234). No specific references to Herbert.

**420. Mourgues, Odette de.** *Metaphysical Baroque & Précieux Poetry.* Oxford: Clarendon Press. vii, 184p.

Compares French poets whom the author considers "metaphysical"—a term that she distinguishes from "baroque" and "précieux"—and certain late sixteenth- and early seventeenth-century English poets, including Herbert. Argues that "there exists in French poetry, not a metaphysical school, but a metaphysical 'line' beginning as early as 1544 with Scève's *Délie,* dodging the Pléiade, running in an underground way through scientific poetry, coming to the surface again at the end of the sixteenth century and giving its last scattered manifestations in some minor poets of the mid-seventeenth century" (p. 10). Shows how Herbert is metaphysical, not baroque. Briefly compares Herbert with Jean de La Ceppède.

**421. Noakes, Aubrey.** "The Mother of George Herbert." *ContempR* 183:39–45.
Appreciative biographical sketch of Magdalene Herbert. Comments also on the life of George Herbert and Sir John Danvers. Includes a detailed description of Danvers's house.

**422. Perkins, David.** "Johnson on Wit and Metaphysical Poetry." *ELH* 20:200–217.
Reevaluates Dr. Johnson's attitude toward metaphysical poetry, especially his "*favorable* approach to qualities—such as 'wit' and 'novelty' in the uses of imagery and language—that are now commonly associated with the 'metaphysical' style" (p. 201). Points out the value that Johnson places on "intellectual activity in the language of poetry" (p. 202) and on wit. Redefines Johnson's concept of wit. Notes that Johnson quotes Herbert seventy-eight times in the *Dictionary*. Maintains that, although Johnson's admiration for the metaphysical poets was not complete or without certain reservations, it was "strong enough, however, to make him the first critic to analyze and define them—in a sense, even to resurrect and justify them critically" (p. 217).

**423. Ross, Malcolm M.** "A Note on the Metaphysicals." *HudR* 6:106–13.
Discusses the decline of Christian poetic sensibility in the seventeenth century. Argues that the change can best be seen in "those Christian symbols which at one and the same time are rooted in dogma and which convey—or seek to convey—the immediate sense of existence" (p. 107). Comments on the breakdown of the Christian symbol from analogy to mere metaphor as a result of the reform of Christian dogma. Maintains that in Anglican poetry, such as Herbert's, "hovering precariously as it must between Catholic and Protestant symbol, that one is able to see most clearly a far-reaching crisis in the Christian aesthetic" (p. 107). Comments on Herbert's eucharistic theology as reflected in his poetry and shows that in these poems one can observe "analogical language dissolving into simple metaphor" (p. 111). Concludes that, in Herbert, "metaphor succeeds analogy with the immediacy of a first echo—and with the poignant loveliness of something very near yet very far because irretrievable" (p. 112).

**424. Thornton, Robert D.** "Polyphiloprogenitive: The Sapient Sutlers." *Anglican Theological Review* 35:28–36.
Comments on Herbert's views on preachers and preaching, especially on his concept of the Word. Argues that "The Windows" may be the primary impulse for T. S. Eliot's "Sunday Morning Service" and maintains that "no poem written in the more than three hundred years since 'The Windows' seems so close to Herbert's" (p. 30). Compares the two poems and compares Herbert's and Eliot's views on the Word: "Both emphasize the thought that no man can presume to be a Christian and certainly not presume to be a priest of God until he had learned of pride and humility" and that "he cannot learn of these until he has gone back to the study of the Word" (p. 33).

# 1954

**425. Anon.** "George Herbert." *TLS*, 16 April, pp. 241–42.

Essay occasioned by the publication of Margaret Bottrall's study (entry 427). Presents a general view of Herbert's personality, poetry, and prose. Compares and contrasts Herbert with Donne, noting, for instance, that "nearly all the characteristics of Donne's poetic method can be found in George Herbert—less complex, less strident, no doubt, but at the same time less violent, less deliberately idiosyncratic" (p. 241). Maintains that, unlike Donne, Herbert's inner tension "was the outcome of his awareness of spiritual inadequacy," not guilt, and "of his own intense conviction that at the heart of things there was no conflict at all" (p. 241). Briefly comments on *A Priest to the Temple*, especially Herbert's views on preaching and the use of language. Points out also that Herbert, unlike Donne, uses the metaphysical conceit, not because it figures forth skepticism and doubt, but rather because it shows "a sense of coherence, a sense of harmony at the centre of which was no incomprehensibility but only the One Incomprehensible" (p. 242). Finds music a key to understanding Herbert's art and contrasts Herbert's uses of paradox with those of Donne.

**426. Akrigg, G. P. V.** "George Herbert's 'Caller.'" *N&Q* 199:17.

Maintains that, since the major action of "The Collar" is the calling that occurs in the last few lines of the poem, perhaps Herbert originally entitled it "The Caller" and a copyist made a mistake in transcription.

**427. Bottrall, Margaret.** *George Herbert.* London: John Murray. 153p.

Reprinted, Folcroft, Pa.: Folcroft Library Editions, 1971; Norwood, Pa.: Norwood Editions, 1975; Philadelphia: Richard West, 1977.

Chapter 6, "Herbert's Craftsmanship," reprinted in *Seventeenth Century English Poetry: Modern Essays in Criticism*, edited by William Keast (entry 584), 238–51.

Chapter 1, "The Layman" (pp. 1–24), calls Herbert a great poet but not a major one: "His greatness lies in the way he handles great concepts" (p. 1). Maintains that in poetical theory Herbert is closer to Sidney than to Donne: "Herbert's wit was fired not by the example of Donne but by the paradoxical nature of Christianity itself" (p. 2). Comments on the influences of Anglicanism, music, and classical studies on Herbert. Chapter 2, "The Priest" (pp. 25–48), outlines Herbert's life as a priest and comments on his marriage to Jane Danvers and his friendship with Nicholas Ferrar. Chapter 3, "Literary Remains" (pp. 49–66), gives a bibliographical survey of Herbert's writings, both poetry and prose, Latin and English. Discusses the themes and structure of *The Temple*. Chapter 4, "The Country Parson" (pp. 67–82), discusses Herbert's posthumously published pastoral treatise and calls it "a practical treatise, in which Herbert explores the methods by which a contemporary parson could strengthen the hold of the established church upon the hearts and minds of the people of rural England" (p. 68). Sketches the historical and religious context of the work. For instance, points out that Herbert stresses the need for public worship because the reformed liturgy had not yet become fully familiar to the rural folk. Surveys major themes in *The Country Parson* and relates them to Herbert's poetry: "Coming to *The Country Parson* with Herbert's poetry already in mind, we recognize occasional similarities of phrasing as well as constant similarities of temper" (p. 79). Chapter 5, "Herbert's Themes" (pp. 83–98), comments on Herbert's particularly Christian uses of analogy and metaphor ("his constant tendency to co-ordinate and harmonize" [p.

84]) and his fundamentally orthodox view of the world as "a divinely organized harmony" (p. 85). Maintains that "his most frequent and dearest theme is the redemptive love of Christ" (p. 88). Comments on the traditional sources of Herbert's imagery, especially the Bible and typology. Compares Herbert with Hopkins. Chapter 6, "Herbert's Craftsmanship" (pp. 99–116), discusses Herbert's originality, experimentation, and economy in meter, forms, structures, "his architectonic skill" (p. 99). Presents the tension in Herbert between elaboration and ingenuity and his conscious striving for simplicity and directness. Comments on the musicality of much of Herbert's verse and his colloquial rhythms. Discusses the complex, conceptual, yet unobtrusive nature of Herbert's imagery, especially pointing out the influence of the Bible and emblem books. Chapter 7, "Literary Affinities" (pp. 117–33), comments on the influence of Donne and maintains that Herbert's indebtedness to Donne has been exaggerated. Compares Herbert also with Lord Herbert of Cherbury, Jonson, Wyatt, and especially Sidney. Chapter 8, "The Christian Poet" (pp. 134–47), discusses the particular temper of Herbert's Christian vision, his general disinterest in the purely speculative issues of theology, and his joy and self-confident devotional spirit. Compares the religious sensibility of Herbert with that of Crashaw, Vaughan, and Christopher Harvey. Outlines briefly Herbert's reputation and concludes that "today Herbert's reputation is higher than it has been since the end of the seventeenth century" (p. 146). Selected bibliography.

Reviews:

Anon. *Listener* 51 (1954): 1105
Anon. *TLS*, 16 April 1954, pp. 241–42
Robert Ellrodt, *EA* 7 (1954): 419–21
Louis MacNeice, *London Magazine* 1, no. 7 (1954): 74–76
Edwin Muir, *Observer*, 16 May 1954, p. 11
K. Williamson, *SN* 27 (1956): 163–66

**428. Cruttwell, Patrick.** *The Shakespearean Moment and Its Place in the Poetry of the 17th Century*. London: Chatto & Windus; New York: Columbia University Press. 262p.

Reprinted, 1955, 1970; New York: Vintage Books, 1960.

Argues that at the end of the sixteenth century Shakespeare and the metaphysical poets were participating with the same qualities in the richest moment in English poetry: "The mature Shakespearean or metaphysical style—which, it must be repeated, is the same style used for different purposes and in different *milieux*—emerged in the last years of the sixteenth century and remained the most fruitful style for the first few decades of the next" (p. 73). Discusses the conditions of life that allowed the building of bridges between all subjects and things and elaborates on what caused the end of the metaphysical style—Puritanism, the Commonwealth Interregnum, and the resulting differences in thinking about the human condition. Several references to Herbert but no extended discussion. Briefly contrasts Herbert and Donne and also contrasts Herbert and other representatives of the "Shakespearean moment" with the Puritans and points out that when the former express "an ascetic revulsion from and rejection of the sensuous, their asceticism seems to express itself, paradoxically, in thoroughly sensuous terms, so that the physical world has returned, as it were, by a backdoor" (p. 140). Sees Herbert's use of domestic imagery and colloquial language as a reflection of the "Shakespearean moment." Briefly contrasts Herbert and Lord Herbert of Cherbury. The conclusion divides the age into two great types of mind and places Herbert on the side represented by Anglo-Catholicism, traditional medieval theology, native popular art, sensuousness allowed to permeate all things, courtly splendor, attempts to preserve what remained of the medieval Continental unity, monarchist sympathies and a hierarchical view of society, pessimism and skepticism about the possibility of human improvement, and a dramatic and tragic sense (pp. 252–53).

**429. Emslie, Macdonald.** "Herbert's 'Jordan I.'" *Expl* 12:item 35.

Line-by-line explication of "Jordan (I)." Comments on such phrases as "false hair" (line 1), "winding stair" (line 3), "painted chair" (line 5), and "Catching the sense at two removes" (line 10). Sees the poem as an attack on those who make the writing of religious verse "over-elaborate or who convey religious themes through pastoral allegory." Comments on possible Platonic elements in the poem.

**430. Lawrence, Ralph.** "The English Hymn." *E&S* n.s. 7:105–22.

Discusses the development of the English hymn. Maintains that the hymn, as we know it, did not fully emerge until 1623 with Wither's *Hymnes and Songs of the Church* and that it was not until 1707 that "the first authentic hymnal appeared: Dr. Isaac Watts's *Hymns and Spiritual Songs in Three Books*" (p. 106). Points out the main differences between a religious poem and a hymn and claims that Herbert's "The Elixir," when sung, loses much of its charm. Argues that the seventeenth century, while producing some hymns of rare distinction, "was primarily an age of Psalters, these being translations made from the Genevan Psalters in metrical form" (p. 106). Maintains that there are some affinities between John Keble and Herbert but that *The Christian Year* "is far inferior to *The Temple*" (p. 115).

**431. Martz, Louis L.** *The Poetry of Meditation: A Study in English Religious Literature of the Seventeenth Century.* (Yale Studies in English, vol. 125.) New Haven: Yale University Press. London: Oxford University Press. xiv, 375p.

Rev. ed., 1962, 1969, 1978.

Pages 135–44 reprinted in *The Modern Critical Spectrum*, edited by Gerald Jay Goldberg and Nancy Marner Goldberg (Englewood Cliffs, N.J.: Prentice-Hall, 1962), 244–50.

Pages 211–48 (with revisions from the 2d ed.) reprinted in *Seventeenth Century English Poetry: Modern Essays in Criticism*, edited by William Keast (entry 584), 144–74, rev. ed. (entry 879), 118–51.

Pages 220–23 and 228–48 reprinted in *John Donne: A Collection of Critical Essays*, edited by Helen Gardner (Englewood Cliffs, N.J.: Prentice-Hall, 1962), 152–70.

Announces that the primary purpose of this study is "to modify the view of literary history which sees a 'Donne tradition' in English religious poetry" (p. 3). Maintains instead "a 'meditative tradition' which found its first notable example not in Donne but in Robert Southwell" (p. 3). Argues that the metaphysical poets, though obviously widely different, are "drawn together by resemblances that result, basically, from the common practice of certain methods of religious meditation" (p. 2). Mentions Herbert throughout and devotes two complete chapters to him: (1) chapter 7, "George Herbert: In the Presence of a Friend," discusses the influence of, and Herbert's affinities to, St. François de Sales, Sir Philip Sidney (especially his translations of the psalms), the *Imitation of Christ*, and Girolamo Savonarola; (2) chapter 8, "George Herbert: The Unity of *The Temple*," argues that *The Temple* has a structure built primarily upon the art of mental communion. Other important issues discussed in relation to Herbert: (1) the uses of meditative structure in Herbert's poems, (2) "The Sacrifice" as a meditation on the liturgy of Holy Week, (3) devotion to the Virgin

Mary, (4) the influence of the method of self-examination, especially the *Spiritual Combat* of Lorenzo Scupoli, (5) the art of sacred parody, the literature of tears, and various meditations on death. In addition to those already mentioned, Herbert is compared and contrasted with Donne, Southwell, Vaughan, and Crashaw.

**432. Maycock, Alan.** *Chronicles of Little Gidding.* London: SPCK. 120p.

Presents "an account, first of the events covered by the twenty years between Nicholas's death in 1637 and the death of John Ferrar in 1657, and then of various episodes and happenings connected with Little Gidding which take us on almost to the middle of the eighteenth century" (p. 1). Several references to Herbert. Points out that John Ferrar's accounts for 1649 show that he sent to various settlers in Virginia no less than 197 books, including copies of Herbert's poems. In a letter to his son, John Ferrar commented on the friendship between Nicholas Ferrar and Herbert, "your uncle's most dear friend (of whom it was said by them that knew them both there was one soul in two bodies)" (p. 89). Maintains that it was perhaps the publication of *The Country Parson* in 1652, with an introduction by Barnabas Oley, that determined John Ferrar to write his own short life of Nicholas Ferrar in 1653 or 1654.

**433. Moloney, Michael F.** "A Suggested Gloss for Herbert's 'Box Where Sweets . . . .'" *N&Q* 199:50.

Maintains that "A box where sweets compacted lie" in "Vertue" may not be a box of perfumes, as Hutchinson suggests (entry 266), but a music box.

**434. Ross, Malcolm MacKenzie.** *Poetry and Dogma: The Transfiguration of Eucharistic Symbols in Seventeenth Century English Poetry.* New Brunswick: Rutgers University Press. xii, 256p.

Reprinted, 1969.

Studies "some of the consequences for religious poetry in England of the Protestant revision of Eucharistic dogma" and maintains that "the dogmatic symbolism of the traditional Eucharistic rite had nourished the analogical mode of poetic symbol, indeed had effected imaginatively a poetic knowledge of the participation (each with the other) of the natural, the historical, and the divine orders" (p. vii). Reprints "George Herbert and the Humanist Tradition" (entry 328) (pp. 135–57). Mentions Herbert frequently throughout this study of the influence of the revolution in Christian dogma on the poetic act. Sees in Herbert the breakdown of the analogical symbol. Argues that there is a "certain tension which obtains in his work between a Catholic sensibility and an urgent, if uneasy Protestant dogmatism" (p. 176). Maintains that Herbert is linked to the Catholic tradition "not so much by his use of traditional typology and iconography as by his intense and immediate feeling for the Person of Christ" (p. 176). Points out a number of Catholic and even Counter-Reformation elements in Herbert's art but sees his Protestant views on the Eucharist as "the spectacle of analogical symbol dissolving into simple metaphor" (p. 181). Argues that Herbert's rhetoric is "a displaced rhetoric, a Catholic rhetoric Protestantized but always looking backward" and suggests that "it is the end-point of a moving cycle, of a steady process of deterioration in the analogical symbol from Shakespeare onwards, a cycle in poetry reflecting a decline in dogma and in habits of mind and heart that were rooted in dogma" (p. 219).

**435. Summers, Joseph H.** *George Herbert: His Religion and Art.* Cambridge, Mass.: Harvard University Press; London: Chatto & Windus. 247p.

Reprinted, 1968.

Reprinted, Binghamton, N.Y.: Medieval & Renaissance Texts & Studies, 1981.

Chapter 4, "The Conception of Form," first appeared as "Herbert's Form" (entry 387). Reprinted in *The Metaphysical Poets: Key Essays on Metaphysical Poetry and the Major Metaphysical Poets*, edited by Frank Kermode (entry 795), 230–51; *The Metaphysical Poets: A Selection of Critical Essays*, edited by Gerald Hammond (entry 985), 157–81.

Chapter 6, "The Poem as Hieroglyph," reprinted in *Seventeenth Century English Poetry: Modern Essays in Criticism*, edited by William Keast (entry 584), 215–37, rev. ed. (entry 879), 225–47.

A portion of chapter 6 reprinted in *George Herbert and the Seventeenth-Century Religious Poets: Authoritative Texts/Criticism*, edited by Mario Di Cesare (entry 1140), 255–70.

Full-scale study of Herbert's religion as reflected in his poetry, and an interpretation of the poetry in the light of his religious convictions and sensibilities. Explores the symbolism and traditions of the Church that inform Herbert's art. Announces that "the major assumption of this book" is that George Herbert "is one of the best lyric poets who has written in the English language" (p. 7). The book is divided into three major sections: the first three chapters consider Herbert's poetic reputation, his life, and his religious thought and sensibility; chapters 4 and 5 discuss Herbert's theories of form and language, "both basic to his poetic and religious practice" (p. 7); and the final section applies these concepts to the poems. Chapter 1, "Time and *The Temple*" (pp. 11–27), surveys Herbert's reputation and influence as a poet both in his own time and later. Maintains that in his own day, "except for John Cleveland, he was the most popular of the so-called 'metaphysical poets,' sacred or profane" (p. 11). Argues that art and religion are inextricably woven together in *The Temple*. Chapter 2, "The Life" (pp. 28–48), rejects the notion that Herbert was a simple, naive saint and mystic and presents him as a devout, sophisticated, complex man of his times. Questions a strict autobiographical reading of the poems. Chapter 3, "Religion" (pp. 49–69), surveys the diversity of religious opinion in England in the early seventeenth century and presents Herbert's religious thought and sensibilities as reflected in his poems, translations, and prose works. Chapter 4, "The Conception of Form" (pp. 73–94), argues that Herbert's use of form in the poetry reflects his religious convictions, his "analogical habit of mind and the belief that order, measure, proportion, and harmony are both divine and beautiful" (p. 76). Discusses the significance of the arrangement of the poems in *The Temple* and rejects Palmer's reordering: "The composition of the poems, imitative as they were of that ordering which he had experienced and which he hoped to experience again, was the act of a craftsman who shapes the imperfect materials of his own suffering as well as joy into a pattern symbolic of divine order" (p. 94). Chapter 5, "The Proper Language" (pp. 95–119), surveys Herbert's views on the nature and function of language, especially "the implication that the beauty of language, like the soul's, can live only if it is 'lost' to the proper object" (p. 119). Comments on Herbert's love of language, which was always kept in check by rational control, and points out his "insistence on propriety and the equal insistence that language is finally unimportant when compared with the spirit" (p. 119). Chapter 6, "The Poem as Hieroglyph" (pp. 123–46), discusses Herbert's "art which conceals art" (p. 135). Maintains that "the hieroglyph represents to Herbert a fusion of the spiritual and material, of the rational and sensuous, in the essential terms of formal relationships" (p. 145). Argues that the pattern poems are the most developed of hieroglyphs. Chapter 7, "Verse and Speech" (pp. 147–55), discusses Herbert's metrical inventiveness and his uses of counterpoint, rhythm, sound, and diction. Maintains

that "in Herbert's poems subject and image do not determine speech; they are transformed by it" (p. 152). Chapter 8, "Music" (pp. 156–70), comments on Herbert's lifelong interest in music and his uses of musical effects and metaphors. Suggests that music best explains the sound patterns, tone, and form in many of the poems, noting that "about a fourth of the poems in *The Temple* concern music directly" (p. 157). Chapter 9, "Allegory and Sonnet: A Traditional Mode and a Traditional Form" (pp. 171–84), discusses Herbert's experimentation with the sonnet ("he sought to transform and to revitalize the conventional so as to make it freshly available to serious poetry" [p. 171]) and his complex uses of allegory, especially in its then-popular Christian form. Chapter 10, "Conclusions" (pp. 185–90), presents a summary of several major points about Herbert's art. Maintains, for example, that "we can fully realize Herbert's poetic achievement—or almost any one poem in *The Temple*—only within the light of ideas, beliefs, and conventions of early seventeenth-century England" (p. 185) and that "for Herbert, Christianity provided the means of giving order and universal significance to his personal experience" (p. 186). Appendix A, "Mr Herbert's Temple & Church Militant Explained and Improved" (pp. 191–94) discusses George Ryley's annotations and explanations of the poems in *The Temple* (1714/1715), which, though primarily theological, "often provide the key to many of the passages and poems which are difficult for the modern reader of Herbert" (p. 191). Appendix B, "Bacon and Herbert" (pp. 195–97), briefly discusses the relationship between the two men, stressing the areas of their agreement on matters of religion and morality. Notes (pp. 198–237). Index (pp. 239–47).
Reviews:
Anon. *Listener* 51 (1954): 1105
Anon. *SCN* 12 (1954): 27
Anon. *TLS*, 4 June 1954, p. 358
Edwin Muir, *Observer*, 16 May 1954, p. 11
Rosemond Tuve, *JEGP* 54 (1955): 284–85
Charles M. Coffin, *YR* 44 (1955): 623–32
Jackson I. Cope, *MLN* 70 (1955): 55–57
Robert Ellrodt, *EA* 8 (1955): 157–59
L. C. Knights, *SR* 63 (1955): 480–84
Geoffrey Bullough, *MP* 53 (1956): 277–78
C. G. Thayer, *Books Abroad* 29 (1956): 227
K. Williamson, *SN* 27 (1956): 163–66
Louis MacNeice, *London Magazine* 1, no. 7 (1954): 74–76
Anon. *The Economist* 171 (1954): 706
Andrew Wordsworth, *New Statesman and Nation* n.s. 47 (1954): 762–64
Review of 1981 reprint: Louis L. Martz, *GHJ* 5 (1981–1982): 79–86

**436. Vaughan Williams, Ralph.** *Hodie (This Day): A Christmas Cantata.* For soprano, tenor, and baritone soli, chorus, and orchestra. Pianoforte arrangement by Roy Douglas. London: Oxford University Press. x, 100p.
Reprinted, 1967.
Includes a musical setting of the second part of "Christmas" (pp. 52–55) for baritone solo. First performed at the Three Chorus Festival, Worcester, on 8 September 1954.

**437. Willy, Margaret.** "The Poetry of Donne: Its Interest and Influence Today." *E&S* n.s. 7:78–104.

Discusses likenesses between the metaphysical poets, particularly Donne, and certain modern poets. Maintains that the kinship between the seventeenth and the twentieth centuries "penetrates far deeper than that relatively superficial kind: rooted as it is in broadly similar social conditions, which, in the literature of both ages, evoked certain responses that correspond strikingly in spirit and technique" (pp. 79–80). Focuses on Donne but also mentions Herbert. Comments briefly on the affinities between Herbert and Hopkins.

**438. Young, Simon.** "George Herbert." *TLS*, 15 January, p. 41.
Requests information on Herbert for a projected biography.


# *1955*


**439. Bairstow, Edward Cuthbert.** "Peace" and "L'Envoy," in *Five Poems of the Spirits*, for Baritone Solo, Chorus, and Orchestra, 13–19, 26–29. London: Novello.
Musical setting of "Peace" (for mixed voice chorus) and "L'Envoy" (for baritone solo and optional mixed voice chorus).

**440. Blunden, Edmund.** "Some Seventeenth-Century Latin Poems by English Writers." *UTQ* 25:10–22.
Translates into English two Latin poems by Herbert: "On Sacred Music" ("De Musicâ Sacrâ") and "To Pallas Athene" ("Innupta Pallas, nata Diespitre"). General comments on Herbert's Latin verse. Maintains that in these poems, "which amount to about a fourth part of Herbert's whole extant works, a view of Herbert is found which is not quite that of the poems in English" (p. 12). Comments in particular on *Parentalia*. Translations also of Donne, Crashaw, and Milton.

**441.** Item dropped.

**442. Bush, Douglas.** "Seventeenth-Century Poets and the Twentieth Century." *Annual Bulletin of the Modern Humanities Research Association* 27:16–28.
Comments on the revival of interest in the metaphysical poets, especially Donne, from the nineteenth century through the twentieth century and gives reasons for the extraordinary attention given the metaphysical poets by both scholars and practicing poets, especially during the 1920s and 1930s, and for the decline of interest since that period, especially among practicing poets. Considers also the effects of the metaphysical revival on the fate of Milton in the twentieth century and concludes that Milton, "far from having been dislodged from his throne, appears to sit more securely than ever on a throne that has partly new and even more solid foundations" (p. 26). Maintains that "amateur criticism restored Donne and banished Milton, scholarly criticism kept Donne and restored Milton" (pp. 26–27). No specific comment on Herbert.

**443. Coleridge, Samuel Taylor.** *Coleridge on the Seventeenth Century.* Edited by Roberta Florence Brinkley with an introductory essay by Louis I. Bredvold. Durham, N.C.: Duke University Press. xxxviii, 704p.
Reprinted, New York: Greenwood Press, 1968.

Selections reprinted in *The Metaphysical Poets: A Selection of Critical Essays*, edited by Gerald Hammond (entry 985), 59–60.

Collection of Coleridge's comments on the seventeenth century arranged under seven headings: (1) the seventeenth century in general, (2) the philosophers, (3) the divines, (4) science, (5) literary prose, (6) poetry, and (7) the drama. Several references to Herbert, whom Coleridge calls "the every way excellent George Herbert" (p. 275). Includes a collection of Coleridge's specific comments on Herbert (pp. 533–40). In a letter to W. Collins, Coleridge remarks: "I find more substantial comfort now in pious George Herbert's 'Temple' . . . than in all the poetry since the poems of Milton" (p. 533).

**444. Davenport, A.** "George Herbert and Ovid." *N&Q* 200:98.

Points out that the sequence of thought in Herbert's "Vertue" occurs in Ovid's *Ars Amatoria*, book 2, lines 111 ff. Notes that it "is worth pointing out since it enables us to watch Herbert's imagination in the art of developing and enriching the Ovidian outline."

**445. Duncan-Jones, Elsie.** "Benlowes's Borrowings from George Herbert." *RES* n.s. 6:179–80.

Points out two possible borrowings from Herbert in Edward Benlowes's *Theophilia*: (1) canto 2, line 91 echoes lines from "Bitter-sweet" and (2) canto 9, line 17 appropriates a line from the first verse of *The Church-Porch*.

**446. Esch, Arno.** "Zum Gedichtaufbau von George Herbert," in *Englische religiöse Lyrik des 17. Jahrhunderts: Studien zu Donne, Herbert, Crashaw, Vaughan*, 69–96. (Buchreihe der Anglia Zeitschrift für englische Philologie, 5.) Tübingen: Max Niemeyer. xi, 225p.

Studies the problems of religious poetry of the period by analyzing and comparing the works of individual poets. Chapter 3 (pp. 11–27) deals specifically with Herbert's poetry, especially with various poetic structures. Classifies Herbert's poems into five main types: (1) chain poems (those in which a stanza could be added or subtracted or possibly stanzas could be interchanged without damaging the poem); (2) definition poems (such as "Prayer (I)"); (3) poems based on verbal or visual patterns (such as "Easter-wings" and "Paradise"); (4) poems clearly symmetrical in structure, often built on antithesis, with two main parts (such as "Death"); (5) poems containing a tripartite structure. Argues that in the last category are found Herbert's best poems and maintains that this structure suggests the influence of Quintilian's rhetoric, especially as it was used by the early Fathers of the Church in their sermons. Analyzes a number of poems in this last category, including "The Bunch of Grapes," "Peace," "Divinitie," "Redemption," "Love (III)," "Miserie," "Mortification," "Discipline," "Jesu," "Life," "Aaron," "The Collar," and "The Quip."

**447. Groom, Bernard.** "The Spenserian Tradition and Its Rivals to 1660," in *The Diction of Poetry from Spenser to Bridges*, 48–73. Toronto: University of Toronto Press; London: Geoffrey Cumberlege, Oxford University Press.

Comments briefly on Herbert's "classical neatness and conciseness of style" (p. 62) and on "the controlled fervour and the precision of his unaspiring style" (p. 63). Maintains that Herbert's chief effects "come from some simple phrase tellingly reserved, unerringly placed" (p. 63). Contends also that Herbert's diction is plain, so that "those who do not enter into the spirit of his poetry find it sometimes 'quaint'" (p. 63). Briefly compares Herbert and Vaughan.

**448. Herbert, George.** *George Herbert of Bemerton: A Selection from "The Temple."* With an introduction by Frances Forrest. Salisbury: Printed for the Rector and Churchwardens by the Salisbury Times Co. 48p.

Booklet intended for visitors to Bemerton that includes a biographical sketch of Herbert and a very general evaluation of his poetry (pp. 5–16), followed by an anthology of thirty-six poems (pp. 17–48). Describes in some detail Bemerton, St. Andrew's Church, and the Rectory. Maintains that Herbert's poems are interesting primarily because they reveal the holiness of the poet and points out that "for all their occasional grotesque metaphor or jarring comparison Herbert's poems are nearly always easy to apprehend, and with the spiritual perception of the mystic reveal not only the poet, but the musician and the orator whose ear rejoices in the sense of decadence and in the balance of line" (pp. 8–9).

**449. Hooper, A[lfred] G[ifford], and C[harles] J[ohn] D[errick] Harvey.** "George Herbert," in *Poems for Discussion: With Commentaries and Questions*, 17–28. Cape Town: Oxford University Press.

Reprinted, 1958.

Line-by-line explications of "The Collar" (pp. 18–23) and of "Love (III)" (pp. 24–26). Points out that the spiritual conflicts presented in "The Collar" are "beautifully suggested by the imagery, and sustained by the rhythm" (p. 22) of the poem and calls attention to Herbert's use of biblical language. Compares and contrasts the tone, imagery, and diction of "Love (III)" and Donne's "Batter my heart." Shows how Herbert's poem follows his usual pattern of development—"hesitation, reassurance, acceptance, and submission" (p. 25) and maintains that it thus becomes "the record of the gradual growth of self-respect" (pp. 25–26) that the speaker develops as he discovers God's acceptance of and love for him.

**450. Rosenthal, M. L., and A. J. M. Smith.** *Exploring Poetry.* New York: Macmillan Co. xli, 758p.

Includes a brief discussion of "Vertue" (pp. 415–17), commenting especially on Herbert's figures of speech and on what the authors call the process of elimination. Comments also on "The Pulley" (pp. 544–45), especially on its concentrated intellectual manner and dramatic elements. Several briefer references and questions on other poems.

**451. Sells, Arthur Lytton.** "Southwell," in *The Italian Influence in English Poetry: From Chaucer to Southwell*, 306–35. Bloomington: Indiana University Press.

Brief comments on the possible influence of Southwell and the spirit of the Counter-Reformation on Herbert's poetry: "It was through the intermediary of Southwell, whose works were widely read and admired in England, that the better literary theories of the Counter-Reformation entered into the fabric of Anglican poetry as well as of Catholic" (p. 311). Suggests several close parallels between Herbert's poetry and that of Southwell.

**452. Sypher, Wylie.** *Four Stages of Renaissance Style: Transformations in Art and Literature, 1400–1700.* (Anchor A44.) Garden City, N.Y.: Doubleday & Co. 312p.

Reprinted, Gloucester, Mass.: Peter Smith, 1978.

Studies the development of various Renaissance styles from 1400 to 1700, stressing relationships between literature and the fine arts. The metaphysical poets are discussed as examples of the mannerist style. Maintains that in art history, mannerism "represents a 'formal dissolution of a style'—the style of renaissance art founded upon the concepts of proportion and harmony and unity" (p. 102), but that in literature, this style exemplifies Eliot's notion of "dissociation of sensibility" and Grierson's idea that Donne and the metaphysical poets "are 'more aware of disintegration than of comprehensive harmony'" (p. 103). Several references to Herbert. Comments on his tension between "calm, assured piety and his agitated awareness of things in the world" (p. 169), discusses his use of metaphor and image, and briefly compares him with Crashaw.

**453. Watson, George.** "Hobbes and the Metaphysical Conceit." *JHI* 16:558–62.
Argues that the metaphysical conceit was killed by a change in literary theory and illustrates this change by referring to the critical writings of Hobbes. Maintains that, in time, the conceit lost its intellectual force and was dismissed as mere sound. No specific mention of Herbert. For a reply, see T. M. Gang (entry 463).

**454. Wickes, George.** "George Herbert's Views on Poetry." *Revue de Langues Vivantes* (Brussels) 21:344–52.
Collects various scattered statements concerning Herbert's view of poetry as reflected in his poems: "No less than one quarter of his poems reflect his preoccupation with his role as poet" (p. 345). Also finds similar comments in *A Priest to the Temple*. Considers two main aspects of Herbert's poetic theory: his concern with content and his conscious efforts in technique. Points out some of the more explicit statements and themes that reflect Herbert's view on the uses of poetry in the religious life and also comments on the less explicit views on poetic techniques and tastes. Comments on Herbert's uses of wit and on the highly pictorial quality of his verse. Maintains that the essential principle of his poetry is "to inform and inflame or—to use the characteristic seventeenth century expression of Nicholas Ferrar—to «enrich the World with pleasure and piety»" (p. 352).

# 1956

**455. Britten, Benjamin.** *Antiphon for Choir (with optional Soloists) and Organ.* New York: Boosey & Hawkes. 14p.
Musical setting of "Antiphon (II)" written for the centenary of St. Michael's College, Tenbury.

**456. Compton-Rickett, Arthur.** "The English Renascence," in *A History of English Literature from Earliest Times to 1916*, 73–190. London, Edinburgh, Paris, Melbourne, Toronto, New York: Thomas Nelson and Sons.
Reprinted, 1958, 1964.
Biographical note on Herbert and brief comment on his poetry. Notes that "of all the school of Donne he is the most widely read, by reason of his clearness of presentment and his happy knack for using conceits sufficiently obvious to most people" (p. 186). Maintains that Herbert's treatment of religious themes "has the simple, unstudied earnestness of Longfellow" and that his poetry exhibits "a quaintness and daintiness characteristic of the time" (p. 186). Claims that "the discerning reader will note also a welcome salt of humour" in Herbert's poetry "that preserved him from the extravagance into which so many of his contemporaries fell" (p. 186). Reproduces "The World" as an example of Herbert's art.

**457. Cox, R. G.** "A Survey of Literature from Donne to Marvell," in *From Donne to Marvell*, edited by Boris Ford, 43–85. (The Pelican Guide to English Literature, vol. 3.) London and Baltimore: Penguin Books.

Reprinted several times (with minor revisions).

Broad survey of poetry and prose from Donne to Marvell. Discusses Herbert in a subsection entitled "The Metaphysical Manner and Religious Poetry" (pp. 54–59). Compares Herbert with Donne, Crashaw, Quarles, Vaughan, and Marvell. Comments briefly on those elements usually associated with Herbert's verse: courtly urbanity of language, allegorical vividness, musical verse forms, neatness, homely wit, intensity, effects of surprise, control of tone, dramatic sense, purity of diction, proverbial and colloquial uses of language, and so on. Maintains that Herbert's best work "embodies the religious temper of the seventeenth century at its finest and most humane" (p. 57).

**458. Denonain, Jean-Jacques.** *Thèmes et formes de la poésie "métaphysique": Étude d'un aspect de la littérature anglaise au dix-septième siècle.* (Publications de la faculté des lettres d'Alger, 28.) Paris: Presses universitaires de France. 548p.

In the introduction (pp. 5–18) states that his purpose is to define as precisely as possible the nature of metaphysical poetry and challenges several of the better-known definitions. The book is divided into five major parts: (1) a tentative definition of metaphysical poetry (pp. 21–95); (2) an analysis of major themes in metaphysical poetry (pp. 99–326); (3) a discussion of the psychological processes by which the themes of the poetry are developed and expanded (pp. 329–64); (4) a study of poetic forms utilized by the metaphysical poets (pp. 367–449); and (5) a conclusion that seeks to discern the unifying characteristics of metaphysical poetry (pp. 453–80). Three sections of the book deal specifically with Herbert: (1) the religious themes of George Herbert: meditations on religious occasions and theological themes, pain of sin, ingratitude toward God and rebellion, contrition and submission to the will of God, prayer, actions of grace, worship, mystical effusions, blind confidence in the intercession of Christ, proselytism (pp. 185–220); (2) images, metaphor, and conceit in Herbert (pp. 389–93); and (3) poetic technique in Herbert (pp. 426–36). Among the several appendixes, two deal specifically with Herbert: (1) the chronology of George Herbert (pp. 485–86) and (2) the structure of prosody in Herbert (pp. 505–10). Some negative attitudes expressed: "A la médiocrité de l'inspiration, Herbert ajoute un mauvais goût impardonnable dans ses conceits, même si l'on tient compte de la psychologie et des habitudes du temps" (p. 393). Selected bibliography.

**459. Enright, D. J.** "George Herbert and the Devotional Poets," in *From Donne to Marvell*, edited by Boris Ford, 142–59. (The Pelican Guide to English Literature, vol. 3.) London and Baltimore: Penguin Books.

Reprinted several times (with minor revisions).

Calls Herbert "one of the strongest poetic personalities in English" (p. 142). Comments on Herbert's quiet tone; his uses of homely imagery and rhetoric; his combining of courtly and popular elements; and his sense of drama, immediacy, and intimacy. Outlines the major themes of Herbert's poetry: "foremost among them are the Incarnation, the Passion and the Redemption" (p. 145). Maintains that the most serious criticism that can be leveled against Herbert is "the rather clumsy way in which the scales are occasionally weighted against earthly pleasures as opposed to heavenly bliss" (p. 146). Compares and contrasts Herbert with Vaughan and Crashaw.

**460. Ford, Boris, ed.** *From Donne to Marvell.* (The Pelican Guide to English Literature, vol. 3.) London and Baltimore: Penguin Books. 277p.

Reprinted several times (with minor revisions).

Mentions Herbert throughout this collection of original essays on various seventeenth-century topics. Essays in which Herbert is given special consideration have been entered separately in this bibliography (see entries 457, 459). Selective bibliography of Herbert and Herbert criticism (pp. 261–62).

**461. Frankenberg, Lloyd.** *Invitation to Poetry: A Round of Poems from John Skelton to Dylan Thomas Arranged with Comments.* Garden City, N.Y.: Doubleday & Co. 414p.

Brief critical comments on "A true Hymne" (pp. 62–63) and on "Vertue" (pp. 163–64).

**462. Fukuchi, Shiro.** "Keijijo-ha no Seija George Herbert" [George Herbert: Saint of the Metaphysical School]. *Mie Kenritsu Daigaku Kenkyu Nempo* [Bulletin of the Mie Prefectural University] vol. 2, no. 2 (March): 27–42.

Reprinted in *Eikoku Ju-na-na-seiki keiji-jo shijin* [English Seventeenth-Century Metaphysical Poets] (privately printed, 1980), 123–47.

General survey of Herbert's life and poetry. Views Herbert as a "saint" of the Metaphysical School. Follows closely Walton's *Life*.

**463. Gang, T. M.** "Hobbes and the Metaphysical Conceit: A Reply." *JHI* 17:418–21.

In part a reply to George Watson (entry 453). Challenges Watson's interpretation of Hobbes's critical theory. Second part of the essay is devoted to a discussion of the metaphysical conceit. Maintains that Herbert and Donne, "even when they do not use the terminology of metaphysics, play with concepts in a manner which they have learnt from the metaphysicians" (p. 419). Claims that it was possible for metaphysical poets "to use the language and assumptions of metaphysics because they believed these to have a validity" (p. 419). Points out, however, that "to play on ideas which have become meaningless is pointless" and maintains that "this, surely, is what happened in the fifties and sixties of the seventeenth century: both the verbiage and the general method had become, or were fast becoming, meaningless" (p. 419). Argues that what makes a conceit "metaphysical" is "not the wildness of the comparison, but the fact that the comparison is between a concrete thing and an abstraction, and that the double meanings are produced by taking the concrete part of the comparison 'seriously,' that is, writing literally about the vehicle of the metaphor" (p. 421). Points out that in Herbert's poetry "the non-literal language that is treated literally is often the language of the Bible, the Prayer-book, and common proverbial expressions" (p. 421).

**464. Herbert, George.** *The Country Parson and Selected Poems by George Herbert,* edited by Hugh Martin. (A Treasury of Christian Books Series.) London: SCM Press. 126p.

Contains a biographical introduction with brief critical comment on *The Country Parson* and the poems (pp. 7–10). Calls Herbert "the father of the religious lyric" (p. 8). Maintains that *The Country Parson* "has no clear scheme and seems uncompleted" but notes that "it is straightforward and business-like, in striking contrast to the poems" (pp. 9–10). Reprints *The Country Parson* (pp. 11–96) and selected poems (pp. 97–126) without notes or commentary.

**465. Hilberry, Conrad.** "Two Cruxes in George Herbert's 'Redemption.'" *N&Q* 201:514.

Comments on the phrase *small-rented lease* in "Redemption" (line 4) and sees a possible biographical reference in the first quatrain: "Herbert, in taking orders and committing himself later to parochial life, was certainly cancelling an old lease in which he had not thrived and accepting a new 'small-rented' one in its place." Gives several possible interpretations of the use of the word *land* (line 7): (1) land=dust, man; (2) land=Christ; (3) land=Eden and, typologically, Calvary.

**466. Jarrell, Randall.** "The Schools of Yesteryear: A One-sided Dialogue." *New Republic*, 19 November, pp. 13–17.

Reprinted in *Writing from Experience*, edited by Raymond C. Palmer, James A. Lowrie, and John F. Speer (Ames: Iowa State College Press, 1957), 78–89.

An imaginary dialogue between a certain Alvin and his Uncle Wadsworth in which the elder recalls that Alvin's great grandfather first read Herbert's "Sunday" in *Appleton's Fifth Reader* while Alvin himself was more likely to encounter it in his sophomore year in college. Uncle Wadsworth then interprets several lines of the poem to a confused Alvin.

**467. Koretz, Gene M.** "The Rhyme Scheme in Herbert's 'Man.'" *N&Q* 201:144–46.

Discusses the intricate design and formal order in "Man." Points out that, of all the poems in *The Temple*, "Man" "is the only one in which the rhyme scheme is consistently varied in stanzas of equal lengths" (p. 145). Shows how the formal symmetry of the poem is related to the poem's subject: "Since man occupied the central position in the chain of being, serving as mediator between the material and spiritual realms, and since the natural world was created for his sustenance and pleasure, the poem provides a comprehensive treatment of the whole of creation with relation to man. Implicit in the world-picture which Herbert presents are the concepts of unity enveloping diversity, order governing abundance and variety—and it is these concepts which the poet has sought to embody in the poem's structure" (p. 145).

**468. Korninger, Siegfried.** *Die Naturaufassung in der englischen Dichtung des 17. Jahrhunderts.* (Weiner Beiträge zur englischen Philologie, 64.) Vienna and Stuttgart: Wilhelm Braumüller. 260p.

Discusses changing attitudes toward nature in the seventeenth century. Uses poetry as the source material for studying two major groups of questions: (1) how does man face his environment, what does he understand of it, and how does he depict it? and (2) to what extent is man's attitude toward nature expressed in his poetic works, and what inspirations and artistic impulses does the poetry derive from the investigation of nature? Finds in Herbert's poetry an interest in nature and natural phenomena, which he shares with most of his contemporaries. Many illustrations drawn from Herbert's poetry.

**469. Lamson, Roy, and Hallett Smith, eds.** "George Herbert," in *Renaissance England: Poetry and Prose from the Reformation to the Restoration*, 886–906. New York: W. W. Norton and Co.

An expanded edition of *The Golden Hind* (New York: W. W. Norton, 1942), the editors' anthology of Elizabethan poetry and prose.

Calls Herbert "a poet of great clarity, vividness, and intensity" and "a most sensitive portrayer of moods" (p. 886). Presents a thumbnail sketch of Herbert's life, notes the influence of both Donne and Sidney, and comments very generally on Herbert's poetry (pp. 886–87). Thirteen selections from *The Temple* with explanatory notes (pp. 888–906).

**470. Manning, Stephen.** "Herbert's 'The Pearl,' 38." *Expl* 14:item 25.

Explicates Herbert's symbolic uses of the silk twist in line 38 of "The Pearl" and concludes that symbolically the silk twist "is faith, by which God both conducts and teaches man how to climb to Him." Supports such a reading by referring to the commentaries of Rabanus Maurus, Rupertus of Deutz, and the English translator of Bèze.

**471. Rao, A. V.** "The Religious and Meditative Poetry of England." *Prabuddha Bharata; or Awakened India* (Calcutta), pp. 139–42.

Briefly comments on some of the major devotional and mystical poets of England from the thirteenth century to T. S. Eliot. Assures Indian readers that "a rich vein of religious, devotional, and meditative poetry runs through the literature of England, though at first sight it would seem incredible, because the English people have been looked on as fighters, colonizers, empire-builders, sturdy John Bulls, a 'nation of shopkeepers,' and what not—anything but mystics and devotional poets" (p. 139). Briefly mentions Herbert and maintains that he is simpler than Donne, "though not altogether free of 'wit' " (p. 141).

**472. Smith, A. J.** "An Examination of Some Claims for Ramism." *RES* n.s. 7:348–59.

Reprinted in *Essential Articles for the Study of John Donne's Poetry*, edited by John R. Roberts (Hamden, Conn.: Archon Books, 1975), 178–88.

Challenges Rosemond Tuve's claim in *Elizabethan and Metaphysical Imagery: Renaissance Poetic and Twentieth-Century Critics* (entry 330) that Ramism "provides a satisfactory explanation not only of certain major elements in so-called 'Metaphysical' poetry, but even of the very thought processes of the greatest 'Metaphysical' poet, Donne" (p. 348). Discusses the nature of Ramism, in particular its relation to verse. Concludes that "too much has been made of the attempt at reform in teaching method called Ramism, in itself and as an influence" and that "for the true explanation of 'Metaphysical' qualities and techniques one need seek no farther than the great sixteenth-century tradition of which Ramism was but a backwater—that of *wit* as it was developed in conventional rhetoric" (p. 359). No specific mention of Herbert. For a reply, see George Watson (entry 505).

**473. Tillyard, E. M. W.** *The Metaphysicals and Milton.* London: Chatto & Windus. vii, 87p.

Reprinted, 1960, 1965; Westport, Conn.: Greenwood Press, 1975.

Examines the supposed opposition between the metaphysicals and Milton. Maintains that Milton was "a great figure looking back to the Middle Ages and forward to the spirit and achievements of eighteenth-century puritanism" but argues that "his larger surprises and ironies are in harmony with the requirements of his age" (p. 74). Maintains that "he is more like Jonson and Marvell than he is like Donne and Crashaw" and argues that Donne, on the other hand, "was a great innovator but with a narrower, more personal talent" (p. 74). Rejects the notion of a "school of Donne" and claims that Herbert is closer to Milton "in many motions of his mind" (p. 2) than he is to Donne. Maintains that Donne's "direct influence on Herbert was undoubted but it extended to a smaller proportion of his poems than is often thought" (p. 58).

**474. Wellek, René.** "The Criticism of T. S. Eliot." *SR* 64:398–443.

Reviews Eliot's basic comments on the metaphysical poets (pp. 437–40) and points out that, although his criticism has proved to be an important impetus to the so-called metaphysical revival, his ideas are, for the most part, neither original nor consistent and that he is the first critic to link the metaphysical poets so definitely with the French symbolists. Briefly comments on Eliot's evaluation of Herbert: "He rates Herbert more high [than Donne] as a great master of language, as a sincere devotional poet, as an anatomist of feeling, as a trained theologian, and as a man who, in his short life, went much further along the road to humility than Donne" (p. 439). Notes Eliot's insistence that *The Temple* be considered "as a continuous religious meditation with a planned, intellectual framework" (p. 439). Maintains that Eliot considers Vaughan inferior to Herbert.

**475. Wilcock, J. R.** "George Herbert," in *Poetas líricos ingleses*, selección de Ricardo Baeza; estudio preliminar por Silvina Ocampo, 87–90. (Clásicos Jackson, vol. 34.) Buenos Aires: W. M. Jackson.

Brief introduction to Herbert's life and work (p. 87), followed by Spanish prose translations of "Sinne (I)," "Giddinesse," "The Collar," and "The Flower" (pp. 87–90), without notes or commentary.

# 1957

**476. Collmer, Robert G.** "Herbert's 'Businesse,' 15–30." *Expl* 16:item 11.

Comments on five different possible meanings for, or kinds of, death in lines 20–30 of "Businesse": "(I) redemptive, or Christ's; (II) spiritual, that is, separation of the human being from God in this life; (III) eternal, that is, separation of the human in the future life; (IV) transformatory, or separation of the soul from the world and sin, which is achieved by applying the merits of Christ's crucifixion and resurrection to the soul; (V) natural, separation of the soul from the body."

**477. Gardner, Helen, ed.** *The Metaphysical Poets*. Selected and edited by Helen Gardner. Baltimore: Penguin Books. 328p.

Reprinted, 1959, 1961, 1963, 1964, 1966.

2d ed., London: Oxford University Press, 1967; rpt., 1967, 1972.

3d ed., 1975.

Pages xix-xxiv reprinted in *Seventeenth Century English Poetry: Modern Essays in Criticism*, edited by William Keast (entry 584), 50–62, rev. ed. (entry 879), 32–44.

An anthology of metaphysical poetry in which Herbert is represented by twenty-four poems (pp. 118–40). Selected bibliography (p. 303) and biographical notes (pp. 304–20). The introduction outlines and comments on the major characteristics of metaphysical poetry, especially its concentration, its uses of the conceit, its argumentative and persuasive tone and structure, its dramatic elements, its strong sense of the real and actual, its individuality, and so forth. Comments briefly on "Mortification," stressing Herbert's individuality in treating "the old theme of the stages of human life and the traditional lessons of the *Ars Moriendi*" (p. 27).

**478. Gregory, Horace, and Zaturenska Marya, eds.** *The Mentor Book of Religious Verse*. (A Mentor Book.) New York: New American Library of World Literature. xxviii, 238p.

Anthology of religious verse arranged according to the liturgical calendar. In the introduction (pp. xv-xxviii) comments on the rediscovery and appreciation of religious poetry in the twentieth century. Comments briefly on how much Herbert was appreciated by Coleridge, Emerson, and Emily Dickinson. Includes seven poems by Herbert.

**479. Kermode, Frank.** " 'Dissociation of Sensibility': Modern Symbolist Readings of Literary History," in *Romantic Image*, 138–61. London: Routledge and Kegan Paul.

The relevant parts of this chapter that deal with the metaphysical poets and the seventeenth century appear in much expanded form in "Dissociation of Sensibility" (entry 480).

**480.** ———. "Dissociation of Sensibility." *KR* 19:169–94.

Reprinted in *Essential Articles for the Study of John Donne's Poetry*, edited by John R. Roberts (Hamden, Conn.: Archon Books, 1975), 66–82.

Challenges Eliot's theory of "dissociation of sensibility" and points out that the tension between reason and theological truth was not solely confined to, nor begun in, seventeenth-century England. Maintains that as far as poetry is concerned, especially metaphysical poetry, the theory is simply an "attempt on the part of Symbolists to find an historical justification for their poetics" (p. 194). Discusses how the term and concept are closely related to the twentieth-century revival of metaphysical poetry. No specific references to Herbert. In a much-revised form, the same ground is covered in " 'Dissociation of Sensibility': Modern Symbolist Readings of Literary History" (entry 479).

**481. Kusunose, Toshihiko.** "George Herbert no Seikaku to Shiso" [George Herbert's Character and Thought]. *Kanseigakuin Daigaku Eibei Bungaku* [English and American Literature, Kanseigakuin University], vol. 2, no. 2:69–84.

Discusses the character and thought of Herbert, especially his views of nature, man, and poetry.

**482. Levang, Dwight.** "George Herbert's 'The Church Militant' and the Chances of History." *PQ* 36:265–68.

Points out that Samuel Ward of Ipswich, a Puritan preacher, was imprisoned in 1635 for making a statement in a sermon that is strikingly close to lines 235–36 of *The Church Militant* ("Religion stands on tip-toe in our land, / Readie to passe to the *American* strand.")

**483. Miles, Josephine.** *Eras & Modes in English Poetry*. Berkeley and Los Angeles: University of California Press; London: Cambridge University Press. xi, 233p.

Rev. ed., 1964.

Chapter 1 is a reprint of "Eras of English Poetry," *PMLA* 70 (1955): 853–75.

Questions the theory of dividing English poetry arbitrarily into historical periods and defines three recurrent modes in poetry based upon the various kinds of sentence structure and word usage favored by English poets: the clausal or predicative, the phrasal or sublime, and the balanced or classical. Considers the clausal or active predicative mode as the most English and traces it to Chaucer. In this mode one finds such a variety of poets as Chaucer, Skelton, Wyatt, Sidney, Donne, Jonson, Herrick, Herbert, Cowley, Coleridge, Byron, Browning, Hardy, Cummings, Frost, and Auden. The clausal mode lends itself to passionate argumentation, natural discourse in verse, abrupt movement, clausal connectives, and a preponderance of verbs over adjectives.

In appendix A (pp. 215–30) shows, by means of a statistical table, that Herbert belongs to the clausal mode. Chapter 2, "The Language of the Donne Tradition" (pp. 20–32), is a revision of an article by the same title in *KR* 13 (1951): 37–49. Although Herbert is not directly mentioned in this chapter, many of the general observations could be applied to his poetry.

**484. Moloney, Michael F.** "A Note on Herbert's 'Season'd Timber.'" *N&Q* 202:434–35.

Comments on stanza 4 of "Vertue" to illustrate the complexity of Herbert's "imagistic texture." Maintains that the "primary likeness which Herbert wishes to stress between the virtuous soul and seasoned timber is . . . that just as the latter resists the structural strains placed upon it without warping or bowing, so the former resists with complete integrity the burden of temptation" (p. 435). Shows how a "simple simile . . . veils a subtle metonymy" (p. 435).

**485. Oxford University. Bodleian Library.** *English Literature in the Seventeenth Century: Guide to an Exhibition held in 1957.* Oxford: Bodleian Library. 167p.

Guide to an exhibition of seventeenth-century books and manuscripts in the Bodleian (including three that were borrowed) that were "read then or now for their literary merit" (p. 5). Includes a copy of the second state of the first edition of *The Temple* (number 39) and the manuscript of the poems owned by Archbishop Sancroft (number 41). Points out that the copy of *The Temple* was bought in 1854 for two guineas out of the bequest of Robert Mason and comments in some detail on the manuscript, noting that the Williams Library manuscript, not the Sancroft, is more likely the one that Herbert gave Edmund Duncon in 1633.

**486. Scott, A. F.** *The Poet's Craft: A Course in the Critical Appreciation of Poetry.* Cambridge: University Press. xi, 219p.

Divided into five sections: (1) reproductions of a number of manuscript poems, many of them original drafts, often showing the poets' corrections; (2) first published versions of several poems with more widely accepted revisions; (3) raw materials used by several poets (North, Golding, etc.); (4) several translations of Greek and Latin poems into English by different hands; and (5) a number of unsigned poems grouped together for comparison and contrast. Reproduces Herbert's "Perfection" ("The Elixir") from the Williams MS (pp. 4–5) and includes "Love (III)" in the fifth section.

**487. Taylor, Ivan Earle.** "Cavalier Sophistication in the Poetry of George Herbert." *Anglican Theological Review* 39:229–43.

Challenges the notion that Herbert is a "plastic saint" and argues that in his poetry he "gives evidence of being basically a cavalier; that is to say, a courtly seventeenth century aristocrat concerned to a remarkable degree with interests generally associated with the cavaliers: wine, game, women, sophisticated conversation, dress, and the like" (p. 230). Classifies and discusses under four major headings the images, allusions, and metaphors in Herbert's poetry "that reveal him as a true cavalier and sophisticate": (1) stewardship and the ways the lord of a manor relates to his tenants concerning such matters as the proper uses of grants and leases; considerations of court life, great places, and proper upbringing of a gentleman; (2) rich clothing, silks, weaving knots, and so forth; (3) wine, drinking, eating, and so forth; (4) wit, courtesy, love dalliance, the art of language. Argues that "there are, moreover, many references, here and there throughout the poems, to such sophisticated activities as gambling, falconry, gardening, to jewels and perfumes, and, of course, to music" (pp. 230–31).

# 1958

**488. Adams, Robert M.** "Metaphysical Poets, Ancient and Modern," in *Strains of Discord: Studies in Literary Openness*, 105–45. Ithaca, N.Y.: Cornell University Press.

Maintains that the most distinguishing feature of metaphysical poetry is wit, a "wit based upon a difficult metaphor, intellectual or abstract in its nexus, rather than naturalistic, involving more often an esoteric analogy than a superficial, single-level physical resemblance, and giving always the sense of a difficulty overcome" (p. 107). Comments on the dramatic element in Herbert's poetry: Herbert, Donne, and Marvell are poets "who play with a contrast between spheres of existence: the microcosm and the macrocosm or the stadium of heavenly simplicity and that of worldly complexity or the sphere of contemplation and the sphere of action" (p. 111). Concludes that their style is metaphysical "precisely as it juxtaposes points of view which are in some ways compatible, in others not—as it carries out a juxtaposition which involves a strain" (p. 111). In a subsection of the essay entitled "Auden and Herbert," compares the simplicity of style, the seemingly artless quality, and the quiet and graceful tone of Herbert's poetry with the strenuous, difficult, allusive, and restless quality of the metaphysical verse of Auden and Empson. Comments on Herbert's deliberate and inventive devices for achieving simplicity, especially his uses of shaped verse and stanzaic patterns. Calls "Love (III)" an exquisite example of "a metaphysical poem so close to metaphysical reality that it needs no impurities of style, no dramatization or assertion of self; yet its very comportment, its quiet and easy grace, are dramatically eloquent" (p. 124).

**489. Adler, Jacob H.** "Form and Meaning in Herbert's 'Discipline.'" *N&Q* 203:240–43.

Shows through a stanza-by-stanza analysis of "Discipline" that, "in spite of an apparent (and in a sense genuine) simplicity and austerity, the effect of the poem is both complex and powerful" (p. 243). Points out how various elements in the poem contribute to the total effect: "The short lines with end-pause; the particularly short third lines; the direct word order and easy-seeming rime; the rod and the vivid imagery of love as a man of war which are together expressive of the central idea of the poem; the first and last stanzas, which need to be similar and need to be different: all contribute to the tension between two conflicting emotions toward God which the poem builds up and resolves" (p. 243).

**490. Burgess, Anthony [John Burgess Wilson].** "The Age of Milton: End of a Period," in *English Literature: A Survey for Students*, 131–53. London: Longman, Green, & Co.

New edition, 1974.

Calls Herbert the greatest of the Anglican poets and maintains that "The Collar" "catches some of the tones of the Elizabethan dramatists in its irregular rhymed verse" and that the end of the poem contains "a fine dramatic surprise" (p. 139). Regards Herbert as a mystic and notes that his mysticism, as reflected in "Love (III)," is "gentle and homely" (p. 140).

**491. Broderick, John C.** "The Date and Source of Emerson's 'Grace.'" *MLN* 73:91–95.

Amplifies Norman A. Brittin's comments (entry 197) on the thematic and stylistic resemblances between Emerson's "Grace" and Herbert's "Sinne (I)." Argues that Emerson made "Grace" his own "by modifying Herbert's devout lament over the power of sin into a hymn of thanksgiving with a characteristically optimistic theme" (p. 95). Points out that Emerson may have read Herbert's poem in Coleridge's *Aids to Reflection*, where it appeared under the title "Graces vouchsafed in a Christian Land."

**492. Bush, Douglas.** "Tradition and Experience," in *Literature and Belief*, edited by M. H. Abrams, 31–52. (English Institute Essays, 1957.) New York: Columbia University Press.

Reprinted in *Engaged and Disengaged* (Cambridge, Mass.: Harvard University Press, 1966), 143–63.

Discusses non-Christian responses to, and experience of, poetry that is firmly rooted in Christian belief. Makes several references to Herbert by way of illustration. Argues that "the great poetry of religious meditation, the poetry that really comes home to modern readers who do not share the beliefs it embodies, is that which extends beyond the particular creed and personality of its author, which grows out of and embraces general human experience" (pp. 40–41). Maintains that such an appeal is what the modern reader finds in Herbert: Herbert's "greater poems are greater because they deal with worldly allurements, rebellious self-will, the desire for discipline and humility and for the renewal of spiritual energy, with conflicts and aspirations and defeats and victories that belong to all human life" (p. 39). Contrasts Herbert's modern appeal with that of Donne and Crashaw.

**493. Evans, G. Blakemore.** "George Herbert's 'Jordan.'" *N&Q* 203:215.

Supports the interpretation of the title of Herbert's two Jordan poems put forward by Grosart: "(a) That he was crossing into the Promised Land; (b) That thereupon Jordan was to be his Helicon—the Lord, not the Nine Muses, the source of his inspiration" (p. 215). Supports this position by references to Christopher Harvey's *The Synagogue* (2d ed., 1647) and to anonymous lines appearing in a memorial poem included in Herbert's *The Temple* (10th ed., 1674): "In both passages, with specific reference to Herbert's poetry, we find a sacred height . . . compared to Parnassus, and Christ's blood . . . to an implied Helicon" (p. 215).

**494. Hagstrum, Jean H.** "The 'Baroque' Century," in *The Sister Arts: The Tradition of Literary Pictorialism and English Poetry from Dryden to Gray*, 93–128. Chicago: University of Chicago Press.

Comments on the emblematic quality of Herbert's poetry and calls him "the most emblematic of poets" (p. 100). Notes that the titles of many of Herbert's poems "are graphic in an emblematic way and seem almost to take the place of engraved design" (p. 98); that "The Posie" "even uses the technical language of the device or impresa" (p. 98); and that "the graphically conceived icon in Herbert's verse often provides its organizing form" (p. 100). Maintains that *The Temple* "resembles a book of *imagini*, like Cesare Ripa's *Iconologia*": "Herbert's collection of poems represents the same kind of subject, limited of course to the church, its symbols and its seasons, its feasts and its fasts" (p. 99). Recognizes that the symbolic and metaphysical meanings of objects, rather than the objects themselves, are the concern of Herbert's poetry, but maintains that, because of Herbert's emblematic method, he "belongs to the iconic and pictorialist tradition" (p. 100).

**495. Hilberry, Conrad.** "Herbert's 'Dooms-day.'" *Expl* 16:item 24.

Outlines the basic argument of "Dooms-day," which is a "striking illustration of George Herbert's very sure control of tone: the first four stanzas are a bizarre, partly comic plea for an early Doomsday; then the last stanza shifts the tone slightly and unfolds a new center of seriously religious meaning."

**496. Joselyn, Sister M.** "Herbert and Hopkins: Two Lyrics." *Renascence* 10:192–95.

Compares and contrasts Herbert's "Affliction (I)" and G. M. Hopkins's "Carrion Comfort" and maintains that the subject of both poems is similar: "A trial of faith more or less intense . . . favorably resolved at the end though at the cost of severe personal sacrifice" (p. 192). Yet points out that, "in tenor and decorum, every nuance and strategy of feeling, the two poems could hardly differ more" (p. 192). Presents a close reading of Herbert's poem.

**497. Mitton, C. Leslie.** "George Herbert's 'The Country Parson.'" *Expository Times* 69:113–15.

Appreciative essay on *The Country Parson* by a clergyman. Stresses that even today Herbert's book "is particularly applicable to the minister, but words of homely wisdom abound, many of which are also of significance for every one who seeks to live the Christian life" (p. 114).

**498. Muraoka, Isamu.** *Eishi no Sugata—Ju-Na-Na-Seiki Eishi no Image* [Imagery of English Poems of the Seventeenth Century]. Tokyo: Kenkyusha.

Argues that Herbert was influenced by Donne's uses of wit and imagery and stresses that Herbert characteristically used images drawn from the everyday and domestic world.

**499. Novarr, David.** *The Making of Walton's Lives.* (Cornell Studies in English, edited by M. H. Abrams, Francis E. Mineka, and William M. Sale, Jr., 41.) Ithaca, N.Y.: Cornell University Press. xvi, 527p.

Discusses Walton's biographical methodology and makes important comments on the various subjects of the *Lives.* Mentions Herbert throughout, especially in the sections devoted to Donne. Chapter 10, "The 'Almost Incredible Story' of George Herbert," is devoted to the *Life of Herbert* (1670) and its subsequent revisions. Comments on Walton's long interest in Herbert before the writing of the *Life.* Outlines Walton's intention, point of view, and sources in writing the biography. Concludes that Walton "had put a halo about Herbert's head, had made a case that the halo glorified even noble and learned heads, and had shown the clergy precisely how they, too, could obtain halos. His revisions serve only to show that he was himself pleased by his accomplishment" (p. 361). Shows that Walton did not "go to great trouble to get detailed biographical information" and that thus the *Life* is "full of inaccuracies and gaps" (p. 488). Shows how Walton used Herbert's poetry and prose to create a portrait of Herbert as "a prototype of the good parson" (p. 488). Appendix B, "Walton and the Poems about Donne's Seal" (pp. 503–6), comments on Herbert's reply. Appendix D, "The Publication of the *Life of Herbert*" (pp. 510–12), presents bibliographical information. Appendix F, "Walton on Herbert's Resignation of His Fellowship" (pp. 516–20), discusses Walton's reason for dropping his reference to Herbert's resignation of his fellowship.

**500. Pietrkiewicz, Jerzy, ed. and trans.** "George Herbert," in *Antologia liryki angielskiej (1300–1950)*, 70–73. London: Veritas Foundation Press.

Reproduces "Death" and "Vertue" with Polish translations on facing pages, without commentary.

**501. Ricart, Domingo.** *Juan de Valdés y el pensamiento religioso europeo en los siglos xvi y xvii.* Durango, Mexico: El Colegio de México; Lawrence: University of Kansas. 139p.

Maintains that until Nicholas Ferrar's translation of the *Consideraciones*, Juan de Valdés was unknown in England. Comments on the friendship between Herbert and Ferrar and discusses Herbert's *Briefe Notes on Valdesso's Considerations*. Maintains that Herbert's reactions to the Spanish writer are those of a professional theologian and an orthodox member of the Anglican Church. Notes that, although Herbert's poetry reflects a very solid intellect and a concern for theology, his *Briefe Notes* are his only formal contribution to speculative and doctrinal theology. Argues that Herbert's theology and his poetry rest upon the authority of the Church, not upon any mystical inspiration, and calls Herbert an exquisite representative of Anglican piety. Comments on Herbert's reservations about some of the points in the *Consideraciones* but notes that he regarded Valdés as a genuine Christian reformer.

**502. Rickey, Mary Ellen.** "Rhymecraft in Edward and George Herbert." *JEGP* 57:502–11.

Proposes "to examine the range of rhyme designs used by both men and to determine what light, if any, can be cast on the relationship of their rhymecraft" (p. 502). Presents a tabulation of the "rhyme formulas and number of nonrepeated stanza forms" employed by each (pp. 503–4). Shows that "George Herbert uses 48 rhyme plans in 169 stanzas while Edward Herbert uses 44 rhyme plans in 62 stanzas" (p. 504). Points out that such innovators as Campion, Donne, Southwell, and Raleigh cannot match the Herberts in range of pattern. Enumerates some of the so-called oddities of Herbert's verse found in the earlier work of Edward Herbert—for instance, the hieroglyphic (shaped poem), the convention of the echo, the use of a shift in stanza form within a poem, and the use of rare or unknown stanza forms. Shows that Edward's experimentation with rhyme and his ingenuity are more extensive than George's and concludes that the younger brother appropriated some formal qualities from the older brother: "It is especially curious that several of the highly wrought lyrics of holy Mr. Herbert should have been suggested to him by the more flippant verse of Lord Herbert of Cherbury" (p. 511).

**503. Wardropper, Bruce.** "El siglo XVI: La divinización de la poesía culta," in *Historia de la poesia lirica a lo divino en la cristiandad occidental*, 255–301. Madrid: Revista de Occidente.

Briefly discusses Herbert's conversion of the themes and techniques of secular (and even erotic) poetry to the service of sacred poetry and comments, in particular, on "A Parodie" (pp. 297–300). Notes that in the poem Herbert "imita a la perfección la complicada estructura rítmica de su modelo, pero mantiene una vez pasados los primeros versos" (p. 298).

**504. Warnke, Frank J.** "Jan Luyken: A Dutch Metaphysical Poet." *CL* 10:45–54.

Argues that metaphysical poetry "constitutes a style, unlike the continental baroque, and that this style is not limited to English poetry" (p. 46). Maintains that "no body of continental verse demonstrates more tellingly the presence of this analogous something than does the religious poetry of the seventeenth-century Dutchman Jan Luyken (1649–1712)" (p. 46). Compares and contrasts Luyken with Herbert and maintains that the Dutch poet is more closely related to Vaughan or Traherne than he is to Herbert or Donne: he belongs "to that last phase of metaphysical poetry, in which the traditional view of the world expresses itself through a meditative attention

to observed nature, an attention which in many ways anticipates that of those romantics who a century and a half later were also to look for the Creator in the creation"
(pp. 53–54).

**505. Watson, George.** "Ramus, Miss Tuve, and the New Petromachia." *MP*
55:259–62.
Challenges in part A. J. Smith's attack (entry 472) on Rosemond Tuve's claims for
Ramism in her *Elizabethan and Metaphysical Imagery: Renaissance Poetic and Twentieth-Century Critics* (entry 330). Agrees with Smith that Tuve's argument is "too
ambitious and will not stand" (p. 260) but concludes that Ramism, "as far as the
English were concerned, was a quick handbook for logic with Cambridge and Puritan
associations" (p. 262). Maintains that "it is still not clear that there is any need to seek
a connection between Ramism and English poetry; but, if one must be sought at all,
the neo-Ramists might surely have found a happier hunting-ground than the poems of
men as un-puritanical and unsimple as the English metaphysicals" (p. 262). No
specific mention of Herbert.

**506. Wilson, Edward M.** "Spanish and English Poetry of the Seventeenth Century." *Journal of Ecclesiastical History* 9:38–53.
Announces his intent "to show that there was unity as well as diversity in two
contemporary religious literatures and to hint at the sources of that unity" (p. 38).
Maintains that "in each country there was a common way to express religious truths
in vivid everyday terms" and that this "was partly due to the fact that both countries
had a medieval heritage in common, but still more to the fact that a devotional
literature spread from Spain through Roman Catholic Europe into England in spite of
fundamental differences of religious belief and practice" (p. 53). Discusses the art of
sacred parody and the uses of divine analogy (or continued metaphor) in English and
Spanish devotional poetry. Notes Herbert's parody of Sidney and calls "Redemption"
the best example of the continued metaphor in English. Compares Herbert briefly
with Alonso de Ledesma, Lope de Vega, and Valdivielso. Comments on possible
Spanish influence on Herbert and discusses also the influence of the art of discursive
meditation on the poets of the period.

# 1959

**507. Attal, Jean-Pierre.** "Qu'est-ce que la poésie 'métaphysique'?" *Critique* (Paris)
15:682–707.
Review of six critical studies: (1) Denonain's *Thèmes et formes de la poésie "métaphysique"* (entry 458); (2) Odette de Mourgues's *Metaphysical Baroque and Précieux
Poetry* (entry 420); (3) Alan Boase's *Sponde* (Geneva: Pierre Cailler, 1949); (4)
Boase's "Poètes anglais et français de l'epoque baroque" (entry 343); (5) Joan Bennett's *Four Metaphysical Poets* (entry 174); (6) T. S. Eliot's "The Metaphysical Poets"
(entry 70). Maintains that metaphysical poetry is indeed metaphysical in that it deals
with first principles and first causes, that it is above all concerned with truth rather
than with beauty, and that it scorns the heritage of the classics and traditional poetic
phraseology: "Ils se sont tournés vers le quotidien et le familier pour atteindre le
«réel»" (p. 706). Compares Herbert and Donne: "Alors que Donne soumet l'apparence au sacré (ce qui explique en partie sa liberté d'images qui n'ont qu'un but:

signifier ce sacré), Herbert et Vaughan la soumettent plutôt au divin; l'apparence est pour eux «l'inépuisable livret d'une inépuisable musique»" (p. 702).

**508. Bald, R. C., ed.** *Seventeenth-Century English Poetry.* (The Harper English Literature Series.) New York: Harper Brothers. ix, 591p.

Maintains that "the religious lyricists of the century looked to Herbert rather than to Donne as their master" (p. 26). Briefly contrasts Herbert and Donne and notes that Herbert's admirers frequently imitated his "delight in accumulating a whole series of images to describe his theme," as in "Sunday" and "Prayer (I)," and "his invention of parables (perhaps to compensate for his renunciation of allegory) such as form the substance of his best-known poems," "Redemption," "The Collar," and "The Pulley" (p. 26). Notes Herbert's influence on Crashaw and Vaughan and comments briefly on his use of emblems. Biographical sketch, bibliographical note, and sixteen of Herbert's poems, with brief explanatory notes (pp. 219–30).

**509. Boyd, George W.** "What Is 'Metaphysical' Poetry?" *MissQ* 12:13–21.

Traces the meaning of the term *metaphysical poetry* from Dryden to the present, "taking account of its sometimes gradual, sometimes drastic shifting and giving especial attention to the wide-ranging discussion of the subject in the criticism of the past decade" (p. 13). Maintains that the "classic definition and delineation of metaphysical poetry laid down by Messrs. Grierson, Eliot, and Williamson . . . has not been superseded in modern criticism" (p. 21). Sees the work of Joseph Mazzeo and Louis Martz as possible new directions. No specific mention of Herbert.

**510. Chute, Marchette.** *Two Gentle Men: The Lives of George Herbert and Robert Herrick.* New York: E. P. Dutton & Co. 319p.

Reprinted, London: Secker & Warburg, 1960.

Part 1 (pp. 11–152) presents a biographical account of Herbert for the common reader with brief critical comments on his poetry, which is seen primarily as autobiographical. Appendix: "Walton's Biography of Herbert" (pp. 277–82) comments on Walton's intention and methodology in the *Lives.* Challenges in particular Walton's contention that Herbert entered politics because of worldly ambition, a "case of manipulation, one that adds a great deal to the effectiveness of the story of a saint who forsook the world but one which has no support outside of Walton's pages" (p. 279). Also questions Walton's account of the reasons Herbert became a deacon. Bibliography (pp. 283–97). See also entry 511.

**511. ———.** "A Biographer and Two Dear Friends She Never Met." *New York Herald Tribune Book Review,* 27 December, pp. 1, 11.

Explains why she enjoyed writing *Two Gentle Men: The Lives of George Herbert and Robert Herrick* (entry 510): "I already knew, before I began the book, that I loved them both as poets but after I made their acquaintance I found I loved them as people too" (p. 1). Biographical sketch of Herbert and Herrick.

**512. Colie, Rosalie L.** "Constantijn Huygens and the Metaphysical Mode." *GR* 34:59–73.

Examines the religious verse of Huygens, the Dutch translator of Donne's poems, to determine the validity of Huygens's claim of being a metaphysical poet. Points out a number of parallels between Huygens and the metaphysical poets and concludes that his "religious poetic, his mode of metaphoric usage, his choice of meter, all show the poet's persuasive belief in God's original wit and in his own lesser wit, set to sing his praises of God's creativity, working simultaneously in the physical and spiritual worlds of which metaphysical poetry is made" (p. 73). Notes that Huygens possessed a copy of Herbert's poetry and finds many parallels between the religious verse of Huygens and that of Herbert, especially echoes of "The Flower," "The Collar," "The Sacrifice," "Christmas," "The H. Scriptures (II)," and "Jordan (II)." Maintains that Huygens, like Herbert, "managed to maintain in his poems an intellectual tension rising from his awareness of the necessarily paradoxical bases of his religious life and to force upon his readers a sharp and articulate religious understanding" (p. 67).

**513. Drew, Elizabeth.** *Poetry: A Modern Guide to Its Understanding and Enjoyment.* New York: W. W. Norton & Co. 287p.

Brief explication of "Love (III)" (pp. 245–47). Calls the poem "a little symbolic drama of personal experience, where the Christian ethic shines out in all its simple beauty" (p. 245). Brief mention of "Vertue" (p. 107) and "The Flower" (p. 142).

**514. Duncan, Joseph E.** *The Revival of Metaphysical Poetry: The History of a Style, 1800 to the Present.* Minneapolis: University of Minnesota Press. 227p. Reprinted, New York: Octagon Books, 1969.

General review of the critical reputation of the metaphysical poets from their own time to the present. Emphasizes "the line of successive interpretations rather than individual evaluations, and treats poetic style as a vital force guiding creative efforts in a later period" (p. 5). Attempts to show in what ways "the metaphysical style, as it was interpreted and varied through successive periods, was both like and unlike the metaphysical style of the seventeenth century" (p. 4). Divided into ten chapters: (1) "The Early Conceptions of Metaphysical Poetry" (pp. 6–28); (2) "Seeds of Revival" (pp. 29–49); (3) "John Donne and Robert Browning" (pp. 50–68); (4) "The Beginnings of the Revival in America" (pp. 69–88); (5) "The Catholic Revival and the Metaphysicals" (pp. 89–112); (6) "The Metaphysical Revival: 1872–1912" (pp. 113–29); (7) "Yeats, Donne and the Metaphysicals" (pp. 130–42); (8) "Eliot and the Twentieth-Century Revival" (pp. 143–64); (9) "Metaphysicals and Critics since 1912" (pp. 165–81); and (10) "Metaphysical Florescence" (pp. 182–202). Chapter 3 first appeared as "The Intellectual Kinship of John Donne and Robert Browning" in *SP* 50 (1953): 81–100, here slightly revised; chapter 6 first appeared as "The Revival of Metaphysical Poetry, 1872–1912" (entry 415), here slightly revised. Many references throughout to Herbert. Comments on Herbert's influence on many later poets and surveys the appreciative evaluation of him by many notables, including Coleridge, Margaret Fuller, Emerson, Lowell, and especially John Keble, G. M. Hopkins, Francis Thompson, and Yeats.

**515. Emerson, Ralph Waldo.** "Ben Jonson, Herrick, Herbert, Wotton," in *Early Lectures of Ralph Waldo Emerson,* vol. 1 (1833–1886), edited by Stephen E. Whicher and Robert E. Spiller, 337–55. Cambridge, Mass.: Harvard University Press.

Presents Emerson's lecture to the Society for the Diffusion of Useful Knowledge at the Masonic Temple in Boston on 31 December 1835. The editors suggest that Emerson's choice of writers for this lecture may have been in part motivated by his concern at the time about the function of language as symbol, noting that as early as 1831 Emerson, in the *Journal*, had commented on Herbert's use of language. In the lecture, Emerson calls Herbert "a striking example of the power of exalted thought to melt and bend language to its fits of expression" (p. 350) and maintains that Herbert excels "in exciting that feeling we call the moral sublime" (p. 352). Praises Herbert's diction and quotes from "Vertue," "Confession," "The Elixir," "Providence," and "Affliction (I)."

**516. Gamberini, Spartaco.** *Poeti metafisici e cavalieri in Inghilterra.* (Biblioteca dell' «Archivium Romanicum»: Serie 1: Storia-letteratura-paleografia, vol. 60.) Florence: Leo S. Olschki. 269p.

Discriminates between such critical terms as *wit, conceit, metaphysical poetry, euphuism, baroque,* and *mannerism.* Compares and contrasts Donne, Jonson, and Chapman as leaders of different poetic schools. Presents a general survey of Herbert's work for an Italian audience (pp. 83–92). Comments primarily on the thematic concerns of Herbert's poetry and on his religious sensibilities. Calls *The Temple* "il diario intimo che con scrupolosa esattezza annota ogni moto dell'anima" and suggests that "forse per questo scrupolo di verità, nell'ansia di osservare e definire ogni stato d'animo, nel non permettere mai il minimo abbandono, la poesia del Herbert non è lirica, intendendo questo genere come canto, abbandono alato all'empìto del sentimento. Manca la lirica, c'è la preghiera, l'analisi, l'introspezione, l'argomentazione, ma non il canto" (p. 86). Compares Herbert with Lyly, Benlowes, Lord Herbert, and especially Vaughan.

**517. Hart, A. Tindall.** "Saints and Sinners," in *The Country Clergy in Elizabethan & Stuart Times, 1558–1660,* 137–64. London: Phoenix House.

Biographical account of Herbert as a Laudian clergyman. Outlines some of his main tenets concerning the living of a Christian life, especially as these apply to a country parson.

**518. Honda, Kin-ichiro.** "George Herbert no kami ni tsuite—*The Temple* no ichi kosatsu" [On George Herbert's God—A Study of *The Temple*], in *Kashiwagura kyoju Kanreki kinen Rombun-shu* [Essays in Honor of the Sixtieth Anniversary of the Birth of Professor Kashiwagura], 24–36. Tokyo: Kenkyusha.

Argues that the primary characteristic of God that Herbert focuses on in his verse is His love for man and maintains that, despite a life of internal conflicts, Herbert was finally assured of his salvation. Discusses Herbert's fascination with the paradox of the Incarnation.

**519. Rathmell, J. C. A.** "Hopkins, Ruskin and the Sidney Psalter." *London Magazine* 6:51–66.

Primarily discusses the influence of the *Sidney Psalter* on G. M. Hopkins, especially on his "terrible sonnets." Maintains that Herbert also owes a great deal to the *Psalter* and briefly comments on Herbert's influence on Hopkins. Sees the modern metaphysical revival beginning, not in 1912 with the publication of Grierson's edition of Donne, but in the 1860s with Ruskin's and Hopkins's great admiration for Herbert.

**520. Richmond, H. M.** "The Intangible Mistress." *MP* 56:217–23.

Discusses various treatments of the theme of the unknown or unknowable mistress, a stock theme of Renaissance poetry, as a way of distinguishing what is genuinely metaphysical in so-called metaphysical poetry. Only incidentally comments on Herbert. Maintains that "prettily conceited verse dealing with quaint situations is particularly a Caroline specialty" and that "to this vein many of the poems of George Herbert, for example, could be more readily assimilated than to that of Donne's verse, to the stringent scholasticism of which they offer no parallel" (p. 222). Maintains also that Herbert, although he writes religious poems exclusively, gives one a "more secular sense of delight than is produced by the intense scrutiny to which Donne subjects even pagan themes" (p. 222).

**521.** [**Smith, A. J.**] "Anglicanism and the Poets." *TLS*, 20 March, Religious Books Section, pp. i-ii.

Comments on the great diversity of Anglican poets and maintains that many of them, though not always agreeing on points of doctrine, often seem to share "an understanding of the peculiarly indefinable Anglican temperament" (p. i). Maintains that the local nature of the Anglican Church accounts for a great deal of this diversity: "The ability of Anglican poets . . . to take upon them the prevailing attitudes of their age can occasionally make clear distinctions difficult, and the absence of an inflexible orthodox line has led many critics into what in one sense are almost bizarre comparisons between, for example, Wordsworth and Vaughan, for intellectually these poets differ greatly" (p. i). Several references to Herbert by way of illustrating the Anglican temperament of the seventeenth century.

**522. Tuve, Rosemond.** "George Herbert and *Caritas*." *JWCI* 22:303–31.

Reprinted in *Essays by Rosemond Tuve*, edited by Thomas P. Roche, Jr. (Princeton: Princeton University Press, 1970), 167–206.

Discusses the nature of Christian love in Herbert's poems and shows the intellectual fineness of his theology of love. Maintains that the primary conflict in Herbert is not between his secular ambitions and his religious calling but rather between his will and the demands of God's love. Notes that his fundamental torment is that he does not fully respond to God's love. Points out that Herbert writes "much more of God's love for man than of what man's love to God should be" (p. 308). States that Herbert "celebrates in poem after poem God's love for man, Agape, and the single revelation of it in Christ's Incarnation and Passion" (p. 314). Comments on various distinctions that must be made between secular poetry and Herbert's religious love poetry. For example, unlike the secular love poet, Herbert "never mentions, or implies, or fears, that his love is unrequited" (p. 310); likewise, he is "so entirely convinced and aware of the boundless love received from the one he loves that this is a *datum* in the most unhappy, the most tormented of the poems" (p. 311).

**523. Untermeyer, Louis.** "After the Renaissance," in *Lives of the Poets: The Story of One Thousand Years of English and American Poetry*, 137–69. New York: Simon & Shuster.

Biographical sketch of Herbert. Comments on his poetry's playfulness, piety, double meanings, metaphorical ingenuity, wit, and technical experimentation. Calls the poetry "a union of play and passion which allows Herbert to embody his most profound reflections in anagrams and acrostics, shaped stanzas, and picture poems" (p. 139). Comments on the "fusion of solemnity and virtuosity" (p. 140) and notes, "quiet, alternately courtly and colloquial, this is a poetry which begins in wonder and ends in certainty" (p. 142).

# *1960*

**524. Allen, Don Cameron.** "George Herbert: 'The Rose,'" in *Image and Meaning: Metaphoric Traditions in Renaissance Poetry*, 67–79. Baltimore: Johns Hopkins Press.

Rev. and enlarged ed., 1968.

Discusses the classical and Christian symbolic uses of the rose that inform Herbert's poem "The Rose." Shows that Herbert "brings in the Christian meanings of the flower and permits the pagan rose to be contrasted with the spiritual one" (p. 68). Notes that in antiquity the rose had a double metaphoric tradition: it not only stood for transient worldliness but also represented drunken revelry and riot, and thus, to some early Christians, the rose was a sign of the deceits of the world. Observes that later the rose was transformed into a symbol of love and virginity and a sign of those who scorned the world, especially the martyrs, and that the rose was particularly associated with the Virgin Mary and ultimately with Christ, who, from the twelfth century on was often called the mystic rose. Shows that in Herbert's poem "the rose of fleeting worldly pleasure is also the Christian and his God, a God who is love, but who is also judge and sentencer. So there are two flowers, an earthly one and a heavenly one; and on this doctrine of the rose, the poem of Herbert rests" (pp. 78–79).

**525. Bennett, Joan.** *Four Metaphysical Poets: Donne, Herbert, Vaughan, Crashaw. With an Anthology of Their Poetry Especially Selected for The Vintage Edition.* New York: Vintage Books. xii, 233, viip.

Reprinted, 1965.

Reprints the corrected second edition (1957) of *Four Metaphysical Poets: Donne, Herbert, Vaughan, Crashaw* (first published in 1934, entry 174), adding selections from their poetry. Includes twenty-six poems by Herbert (pp. 173–98) without notes or additional commentary.

**526. Crossett, John.** "Did Johnson Mean 'Paraphysical'?" *Boston University Studies in English* 4:121–24.

Maintains that, if one studies Dr. Johnson's dictionary as well as his general critical vocabulary, a vocabulary often taken from Longinus, it is possible to trace the origin and the precise meaning of the term *metaphysical* as Johnson used it in *The Lives of the Poets.* Concludes that Johnson merely "substituted 'metaphysical' for the non-existent 'paraphysical,' willingly or otherwise accepting the confusion in the exact meanings of *meta* and *para*; and that he wished 'metaphysical' to express the notion of deviating from nature by being excessive and contrary to nature" (p. 124). Maintains that Johnson's main criticism of the metaphysical poets was "that they did violate nature; the word that he chose to categorize them was intended to convey this notion" (p. 124).

**527. Daiches, David.** "Poetry after Spenser: The Jonsonian and the Metaphysical Traditions," in *A Critical History of English Literature,* 1:346–89. New York: Ronald Press Co.

2d ed., London: Secker & Warburg, 1969; rpt., New York: Ronald Press, 1970.

General survey and evaluation of Herbert's poetry (pp. 368–71). Calls Herbert "the finest of the religious 'metaphysicals'" and maintains that his poems reflect an inner tension between "worldly wit and sophistication" and "true Christian devotion" (p. 368). Maintains that Herbert explores, "with a combination of colloquial ease and emblematic cunning, the significance of the main symbols and beliefs of Protestant Christianity" (p. 386). Notes that, although Herbert sometimes strikes a Calvinistic note, he was faithful to the forms of worship of Anglicanism. Compares and contrasts Herbert's style to those of Sidney, Wyatt, Quarles, and Donne. Points out that Herbert "uses musical devices and analogies to a greater extent than any other of the metaphysical poets" (p. 369) and that "the combination of shock and repose in Herbert's poetry is something difficult to parallel in English literature" (p. 370). Praises Herbert's craftsmanship and comments briefly on "Easter-wings," "Deniall," and "The Collar."

**528. Ellrodt, Robert.** *L'Inspiration personnelle et l'esprit du temps chez les poètes métaphysiques anglais.* Paris: José Corti. 2 parts in 3 vols. 459p; 491p; 435p. Part 1 (vols. 1–2): 2d ed. (with new bibliography), 1973.

General introduction (pp. 14–77) reviews various definitions of metaphysical poetry using historical, stylistic, and psychological approaches and dismisses each as inadequate. Presents a tentative definition of metaphysical poetry and concludes that, since the metaphysical conceit comes from "la perplexité de l'esprit en présence des contradictions inhérentes à l'existence," Herbert, Donne, and Marvell "sont les vrais «poètes métaphysiques,» car leur poésie reproduit la démarche même et l'inquiétude du métaphysicien" (p. 30). Part 1, "Les Structures fondamentales de l'inspiration personnelle," is divided into two volumes. Volume 1, "John Donne et les poètes de la tradition chrétienne," is further subdivided into two books: "John Donne" (pp. 80–264) and "Les Poètes de la tradition chrétienne" (pp. 265–452). In the second book, one chapter is specifically devoted to Herbert (pp. 267–373). This chapter has four major sections: (1) "Le temps et l'espace," (2) "Modes de conscience et de sensibilité," (3) "Modes de pensée et formes d'expression," and (4) "Donne et Herbert, poètes métaphysiques." Throughout the chapter the author contrasts and compares Herbert to Donne. States that "l'habitude de penser sur deux plans à la fois, la perception simultanée de vérités parallèles et contraires, indissociables et distinctes, telle est la «forme» d'esprit qui apparente Donne et Herbert" (p. 341). Comments specifically on Donne's and Herbert's perceptions of time and space; discusses the autobiographical elements in the poetry of each; contrasts and compares Donne's and Herbert's uses of hyperbole, litotes, paradox, and irony; comments in detail on Herbert's attitude toward the Eucharist and compares it with the Calvinistic position; and evaluates the applicability of the term *metaphysical* to Herbert. In the last section of this chapter Herbert is contrasted with Crashaw (pp. 375–452). Volume 2 of part 1 is divided into two books: "Poètes de transition" (pp. 9–170) and "Poètes mystiques" (pp. 171–399). Throughout Herbert is compared to Lord Herbert of Cherbury, Cowley, Marvell, Vaughan, and Traherne. Three tables summarize the major characteristics of the metaphysical poets (pp. 411–12, 416, 422). In part 2 (pp. 9–400) the author discusses the social, psychological, and literary origins of metaphysical poetry at the turn of the sixteenth century.

**529. Herbert, George.** *Selected Poems of George Herbert, with a few representative poems by his contemporaries,* edited by Douglas Brown. London: Hutchinson Educational. 160p.

Prefatory note (pp. 5–6); contents (pp. 7–9); short biographical portrait (pp. 11–15); early records: selections from Walton's *Life* and Nicholas Ferrar's preface to *The Temple* (pp. 16–21); a note on the social and literary setting (pp. 22–25); selections from Herbert's poetry as well as a few poems by other sixteenth- and seventeenth-century poets, arranged into four major groups: hymns and anthems, his quick-piercing mind, the many spiritual conflicts, and poetry of meditation (pp. 27–100); critical commentary and notes on each section and on individual poems (pp. 101–50); short bibliography (p. 151), and glossary (pp. 153–60).

**530. Honda, Kin-ichiro.** "George Herbert no Geijutsu—Shijin to shite no shisei ni terashite" [George Herbert's Art—Referring to his Attitude as a Poet], in *Hok-*

*kaido Daigaku Gaikokugo Gaikoku Bungaku Kenkyu* [Studies in Foreign Language and Literature, Hokkaido University] no. 7 (March): 45–56.

Considers Herbert's attitude and artistic techniques as a poet. Argues that Herbert's poetry is the action of his prayer and the record of his love of God. Asserts that Herbert expressed his love of God in the verse form most suitable for each poem, using familiar images.

**531. Hughes, Richard E.** "Conceptual Form and Varieties of Religious Experience in the Poetry of George Herbert." *Greyfriar: Siena Studies in Literature* 3:3–12.

Discusses the idea of form as concept and argues that Herbert's works "*de facto* are more a question of concept than precept" and that "there is a tense ambivalence in Herbert's poetry which can be seen once we extend behind the disciplinary elements of his forms to the concepts which his forms embody" (p. 6). States that "a single, consecrated subject matter; an edifying and persuasive intention; poetry as recapitulation: behind all of these lies one concept. This concept might be generally termed the rhetorical viewpoint" (p. 6). Maintains that Herbert's rhetorically oriented conceptualism consists of three main ingredients: (1) a belief in probability; (2) "the belief that probability gives grounds for action, and that reasonable men will act on probability, once it is presented" (p. 7); and (3) "the belief that isolated phenomena, experiences, perceptions find their real value when they can be absorbed into or subordinated to the abstract realm of probability" (p. 7). Argues that the "temptation in criticizing Herbert is to overstress the orderliness of his poetry, and to overlook the rich complexity of the concept which lies behind that orderliness" (p. 9). Discusses the techniques of Herbert's rhetoric, especially commenting on his uses of figures and tropes. Comments in some detail on "Redemption," "The Collar," "Christmas," "Easter," and "The Pilgrimage" as poems that involve the search for God, in which Herbert "combines two varieties of religious experience, and moves from a detached, intellectualized expression into an expression of simultaneous realities" (p. 11).

**532. Knieger, Bernard.** "The Religious Verse of George Herbert." *CLAJ* 4:138–47.

Maintains that Herbert's poems do not "merely dramatize the philosophy of an Anglican priest" but rather "illuminate the situation of all men" (p. 138). Discusses some of the major themes of Herbert's spiritual struggle. Remarks on the extensive use of business imagery in Herbert's poems of conflict, such as "Jordan (II)," "Affliction (I)," "The Pearl," and "Redemption." Concludes that "because 'selling' and 'buying' are to him very strong symbols for states of impotency and value respectively, because he conceives the relation between God and man as almost expressible in legal terms, and because he is so intimate and confident in his intercourse with God that he can employ even the language of business when talking to Him and about Him, for all these reasons George Herbert employs business imagery with telling effect" (p. 147).

**533. Leach, Elsie.** "More Seventeenth-Century Admirers of Herbert." *N&Q* 205:62–63.

Notes certain seventeenth-century admirers and imitators of Herbert not mentioned in Hutchinson's edition (entry 266), including Thomas Washbourne in *Divine Poems* (1654), John Rawlet in *Poetick Miscellanie* (1687), Samuel Speed in *Prison-Pietie: Or, Meditations Divine and Moral* (1677), Richard Baxter in *Poetical Fragments* (1681), Daniel Baker in *Poems upon Several Occasions* (1697), W. S. in *The Poems of Ben. Jonson Junior, Being a Miscelanie of Seriousnes, Wit, Mirth, and Mysterie* (1672), and

John Hall in *Jacobs Ladder: or, the Devout Souls Ascention to Heaven, in Prayers, Thanksgivings, and Praises* (2d ed., 1676).

**534.** ———. "Lydgate's 'The Dolerous Pyte of Crystes Passioun' and Herbert's 'The Sacrifice.'" *N&Q* 205:421.

Points out parallels between Herbert's "The Sacrifice" and Lydgate's "The Dolerous Pyte of Crystes Passioun" (Early English Text Society, extra series 107 [1911]:250–52), especially the complaint. Maintains that this is the only medieval poem that renders into English the specific complaint used by Herbert.

**535. Martz, Louis L.** Foreword to *The Poems of Edward Taylor*, edited by Donald E. Stanford, xiii–xxxvii. New Haven: Yale University Press.

Reprinted in *The Poem of the Mind: Essays on Poetry, English and American* (entry 706), 54–81.

Compares and contrasts Herbert and Taylor, pointing out the pervading influence of Herbert, especially on *Preparatory Meditations*. Relates both Herbert and Taylor to the larger meditative tradition but also points out specific echoes and borrowings from Herbert. Concludes that Taylor "appears to have had a mind saturated with Herbert's poetry, and the result is that a thousand tantalizing echoes of Herbert remain for the most part untraceable because the meditative voice of Herbert has been merged with Taylor's own peculiar voice" (p. xiv). Rejects the notion that Taylor is "a quaint primitive who somehow, despite the Indians, managed to stammer out his rude verses well enough to win the title of 'our best Colonial poet'" (p. xviii).

**536. Miles, Josephine.** *Renaissance, Eighteenth-Century, and Modern Language in English Poetry: A Tabular View.* Berkeley and Los Angeles: University of California Press. iii, 73p.

Presents information gathered from two hundred poets, from Chaucer to the present, "in such a way as to suggest the basic patterns of relation between poet and poet in the use of language, and at the same time to provide the most straightforward chronological arrangement of materials for those who may have other questions to ask, about single poets, single eras, single types, or single terms" (p. 1). Tabulates Herbert's use of language, pointing out, for instance, the number of nouns, adjectives, and verbs in the first one thousand lines of *The Temple* (through "Mattens" in Hutchinson's edition [entry 266]). Lists the most frequently used adjectives, nouns, and verbs in Herbert's verse.

**537. Montgomery, Robert L., Jr.** "The Province of Allegory in George Herbert's Verse." *TSLL* 1:457–72.

Reprinted in *Essential Articles for the Study of George Herbert's Poetry*, edited by John R. Roberts (entry 1216), 114–28.

Discusses the allegorical elements in Herbert's symbolic method. Argues that basically his symbols are analogies. Distinguishes between the meditative and allegorical modes and attempts to define the allegorical elements of Herbert's method and to indicate which of his poems can be properly labeled allegorical. Maintains that "the fable is the core of Herbert's allegorical method" (p. 463) and points out three criteria for distinguishing his allegorical lyrics: "A fable (or fiction structure) in control of the poem, the symbolic character of the fable, and fantasy or conceit" (p. 465). Concludes that "allegory as a kind of larger symbol and vital form, is, in Herbert's hands, his most versatile tool" (p. 472).

**538. Pettet, E. C.** *Of Paradise and Light: A Study of Vaughan's Silex Scintillans.* Cambridge: University Press. x, 216p.

Throughout this study, Herbert's influence on Vaughan is discussed and specific borrowings, echoes, and parallels are documented. Chapter 3, "Herbert's Poetry" (pp. 51–70), traces the extent and specific nature of Herbert's influence on *Silex Scintillans*. Notes the general inspiration that Vaughan got from Herbert and comments on features of his style as well as on direct borrowings of specific images, titles, metrical forms, and even lines and half-lines from *The Temple*. Particularly sees Herbert's influence in Vaughan's use of homely images and metaphors. Argues, however, that "in theme, attitude, and spirit" the poems in *Silex Scintillans* "owe little to Herbert" (p. 52). Concludes this survey by remarking: "All considered, there is little doubt that Herbert's poetry exercised an immense influence on the composition of *Silex Scintillans*. On the other hand, in spite of this great indebtedness to *The Temple*, Vaughan's work, particularly the flower of it, remains richly individual and, in all that essentially matters, entirely distinctive from Herbert's. Certainly the two writers can be regarded as true poetic twins; but, like Coleridge and Wordsworth, they are twins of the dissimilar type" (p. 70).

**539. Schlauch, Margaret.** "Angielscy poeci metafizyczni XVII wieku" [English Metaphysical Poets in the Seventeenth Century]. *PHum* 4–5:47–74.

Discusses the nature of metaphysical poetry and maintains that its main features are intensity, ecstasy, animation, and a particular sensibility. Briefly discusses Herbert as a metaphysical poet, attributing his piety and its poetic expression in part to his upbringing and particularly to his mother's influence. Notes the highly metaphorical nature of the language in "Prayer (I)" and comments on the dramatic elements in "The Collar." Translates into Polish prose "Redemption," calling it highly characteristic of metaphysical poetry and praising its central conceit.

**540. Stambler, Elizabeth.** "The Unity of Herbert's 'Temple.'" *Cross Currents* 10:251–66.

Reprinted in *Essential Articles for the Study of George Herbert's Poetry*, edited by John R. Roberts (entry 1216), 328–50.

Challenges in part the attempts of Louis Martz (*The Poetry of Meditation: A Study in English Religious Literature of the Seventeenth Century*, entry 431) and Joseph Summers (*George Herbert: His Religion and Art*, entry 435) to account for the unity of *The Temple* resemble lyrics of the courtly love tradition" (p. 252). Finds "resemblances in several important details and in two fairly large general themes, the poetry—the *Vita Nuova*, Petrarch's *Rime*, *Astrophel and Stella*—as individual poems of *The Temple* resemble lyrics of the courtly love tradition" (p. 252). Finds "resemblances in several important details and in two fairly large general themes, the theme of loss and the theme of discipline which brings the protagonist at last to a condition of purified desire" (p. 252). Discusses such unifying details as the dramatic persona; the unceasing shifts of states of feeling that record a wide range of emotion; Herbert's references to *The Temple* as a whole and to his desire that single poems be placed within the context of the whole; the unifying effect of the title of the volume; the flow of time and the ordered chronology of the poems; the chain of images in the first fourteen poems, in which the protagonist is transformed from an inanimate object to an animate one; the recurring images, especially sun-stone, measure, and eyes. Agrees that Herbert's "reordering and revitalizing of the form of the courtly love volume is an entirely characteristic display of his talent, on the same principle as his utilization of Christian typologies or tracts of meditation" (p. 252).

# *1961*

**541. Alvarez, A.** *The School of Donne.* London: Chatto & Windus; New York: Pantheon Books. 202p.

Reprinted, New York: Pantheon Books, 1962; New York: New American Library, 1967; London: Chatto & Windus, 1970.

Announces his intent "to show how Donne affected the language and form of poetry in a way that is still peculiarly meaningful to us, and is rapidly becoming yet more meaningful" and "to define a kind of intelligence which, though it was first expressed at the end of the sixteenth century, is still vital and urgent" (p. 12). Argues for the notion of a "School of Donne," united not so much by poetical methods and techniques as by the intellectual attitude and tone that formed it: the desire to portray dramatically in poetry the complexities of thought and feeling. Chapter 3, "The Poetry of Religious Experience" (pp. 67–90), deals specifically with Herbert (pp. 67–83) and Vaughan (pp. 83–90). Calls Herbert the "only poet to use Donne's discoveries for wholly original ends" (p. 67). Remarks on Herbert's debt to Donne ("but his debt is nowhere as specific as that of the other Metaphysicals" [p. 68]), especially his peculiar intensity and his use of common, conversational language in religious verse. Notes, however, definite ways in which Herbert differs from Donne, for example, in his uses of the Bible, in his wit, and in his complex simplicity. Sees Herbert's simplicity, however, as "not the measure by which he fell short of Donne, but of the distance he went beyond him" (p. 70) and argues that Herbert's wit and ingenuity are best seen in his inventive verse forms. Concludes that Herbert's "contribution to religious poetry is large and his own. But the ground in which it could flower had been cleared by Donne" (p. 83). Comments specifically on "Jordan (I)," "The Forerunners," "Home," "The Pearl," and "Love (III)." Compares Herbert also with Crashaw, Vaughan, Marvell, Cowley, Hopkins, and Southwell.

**542. Arai, Akira.** "George Herbert no Shiron to sono Jissen" [George Herbert's Poetics and Its Practice]. *Eigo Kyoiku* [English Teachers' Magazine] 9, no. 11 (February): 694–97.

Praises the element of Christian simplicity found in Herbert's verse.

**543. Bamonte, Gerardo.** "La poesia barocca in Inghilterra," in *Poeti dell'età barocca*, with a preface by Giancinto Spagnoletti, 523–637, 656–57. (Collezione Fenice, diretta da Attilio Bertolucci, 49.) Parma: Ugo Guanda.

A general discussion of English baroque poetry (pp. 523–35), followed by selections from the poets, with Italian translations on facing pages (pp. 536–637). Includes Herbert's "Easter-wings," "The Windows," "Jesu," "The Collar," "Love (III)," and "Redemption" (pp. 562–75). Discusses briefly Herbert's inner struggles with the attractions of the world and maintains that the principal theme of his poetry is "la psicologia delle sue esperienze religiose" (p. 529). Comments on his use of metaphor, images, everyday diction, and shaped verse. Calls "The Collar" Herbert's most inspired poem. Biographical note (p. 656).

**544. Banzer, Judith.** "'Compound Manner': Emily Dickinson and the Metaphysical Poets." *AL* 32:417–33.

Argues that Dickinson, like Herbert and the other metaphysical poets, "practiced the metaphysical awareness of the unity of experience" and maintains that "the discipline that wrought many of her poems was the metaphysical one of a 'Compound Vision' by which the eternal is argued from the transient, the foreign explained by the familiar, and fact illuminated by mystery" (p. 417). Comments on Dickinson's familiarity with the metaphysical poets ("her pencil-markings of several poems argue close attention to their vision and technique") and shows that her poems themselves are "the crucial argument for her knowledge of Donne or Herbert" (p. 418). Points out many similarities between Herbert and Dickinson, especially their uses of material conceits to illustrate transcendent realities, their uses of "homely images of safe enclosure" (p. 421), and their reflective practices, "which put Herbert forever in the divine presence" and result in "Emily's habit of strolling with Eternity" (p. 423). Sees both poets as in the meditative mode and suggests specific echoes of Herbert in Dickinson's poetry.

**545. Blum, Irving D.** "The Paradox of Money Imagery in English Renaissance Poetry." *Studies in the Renaissance* 8:144–54.

Argues against the somewhat standard opinion that money imagery is used in Renaissance poetry only to depict "the crass, prosaic details of existence" (p. 144) and gives a number of examples to show that often money imagery" is used "to cast light upon all facets of life—the beautiful and the ugly, the generous and the miserly, the good and the evil" (p. 145). Maintains that such images "remain well within the Petrarchian and Spenserian conventions and, indeed, well within the poetic tradition of the entire English Renaissance" (pp. 144–45). Comments on such usage in Spenser, Gascoigne, Wyatt, Sidney, Daniel, Shakespeare, Chapman, Donne, and Herbert. Remarks that, like many others, Herbert did not "scorn to borrow the qualities of money to define fanciful things in metaphor, while expressing disdain for wealth in literal references" (p. 153). Shows Herbert's rejection of money in "Avarice" but notes his metaphorical uses of it in *The Church-Porch* (lines 1–2, 109–10, 429–30) and "The Pearl."

**546. Collmer, Robert G.** "The Meditation on Death and Its Appearance in Metaphysical Poetry." *Neophil* 45:323–33.

Discusses the *meditatio mortis* tradition and comments on some of its appearances in the poetry of Herbert, Donne, Vaughan, and Crashaw. Shows a number of ways in which Herbert's attitude toward death is reflected in his poetry, especially in "Repentance," "Church-monuments," and "Mortification." Notes that Herbert, unlike Donne and Vaughan, does not present descriptions of the more gruesome aspects of death.

**547. Dalglish, Jack.** *Eight Metaphysical Poets.* Edited with an introduction and notes by Jack Dalglish. New York: Macmillan Co.; London: Heinemann. viii, 184p.

Reprinted, 1963, 1965, 1970.

General introduction to the nature and style of metaphysical poetry (pp. 1–10). Considers the intellectual and introspective nature of much metaphysical poetry, its fusion of thought and feeling, its uses of imagery and conceits, its verse movement and dramatic qualities, and so on. Anthologizes selections from Donne, Herbert, Carew, Crashaw, Vaughan, King, Marvell, and Cowley (pp. 11–126). Herbert is represented by sixteen poems with commentary and notes on individual poems. The notes for Herbert (pp. 137–47) include a biographical sketch and a brief essay on general characteristics of his poetry, such as his themes, conversational tone, uses of complex metrical forms, technical skill and inventiveness, and uses of imagery and the conceit.

**548. Fletcher, Harris Francis.** "Appendix II: Holdsworth's 'Directions for a Student in the Universitie,'" in *The Intellectual Development of John Milton*, vol. 2, *The Cambridge University Period, 1625–32*, 623–64. Urbana: University of Illinois Press.

Reproduces an Emmanuel College manuscript (MS. 1.2.27 [1]) that contains a course of study for undergraduates at Cambridge (about 1637) designed by Richard Holdsworth (Oldsworth) (1590–1649), Master of Emmanuel College from 1637 to 1639. Holdsworth includes in a list of suggested readings Herbert's *The Temple*.

**549. Gaskell, Ronald.** "Herbert's 'Vanitie.'" *CritQ* 3:313–15.

Briefly compares Herbert and Jonson and concludes that Herbert's is "a discipline more deeply moral, more completely a discipline of sensibility" (p. 313). Presents a close reading of "Vanitie (I)," commenting on Herbert's sensitive use of language and technical subtleties. Briefly compares Herbert to Keats. For three replies, see John Blackie, E. P. Smith, and Ronald Gaskell (entry 573).

**550. Hart, Jeffrey.** "Herbert's *The Collar* Re-Read." *Boston University Studies in English* 5:65–73.

Reprinted in *Seventeenth Century English Poetry: Modern Essays in Criticism*, edited by William Keast (rev. ed., entry 879), 248–56; *Essential Articles for the Study of George Herbert's Poetry*, edited by John R. Roberts (entry 1216), 453–60.

Maintains that to see "The Collar" only in terms of "the struggle between discipline and pleasure, between the duties of a clergyman and the satisfactions to be derived from the natural life," or "the struggle between God's will and the speaker's rebellious Heart" (p. 66), is to miss the full complexity and import of the poem. Reads the poem "in the context of Herbert's other poems, and with reference to the tradition which informs his imagery with meaning" and sees the poem as representing "in psychological terms the events of the Christian moral drama—the Fall, the Atonement, and the Redemption" (p. 66). Describes the moral events of the poem: "Just as the moral disorder entailed by the rebellious Adam and Eve was overcome by Christ's sacrifice, so the moral disorder of the speaker's rebellion is to be finally overcome by the sacrament of the Eucharist" (p. 66). Maintains that "the brilliance of the poem lies in the fact that it expresses rebellion and atonement in the same vocabulary, and by so doing epitomizes its central idea: that rebellion necessarily entails, because of God's justice and mercy, atonement" (p. 66). Presents a detailed reading of the poem and comments on its structure and form; its uses of images, puns, symbols, and double entendre; and its dramatic development.

**551. Herbert, George.** *The Poems of George Herbert*. With an introduction by Helen Gardner. (The World's Classics, no. 109.) 2d ed. London, New York, Toronto: Oxford University Press. xxi, 285p.

Reprinted, 1964, 1967, 1969, 1972, 1974. (The text of this edition is based on Hutchinson's text [entry 266]. An earlier edition in this series was edited by Arthur Waugh in 1907 and was based on Grosart's text [entry 16]).

Contents (pp. v-xiii); introduction by Helen Gardner (pp. xv-xx); bibliographical note (p. xxi); text of *The Temple* (pp. 1–189); English poems in the Williams MS not included in *The Temple* (pp. 191–96); poems from Walton's *Lives* (pp. 197–98); doubtful poems (pp. 199–214); *Musae Responsoriae* (pp. 215–36); *Passio Discerpta* (pp. 237–42); *Lucus* (pp. 243–56); *Memoriae Matris Sacrum* (pp. 257–68); *Alia Poemata Latina* (pp. 269–77); appendix: Andrew Melville's *Pro Supplici Evangelicorum Ministrorum in Anglia* (pp. 279–85). In the introduction Gardner comments on the general characteristics of Herbert's poetry, such as its grace of style, wit, intellectual vivacity, sincerity, precision and design, and the range of verse forms. Praises Herbert's "spiritual subtlety and delicacy" (p. xix) and maintains that "few devotional poets so exercise the mind" (p. xx). Comments briefly on the arrangement of the poems in *The Temple*, rejects the notion that the poems are simply a narrative account of the poet's spiritual progress, and concludes that, excluding some poems in the opening and the conclusion of the volume, "the connexions from poem to poem are not systematic: they are subtle relations of theme and mood and thought, groups of poems forming variations on the ground theme of the book, the love of God for man" (p. xviii). Maintains that "the source of the struggles in *The Temple* does not lie in a conflict between the world and a call to serve God at his altar; but in the difficulty of learning to say truly in any calling 'Thy will be done'" (p. xvii). Comments also briefly on Herbert's reputation.

552. ———. "A Priest to the Temple, or the Country Parson: His Character and Rule of Holy Life," in *Five Pastorals*, abridged and edited with introductions by Thomas Wood, 75–140. London: SPCK.
 Presents in the introduction (pp. 79–93) a biographical sketch of Herbert, commenting on his religious attitudes and sensibilities as reflected in *A Priest to the Temple*. Surveys the religious temper of the times, the state of the English clergy, and the problems of episcopal discipline in the first half of the seventeenth century. Discusses the spiritual soundess of *A Priest to the Temple* and surveys its early publication history and reception. Reproduces the text of *A Priest to the Temple* (pp. 94–140).

553. Hollander, John. "'The Sacred Organ's Praise,'" in *The Untuning of the Sky: Ideas of Music in English Poetry, 1500–1700*, 245–331. Princeton: Princeton University Press.
 Reprinted, 1970.
 "Herbert's Musical Temper" (pp. 288–94) discusses the wide range of musical images, puns, conceits, and terminology as well as the more generalized musical effects in Herbert's poetry. Maintains that the musical conceit "is seldom unconnected with some other, more central and governing one in each poem. It is as if the image of music were always running along beneath the surface of all of Herbert's poems, breaking out here and there like the eruption of some underground stream, but exercising always an informing, nourishing function" (p. 294). Argues that Herbert's "almost constant use of 'sing' for 'pray' represents a personal as well as a conventional figure; it is the actual image of the poet-divine playing and singing in secluded retirement that lurks behind so many of the musical conceits in his poetry" (p. 288). Comments specifically on "The Thanksgiving," "The Temper (I)," "Repentance," "Deniall," "The Quip," "Ephes.iv.30," "Dooms-day," "Easter," and "Easter-wings."

554. Howarth, R. G. "Notes on Vaughan." *N&Q* 206:184–85.
 Rejects A. H. Bullen's suggestion in *More Lyrics from the Song-books of the Elizabethan Age* (1888) that the poem beginning "Yet if his majesty our sovereign lord" is by Vaughan. Maintains that it resembles Herbert but is inferior and more likely the work of one of Herbert's many imitators. Also suggests that the poem "Cry, bold but blessed thief," which Norman Ault includes in his *Poets' Life of Christ* (entry 79) and his *Seventeenth-Century Lyrics* (London, New York: Longmans, Green and Co., 1928) may be by Herbert, but again thinks that it is doubtful.

555. Hughes, R. E. "George Herbert's Rhetorical World." *Criticism* 3:86–94.

Reprinted in *Essential Articles for the Study of George Herbert's Poetry*, edited by John R. Roberts (entry 1216), 105–13.

Argues that "a commitment to rhetoric, instead of limiting a writer to a learned facility, actually involves him in a complex frame of reference, that rhetoric, properly defined, might better be called a *weltanschauung* than a *discipline*; and that to view rhetoric in this light is a considerable help in understanding and appreciating much of the poetry of George Herbert" (p. 86). First discusses rhetoric generically and theoretically and then applies his conclusions specifically and analytically to some of Herbert's poems, particularly "Prayer (I)," "The Agonie," "Redemption," "Christmas," "Easter," and "The Pilgrimage." Primarily concerned with showing that in Herbert's poetry "rhetoric is not simply technique, not simply discipline, but is a way of looking at experience and ideas" (p. 88). Comments on Herbert's use of allegory as a way of subordinating "the specious world of appearances to the real world of abstractions" (p. 88). Maintains that all Herbert's themes are related to the probability of the communion between the human spirit and God and that all his poetry insists "on this probability; and if he could not *prove* that probability, as a logician might, he could *demonstrate* it, as a rhetorician would: through trope, which presented both the attributes and the uniqueness of God" (p. 88).

**556. Izzo, Carlo.** "Il periodo post-shakespeariano," in *Storia della letteratura inglese*, vol. 1, *Dalle origini alla restaurazione*, 415–515. (Storia delle letterature di tutto il mondo, directed by Antonio Viscardi.) Milan: Nuova accademia editrice.

Brief introduction to Herbert's life, poetry, and prose (pp. 478–80). Maintains that "Vertue" is Herbert's most celebrated poem and offers a prose translation of it into Italian. Contrasts Herbert and Donne and observes that Herbert "nei momenti migliori egli è tuttavia capace d'una semplicità di linguaggio che non si può certo far risalire all'iniziatore della moda «metafisica», e che conferisce ai suoi versi un carattere autonomo ben definito, più gradevole, spesso, di quanto non siano le non sempre felici astruserie dei «metafisici» più spinti" (p. 479).

**557. Leishman, J. B.** *Themes and Variations in Shakespeare's Sonnets*. London: Hutchinson & Co. 254p.

Comments on the "religiousness" of Shakespeare's sonnets and sees an affinity between them and Herbert's poetry, especially in their uses of the theme of "compensation": "I can find nothing in other love-poetry really comparable with his [Shakespeare's] many variations on the theme of what I have called 'compensation', and I think the only things in other poetry of which they really 'remind' me are some of those poems where George Herbert expresses, or, as it were, revivifies his conviction that his 'pearl of great price' is a more than sufficient compensation for all that either he himself or the world may have supposed him to have resigned or forgone" (p. 216). Maintains that some of Donne's more serious love poems may have served as stylistic models for Herbert's religious love poems. Briefly comments on Palmer's attempt to reorder Herbert's *The Temple* to make it fit a notion of spiritual biography and quotes Aldous Huxley's comment about Herbert's poetry reflecting "inner weather" (entry 149).

**558. Lievsay, John Leon.** *Stefano Guazzo and the English Renaissance, 1575–1675*. Chapel Hill: University of North Carolina Press. xii, 344p.

Discusses Guazzo's contribution to English proverb lore and presents a list of more than fifty of the so-called outlandish (foreign) proverbs in G. H.'s *Witts Recreation. Selected from the finest Fancies of Moderne Muses. With a Thousand Outlandish Proverbs* (1640), often attributed to Herbert, that can be found in either Guazzo's

*Civil conversatione* or his *Dialoghi piacevole*. Maintains that the writer of *Witts Recreation* adapted the proverbs either directly from Guazzo or perhaps indirectly from Florio's *Second Frutes*. Points out that proverbs from *Witts Recreation* also appear in *Comes Facundus in Via: The Fellow-Traveler* (1658) and in N. R.'s *Proverbs English, French, Dutch, Italian, and Spanish. All Englished and Alphabetically Digested* (1659). Calls the latter "a shameless steal from the *Outlandish Proverbs*" (p. 321).

**559. Pagnini, Marcello, ed.** *Lirici carolini e repubblicani.* (Collana di letterature moderne, 15.) Naples: Edizione scientifiche italiane. xii, 420p.
Anthology of seventeenth-century English poetry for the Italian reader. Includes a general introduction to the lyrical poetry of the period as well as critical comment on each of the poets included (pp. 3–40). Textual note (pp. 41–42) and a selected bibliography of critical works on the period and on individual poets (pp. 43–51). Herbert is represented by twenty poems and by a biographical sketch and bibliographical note (pp. 129–60).

**560. Peckham, Morse, and Seymour Chatman.** *Word, Meaning, Poem.* New York: Thomas Y. Crowell Co. xx, 683p.
Presents syntactic and lexical glosses for "Man" (pp. 209–17), followed by a detailed critical analysis of the poem (pp. 218–22). Maintains that "the structure of the poem is argument inside of informal meditation, not a continuous application of the mind to the contemplation of some religious truth, but rather the discovery of a religious truth by the analysis of a truism" and that, "by an intellectual process, the speaker humbles the intellect and thus dramatizes how an individual may use all his intellectual resources to arrive at a profound but willing and joyous abasement before the Deity" (p. 222). Presents also lexical glosses for "The Collar" and "Mortification" (pp. 408–11).

**561. Reeves, James.** "The Seventeenth Century: Donne and the Metaphysicals," in *A Short History of English Poetry, 1340–1940*, 75–88. London: Heinemann.
Reprinted, New York: E. P. Dutton, 1962, 1964.
Brief introduction to Herbert's life and poetry. Maintains that, "though we may not like the fantastic element in his poems, their homely and sometimes naïve conceits, we cannot but be moved by their sincerity, by the charity and sweetness of their tone, and by their grave and unaffected simplicity" (pp. 81–82). Singles out "Redemption" as an example of Herbert's "quiet naturalness" and his ability to reproduce "intimate and unaffected speech rhythm" (p. 82).

**562. Sanders, Wilbur.** "Herbert and the Scholars." *Melbourne Critical Review* 4:102–11.
Explores the question "of how far Herbert's poetry depended upon his predecessors, upon contemporary religious thought, and upon traditional and liturgical symbolism" (p. 102) by examining the work of four recent critics: Louis Martz (*The Poetry of Meditation: A Study in English Religious Literature of the Seventeenth Century*, entry 431), Rosemary Freeman (*English Emblem Books*, entry 337), Rosemond Tuve (*A Reading of George Herbert*, entry 409), and Malcolm MacKenzie Ross (*Poetry and Dogma: The Transfiguration of Eucharistic Symbols in Seventeenth Century English Poetry*, entry 434). Argues that Martz, Tuve, and Freeman overstate their cases in claiming that Herbert's cultural environment made his poetry possible and maintains that "poetry cannot be discussed at all except in terms of its meaning to

us now" (p. 108). Agrees with Ross that Herbert was "caught in a process of social decay which reinforces his natural impulse away from a comprehensive humanism into a defensive and personal mysticism" (p. 110) and maintains that actually Herbert "estranged himself from the intellectual currents of his time and committed himself to a deliberate reaction" (p. 111).

**563. Sanesi, Roberto, ed.** "George Herbert (1593–1633)," in *Poeti metafisici inglesi del Seicento*, 107–29, 258–62. (Collezione Fenice, gen. ed., Attilio Bertolucci, no. 45.) Parma: Guanda.
2d ed. (revised and augmented), 1976.
Anthologizes "The Altar," "Easter-wings," "Church-monuments," "The Church-floore," "The Windows," "Frailtie," "Vertue," "The Bunch of Grapes," "Josephs coat," "Aaron," and "Death" with Italian translations on facing pages (pp. 108–29). In the notes (pp. 258–62) gives a biographical sketch of Herbert, a brief bibliography, and notes on individual poems. In the second edition adds "Nature," "Jordan (I)," "Deniall," "Vanitie (I)," "Jordan (II)," "Hope," and "Artillerie."

**564. Souris, André, comp. and arr.** *Poèmes de Donne, Herbert et Crashaw mis en musique par leurs contemporains G. Coperario, A. Ferrabosco, J. Wilson, W. Corkine, J. Hilton.* Transcriptions et réalisation par André Souris après des recherches effectuées sur les sources par John Cutts. Introduction par Jean Jacquot. Paris: Editions du centre national de la recherche scientifique. xix, 26p.
Comments briefly in the introduction on Herbert's interest in music and the importance of music in his poetry (pp. x-xi). Presents John Wilson's musical setting for "Content" (Bodleian Library Ms. Mus. b. 1, ff. 50v–51).

**565. Sudo, Nobuo.** "George Herbert no Shi to Shukyo" [The Poetry and Religion of George Herbert], in *Eikoku no Shukyo Bungaku* [English Religious Literature], 78–99. Tokyo: Shinozaki Shorin.
Reprinted in *17–Seiki Eibungaku ni Okeru Christian Humanism* [Christian Humanism in Seventeenth-Century English Literature] (Tokyo: Yugakusha, 1971), 41–73.
Discusses *The Temple* in terms of Christian humanism, maintaining that love is at the center of Herbert's Christianity and arguing that Herbert portrays a God of loving kindness and tender mercy.

**566. Tuve, Rosemond.** "Sacred 'Parody' of Love Poetry, and Herbert." *Studies in the Renaissance* 8:249–90.
Reprinted in *Essays by Rosemond Tuve*, edited by Thomas P. Roche, Jr. (Princeton: Princeton University Press, 1970), 207–51; *Essential Articles for the Study of George Herbert's Poetry*, edited by John R. Roberts (entry 1216), 129–59.
Discusses some conceptions of Herbert and his predecessors concerning the relationship between sacred and profane love poetry. Comments in detail on Herbert's "A Parodie," a sacred parody of William Herbert, third earl of Pembroke's poem "Soules joy, now I am gone" (sometimes attributed to Donne). Discusses various Renaissance meanings of the word *parody* and concludes that "not any of these descriptions accurately describes the relation Herbert's poem bears to its original" (p. 251). Argues that there "is a parallelism between the two poems extending throughout their length, but it is not conceptual, and . . . had little to do . . . with 'turning' another poet's sense and thus obliquely commenting thereon, or with the intention of substituting good love for bad by displacing naughty verses" (p. 254). Maintains rather that the word

*parody* in Herbert's title is a musical term and implies that Herbert set his words to the same musical setting that Pembroke had used for his verse. Points out numerous contemporary and earlier examples of this practice of using secular music for sacred verse and vice versa without the intention of converting the one to the other. The author indicates that she has been unable to find the exact piece of music presumably used by both Herbert and Pembroke but describes how she searched for it and the problems involved. Makes a close comparison between the two poems and shows that Herbert's poem, in spite of some obvious parallelism, is on an entirely different subject than Pembroke's: these comparisons "demonstrate usefully the nature of a parodic relation which imitates *form*, and is unarguably divorced from the interest in evoking conceptual ambiguities which we attribute to practically all literary interaction of the sacred and the profane" (p. 285). Presents a hypothetical setting with music for both poems in order to illustrate the effects of musical parody.

**567. Warnke, Frank J.** *European Metaphysical Poetry.* (The Elizabethan Club Series, 2.) New Haven and London: Yale University Press. xi, 317p.
Reprinted, 1974.
Anthology of French, German, Dutch, Spanish, and Italian metaphysical poetry. The introduction (pp. 1–86) distinguishes between baroque and metaphysical style. The latter is considered as one of several related styles that can be seen within the generic category of the baroque. Maintains that the European metaphysical poets show "the extent to which not only the Baroque style but also its Metaphysical variation ought to be regarded as international phenomena, further manifestations of the real unity of our culture" (p. 4). States that "metaphysical poetry is associated in the minds of its readers with the work of one man, John Donne. Yet, since every poet has his individual voice as well as his adherence to a collective style, one cannot simply make a touchstone of Donne's style in determining what poetry is Metaphysical; certain of his crucial themes, techniques, and emphases will occur in all Metaphysical poetry, but others will not. Metaphysical poetry has, when tried on the ear, a 'metaphysical' sound; that is to say, it sounds significantly like the poetry of John Donne. But each Metaphysical poet has also the unique sound of the individual poet" (p. 5). Discusses some of the characteristics of Donne's style but throughout compares and contrasts Herbert with Donne, Crashaw, Vaughan, and Marvell. Argues that all the metaphysical poets "display differing aims and differing sensibilities; they are united by a set of shared stylistic traits—ingenious metaphor, consistent intellectuality, radically all-inclusive diction, and colloquial tone—and, ultimately, by a shared habit of vision—the tendency to view their experience in the light of total reality, with a consequent concern for metaphysical problems and contradictions" (p. 21). Comments on specific features of Herbert's poetry: its ingenuity and intellectuality; its uses of paradox and homely images; its didacticism and simplicity; its uses of allegory, conceit, and concrete diction; its functional structure; and so on. Compares Herbert to European poets such as Friedrich von Speè, Heiman Dullaert, Jean de La Ceppède, Jean-Baptiste Chassignet, Paul Fleming, Jacobus Revius, Constantijn Huygens, Martin Opitz, Lope de Vega, Jean de Sponde, and Jan Luyken.

**568. Williamson, George.** "Caroline Wit," in *The Proper Wit of Poetry*, 43–62. Chicago: University of Chicago Press.
Traces the changing concept of wit from the Jacobean era through the Caroline and Interregnum periods to the Augustan Age and attempts to indicate what particular fashions prevailed, how each generation understood the nature and function of wit in a slightly different way, and how finally there was a gradual separation of the face-

tious and the serious, of nature and fancy. Comments briefly on Herbert's commitment to simplicity and on his more ingenious uses of wit and accounts for this by suggesting that Herbert believed that the poet must use the "bait of pleasure" to win his readers.

# *1962*

**569. Adams, Robert M.** "George Herbert," in *The Norton Anthology of English Literature*, edited by M. H. Abrams, 1:830–42. New York: W. W. Norton and Co.
  2d ed., 1968; 3d ed., 1974; 4th ed., 1979.
  5th ed., with new introduction by Barbara Lewalski, 1986.
  Biographical and critical introduction (pp. 830–31), followed by sixteen selections from Herbert's poetry, with explanatory notes (pp. 831–42). Maintains that, "as a poet, Herbert is quiet, inward, subtle, graceful, and neat" and points out that "he delights in using quaint devices and homely images" and that "his spiritual feeling is to an extraordinary degree pure and fresh and free" (p. 830). Notes that, whereas Donne is "a poet of religious doubt, of strain, of anxiety," Herbert is "the poet of religious faith, of submission, of acceptance" (p. 830). Maintains that Herbert "is never flashy, nor even strongly dramatic" but rather, "like the church he served, he is devoted to the quiet middle way" (p. 830). Concludes that Herbert's poetry "is like the parish church—an intricate, ancient structure, rich in traditional designs, which is open for the humblest and simplest person to enter" (p. 831). The second, third, and fourth editions make only minor changes in the introduction and in the selections of verse presented.

**570. Allen, Ward Sykes.** "A Note upon George Herbert's 'The Pearl. Matth. 13.45.'" *N&Q* 207:212–13.
  Argues that the allusion in "The Pearl" to the head and pipes that feed the press (lines 1–2) may have been suggested by an interpretation of Zech. 4.12 in the preface to the Authorized Version of the Bible. "Translators to the Reader" notes that "if you ask what they had before them, truly it was the *Hebrew* text of the Old Testament, the *Greek* of the New. These are the two golden pipes, or rather conduits, wherethrough the olive branches empty themselves into the gold" (p. 212). Points out several other images in the preface that suggest images in Herbert's poem.

**571. Austin, Allen C.** "T. S. Eliot's Theory of Dissociation." *CE* 23:309–12.
  Argues that Eliot's theory of dissociation of sensibility has been variously misunderstood by modern critics, especially F. W. Bateson, Basil Willey, Frank Kermode, and W. K. Wimsatt, Jr. Maintains that Eliot primarily laments the split that occurred in the seventeenth century between wit and emotion, ideas and images, and language and sensibility. Maintains that Eliot "is lamenting the loss of intellectual poetry, the amalgamation of intellectual and emotional experience" (p. 311). No specific references to Herbert.

**572. Beaurline, L. A.** "Dudley North's Criticism of Metaphysical Poetry." *HLQ* 25:299–313.
  Comments on a now-forgotten essay on the various fashions of seventeenth-century poetry by Dudley North (1581–1666) published in his collected writings, entitled

*A Forest of Varieties* (1645). Reproduces the text of this essay, one of the few contemporary statements about early seventeenth-century poetry. Argues that North's essay "is in direct contradiction to Miss Tuve's theory that fashionable Jacobean poetry was basically the same in theory and practice as Elizabethan poetry" and points out that North objects strongly that "the new poetry violates propriety in amatory verse" (p. 299). No specific references to Herbert.

**573. Blackie, John, E. P. Smith, and Ronald Gaskell.** "Herbert's 'Vanitie.'" *CritQ* 4:80–81.

Two replies and an answer by the author to Ronald Gaskell's essay, "Herbert's 'Vanitie'" (entry 549). Blackie objects to Gaskell's suggestion that Herbert misused the word *mellowing* in the fourth stanza of the poem. Shows that it meant "soft, loamy, rich" as applied to soil and that "this is precisely the ultimate effect that frost has on soil" (p. 80). Smith objects more generally to Gaskell's reading of the poem, specifically dislikes Gaskell's emphasis "on the parallels between the openings of the first three stanzas . . . when one ignores . . . those between the second halves of each of these stanzas" (p. 80), and believes that an understanding of the sexual overtones in the poem is crucial to an understanding of its complex theme. Gaskell, in his answer, agrees with Blackie's point and agrees with Smith that the sexual overtones are present in the third stanza.

**574. Bowers, Fredson.** "Herbert's Sequential Imagery: 'The Temper.'" *MP* 59:202–13.

Reprinted in *Essential Articles for the Study of George Herbert's Poetry*, edited by John R. Roberts (entry 1216), 231–48.

Argues that the order of the poems in *The Temple* "is not random but is planned according to developing sequences that work out major themes" and that "within these sequential poems Herbert develops clusters of images that are appropriate not only for the poem in which they appear but also—in some sense—exist coincidentally with the individual poems and apply independently to the great central theme of the section and then of *The Temple*" (p. 202). Comments on the "narrative continuity" of one such sequence but maintains that "more continuity is discoverable in the poems of this sequence than is found merely in the progression of formal ideas or in links at end and beginning" (p. 203). Finds especially significant "the development of certain strains of images that independently form a commentary on the announced theme for any poem" (p. 203). Illustrates this Herbertian device by comments on "The Temper (I)," especially on "some of the accumulated meanings of the title . . . as they are worked out either in the poem itself or as ascertainably present from the evidence of the preceding sequential imagery" (p. 203).

**575. Bradner, Leicester.** "New Poems by George Herbert: The Cambridge Latin Gratulatory Anthology of 1613." *Renaissance News* 15:208–11.

Announces the discovery of two heretofore unknown Latin poems by Herbert: one on the visit of Frederick, the Elector Palatine, and Prince Charles to Cambridge University in 1613; the other an epithalamium for Frederick and Princess Elizabeth, daughter of James I, who were married on 14 February 1613. The poems were found in a two-part volume, originally in Frederick's library but now at the Vatican (MS. Palat. lat. 1736). Notes that there were approximately sixty contributors to the volume, including, in addition to Herbert, Giles Fletcher and William Gager. Reproduces the two Latin poems by Herbert and comments briefly on each.

**576. Duckles, Vincent.** "John Jenkins's Settings of Lyrics by George Herbert." *Musical Quarterly* 48:461–75.

Comments briefly on Herbert's interest in music and his extensive use of musical imagery in his poetry. Notes that there is a "surprising lack of Herbert lyrics set to music by his contemporaries" (p. 462). Comments primarily on a set of partbooks found in the library of Christ Church College, Oxford (MSS. 736–38) that contains six lyrics from *The Temple* with musical settings by John Jenkins and states that "these are the earliest known examples of Herbert's lyrics set to music" (p. 462). The six settings include (1) "The shephards sing, but shall I silent be" (strophe 2 of "Christmas"); (2) "Awake, sad heart, whom sorrow ever drowns" (from "The Dawning"); (3) "O take thy lute and tune it" (last three stanzas of "Ephes.iv.30"); (4) "And art Thou grieved, sweet and sacred Dove" (first three stanzas of "Ephes.iv.30"); (5) "Then with our trinity of light" (last four stanzas of "The Starre"); and (6) "Bright spark, shot from a brighter place" (first four stanzas of "The Starre"). Analyzes the musical settings and argues that "our appreciation of George Herbert is not complete until we have experienced his poetry within the framework provided by John Jenkins's music" (p. 475). Illustrations.

**577. Eliot, T. S.** *George Herbert.* (Writers and Their Works, no. 152.) London: Longmans, Green and Co. 36p.

Reprinted, 1968.

American ed., Lincoln: University of Nebraska Press, 1964. This edition includes, in addition to Eliot's study, Frank Kermode's *John Donne* (1957) and Margaret Willy's *Three Metaphysical Poets: Richard Crashaw, Henry Vaughan, Thomas Traherne* (1961).

Pages 15–25 reprinted in *George Herbert and the Seventeenth-Century Religious Poets: Authoritative Texts/Criticism*, edited by Mario Di Cesare (entry 1140), 236–42.

Reprinted in *British Writers*, edited under the auspices of the British Council, Ian Scott-Kilvert, general editor, vol. 2, *Thomas Middleton to George Farquhar* (New York: Charles Scribner's Sons, 1979), 117–30.

Divided into three sections. (1) A biographical sketch of Herbert that asserts that "to think of Herbert as a poet of a placid and comfortable piety is to misunderstand utterly the man and his poems" (p. 14). (2) Calls *The Temple* "a coherent sequence of poems setting down the fluctuations of emotion between despair and bliss, between agitation and serenity, and the discipline of suffering which leads to peace of spirit" (p. 23) and insists that "we cannot judge Herbert, or savour fully his genius and his art, by a selection to be found in an anthology; we must study *The Temple* as a whole" (p. 15). Calls Herbert a major poet in his own right who should not be unfavorably compared with Donne. Compares Donne's "Batter my heart" and Herbert's "Prayer (I)" in order to show their differences: "Both men were highly intellectual, both men had keen sensibility: but in Donne thought seems in control of feeling, and in Herbert feeling seems in control of thought" (p. 17). Notes that in Donne there is "much more of the *orator*; whereas Herbert . . . has a much more intimate tone of speech" (p. 18). Calls Donne's poetry witty; Herbert's, "magical" (p. 18). Yet claims that Herbert is "closer in spirit to Donne than is any other of 'the school of Donne'" (p. 20). Comments on the exclusively religious subject matter of Herbert's poetry and insists that his poems are valuable, even to the nonbeliever, precisely because of their content: "The poems form a record of spiritual struggle which should touch the feeling, and enlarge the understanding of those readers also who hold no religious belief and find themselves unmoved by religious emotion" (p. 19). (3) Returns to a comparison

of Herbert and Donne, pointing out a number of lines that remind the reader of their relationship, yet pointing out that Herbert's originality and resourcefulness of invention in metrical forms have "no parallel in English poetry" (p. 31). Selected bibliography (pp. 35–36).
Reviews:
Helen Gardner, *Listener* 68 (1962): 1099, 1101
William Empson, *New Statesman*, n.s. 65 (1963): 18
James McAuley, *Quadrant* (Sydney) 7 (1963): 94

**578. Grieder, Theodore.** "Philip Pain's 'Daily Meditations' and the Poetry of George Herbert." *N&Q* 207:213–15.
Points out possible borrowings from Herbert's poetry in the *Daily Meditations* (1668) of Philip Pain, a somewhat obscure American Puritan poet. Notes that Pain uses the form of several of Herbert's poems, certain meters and rhythms, as well as specific images and figures. For a reply, see Norman Farmer (entry 631).

**579. Hachiya, Akio.** "Herbert's 'Vertue.'" [Herbert's "Vertue"]. *Eibungaku Techo* no. 7:29–30.
Translates "Vertue" into Japanese and briefly discusses it.

**580. Herbert, George.** *Herbert*. Selected, with an introduction and notes by Dudley Fitts. (The Laurel Poetry Series.) New York: Dell Publishing Co. 191p.
Reprinted, 1966.
Introduction (pp. 9–22); bibliography (pp. 22–23); chronology (pp. 24–25); note on the text (p. 26); selection from the English poems based primarily on Hutchinson's text (entry 266) with minor alterations (pp. 27–185); notes on individual poems (pp. 186–91). Maintains in the introduction that Herbert is more admired today than read, primarily because the modern reader is often embarrassed or bored "by the expression of so direct and personal a faith as Herbert's was" (p. 10), especially since his poetry lacks the rhetorical splendor, sensationalism, and mystical rhapsody of more popular metaphysical poets. Argues that *The Temple* has something to say to the modern reader because it presents "an important human argument: a man's attempt to discover himself, to define and to refine away what is selfish and vacillating and cowardly in his nature, to fix a goal for his life's course, and to submit himself to the demands imposed by that goal" even if Herbert's way of doing these things "is stated in terms of a specific religious system" (p. 13). Comments on Herbert's complex simplicity, especially as reflected in such poems as "Love unknown" and "Love (III)" as well as in his stanzaic inventiveness and artistry.

**581. ———.** *Select Hymns Taken Out of Mr. Herbert's Temple (1697)*. With an introduction by William E. Stephenson. (Augustan Reprint Society, no. 98.) Los Angeles: William Andrews Clark Memorial Library, University of California. vii, 45p.
Reprinted, Millwood, N.Y.: Kraus Reprint Co., 1975.
Facsimile edition of *Select Hymns*, first published by Thomas Parkhurst, the well-known Presbyterian bookseller, in 1697, and currently in Dr. Williams's Library, London. The adapter is unknown but his intention is to turn some thirty-two of Herbert's poems into hymns "suitable for congregational singing by the nonconformist worshippers known as Dissenters" (p. i). In the introduction points out that the collection "shows clearly which elements of Herbert's poetry a later age valued" (p. i). Outlines the state of congregational singing in the 1690s among the Dissenters. Main-

tains that the adapter chose the poems to be included on the basis of their themes rather than their stanzaic patterns.

**582. Hopkins, Kenneth.** *English Poetry: A Short History.* Philadelphia and New York: J. B. Lippincott. 568p.

Reprinted, Carbondale: Southern Illinois University Press, 1969.

Comments briefly on Herbert's reputation, life, and poetry and maintains that "today he is again firmly established as the great celebrator of the Church of England" (p. 114). Notes Herbert's use of "outlandish conceits and images in conveying ideas not necessarily complex in themselves" and maintains that many of his poems "are too consciously quaint and 'conceited' to please a later age (his own time had a taste for verbal dexterity) but over and over he has the note that rings of a permanent truth" (pp. 114–15). Briefly compares and/or contrasts Herbert to Spenser, Phineas Fletcher, Donne, Vaughan, Crashaw, Thomas Campion, and Christina Rossetti.

**583. Jennings, Elizabeth.** "The Lyric Intervention: Herbert and Vaughan," in *Every Changing Shape*, 72–82. London, Philadelphia: Dufour Editions.

Sees Herbert primarily as a mystical poet, a visionary. Comments through examples drawn from Herbert's poems on the nature of his religious experience: "He explored and depicted all the stages of approach to God, from the articulate, discursive prayer of the beginner to the wordless prayer of the man far advanced in the spiritual life" (p. 74). Points out major features of Herbert's verse: its simplicity, directness, wide range of images, use of paradox, colloquial diction, and especially its dramatic elements. Sees the dominating theme of all Herbert's poetry as one of "flight from and return to God" (p. 73). Briefly compares and contrasts Herbert and Vaughan.

**584. Keast, William R., ed.** *Seventeenth Century English Poetry: Modern Essays in Criticism.* (A Galaxy Book, 89.) New York: Oxford University Press. 434p.

Rev. ed., 1971 (entry 879).

Collection of previously published items. Includes five general essays on metaphysical poetry: (1) H. J. C. Grierson, "Metaphysical Poetry," from *Metaphysical Lyrics & Poems of the Seventeenth Century* (entry 73), pp. xiii-xxxviii; (2) T. S. Eliot, "The Metaphysical Poets" (entry 70); (3) F. R. Leavis, "The Line of Wit," from *Revaluation: Tradition & Development in English Poetry* (London: Chatto & Windus, 1936, 1949; New York: W. W. Norton Co., 1947), pp. 10–36; (4) Helen Gardner, "The Metaphysical Poets," from *The Metaphysical Poets* (entry 477), pp. xix-xxxiv; (5) Joseph Anthony Mazzeo, "A Critique of Some Modern Theories of Metaphysical Poetry" (entry 404). Includes two essays specifically on Herbert: (1) Joseph H. Summers, "The Poem as Hieroglyph," from *George Herbert: His Religion and Art* (entry 435), pp. 123–46; (2) Margaret Bottrall, "Herbert's Craftsmanship," from *George Herbert* (entry 427), pp. 99–116.

**585. Leach, Elsie.** "Yeats's 'A Friend's Illness' and Herbert's 'Vertue.'" *N&Q* 207:215.

Maintains that Yeats's "A Friend's Illness," written for Lady Gregory, contains several possible echoes from "Vertue."

**586. Lott, Bernard.** "M. E. *Drinken* and *Drink* in George Herbert." *Indian Journal of English Studies* (Calcutta) 3:132–34.

Challenges Rosemond Tuve's interpretation (*A Reading of George Herbert*, entry 409) of a line in a medieval religious lyric ("And thou wyth eysyl drinkest to me").

Tuve claims that the line resembles Herbert's colloquial style for exalted subjects and interprets the line by saying that "the vinegar as a kind of toast which 'thou drinkest to me' is typical of what happens in this tradition, and long before Herbert used it" (p. 133). Lott argues that such an interpretation is "unscriptural and makes no good sense" but that "*drink* used causatively to mean 'to hand or present a person beverage for his use; to give drink to' is well attested, and gives the correct meaning here" (p. 133).

**587. Praz, Mario.** "Il barocco in Inghilterra," in *Manierismo, barocco, rococò: Concetti e termini*, 129–46. (Problemi attuali di scienza e di cultura, no. 52.) Rome: Accademia nazionale dei Lincei.

Translated into English in *MP* 61 (1964): 169–79.

Maintains that the baroque was essentially alien to English sensibility and taste but that Milton, Crashaw, Beaumont and Fletcher, and Dryden were to differing degrees influenced by baroque models. Sees Donne as a mannerist, not a baroque poet. No specific comment on Herbert. Discusses the revival of interest in metaphysical poetry in the twentieth century.

**588. Rauter, Herbert.** "Eine Anleihe Sternes bei George Herbert." *Anglia* 80:290–94.

Maintains that Sterne was familiar with Herbert's work and that in at least two places in *Tristram Shandy* he is influenced by Herbert: (1) Walter Shandy's comments on jest and wit in chapter 5 reflect strophe 40 of *The Church-Porch*, and (2) the character of Yorkic is influenced by Herbert's *The Country Parson*, as is especially reflected in Yorkic's comments on the catechism.

**589. Rees, T. R.** "T. S. Eliot, Rémy de Gourmont, and Dissociation of Sensibility," in *Studies in Comparative Literature*, edited by Waldo F. McNeir, 186–98. (Louisiana State University Studies: Humanities Series, no. 11.) Baton Rouge: Louisiana State University Press.

Reviews the modern critical controversy over Eliot's concept of "dissociation of sensibility," especially F. W. Bateson's attack (see entries 374, 394), and attempts to explain and defend Eliot's use of the term in the light of its Continental sources, especially the work of Rémy de Gourmont. No specific references to Herbert.

**590. Rickey, Mary Ellen.** "Vaughan, *The Temple*, and Poetic Form." *SP* 59:162–70.

Demonstrates that Vaughan's borrowings from Herbert "are structural as well as verbal" (p. 170) and that they appear in the early secular poems as well as in *Silex Scintillans*. Discusses a number of Vaughan's poems in which he "plays tricks with rhymes which are clearly Herbertian" and points out several poems "in which only a part is modeled on the poems in *The Temple*" (p. 163). Compares and contrasts, for instance, Herbert's use of rhyme irregularities that are finally normalized in the end of the poem in "Antiphon (II)" and "Deniall" with Vaughan's imitation of this device in "Disorder" and "Frailty"; Herbert's use of rhymes that double back on themselves to form a veritable wreath of verses in "A Wreath" and Vaughan's use of the same form in his "The Wreath"; and Herbert's uses of a system of triads in "Trinitie Sunday" and Vaughan's adaptation of the form in his "Trinity Sunday." Discusses a number of poems in which Vaughan does not appropriate whole rhyme schemes from Herbert but uses "Herbertian stanza forms with few distinct traces of the theme for which Herbert uses them" (p. 166).

**591. Sanders, Wilbur.** "'Childhood Is Health': The Divine Poetry of George Herbert." *Melbourne Critical Review* 5:3–15.

Challenges critics, like L. C. Knights and Rosemond Tuve, who maintain that Herbert "is not only a good, competent poet, but a great one" (p. 3). Argues that many of Herbert's poems are "drastically flawed," "sound stuffy and churchy, deal too largely in abstractions, and abound in examples of what one could call a sort of verbal imprecision" (p. 3). Maintains that much of Herbert's poetry is "poetical exhibitionism disguised thinly as piety" (p. 4); regards his simplicity as "simulated simplicity, the uncritical adoption of a simple 'manner'" (p. 4) and "an effort of self-abasement which ends in a new and pernicious form of self-aggrandizement, a type of poetic exhibitionism before an indulgent and pious audience" (p. 5); maintains that Herbert's "preoccupation with subjective experience . . . frequently lands him in sentimentality" (p. 6); and concludes that Herbert "displays more negative submission than positive assent" to the notion of a divinely appointed order in the universe and that "his doubts and his beliefs are never brought into any comprehensive concord" (p. 13). Presents critical evaluations of "The Collar," "Affliction (I)," "Love (III)," "The Pearl," and "The Forerunners."

**592. Sloane, William.** "George Herbert's Reputation, 1650–1710: Good Reading for the Young." *N&Q* 207:213.

Points out six pieces of evidence to show that children of different religious preferences and social classes were urged to read Herbert's poetry during the period 1650–1700: (1) an undated letter from Peter Sterry, chaplain to Cromwell, to his son; (2) Henry Delaune in *Patrikon doron. Or a legacy to his sons* (1651; rev. and enlarged, 1657); (3) Charles Hoole in 1660; (4) Thomas White in *A little book for little children* (1674); (5) Dr. Thomas Willis in *The key to knowledg opening the principles of religion; and the path of life, directing the practice of true pietie; design'd for the conduct of children and servants, in the right way to heaven and happiness* (1682); and (6) Joseph Downing in *The Young Christian's Library* (1710). Concludes that the "sophisticated eighteenth-century reader was presumably content to relegate Herbert to the nursery and the servants' quarters."

**593. Starkman, Miriam K.** "Noble Numbers and the Poetry of Devotion," in *Reason and Imagination: Studies in the History of Ideas, 1600–1800*, edited by J. A. Mazzeo, 1–27. New York: Columbia University Press; London: Routledge & Kegan Paul.

Primarily a critical examination and defense of Herrick's *Noble Numbers*. However, throughout Herrick is compared to Herbert as a devotional poet. Dislikes the term *religious metaphysical* and argues that a more critically appropriate term would be *poetry of devotion*, which is more "hospitable to the symbolic, the meditational, and the emblematic" elements of the religious poetry of the period; which allows "for the various figurative modes that were actually employed, for genres from the couplet to the epic"; which allows room "for the didactic couplet as well as the affective prayer"; and which "is susceptible of being used with historical as well as intrinsic signification" (p. 23). Mentions Herbert's use of gnomic verse in *The Church-porch* and suggests that he may have been influenced by Southwell or perhaps even by the so-called wisdom poetry of collections such as *Tottel's Miscellany*.

**594. Story, G. M.** "Herbert's *Inventa Bellica*: A New Manuscript." *MP* 59:270–72.

Announces the discovery of a manuscript in Chetham's Library, Manchester (Mun. A.3.48), that includes a text of Herbert's "Inventa Bellica." Describes the manuscript and argues that it "offers a text which throws further light on the claims of *Inventa Bellica* to preference over Herbert's unrevised *Triumphus Mortis* and should help to restore the polished version to its proper place in the poet's canon" (p. 270). Presents a transcription of "Inventa Bellica" from the Chetham manuscript (pp. 271–72).

**595. Swardson, H. R.** "George Herbert's Language of Devotion," in *Poetry and the Fountain of Light: Observations on the Conflict between Christian and Classical Traditions in Seventeenth-Century Poetry*, 64–82. Columbia: University of Missouri Press; London: G. Allen & Unwin.

Argues that, although Herbert, like Donne, banished classical mythology from his poetry and stands in "a kind of negative relation to poetry in the classical literary tradition" (p. 64), "in the broad sense of 'classical' Herbert's poetry does reflect intensely one aspect of the tension between the Christian tradition and the classical tradition: the opposition between spiritual sincerity and skill in poetry, or, more crudely, between simple truth and contrived art" (p. 81). Notes that, although Herbert is often praised for his simplicity and straightforwardness, in practice he does not often follow his own advice to say simply, "My God, My King." Maintains that "his plain intention is always curled with metaphors, even in the very poems that reject this strategy" (p. 73). Argues that only occasionally is Herbert able to relax this sense of tension and conflict; more often he shows a general distrust of sensuous and ornate images as well as of the more ingenious forms of wit and rhetoric. Comments on "Jordan (I) and (II)," "The Forerunners," "Sunday," "The Pearl," "The Collar," "Deniall," and "The Flower."

**596. Walker, John David.** "The Architectonics of George Herbert's *The Temple*." *ELH* 29:289–305.

Argues that not only the physical structure of the Hebraic temple but also the complex symbolism associated with it were significant influences on the structure of *The Temple*. Comments on the tripartite division of *The Temple* (*The Church-Porch*, *The Church*, *The Church Militant*) and sees in this division (1) a spatial architectural analogy with the Hebraic temple (porch, holy place, holy of holies), (2) a possible cosmological and symbolic interpretation based on this architectural division and derived from various Church Fathers and early Christian writers (the lower, middle, and upper regions of the cosmos, in other words, the earth, heaven, and heaven of heavens), and (3) a tripartite temporal structure of Christian progression (youth, maturity, old age and death, or, more profoundly, "from primal obedience to Christ, to maturity in affliction, to the ultimate destiny of union with God" [p. 291]).

**597. Williamson, Karina.** "Herbert's Reputation in the Eighteenth Century." *PQ* 41:769–75.

Assesses Herbert's popularity during the eighteenth century in order to show that there were admirers "who, against all the weight of literary fashion, continued to honor and perpetuate his name" (p. 770). Lists editions of Herbert's poetry and collections in which his poems appeared during the period and presents favorable comments by a number of admirers, most of whom were churchmen and/or hymn collectors whose "respect for his writing sprang less from literary judgments than from religious sympathy" (p. 772). Points out that Herbert "was read (or sung or paraphrased), it seems, not for the virtues of his style but rather in spite of them, for the truth of his rendering of Christian attitudes and beliefs" (p. 772). Supports this position by commenting on the many adaptations, changes, and mutilations made in the poems to suit various eighteenth-century tastes, especially those made by Wesley.

**598. Wolfe, Jane E.** "George Herbert's 'Assurance.'" *CLAJ* 5:213–22.

Views "Assurance" as "a most vital and significant chapter" in Herbert's spiritual development, one that "may not be omitted from a spiritual biography which one would desire to intuit from a reading of his poems" (p. 222). Argues that in the poem Herbert "expressed most firmly and with unmistakable finality" his "full assurance of his salvation" and "his unqualified acceptance by God" (p. 213). Presents a detailed, stanza-by-stanza analysis of the dramatic argument of the poem and comments on several important elements, especially its skillful uses of tone and its many biblical echoes in both imagery and diction.

# *1963*

**599. Adams, Hazard.** "Metaphysical Poetry: Argument into Drama," in *The Context of Poetry*, 75–99. Boston: Little, Brown & Co.

Discusses some of the general characteristics of metaphysical poetry (diction, rhythms, conceits, wit) and stresses the dramatic elements. Comments briefly on Herbert as a religious poet who "developed drama out of traditional theological paradoxes" (p. 93). Maintains that Herbert's complexity is, for the most part, "that of traditional religious analogies and emblems, of allegory, which often explains its own meaning" (p. 94).

**600. Cohen, J. M.** *The Baroque Lyric.* London: Hutchinson University Library. 207p.

Comments on Herbert's uses of typology, the sources of his imagery (such as traditional architecture, the liturgy, medieval poetry, iconography), the uses of music and auditory imagery, and the architectural complexity of *The Temple*. Places Herbert's poetry "on the borderline between the religious and the mystical": "For while it speaks of deep personal experience, it invariably does so in the context of church doctrine" (p. 177). Likewise, maintains that Herbert's poetry "expresses a supreme paradox: it is personal and impersonal at the same time, because when he writes as a poet, it is with that part of himself which is immortal man" (p. 174). Compares and contrasts Herbert with Donne, Crashaw, Vaughan, Lope de Vega, Jean de La Ceppède, Argensola, Malherbe, and Bach.

**601. Colie, R. L.** "*Logos* in *The Temple*: George Herbert and the Shape of Content." *JWCI* 26:327–42.

Reprinted as chapter 6 in *Paradoxia Epidemica: The Renaissance Tradition of Paradox* (entry 689), 190–215.

Maintains that "it is in the speculum of the great mystical, self-explanatory notion of the divine *logos* . . . that Herbert's poetry may be most helpfully reflected" and that "the difficulties involved in the doctrine of the *logos*, once understood in relation to Herbert's verse, may clarify some of the content and method of that verse and serve as a model, an emblem, for the difficulties inherent in both his subject-matter and his method" (p. 328). Examines in some detail with many examples drawn from numerous poems "the uses of the Word, intradeical and extradeical, in Herbert's verse," and tests the hypothesis "that from his manipulation of the paradoxes inherent in the *logos*-doctrine we can read the problems in his verse and his versing" (p. 329).

**602. Cubeta, Paul M.** "Ben Jonson's Religious Lyrics." *JEGP* 62:96–110.

Finds a number of resemblances between Jonson's religious lyrics and Herbert's, especially certain tonal qualities. Maintains that Jonson's "A Hymne to God the Father" reminds one of Herbert's "Discipline" and that the diction and sentence structure of "To Heaven" point "ahead a few years to Herbert's easy, relaxed rhythms" (p. 109).

**603. Daniels, Edgar F.** "George Herbert's 'Balm and Bay'—Synonyms?" *SCN* 20:63, item 205.

Comments on Herbert's use of the phrase *balm and bay* in "Sunday" (line 5). Rejects previous interpretations of *bay* and argues that the word "is intended as an alliterative synonym of *balm*, in the old rhetorical tradition of 'might and main' and 'vim and vigor.'" Maintains that the whole phrase simply means "the easement of care." Supports this interpretation by reference to George Ryley's commentary in *Mr Herbert's Temple & Church Militant Explained & Improved* as well as by reference to Herbert's use of a similar rhetorical device in *A Priest to the Temple*.

**604. Empson, William.** "Herbert's Quaintness." *New Statesman* n.s. 65:18.

Primarily a review of T. S. Eliot's *George Herbert* (entry 577). In particular, Empson responds to Eliot's dismissal of his comments on "The Sacrifice," which first appeared in *Seven Types of Ambiguity* (entry 131) and which were severely challenged by Rosemond Tuve in *A Reading of George Herbert* (entry 409). Reasserts his original argument, insists that the ambiguities of the poem spoil it, and maintains that it demonstrates Herbert's own embarrassment about the paradoxes of Christianity. Explains his original position in more detail, while at the same time admitting that it was probably a mistake "to drag in Freud" and that several of the more outrageous puns that he pointed out originally are clearly impossible.

**605. Freeman, Rosemary.** "Parody as a Literary Form: George Herbert and Wilfred Owen." *EIC* 13:307–22.

Comments on Herbert's "A Parodie" as an example of a poem that uses the formulas of love poetry but redirects them to the service of religion. Argues that this "transference of profane to sacred use is a constantly recurring feature in Herbert's work; much of it reflects the form and feeling of love poetry, now directed to a personal God" (p. 309). Comments on "Jordan (I)" and "Jordan (II)" as "examples of literary criticism from Herbert in which judgment is passed on the subjects of contemporary verse" (p. 310) and that serve as an apologia for Herbert's approach. Observes that in "Dulnesse" Herbert "remains very close to the idiom of secular love lyrics so that it enables the poem to work on two planes at once" (p. 313). Mentions other poems in which "the achievements of amatory verse are imitated yet made merely contributory" (p. 315), such as "The Glance," "The Answer," "Clasping of hands," and "Mans medley." In the second part of the essay comments on Wilfred Owens's war poetry, which, like Herbert's, combines the "evocative style of contemporary love poetry with a more serious subject" (p. 315).

**606. Fryxell, Lucy Dickinson.** "George Herbert: Anti-Metaphysical Poet?" *Discourse* (Concordia College) 6:293–99.

Comments on the tension in Herbert between simplicity and conscious artistry and argues that he "was pulled in two directions in his attitude toward the language appropriate for religious poetry" (p. 295). Maintains that Herbert sees poetry as a means of leading men to God and thus recognizes the merits of simplicity and plainness, but he also sees poetry as prayer and thus recognizes that "the finest language that the human mind can invent is the best choice for reflecting God's infinite beauty" (p. 298). Concludes that, although Herbert distrusts the wit and ingenuity that modern critics focus on in his poetry, he is, nonetheless, much concerned about art and art forms: "To him the poet is the artist working for God, and in the orientation toward God anything that calls attention and admiration to the workmanship is inappropriate; but his integrity as an artist requires that he use the best materials available to him, and that he employ those materials with the greatest skill of which he is capable" (p. 298). Maintains that Herbert would disapprove of the inordinate attention given to his artistry, wit, and ingenuity by modern critics: "He would feel that his search for the best way of expressing 'Thou art still my God' has become perhaps a stumbling block to the fulfillment of one purpose of his poems" (p. 298).

**607. Hastings, Robert.** "'Easter Wings' as a Model of Herbert's Method." *Thoth* 4:15–23.

Presents a detailed explication of "Easter-wings" in order "to show that in its form, especially in its structure, diction, and imagery, the poem may be made to serve as a model of Herbert's emblematic mode of expression" (p. 15). Argues that the main theme of the poem is "one of alienation from God through sin, and redemption from sin through faith in the risen Christ, evidenced in the form of the paradox, that sin and its effects are made, for the believer, the very instruments of God's purposes, through the atonement of Christ's passion and the power of His spirit" (p. 16). Comments in detail on formal characteristics of the poem that reinforce its theme—the visual patterns, structure, rhyme scheme, line lengths, metrics, images, metaphors, and diction—and shows that its typological or emblematic characteristics are typical of Herbert's poetry in general.

**608. Herbert, George.** *George Herbert.* Selected by David Herbert. (Pocket Poets.) London: Vista Books. 48p.

Selection of forty-one poems from *The Temple* with no notes and no commentary. One-page introduction to Herbert's life and poetry by David Herbert.

**609. Joselyn, Sister M.** "Herbert and Muir: Pilgrims of Their Age." *Renascence* 15:127–32.

Compares and contrasts Herbert and Edwin Muir. Maintains that they resemble each other in their "tendency toward paradox, prevailing sweetness of tone, use of narrative situations to reveal moral or spiritual truths, self-conscious dialogue with the Deity, frequent use of the quatrain, simple diction and so on" but that their great difference "lies in the degree of certainty with which each is able to close off the dialogue with conscience—or God" (p. 127). Discusses a number of Muir's poems that in varying degrees resemble or differ from Herbert's and sees each poet as reflecting the religious sensibility and tensions of his age.

**610. Kranz, Gisbert.** "George Herbert: Ein Dichter des Anglikanertums." *Hochland* 55:235–46.

General introduction to Herbert for the German reader. Brief history of Herbert's influence on poets of his own time as well as on later poets. Biographical sketch. Maintains that "in Herberts Dichtung ist das Christliche nicht ohne Verständnis des Künstlerischen, das Künstlerische nichte ohne Verständnis des Christlichen zu erfassen" (p. 237). Presents a brief analysis of the major structure and symbols of *The Temple* and compares the musical quality of Herbert's poetry with that of Donne.

**611. Kuna, F. M.** "T. S. Eliot's Dissociation of Sensibility and the Critics of Metaphysical Poetry." *EIC* 13:241–52.

Shows that dissociation of sensibility is simply "a poetic theory, and nothing more, which cannot be applied to any poetry written before the eighteenth century without distorting all historical truth, and which must not be separated from its original context" (p. 243). Argues that Eliot's concept can be applied only to modern poetry and that it is primarily the result of Eliot's theorizing about the nature of his own early poetry. No specific reference to Herbert.

612. **Leach, Elsie.** "Some Commercial Terms in Seventeenth-Century Poetry." *N&Q* 298:414.
Points out that Herbert's use of the business term *market-money* in *The Church-Porch* (line 375) antedates the first recorded instance in the *OED* (1891).

613. **Martz, Louis L., ed.** *The Meditative Poem: An Anthology of Seventeenth-Century Verse.* With an introduction and notes. (Anchor Seventeenth-Century Series, AC6.) Garden City, N.Y.: Doubleday & Co. xxxii, 566p.
Reprinted in hardback (Stuart Editions), New York: New York University Press, 1963.
Rev. ed., *The Anchor Anthology of Seventeenth-Century Verse*, vol. 1 (Garden City, N.Y.: Doubleday & Co., 1969); reprinted as *English Seventeenth-Century Verse*, vol. 1 (1973).
Introduction to *The Meditative Poem* partially reprinted in *The Poem of the Mind: Essays on Poetry, English and American* (entry 706), 33–53.
In the introduction (pp. xvii–xxxii) distinguishes between metaphysical and meditative poetry and outlines the essential features of the meditative mode, suggesting that "the central meditative action consists of an interior drama, in which a man projects a self upon a mental stage, and there comes to understand that self in the light of a divine presence" (p. xxxi). Includes sixty-eight poems by Herbert (pp. 141–229) with commentary and notes (pp. 534–38).

614. **Pérez Gállego, Cándido.** "La iglesia anglicana como estructura y símbolo en George Herbert." *RL* 23:117–21.
Argues that the symbol of the Christian Church confers unity on *The Temple*. Discusses the significance of the Church as both a physical and a spiritual symbol: "Un símbolo: la Iglesia. Pero un símbolo de doble significacion, puesto que además de tener entidad en el poema va alvergando todos los momentos de arrepentimiento que en ella ocurren. Después, una Iglesia real, con una arquitectura visible y concreta. *The Temple* es un gran edificio religioso, de nobles armonías, donde los esfuerzos del autor consisten en conjugar la materialidad del símbolo—un templo—con el camino que conduce al estado de la gracia" (p. 121).

615. **Rickey, Mary Ellen.** "Herbert's Technical Development." *JEGP* 62:745–60.
Reprinted in much revised form as chapter 4 of *Utmost Art: Complexity in the Verse of George Herbert* (entry 713), 103–47.
Reprinted in *Essential Articles for the Study of George Herbert's Poetry*, edited by John R. Roberts (entry 1216), 311–26.
Studies Herbert's poetry "to show that a number of formal differences between his early and later work exist, and that these differences are sufficiently alike in kind to enable one to see a concerted direction in which his writing was moving at the time of his death" (p. 745). Examines "the differences between the sixty-nine 'earlier' poems [in the Williams MS] and the additional 'later' poems which appeared in *The Temple* in 1633" (p. 745). Maintains that, although all Herbert's poems exhibit more sim-

ilarities than differences, the following significant changes occur: (1) an increasing use of figurative titles, due to Herbert's realization that a title "could function much like an additional, and highly desirable, unit of imagery" (p. 747); (2) the use of more than one stanza form in a single poem; (3) a decreasing production of sonnets, probably accounted for by Herbert's interest in more original stanza forms; (4) the use of different kinds of hieroglyphs, "moving away from absolute physical imitation of the topic of his verse, to what might be called a 'semi-hieroglyphic,' in which some less conspicuous formal quality reinforces the matter of the poem" (p. 749); (5) an increasing number of so-called contrapuntal poems: of the poems in the Williams manuscript only 47 percent are contrapuntal whereas 64 percent of the new poems in *The Temple* fit this category; (6) an increasing use of longer and more elaborate stanza forms; (7) an increasingly careful use of feminine endings, which Herbert came to regard "as expressing weakness and disorder" (p. 751) and to use for conscious effects; (8) an increasing use of stanza linking; and (9) an increasingly careful use of variation for dramatic purposes, with a rather detailed comment on the complexity of variations in "The Collar." Concludes that the differences between the "early" and "later" poems show Herbert's "increasingly fine and delicate control of the adjustment of form to substance as well as a more subtle approach to this adjustment" (p. 760).

**616. Sito, Jerzy S.** "George Herbert," in *Śmierć i miłość: Mala antologia poezji wedlug tekstów angieskich mistrzów, przyjaciól, rywali wrogów i naśladowców Johna Donne'a* [Death and Love: A Small Anthology of Poetry Based on the Works of the English Forerunners, Friends, Rivals, Enemies and Followers of John Donne], 61–67. [Warsaw]: Czytelnik.
Translates into Polish (without notes or commentary) "Easter-wings," "Love (III)," "Death," "Vertue," and "Deniall."

**617. Sparrow, John.** "Hymns and Poetry." *TLS*, 11 January, p. 32.
Points out that several poems by Herbert, Donne, Crashaw, and other religious poets of the period are adapted for congregational singing and included in the *Collection of Hymns* (London, 1754), edited by John Gambold for the "Brethren's Church" of the Moravians. Also points out that two of Herbert's poems are printed with musical settings in Playford's *Harmonia Sacra* (book 1). See also entry 640.

**618. Swanston, Hamish.** "The Second 'Temple.'" *DUJ* 25:14–22.
Reexamines the affinity between Herbert and Crashaw, commenting on certain technical features that both exhibit (such as use of language, means of manipulating the metaphor, recurring verbal patterns) and pointing out similar constructive elements (especially their uses of the conceit). Notes the similarity of their general attitudes toward sensible and suprasensible objects. Does not suggest that Herbert "is a fully developed baroque poet, but merely that he could have given encouragement to Crashaw" (p. 17). States that a number of critics in both the seventeenth and eighteenth centuries recognized the many affinities between the two poets.

**619. Watson, George.** "The Fabric of Herbert's *Temple*." *JWCI* 26:354–58.
Comments on Herbert's "audacity" in his use of God-mistress analogies, original metrical and stanzaic patterns, puns, figure poems, and other stylistic devices and maintains that this "intense and ostentatious use of technique encourages the reader to seek deliberation elsewhere in *The Temple*, even where it has not hitherto been sought—in the title and order of the poems" (p. 355). Maintains that the temple that

Herbert has in mind is not a parish church or specific building but rather that he is using the term metaphorically to describe himself as a priest: "The temple, for Herbert, signified his final commitment to the priestly life and his submission to divine love" (p. 357). Concludes that Herbert "lacked the temperament to build a whole collection of poems united by a single 'emblem' or visual image" (p. 357) but that there are "some grounds for thinking that the opening of *The Temple*, at least, was designed to exemplify the titular metaphor" (p. 356).

**620. Witherspoon, Alexander M., and Frank Warnke, eds.** *Seventeenth-Century Prose and Poetry.* 2d ed. New York, Chicago, Burlingame: Harcourt, Brace & World. xxvi, 1094p.

First ed., edited by Robert P. T. Coffin and Alexander M. Witherspoon, entry 313; reprinted, 1957; 2d enlarged ed., 1982.

Revised edition, including new introductions and new selections of verse. Includes general introductions to seventeenth-century prose (pp. 3–17) and poetry (pp. 707–18), with selected bibliographies; a brief introduction to Herbert's life, followed by excerpts from *A Priest to the Temple* (pp. 216–21); and a general introduction to Herbert's poetry, followed by thirty-nine poems (or selections from poems), with brief explanatory notes (pp. 842–59). Calls Herbert "a towering figure in Baroque poetry," "perhaps the finest devotional poet in our language," and "remarkable for his artistic originality" (p. 842). Maintains that "perhaps no other English poet of the age develops to as intense a degree as he the identification of matter and manner characteristic of much Baroque art" (p. 842). Comments on the variety of the poems: "Herbert's subject is single and simple, but in his treatment he marshals all the poetic techniques known to the most various age of English poetry" (p. 842). Briefly compares and/or contrasts Herbert to Donne, Crashaw, Vaughan, and Edward Taylor.

# 1964

**621. Attal, Jean-Pierre.** "L'image 'métaphysique.'" *Mercure de France* 351:270–95.

Defines the metaphysical image as one that gives spiritual significance to things, joins disparate phenomena, creates surprising effects, causes the reader to reason, and opposes the abstract and the concrete. Maintains that the poet who creates metaphysical images is more a beholder than a participant in life. Contends that the metaphysical image has flourished from the sixteenth century onward because of the secularization of life. Comments on Scève, Bunyan, Poe, and Raymond Roussel and maintains that Donne, more than Herbert, composed metaphysical images.

**622. Berry, Lloyd E., comp.** *A Bibliography of Studies in Metaphysical Poetry, 1939–1960.* Madison: University of Wisconsin Press. xi, 99p.

A continuation of Theodore Spencer and Mark Van Doren's *Studies in Metaphysical Poetry: Two Essays and a Bibliography* (entry 242). Lists 1,147 critical studies on metaphysical poetry from 1939 to 1960. Notes that "entries were compiled after a search of more than 1000 journals, about 480 of which are not listed in the PMLA bibliography" (jacket). No annotations. There are 102 items specifically on Herbert, all of which are included in this bibliography.

**623. Blanchard, Margaret M.** "The Leap into Darkness: Donne, Herbert, and God." *Renascence* 17:38–50.

Contrasts the religious sensibilities of Herbert and Donne as they are reflected in the poetry. Studies the tone and the visual and auditory images in the work of each poet and concludes that Herbert's relationship to God tends to be a very personal and intimate one, whereas Donne's tends to be more objective. Notes that in Herbert's poetry God speaks and is more often directly addressed than in Donne's poetry: "Herbert's religious poetry, enriched by the presence and voice of God, does then speak of a more significant spiritual relationship than does Donne's more objective poetry; this is not to say that Donne's struggle with a silent God is less gripping to us on a human level" (p. 50).

**624. Broadbent, J. B.** *Poetic Love.* London: Chatto & Windus. vii, 310p.
Presents a history of love poetry from the twelfth century to the Enlightenment primarily in terms of the problem of duality of the body and soul. Argues that the metaphysical poets separate the spheres of sacred and human love, even though they use human love as a metaphor of divine love. Comments on Herbert as a religious love poet and calls him a "Christian in the deepest Pauline and Augustinian sense" (p. 107). Praises Herbert's poems as being "remarkable for their variety of little genres, and of levels of religious experience" (p. 108). Argues that Herbert's poetry, unlike Donne's, is musical and defines the quality of its music. Maintains that both Herbert and Donne in their poetry are less concerned with presenting the transcendent God than with dramatizing "a struggle between God and themselves" (p. 95). Points out a central paradox of Herbert's poems: "For all their intricate artistry, they do not present themselves (as Milton's obtrusively do) as art, but present rather the divinity which they affirm" (p. 112). Compares and contrasts Herbert with Donne, Hopkins, and Eliot.

**625. Chadwick, Owen.** *The Reformation.* (Pelican History of the Church, vol. 3.) Baltimore: Penguin Books. 463p.
Reprinted, London: Hodder & Stoughton. Grand Rapids, Mich.: Eerdmans, 1965; Harmondsworth: Penguin, 1968, 1972.
Mentions Herbert in several instances. Briefly comments on "The British Church," pointing out that Herbert's assertion in the last line of the poem ("And none but thee") "is the claim to a uniquely favoured reformation" and that "evidently the poet is not so much concerned with truth as a sign of this favour" (p. 226). Briefly contrasts *A Priest to the Temple* and St. Charles Borromeo's *Instruction to a Pastor* to illustrate "a certain antithesis between the pastor of the Reformation and the pastor of the Counter-Reformation" (p. 408). Notes that a friend of Herbert attempted to dissuade him from entering the priesthood by pointing out that the position of a clergyman was beneath him in the light of his family, education, and intellectual abilities. Briefly notes Herbert's love of music.

**626. Cummins, Richard.** *Rise Heart, Thy Lord Is Risen.* (The Westminster Choir College Library Series, edited by David Stanley York, 312–40576.) Bryn Mawr, Pa.: Theodore Presser Co. 11p.
Musical setting of the first eighteen lines of "Easter" for four-part women's voices (SSAA), with alto solo and organ.

**627. Daniels, Edgar F.** "Herbert's 'The Quip,' 23." *Expl* 23:item 7.
Comments on the first half of line 23 of "The Quip" ("Speak not at large"). Disagrees with those who interpret "at large" as meaning "in a general way" and argues that the phrase more appropriately means "at length, in full, fully." "It is the

main point of the poem that God's reply is to be a 'quip,' a short stinging statement, and so He is urged not to speak at length in a point-by-point refutation but to answer everything in a single sentence."

**628.** ———. "Herbert's 'The Quip,' Line 23: 'Say, I Am Thine.'" *ELN* 2:10–12.

Points out that line 23 of "The Quip" is ambiguous and can be read either "say that I (man) am Thine (God's)," as Palmer suggests, or "say, 'I (God) am thine (man's).'" Argues that the thematic unity of the poem "is possible only if the half-line is read as a direct quotation: God's quip is the climactic statement of the poem, minimizing the rewards of the world (beauty, money, glory, and intellectual association) by placing God himself in the balance against them" (p. 12).

**629. Ellrodt, Robert.** "Scientific Curiosity and Metaphysical Poetry." *MP* 61:180–97.

Accounts for the prevailing scientific curiosity in metaphysical poetry and for the differences in the use of science among the various poets. Points out that Herbert "deplored that man's attention should stray through the Creation instead of turning to the Creator" (p. 195) but that he did not hold science in contempt. Maintains that, unlike Donne, Herbert "seems ingenuously persuaded that man's intelligence can penetrate any mystery in Nature" and thus "only disowns the search of the scientist because it does not lead man to God" (p. 195). Argues that, like Bacon, Herbert separated science from religion, but for an entirely different reason: Bacon "wished to free philosophy from theological fetters" while Herbert "would rather free the Christian from intellectual subtleties" (p. 195). Concedes that Herbert is not hostile to natural philosophy nor views learning as useless but recognizes "the *human* value of science" (p. 195). Argues that Herbert's "underlying rationality kept him from wholly surrendering to emotion, ecstasy, or wonder" (pp. 195–96), and thus he is "like Donne and unlike Crashaw in stressing paradox rather than mystery or miracle" (p. 196). Points out specific examples of Herbert's admittedly sparing use of scientific images.

**630. England, Martha Winburn.** "The First Wesley Hymn Book." *Bulletin of the New York Public Library* 68:225–38.

Reprinted in *Hymns Unbidden: Donne, Herbert, Blake, Emily Dickinson, and the Hymnographers,* by Martha Winburn England and John Sparrow (New York: Public Library, 1966), 31–42.

Comments on the adaptations of poems from *The Temple* in John Wesley's *A Collection of Psalms and Hymns* (published in Charleston, S.C., in 1737). Discusses Wesley's great admiration of Herbert as evidenced in his collections of hymns, his publication of Walton's *Life of Herbert* in 1753, and his publication of selections from Herbert's poems in 1773.

**631. Farmer, Norman, Jr.** "The Literary Borrowings of Philip Pain." *N&Q* 209:465–67.

In part a reply to Theodore Grieder (entry 578). Argues that Philip Pain, a minor American Puritan poet, "probably knew his Quarles better than his Herbert" (p. 467). Discusses the relative popularity of the two seventeenth-century English poets and concludes that we can "ill-afford to reject the possibility that Pain had as great a working familiarity with Quarles as with Herbert" (p. 466). Shows that many of the so-called borrowings, both general and specific, attributed to Herbert can also be found in Quarles.

**632. Fisch, Harold.** "Hebraic Poetry," in *Jerusalem and Albion: The Hebraic Factor in Seventeenth-Century Literature*, 56–62. New York: Schocken Books.

Discusses the biblical lineage of Herbert's poetry. Points out that Herbert's meditative poetry "has its roots deep in the Psalter, and its simplicity is that of the Psalmist" (p. 57). Maintains that psalms are typically "a song for two voices addressing one another in the intimate drama of the covenant-relation" (p. 59) and sees this dialectical strain as typical of much of Herbert's poetry: "His characteristic poetry reveals a certain tension owing to the juxtaposition either in sequences or in balance of the various opposing forces of the religious life" (p. 61). Maintains that Herbert may be more appropriately called a "dialogic" poet rather than a metaphysical poet. Describes Herbert's poetry as meditative poetry that is "strenuous, earnest, and controlled; it brings together the various powers of the soul into a unity—the contemplative and active, the rational and the emotional" (p. 60). Comments briefly on Herbert's rendering of Psalm 23 and several other poems, including "An Offering," "Complaining," and "The Collar."

**633. Howarth, R. G.** "The Chronology of George Herbert's Poems," in *A Pot of Gillyflowers: Studies and Notes*, 82–83. Cape Town, South Africa.

Evaluates Palmer's attempt to date and to arrange Herbert's poems in chronological order (entry 2) and Hutchinson's objections to such an ordering (entry 266). Maintains that when one considers "Jordan (II)," in which Herbert renounces his earlier excesses in poetry, "it will be found that Palmer's order is fairly well borne out; though he may, as Hutchinson declares he does, inadvisedly separate some related pieces" (p. 83).

**634. Hughes, Richard E.** "George Herbert and the Incarnation." *Cithara* 4:22–32.

Reprinted in *Essential Articles for the Study of George Herbert's Poetry*, edited by John R. Roberts (entry 1216), 52–62.

Maintains that the central issue in Herbert's poetry is the Incarnation and argues that Herbert "did not merely write *about* the Incarnation: he saw poetry itself as a miniature version of the Incarnation, and each divine poem as a microcosm of the Incarnation" (p. 24). Thus, the "doctrine provided Herbert, not only with subject, but with form, technique and meaning" (p. 24). Comments on Herbert's sacramental sense, his delight in order, his uses of music, and his understanding of the tradition of the Logos as part of his incarnational view. Presents a detailed reading of "Love (III)" in order to demonstrate "how Herbert fashions his poetry so that the entire poetic process becomes incarnative" (p. 29).

**635. Kenner, Hugh, ed.** "George Herbert," in *Seventeenth Century Poetry: The Schools of Donne and Jonson*, 199–225. New York: Holt, Rinehart and Winston.

Brief introductory note on Herbert and a selection of twenty-eight poems with short explanatory notes.

**636. Kusunose, Toshihiko.** "George Herbert no Sei to Shin" [Life and Faith of George Herbert] *Kanseigakuin Daigaku Ronko* [Bulletin of the Kanseigakuin University] 11 (September): 195–208.

Discusses the life and faith of George Herbert, comparing and contrasting his verse to Donne's.

**637. Melchiori, Giorgio.** *Poeti metafisci inglesi del Seicento.* (Scala reale. Antologie letterarie, no. 4.) Milan: Casa Editrice Dr. Francesco Vallardi. 673p.

Brief introduction to Herbert's life and poetry (pp. 267–68). Calls Herbert a mannerist and suggests that "in lui davvero si trova quella precaria e sottilmente bilanciata fusione del colloquiale e del cosmico, di pensiero e sentimento, che è la caratteristica più genuina della grande poesia «metafisica» del primo Seicento; fusione che già apparirà imperfetta nella fase barocca di questa poesia, in poeti come Crashaw e Cowley" (p. 268). Selected bibliography (p. 269). Includes Italian translations of thirty-five of Herbert's English poems, with the English version at the foot of the page (pp. 271–316). In "Appendice: Versi Latini," includes Italian translations of six of Herbert's Latin verses, with the Latin version at the foot of the page (pp. 585–95). Notes to the English poems (pp. 646–49); notes to the Latin poems (pp. 661–62).

**638. Muraoka, Isamu.** "George Herbert to Dionysius Areopagita" [George Herbert and Dionysius the Areopagite], in *Eibungaku Shiron* [Essays in English Literature in Honor of the 77th Anniversary of the Birth of Professor Kochi Doi], 30–40. Tokyo: Kenkyusha.

Points out that Herbert used in his poetry the simplest and homeliest images of the simplest everyday things. Asserts that this aspect of his imagery reflects the influence of Dionysius the Areopagite. Concludes that Herbert was a devoted admirer of Dionysius the Areopagite, who believed in the use of dissimilar and incongruous images to express the nature of God, and that he attached importance to Dionysius's theory of symbolism and put it into practice.

**639. Prasad, Vishnideo.** "Metaphysical Poetry and Poetic Maturity." *Jammu and Kashmir University Review* 7:47–62.

Discusses certain major characteristics of metaphysical poetry, especially its emotional intensity and presentation of inner conflict, its impersonality, its highly dramatic features, and its reflection of a unified sensibility, and argues that metaphysical poetry is "great" (or "mature") poetry, unlike the "immature" poetry of such poets as Shelley, Gray, Collins, Tennyson, and Dryden. Maintains that in metaphysical poetry one finds a "fine blend of a powerful impulse with keen critical intelligence" and argues that "mature poetry is always the result of such a find blend of the two faculties in a poet" (p. 55). Praises Herbert throughout, especially his poetic craftsmanship, his uses of ordinary diction, and his ability to create a conversational tone in his poems.

**640. Sparrow, John.** "George Herbert and John Donne among the Moravians." *Bulletin of the New York Public Library* 68:625–53.

Reprinted in *Hymns Unbidden: Donne, Herbert, Blake, Emily Dickinson and the Hymnographers* by Martha Winburn England and John Sparrow (New York: Public Library, 1966), 1–28.

Comments on John Wesley's lifelong admiration for Herbert's poetry, evidenced by his including several poems (somewhat abridged) from *The Temple* in his *Collection of Moral and Sacred Poems* (1744) and also by his publishing in 1773, when he was seventy years old, a collection of twenty-three poems (again abridged) entitled *Select Parts of Mr. Herbert's Sacred Poems*. Notes that Wesley adapted six of Herbert's poems for congregational singing in 1737 and another six in 1738. Notes also that in 1739 John and Charles Wesley published their *Hymns and Sacred Poems* and that "of the 138 pieces in this book, no fewer than forty-two were adaptations from Herbert (including ten of the twelve that he had already published); all were designated as being 'From *Herbert*,' and in almost every case they retained their original titles" (p. 626). Comments also on the Moravian hymnbook *A Collection of Hymns* (1754), which included thirty poems by Herbert, only ten of which had been previously adapted by Wesley. Compares Wesley's adaptations with those of the Moravian collection.

**641. Sugimoto, Ryutaro.** "Crashaw no Shi—Donne, Herbert to no Rekansei" [Crashaw's poetry in relationship to Donne and Herbert] *Osaka Shiritsu Daigaku Bungaku kai Jinbun Kenkyu* [Studies in the Humanities, Osaka Municipal University] 15, no. 3:23–34.
Compares and contrasts the poetry of Crashaw, Herbert, and Donne, focusing on their uses of imagery and their treatments of love.

**642. Warner, Oliver.** "George Herbert," in *English Literature: A Portrait Gallery*, 28–29. London: Chatto & Windus.
Biographical sketch and an engraved portrait of Herbert based on a drawing by Robert White. The portrait first appeared in Walton's *Life* (1670). Notes that it is "the only representation of Herbert to have survived" (p. 28).

**643. Warnke, Frank J.** "Sacred Play: Baroque Poetic Style." *JAAC* 22:455–64.
Discusses how intellectual play, dramatic projection, and mythic embodiment coexist in the work of certain English and Continental baroque poets, including Herbert. Suggests an approach to baroque poetry, "a way which may conceivably help us understand how a poem may be both serious and not serious, and how its style may partake simultaneously of the frivolous, the dramatic, and the profound" (p. 455). Comments briefly on Herbert's uses of intellectual play: anagrams, acrostics, pattern poems, and various technical effects achieved by the very form of the poem (as, for example, in "Deniall" or "Trinitie Sunday"). Maintains that in *The Temple*, Herbert "plays at the game of salvation—all in the most serious possible manner" and that his art is "an experience of the spirit which, being different from life, affords a ground from which to perceive and celebrate life" (p. 463). Briefly compares Herbert's poetry to Bach's *Musikalisches Opfer*, in which "a joyful mirthful virtuosity is at the service of devout religious sensibility, and serves it best by being joyous and mirthful" (p. 463).

# *1965*

**644. Allchin, F. R.** "George Herbert's 'Rope of Sands.'" *TLS*, 6 May, p. 356.
Queries Geoffrey Tillotson (entry 683) and James Kinsley (entry 662) about a possible link between Herbert and "his senior contemporary in North India, Tulsī Dās, who wrote of a vain task as 'twining a rope of dust specks with which to bind a lordly elephant'" (p. 356).

**645. Beaty, Jerome, and William H. Matchett.** *Poetry: From Statement to Meaning.* New York: Oxford University Press. 353p.
General introduction to the study of poetry. Briefly comments on the originality and experimental quality of Herbert's stanzaic forms. Mentions "The Altar" (p. 105), "Easter-wings" (p. 323), and "The Flower" (pp. 323–24).

**646. Bement, Peter.** "George Herbert's 'Rope of Sands.'" *TLS*, 29 April, p. 331.
Reply to Geoffrey Tillotson (entry 683). Points out that on at least three occasions Chapman used phrases very similar to Herbert's *rope of sands*. Maintains that Chap-

man's source is likely Erasmus's *Adagia* and notes that this is pointed out by Frank L. Schoell in *Etudes sur l'humanisme continental en Angleterre à la fin de la renaissance* (Paris: Champion, 1926), 50–51.

**647. Bouyer, Louis.** "Le Protestantisme après les Réformateurs et les débuts de l'Anglicanisme," in *La Spiritualité orthodoxe et la Spiritualité protestante et anglicane*, 137–225. (Histoire de la spiritualité chrétienne, vol. 3, ed. Louis Bouyer, Jean LeClercq, François Vandenbroucke, and Louis Cognet.) Paris: Aubier.

Translated into English by Barbara Wall (London: Burns & Oates; New York: Desclée Co., 1969; rpt., New York: The Seabury Press, 1982).

Briefly discusses Herbert's life and his commitment to Anglicanism and points out that *The Temple* vividly records Herbert's personal inner tensions. Comments in particular on the religious sensibility reflected in "The Collar," "Aaron," "The Odour," "Home," and "The Banquet." Maintains that the effect of Herbert's kind of piety can be clearly seen in Vaughan's poems.

**648. Coleman, Marion Moore.** "George Herbert's 'Rope of Sands.'" *TLS*, 29 April, p. 331.

Reply to Geoffrey Tillotson (entry 683). Points out the use of the phrase *rope of sands* in Adam Mickiewicz's poem "Pani Twardowska." Notes that the Twardowski legend is a combination of the Faust and Tyll Eulenspiegel legends.

**649. Collmer, Robert G.** "The Function of Death in Certain Metaphysical Poems." *McNR* 16:25–32.

Reprinted in *BSE* (entry 690).

Discusses the treatment of death in the poetry of Herbert, Donne, Vaughan, and Crashaw. Maintains that Herbert, in contrast to Donne, emphasizes in his poetry "unitive death, not divisive death" (p. 28) and views death simply "as part of God's system" (p. 29). Concludes that Herbert "did not view death as a frightful experience; he said virtually nothing about the physical ravages of death" (p. 28). Maintains that Herbert is "closer to Crashaw than to any other metaphysical poet in his belief that death is primarily positive" (p. 29).

**650. Daniels, Edgar F.** "Herbert's 'The Quip,' Line 15: A 'De-Explication.'" *AN&Q* 3:115–16.

Argues that line 15 of "The Quip" ("He scarce allow'd me half an eie") has been overread by both Palmer and Hutchinson and that if it is allowed "to have its simple say without these exegeses, it makes excellent sense and verse" (p. 116). Maintains that glory personified, like the other personified appeals in the poem, shows his general contempt for the poet in his own characteristic way: "Conceived as a pompous person walking past the poet, he does not condescend to give him a glance" (p. 116).

**651. Derry, Warren.** "George Herbert's 'Rope of Sands.'" *TLS*, 29 April, p. 331.

Reply to Geoffrey Tillotson (entry 683). Points out the proverbial nature of the phrase *rope of sands* for expressing the notion of vain labor. Finds use of it in the works of Lucius Junius Columella.

**652. Eliot, T. S.** "To Criticize the Critic," in *To Criticize the Critic and Other Writings*, 11–26. New York: Farrar, Straus & Giroux.

Eliot comments on his role in the modern revival of interest in metaphysical poetry: "I think that if I wrote well about the metaphysical poets, it was because they were poets who had inspired me. And if I can be said to have had an influence whatever in promoting a wider interest in them, it was simply because no previous poet who had praised these poets had been so deeply influenced by them as I had been" (p. 22). He adds: "As the taste for my own poetry spread, so did the taste for the poets to whom I owed the greatest debt and about whom I had written. Their poetry, and mine, were congenial to that age. I sometimes wonder whether that age is not coming to an end" (p. 22). Comments that for pure delight and pleasure he turns now more and more to the poems of Herbert, rather than to those of Donne: "This does not necessarily involve a judgment of relative greatness: it is merely that what has best responded to my need in middle and later age is different from the nourishment I needed in my youth" (p. 23).

**653. Endicott, Annabel M.** "The Structure of George Herbert's *Temple*: A Reconsideration." *UTQ* 34:226–37.

Reprinted in *Essential Articles for the Study of George Herbert's Poetry*, edited by John R. Roberts (entry 1216), 351–62.

Announces that the purpose of this essay is "to deny emphatically the structural analogy between Herbert's *Temple* and the Hebrew one" as suggested by John David Walker (entry 596), "to provide some additional knowledge about the use of this symbol in the Renaissance, and to show that Herbert would almost certainly have been aware of its complexities and its disadvantages" (p. 226). Comments on the traditional typology of the temple as found in the works of Joseph Hall, Donne, and Guillaume Du Bartas to show not only that the image was a common one in the Renaissance but also that "the tradition itself was by no means simple, and allowed much scope for individuality" (p. 233). Discusses "just how much of the *Hebraic* nature of the Temple could be implied by Herbert's use of the name" (p. 232). Concludes that, if one demands an overall pattern for *The Temple*, then a "three-fold structure of didactic, lyrical, and satirical poems" (p. 236) would be more appropriate than any attempt to impose the structure of the Hebraic temple onto this diverse collection of poems.

**654. Gorlier, Claudio.** "Il poeta e la nuova alchimia (II)." *Paragone* n.s. 16, no. 184:43–80.

Suggests that, together with Donne, Herbert represents the highest moment of metaphysical poetry and that, after him, metaphysical wit tends to disintegrate. Distinguishes between baroque and mannerist and maintains that both Donne and Herbert are mannerists, whereas Crashaw and Marvell are baroque poets. Explains, however, that there are significant differences even in the mannerist movement and contrasts the religious sensibilities and artistic techniques of Donne and Herbert. Maintains that Donne's religious poems always have a touch of Anglican compromise and caution about them, whereas Herbert's are more intense, more dramatic, and less intellectual. Comments briefly on Herbert's religious views in "The Agonie" and his artistic concerns in "Jordan (II)" and suggests that "The Quidditie" is an essential poem in understanding his art. Comments on the visual dimension of *The Temple* and its architectonics. Briefly compares and/or contrasts Herbert to Bach, Campanella, and Vaughan.

**655. Greenwood, E. B.** "George Herbert's Sonnet 'Prayer': A Stylistic Study." *EIC* 15:27–45.

A portion reprinted in *George Herbert and the Seventeenth-Century Religious Poets: Authoritative Texts/Criticism*, edited by Mario Di Cesare (entry 1140), 249–55.

Detailed stylistic analysis of "Prayer (I)" in which the critic attempts "to marry the old rhetoric" with the "new linguistics founded by Saussure and the stylistics of Alonso" (pp. 27–28). Sees Herbert's sonnet as "a kind of *mimesis* of inner speech" (p. 29) and argues that its structure exemplifies the central point of the poem, namely that "we can only understand 'something' of it [prayer], not everything" (p. 42). Comments also on the rhetorical features (such as the use of asyndeton—the omission of conjunctives), the highly concentrated metaphors, and various rhythmic and phonetic characteristics. Explains some of the more important metaphors in the poem. Includes an appendix on apposition as a mode of expression. See also Helen Vendler's review of *Essays on Style and Language: Linguistic and Critical Approaches to Literary Styles*, edited by Roger Fowler, *EIC* 16 (1966): 457–63; and Greenwood (entry 725).

**656. Grennen, Joseph E.** "George Herbert," in *The Poetry of John Donne and the Metaphysical Poets*, 55–58. (Monarch Notes and Study Guides.) New York: Monarch Press.

Biographical note on Herbert followed by brief paraphrases of and/or critical comments on "The Collar," "The Pulley," "The Altar," "Redemption," "Easter-wings," and "Jordan (II)."

**657. Herbert, George.** *The Latin Poetry of George Herbert: A Bilingual Edition.* Translated by Mark McCloskey and Paul R. Murphy. Athens: Ohio University Press. vii, 181p.

Introduction (pp. v–vii); contents (pp. viii–ix); Herbert's Latin and Greek poems (Hutchinson's text [entry 266]) with English translations on facing pages (pp. 1–175); notes (pp. 177–81). In the introduction the translators point out that Herbert's Latin poetry "is not only in the tradition of the Anglo-Latin poetry of his time, but it also reveals significant and little-known sides of his character and style" (p. v). Brief comments on the Anglo-Latin tradition.

Reviews:

Leicester Bradner, *Renaissance News* 18 (1965): 348–49
Richard T. Bruere, *CP* 60 (1965): 272–75
Barney Childs, *AQ* 21 (1965): 284
Harry C. Schnur, *CJ* 61 (1965): 137–38
John R. Mulder, *SCN* 24 (1966): 3–4
George W. Williams, *SAQ* 65 (1966): 295–96

**658. Hunter, Jim.** "George Herbert," in *The Metaphysical Poets*, 108–24. (Literature in Perspective.) London: Evans Brothers.

Reprinted, 1968, 1972.

Biographical account and general survey of Herbert's poetry. Comments primarily on the ingenuity and wit of his poems: "They are technically some of the most complex in English" (p. 111). Includes brief critical comments on several individual poems, especially "The Collar" ("for all its serious intention it must have given Herbert some amusement to create" [p. 114]), "Church-monuments" ("his finest hieroglyph" [p. 115]), "The Pearl," "Frailtie," and "The Forerunners." Stresses Herbert's variety and asks that one's evaluation of Donne not be used to misjudge Herbert, "who is one of the best English poets in most things, and the best of all in some things" (p. 122).

**659. Inglis, Fred, ed.** *English Poetry, 1550–1660.* London: Methuen & Co. xix, 242p.

Anthology that includes twenty-one of Herbert's poems (pp. 145–64), brief notes (p. 220), and a biographical sketch (p. 226). The introduction to the poetry of the period (pp. 1–36) mentions Herbert throughout.

**660. Jaeger, Hasso.** "La Mystique protestante et anglicane," in *La Mystique et les mystiques*, ed. André Ravier, 257–407. Paris: Deslée De Brouwer.

Discusses Herbert's spirituality as it is revealed in his poems: "Son génie poétique lui permet d'exprimer la réalité spirituelle de la grâce intérieure avec une force souveraine" so that, in fact, his poetry becomes "le dialogue intime entre son âme et Dieu" (p. 368). Observes that his poems reflect the joys and sufferings of one undergoing spiritual purification and regeneration.

**661. Jennings, Elizabeth.** "The Seventeenth Century," in *Christianity and Poetry*, 48–63. (Faith and Fact Books, 122.) London: Burns & Oates.

General survey of religious poetry in England during the seventeenth century. Calls Herbert "the most satisfying minor poet of the whole seventeenth century" (p. 53). Maintains that "Love (III)" is "one of the most exquisitely simple poems in English about Holy Communion" (p. 54).

**662. Kinsley, James.** "George Herbert's 'Rope of Sands.'" *TLS* 29 April, p. 331.

Reply to Geoffrey Tillotson (entry 683). Points out that *rope of sands* is proverbial for "something having no coherence or binding power." See also F. R. Allchin (entry 644).

**663. Kirkwood, James J., and George Walton Williams.** "*Anneal'd* as Baptism in Herbert's 'Love-Joy.'" *AN&Q* 4:3–4.

Suggests that the word *anneal'd* in line 3 of "Love-joy" may be a pun on *aneled* (anointed) and thus may refer to the holy oil of chrism used from earliest Christian times in the administering of the sacrament of Baptism. Points out various typological connections in the poem.

**664. Kishimoto, Yoshiyasu.** "George Herbert no Kuno to Sono Shiteki Hyogen— Shishu *The Temple* yori" [George Herbert's Affliction and Its Poetic Expression in *The Temple*]. *Baika Joshi Daigaku Bungakubu Kiyo* [Bulletin of the Faculty of Humanities, Baika Women's College] 2:1–18.

Argues that Herbert expresses his spiritual conflicts in most of his poems, using clear, simple images and a calm tone.

**665. Leighton, Kenneth.** *Let All the World in Every Corner Sing*. London: Novello & Co. 12p.

Musical setting of "Antiphon (I)." Anthem for four-part mixed voices (SATB) and organ commissioned for the Church of St. Matthew, Northampton, and first performed on the Eve of the feast of St. Matthew, 20 September 1965, under the direction of Michael Nicholas.

**666. Leiter, Louis H.** "George Herbert's Anagram." *CE* 26:543–44.

Explication of "Anagram of the Virgin Marie." Argues that, although at first the poem appears "to be only a trick, only a joke or oddity," it captures "the essence of a particular kind of poetic sensibility" (p. 543) and "performs a sacrament of prophecy and praise" (p. 544). For a reply, see Robert E. Reiter (entry 712).

**667. Lucas, F. L.** "George Herbert's 'Rope of Sands.'" *TLS*, 29 April, p. 331.

Reply to Geoffrey Tillotson (entry 683). Points out a Cornish legend of the wicked Tregeagle who was condemned to make ropes of sand. Also points out that *The Oxford Dictionary of English Proverbs* includes ten examples (including Erasmus and Samuel Butler's *Hudibras*) and that the phrase was proverbial in the seventeenth century for performing futile tasks. Challenges Tillotson's suggestion that Ruskin had Herbert in mind when he used the phrase.

**668. MacCaffrey, Isabel G.** "The Meditative Paradigm." *ELH* 32:388–407.

Evaluates Louis Martz's *The Paradise Within: Studies in Vaughan, Traherne, and Milton* (New Haven: Yale University Press, 1964) in which Martz discusses the effects of the Augustinian meditative tradition on the three poets. Disagrees with the notion that the meditative poem forms a specific genre but maintains that what Martz describes is "a literary paradigm, convention, or fiction in which a particular kind of thematic concern expresses itself habitually in—implies or demands—particular structural characteristics" (p. 390). Comments on two distinct meditative traditions, "one concerned with eucharistic and liturgical emblems, the other with a fictive 'landscape of the soul'" (p. 394). Compares Herbert briefly with Vaughan in the light of these traditions.

**669. MacNeice, Louis.** *Varieties of Parables.* Cambridge: University Press. vii, 156p.

Several references to Herbert throughout, especially to his overt parable poems (such as "Redemption"), his uses of the plain style and of traditional symbols, and his skillful uses of allegory and paradox. Maintains that Herbert "is not only less strained or straining than the other so-called Metaphysical poets, but a good deal less 'poetical' than certain prose writers of the period such as Jeremy Taylor and Sir Thomas Browne" (p. 47). Maintains that Herbert anticipates Bunyan and has clear links with Spenser.

**670. Mohanty, Harendra Prasad.** "George Herbert's 'The Collar.'" *Indian Journal of English Studies* 6:114–16.

Argues that the poem "presents a metaphysical ambivalence, the opposition between renunciation and enjoyment, submission to collar and revolt from commitment" (p. 114). Sees a double conflict at the heart of the poem, "one positive, the other negative, one the attraction of the senses, the other the illusory nature of the divine" (p. 115). Praises elements in the poem such as its complexity, dramatic tension, wide-ranging imagery, and colloquial speech rhythms: "Only the mood is turbulent but everything else is controlled, bound in the tight organization of balances, rhythmic stresses, half-rhymes, internal rhymes, alliterations, and onomatopoeia" (p. 116).

**671. Ogoshi, Kazuzo.** "Yagi to Kinobori" [The Buck and Tree Climbing]. *EigoS* 111, no. 3 (March): 138–39.

Mentions the dispute between William Empson (*Seven Types of Ambiguity*, entry 131) and Rosemond Tuve (*A Reading of George Herbert*, entry 409) regarding the interpretation of "The Sacrifice."

**672. Ostriker, Alicia.** "Song and Speech in the Metrics of George Herbert." *PMLA* 80:62–68.

Reprinted in *Essential Articles for the Study of George Herbert's Poetry*, edited by John R. Roberts (entry 1216), 298–310.

Accounts for the various paradoxes in Herbert's poetry "by isolating in metrical terms, the apparently irreconcilable modes of 'song' and 'speech' which have been observed in Herbert by several critics, notably Joseph H. Summers; by discovering what conventions they derive from and how Herbert used and changed what he learned from others; and by showing how the prosodic causes serve as instruments of an overall poetic vision in *The Temple*" (p. 62). Comments on the pervasive influence of the Elizabethan song on Herbert and argues that its most significant influence "lies in the structuring of his stanza-patterns, in which one finds the most important metrical qualities cultivated by the lyricists: complexity and variety, strictness of form, and concurrence of sound with sense" (p. 62). Discusses also the speech elements in Herbert's verse by examining his uses of blank verse, especially "how he used, or abstained from using, the tricks of accentual variety, caesural irregularity, and overflow, common to blank verse" (p. 66). Maintains that "the 'song' elements in Herbert's prosody are supplied by the structure of his stanza patterns; while the 'speech' elements are given by internal rhythmic variation" and concludes that "the poet's treatment of stanza and rhythm helps produce not only his mingled voices of singing and speaking, but affects every aspect of his poetic expression" (p. 68).

**673. Pacey, Desmond.** "Easter Homage to George Herbert." *The Atlantic Advocate* 55:40–44.
Appreciative sketch of Herbert's life and personality. Describes a visit to Salisbury and Bemerton. Five photographs.

**674. Peel, Donald F.** "Syncretistic Elements in Seventeenth Century Metaphysical Poetry." *Northwest Missouri State College Studies* 29, no. 2:3–20.
Considers the effects of the "new philosophy" in the development of metaphysical poetry: "The poetry was born in the disintegration of medieval scholasticism as a universal mode of thought" but, "whereas the scientists hailed that destruction as a victory, the poets saw the moral vacuum so created was not being adequately filled by the 'new philosophy'" (p. 3). Mentions Herbert in several instances, primarily by way of illustration. Concludes that the metaphysical poets, unlike the positivistic scientists, "were more constructive than destructive, more interested in holding up an affirmative ideal than in exposing the false" (p. 20). Concludes that, aware of the tensions and problems created by the new science, the metaphysical poets actively addressed themselves to solving the moral dilemma created by the destruction of the old system.

**675. Purcell, Henry.** "With Sick and Famished Eyes" (Words by George Herbert), in *The Works of Henry Purcell*, vol. 30, *Sacred Music*, part 4, *Songs and Vocal Ensemble Music*, edited by Anthony Lewis and Nigel Fortune, 94–97. London: Novello and Co.
Presents Purcell's musical adaptation of certain stanzas of Herbert's "Longing."

**676. Randall, Julia.** "A Theme of Herbert's," in *The Puritan Carpenter*, 17. (Contemporary Poetry Series.) Chapel Hill: University of North Carolina Press.
Original three-stanza poem roughly based on "Affliction (I)."

**677. Scheurle, William H.** "A Reading of George Herbert's 'Content.'" *LangQ* 4, nos. 1–2:37–39.
Detailed analysis of "Content" in order to examine the spirit of Herbert's religious humility and "to show that the language, figures, and images used by Herbert belonged to a general storehouse of terms and beliefs utilized by other divines of the period" (p. 37).

**678. Scoular, Kitty W.** "Natural Magic," in *Natural Magic: Studies in the Presentation of Nature in English Poetry from Spenser to Marvell*, 1–35. Oxford: Clarendon Press.

Comments on the response of sixteenth- and seventeenth-century poets to the natural world. Points out, for example, that such poems as Herbert's "Peace" and "The Search" reflect the common notion of searching for a hidden God among his creatures, observing that "such colloquies with the creatures were made familiar in meditative practice" and that "lying behind them is the knowledge of Biblical conversations between man and beast, such as Job xii, and the search of the lover for the beloved in *Canticles*" (p. 19). Notes that "among nature's riddles, providence was regarded as one of the strangest" (p. 32) and briefly comments on how Herbert adopts "a deliberately paradoxical style" (p. 33) to deal with the subject in "Providence."

**679. Sito, Jerzy S.** "Waska ścieżka—do ciebie" [The Narrow Path to You]. *Twórczość* 5:37–41.

Associates both George Herbert and Edward, Lord Herbert of Cherbury, with the "School of Donne" but maintains that George is undoubtedly the superior poet. Contrasts the two brothers and presents a biographical sketch of each and a very general survey of their works. Bases his biography of George Herbert on Walton's account and highlights the saintly personality of the Bemerton poet. Notes that the Herbert family came from Norman ancestry and thus was one of the oldest in Britain. Presents a very brief analysis of the characteristics of George Herbert's poetry and comments on the importance of music in shaping his art and his writing of pattern poems.

**680. Steese, Peter.** "Herbert and Crashaw: Two Paraphrases of the Twenty-Third Psalm." *Journal of Bible and Religion* 33:137–41.

Compares Herbert's and Crashaw's paraphrases of Psalm 23 and contrasts their achievements in this genre with the rendition of Sternhold and Hopkins. Shows that Herbert "closely follows the simple dignity of the Scriptures, yet he uses words and phrases which bring various interpretations to the mind of the reader and at the same time creates a sense of poetic unity" (p. 139). Maintains that both Herbert's and Crashaw's paraphrases "represent a level of achievement seldom equalled in the history of the genre" (p. 141).

**681. Stravinsky, Igor.** "Memories of T. S. Eliot." *Esquire*, August, pp. 92–93.

Stravinsky reports that Eliot said to him that the best parts of his essay on Herbert were the quotations and that he regretted "he had not had a 'sense of his audience' while writing it—though he certainly knew his audiences were the English 'lit' departments of several hundred thousand American universities" (p. 92). Also reports that Eliot announced, "Herbert is a great poet" and "one of a very few I can read again and again" (p. 92).

**682. Thorpe, James.** "Herbert's 'Love (III).'" *Expl* 24:item 16.

Maintains that "Love (III)" is not only related to the service of Holy Communion but "is in fact a dramatization of the central portion of that service, from the Exhortation following the offertory through the Administration of the Elements." Presents, through detailed allusions to *The Book of Common Prayer*, an allegorical interpretation of the poem in which the Eucharist is figured as a feast. Argues that the poem allows for a four-fold interpretation as found in medieval scriptural exegesis: (1) literal (simply the invitation to dinner), (2) allegorical (the eucharistic feast), (3) tropological (a dialogue between the soul and love), and (4) anagogical (the reception of the soul into heaven).

**683. Tillotson, Geoffrey.** "George Herbert's 'Rope of Sands.'" *TLS*, 22 April, p. 320.

Comments on the phrase *rope of sands* in line 22 of "The Collar." Points out that in his *Royal Academy Notes* Ruskin uses the phrase. Notes that Ruskin's editors, E. Cook and A. Weddeburn, apparently unaware of the Herbert allusion, refer the reader to Scott's notes on his *Lay of the Last Minstrel*, which contain a reference to a certain Michael Scott, a thirteenth-century scholar and magician, who tells of keeping a demon busy by engaging him "in the hopeless and endless task of making ropes out of sea-sand." Tillotson states that he has been unable to discover how Herbert may have come onto the legend. For replies, see F. R. Allchin (entry 644), Peter Bement (entry 646), Marion Moore Coleman (entry 648), Warren Derry (entry 651), James Kinsley (entry 662), and F. L. Lucas (entry 667).

**684. Wagner, Linda Welshimer.** "Donne's Secular and Religious Poetry." *Lock Haven Review* no. 7:13–22.

Compares Herbert's "The Flower," Vaughan's "The Flower," and Donne's "The Blossom" and "Holy Sonnet II," "poems related through subject matter rather than through category" (p. 13), in order to show various likenesses and differences. Maintains that Herbert's poems "combine elements of metaphysical religious poetry and the personally urgent lyric creating a unified expression of devout, almost passionate, belief" (p. 16). Argues that the chief parallel among the three poets is their pervasive conversational tone and that the chief differences "stem from the poets' concepts of nature as well as their religious beliefs" (p. 20). Concludes that a study of the four poems highlights Donne's influence on Herbert and Vaughan: "In their choice of images, point of view, poetic craft, and positive expression of feelings, these later poets couple techniques of both Donne's secular and religious poems" (pp. 21–22). Agrees with Helen Gardner's statement that Herbert's poems "can be regarded as a species of love poetry" (p. 22).

**685. Whiting, Paul.** "Two Notes on George Herbert." *N&Q* 210:130–31.

(1) Comments on stanza 51 of "The Sacrifice." Argues that Herbert is not merely restating a conventional concept when he describes Christ, the new apple, nailed to the "dry tree" of the cross; actually, through this image the "sin-tree" (the tree of knowledge of good and evil) becomes transformed into the "life-tree" (the tree of life also found in the Garden): "The Eden-fruit brought death, but the new apple, which is Christ, brings life" (p. 130). Concludes that Herbert has "extended the meaning area of an apparently traditional concept, and only a reading that bears in mind the familiar Scriptural background involved will really be adequate" (p. 130). (2) Comments on lines 9–12 of "Easter." Maintains that in the image of Christ stretched out on the cross, which is likened to the fine tuning of a musical instrument, "we see that the sinews are stretched not only in order to temper them correctly, but specifically to reach a key high enough for the adequate celebration of 'this most high day'" (p. 131). Points out that church music in Herbert's day was in a high key.

**686. Woodhouse, A. S. P.** "The Seventeenth Century: Donne and His Successors," in *The Poet and His Faith: Religion and Poetry in England from Spenser to Eliot and Auden*, 42–89. Chicago and London: University of Chicago Press.

Comments on the general conditions of English religion and poetry in the seventeenth century that made the period such an important one for religious verse. Contrasts the lives and the religious sensibilities of Herbert and Donne. Sees Herbert's struggle as primarily one against the attractions of the world while Donne's was with "the world, the flesh, and the devil of doubt and cynicism" (p. 67). Maintains that in temper and attitude Herbert resembles John Keble. Briefly discusses the influence of Herbert on Crashaw and Vaughan.

# *1966*

**687. Breen, Timothy Hall.** "The Non-Existent Controversy: Puritan and Anglican Attitudes on Work and Wealth, 1600–1640." *Church History* 35:273–87.

Rejects the notion that early seventeenth-century Anglicanism, in contrast to Puritanism, supported a non-commercial, feudal ethic and argues that Anglican and Puritan attitudes on work and wealth did not greatly differ: "Neither theology monopolized the discussion of the labor discipline, and no man sought Puritan preaching between 1600 and 1640, because he did not hear industry and diligence properly extolled by the Anglican clergy" (p. 287). Maintains that, on the whole, "both theologies defended conservative economic attitudes" and that "it is difficult to find evidence on either side of a new morality blessing the increase of riches" (p. 283). Contends that Herbert, like other Anglicans of the time, was as much a part of his changing world as were the Puritans. Notes several examples in *Outlandish Proverbs* that encourage industry and condemn idleness and sees similarities between the collection and Benjamin Franklin's *Poor Richard* almanacs. Observes that in "Employment (I)" Herbert "describes the world in term of pure and continual act" and shows that "man should ever be industrious if he intended to live harmoniously with God's order" (p. 278).

**688. Charles, Amy M.** "The Manuscript Poems," in *The Shorter Poems of Ralph Knevet: A Critical Edition*, 49–74. Columbus: Ohio State University Press.

Comments on Herbert's influence on Ralph Knevet and maintains that Knevet "was not content to be a mere imitator of Herbert: the *Temple* served more often as a general guide than as a specific model" (p. 64). Points out that of the eighty-two poems in *A Gallery to the Temple* there are only three "direct imitations" of Herbert but that "repeatedly Knevet has caught Herbert's manner or tone" (p. 64). Observes that, unlike Herbert, Knevet "does not cover a wide span of the Christian year" but rather "dwells on certain events commemorated in Christian ceremony that are the essence of his belief" (pp. 64–65); that he fails to follow Herbert's example of avoiding in his devotional poems the use of classical allusion; and that, although he "shares some of Herbert's appreciation of simplicity," Knevet's diction is "generally less restrained" and "more diffuse than Herbert's" (p. 66).

**689. Colie, Rosalie L.** *Paradoxia Epidemica: The Renaissance Tradition of Paradox.* Princeton: Princeton University Press. xx, 553p.

Reprinted, Hamden, Conn.: Archon Books, 1976.

Chapter 6, "*Logos* in *The Temple*" (pp. 190–215), first appeared in *JWCI* (entry 601).

Mentions Herbert throughout. Comments on the use of "rhopographical" images (images of "insignificant objects, odds and ends") and "rhypological" images (images of low and sordid things) in Herbert's poetry. Points out that Dionysius the Areopagite recommends such images as "appropriate to attempt comprehension of the divine essence" (p. 25) and that their use was practiced by certain Hellenistic painters. Argues that this tradition explains "the curious habit of devotional poets' using 'low things' in immediate juxtaposition to the highest, such as Herbert's likeness of Christ to a bag, or of God to a coconut, and Donne's of the flea's triple life to the Trinity" (p.25).

**690. Collmer, Robert G.** "The Function of Death in Certain Metaphysical Poems." *BSE* 6:147–56.
First appeared in *McNR* (entry 649).

**691. Curtis, Jared R.** "William Wordsworth and English Poetry of the Sixteenth and Seventeenth Centuries." *Cornell Library Journal* 1:28–39.
Comments briefly on Wordsworth's acquaintance with Herbert's poetry and prose. Notes that Wordsworth owned a copy of *Herbert's Remains* (1652) and that he refers to *The Country Parson* in "Sacred Religion." Questions whether Wordsworth knew *The Temple* but maintains that Wordsworth's concept of his own great work as a cathedral may have been derived from Herbert. Points out also that Emerson saw certain resemblances between Herbert's "Constancie" and Wordsworth's "Character of a Happy Warrior" but maintains that the similarities are extremely slight.

**692. Daniells, Roy.** "The Mannerist Element in English Literature." *UTQ* 36:1–11.
Briefly discusses certain manneristic elements in Herbert's poetry, especially the note of striving for the moment of divine illumination. Maintains that Herbert's poetry is often a record of an experience "which is more than conventionally devotional and less than mystical" and that what he achieves is "the sudden vision of a transcendental world, of a highly personal kind and of great delicacy," although he is "'ever in warres' and must rise to each instant of serenity by a fresh effort of dedication" (p. 8).

**693. Endicott, Annabel M.** "'The Soul in Paraphrase': George Herbert's 'Library.'" *Renaissance News* 19:14–16.
Argues that the paradox of "The Parson's Library" in *A Priest to the Temple* may come from one of Donne's sermons on the penitential psalms (tentatively assigned by Donne's editors to the winter of 1624–1625). Speculates on "whether Donne's linking of David and Solomon, poet and preacher, sheds any new light on the relationship between *A Priest to the Temple* and *The Temple*" (p. 15) and maintains that "*The Temple*, by combining the functions of David and Solomon, becomes an act of public worship, rather than of private devotion; the full appropriateness of its title becomes clearer; and the reader is spared the frequently embarrassing sensation that he may be eavesdropping on the intimate conversation between a man and his God" (p. 16).

**694. Fitts, Dudley.** "The Collar," in *Master Poems of the English Language*, edited by Oscar Williams, 147–51. New York: Trident Press.
Calls "The Collar" "a miniature drama of revolt against moral authority, a brief violence stilled by a single word almost before it has got well under way" (p. 149). Rejects autobiographical readings of the poem: "The predicament is general: every one of us has known the collar and has longed to slip it. If we were passionate enough, and metrists sufficiently accomplished, we might write the first thirty-two lines of 'The Collar'; so far, it is a superbly adolescent outburst. It is in the last four lines however—indeed, in the last five words—that we watch the transformation into superb poetry"

(pp. 150–51). Comments on the technical finesse of the poem and praises Herbert's control.

**695. Funato, Hideo.** "George Herbert no Eucharist Poems" [Eucharistic Poems of George Herbert]. *Rikkyo Daigaku Eibei Bungaku* (English and American Literature, Rikkyo University) no. 27 (March): 15–33.
Points out that Herbert had a great interest in the two sacraments of Baptism and the Eucharist and notes that images of food and meals appear frequently in his verse.

**696. Gardner, Helen.** "The Titles of Donne's Poems," in *Friendship's Garland: Essays Presented to Mario Praz on His Seventieth Birthday*, 189–207. (Storia e letteratura: Raccolta di studi e testi, 106.) Rome: Edizioni di storia e letteratura.
Maintains that Herbert was the first poet to use titles as "an opportunity for embellishing the poem by the witty aptness of its title" (p. 190). Points out that many of his titles have "an enigmatic, or emblematic, or witty turn" (p. 191). Comments specifically on "The Pulley," the title of which "provides us with an image analogous to the image of the poem, but entirely distinct and unhinted at in the poem," and "The Temper (I) and (II)," the titles of which take "an image from the working of metal, with a pun on human temper, or temperament, to characterize two poems that tell of God's 'tempering' of man's soul" (p. 191).

**697. Hanley, Sara William.** "George Herbert's 'Ana $\left\{\begin{array}{c}\text{Mary}\\\text{Army}\end{array}\right\}$ gram.'" *ELN* 4:16–19.
Points out that in the 1633 edition of *The Temple* the two-line anagram was moved (perhaps by Herbert himself) from its original position between "Church-musick" and "Church-lock and key" and placed between "Avarice" and "To all Angels and Saints." Argues that the poem in its present context takes on additional meaning and that, in fact, in the three poems "we have a tightly knit group, united not in a gradually developing sequence but as a strikingly contrasted pair of poems linked by a third poem placed deliberately between them" (p. 19). Discusses the imagery, wit, conceit, and general cleverness of the anagram.

**698. ———.** "Herbert's 'Frailtie.'" *Expl* 25:item 18.
Sees echoes of the *Spiritual Exercises* of St. Ignatius Loyola in the tripartite structure of "Frailtie" (the three stanzas corresponding to the exercise of the memory, understanding, and will) and in the reference in lines 9–10 to "both Regiments; / The worlds, and thine" (similar to Ignatius's meditation on the Two Standards).

**699. Himuro, Misako.** "George Herbert—sono Hito to shi" [George Herbert—Man and his Poetry]. *Seiki* [Century] no. 194 (July): 65–67.
Comments on the special character and quality of Herbert's verse.

**700. ———.** "*Silex Scintillans* no Shizen—Herbert tono Kanren ni oite" [Nature in *Silex Scintillans*—with special reference to Herbert]. *Eibungaku* [English Literature, English Literary Society of Waseda University] no. 29 (December): 17–39.
Compares and contrasts Herbert and Vaughan, centering on their views of nature.

**701. Knepprath, H. E.** "George Herbert: University Orator and Country Parson." *Southern Speech Journal* 32:105–12.
Comments on Herbert's activities and achievements as a student, teacher, and practitioner of the art of public speaking. Argues that Herbert's views on the purpose

and means of rhetoric changed when he became a country parson: "He found that what constitutes gravity, elevation, transparency, and conciseness in a speech depends not so much on the niceties of invention, arrangement, and language as taught by sixteenth- and seventeenth-century logic and rhetoric as it does upon an understanding of the nature and beliefs of an audience" (p. 112). Examines the few comments on rhetoric found in *The Country Parson*.

**702. Knieger, Bernard.** "The Purchase-Sale: Patterns of Business Imagery in the Poetry of George Herbert." *SEL* 6:111–24.

Demonstrates with many examples drawn from the poems that Herbert frequently uses commercial imagery "to express the very heart of his devotional experience" (p. 111). Argues that such business terms as *debtor, creditor, debt, purchase, sold, commerce, expense, wages, price, profit*, and *business* "play a crucial role in Herbert's strategy of communication" (p. 112). Points out, as an example, that Herbert's "use of *selling* is representative of his employment of business-commercial terminology," for though "he characteristically uses this concept in a seemingly-pejorative sense (in the context of betrayal), this same term simultaneously incorporates within itself the magnitude of God's love for mankind as exemplified by his voluntarily subjecting himself to the utmost degradation for man's sake: from this point of view, paradoxically, the term could not have a more positive content" (pp. 116–17). Suggests that Herbert may have been influenced by his observance of the immense expansion of English commerce during his own day, by the Puritan work ethic, and by the use of such imagery in the Bible. Argues that in part his usage is shaped by his "conception of the blood-sacrifice of Christ: that is, Herbert conceived of the crucifixion as a purchase-sale in which Christ, going about God's business, purchased (for man) mankind's salvation at the cost of His own degradation and agony" (p. 111). Also argues that Herbert "conceives of commerce and of business employment as useful or potentially useful activities, indeed a sign of God's providence" (p. 124).

**703. ——.** "Teaching George Herbert in Israel—and in America? *CLAJ* 10:143–48.

Concerned with making Herbert's poetry acceptable and meaningful for modern students, whether Israeli or American, who do not share Herbert's religious beliefs or his commitment to otherworldliness. Maintains that the teacher of Herbert must emphasize close critical readings of the poems and must point out their universality: "We must relate the psychological conflicts and the specific religious concerns of Herbert to our own psychological conflicts and our search for centers of value while simultaneously demonstrating the artistic achievement of one of the masters of English verse" (p. 148). Illustrates this approach by presenting a series of questions for the study of "Vertue." Comments on "Vanitie (I)" and "The Pearl" as being central to an understanding of Herbert's universality.

**704. La Guardia, Eric.** "Figural Imitation in English Renaissance Poetry," in *Actes du IVe Congrès de l'Association Internationale de Litterature Comparée*, edited by François Jost, 844–54. The Hague and Paris: Mouton and Co.

Compares and contrasts medieval and Renaissance figuralism. Comments on the special character of Renaissance figuralism, maintaining that the Renaissance poet participated in two worlds, the ideal and the mundane, or to use Sidney's terms, the golden and the brazen. Illustrates his arguments by commenting on the treatment of nature, love, and art in a number of Renaissance poems. Briefly comments on Herbert's "Jordan (II)," suggesting that "love" becomes a figura in the poem.

705. McGill, William J., Jr. "George Herbert's View of the Eucharist." *Lock Haven Review* no. 8:16–24.

Comments on Herbert's theology and his religious sensibility, particularly on his eucharistic theology. Argues that an examination of Herbert's eucharistic theology, as found in his poems and in *The Country Parson*, "shows that while he rejects out of hand certain doctrines [such as transubstantiation and impanation], he does not propose any substitute dogmatic formulation" (p. 24). Maintains that Herbert clearly believes in the Real Presence but "he declines to speculate further, thus reflecting one of the principal characteristics of the Church to which he belonged, his primary concern for God's grace and man's salvation, and his preoccupation with the tasks of devotion" (p. 24). Argues, however, that Herbert's piety was "intensely liturgical, even sacramental, in its expression" and that "it was in the eucharist that it had its fullest manifestation" (p. 24).

706. Martz, Louis L. *The Poem of the Mind: Essays on Poetry, English and American.* New York: Oxford University Press. xiii, 231p.

Reprinted in paperback, 1969.

Collection of previously published essays and one essentially new essay that discuss poetry "of the interior life, where the mind, actually aware of an outer world of drifting, unstable forms, finds within itself the power to create coherence and significance" (p. ix). Three essays discuss Herbert. Chapter 3, "Meditative Action and 'The Metaphysick Style'" (pp. 33–53), in a shorter version, first appeared in the introduction to *The Meditative Poem: An Anthology of Seventeenth-Century Verse* (entry 613) and also includes material from an essay on Donne in *Master Poems of the English Language*, edited by Oscar Williams (New York: Trident Press, 1966). Discusses the nature of meditative action in seventeenth-century English poetry and distinguishes between meditative action and metaphysical style. Maintains that Herbert is linked to Donne not so much by style as by their both sharing the meditative mode. Chapter 4, "Edward Taylor: Preparatory Meditations" (pp. 54–81) originally appeared in the foreword to Donald E. Stanford's edition of *The Poems of Edward Taylor* (entry 535). Comments on the influence of Herbert on Taylor and shows how the two poets differ in their uses of metrics, diction, imagery, and so forth. Chapter 5, "Whitman and Dickinson: Two Aspects of the Self" (pp. 82–104), essentially a new essay, includes passages from a review-article on Thomas Johnson's edition of Emily Dickinson's poems (1955) in *UTQ* 26 (1957): 556–65. Brief comparison of Herbert and Dickinson.

707. Miles, Josephine, and Hanan C. Selvin. "A Factor Analysis of the Vocabulary of Poetry in the Seventeenth Century," in *The Computer and Literary Style: Introductory Essays and Studies*, edited by Jacob Leed, 116–27. (Kent Studies in English, no. 2.) Kent, Ohio: Kent State University Press.

Reprinted in *The Metaphysical Poets*, edited by Gerald Hammond (entry 985), 182–96.

Presents a "factor analysis of the sixty nouns, adjectives, and verbs used at least ten times in a consecutive thousand lines by each of at least thirty poets in the seventeenth century" to see if such an analysis will reveal "a number of factors useful for characterizing certain groups of poets and poetic habits of style" (p. 116). Includes Herbert's *The Church*. Shows, for example, that Donne's word usage has much in common with that of such poets as Carew and Shirley and "least with Herbert, Wither, and Milton" (p. 121). Argues that certain emphases become more obvious through such a study than they do in literary histories, such as "the primacy of the Donne tradition;

the ethical allegiance of Herbert to Jonson; the early innovative forces of Sandys and Quarles toward the Biblical aesthetic; and the isolation of Vaughan from his religious confrères, in contrast to the surprising general continuity in Prior and Pomfret" (p. 125).

**708. Mollenkott, Virginia Ramey.** "George Herbert's Life of Love of God." *Christianity Today* 10, no. 24:11–13.
Laments the fact that Herbert is not read or appreciated by modern evangelicals. Points out that in the seventeenth and eighteenth centuries he was greatly respected by Nonconformists. Outlines some of the main features of Herbert's religious sensibility as reflected in his poetry. Maintains that "the most important insight that Herbert's poetry offers the twentieth-century evangelical is his concept of organic Christian living" (p. 12) and that "it was precisely Herbert's Christocentricity that made him most completely himself as a creative individual" (p. 13).

**709. ———.** "The Many and the One in George Herbert's 'Providence.'" *CLAJ* 10:34–41.
Argues that "Providence" is Herbert's "equivalent to Spenser's 'Cantos of Mutabilitie' or to Hopkins' 'Pied Beauty' and its central motif is that of the One in the Many and the Many in the One" (p. 34). Maintains that Herbert found his theme of the oneness of Providence behind the multiplicity of phenomena" (p. 35) in the Apocrypha, specifically in the Wisdom of Solomon 8:1. Presents a detailed reading of the poem.

**710. Morita, Katsumi.** "Imagery and Themes in George Herbert's Poems— 'Prayer (I)' and *The Temple* (I)." *Ehime Daigaku Kiyo*, part I (Bulletin of Ehime University) 12 (December): 103–17.
Part 1 of a three-part series. Points out that "'Prayer (I)' is of special significance in that it includes metaphor and imagery used to figure forth the main thought in *The Temple*" (p. 103). Shows how the imagery of this poem is developed in other poems such as "Gratefulnesse," "Businesse," "Sion," "Affliction (I)," "The Search," "Love (III)," "The Pilgrimage," "Home," "Man," "Miserie," "Longing," "Mans medley," "Coloss.iii.3," "Vanitie (II)," "Easter-wings," "Whitsunday," "The Flower," "The Storm," and "The Altar." For parts 2 and 3, see entries 733 and 921.

**711. Pennel, Charles A., and William P. Williams.** "The Unity of *The Temple*." *XUS* 5:37–45.
Comments on the unity of the central portion of *The Temple*, "that portion which follows the purification on the porch and the sacramental celebration of the first fourteen poems in 'The Church' and which precedes the group of poems on 'last things' with which 'The Church' closes" (p. 37). Maintains that Herbert "patterned the poems which lead from the sacrament to death and judgment as a pilgrimage" and that "the progress of the pilgrim soul, under the care of Christ's church, is the *leitmotif* of the central portion of *The Temple*" (p. 38). Traces out this design and maintains that "The Pilgrimage," although not a "key" to *The Temple*, offers "itself as a useful trope for illuminating 'The Church'" (p. 39).

**712. Reiter, Robert E.** "George Herbert's 'Anagram': A Reply to Professor Leiter." *CE* 28:59–60.
In part a reply to Louis H. Leiter (entry 666). Comments on the phrase *pitch His tent* in "Anagram of the Virgin Marie." Points out that in the Greek version of John

1:14 (usually translated as "and the word was made flesh and dwelt among us") the verb *eskenosen* literally means *pitched a tent*. Argues that "the wit of the poem, the appropriateness of the anagram, and the meaning of the poem are directly dependent upon the literal meaning of the Greek text" (p. 60).

**713. Rickey, Mary Ellen.** *Utmost Art: Complexity in the Verse of George Herbert.* Lexington: University of Kentucky Press. xv, 200p.

Part of chapter 4 originally appeared as "Herbert's Technical Development" (entry 615).

Proposes "to examine the nearly paradoxical co-existence of complexity and seeming simplicity in Herbert's English poetry, to point out tropological materials hitherto overlooked, and, by exploring the development of his art and his own statements about the nature of divine poetry, to show his endeavor to concentrate a great store of motifs in small and unpretentious verses" (pp. xiv-xv). Chapter 1, "The Classical Materials" (pp. 1–58), argues that Herbert used many classical allusions, images, and motifs and that he used these "as tellingly as he did his familiarity with the English Church, the natural world, or the teachings of the Fathers" (p. 2). Maintains that, unlike his Elizabethan predecessors and many of his contemporaries, Herbert weaves these materials so skillfully into the texture of his verse that the modern reader may miss them altogether. Cites numerous examples of Herbert's use of classical materials and maintains that his main purpose for using them is "the consistent demonstration of the degree to which the happiness of the Christian surpasses that of the pre-Christian, or natural, man and of the contrast between God's total concern for His creatures and the meretricious activities of the deities of the ancients" (p. 57). Concludes that Herbert once again "demonstrates the propriety of subordinating the natural to the divine" (p. 58). Chapter 2, "Sacred Quibbles" (pp. 59–91), maintains that Herbert's serious puns and witty quibbles "constitute a weightier component of his verse than is generally conceded" (p. 60). Points out many examples to show that, unlike Donne, who "moves freely from one trope to another," Herbert frequently sustains in one poem two or more metaphorical systems simultaneously, thus allowing him "to sound his imagerial notes in polyphonic fashion" (p. 60). Presents a partial catalogue of Herbert's uses of serious puns "which briefly introduce new metaphorical dimensions by overlapping two or more figures" (p. 72) and argues that for Herbert "the neatness of the pun made possible the balance and harmony of some of his best poems" (p. 91). Chapter 3, "Quiddities: The Titles" (pp. 92–102), comments on Herbert's highly original uses of titles for the poems of *The Temple*. Cites a number of examples to show both the often-missed metaphorical complexity of many of his titles and the spareness of many others, which "set off the richness of the arguments within the poems" (p. 102). Chapter 4, "Time's Pruning Knife: The Development" (pp. 103–47), reviews several aspects of Herbert's development as a poet by comparing the first and second halves of *The Temple*, by comparing the poems in the Williams MS with those written later, and by commenting on the revisions in the Williams MS. Discusses Herbert's increasingly mature handling of imagery and invention and argues that "the nature of Herbert's revisions, his increasingly fine discipline of his imagery, and his progressive shifting from literal to metaphorical titles—suggest a gradual change in his conception of the devotional lyric" (p. 120). Illustrates that when "one examines the early and late sections of *The Temple*, he does indeed find that the two groups contain different *kinds* of poems" (p. 120). Comments also on Herbert's mastery of versification and his highly original stanzaic inventions to show that, like the changes in his handling of imagery, his prosodic mutations also "evince his steady pursuit of precision and concentration of idea" (p. 134). Chapter 5, "The

Clothing of the Sonne: Complexity in Apparent Simplicity" (pp. 148–79), discusses Herbert's theory of poetry and comments on his complex simplicity. Argues that it is "a kind of simplicity on our part, as well as myopia, if, noting that Herbert is genuinely holy, we insist on reading his verse as jejune. For its primary impact to be one of lowly-hearted praise is precisely what he intended; and a refusal to recognize that a well-equipped adult mind has been painstakingly disciplined to make this humility possible springs from our obstinacy, not Herbert's deficiency" (p. 178). Appendix: "Herbert and William Alabaster" (pp. 180–84) comments on resemblances between the two poets, points out specific parallels, and suggests that Herbert may have known Alabaster's English poetry in manuscript. Notes (pp. 185–95); index (pp. 196–200).
Reviews:
W. A. Armstrong, *English* 16 (1967): 148–49
B. Drake, *JEGP* 66 (1967): 452–55
G. L. Finney, *RenQ* 20 (1967): 69–71
John R. Mulder, *SCN* 26 (1968): 9–10
H. L. Richmond, *CL* 22 (1970): 81–85

**714. Stewart, Stanley.** *The Enclosed Garden: The Tradition and the Image in Seventeenth-Century Poetry.* Madison, Milwaukee, London: University of Wisconsin Press. xiv, 226p.
Considers the figure of the enclosed garden as it appeared in the poetry of the late sixteenth and seventeenth centuries. Argues that this tradition is the proper context for an understanding of such poems as Herbert's "Paradise" and Marvell's "The Garden." Shows the extensive use of the tradition, based on the allegorization of the Song of Songs, in Herbert's poetry. Discusses also Herbert's uses of time in his poetry. Mentions Herbert throughout with specific comments on individual poems, including "Paradise," "The Thanksgiving," "Longing," "The Flower," "The Crosse," "Evensong," "Life," "Time," "Sunday," "Employment (I)," and "In Solarium."

**715. ———.** "Time and *The Temple.*" *SEL* 6:97–110.
Reprinted in *Essential Articles for the Study of George Herbert's Poetry*, edited by John R. Roberts (entry 1216), 363–73.
Discusses the structural integrity of *The Temple*, especially the function of *The Church Militant* in the design of the whole. Maintains that the placement of *The Church Militant* "is a hieroglyphic of a temporal relation" and argues that "the absence of intensity in 'Church Militant,' like that in 'Church Porch', cannot be detached from the function of the poem within the larger structure" (p. 105). Contends that, unlike the voice in *The Church*, which reflects the anxieties and struggles of man with time (and thus change), the speaker in *The Church Militant* "sees the world with the vision of one in a state outside of life, a state which was achieved by the proper redemption of time" (p. 105). Argues that *The Church Militant* is "an apocalyptic poem" and that "its tone is detached and austere because its speaker sees the past, the present, and the future with equal clarity" (p. 105). Concludes that *The Church Militant*, unlike *The Church*, which portrays the struggles of man in time, is concerned "with the movement of the Church throughout all time" (p. 105).

# 1967

**716. Barnes, T. R.** "The Seventeenth Century," in *English Verse: Voice and Movement from Wyatt to Yeats*, 58–116. Cambridge: University Press.

Comments briefly on some of the major elements of Herbert's verse, especially the conceits, concentration, colloquial tone, dramatic elements, rhythms, music, rejection of the pastoral, complexity, and so forth. Presents a close reading of "The Windows" and "Jordan (I)."

**717. Block, Haskell M.** "The Alleged Parallel of Metaphysical and Symbolist Poetry." *CLS* 4:145–59.
Reprinted in *Comparative Literature: Matter and Method*, edited by Alfred Owen Aldridge (Urbana: University of Illinois Press, 1969), 90–105.
Denies that there is a basic parallel between metaphysical and symbolist poetry. Tries to account for the alleged likenesses by reviewing the criticism of T. S. Eliot, Cleanth Brooks, and others. Discusses also those critics who deny the likeness and suggests properties of both kinds of poetry that prove them basically unlike. No specific reference to Herbert.

**718. Brown, William J.** "Herbert's 'The Collar' and Shakespeare's *1 Henry IV*." *AN&Q* 6:51–53.
Comments on the pun *collar-choler* in Herbert's poem. Argues that at the beginning of the poem "the *cause* of his unhappiness is felt to be the 'collar,' whereas in truth it is his 'choler. ' When, in the final stanza, the anger of his rebellion is seen in perspective as a childish tantrum, the implication is that true happiness lies in submission to the will of God—in acceptance of the 'collar'" (p. 51). Comments on Shakespeare's pun on *collar-choler* in *1 Henry IV* and notes correspondences between Herbert's poem and the play: the pun "with the idea of religious restraint and sobriety as responsible for blasting the joys of youth is unusual and reinforced by strong verb similarities: blow, sigh, and abroad" (p. 52). Poses the question of whether Herbert had Shakespeare's play in mind while composing his poem.

**719. Champion, Larry S.** "Body Versus Soul in George Herbert's 'The Collar.'" *Style* 1:131–37.
Argues that "The Collar" is not simply a continuous statement of rebellion but is rather "a carefully articulated dialogue between the body and the soul" (p. 131). Divides the poem into four sections: (1) lines 1–16 (the body rebels); (2) lines 17–26 (the soul replies); (3) lines 27–32 (the body replies to the soul's reply); and (4) lines 33–36 (God's command for humility is set forth through the soul, and the body, "its audacity obliterated by the simple command, presents itself in childlike obedience" [p. 133]). Shows how the narrative, the metrical structure, and the imagery combine to support such a reading and argues that the ending of the poem is neither a surprise nor an abrupt conclusion.

**720. Charles, Amy M.** "George Herbert: Priest, Poet, Musician." *Journal of the Viola da Gamba Society of America* 4:27–36.
Reprinted in *Essential Articles for the Study of George Herbert's Poetry*, edited by John R. Roberts (entry 1216), 249–57.
Discusses the subtlety, complexity, and pervasiveness of music in Herbert's poetry and comments on the central role that it played in his life: "In a very real sense, music *was* Herbert's sustenance on earth and its upward movement his most treasured avenue to God" (p. 36). Points out that, although there are numerous musical allusions in Herbert's poetry, his "open use of musical language and imagery is less than would be expected, if one looks only for the terms in a musical glossary" (p. 27). Notes, for example, that Herbert mentions the viol only once (in *The Country Parson*)

yet figures of tuning and strings "provide some of Herbert's most effective musical figures" (p. 28). Cautions against finding musical allusions where none were intended (such as references to "measure," "score," "springs"). Points out that, although many of Herbert's poems were set to music by later musicians, few of his hymns and anthems are in general use today as hymns, primarily because of their stanzaic complexities and subtleties. Comments on Herbert's skillful uses of sound in his poetry and maintains that "it is doubtful that he would have used them so widely had his sense of the sound of words not been developed and refined by his music" (p. 35).

**721. Davis, Bernard, and Elizabeth Davis, eds.** *Poets of the Early Seventeenth Century.* (Routledge English Texts, ed. T. S. Dorsch.) London: Routledge and Kegan Paul. x, 246p.

Includes a general introduction to early seventeenth-century English poetry (pp. 1–6); twenty-four poems by Herbert (pp. 53–72); and a biographical sketch of the poet and a brief introduction to his poems (pp. 193–95), followed by notes to the poems (pp. 195–201). Calls *The Temple* "a unique monument to the faith, worship, and liturgy of the Anglican Church" (p. 194) and observes that the major theme of Herbert's poetry is "one of assurance in the power of Divine mercy and redemption to strengthen and perfect human frailty" (p. 195). Praises the simplicity and sincerity of Herbert's poems and briefly compares and contrasts them to Donne's.

**722. Ferry, Anne Davidson, ed.** *Religious Prose of Seventeenth-Century England.* (Borzoi Anthology of 17th-Century English Literature, vol. 5.) New York: Alfred A. Knopf. 258p.

Includes a general critical introduction to the nature and varieties of religious prose during the period (pp. 3–29). Reproduces chapter 7 of Herbert's *A Priest to the Temple* (pp. 241–43).

**723. Foster, D. W.** "George Herbert." *Theology* (London) 70:68–76.

An appreciative essay that comments on Herbert's modern relevancy: "He gives us depth, complication, and immediacy of experience" (p. 73). Argues that Herbert's sanctity, though real, is "far removed from *sancta simplicitas*" (p. 69) and attempts to demythologize accounts of Herbert's life. Comments on the complex religious sensibility and poetic excellence of Herbert's verse and suggests that the modern reader can respond to Herbert in the same way that he can to "the life and work of Gandhi, Dolci, or Pope John without necessarily sharing their tenets" (p. 70). Discusses briefly the comprehensive biblical symbolism that informs Herbert's poetry and exemplifies this richness by commenting on "Affliction (I)." Contrasts Herbert and Keble.

**724. French, Roberts W.** "Herbert's 'Vertue.'" *Expl* 26:item 4.

Discusses the meaning of the word *coal* in the last stanza of "Vertue" and argues that it should be taken in the sense of "glowing coal" or "redhot coal" rather than "cinder" or "ashes" in order to sustain the main simile of the stanza. For a reply, see Dan S. Collins (entry 785).

**725. Greenwood, E. B.** "Putting the 'Romance' Back into Stylistics: A Reply to Helen Vendler." *EIC* 17:256–57.

Reply to Helen Vendler's review of *Essays on Style and Language: Linguistic and Critical Approaches to Literary Styles,* edited by Roger Fowler, in *EIC* 16 (1966): 457–63. Defends his reading of Herbert's "Prayer (I)" (entry 655).

**726. Herbert, George.** *A Choice of George Herbert's Verse.* Selected with an introduction by R. S. Thomas. London: Faber and Faber. 95p.

Presents a biographical sketch of Herbert and relates him to the historical period. Sees Herbert as a reflection of the best in seventeenth-century Anglican sensibility. Maintains that Herbert's relevance to the modern world "is bound up with the relevance of Christianity, and with the possibility of a fruitful relationship between Christianity and poetry" (p. 15) and that he "commands a way of life for the individual that is still viable" (p. 17). Selections from *The Temple* and from Walton's *Life*.

727. ———. *George Herbert: Selected Poetry*, edited by Joseph H. Summers. (Signet Classic Poetry Series, edited by John Hollander.) New York and Toronto: American Library; London: New English Library. xxxviii, 288p.
    Contents (pp. v-viii). Introduction by Joseph H. Summers (pp. ixxxvii). A general note on the text by John Hollander (p. xxix). A note on this edition (pp. xxxi-xxxiii). Chronology (pp. xxxv-xxxvi). Selected bibliography (pp. xxxvii-xxxviii). *The Temple* (pp. 41–265). Poems from the Williams MS excluded from *The Temple* (pp. 267–75). Poems from Walton's *Lives* (pp. 277–78). Translations of Herbert's Latin poems (pp. 279–80). Doubtful poems (pp. 281–84). Index of first lines (pp. 285–88). In the introduction, Summers calls Herbert "the author of the best extended collection of religious lyrics in English, a man whose art is as unquestionable as is his spiritual authenticity" (p. ix). Notes ways for the inexperienced reader to approach the poems of Herbert. Comments primarily on *The Church-Porch* because it is most likely to present problems to the reader. Bases his text of the poems primarily on Hutchinson's edition (entry 266). Includes explanatory notes.

728. **Honda, Kin-ichiro.** "Herbert to Milton no Kyori—Futatsu no Shikan wo Jiku toshite" [Herbert and Milton—Two Attitudes towards Poetry]. *Hokkaido Daigaku Gaikokugo Gaikoku Bungaku Kenkyu* [Studies in Foreign Language and Literature, Hokkaido University] 14:37–70.
    Contrasts Herbert's and Milton's theories of poetic composition. Characterizes Herbert's poems as records of personal dialogues with God and sees Milton's verse as more didactic.

729. **Kawata, Akira.** "George Herbert no Shukyo-shi—sono Riron to Jissai" [George Herbert's Religious Poetry: His Theory and Practice]. *Ichinoseki Kosen Kenkyu Kiyo* [Bulletin of Ichinoseki Technical College] no. 1 (March): 14–24.
    Considers Herbert's theory and practice of composing religious verse. Points out that, while he sought simplicity and plainness of style, he did not always achieve them in his verse. Argues, however, that Herbert does not reject the use of wit and invention in poetry, as long as they are put to proper use in a spiritually sincere celebration of God.

730. **Lever, Tresham.** "Charles I and the Herberts," in *The Herberts of Wilton*, 97–117. London: John Murray.
    Comments on Herbert's kinsman and patron, William Herbert, third earl of Pembroke, who, in 1620, according to Walton, exerted his influence in order to obtain for Herbert the office of Public Orator at Cambridge and who later contributed money to assist Herbert with the restoration of the little church at Leighton Bromswold. Points out that, according to Walton, after William Herbert's death, his brother, Philip Herbert, fourth earl of Pembroke, succeeded in persuading King Charles I to bestow on Herbert the rectory of Fugglestone-with-Bemerton.

731. **Miles, Josephine.** *Style and Proportion: The Language of Prose and Poetry.* Boston: Little, Brown and Co. ix, 212p.

Discusses how "words and structures of language in literature differ from era to era, from place to place, from kind to kind" in order "to gain a more general view of literary styles of language" (p. v). Analyzes sixty poetical texts and sixty prose texts, including Herbert's *The Church* (through "Mattens").

**732. Mollenkott, Virginia R.** "Christian Humanism Through the Centuries," in *Adamant and Stone Chips: A Christian Humanist Approach to Knowledge,* 31–52. Waco, Tex.: Word Books.
Maintains that Herbert's "The Elixir" "admirably summarizes the Christian humanist approach to life, to the environment and the duties of this world" (p. 50). Points out three detriments to Christian living: activism, secularism, and fragmentation. Maintains that Richard Sibbes alludes to Herbert's central metaphor in his *A Learned Commentary* (1656).

**733. Morita, Katsumi.** "Imagery and Themes in George Herbert's Poems—'Prayer (I)' and *The Temple* (2)." *Ehime Daigaku Kiyo* (part 1) [Bulletin of Ehima University] 13 (December): 73–86.
Part 2 of a three-part series of articles. Points out that images of the Eucharist are prominent in Herbert's poetry. Comments on the images in "The Bunch of Grapes," "The Agonie," "Superliminare," "The Invitation," "Peace," "The Banquet," "Longing," "The Sacrifice," "Sunday," and "The Familie." For parts 1 and 3, see entries 710 and 921.

**734. Nomachi, Susumu.** "George Herbert: Man's Innate Trust in the Eternal." *The Annual Collection of Critical Studies* (Gaskushuin University, Tokyo) 14:1–51.
Comments on Donne's influence on Herbert and contrasts their spiritual sensibilities and inner conflicts: "While Donne's was a furious battle in which external elements participated, Herbert's was a conflict of introspection; his was the sort of question to be dealt with in his own breast, hidden from vulgar eyes" (p. 3). Discusses Herbert's interest in concrete things, his refinement of taste, and his love of neatness and sees these qualities as reflecting a feminine element in Herbert's nature. Points out a number of manifestations of Herbert's feminine character in the language of his poems and in his verse forms and rhyme schemes. Comments on Herbert's dualism in his response to the world outside himself and to the various competing antitheses in his own mind. Contrasts Herbert's view of beauty and order with the views of Donne and Vaughan and suggests that Herbert's sense of orderliness and his attention to minute detail may have been influenced by his mother. Analyzes in detail "Prayer (I)" as an example of Herbert's feminine mind and method and comments on *The Church-Porch* and "Discipline" as examples of Herbert's intuitive manner. Concludes by discussing the development of Herbert's thought, especially his idea of God and death, and maintains that "the minute care, feminine in its essential character, for the matters of daily life, never for a moment deserted Herbert's mind" (p. 51).

**735. Peterson, Douglas L.** *The English Lyric from Wyatt to Donne: A History of the Plain and Eloquent Styles.* Princeton: Princeton University Press. vi, 391p.
Traces the development of the lyric during the sixteenth century, stressing the medieval origins of the plain and eloquent styles and accounting for the changes and relative importance of both. Sees Herbert as a master of the plain style and maintains that he—along with Vaughan, Traherne, Crashaw, and other devotional poets of the seventeenth century—continues "a tradition of anticourtly and otherworldly verse

originating in the simple didactic poetry of the Middle Ages and becoming in the seventeenth century the dominant and most vigorous mode of English lyric" (pp. 356–57). Maintains that Herbert, like Donne, was strongly opposed to "studied eloquence as well as courtly love poetry" and that he "avoids those schemes which in the sonnets contribute to the mellifluousness of the sugared style" (p. 240). Several references to Herbert and to individual poems throughout.

**736. Poggi, Valentina.** *George Herbert.* (Testi e saggi di letterature moderne, 10.) Bologna: Casa Editrice Prof. Riccardo Pàtron. 263p.
 Divided into three major chapters: (1) "Il poeta di Dio" (pp. 13–130); (2) "Finito e infinito in *The Temple*" (pp. 131–201); and (3) "Il 'Final Twist'" (pp. 203–52). Chapter 1 is subdivided into three sections. (1) "Il sacro ministero della poesia" presents a biographical sketch of Herbert, discusses the major themes of his poetry, and comments on the relationship between poetic language and the expression of religious sentiments in his poems. (2) "Il volto di Dio" surveys Herbert's presentation of God in the poems and maintains that he views God primarily as a friend rather than as a lover or a father. (3) "La condizione umana" comments on man's relationship to God in Herbert's poetry and maintains that the image of dust is a major key to understanding *The Temple*. Presents a detailed reading of "Easter-wings." Chapter 2 is subdivided into two sections. (1) "Il senso dello spazio e l'angoscia del vuoto" considers the theme of temptation in *The Temple* and concludes that Herbert views temptation as a condition of man's free will. Contends that Herbert associates open spaces and freedom of movement with danger and temptation. (2) "La misura del posto e la casa interiore" maintains that Herbert associates joy and peace with confined spaces. Chapter 3 describes this poetic closure in Herbert's poems, especially his use of surprise endings and reversals. Presents a close reading of "Affliction (I)," "Redemption," "Prayer (I)," "Frailtie," "Constancie," "The Collar," "The Pulley," "The Flower," and "Sinne (I)." Selected bibliography (pp. 253–57).
Reviews:
Robert Ellrodt, *EA* 22 (1969): 424–26
H. M. Richmond, *CL* 22 (1970): 81–85

**737. Reilly, R. J.** "God, Man, and Literature." *Thought* 42:561–83.
 Maintains that "since the writer's felt apprehension of his relationship to God shapes his literary imagination, it might well be used as a principle of classification of literature" (p. 561). Outlines five basic categories: (1) "the 'rapt' writers, those who have a sense, or awareness, of their intimate union with God" (p. 568); (2) "the 'excited' writers, those who also apprehend that the relationship between God and man is an intimate one, but whose apprehension is more intellectual than that of the writers in Group I" (p. 568); (3) "the 'normal' writers or 'humanistic' writers, those who accept the close relationship posited for them by their religions or philosophies but for whom the relationship is not existentially central" (p. 568); (4) "the writers in whose work there is less than normal recognition of the relationship, whether or not their religion or philosophy posits such a relationship" (p. 568); and (5) "the 'fervid deniers' of the relationship" (p. 568). Places Herbert in the second category.

**738. Roscelli, William John.** "The Metaphysical Milton (1625–1631)." *TSLL* 8:463–84.
 Comments on the possible influence of the metaphysical poets on Milton and concludes that "(1) in at least six English poems which he composed between 1625 and 1631 and which have survived, Milton does employ images which can properly

be considered metaphysical; (2) the use of metaphysical images, in general, is restricted to poems whose ostensible subject is death; (3) some of these metaphysical images find parallels in the poems of George Herbert, but the echoes are not so strong as to suggest direct influence; (4) the internal evidence provided by the English poems substantially confirms Raleigh's judgment that Milton was 'untouched' by Donne" (p. 484). Maintains that the differences between Milton and Herbert are not so great as those between Milton and Donne. Sees specific resemblances between stanza 5 of "On the Death of a fair Infant" and Herbert's "Death," between the proem of "On the Morning of Christ's Nativity" and Herbert's "Christmas," and between lines 79–82 of "On the Morning of Christ's Nativity" and Herbert's "Whitsunday," lines 13–16.

**739. Ruthven, Grey.** *For George Herbert.* Cambridge, Mass.: Pym-Randall Press. unpaged.
An original five-stanza poem on Herbert.

**740. Starkman, Miriam K., ed.** *Seventeenth-Century English Poetry*, vol. 1. (Borzoi Anthology of 17th-Century English Literature, vol. 1.) New York: Alfred A. Knopf. xiii, 294, viiip.
Includes a general critical introduction to metaphysical poetry (pp. 3–24). Calls Herbert "the source and well-spring of devotional poetry for the seventeenth century" (p. 8). Outlines the major themes of *The Temple* and comments on the influences that shaped Herbert's art, such as the liturgy, iconography, emblem books, and music. Contrasts Herbert briefly with Donne and Vaughan. Presents a biographical sketch of Herbert (p. 111) and reproduces fifty-five poems from *The Temple* (pp. 112–60), with brief explanatory notes. Selected bibliography (p. 292).

**741. Syudo, Tomoko.** "St. Mary Magdelene wo megutte—Herbert to Crashaw" [St. Mary Magdelene—Herbert and Crashaw]. *Shokei Jogakuin Tandai Kenkyu Hokoku-shu* [Bulletin of the Shokei Women's Junior College] no. 14 (October): 13–28.
Compares the faith, serenity, and chaste simplicity of Herbert's "Marie Magdalene" with Crashaw's feverish, complex, ecstatic treatment of the saint in "The Weeper."

**742. Tayler, Edward W., ed.** *Literary Criticism of Seventeenth-Century England.* (Borzoi Anthology of 17th-Century English Literature, vol. 4.) New York: Alfred A. Knopf. xii, 427, vp.
Includes a general critical introduction to the literary criticism of the seventeenth century (pp. 3–32). Presents a brief introduction to Herbert (pp. 259–60) and reproduces "My God, where is that ancient heat towards thee," "Love (II)," "Jordan (I) and (II)," and "A Wreath" (pp. 260–62), all poems that deal with the relationship of poetry and religion.

**743. Weiss, Wolfgang.** "Note On Herbert's 'The Collar.'" *N&Q* n.s. 15, 212:93.
Maintains that both the image of the collar in the title and the images *rope of sands* and *good cable* in the poem "express the idea of thraldom in the relationship of god and man" and are derived from the old etymology of the word *religio* (*ligare*, to bind).

**744. Whitlock, Baird W.** "From the Counter-Renaissance to the Baroque." *BuR* 15:46–60.
Discusses certain differences between sixteenth-century and seventeenth-century art forms, between the Counter-Renaissance (ca. 1520–1620) and the baroque (ca.

1620–1720). Maintains that Donne and Herbert "represent the shift that took place between the two periods" (p. 48). Points out, for example, that "both created a new poetic form in nearly every poem they wrote, but Donne's metrical and rhyme innovations very seldom add to the unification or meaning of the whole poem, whereas Herbert's variations almost without exception do" (p. 48). Considers Herbert as a baroque poet and sees *The Temple* as offering "good evidence of the manner in which the Baroque poet sought to organize his previously separate works into a more unified sequence than the mere chronological or even haphazard collections of the previous century" (p. 57). Mentions briefly the formal methods of unification found in "Man," "The Collar," "The Church-floore," and *The Church-Porch.*

**745. Williamson, George.** *Six Metaphysical Poets: A Reader's Guide.* New York: Farrar, Straus and Giroux. 274p.

Published in England under the title *A Reader's Guide to The Metaphysical Poets: John Donne, George Herbert, Richard Crashaw, Abraham Cowley, Henry Vaughan, Andrew Marvell* (London: Thames and Hudson, 1968).

Paperback edition, 1968, reissued several times.

General introduction to Herbert's life and poetry (pp. 94–118). Includes prose summaries of the arguments of sixteen major poems. Comments primarily on Herbert's wit and ingenuity and notes that "he seems to have found his mode of wit or rhetoric in the Bible, or its familiar illustration" (p. 102). Maintains that Christ's parables "also supply the key to Herbert's poetry in method, imagery, and diction" (p. 102). Contends that Herbert "is more like Donne than appears on the surface" (p. 118). Brief bibliography (pp. 263–65).

**746. Winters, Yvor.** "Aspects of the Short Poem in the English Renaissance," in *Forms of Discovery,* 1–120. Chicago: Alan Swallow.

Critical discussion of "Church-monuments" (pp. 83–88). Calls the poem "the last word in the sophistication of the plain style" and one of "the most impressive short poems in the English Renaissance" (p. 84). Praises its "quiet profundity" and "impeccable organization" (p. 87). Comments in some detail on the relationships between the syntax of the poem and its lines and between the syntax and the stanzaic form and considers such matters as enjambment, punctuation, sentence lengths, rhythm, diction, metaphor, and tone. Notes that the poem has no exclusively Christian references: "The poem deals with the vanity of life and the necessity of preparing for death" (p. 86). Maintains that in many respects the poem is uncharacteristic of Herbert's poetry, much of which is marred by "cloying and almost infantile pietism" that "leads him into abject clichés" (p. 88).

**747. Ziegelmaier, Gregory.** "Liturgical Symbol and Reality in the Poetry of George Herbert." *ABR* 18:344–53.

Comments on pervasive liturgical elements in Herbert's poetry, many of which are hidden from the modern reader unfamiliar with both the liturgy itself and the habit of mind it produces and reflects. Maintains that Herbert turns to the liturgy "sometimes for its power to concentrate dogma, but more often for its emotional effects" (p. 345). Contends that Herbert's "originality is more devotional than strictly liturgical" (p. 349). Concludes that Herbert "intuitively finds the objects proper to his sense and turns them into praise: the rhythms and colors of the emblems, sculpture, vestments, the music of song and organ, of smell, of the upward wreathing of incense; the use of body in gestures and movements in the handling of material things used in worship; the use of the lips in the mystery of words" (p. 353). Notes also that "his words have their spirit, their evocative power; gestures their vitality, meaning" and that "for those students for whom sacrifice and altar are realities, the liturgical element in George Herbert preserves its reality too" (p. 353).

# *1968*

**748. Bercovitch, Sacvan.** "Empedocles in the English Renaissance." *SP* 65:67–80.

Briefly discusses the influence of Empedocles on Herbert. Argues that the fifth-century Greek philosopher had "an appreciable effect" (p. 79) on Herbert's thought. Maintains, for instance, that in "Affliction (IV)" Herbert "evokes the Empedoclean vision of man in our world-in-strife" (p. 78).

**749. Buchloh, Paul Gerhard.** "George Herbert: The Pulley," in *Die englische Lyrik: Von der Renaissance bis zur Gegenwart*, edited by Karl Heinz Göller, 1:159–65. Düsseldorf: August Bagel.

Detailed explication of "The Pulley." Argues that the basic conceit of the poem is built upon an altered version of the Greek myth of the box of Pandora. Stresses that God is presented in the poem in very human terms. German prose translation of the poem.

**750. Buckley, Vincent.** *Poetry and the Sacred.* New York: Barnes and Noble; London: Chatto & Windus. 244p.

Discusses "the variety of modes and directions which the religious impulse in literature may take" (p. 3). Calls Herbert and Hopkins "the two most centrally religious poets in the language" (p. 1). Comments briefly on the dramatic elements of Herbert's poetry and maintains that Herbert's drama is basically rhetorical: it is "the drama of contrived imaginative situations" (p. 31). Does not suggest that "Herbert did not feel the dramas he proposes in his poetry" but maintains that "the dramatic forms in which he proposes them are at a large remove from his initial feeling of them" (p. 31). Laments that Herbert's dramatic poems have become widely regarded as a prototype for Christian poetry. Contrasts Herbert with a number of religious poets, especially Greville, Donne, Henry King, Wordsworth, Hopkins, Dylan Thomas, and Theodore Roethke.

**751. Caldwell, Harry B., Edward E. Samaha, Jr., and Donna G. Fricke, comps.** "George Herbert: A Recent Bibliography, 1960–1967." *SCN* 26:54–56.

Lists 138 items on Herbert published between 1960 and 1967. No annotations. Divided into five sections: (1) editions and anthologies, (2) milieu and general studies, (3) theme and structure, (4) analyses of individual poems, and (5) miscellaneous. See also Humphrey Tonkin, "A Bibliography of George Herbert 1960–1967: Addenda" (entry 812).

**752. Carnes, Valerie.** "The Unity of George Herbert's *The Temple*: A Reconsideration." *ELH* 35:505–26.

Reprinted in *Essential Articles for the Study of George Herbert's Poetry*, edited by John R. Roberts (entry 1216), 374–92.

Maintains that the tripartite division of *The Temple* derives its thematic unity from an extended metaphor or analogy between religion and art, between man's religious and aesthetic activities. Argues that in *The Church-Porch* the persona is seen as the preacher expressing the revealed Word of God; in *The Church* the persona is viewed as the poet who expresses through his art the Word; and in *The Church Militant* the speaker is seen as the redeemed soul that unites the secular word and the sacred Word. Finds a parallel movement from didactic image, to symbol, to myth. Contends that man's recreation of this cycle in his attempts to communicate with God prefigures man's ultimate reconciliation of his soul to God.

753. **Cooper, John R.** "Walton's Borrowings," in *The Art of The Compleat Angler*, 138–65. Durham: Duke University Press.
Points out that in *The Compleat Angler* Walton borrowed the thirty-sixth, eighth, and seventh stanzas from "Providence" (slightly altered) and made of them "a well-ordered statement that gives a religious point to his catalogues of marvelous fish and rivers" (p. 160).

754. **Davies, H. Neville.** "Sweet Music in Herbert's 'Easter.'" *N&Q* 213:95–96.
Comments on the appropriateness of lines 11–12 of "Easter" ("His stretched sinews taught all strings, what key / Is best to celebrate this most high day") and points out the commonly accepted notion in the seventeenth century that a high musical key was associated with sweetness and love. Argues that the music that "may be played on a fully stretched string was known primarily not for its suitability for devotional use *per se*, but for its *sweetness*" (p. 95). Finds an analogue in Lyly's *Euphues*. Notes also the familiar reference to Christ as *Jesu dulcissime* and points out that "the sweet music produced by Christ when stretched on the Cross is a particular idea which would have been well known to Herbert and his contemporaries" (p. 95). Concludes that Herbert's "sweet music is, therefore, the fittest with which to celebrate the triumph of love over sin and death, for through its sweetness the hearer could ecstatically experience the love of God" (p. 96).

755. **Goldknopf, David.** "The Disintegration of Symbol in a Meditative Poet." *CE* 30:48–59.
Discusses the disintegration of symbol in the poetry of Vaughan and especially Traherne "as an access route to a consideration of how symbols in general operate" (p. 48). Observes that in Herbert's poetry "powerful images are used repeatedly, usually in a religious context yet with extraordinary vividness" and that, "in fact, the imagery often gives the religious sense an almost shocking materiality" (p. 51). Notes in particular, the prevalence of blood imagery in the poetry of "this gentle, near-sainted man" and maintains that "one cannot carry imagism much farther than the shaped poem" (p. 51). Briefly contrasts "H. Baptisme (II)" with Vaughan's "The Retreat" and Traherne's "The Preparative"—all poems that deal with "the grace of infancy by reason of the pre-existence of the soul" (p. 51). Notes that in the poetry of Herbert and Donne "an anti-sensuous philosophical statement is often propounded in a sensuous terminology, and tension between, one might say, ideology and physiology becomes part of the overall meaning of the poetry," whereas "only traces of this dialectic struggle are found in the poetry of Vaughan and Traherne, for the imagistic bonds with nature have dissolved almost entirely" (p. 52).

756. **Gorlier, Claudio.** "La Poesia di George Herbert," in *La Poesia metafisica inglese*, 81–105. (Biblioteca di studi inglesi e americani, 1.) Milan: La Goliardica.
Biographical sketch of Herbert and a critical evaluation of the poetry, stressing its dramatic elements. Comments on the major themes of Herbert's poetry and sees the

major tension in the poems as being between God and man. Prose translations of "The Altar," "Jordan (II)," "Discipline," "Love (III)," "Death," "Artillerie," "The Pearl," and "Redemption" by Giorgio Melchiori with brief explications and comments on each.

**757. Hanley, Sara William.** "Temples in *The Temple*: George Herbert's Study of the Church." *SEL* 8:121–35.

Argues that the title, *The Temple*, is a major metaphor that gives unity to the whole volume as well as to clusters of individual poems within the work: "*The Temple* is, literally, a book about temples, and the plot of the book concerns man's gradual efforts to 'enter' the temple of his own soul, the temple of his Christian Church, and the eternal temple of the people of God, finding at the center of each temple the God who created it and inhabits it" (p. 122). Comments in detail on a group of tightly knit poems beginning with "Mattens" and ending with "Trinitie Sunday" and maintains that this cluster of poems presents a discussion "of the nature of the Church, the source of grace" (p. 123). Sees "Mattens," "Sinne," and "Even-song" as studies and examples of the Church's prayer; maintains that the five so-called furniture poems that follow "focus attention on the symbol of the Church as heart, as building, as body of the faithful, and as the New Jerusalem"; and contends that the final poem in the sequence, "Trinitie Sunday," celebrates this major feast of the Church "with a litany-like prayer" (p. 121). Concludes that the "furniture poems" are not inferior, as has been suggested, but rather form an essential part of *The Temple*.

**758. Harbinson, M. J.** "A Crux in Herbert's 'The Sacrifice.'" *N&Q* 213:96–98.

Interprets lines 121–24 of "The Sacrifice" ("Why, Caesar is their onely King, not I: / He clave the stonie rock, when they were drie; / But surely not their hearts, as I well trie: / Was ever grief, &c.). Maintains that certain passages in Josephus's *Antiquities of the Jews* provide a key to this puzzling stanza. Notes that in a passage preceding the only reference to Christ in Josephus, the historian describes the force that Pilate (acting as Caesar's delegate) used to put down a riot begun by the Jews when he attempted to build conduits to bring water into Jerusalem. Argues that "an illuminating parallel then appears between Pilate as Caesar's procurator dealing with the mob rioting over taxes spent on the aqueduct, and Pilate as Caesar's procurator dealing with the mob calling for Christ's death" (p. 98). Also notes that Pilate's method of dealing with the mob in both cases "has obvious relevance to the nature of imperial power" and that "peace must be bought at the lowest price—contrast the price Christ is willing to pay" (p. 98). Maintains that Herbert was most likely familiar with these passages from Josephus.

**759. Herbert, George.** *The Temple* (1633). (Scolar Press Facsimile.) Menston, Eng.: Scolar Press. 11, 195p.

Facsimile of the 1633 edition (original size) of *The Temple* (British Museum: Shelfmark C 58.a.26). Brief bibliographical introduction. *Short-Title Catalogue* 13183.

**760. Himuro, Misako.** "Allegorical Poems of George Herbert." *Eibungaku* [English Literature, English Literary Society of Waseda University] no. 33 (December): 117–30.

Discusses Herbert's use of allegory, commenting particularly on "Humilitie."

**761. Honig, Edwin, and Oscar Williams, eds.** *The Major Metaphysical Poets of the Seventeenth Century: John Donne, George Herbert, Richard Crashaw, and Andrew Marvell.* New York: Washington Square Press. 902p.

Includes a detailed critical introduction to metaphysical poetry (pp. 1–33) by Edwin Honig. The Herbert section (pp. 321–501) contains a biographical sketch, *The Temple*, English poems not included in *The Temple*, and poems from Walton's *Lives*. Selected bibliography prepared by Milton Miller and Beverly Goldberg (pp. 867–77).

**762. Howard, Thomas T.** "Herbert and Crashaw: Notes on Meditative Focus." *Gordon Review* 11:79–98.

Maintains that, although both Herbert and Crashaw were products of a similar religious tradition and shared a devotion to the liturgy, the sacraments, and spiritual meditation, there is a fundamental difference between the two poets: "Whereas Herbert's vision of religion and the world was a truly sacramental one, albeit tempered with an Anglican reticence about becoming too baroque, Crashaw felt at home in the excruciating physical forms of Counter-Reformation meditation, an idea which is borne out in his shift to Rome as well as his poetic focus" (p. 84). Argues that Herbert's "devotional and meditative posture takes the form of scrutiny, analysis, self-calumny, dialogue with God, reflection on the implications of grace, and so forth, with the full consciousness of liturgical and traditional forms and the significance of ecclesiastical ornament, the figural, and sacramental understanding of the creation as 'God-bearing images'"; whereas Crashaw "is disposed to adoration, and baroque elaboration of objects of veneration as though by the artistic expansion of the object the soul will be that much the more impressed and aware of its overwhelming debt of gratitude" (p. 84). Comments on a number of Herbert's poems in order to illustrate the nature of his religious convictions and sensibilities and then contrasts these with Crashaw's.

**763. Jerome, Judson.** *Poetry: Premeditated Art.* Boston: Houghton Mifflin. xxxiv, 542p.

Comments briefly on "Prayer (I)," pointing out that the poem contains no complete sentence and that "the communication is entirely by means of a succession of images" (p. 154). Presents a critical analysis of the theme and style of "The Collar," comparing and contrasting the poem to Milton's "On His Blindness" and Donne"s "Batter My Heart" (pp. 292–303). Calls "The Collar" baroque and claims that it "zig-zags, twists, tangles and uncoils like a spastic serpent" (p. 294). Maintains that in the poems Herbert is "Dionysian" and that he "wrestles with his angel and falls panting" (pp. 294–95). Reproduces, in addition to "Prayer (I)" and "The Collar," "Love (III)" and "The Pulley" (pp. 412–13).

**764. Kawata, Akira.** "George Herbert no *The Temple*—Yotei no Kyogi wo Megutte" [George Herbert's *The Temple* with Special Reference to the Doctrine of Predestination]. *Ichinoseki Kosen Kenkyu Kiyo* [Bulletin of the Ichinoseki Technical College] no. 2 (March): 85–98.

Examines in detail "The Water-course," as well as several other poems in *The Temple* that refer to God's providence or Christ's redemptive action, arguing that Herbert had accepted the doctrine of predestination. Concedes that Herbert's belief in predestination is not expressed as clearly as Calvin's but should not be overlooked.

**765. Levitt, Paul M., and Kenneth G. Johnston.** "Herbert's 'The Collar' and the Story of Job." *PLL* 4:329–30.

Points out striking similarities in both the dramatic situation and the imagery of "The Collar" and the Book of Job. Notes, for example, that both the speaker of the poem and Job are rebels "against the austerities inherent in a life of denial and obedience" (p. 329), both weep and sigh in their trials, neither fully rejects God though both question God's providence, and "the faith of both men is confirmed when they hear the voice of God" (p. 330). Maintains that even the reversal of Herbert's last line recalls Job's exclamation, "Thou shalt call, and I will answer thee." Also points out several possible parallel images.

**766. Lloyd, J. D. K.** "The Architect of the Herbert Monument at Montgomery." *Montgomeryshire Collections* 59:138–40.
Identifies the architect of the tomb of Sir Richard Herbert, father of George Herbert, in Montgomery Church as Walter Hancock. For a detailed account and description of the tomb, see J. D. K. Lloyd (entry 365).

**767. Metteden, A. K.** "On Reading Old Poets." *NigM* 98:251–57.
Presents a selection of "old masters" for the pleasure of his reading audience, including "The Pulley" and lines from "Man." Includes a biographical note on Herbert, whom he calls "one of the first and greatest Metaphysical poets" (p. 257).

**768. Murrin, Michael.** "Poetry as Literary Criticism." *MP* 65:202–7.
Comments on "Jordan (II)" as literary criticism and maintains that the poem is written "in a metaphysical style and that it represents a negative judgment on that style, presented as if it were on stage in a dramatic action, where a problem is set up and answered in eighteen lines" (p. 202). Also comments on "Jordan (I)," calling it an allegorical poem that attacks allegory. Concludes that Herbert "deliberately wrote an allegorical poem when he was attacking allegory, just as he wrote metaphysically when attacking metaphysical poetry" (p. 203). Warns that the modern critic, therefore, "must consider the whole poem, both form and content, as a complex critical statement" (p. 206).

**769. Okuyama, Toshimi.** "Herbert kara Vaughan e—Hitotsu no Yoshiki no Hokai—Easter Poems o Chushin ni shite" [From Herbert to Vaughan—The Breakdown of a Style—Centering on Easter Poems]. *Akita Daigaku Kyoiku Gakubu Kenkyu Kiyo. Jimbunkagaku. Shakaikagaku.* [Bulletin of the Faculty of Education, Akita University] 18 (February): 13–24.
Compares and contrasts Herbert and Vaughan, with special reference to their Easter poems.

**770. Rawlinson, D. H.** *The Practice of Criticism.* Cambridge: Cambridge University Press. xvii, 229p.
In chapter 9, "Emotion and Emotionality: Herbert's 'Life' and E. B. Browning's 'Irreparableness'" (pp. 67–72) contrasts "writing which has the modesty, delicacy and humour of a sensitive man who knows the relative worth of what he is saying, and writing in which feeling is simulated or worked up for the occasion" (p. 68). Contrasts Herbert's "Life" with Elizabeth Barrett Browning's "Irreparableness," stressing that Herbert, "writing a 'slight,' unpretentious poem can be, in a modest way, genuinely profound" and that his profundity "is closely bound up with the success of every detail of the poem," whereas Browning's poem is marred by "pseudo-profundities and [an] inflated manner" (p. 72). In chapter 10, "Meaning Stated and Meaning Created: Two More Herbert Poems" (pp. 73–77), comments on Herbert's "The Collar" as an example of "meaning 'actually presented'" and on his "Nature" as an example of "meaning 'talked about'" (p. 73). Argues that, when Herbert fails as a poet, it is because he "has not entered fully into the poem, which remains an

external conception, coherent but too neatly put together, his store of metaphors and 'little allegories' (as Grierson aptly calls them) easily sustaining a respectable level of interest but no more" (p. 73).

**771. Ryan, Thomas A.** "The Poetry of John Danforth." *PAAS* 78:129–93.
Briefly points out that John Danforth (1660–1730), a minor Puritan poet, alludes to Herbert's "Anagram of the Virgin Marie" in his elegy on Mrs. Mary Gerrish. Maintains that such an allusion shows that the Puritans "had no qualms about reading or even quoting such Anglican poets of the time as Herbert or Quarles" (p. 133).

**772. Smith, Barbara Herrnstein.** *Poetic Closure: A Study of How Poems End.* Chicago and London: University of Chicago Press. xvi, 289p.
Discusses the relationship of thematic structure to poetic closure in "Vertue" (pp. 67–70): "What gives this poem so much of its power is the fact that so many elements in its formal and thematic structure conspire to bring about closure at the conclusion of the *third* stanza" (p. 69). Points out that the fourth stanza, however, "is hardly anticlimactic: on the contrary, it has the effect, entirely appropriate to its theme, of a revelation—that which is known beyond what can be demonstrated logically" (p. 69). Discusses briefly three major principles of thematic structure in "Mortification": "Two of them are sequential, one being a series, the other a logical development" and "the third principle, a recurrent conceit, is in effect paratactic" (p. 113). Shows how the conclusion of the poem "derives its expressive power and stability from the complex relation of these three principles and from other nonstructural elements as well" (p. 113). Comments also on the sequential structure and the allegorical elements of "Redemption" and calls its conclusion "extraordinarily moving": "As the reader is drawn into the allegorical world of tenants and property transactions, he follows the events as in a fictional narration—even though their religious significance is always apparent"; thus "the conclusion is experienced with a double shock of surprise and recognition" (pp. 125–26).

**773. Stein, Arnold.** *George Herbert's Lyrics.* Baltimore: Johns Hopkins Press. xliv, 221p.
Condensed version of chapter 1 published in *The Poetic Tradition: Essays on Greek, Latin, and English Poetry*, edited by Don Cameron Allen and Henry T. Rowell (entry 774), pp. 99–122.
A shorter version of chapter 1 reprinted in *Seventeenth Century English Poetry: Modern Essays in Criticism*, edited by William Keast (rev. ed., entry 879), pp. 257–78.
Chapter 2 published as "George Herbert's Prosody" (entry 775).
Announces that the purpose of this study is to demonstrate "why Herbert is one of the great masters of lyric poetry" (p. vii) and to show that his lyrics "are the expression of a complex and subtle mind, uniquely aware of itself and its fertile deceptions yet trusting the depths of feeling, and trusting his own power to invent and order imaginative explorations of personal experience" (p. viii). Divided into five sections. Introduction (pp. xiii-xliv) briefly outlines the history of the plain style from its classical origins through the early Christian era to the seventeenth century and locates the metaphysicals in this tradition. Argues that the plain style, although based on the natural rhythms of speech, has always depended on careful artistry and discipline and is not necessarily free from obscurity. Chapter 1, "The Art of Plainness" (pp. 1–44), discusses Herbert's attitude toward poetry and argues that his art of plainness "is an

art, not a summary feature" (p. 44). Shows that one of Herbert's major themes is poetry itself. Analyzes the tension between Herbert's desire for simplicity and sincerity and his need to use rhetoric, metaphor, and language in order to create poems. Demonstrates that his art of plainness "does not bear a single stamp, and his arguments with God are conducted with great freedom and inventiveness" (p. 26). Maintains that the major devices of Herbert's plainness are "not traditional figures but psychological gestures and movements" (p. 27). Illustrates the range of Herbert's art of plainness by closely examining "The Temper (I)," "The Pearl," and "Death" and argues that the power of the plain style "lies in the passion excluded, in the resistance mastered, and in the deliberate grace of saying difficult things with ease" (p. 43). Chapter 2, "The Movement of Words" (pp. 45–84), discusses "the basis of Herbert's metrical rhetoric, the expressive movement of words by which he brings into focus and controls the particular discriminations of his meanings" (p. 45). Primarily comments on stress, juncture, and phrasing and shows that Herbert's metrical style "is characterized by the frequency of its colloquial phrasing and by the inventive ease with which he adjusts colloquial and metric phrasing to each other" (p. 53). Shows how stress, juncture, and phrasing "work together to create an order of separate and overlapping forms" and how "the balance between apparently independent, informal elements and apparently controlled formal elements is capable of endless variation" (p. 58). Discusses and illustrates certain primary patterns: advancing intensity of stress, loosening and contracting of rhythmical movements, and augmenting or diminishing of established patterns. Maintains that Herbert's "techniques for ordering the movement of language are significant in themselves" and "resemble metaphor in both establishing and discovering meanings" (p. 84). Chapter 3, "Complaint, Praise, and Love" (pp. 85–135), discusses complaint, praise, and love "in part as the subjects of [Herbert's] poetry, in part as thematic ideas which move and develop in their own characteristic ways but which are significantly related to each other" (p. 85). Points out that one of the primary causes for complaint in Herbert's poetry is the grief that man feels when he confronts his failure to love God fully. Argues that Herbert's "lyric gifts are not fully engaged by lament pure and simple" (p. 96), since "the expression of pain and longing is always qualified by something else—by his disciplined detachment, by his imaginative ability to perceive and relate what he finds real within and without himself" (p. 97). Shows that in Herbert's poetry "every complaint is also, more or less, a declaration of praise and love" (p. 97). Examines various difficulties that the religious poet encounters in his attempt to praise God and especially comments on Herbert's "master metaphor of praise, music, an art that for him not only expresses but represents both meaning and feeling" (p. 110). Maintains that Herbert approaches his central theme of love in three ways: (1) a movement away from love, an effort to escape; (2) a movement toward love, aiming to force love; and (3) contemplation of love. Chapter 4, "Questions of Style and Form" (pp. 137–210), points out that Herbert does not often repeat the situations and plots of his most significant poems and maintains that he consistently keeps a delicate balance between "the elements of individuality and freedom" and "the commitment to significant form and specific beliefs" (p. 139). Compares the earlier and revised versions of "The Elixir" and "Easter" so that "we can gain some insight into what did and did not satisfy Herbert in terms of a whole poem" (p. 139). Analyzes a number of individual poems in terms of closed form (poems that turn back and close in on themselves, such as "A Wreath," "Sinnes round," "H. Baptisme (II)," and "Aaron") and in terms of open form (poems that have an expanding movement outward, such as "Easter-wings," "Trinitie Sunday," and "The Odour"). Offers detailed explications of "Mor-

tification," "Life," "Vertue," "Love (III)," and "The Flower." Concludes by commenting briefly on Herbert's attitude toward the imagination and by suggesting that Herbert "is a splendid master of that basic illusion upon which his poetry depends, that the language and forms of art are only another, if better, way to talk naturally" (p. 208).
Reviews:
Margaret Bottrall, *ELN* 6 (1969): 207–9
Edward E. Ericson, Jr., *SCN* 27 (1969): 8–9
J. McGann, *Poetry* (Chicago) 115 (1969): 196–201
Philip C. McGuire, *JEGP* 68 (1969): 696–99
H. M. Richmond, *Renaissance Quarterly* 22 (1969): 202–3
C. C. Brown, *RES* 21 (1970): 206–8
Louis L. Martz, *MLQ* 31 (1970): 252–60
G. Thomas, *English* 19 (1970): 26–27

774. ———. "George Herbert: The Art of Plainness," in *The Poetic Tradition: Essays on Greek, Latin, and English Poetry*, edited by Don Cameron Allen and Henry T. Rowell, 99–122. (Percy Graeme Turnbull Memorial Lectures on Poetry.) Baltimore: Johns Hopkins Press.
Reprinted in revised form in *George Herbert's Lyrics* (entry 773), 1–44.
Reprinted in *Essential Articles for the Study of George Herbert's Poetry*, edited by John R. Roberts (entry 1216), 160–80; and *Seventeenth Century English Poetry: Modern Essays in Criticism*, edited by William R. Keast, rev. ed. (entry 879), 257–78.
Comments on the complexity of Herbert's plain style and his mastery of the rhetoric of sincerity (the "art by which he may tell the truth to himself and God" [p. 107]). Argues that Herbert "does not give us a single, consistent attitude toward expression, that his art of plainness does not bear a single stamp, and that his arguments with God are conducted with great freedom and inventiveness" (p. 106); thus, when "we take a single example as our model to copy, we become aware of statements on the other side and of stylistic demonstrations that force us to widen our definitions" (pp. 106–7). Maintains that Herbert achieves his rhetoric of sincerity not primarily by traditional figures but by "psychological gestures and movements" (p. 107). Illustrates Herbert's art of plainness by commenting in detail on "The Temper (I)," "The Pearl," and "Death." Argues that the power of the plain style "lies in the passion excluded, in the resistance mastered, and in the deliberate grace of saying difficult things with ease" (p. 121). Evaluates Coleridge's comments on Herbert and maintains that two important points emerge: "First, it is clear that Herbert is a master who draws a leading thought through authentic obstacles which both test and refine the ultimate expression of that thought" and, "secondly, the rhetorical proof of character lies in the poet's convincing demonstration that *he* becomes what he says, that the flow and shape of his words lead to a unity of eloquence and wisdom, and that he is at the expressive center of what he concludes" (p. 122).

775. ———. "George Herbert's Prosody." *Lang&S* 1:1–38.
Reprinted in revised form in *George Herbert's Lyrics* (entry 773), 45–84; and in *Perspectives in Poetry*, edited by James L. Calderwood and Harold E. Toliver (New York: Oxford University Press, 1968), 169–77.
Studies "the basis of Herbert's metrical rhetoric, the expressive movement of words by which he brings into focus and controls the particular discriminations of his meanings" (p. 1). Argues that Herbert's techniques "for ordering the movement of

language are significant in themselves" (p. 38). Shows how Herbert sets up a tension between colloquial and metrical phrasing and how each phrase is fully sensitive to those that follow or precede it: "Stress, juncture, and phrasing work together, then, and create an order of separate and overlapping forms which may express the fullest possible variety or may give concentrated prominence to a limited range of effects" (p. 9). Comments on the loosening and contracting of rhythmical movement in Herbert's poetry, pointing out "the ways in which the rhythmic flow of emphasis resembles the power of metaphor to control and establish meaning while discovering new and unexpected meanings" (p. 34). Scans numerous lines from individual poems to illustrate his points and presents an extended discussion of "Employment (I)" and "The Crosse."

776. **Unrau, John.** "Three Notes on George Herbert." *N&Q* 213:94–95.
(1) Comments on the use of *thankfull glasse* in "The H. Scriptures (I)," lines 8–9. Maintains that Herbert is referring to a mirror, perhaps a wish-fulfilling mirror as described by Girolamo Cardano (Cardanus) in *De Rerum Varietate Libri XVII* (1557). Notes that, if this is Herbert's intent, *thankfull* should be interpreted as *pleasing* or *agreeable*. (2) Maintains that Herbert's allusion to *ebony box* in "Evensong," lines 21–23, may refer to the well-known medicinal properties of ebony and that the lines may thus be interpreted to read: "Just as poisonous liquids are rendered harmless by enclosure in a box of ebony, so the frustrations and tensions of the day, described by Herbert in the preceding stanza, are neutralized by night and sleep" (p. 94). Finds a similar use of ebony in Arthur Golding's translation of *The excellent and pleasant worke of Julius Solinus* (1587). (3) Comments on lines 37–45 of "Love unknown." Points out that Pliny, Solinus, and several Elizabethan and seventeenth-century writers comment on the idea that only blood is "capable of softening the otherwise indestructible diamond" (p. 94). Notes the use of the idea in Thomas Johnson's *Cornucopiae, or diuers secrets* (1595) and in Donald Lupton's *Emblems of rarieties* (1636).

777. **Walcutt, Charles Child, and J. Edwin Whitesell, eds.** "Herbert," in *The Explicator Cyclopedia*, 2:147–57. Chicago: Quadrangle Books.
Reprints *Explicator* articles on the following poems by Herbert: (1) "Businesse" (Robert G. Collmer, entry 476); (2) "The Collar" (Dan S. Norton, entries 296, 306; T. O. Mabbott, entry 294; Jack M. Bickham, entry 376); (3) "Dooms-day" (Conrad Hilberry, entry 495); (4) "Jordan" (Sheldon P. Zitner, entry 373; Frances Eldredge, entry 400; Macdonald Emslie, entry 429); (5) "The Pearl" (Stephen Manning, entry 470); (6) "The Pulley" (D. S. Mead, entry 303); (7) "Redemption" (Bernard Knieger, entry 416); (8) "Trinitie Sunday" (Joseph H. Summers, entry 407); (9) "Vertue" (Herbert Marshall McLuhan, entry 280; Edwin B. Benjamin, entry 358).

778. **Whitlock, Baird W.** "The Baroque Characteristics of the Poetry of George Herbert." *Cithara* 7:30–40.
Argues that Herbert, not Crashaw, is "the most typical English baroque poet" (p. 30) and maintains that "to study the characteristics of the Baroque without seeing George Herbert as a central figure in the movement is to miss most that is central to the concept" (p. 39). Cites twelve generally accepted major characteristics of baroque art and illustrates each with specific examples from Herbert's poems. Comments on such baroque elements as the insistence on achieving unity "by form rather than *in* form" (p. 30), the sacramental sense of art being an "outward sign of an inward grace," the rejection of classical forms, the movement from closed to open form and

from clarity to obscurity or relative clarity, the indirect method of progression or "serpentine approach to beauty" (p. 37), the preference for small size, the quest for illusion, and the belief in the unity of all the arts.

# *1969*

**779. Anon.** "Weekend Competition 2053." *New Statesman* n.s. 78:95.

Reports that a pub is to be opened at Bemerton to encourage churchgoing. Invites competitors "to compose verses by Herbert on this new development, or by other literary figures on places associated with them which may be similarly refurbished: e.g. Tennyson on the conversion of Farringford into a hotel, Wordsworth on the Labour Exchange that now occupies the Cockermouth birthplace, etc." Reproduces four poems submitted to the competition.

**780. Armour, Richard.** *English Lit Relit: A short history of English literature from the Precursors (before swearing) to the Pre-Raphaelites and a little after, intended to help students see the thing through, or see through the thing, and omitting nothing unimportant.* Irreverently illustrated by Campbell Grant. New York: McGraw-Hill. 151p.

Humorous treatment of Herbert (pp. 35–36): "Herbert died of consumption from living in a house with a leaky roof. He thought of telling someone of the condition of the place, but shrank from saying such a thing as 'This damp house'" (p. 36).

**781. Asals, Heather.** "George Herbert and Hugh of St. Victor's 'Soliloquium de Arrha Animae.'" *N&Q* 214:368–70.

Maintains that Herbert is drawing on a well-established tradition when he employs money imagery in *The Temple* and specifically points out that "the function of the governing money image in Herbert's 'Dialogue' quite exactly parallels the function of the money image in Hugh's *Soliloquium*" (p. 369). Also suggests that Herbert may have found in the *Soliloquium* a model for the numerous internal dialogues in *The Temple*.

**782. ———.** "The Voice of George Herbert's 'The Church.'" *ELH* 36:511–28.

Reprinted in *Essential Articles for the Study of George Herbert's Poetry*, edited by John R. Roberts (entry 1216), 393–407.

Argues that the psalms and the pre-1633 Christian commentaries on the psalms (especially those of St. Augustine) exercised a much more profound influence on *The Church* than has been usually recognized. Points out many verbal echoes from the psalms but argues that this kind of influence is minimal in comparison to more significant considerations. Notes that the voice in the psalms was often identified by the Christian commentators as that of Christ's Body or of the Church and argues that this identification enables Herbert to create a plural identity for the speaker of *The Church*: "By echoing the voice of the Psalmist, Herbert expands the dimensions of the 'I' of his poetry" (p. 513). Concludes that the multiple speakers in the poems (Christ, David, the Christian, everyman, and so on) are really all various voices of one voice, the Church, and likewise all the various voices "are the voice of one man—all the 'I's are one 'I'" (p. 516). Shows how this concept explains the many shifts in point of view found between the poems and even within the same poem. Comments also on how the concepts of affliction and suffering in *The Church* are shaped by the views expressed by the Christian commentators on the psalms: "As the voice of the Church is one with the voice of Christ, so also are the complaints of the Church one with the complaints of Christ" (p. 519)" Explains how "the development of 'The Church' dramatizes the gradual acknowledgment by the speakers in 'The Church' of the fact that the real speaker in all the poems is the voice of 'The Church'" (p. 519). Also compares Herbert's uses of verb tense with Hebrew usage, pointing out that, in Hebrew, tense is not related to time but to the kind of action described, completed or not completed. Argues, for example, that the use of the past tense in "Love (III)" "is meant to be seen as a figure of speech declaring the fact that the reconciliation of 'The Church' with God in God's time is as sure as done" (p. 525), and likewise Herbert's various pleas in the poems that God remember him "are not ultimately requests but figures expressing the condition of 'The Church' in this world" (p. 527).

**783. Bagg, Robert.** "The Electromagnet and the Shred of Platinum." *Arion* 8:407–29.

Argues that Reuben Arthur Brower's *The Fields of Light: An Experiment in Critical Reading* (entry 378) exemplifies the serious limitations of Eliot's impersonal theory and insists that "personality is the organizing vitality of art" and that Eliot's theory "is a menace whenever it stops us from realizing that the greatness of a poem like 'Love' is in its power to convince us, by its inexhaustible nuance of experience beyond the power of the artist to will, that its voice is not an ad hoc construction, but a mode of being" (p. 429). Presents a brief Freudian reading of "Love (III)," maintaining that the primary appeal of the poem "is the almost geisha-like care and thoughtfulness of Love; shyness and unworthiness before Christ is felt as unworthiness in an encounter full of sexual ambience" (p. 428). Contends that Christ is seen metaphorically as a woman appearing in a dream to soothe the sexual anxiety of the poet, all of which is a metaphor for Christ's power.

**784. Clements, A. L.** *The Mystical Poetry of Thomas Traherne.* Cambridge, Mass.: Harvard University Press. x, 232p.

Comments throughout on Herbert's influence on Traherne, calling him "perhaps the single major literary influence on Traherne" (p. 95), and in several places compares and contrasts the two poets. Briefly discusses Herbert's use of dwelling-place and kingship symbolism and his use of the biblical technique of repetition.

**785. Collins, Dan S.** "Herbert's 'Vertue.'" *Expl* 27:item 50.

Reply to Roberts W. French (entry 724). Maintains that in stanza 4 of "Vertue" Herbert has in mind "live coal," which permits him "to distinguish the dead cinder into which the world of flesh turns at death from the live coal which yet glows in the center ('chiefly') of the mass." Maintains also that the best gloss of the image is stanza 2 of "Employment (II)."

**786. Crum, Margaret, ed.** *First-Line Index of English Poetry 1500–1800 in Manuscripts of the Bodleian Library Oxford.* 2 vols. New York: Index Committee of the Modern Language Association; Oxford: Clarendon Press. x, 1–630; 631–1257p.

First-line index of English poetry (1500–1800) in manuscripts of the Bodleian up to 1961. Five indexes: (1) Bodleian manuscripts listed by shelf marks; (2) index of authors; (3) index of names mentioned; (4) index of authors of works translated, paraphrased, or imitated; and (5) index of references to composers of settings and tunes named or quoted. Includes thirty-three main entries for Herbert.

**787. Denis, Yves.** "Poèmes métaphysiques." *NRF* 17:235–46.

General introduction to the nature of metaphysical poetry. Includes a biographical sketch of Herbert and translations of "Redemption" and "Love (III)" into French (pp. 241–43).

**788. Dolan, Paul J.** "Herbert's Dialogue with God." *Anglican Theological Review* 51:125–32.

Through an examination of the various stances and attitudes of the speaker and listener in "Dialogue," "The Temper (I)," "Discipline," "Christmas," "The Thanksgiving," and "The Collar," shows that one of the distinctive characteristics of Herbert's poetry is his skillful use of the dialogue mode and maintains that those poems "concerned with God's bargain with man or the contractual conditions of salvation" (p. 125) are particularly important "because these reveal most distinctly the nature of Herbert's concept of man's relationship to God Whom he petitions and the God to Whom he repents" (p. 126).

**789. Ericson, Edward E., Jr.** "A Structural Approach to Imagery." *Style* 3:227–47.

Analyzes "the external structure and arrangement of images" (p. 227) in order to "tell us something about the methods which a particular poet employed in constructing his poems—or at least the imagistic pattern within his poems" (p. 228). Comments on the structural types of Herbert's imagery as a way of illustrating the general approach and classifies his images into several categories: simple, extended, running, images within images, images within images within images, and images within images within images within images. Examines the structural patterns of images in "Prayer (I)," "Grief," "Vanitie (I)," "Mortification," "The Rose," "The World," "The Pilgrimage," "Redemption," "Artillerie," "Assurance," "Church-rents and schismes," and "The Bag." Maintains that most of the poems can be divided into two major patterns: (1) those that "are unified from beginning to end through the use of imagery" and (2) those that use "separate blocks of images connected end to end" (p. 229). Notes that most of Herbert's poems fall into the second category but argues that the best poems fall into the first.

**790. Fogelman, Roger.** "Revision and Improvement in George Herbert's *The Temple*." *NR* 1:65–85.

Comments on the nature of Herbert's revision of several of the poems in *The Temple*. Argues that "a comparison of certain poems in the Williams MS and the Bodleian MS shows that Herbert's revisions were inspired, on occasion, by the wording and imagery of other of his poems" (p. 78) and that the revisions "show the development of significant attitudes in Herbert's religious thought," especially "an emphasis upon the positive aspects of the human condition, and a deepening awareness of the general or universal nature of man's relation to his fellow-man and to God" (p. 79). Comments in particular on the revision of "Easter," "Whitsunday," "Praise (I)," and certain lines in *The Church-Porch*, "Faith," and "The Sacrifice."

**791. Forsyth, R. A.** "Herbert, Clough, and Their Church-Windows." *VP* 7:17–30.

Suggests that Herbert's "The Windows" is a possible source for the unusual window imagery in Arthur Hugh Clough's "Epi-straussium." Argues that Clough's poem does not simply echo Herbert's in material or style and is not simply a parody of a Victorian reworking of a seventeenth-century poem; rather, maintains that Clough uses the imagery of Herbert's poem to underline his own religious beliefs. Argues that in "The Windows" Herbert says that it is only by becoming Christ-like that man can become the true Christian and that Clough, in his poem, ironically finds that his rejection of the historical Jesus does not destroy his religious beliefs but allows him to discover more readily and more clearly essential Christianity. Contains a close reading of "The Windows."

**792. Honda, Kin-ichiro.** *H. J. C. Grierson: Keijijo-shijin Ron* [Japanese translation of H. J. C. Grierson's "Introduction" to *Metaphysical Lyrics and Poems of the Seventeenth Century, Donne to Butler* (1921)]. Tokyo: Hokuseido Shoten. 216p.

Includes explanatory notes in Japanese and Honda's essay "An Historical Survey of the Revival of Critical Interest in the Metaphysical Poets" as an appendix.

**793. Huntley, Frank L.** "Dr. Johnson and Metaphysical Wit; or, *Discordia concors* Yoked and Balanced." *Papers of the Midwest Modern Language Association* 1:103–12.

Views the metaphysical poets from Dr. Johnson's perspective, primarily by explaining Johnson's use of the phrase *discordia concors*. Distinguishes between "two modes of imitating world harmony," the classical and the Christian, and "describes and illustrates the difference in feeling and shape that one mode produces in Denham and Pope; and the other, in Donne and Herbert": "One pattern imitates the natural balance between the elements of fission and fusion; the other more daringly combines a lower into a higher value to achieve a third" (p. 104). Argues that "the balanced pattern is Pythagorean and Empedoclean and consists of two's and four's; the yoked pattern is Platonic and Christian, and often appears in three's and five's" (p. 104). Uses the first three stanzas of Herbert's "Easter" and the first four lines of "The H. Scriptures (II)" to illustrate the Christian mode, "an upward struggle from a lower entity to its opposing higher entity in order to achieve a third which is brand new" (p. 110). Maintains that Dr. Johnson is not ridiculing the metaphysicals but views the Augustans and the metaphysicals from a "classical" viewpoint.

**794. Inglis, Fred.** "An Approach to Poetry," in *An Essential Discipline: An Introduction to Literary Criticism*, 47–119. London: Methuen; New York: Barnes and Noble.

Explicates "The Flower" (pp. 77–82). Maintains that in the poem Herbert "establishes a tone and manner of great elegance and great simplicity" and that the elegance comes from the use of "gentle words and natural rhythms, and the completely unforced assurance of argument and progression," while the simplicity "is that of religious maturity" (p. 81). Praises the artistry of the poem, pointing out that "no word is out of place, or ill-mannered; the tone is graceful, thoughtful and resonant, but the subject-matter is illimitable, it is a whole attitude to life" (p. 82).

**795. Kermode, Frank, ed.** *The Metaphysical Poets: Key Essays on Metaphysical Poetry and the Major Metaphysical Poets.* Edited with introduction and commentary by Frank Kermode. (Fawcett Premier Literature and Ideas Series, edited by Irving Howe.) New York: Fawcett Publications. 351p.

General introduction to metaphysical poetry by Frank Kermode (pp. 11–32) with a brief introduction to Herbert (pp. 25–26). Maintains that "Herbert employed traditional pious themes, from the liturgy and from the resources of Biblical typology, with such originality that he created new forms and almost a new tone in English poetry"

(p. 25). Collection of twenty-six previously published essays and/or selections from book-length studies arranged under five major headings: (1) The English Background, (2) Baroque, (3) Metaphysical Poetic, (4) The Major Metaphysical Poets, and (5) Epilogue. Although several items in this collection refer to Herbert and are important in understanding the nature of metaphysical poetry in general, only two are specifically on Herbert: (1) A selection from Walton's *Life of Mr. George Herbert* (pp. 225–29) and (2) Joseph H. Summers's "Herbert's Conception of Form" (pp. 230–51) from *George Herbert: His Religion and Art* (entry 435), pp. 73–94, 219–21.

**796. Krzeczkowski, Henryk, Jerzy S. Sito, and Juliusz Żuławski, eds.** "George Herbert," in *Poeci języka angielskiego* [Poets of the English Language], 1:517–33, 857–59. (Biblioteka poezji i prozy.) Warsaw: Panstwowy Instytut Wydawniczy.
Reprinted, 1971, 1974.
A general introduction to Herbert's life and poetry (pp. 517–18), followed by a selection of seventeen poems, translated into Polish by Jerzy Lowinski, Jerzy S. Sito, Maciej Słomczyński, Aleksander Mierzejewski, and Stefan Stasiak (pp. 518–33), with brief notes (pp. 857–59). Maintains that literary scholars consider Herbert's religious lyrics among the best in the English language.

**797. Lekberg, Sven.** *Let All the World in Every Corner Sing.* New York and London: G. Schirmer. 8p.
Musical setting of "Antiphon (I)" for four-part chorus of mixed voices.

**798. Levitt, Paul M., and Kenneth G. Johnston.** "Herbert's 'The Collar': A Nautical Metaphor." *SP* 66:217–24.
Comments on the "boat-of-the-mind" metaphor, "which enriches, clarifies, and organizes 'The Collar'" (p. 217). Argues that recognition of the pervasive nautical imagery of the poem in no way destroys the standard Christian interpretation but rather shows that Herbert's speaker is proposing "to embark on a worldly voyage" (p. 217). Comments on a possible nautical meaning of the title: "a band (or garland) of rope which helps to support the main mast, to restrain the motion of the mast, and thus to ensure a safe voyage" (p. 218) and notes that, thus, the title suggests it would be "as disastrous for the speaker to renounce his Christian life of discipline, denial, and restraint ('to slip the collar' as the phrase went) as it would be for the sailor to cut the collar supporting the mast" (p. 219). Comments on possible nautical meanings of "the board" (line 1), "abroad" (line 2), "lines" (line 4), "rode" (line 4), "Loose as the winde, as large as store" (line 5), "suit" (line 6), "bayes" (line 14), "garlands" (line 15), "hands" (line 18), "cage" (line 21), "rope of sands" (line 22), "Good cable" (line 24), "Away" (line 27), "deaths head" (line 29). Maintains that Herbert's speaker says "that the religious man must weather a spiritual storm, as it were, before he can arrive at a spiritual calm" and that, when the speaker achieves peace of mind, he "no longer desires to set sail in search of worldly pleasures" (p. 224). For a reply, see D. F. Rauber, "Critics and Collars" (entry 885).

**799. McGuire, Philip C.** "Herbert's Jordan II and the Plain Style." *MichA* 1, no. 3–4:69–74.
Maintains that Herbert's rejection of figures of diction and of stylistic embellishments in "Jordan (II)" was influenced by statements about the proper style for private prayer found in various Renaissance devotional manuals and handbooks on prayer as well as by the tradition of classical plain style. Presents a close reading of "Jordan (II)."

**800. Martz, Louis L.** *The Wit of Love: Donne, Carew, Crashaw, Marvell.* (University of Notre Dame Ward–Phillips Lectures in English Language and Literature, vol. 3.) Notre Dame and London: University of Notre Dame Press. xv, 216p.

Series of four lectures (revised and expanded) first delivered at the University of Notre Dame in March 1968. Only brief references to Herbert. Maintains that Herbert is neither a mannerist nor a baroque poet but that in his poetry he "achieves the perfect harmony of a High Renaissance symbol" (p. 136). Compares briefly the careers of Herbert and Carew (pp. 151–52) and the devotional poetry of Herbert and Crashaw (pp. 136–37) and of Herbert and Marvell (pp. 154–56).

**801. Merrill, Thomas F.** "'The Sacrifice' and the Structure of Religious Language." *Lang&S* 2:275–87.

Reprinted (in slightly different form) as chapter 5 of *Christian Criticism: A Study of Literary God-Talk* (Amsterdam: Rodopi N. V., 1976), 73–85.

Discusses the structure of religious language and maintains that it "is the same as everyday language but *put to a special use*," that use being "communication to and about God" (p. 276). Discusses "The Sacrifice" as an excellent model for analyzing the language of devotional poetry and argues that from a structural analysis of the poem it would seem that the real subject of it "is a crucial piece of Christian dogma— the Hypostatic Union" (p. 287). Disagrees with the conclusions of William Empson and Rosemond Tuve about the poem.

**802. Miner, Earl.** *The Metaphysical Mode from Donne to Cowley.* Princeton: Princeton University Press. xix, 291p.

Pages 118–58 reprinted in *Seventeenth Century English Poetry: Modern Essays in Criticism*, edited by William Keast (rev. ed., entry 879), 45–76.

Pages 99–117 reprinted in *The Metaphysical Poets: A Selection of Critical Essays*, edited by Gerald Hammond (entry 985), 197–214.

Announces that the purpose of this study is "to discriminate poetic features that are particularly important to the Metaphysical style and differences possible within the style: in other words, what is lasting and what changes, what is general to the style and what is peculiar to individual writers" (p. xi). Argues (1) that metaphysical poetry is "private in mode, that it treats time and place in ways describable in terms of the 'dramatic,' the 'narrative,' the 'transcendent,' the 'meditative,' and the 'argumentative'—and that these terms provide in their sequence something of a history of the development of Metaphysical poetry" (p. xi); (2) that "the wit of Metaphysical poetry can be characterized as definition, that is, as those logical or rhetorical processes bringing together or separating (whether in metaphor or idea) matters of similar or opposed classes; and as that dialectic, or those processes, that extend such matters by their relation in logical and rhetorical procedures" (pp. xi-xii); and (3) that "the thematic range of Metaphysical poetry can best be represented in terms of satiric denial and lyric affirmation" (p. xii). Chapter 1, "The Private Mode" (pp. 3–47), argues that the private mode is "the chief 'radical' of Metaphysical poetry, that feature differentiating it from the social and public modes of other poetry written in modern English before the late eighteenth century and the Romantic poets" (p. x). Chapter 2, "Forms of Perception: Time and Place" (pp. 48–117), explores "forms, modes and structures of Metaphysical poems in terms of their version of time and space" (p. x). Chapter 3, "Wit: Definition and Dialectic" (pp. 118–58), defines the "major feature of Metaphysical wit in terms reflecting the poets' use of an older logic and rhetoric" (p. xi). Chapter 4, "Themes: Satire and Song" (pp. 159–213), comments on "the thematic range of Metaphysical poetry in terms of complementary elements," in terms of song and satire, "the former a tendency to affirmation, the latter a tendency to denial, both being capable of expression in lyricism or in satire, or in mixtures" (p. xi). Chapter 5, "Three Poems" (pp. 214–71), examines in detail Donne's "The Perfume," Herbert's "The Flower," and Marvell's "The Nymph complaining for the death of her Faun." Mentions Herbert throughout and compares and contrasts him with Donne, Vaughan, Crashaw, Marvell, Traherne, Cowley, and Quarles. Deals with Herbert's dramatic qualities, his uses of the meditative and emblem traditions, and his particular kind of wit. Comments on "Artillerie," "Bitter-sweet," *The Church-Porch*, "The Collar," "Grace," "Jordan (I)," "Life," "Love (III)," "The Pearl," "Prayer (I)," "The Pulley," "The Quip," "The Sacrifice," "The Temper (I)," and "Vertue" and presents a detailed reading of "The Flower" (pp. 231–46). Relates "The Flower" to the tradition of the poetry of meditation, the emblem tradition, and the tradition of the soul's vicissitudes.

**803. Mulder, John R.** *The Temple of the Mind: Education and Literary Tastes in Seventeenth-Century England.* (Pegasus Backgrounds in English Literature.) New York: Pegasus. viii, 165p.

Mentions Herbert frequently in this background study of significant aspects of seventeenth-century education and sensibility. Argues that, although education does not account for the literature of the period, an understanding of the curriculum helps the modern reader "to recover the way in which Browne or Herbert was read by his contemporaries; and such knowledge is likely to bring us closer to the author's intention" (p. xvii). Chapter 1 discusses the training offered students in language, logic, and rhetoric. Chapter 2 studies the emphasis of the curriculum on logical and dialectical argumentation. Chapter 3 comments on seventeenth-century fondness for word play. Chapter 4 discusses the central role that religion played in the formation of the seventeenth-century reader and writer. Chapter 5 discusses Nowell's *Catechism* as an example and synopsis of religious ideas generally shared by the writers of the period. Chapter 6 outlines the principles of biblical typology and the prevalence of typological thinking in the age. Comments on the rhetorical method of argument in Herbert's "Employment (II)" (pp. 65–66) and his uses of logic and debate in such poems as "Deniall," "The Quidditie," "The Reprisall," "The Thanksgiving," "H. Baptisme (I) and (II)," "The Temper (I) and (II)," "Love (I)," "Church-monuments," and "Church-musick," especially stressing Herbert's arranging of poems in pairs in order to form complex inner relationships. Discusses Herbert's use of titles that have complex and multilevel meanings, especially "The Agonie," "Divinitie," "Unkindnesse," "The Temper (I)," "Mans medley," "The Storm," "The Size," "Redemption," "Businesse," and "Dialogue" (pp. 73–79). Comments on "Man" as reflecting a typical seventeenth-century attitude toward man in the hierarchy of creation (pp. 103–4). Presents examples from *The Temple* to illustrate generally accepted religious notions of the time and argues that an understanding of the nuances of mood and meaning in many of Herbert's poems requires knowledge of generally accepted religious views such as those contained in Nowell's *Catechism* (pp. 115–20). Gives a close reading of "The H. Scriptures (II)" as an example of Herbert's uses of biblical typology (pp. 130–31) and comments on the wide-ranging influence of typological thinking on the structure and design of *The Temple* (pp. 138–41). Maintains that the poems preceding "Coloss.iii.3" "lay the foundations of the doctrines of redemption and the mysteries of faith" and that those following the poem emphasize "the difficulties the Christian encounters in building on these foundations" (p. 142). Contrasts briefly Herbert's and Milton's approaches to typology, arguing that Herbert's interpretation "is reminiscent of the Epistle to the Hebrews, in which Old Testament types prefigure the antitypes of the New, and both in turn anticipate the full revelation of heaven" (p. 146), while Milton recalls the approach of St. Paul.

**804. Murrin, Michael.** "The End of Allegory," in *The Veil of Allegory: Some Notes Toward a Theory of Allegorical Rhetoric in the English Renaissance*, 167–98. Chicago and London: University of Chicago Press.

Briefly discusses Herbert as an allegorist: "He cast his *Temple* in allegorical form and used the traditional metaphors and symbols of the Christian-biblical tradition" (p. 195). Argues that Herbert's style is "simple, his wit restrained, and his allegory depends upon popular symbols, unfamiliar to us but well-known in the seventeenth-century" (p. 195). Maintains that Herbert, "more than anyone perhaps, put into effect the old principle: *ars est celare artem*" and that, as far as the more elaborate forms of allegory are concerned, Herbert "is a sign of the end" (p. 196). Concludes that the allegory that survived the change "was of the simplified, clear type which Herbert used but—after Bunyan—without the profundity of his Christian symbols" (p. 197).

**805. Rothschild, Phillipe de.** "George Herbert, 1593–1633," in *Poèmes élisa-béthains*, 259–75, 389–91. Preface de André Pieyre de Mandiargues. Introduction de Stephen Spender. Notices biographiques de Christopher Ricks. Paris: Seghers.

Brief introduction to Herbert's life and poetry (pp. 259–63), followed by "Easter-wings," "The Church-floore," "Content," "The Flower," "Aaron," "Man," and "Love (III)," with French translations on facing pages (pp. 264–75). Notes and variants on the text, in English and French (pp. 389–91). Calls *The Temple* "un des plus importants volumes de poésie religieuse de la littérature anglaise" (p. 263).

**806. Roy, V[irendra] K[umar], and R. C. Kapoor.** "Metaphysical Poets," in *John Donne and Metaphysical Poetry*, 18–44. Dehli: Doabo House.

General introduction to the major characteristics of metaphysical poetry with brief critical comments on Donne, Herbert, Carew, Crashaw, Vaughan, Marvell, Cowley, and Herrick. Maintains that Herbert's poetry reflects his unflinching faith in the Church of England and is characterized by his conversational tone with God, lack of sentimentality, variety of metrical forms, technical invention, use of everyday images, and economy of expression. Contends that Herbert's conceits are based on a contrast between the dignity of his subject matter and the familiarity of the images that he employs to illustrate it.

**807. Ruthven, K. K.** *The Conceit.* (The Critical Idiom, edited by John D. Jump, vol. 4.) London: Methuen & Co. 70p.

Discusses the word *conceit*, the theoretical basis of conceits, some common types of conceits, and the decline of the conceit. Mentions Herbert throughout and briefly comments on his uses of typology, as evidenced in "The Agonie."

**808. Shawcross, John T., and Ronald David Emma, eds.** *Seventeenth-Century English Poetry.* (Lippincott College English Series.) Philadelphia and New York: J. B. Lippincott Co. xvii, 636p.

Includes a general introduction to seventeenth-century poetry (pp. 1–11) and a general bibliography (pp. 13–15). Presents a brief introduction to Herbert's life and works, with a selected bibliography (pp. 196–98), and reproduces forty-four poems from *The Temple*, with explanatory notes (pp. 198–239).

**809. Shelston, A. J.** "George Herbert's 'Employment (II).'" *Critical Survey* 4:92–95.

Presents a close reading of "Employment (II)" and maintains that it is "fluctuation of mood that provides the major interest as one examines the poem in detail" (p. 95). Argues that the poem develops "in terms of a series of cryptic statements rather than a logical and unified argument" and that the very inconsistencies in it "express its particular truth: its fluctuations are the fluctuations of the experience which it defines" (p. 95).

**810. Tashiro, Tom T.** "English Poets, Egyptian Onions, and the Protestant View of the Eucharist." *JHI* 30:563–78.

Points out that in his fifteenth satire Juvenal says that Egyptians never ate onions because they believed them to be vegetable deities but they were not reluctant to practice cannibalism. Relates how the onion became a symbol of cannibalism and was used by writers to attack the notion of the Eucharist. Argues that in *The Church Militant* Herbert is probably referring to Juvenal's onions when he speaks of the Egyptian "who makes a root his god" (line 115). Observes that, since Herbert viewed the world and history typologically, his reference to Egyptian idolatry is meant to apply to Roman Catholicism as well. Maintains that in lines 127–28 of the poem European statues of enshrined saints also become a "type" of the Egyptian onions. Comments also on Donne's influence on *The Church Militant*, noting that Herbert uses Donne's "characteristic meters, something Herbert never does again," and that many ideas and phrases in the poem "can be traced directly to either the *Metempsychosis* or to the two *Anniversaries*" (p. 572).

**811. Tokson, Elliot H.** "The Image of the Negro in Four Seventeenth-Century Poems." *MLQ* 30:508–22.

Discusses the image of the Negro in Herbert's "Aethiopissa ambit Cestum Diuersi Coloris Virum," Henry Rainolds's "A Blackmore Mayd Wooing a fair Boy," Henry King's "The Boy's answer to the Blackmore," and John Cleveland's "A Fair Nymph Scorning a Black Nymph Boy courting her." Compares and contrasts the poems to show how they dramatize certain major attitudes toward Negroes: "The attitudes suggested by the sympathetic treatment in the poems of Herbert and Rainolds tend to stand out clearly against the popular tendency to view the Negro solely in derogatory terms as unfeeling, ugly, inferior, savage and subhuman; the speakers in the King and Cleveland poems, on the other hand, add to the texture of conceptions that divided the races then, and still to some degree keep them apart today" (p. 522). Maintains that Herbert's poem rises above mere cleverness and "sympathizes imaginatively with its subject, producing a sensitively realized scene" (p. 509): "To be the only poem about secular love written by a religious poet would make this poem unique; to be written in a period in which the very nature of the Negro as a human being was considered questionable makes it remarkable" (p. 510).

**812. Tonkin, Humphrey.** "A Bibliography of George Herbert 1960–1967: Addenda." *SCN* 27:29.

Addenda to "George Herbert: A Recent Bibliography, 1960–1967," compiled by Harry B. Caldwell, Edward E. Samaha, Jr., and Donna G. Fricke (entry 751). Lists eighteen items.

**813. Untermeyer, Louis.** "The Oddities of Poetry," in *The Pursuit of Poetry: A Guide to Its Understanding and Appreciation With an Explanation of Its Forms and a Dictionary of Poetic Terms*, 124–37. New York: Simon and Shuster.

Discusses briefly Herbert's highly experimental forms, his anagrams, acrostics, echo verses, and shaped poems. Maintains that "never has there been a poetry so pious and yet so playful" (p. 124). Brief critical commentary on "Anagram of the Virgin Marie," "Paradise," "Heaven," and "The Altar."

**814. Yoshida, Sachiko.** "George Herbert: *The Temple* ni okeru Naiteki Henka" [George Herbert: His Inner Conflict in *The Temple*]. *Mukigawa Joshi Daigaku Kiyo* (Jimbunkagaku-hen) [Bulletin of the Mukogawa Women's University, Humanities] no. 17 (August): 123–29.

Discusses Herbert's inner conflict and his transition from conflict to resolution in *The Temple*.

# *1970*

**815. Bradbury, Malcolm, and David Palmer, eds.** *Metaphysical Poetry.* (Stratford-Upon-Avon Studies, 11.) London: Edward Arnold; New York: St. Martin's Press. 280p.

Reprinted, 1971.

Collection of ten essays that reflects "the shifts of emphasis that have taken place since the revival of modern interest in 'metaphysical poetry'" and shows that "there is an evident desire to see these poets in new contexts, and to relate them to a more varied and extensive awareness of the different kinds of poetic activity that belongs to this period" (pp. 6–7). Essays in which Herbert is discussed have been entered separately in this bibliography (entries 831, 839, 841).

**816. Carpenter, Margaret.** "From Herbert to Marvell: Poetics in 'A Wreath' and 'The Coronet.'" *JEGP* 69:50–62.

Presents a close reading of Herbert's "A Wreath" and Marvell's "The Coronet" in order to show that, although both poems are similar in a number of respects, they greatly differ and maintains that a study of their dissimilarities reveals a great deal about each poet's achievement. Argues that although both poems deal with "the problem of writing a poem felt by its author to be not truly worthy of God" (p. 51), Herbert asks God to substitute a more fitting poem for his unworthy one, whereas Marvell seeks annihilation of both his poem and his body. Finds two major differences: (1) Marvell "makes more explicit than Herbert the double subject of his poem: the poet-artist in particular and man in general as a creative being and for whom, therefore, the specific poet-artist can be a metaphor" and (2) Marvell "operates primarily by the indirection of ironic implication and suggestion" (p. 61).

**817. Dieckmann, Liselotte.** "Poetic Hieroglyphics," in *Hieroglyphics: The History of a Literary Symbol*, 86–96. St. Louis: Washington University Press.

Maintains that Joseph Summers's chapter 6, "The Poem as Hieroglyph," in *George Herbert: His Religion and Art* (entry 435) is "the most interesting study of the term hieroglyphic in the metaphysical poets" (p. 94). Shows how the term is used metaphorically in the seventeenth century and "has lost its connection with Egypt": "Neither the *Altar* nor the *Wings* by Herbert are Egyptian hieroglyphics, nor did the Egyptians write poetry to explain a visual image or to be considered, formally, as a symbol" (p. 95). Distinguishes between hieroglyph and emblem.

**818. El-Gabalawy, Saad.** "George Herbert's Affinities with the Homiletical Mode." *Humanities Association Bulletin* 21:38–48.

Discusses a number of relationships and common features between Herbert's theory and practice of poetry and the homiletic literature of his day, noting that "there is no division in Herbert's consciousness between his career as a poet who communicates his religious experience and his vocation as a priest who conveys the Word of God to man" (p. 47). Maintains that the preacher and the poet shared similar assumptions about the purpose and function of their respective arts; that they employed similar uses of rhetoric, diction, and imagery; that they attempted to convey a conversational tone and a sense of spontaneous thought; and that they held similar views on the employment of humor, irony, sarcasm, and mimicry and shared a fondness for proverbs.

819. ———. "The Pilgrimage: George Herbert's Favourite Allegorical Technique." *CLAJ* 13:408–19. Comments on a number of Herbert's allegorical poems, especially "The Pilgrimage," "Peace," "Redemption," "Christmas," and "The Bag," "with the intention of showing that the pilgrimage is the poet's favourite allegorical form, demonstrating how he revitalizes this traditional method, with a didactic purpose, to make it a dynamic vehicle freshly available to serious poetry" (p. 408).

820. **Ellrodt, Robert.** "George Herbert and the Religious Lyric," in *English Poetry and Prose, 1540–1674*, edited by Christopher Ricks, 173–205. (History of Literature in the English Language, vol. 2.) London: Barrie & Jenkins.
   Paperback ed., Sphere Books, 1970.
   Reprinted in *Essential Articles for the Study of George Herbert's Poetry*, edited by John R. Roberts (entry 1216), 3–32.
   Discusses Herbert's religious lyric, contrasting his achievement with that of Donne, Crashaw, Vaughan, and Traherne. Maintains that "a strong flavour of individuality is the distinguishing mark and excellence of the religious lyric in seventeenth-century England, as compared with earlier devotional verse or with the Baroque lyric of the Continent" (p. 173). Recognizes the various currents of philosophical and theological thought that shaped Herbert's vision and admits the influence of Donne, the liturgy, the emblem tradition, and so forth, but stresses the individuality of Herbert's imagination and style. Discusses Herbert's intuition of space and time as reflected in his poetry, his individual religious sensibility and mode of devotion, and his unique sense of form.

821. **Enomoto, Kazuyoshi.** "George Herbert to Shinko-shi—Donne kara Herbert e" [George Herbert and Divine Poetry—from Donne to Herbert]. *Aichi Daigaku Bungaku Ronshu* (Studies in Literature, Bulletin of the Faculty of Literature, Aichi University) no. 45 (December): 53–83.
   Discusses Donne's influence on Herbert's poetry, especially on Herbert's use of wit, conceits, rhythm, and meter. Maintains that Donne's example encouraged Herbert to reject traditional forms of devotional poetry and to express his religious experience in a personal and individualistic style. Compares "Thou hast made me," "Batter my heart," and "Oh, to vex me, contraryes meet in one" to Herbert's poems to illustrate the point.

822. **Esch, Arno.** "Die 'metaphysische' Lyrik," in *Epochen der englishchen Lyrik*, edited by Karl Heinz Göller, 100–128. Düsseldorf: August Bagel Verlag.
   A general introduction to metaphysical poetry (pp. 100–104), followed by discussions of individual poets, including Herbert. Attributes the 1920s rebirth of interest in

metaphysical poets to the similarities that the poets of the time perceived between their situation and that of Donne and his contemporaries. Maintains that metaphysical poetry evidences a continuity with Renaissance poetry, not a sudden rupture. Presents a survey of Herbert's life and poetry (pp. 112–17) and comments in particular on his religious attitudes and sensibility. Remarks on the many kinds of poems in *The Temple*—pattern poems, acrostics, sonnets, lyrics, and so on. Praises Herbert's poetry for its simplicity and restraint, its musicality, its highly conscious structure and use of homely, everyday imagery, and its experimentation with form and metrics. Comments on how the stanzaic pattern of the poem or its emblematic title often helps explain or reinforce its meaning.

**823. Farmer, Norman K., Jr.** "A Theory of Genre for Seventeenth-Century Poetry." *Genre* 3:293–317.
Maintains that most critical discussion of seventeenth-century poetry is devoted to the lyric and that other genres tend to be neglected. Presents a theory of genre as a way of laying "the aesthetic foundation for an understanding of seventeenth-century poetry that is based on something other than whether a poem is 'metaphysical' or 'cavalier,' 'classical,' or 'Jonsonian'" and "offers an explanation for the richness of seventeenth-century poetry by showing how the lyric stood in relation to other more public genres commonly practiced at the time and how poets were able to develop the 'I' of the lyric poem with greater facility than their predecessors by virtue of cutting across generic lines and developing the rhetorics of various other modes as well" (p. 312). Maintains also that "our awareness of the relative referentiality and contextuality of the various genres and subgenres of seventeenth-century poetry serves to remind us of some very important cultural factors that led to the development of the lyric" (p. 312). Discusses the nondidactic sacred lyric as one of the specific genres of the seventeenth century and distinguishes it from the secular lyric. Argues that, although the sacred lyric "is a self-enclosed form which invites full play of the reader's critical imagination within the construct of the poem," the "very fact that it is sacred rather than secular poses a problem for the critic who would nonetheless make fine distinctions regarding referentiality" (p. 310). Maintains that Herbert's poems, which primarily deal with the problem of belief, "continually invite their readers to make the referential leap between poem and belief" or "between the poem and the liturgy" (p. 310). Suggests that both Rosemond Tuve's *A Reading of George Herbert* (entry 409) and Arnold Stein's *George Herbert's Lyrics* (entry 773) may mislead the reader into thinking that in order to understand and appreciate Herbert's poems one need only master the various contexts of belief (Tuve) or only focus on the interiorized contexts (Stein).

**824. Fish, Stanley E.** "Letting Go: The Reader in Herbert's Poetry." *ELH* 37:475–94.
Expanded version, "Letting Go: The Dialectic of the Self in Herbert's Poetry," in *Self-Consuming Artifacts: The Experience of Seventeenth-Century Literature* (entry 905), 156–223.
Maintains that the reader is very much a part of the drama and the process in Herbert's poems. Argues that "those problems which engage Herbert's protagonists engage his reader also" and that the poems "are structured so as both to describe an experience and give one, and that experience is, in a very special sense, self-diminishing" (p. 476). Demonstrates that characteristically Herbert asserts in his poems that God is everything and that thus "the claims of other entities to a separate existence, including the claims of the speakers and readers of these poems, must be relinquished"

(p. 478). Argues that Herbert consciously "writes himself out of his poems" so that they become, "quite literally, *God's* word" (p. 479) and that as readers of the poems we are required "to let go first of the terms in which we think (and say), and then of thinking, and finally of (separate) being, in all its manifestations, including Herbert's poetry" (p. 480). Illustrates this thesis through a close reading of "Clasping of hands," "Even-song," "The Holdfast," "A true Hymne," and especially "The Altar."

**825. Gallagher, Michael P.** "Rhetoric, Style, and George Herbert." *ELH* 37:495–516.

Discusses Herbert's poetry "in the light of his professional expertise in the arts of style and language" (p. 495) and attempts "to clarify what the plain style meant in the rhetoric that Herbert knew, examining his own views on style and poetry insofar as we know them, and finally looking at the rhetoric of some of his poems" (p. 496). Maintains that Herbert endorses the classical plain style as it was adapted to Christian rhetoric by St. Augustine in his *De Doctrina Christiana* and shows that for Herbert the plain style "was clearly more than a matter of figures or language or logical structure; it involved moral values and attitudes to experience" (p. 512).

**826. Graff, Gerald.** "Action and Argument," in *Poetic Statement and Critical Dogma*, 112–37. Evanston: Northwestern University Press.

Contrasts the structure and organizational principles of "The Collar" and "Church-monuments." Argues that "The Collar," organized psychologically or associatively, progresses "fitfully from thought to thought, suggesting the spontaneous and unpremeditated process of a mood of spiritual restlessness and rebellion" (p. 113), whereas "Church-monuments" is "explicitly logical, expository, and propositional" (p. 114). Acknowledges, however, that "Church-monuments" is "as much a presentation of the *act* or *process* of thinking and feeling as is 'The Collar'" and that "The Collar," "despite the associative and spontaneous character of its development" (p. 117), owes something to logic and "is ordered with regard to psychological probability—how a person of volatile temperament would be likely to be react under the strain of a strict religious discipline" (p. 118).

**827. Halewood, William H.** "Herbert," in *The Poetry of Grace: Reformation Themes and Structures in English Seventeenth-Century Poetry*, 88–111. New Haven and London: Yale University Press.

Argues that certain Reformation ideas, interests, and attitudes not only shape Herbert's theology and preoccupations but also influence the characteristic forms of his poetry. Maintains, for instance, that the basic situation that Herbert depicts in "The Collar" has striking similarities to Calvin's theology. Maintains that "by appealing to a Reformation reading of life instead of the medieval one that Miss Tuve suggests (though not denying continuities), we secure the double benefit of restoring to Herbert an appropriate intellectual background (a guard against random modernizations) and preserving the modern critic's perception that there is a special element of shock in the poem" (p. 96). Shows how a Reformation reading of life contains the elements of shock, surprise, and paradox. Discusses the specifically Protestant and Augustinian nature of Herbert's poetry, finds a number of elements that could be called "enthusiastic," and thus accounts for Herbert's appeal among the Nonconformists: "His account of the religious life, though attentive to church feasts and occasions and to the Church as an institution . . . , is mainly cast in terms of vivid personal experiences which practitioners of individual religion would recognize and appreciate" (p. 102). Maintains that Herbert's Christology, his stress on the importance of the will, and his strong and precise sense of humility are fully in accord with and informed by Protestant teaching. Calls Herbert's poetry "the poetry of reconciliation" and argues that "the gap between ostensible truth and the truth of God is Herbert's constant theme and is the conceptual basis for a poetic form in which opposites clash violently and subside in reconciliations which are in fact victories for one voice in the dialectic and defeats for the other" (p. 98). Relates Herbert's plain style to his theological views.

**828. Handscombe, R. J.** "George Herbert's 'The Collar': A Study in Frustration." *Lang&S* 3:29–37.

A reading of "The Collar" that employs interpretative stylistics. Sees the poem as "*a linguistic event which demands developing response*" (p. 29). Maintains that in the poem Herbert represents "by way of reflection in language the pain of a crisis in religious conviction through an assault on the reader's faith in his own linguistic competence, a crisis almost as important and painful" (p. 37).

**829. Herbert, George.** *Herbert's Remains. Or Sundry Pieces of that Sweet Singer of The Temple, Mr George Herbert (1652).* (A Scolar Press Facsimile.) Menston, Eng.: Scolar Press. 168, 194p.

Facsimile (original size) of the 1652 *Remains* (Wing H 1515). Includes "A prefatory View of the Life of Mr. Geo. Herbert" (later claimed by Barnabas Oley as his), *A Priest to the Temple, Jacula Prudentum,* two prayers, "Mr. G. Herbert to Master N. F.," three Latin poems, and "An Addition to Apothegmes by Severall Authors" (none of which is by Herbert). Bibliographical note on the volume and on items included.

**830. Himuro, Misako.** "George Herbert Henreki" [A George Herbert Pilgrimage]. *Seiki* [Century] no. 246 (November): 65–72.

Records impressions on a trip to Bemerton.

**831. Hinman, Robert B.** "The Apotheosis of Faust: Poetry and New Philosophy in the Seventeenth Century," in *Metaphysical Poetry,* edited by Malcolm Bradbury and David Palmer, 149–79. (Stratford-Upon-Avon Studies, 11.) New York: St. Martin's Press; London: Edward Arnold.

Rejects the generally accepted twentieth-century view that during the seventeenth century art and science were fundamentally opposed to each other and that the new science had a bad effect on the poetry of the period. Maintains that actually the artists and the new philosophers were "spiritual allies, even if they were not always aware of the alliance, and that despite individual and occasional antagonisms—the total effect of each group on the other was salubrious" (p. 149). Argues that "the same ordering, synthesizing, all encompassing, imaginative surge toward 'reality,' towards as much truth as man can grasp or express, seems evident in such diverse achievements as *The Temple* and *Principia Mathematica*" (p. 156). Shows that Herbert in *The Temple* "is just as much concerned with demonstrating or discovering a pattern where none seems to be as Newton is" and that Herbert's poems "express a kind of spiritual topology in which inside and outside are seen to be one, just as Newton's mathematics express an unseen connection between falling bodies and planetary motions" (p. 157).

**832. Hobsbaum, Philip.** "Consensus and Reconciliation," in *Theory of Criticism,* 115–42. Bloomington and London: Indiana University Press.

Surveys the critical argument, initiated by William Empson (entry 131) and Rosemond Tuve (entry 409), about how "The Sacrifice" should be read. Points out that one school of thought (represented by such critics as Rosemary Freeman and Rosemond Tuve) "considers that no reading is adequate unless it takes in all that probably influenced the poem" while the other (represented by such critics as William Empson and L. C. Knights) "would read the poem as we read the living verse of our own time" (p. 131). Observes that there are a number of critics (such as Margaret Bottrall and Louis Martz) "who find no especial difficulty in coming to terms with both parties" (p. 131).

**833. Huntley, Frank L.** "A Crux in George Herbert's *The Temple.*" *ELN* 8:13–17.

Reprinted in revised and expanded form in "What Happened to Two of Herbert's Poems?" in *Essays in Persuasion: On Seventeenth Century English Literature* (entry 1292), 65–76.

Maintains on the basis of history, manuscript evidence, and close literary analysis that "the poem now so awkwardly entitled 'Church-lock and key' be called what Herbert once called it, 'Prayer,' and that it be read not with 'Church-Monuments' and 'Church-Windows' but in the position where Herbert once placed it, next to that masterful sonnet, 'Prayer the church's banquet . . . something understood'" (p. 17).

**834. Ishii, Shōnosuke.** *Sekai Meishishu Taisei—Igirisu-hen (I)* [An Anthology of World Famous Poems—English Poetry (I)]. Tokyo: Heibonsha.

Translates into Japanese "Jordan (I)," "Vertue," "Life," "The Collar," and "Love (III)" (pp. 121–23).

**835. Lamba, B. P., and R. Jeet Lamba.** "Herbert's 'The Agonie' 9–10." *Expl* 28:item 51.

Maintains that lines 9–10 of "The Agonie" ("A man so wrung with pains, that all his hair, / His skinne, his garments bloudie be") refer to David, not to Christ, as suggested by Rosemond Tuve in *A Reading of George Herbert* (entry 409). For a reply, see Edgar F. Daniels and René Rapin (entry 861).

**836. Leimberg, Inge.** "George Herbert 'The Sinner' der Tempel als Memoria-Gebäude." *Archiv* 206:241–50.

Explicates "The Sinner" in terms of its architectural images, especially in terms of Herbert's use of images of stone, engraving, and quarries. Maintains that "das Thema des Gedichte ist der Verlust und die Wiederherstellung der Ebenbeldlickeit" (p. 243). Also comments on the architectural imagery in *The Temple* in general.

**837. Lloyd, J. D. K.** "Where Was George Herbert Born?" *Archaeologia Cambrensis* 118:139–43.

Notes that there is no positive evidence to support the claim that Herbert was born at Montgomery Castle. Maintains that he was most likely born at Eyton-on-Severn in Shropshire, the home of his maternal grandmother, Lady Margaret Newport. Surmises that Herbert was probably baptized either in the chapel there or in the church in Wroxeter.

**838. McGrath, F. C.** "Herbert's 'The Bunch of Grapes.'" *Expl* 29:item 15.

Explicates "The Bunch of Grapes" to show that in the poem Herbert "has concisely and effectively woven his personal emotional experience and individual destiny with that of all men for all time and has resolved these mutual destinies in the blood of Christ." Notes that through its intricate uses of imagery and diction, the poem distinguishes between the "pre-Christian promise of everlasting joy and the Christian promise of salvation in the crucified and resurrected Christ."

**839. Mahood, M. M.** "Something Understood: The Nature of Herbert's Wit," in *Metaphysical Poetry*, edited by Malcolm Bradbury and David Palmer, 123–47. (Stratford-Upon-Avon Studies, 11.) New York: St. Martin's Press; London: Edward Arnold.

Surveys the range, complexity, and variety of Herbert's wit and shows that a "concern for dramatic form, with ordered movement towards a timely conclusion, guides Herbert in his choice and use of all the technical resources of his poetry: diction, imagery, sentence-structure, stanza forms, rhyme and rhythm" (p. 125). Illustrates generic points with detailed examples drawn from many of the poems, especially "Prayer (I)," "Constancie," "The Pearl," "Love unknown," "Vertue," and "Love (III)."

**840. Mangelsdorf, Sandra R.** "Donne, Herbert, and Vaughan: Some Baroque Features." *Northeast Modern Language Association Newsletter* 2:14–23.

Discusses baroque features in Donne's "The Canonization," Herbert's "Easter-wings," and Vaughan's "Corruption." Using the terminology of Wölfflin and Sypher, finds the following baroque qualities in "Easter-wings": its "exploration of an idea in the variance from man's fall in the first stanza and the speaker's own in the second, organic unity, use of images to reinforce ideas, nearseeing, molding, openness, and dynamism," and especially its "total merging of form with content" (p. 20).

**841. Martz, Louis L.** "The Action of the Self: Devotional Poetry in the Seventeenth Century," in *Metaphysical Poetry*, edited by Malcolm Bradbury and David Palmer, 101–21. (Stratford-Upon-Avon Studies, 11.) New York: St. Martin's Press; London: Edward Arnold.

Maintains that seventeenth-century devotion involved "an active, creative state of mind, a 'poetical' condition" in which "the mind works at high intensity" and that thus devotional poetry should not "be taken to indicate verse of rather limited range, 'merely pious' pieces without much poetic energy" (p. 103). Argues that devotional poetry is the result of "a state of mind created by the 'powers of the soul' in an intense dramatic action, focused upon one central issue" (p. 103). Warns against overestimating the influence of Donne on the development of English devotional poetry and contrasts the instability, tension, and even querulous action of Donne's *Holy Sonnets* with the deeply achieved sense of security and familiar confidence that pervades *The Temple*. Analyzes "Vertue," "Conscience," and other selections from Herbert to contrast the states of mind and resulting poetical techniques of the two poets. Comments in particular on the technique of repetition found throughout *The Temple*: "Upon the fabric established by these repetitions, Herbert weaves an astonishing variety of designs, including some of the boldest familiarity with God found anywhere in literature" (p. 111). Shows that Vaughan's poetry, though often in direct imitation of Herbert's, fails to achieve the same stability and architectural neatness.

**842. Molho, Blanca, and Maurice Molho, eds.** *Poetas ingleses, metafísicos del siglo XVII.* (Preparación de textos originales, Maria Gomis.) Barcelona: Barral Editores. 181p.

General introduction to metaphysical poetry and poets for the Spanish reader with selections from the poetry of Donne, John Fletcher, William Drummond, William Browne, Herbert, James Shirley, Waller, William Cartwright, Crashaw, Lovelace, Marvell, and Vaughan. In the introduction, "Prologo: John Donne y la poesia metafísica" (pp. 11–36), comments on Herbert's spiritual temper as it is reflected in his poems, maintaining that Herbert, "tentado también de pecar por el espíritu, sostiene en su vida una magnífica lucha con la Divinidad siempre victoriosa" (p. 28). Describes Herbert's God as "el Dios de las Batallas" and suggests that "se lanza a la lucha radiante de divino furor; martillea el suplicio del hombre con estallidos de su gozo brutal" (p. 30). Briefly compares and/or contrasts Herbert to Donne, Vaughan, Crashaw, Milton, and Blake. Anthologizes, without notes or commentary, "Nature," "Giddinesse," "The Temper (I)," "The Collar," "The Flower," and "Death" (pp. 108–23), with English and Spanish on facing pages.

**843. Nagasawa, Kunihiro.** "George Herbert Shiron—'Shinzo' no Image Imisuru mono" [What the Image of "Heart" Means—An Essay on George Herbert]. *Ibaraki Daigaku Kyoyobu Kiyo* [Bulletin of the College of General Education, Ibaraki University] 2 (March): 63–75.

Considers the meaning of the image of the heart as a battlefield where God's love struggles with man's sins.

**844. Patterson, Annabel M.** " 'True Nakedness': Elizabethan Sonnets," in *Hermogenes and the Renaissance: Seven Ideas of Style*, 122–52. Princeton: Princeton University Press.

Discusses the importance and possible influence of the Seven Ideas of style contained in *Concerning Ideas* by the second-century rhetorician Hermogenes of Tarsus on Renaissance rhetoric, poetics, and aesthetics. Points out that Herbert specifically mentions Hermogenes in *A Priest to the Temple* and comments on how Herbert deals with and reconciles the Ideas of Beauty and Verity in his poems. Observes that Herbert's sacred lyrics "reject artifice in exactly the same manner as do the sonnets of Sidney and Shakespeare, as part of a poetic stance of sincerity which he can take up or put down as necessary" (p. 148). Argues that in "Jordan (I)," "Jordan (II)," "The Forerunners," and "A true Hymne" Herbert rejects literary artifice. Maintains, however, that these poems "make it clear that Herbert consciously used opposing styles, one of which expresses the basics of his belief in monosyllables, and another which employs 'lovely enchanting language' but which makes exactly the same statements, only 'perhaps with more embellishment,' as he puts it in *The Forerunners*" (p. 151).

**845. Reiter, Robert E.** "George Herbert and His Biographers." *Cithara* 9:18–31.

Discusses the formation and development of the biographical tradition surrounding Herbert and surveys the biographical accounts of Nicholas Ferrar (1633), Barnabas Oley (1652), Walton (1670), George L. Duyckinck (1858), J. J. Daniell (1893), George Herbert Palmer (1905; entry 2), A. G. Hyde (1906; entry 11), F. E. Hutchinson (1941; entry 266), Joseph H. Summers (1954; entry 435), and Marchette Chute (1959; entry 510). Points out that, although various biographers have corrected certain details and minor facts in Walton's biography, "it was really not until 1954 that Joseph Summers radically reinterpreted the life of Herbert and showed that Walton's understanding of Herbert could be wrong" (p. 31). Points out a number of serious lacunae in our present information and notes that "about his activities from his late twenties to about 1633 we still know relatively little" (p. 31).

**846. Stanwood, P. G.** "Poetry Manuscripts of the Seventeenth Century in the Durham Cathedral Library." *DUJ* 31:81–90.

Describes Durham MS. Hunter 27, which contains a translation of Herbert's *The Church Militant* into Latin hexameters and also a Latin verse translation of "Good Friday" by James Leeke (1605–1654), a fellow of Peterhouse. Points out that since Leeke probably completed his translation soon after 1633, he is Herbert's first translator. Reproduces the first sixty-six lines of the translation.

**847. Stein, Arnold.** "Metaphysical Poets." *YR* 59:598–406.

Review article that evaluates Earl Miner's *The Metaphysical Mode from Donne to Cowley* (entry 802), A. L. Clements's *The Mystical Poetry of Thomas Traherne* (entry 784), Ann E. Berthoff's *The Resolved Soul: A Study of Marvell's Major Poems* (Princeton: Princeton University Press, 1970), and Louis L. Martz's *The Wit of Love: Donne, Carew, Crashaw, Marvell* (entry 800).

**848. Strzetelski, Jerzy.** *The English Sonnet: Syntax and Style.* Krakow, Poland: Jagellonian University. 149p.

A study in descriptive linguistics that examines the contribution of syntax to the style of the English sonnet. Announces his intent "to find out what describable formal syntactical features of the sonnets differentiate the style of the English sonneteers from one another" (p. 12). Mentions Herbert in several instances (pp. 25, 26–27, 82, 119, 127, 143). In particular, comments on "Prayer (I)," the only one of the 278 sonnets considered that does not contain a finite verb. Maintains that Herbert's style is more involved and complex than Donne's. Several illustrative tables.

**849. Summers, Joseph H.** "Gentlemen at Home and at Church: Henry King and George Herbert," in *The Heirs of Donne and Jonson*, 76–101. New York and London: Oxford University Press.

Calls *The Temple* "the best and wittiest collection of religious lyrics in English" (p. 88). Comments on *The Church-Porch* and explains its inherent relationship to *The Church*, which is more readily recognized as great poetry. Maintains that *The Church-Porch* is an effective and necessary presentation of the moral life as totally rational and that one of its chief pleasures is in recognizing "memorable formulations of traditional wisdom" (p. 91). Contrasts *The Church-Porch* and *The Church* and sees the latter as introducing the reader to "an almost completely different world of thought and discourse" (p. 96), in which instead of being told about religion the reader finds poems that are "the reflections and creations of a religious life: the hymns, complaints, cries, laments, examinations, quarrels, rejoicings, and promises of a talented poet who was most concerned with the relation of his experience to God's work and Word" (p. 97). Comments on Herbert's effective use of monosyllabic lines, his playfulness and diverse experimentation with form, his rhetorical skill, and his profound simplicity, which often conceals his art. Cites "Love (III)" as a prime example of Herbert's use of rhetoric and Christian persuasion.

**850. ———.** "The Heritage of Donne and Jonson." *UTQ* 39:107–26.

Distrusts the use of the term *metaphysical poets* because it "inevitably results in an emphasis on the influence of Donne and one kind of poetry at the expense of other influences and kinds" (p. 108) of equal interest. Maintains that *heirs of Donne and Jonson* is a preferable term, "not with the implication that later poets had any familial or natural rights or that either Donne or Jonson intended that they should inherit, but in simple recognition that they came to occupy a good deal of the literary estate of their two great predecessors" (p. 108). Maintains that the inheritance "was less important as a fabulously rich collection of specific models than as a suggestion of the possibilities available for individual poets who were willing to explore varying, and even contrasting, speakers, genres, and literary ideals" (p. 126). Outlines the major features of Donne's and Jonson's art, showing the differences as well as the similarities between the two. No specific mention of Herbert.

**851. Vendler, Helen.** "George Herbert's 'Vertue.'" *ArielE* 1:54–70.

Reprinted as chapter 1 of *The Poetry of George Herbert* (entry 1050), 9–24.

Detailed analysis of "Vertue." Shows that the surface simplicity and ease of the poem are deceptive and accounts for the complex, often surprising, and interrelated conceits that lie beneath its surface: "Almost every line in it surprises expectation, though few poems in English seem to unfold themselves with more impersonality, simplicity, and plainness" (p. 55). In order to illustrate the artistic excellence and precision of the poem, the author often rewrites individual lines and stanzas and also compares the poem with Wesley's adaptation of it: "The distinction between the hymn writer, versifying doctrine, and the poet, expressing feeling, is nowhere clearer than in Wesley's revisions of Herbert" (p. 70).

**852.** ———. "The Re-Invented Poem: George Herbert's Alternatives," in *Forms of Lyric: Selected Papers from the English Institute*, edited by Reuben A. Brower, 19–45. New York and London: Columbia University Press.

Reprinted as chapter 2 of *The Poetry of George Herbert* (entry 1050), 25–56.

Reprinted in *Literary Criticism: Idea and Act* (The English Institute, 1939–1972: Selected Essays), edited and with an introduction by W. K. Wimsatt (Berkeley, Los Angeles, London: University of California Press, 1974), 362–81; *Essential Articles for the Study of George Herbert's Poetry*, edited by John R. Roberts (entry 1216), 181–98.

Demonstrates how "a poem by Herbert can repudiate itself, correct itself, rephrase itself, rethink its experience, re-invent its topic" (p. 45). Argues that Herbert's poems are "constantly self-critical poems, which so often reject premises as soon as they are established" (p. 20). Shows that Herbert often uses a traditional image or concept but then frequently "re-invents the poem afresh as he goes along: he is constantly criticizing what he had already written down, and finding the original conception inadequate, whether the original conception be the Church's, the Bible's, or his own" (p. 24). Illustrates the complexity and pervasiveness of this principle, especially in "The Invitation," "Dooms-day," "Prayer (I)," "The Temper (I)," "The Forerunners," "Affliction (I)," "The Flower," and "Love (III)." Concludes that "it is in this free play of ideas that at least part of Herbert's true originality lies" (p. 45).

**853. Vickers, Brian.** *Classical Rhetoric in English Poetry.* London: Macmillan and Co.; New York: St. Martin's Press. 180p.

Mentions Herbert throughout this concise history of rhetoric. Gives examples of Herbert's uses of certain rhetorical figures: (1) *anadiplosis* in "Love (III)," (2) *anaphora* in "Longing," (3) *antanaclasis* in "Church-monuments," (4) *antimetabole* in "Affliction (I)" and "Hope," (5) *asyndeton* in "Good Friday," (6) *auxesis* in "Church-monuments," (7) *epanalepsis* in "Love (I)," (8) *gradatio* in "Justice (I)," "Confession," and "Sinnes round," (9) *paronomasia* in "The Temper (II)," (10) *polyptoton* in "The Forerunners," and (11) *syllepsis* in "Time." Presents a rhetorical analysis of "A Wreath" (pp. 161–63) to show how Herbert "makes a fresh and imaginative use of rhetoric" (p. 164).

**854. Watson, George.** "The Language of the Metaphysicals," in *Literary English Since Shakespeare*, edited by George Watson, 156–74. London, Oxford, New York: Oxford University Press.

Argues that "there is no strictly linguistic way to take intellectual possession of metaphysical poetry, and that this judgment must apply, though in differing measure, to Renaissance and to modern methods of linguistic analyses" (p. 162). Chooses Donne's "Negative Love" and Herbert's "Vertue" to test certain "ancient and accepted assumptions about the ways that language works in them" (p. 162). Comments on a number of common (though not universal) aspects of metaphysical poems: the narrative quality, the use of dramatic monologue, the sense that the poet and the reader share an experience, the coterie nature of much of the language, the uses of argumentation, and so forth. Argues that "the brief history of metaphysical poetry, from the 1590's down to the Restoration, seems to be a progress toward public status" and that "this is a language that begins in relative secrecy among friends, and turns decisively towards public utterance with Herbert's *The Temple*" (p. 170). Comments on literary, philosophical, and moral reasons for the virtual demise of metaphysical poetry after 1660.

**855. Williams, A. M.** Introduction, in *Conversations at Little Gidding. 'On the Retirement of Charles V.' 'On the Austere Life': Dialogues by Members of the Ferrar Family*, xi-lxxxvi. Edited with introduction and notes by A. M. Williams. Cambridge: Cambridge University Press.

An account of the Ferrar family, the life and discipline observed at Little Gidding, and the historical and religious events that shaped the spiritual temper of the community. Briefly points out the close parallels between the careers of Herbert and Nicholas Ferrar. Comments briefly on Herbert's *Briefe Notes on Valdesso's "Considerations"* and the translation of *Discorsi della vita sobria* of Luigi Cornaro.

**856. Williams, R. Darby.** "Two Baroque Poems on Grace: Herbert's 'Paradise' and Milton's 'On Time.'" *Criticism* 12:180–94.

Explicates Herbert's "Paradise" and Milton's "On Time" as "game poems," as "exercises in poetic fancy that intentionally riddle the imagination and challenge the reader to match wits with the poet" (p. 180). Characterizes the "game poet" by "his attempt to transcend ordinary poetic conventions (and often, verbal conventions as well), his intensely self-conscious playfulness, and his willingness to be deliberately obscure for wit's sake" (p. 181). Calls "Paradise" a "cryptic *technopaignion*, an art-plaything with a crossword puzzle-like riddle for the reader to unknit" (p. 182). Shows how the poem operates on two levels: one the clever celebration of the conventional *hortus conclusus* theme and the other an elaborate puzzle developed within the poem that allows the reader to pare certain of the capitalized letters and end up with the statement: I GROW CHRISTS FRIEND.

**857. Winny, James.** "A Critical Examination of Some Metaphysical Poems," in *A Preface to Donne*, 120–52. (Preface Books, edited by Maurice Hussey.) New York: Charles Scribner's Sons; London: Longman Group.

Presents a close reading of Herbert's "Conscience" (pp. 144–45). Primarily contrasts Herbert with Donne, suggesting that, whatever Herbert may have learned from Donne, "he was much closer in feeling and outlook to the writer of the twenty-third Psalm" (p. 145).

# 1971

**858. Blau, Sheridan D.** "The Poet as Casuist: Herbert's 'Church-Porch.'" *Genre* 4:142–52.

Reprinted in *Essential Articles for the Study of George Herbert's Poetry*, edited by John R. Roberts (entry 1216), 408–15.

Discusses the relationship between *The Church-Porch* and *The Church*, accounting for their moral, stylistic, and structural differences by relating the former to the seventeenth-century Anglican practice of case-divinity or casuistry. Notes that in *The Church-Porch* Herbert attempts to define holiness in terms of moral conduct; it is directed "not to the polluted but the perplexed, and it serves as a living guide to the everyday questions of what is right and lawful in particular actions" (p. 145). Maintains that Herbert considered *The Church-Porch* "as a sort of sermon based on practical divinity or casuistry and that its purpose, like that of all sermons, was to prepare its audience for the prayers of 'The Church'" (p. 150).

**859. Bottrall, Margaret.** "Herbert, 1593–1633," in *English Poetry: Select Bibliographical Guides*, edited by A. E. Dyson, 60–75. London and New York: Oxford University Press.
    Evaluative bibliographical essay on Herbert divided into five major sections: (1) texts, (2) critical studies and commentary, (3) biographies and letters, (4) bibliographies, and (5) background reading, followed by a selected listing of items according to the above categories.

**860. Chossonnery, Paul.** "La composition et la signification de *The Temple* de George Herbert." *EA* 24:113–25.
    Reinterprets the meaning of "The Altar" in the light of two of Herbert's Latin poems in *Lucus* and argues that the poem does not refer to a physical altar upon which the remainder of the poems are offered, as suggested by Joseph H. Summers, but rather refers to the fallen condition of man before he embarks on his Christian voyage. Sees "The Sacrifice" as a presentation of Christ, who redeemed fallen man and made his Christian life in the Church possible. Traces this symbolic journey in other poems to show that the main theme of *The Temple* is the problem of salvation: Herbert "allait démontrer à ses lecteurs comment chacun d'eux pouvait faire de son âme un Temple où Dieu pourrait venir habiter" (p. 123). *The Church-Porch* thus is seen as simply a moral treatise that shows those limited virtues that man can achieve without the help of the Church.

**861. Daniels, Edgar F., and René Rapin.** "Herbert's 'The Agonie.'" *Expl* 30:item 16.
    Two separate replies that argue that the man mentioned in the second stanza of "The Agonie" is Christ, not David, as suggested by B. P. Lamba and R. Jeet Lamba (entry 835).

**862. El-Gabalawy, Saad.** "George Herbert and the *Ars Amatoria*." *XUS* 10:28–33.
    Maintains that some modern critics tend to overemphasize the impact of secular love poetry on Herbert's religious lyrics and that "to lay too much stress on it may lead us to disregard the spiritual and ethical connotations of the poet's tears, sighs and complaints, which are, in fact, an integral part of his religious sensibility" (pp. 32–33). Maintains that Herbert would probably have scorned the notion that he was indebted to the love poets and would have argued that "these poets had derived their style and devices from the Hebrew religion" (p. 29). Points out various amatory elements found in the Psalms; in the works of St. Augustine, St. Bernard, St. Anselm, and St. Bonaventure; and in much medieval religious verse, all of which are more likely sources and models for Herbert than are the secular love poets.

**863. ———.** "A Seventeenth-Century Reading of George Herbert." *PLL* 7:159–67.

Maintains that the "Alphabeticall Table," a kind of subject index, composed by an anonymous compiler and found in the 1656 edition of *The Temple* and all subsequent editions up to 1709, provides "a window, or perhaps a loophole, however narrow, through which one may see how the poet was read by a seventeenth-century man attempting to guide the reader of his day" (p. 159). Shows that the index is important because "it classifies systematically some fundamental conceptions and motifs of the poet, provides a key to certain passages and poems, and suggests the age's understanding of *The Temple* as a whole" (p. 159). Maintains that the primary concern of the indexer was "to indicate the universal significance of *The Temple*" and that he "shows little interest in its poetry as a private statement expressing the author's individual experience" but sees *The Temple* "as an objective record of religious thought and feeling, valid for all Christians whatever their persuasions may be" (p. 167).

**864. Enomoto, Kazuyoshi.** "'Bi' to 'Ai' to 'Shin'—George Herbert no Shiteki Taido to 'Jordan' Poems wo Megutte" ["Beauty," "Love" and "Truth"—On George Herbert's Poetic Attitude, with Special Reference to the "Jordan" Poems]. *Aichi Daigaku Bungaku Ronshu* [Studies in Literature, Aichi University] no. 46 (March 1971): 107–32.
Cited in *The Renaissance Bulletin* (Tokyo) 5 (1978): 45. Not available.

**865. Ericson, Edward E., Jr.** "The Holy Mr. Herbert." *Christianity Today* 15 (10 September): 7–11.
Discusses Herbert as "one of the finest exemplars of wholeness and balance in the spiritual life" and as "the devotional poet par excellence" (p. 7). Maintains that, like St. Paul, Herbert recognizes the limitations of human reason and knowledge even though he is a very learned poet and writes poetry informed by learned images: "He felt no need to deny his mind in order to exercise his spirit" (p. 10). Argues that "it is the quality of his intellect" that "refines his devotion and makes his poetry, not a superficial emoting, but a powerful force for the promotion of truly spiritual living" (p. 11).

**866. Fens, K.** "Terzijde Liturgische teksten." *Streven* 24:1068–73.
Uses Herbert's "The Holy Scriptures (II)" as an example of the proper attitude for a religious poet and takes to task the contemporary Dutch religious poets for their views. Ridicules the widespread notion in Holland that contemporary readers cannot understand Scripture and require that it be rewritten in a contemporary idiom, using modern imagery. Concludes by quoting the first stanza of "Church-musick" and maintaining that, although the past is indeed past, the present makes a mistake by responding hostilely to it.

**867. Festugière, A. J.** *George Herbert, poète, saint, anglican (1593–1633).* (Etudes de théologie et d'histoire de la spiritualité, 18.) Paris: Librairie philosophique J. Vrin. 349p.
Primarily sees Herbert as an Anglican saint and stresses the religious influences on his sensibility and art, especially the influence of Calvinism and *The Imitation of Christ.* Maintains that *The Temple* "est *l'Imitation* mise en vers" (p. 11). Chapter 1, "Le cadre politique" (pp. 15–28), discusses the reigns of Elizabeth I, James I, and Charles I. Chapter 2, "Le cadre de la vie temporelle" (pp. 29–43), describes daily life in Herbert's time. Chapter 3, "Le cadre de la vie spirituelle" (pp. 45–145), is divided into three main sections: (1) "The Church-porch" (pp. 45–62) presents a prose

translation of the poem into French with commentary and concludes that the poem was written before 1627, (2) "Le Service Divin du Prayer Book et ses paralleles" (pp. 63–101) compares the Catholic Mass with the Anglican service and comments on the attitudes toward the Mass in Calvin's writings and in *The Imitation,* and (3) "Sources de la spiritualité de Herbert" (pp. 102–45) discusses the role of the sacraments in Herbert's spirituality and concludes that "sa vie spirituelle n'est pas essentiellement sacramentelle" (p. 102). Also comments on the influence of *The Imitation* and the Prayer Book and outlines the relationship between Herbert and the Anglican Church, especially the influence of the liturgical year. Chapter 4, "Vie de George Herbert" (pp. 147–84), presents a biography of Herbert. Chapter 5, "The Country Parson" (pp. 185–216), describes country life and parish life in Herbert's time and presents a French translation of parts of *The Country Parson.* Chapter 6, "Les crises spirituelles de George Herbert" (pp. 263–304), outlines Herbert's conversion, his obsession with sin, and his spiritual vacillations, exemplified by translations of a number of Herbert's poems. Appendix 1, *Le Complete Gentleman* de Henry Peacham" (pp. 305–18), discusses the influence of Peacham on Herbert's work, especially on *The Country Parson.* Appendix 2, "L «Autobiographie» d'Edward, Lord Herbert of Cherbury" (pp. 319–35), points out certain parallels between the *Autobiography* and *The Church-Porch* and *The Country Parson.* Appendix 3, "Le yeoman anglais sous Elizabeth et Jacques I" (pp. 337–49), describes the yeomen of Herbert's parish, their social background, financial status, religious faith, and so forth.
Review:
Anon., *TLS,* 22 September 1972, p. 1099

**868. Fisch, Harold.** "The Tudor Period and Beyond," in *The Dual Image: The Figure of the Jew in English and American Literature,* 25–52. New York: KTAV Publishing House.
    Maintains that "it is in the religious poetry of the seventeenth century that the Christian imagination first seriously evaluates the Jew as a positive figure, or at least first seriously tries to resolve the contradiction between the negative and positive aspects of the traditional portrait" (pp. 39–40) and observes that Herbert's "The Jews" is "the first genuinely and deeply sympathetic poem on the Jew," a poem that is very Christian in all respects but which "breathes a devout love of Israel as the people of God" (p. 40). Calls Herbert "the gentlest of English priests and the most simple, delicate, and masculine of English seventeenth century poets" (p. 40) and notes that his poems owe a great deal to the Hebrew biblical tradition.

**869. Fischer, Hermann, ed.** *Englische Barockgedichte: Englisch und Deutsch.* Stuttgart: Philipp Reclam Jun. 440p.
    General introduction to English baroque poetry (pp. 5–18). Includes "The Windows," "Prayer (I)," "The Starre," "Heaven," "The Altar," "A Wreath," "Love (III)," and "Decay," with German translations on facing pages (pp. 112–23); a biographical note on Herbert (p. 383); and notes on the individual poems (pp. 383–85). Selected bibliography (pp. 417–28).

**870. Gardner, Helen.** "Religious Poetry," in *Religion and Literature,* 121–94. New York: Oxford University Press; London: Faber and Faber.
    Reprinted, 1983.
    Series of three lectures delivered at the University of California at Los Angeles in March 1966: (1) "Religious Poetry: A Definition" (pp. 121–42), (2) Secular and Divine Poetry" (pp. 143–70), and (3) "Seventeenth-Century Religious Poetry" (pp.

171–94). Mentions Herbert only briefly in the first essay, which defines the nature of religious poetry and discusses various forms available to the religious poet at different periods. The third essay surveys English religious verse of the seventeenth century and attempts to account for the fact that this period, perhaps more than any other, was propitious for religious poetry. Denies the assumption that Herbert was greatly influenced by Donne: "There are very few even possible borrowings from Donne in Herbert's poetry and none that are unquestionable" (p. 173) and maintains that the most important bond among the religious poets of the time was the common religious tradition that they shared, especially the practice of discursive meditation. Contrasts Herbert's "The Sacrifice" with the late fifteenth-century "Woefully arrayed" (wrongly attributed to Skelton) and Herbert's "Dialogue" with the medieval "Quia Amore Langueo" to show the marked differences in the religious sensibilities and approaches of the two periods, especially commenting on Herbert's wit. Contrasts also Herbert's "Deniall" with Hopkins's sonnet "I wake and feel the fell of dark, not day" and briefly comments on "Redemption" and "Love (III)." Agrees with Huxley that the majority of Herbert's religious poems are poems of "inner weather." Suggests three things that make seventeenth-century religious poetry appeal to readers of various persuasions: (1) the "poems are made poems, not effusions of feeling" (p. 192); (2) the poetry is highly intellectual, "though full of feeling, emotion, strength of devotion and personal faith, [it] is laced by, and built upon, a scheme of thought, and a universe of discourse that is not the poet's own invention, but has the toughness of systems that have been debated and argued over for centuries"; and (3) the poetry reflects "the unembarrassed boldness and naturalness with which these poets approach their subject, and the freedom with which they bring the experience of daily life, their experience of art, their native powers of mind, their skill in argument and their wit, to play over religious doctrine, religious experience, and religious imperative" (p. 193).

**871. George, Arapara G.** "Metaphysical Poetry," in *Studies in Poetry*, 37–59. New Delhi and London: Heinemann.

Handbook for students and the general reader. Includes a brief introduction to metaphysical poetry, especially to Donne's poems. Herbert is mentioned only in passing. Calls Herbert's poems "short lyrics full of pious aspirations and admirable pictures of nature" (p. 42).

**872. Helsztyński, Stanisław.** "Herbert, George," in *Mały słownik pisarzy angielskich i amerykanskich* [A Concise Dictionary of English and American Writers], edited by Stanisław Helsztyński, 227. Warsaw: Wiedza Powszechna.

Biographical sketch and brief evaluation of Herbert's poetry. Calls it the highest achievement of the English religious lyric in the seventeenth century and points out several major characteristics of Herbert's art, especially his ability to convey deep religious feelings and his effectiveness in employing realistic images that figure forth a complex symbolism.

**873. Herbert, George.** *Selected Poems of George Herbert*. Edited with an introduction, commentary, and notes by Gareth Reeves. (Poetry Bookshelf.) London: Heinemann Educational Books; New York: Barnes and Noble. ix, 171p.

Introduction (pp. 1–31); selected bibliography (p. 32); seventy-two poems selected from *The Temple* and from Walton's *Lives* (pp. 33–109); extracts from *The Country Parson* (pp. 110–18); commentary and notes (pp. 119–66); and index of titles and first lines of poems (pp. 167–71). The introduction contains a biographical sketch and discusses the major characteristics of Herbert's art. Comments on the influences on his poetry, especially the Bible, and on the particular religious sensibility reflected in the poems. Comments in detail on "The Flower" as an example of Herbert's poetic technique and as it compares with Donne's "Loves growth." Also examines in some detail "The Collar," which is called "the supreme example of Herbert's powers of organization and perfection" (p. 29).

**874. Hoyles, John.** *The Waning of the Renaissance, 1640–1740: Studies in the Thought and Poetry of Henry More, John Norris, and Isaac Watts.* (International Archives of the History of Ideas, 39.) The Hague: Martinus Nijhoff. xvii, 265p.

Briefly compares Herbert with John Norris (sometimes called "the last of the metaphysicals") and with Isaac Watts. Comments on *Select Hymnes taken out of Mr Herbert's Temple* (1697), a volume published by the Dissenters for private and family devotions. Maintains that this volume "must have helped crystallise the influence of Herbert into a tradition" (p. 215).

**875. Hughes, Richard E.** "Metaphysical Poetry as Event." *HSL* 3:191–96.

Argues for the development of a "mythico-religious poetics" so that the twentieth-century reader might better understand and appreciate metaphysical poetry: "Writing in a time of anxiety amenable to myth; nurtured by a faith supportive of a sacramental response to reality; accepting the world as a panorama of symbol-saturated events rather than neuter objects: the poets of the earlier seventeenth century were involved in poem, myth and religious insight all at once" (p. 196). Mentions Herbert several times by way of illustration.

**876. Ishii, Shōnosuke.** "George Herbert no 'Kenshin'-ko (I)" [On George Herbert's "The Sacrifice (I)"]. *Shirayuri Joshi Daigaku Kenkyu Kiyo* [The Fleur-de-lis Review: Bulletin of the Shirayuri Women's College] no. 7 (December): 45–72.

Part 1 of a two-part series of articles. Translates "The Sacrifice" into Japanese and discusses its meaning from several points of view, examining its significance within the context of *The Temple*. For part 2, see entry 911.

**877. Johnson, Lee Ann.** "The Relationship of 'The Church Militant' to *The Temple*." *SP* 68:200–206.

Surveys attempts of modern critics to explain the exact relationship of *The Church Militant* to the total design of *The Temple* and finds all of them unconvincing. Maintains that the content and the formal and stylistic characteristics of *The Church Militant* and especially its positioning in the early folios suggest that it should be considered as a separate entity and not as an organic part of the three-part structure of *The Temple*.

**878. Kawata, Akira.** "George Herbert no Shukyo-shi—Humour to no kanren ni oite" [Religious Poetry of George Herbert—In Relation to Humor]. *Fukushima Daigaku Kyoiku Gakubu Ronshu* (Bulletin of the Faculty of Education, Fukushima University) no. 23, pt. 2 (November): 79–90.

Argues against the notion that Herbert is a humorless religious poet of melancholy and gloom. Maintains that his humor is sometimes ironical, sometimes full of wit, and sometimes touches our hearts warmly.

**879. Keast, William R., ed.** *Seventeenth Century English Poetry: Modern Essays in Criticism.* Rev. ed. (A Galaxy Book, 89.) London, Oxford, New York: Oxford University Press. x, 489p.

First published in 1962 (entry 584).

Collection of previously published essays. Five general essays on metaphysical poetry: (1) Herbert J. C. Grierson, "Metaphysical poetry," from *Metaphysical Lyrics & Poems of the Seventeenth Century: Donne to Butler* (entry 73), pp. xiii-xxxviii; (2) T. S. Eliot, "The Metaphysical Poets" (entry 70); (3) Helen Gardner, "The Metaphysical Poets," from *The Metaphysical Poets* (entry 477), pp. xix-xxxiv; (4) Earl Miner, "Wit: Definition and Dialectic," from *The Metaphysical Mode from Donne to Cowley* (entry 802), pp. 118–58; (5) Joseph Anthony Mazzeo, "A Critique of Some Modern Theories of Metaphysical Poetry" (entry 404). Three items specifically on Herbert: (1) Joseph H. Summers, "The Poem as Hieroglyph," from *George Herbert: His Religion and Art* (entry 435), pp. 123–46; (2) Jeffrey Hart, "Herbert's *The Collar* Re-Read" (entry 550); and (3) Arnold Stein, "George Herbert: The Art of Plainness" (entry 774).

**880. Kusunose, Toshihiko.** "George Herbert," in *Shi to Shi—Donne o Meguru Shijin tachi* [Poetry and Faith: Poets Surrounding Donne], 75–105. Tokyo: Keibunsha.

Biographical sketch that maintains that Herbert's various illnesses and diseases are clearly reflected in the poems. Maintains that Herbert is neither a mystic nor a nature poet but sees nature as God's second book of revelation. Comments on the tension between Herbert's sincere desire for simplicity and his rhetorical skill and the tension between the worldly and the sacred as reflected in his poetry. Discusses briefly the religious situation in England during the early seventeenth century and comments on Herbert's religious attitudes. Finds that the poems are characterized by a keen intellectual awareness and an equally fervent faith in God.

**881. Lea, Kathleen.** "The Poetic Powers of Repetition." *PBA* (for 1969) 55:51–76.

Reprinted as a separate monograph, London: Oxford University Press, 1971.

Discusses the variety, delicacy, and force of the rhetorical device of repetition in English poetry. Points out Herbert's skillful use of the device in "The Quip," "The Pearl," "The Bag," "Aaron," "Sinnes round," "Clasping of hands," "A Wreath," "Sighs and Grones," and "The Call."

**882. Mollenkott, Virginia R.** "Experimental Freedom in Herbert's Sonnets." *CSR* 1:109–16.

Disagrees with the idea that Herbert's use of the sonnet is characterized by an unexpected conservatism. Shows that "the sonnets are typical of Herbert's poetic output in their experimental freedom" (p. 116). Maintains that they exhibit a broad range of subject matter and are highly innovative in technique. Discusses the technical aspects of "Love (I)," "The Holdfast," "Josephs coat," and "The Answer."

**883. Orgel, Stephen.** "Affecting the Metaphysics," in *Twentieth-Century Literature in Retrospect*, edited by Reuben A. Brower, 225–45. (Harvard English Studies, 2.) Cambridge, Mass.: Harvard University Press.

Argues that the label *metaphysical* is largely the creation of critics, not of the poets themselves, yet concedes that "from the time 'metaphysical' was first formulated as a critical term its definition has remained relatively constant, but the list of poets whom critics regarded as metaphysical has varied wildly from generation to generation" (p. 226). Presents a brief history of the term and considers how a seventeenth-century reader would have regarded poetry such as Donne's. Shows that "no theory of metaphysical poetry has proved adequate" because "'metaphysical' refers really not to poetry, but to our sensibilities in response to it" (p. 245). Discusses in particular Renaissance concepts of poetic images, especially emblems, stressing that even in emblem books the verbal element is basic: "Renaissance poets tended to think of images as tropes or rhetorical figures, that is, as verbal structures," whereas twentieth-century critics "think of them as *visual* structures" (p. 238). Concludes that "what we find as critics in works of art is largely determined by what we are looking for, and it is one of the functions of criticism to make us look again and again at works of art in ways that are valid but untried," but warns that "we must beware of taking our responses for historical data" (p. 245). Mentions Herbert throughout by way of illustration.

**884. Powell, W. Allen.** "The Nature of George Herbert's Audience as Revealed by Method and Tone in 'The Country Parson' and 'The Temple.'" *Proceedings of the Conference of College Teachers of English of Texas* 36:33–36.

Maintains that the unsophisticated nature of his congregation at Bemerton influenced the method and tone of Herbert's sermons and that, therefore, he consciously avoided both theological controversy and the use of a witty and erudite style. Contends that the reaction of Herbert's audience is revealed in the method and tone of many passages in *The Temple* and primarily in *The Country Parson*: "The simplicity and homeliness of style, the directness of tone, the diplomatic method of reprimanding all wrongdoing, and the uses of images which unmistakably present a spiritual truth all combine to depict the simple faith and devout spirit of George Herbert's humble audience" (p. 36).

**885. Rauber, D. F.** "Critics and Collars." *PCP* 6:50–54.

Reply to P. M. Levitt and K. G. Johnston (entry 798). Rejects the notion that nautical imagery is dominant in "The Collar" and argues that, "when we examine the actual operation of the nautical imagery as presented by Levitt and Johnston, we find that it distorts rather than clarifies, destroys rather than organizes" (p. 51). Calls such criticism free, loose, fragmentary, highly limiting, and inhibiting.

**886. Toliver, Harold E.** "Poetry as Sacred Conveyance in Herbert and Marvell," in *Pastoral Forms and Attitudes*, 116–50. Berkeley, Los Angeles, London: University of California Press.

Contrasts Herbert and Marvell as poets who employ poetry as a sacred conveyance for bringing God to man and man to God. Argues that whereas Marvell typically employs persons, places, nature symbols, and specific historical events as the means for achieving this end, Herbert uses the Christian temple. Maintains that in *The Temple* the poet, the sinner, and the priest "approach communion [with God] in separate ways—through words, cleansing of the heart, and sacraments—but their methods often overlap and reinforce one another" (p. 116). Shows how each of these three "seeks conveyances to bring the mind to Christ and Christ into visible form where his Real Presence may be experienced" (p. 116). Discusses how Herbert transforms various secular forms and modes (the sonnet, the song, and the pastoral) into sacred conveyances and argues that "discovery of an appropriate mode of praise depends upon the poem's receptivity to renewal; as for the sinner, capacity to render praise depends upon the heart's preparation for sanctification and for the priest, upon the validity of the rites he administers" (p. 118). Notes that when "each of these conveyances succeed, Christ, the original of paradise, is rejoined to nature in them" (p. 118). Discusses the means that Herbert employs to make "poetry an enclosed epitome of the world and an incarnation of paradise" and examines some of the "theoretical and practical matters that a concept of sacred poetic and pastoral enclosures involves" (p. 119).

**887. Weinberger, G. J.** "George Herbert's 'The Church Militant.'" *Connecticut Review* 4:49–57.

Argues that *The Church Militant* is not simply a continuation of the two preceding parts of *The Temple* but should be viewed as a companion poem to them. Notes that *The Church-Porch* is an exhortation to seek salvation; *The Church* records the individual's struggles for salvation; and *The Church Militant* "is the same record but is presented as mankind's progress towards salvation through the ages (i.e. historically)" (p. 49). Maintains that the chief protagonist of *The Church Militant* is religion (the Church) and that the principal antagonist is sin. Presents a reading of the poem from this point of view and attempts to account for the differences between it and the two preceding parts of *The Temple*.

**888. West, Michael.** "Ecclesiastical Controversy in George Herbert's 'Peace.'" *RES* 22:445–51.

Rejects the notion that "Peace" is an allegory of human experience or of religious conversion and argues that "it draws upon thoroughly traditional symbolism to comment on ecclesiastical controversies of growing prominence in early seventeenth-century England" (p. 446). Maintains that stanza 1 attacks enthusiastic sects, especially the Seekers; stanza 2 is directed against the Puritans and the Congregationalists; stanza 3 challenges the Erastian position in the Anglican establishment; and the last four stanzas defend orthodoxy and serve as an invitation to participate in the Eucharist of the Anglican Church.

**889. White, Helen C., Ruth C. Wallerstein, Ricardo Quintana, and A. B. Chambers, eds.** "George Herbert," in *Seventeenth-Century Verse and Prose*, vol. 1, *1600–1660*, 270–96. 2d ed. New York: Macmillan; London: Collier-Macmillan.

Revision of the 1951 edition (entry 389), with a new introduction to Herbert and new selections, notes, and bibliography. Presents a general introduction to Herbert's life and poetry (pp. 270–71) and anthologizes forty-seven poems, with brief explanatory notes (pp. 271–96). Maintains that Herbert "has only one subject, the relationship between man and God," but that "the fact is not immediately apparent because Herbert approaches his subject from many different points of view and employs a wide range of poetic styles and forms" (p. 270). Points out that some of the poems "present at least the illusion of plainness, simplicity, and innocence that borders on the homely," while others "depend on devices and conceits fully as ingenious and witty as those of Donne" (p. 270). Observes, however, that in both kinds of poems the reader finds "a firmness of intellectual structure, a precision of phrasing, and an informing craftsmanship" and that in his best poems "there is a perfection of statement seldom equalled, rarely surpassed" (p. 270).

**890. Willy, Margaret, ed.** *The Metaphysical Poets.* (English Library, edited by James Sutherland.) London: Edward Arnold; Columbia: University of South Carolina Press. x, 149p.

An anthology of metaphysical poems that includes a general introduction to metaphysical poetry (pp. 1–11) and seven of Herbert's poems: "Affliction (I)," "The Collar," "The Flower," "The Pulley," "Man," "Redemption," and "Love (III)," with a brief critical introduction and explanatory notes for each (pp. 87–105). Selected bibliography.

**891. Yoshida, Sachiko.** "George Herbert: Bunretsu to Togo" [George Herbert: Discrepancy and Unification]. *Mukogawa Joshi Daigaku Kiyo* (Jimbunkagaku-hen) [Bulletin of Mukogawa Women's University, Humanities] no. 18 (September): 75–82.

Argues that, while Herbert was conscious of his divided self, he made a constant effort to find and praise God and to search for unity in the opposites of love and sin.

# *1972*

**892. Beer, Patricia.** *An Introduction to the Metaphysical Poets.* London and Basingstoke: Macmillan Press; Totowa, N.J.: Rowman & Littlefield. 115p.

General introduction to metaphysical poetry designed primarily for students in their first year of reading for an English honors degree. Divided into seven chapters: (1) The Term "Metaphysical," (2) The Chief Characteristics of Metaphysical Poetry, (3) John Donne, (4) George Herbert, (5) Henry Vaughan, (6) Andrew Marvell, and (7) The Metaphysical Poets and the Twentieth Century. The chapter on Herbert (pp. 55–70) presents a biographical sketch, comments on general features of Herbert's poetry, and suggests ways that modern students might approach the poetry. Also gives a brief critical reading of "Redemption," "Jordan (I)," and "Death."

**893. Brown, C. C., and W. P. Ingoldsby.** "George Herbert's 'Easter Wings.'" *HLQ* 35:131–42.

Reprinted in *Essential Articles for the Study of George Herbert's Poetry*, edited by John R. Roberts (entry 1216), 461–72.

Presents a detailed reading of "Easter-wings," commenting on the artistic integrity of the complex, sophisticated, and precise symbolism of the two wing-shaped stanzas and arguing that the poem "will not yield its meaning unless one reads the visual shape as part of its carefully controlled symbolic language" (p. 131). Maintains that, although the general shape of the poem is Greek in origin, "the precise dimensions [are] Hebrew, so that in writing 'Easter Wings' Herbert opened for himself the problem of defining an attitude toward the pagan and Hebraic sources from which the wings drew some of their meaning" (p. 131). Points out how Herbert skillfully transformed his sources: Simmias's form in *The Greek Anthology*, various Old Testament types, and Plato's metaphor of the winged soul in the *Phaedrus*. Maintains that the primary and controlling text that stands behind the poem is the messianic text in Mal. 4:2. Shows how the metrical and thematic decline and growth of the first stanza enact the fall of mankind and how the metrical and thematic decline and growth of the second stanza enact the speaker's personal experience. Argues that "Easter-wings" may be seen, in fact, as a model of the kind of precise artistic wholeness that Herbert strove for in all his poems.

**894. Brumm, Ursula.** "Edward Taylor and the Poetic Use of Religious Typology," in *Typology and Early American Literature*, edited by Sacvan Bercovitch, 191–206. Amherst: University of Massachusetts Press.

Compares and contrasts Edward Taylor's and Herbert's uses of biblical typology in their poetry: "Herbert's case is indeed relevant: his use of typology, although often more disguised and more integrated esthetically, is comparable to Taylor's and can perhaps help us to a fuller exploration of the problem" (p. 193). Comments specifically on "The Agonie," "Whitsunday," and "The Bunch of Grapes."

**895. Campbell, Jane.** "The *Retrospective* and Some Individual Reputations," in *The* Retrospective Review (*1820–1828*) *and the Revival of Seventeenth-Century Poetry*, 37–56. (Waterloo Lutheran University Monograph Series.) Waterloo, Ont.: Waterloo Lutheran University.

Comments on the important role played by the *Retrospective Review* in the reevaluation of seventeenth-century poetry and poets during the Romantic period. Maintains that Herbert, like Donne and Crashaw, "became better known in the early nineteenth century than he had been in the preceding period" but that "he was still looked down on," with most critics considering him "a good man but a bad poet" (p. 38). Observes that Herbert's poetry was most frequently criticized for its "low" imagery and its "repulsive" conceits and quaintness but was generally admired for its sincerity and piety. Comments briefly on the critical attitudes of Coleridge, Southey, De Quincey, Lamb, and an anonymous *Retrospective* reviewer on Herbert.

**896. Carrive, Lucien.** *La Poésie religieuse anglaise entre 1625 et 1640: Contributions à l'étude de la sensibilité religieuse à l'âge d'or de l'anglicanisme.* Vol. 1. Caen: Assoc. des Pubs. de la Faculté des Lettres et Sciences Humaines de l'Université de Caen. 546p.

Divided into four major sections. (1) "Les poètes religieux et la société" (pp. 15–49) discusses the social background of English religious poets from 1625 to 1640 and maintains that Herbert's poetry "ne se comprend pas si nous ne savons pas que le poète fut éminemment et jusqu'en ses dernières années un homme de cour" (p. 25). (2) "Les principales variétés" (pp. 53–259) comments on such matters as biblical imagery, paraphrases of the psalms, emblems, prayer, spiritual exercises, and mysticism and discusses Herbert's poetry in the light of each of these topics. Maintains that "la plus doué des écrivains de ce temps et ce pays aussi bien par la ferveur de sa foi et l'intensité des sentiments qu'il avait de la présence de Dieu que par l'habileté à utiliser les ressources du style et de la prosodie, ce prêtre au tempérament mystique, ce grand poète «métaphysique» qu'est George Herbert, se sent tenu lui aussi par cette idée de la prière" (p. 169). Nevertheless denies that Herbert is a mystic: "Pour Herbert, comme pour Luther, comme pour Bunyan, la paix et la joie ne viennent pas d'une illumination de la présence de Dieu, mais de la certitude du pardon et de l'amour gratuit de Dieu, cet amour qui ne met point de condition et ne fait pas acception de personne" (p. 248). Disagrees with Louis Martz concerning the dominance of the meditative mode in the period. (3) "Caractères de cette poésie" (pp. 263–339) discusses intellectual and moral aspects of the poetry of the period in general and of Herbert's poetry in particular. Maintains that Herbert, strictly speaking, should perhaps not be considered a "metaphysical" poet: "Il préfère l'affirmation des vérités de sa foi à l'exploration, même poétique, des subtilités et des contradictions de sa doctrine" (p. 267). (4) "Dieu et ses exigences" (pp. 343–513) comments on theological themes and attitudes reflected in the poetry of the period and specifically in Herbert's poetry: God, Christ, the Church, the sacraments, and so forth. Comments on the devotional aspects of the period and their effects on the poets. Bibliography (pp. 515–30). Index.

**897. Charles, Amy.** "The Williams Manuscript and *The Temple.*" *RenP* (for 1971), 59–77.

Reprinted in *Essential Articles for the Study of George Herbert's Poetry*, edited by John R. Roberts (entry 1216), 416–32.

Expresses doubt about whether anyone but Herbert can fully discern the exact reasons for the ordering of the poems in *The Temple*, "because, for one thing, they were not precise, but personal, intuitive, and allusive" (p. 60). Maintains that the Williams MS is "probably more important as a measure of Herbert's development than the more famous Bodleian Manuscript" (p. 59). Points out that, although the Williams MS contains less than half the poems in *The Temple*, it is important "for its earlier versions of many poems, the general three-part division, a scheme of order for the lyrics in 'The Church,' and Herbert's subsequent retention or rejection of some of its features" (p. 59). Compares the two manuscripts and finds the Williams "a skeletal version" of the Bodleian, with a number of significant variations, corrections, reorderings, and expansions. Shows that the final arrangement of the poems was carefully and subtly ordered by Herbert. Comments on how the Bodleian MS grew by accretions, points out that the title, *The Temple*, was probably added by Nicholas Ferrar, and comments on a number of individual revisions and changes. Concludes that at the time Herbert completed the Williams MS he was already an accomplished poet.

**898. Clark, Ira.** " 'Lord, in thee The *beauty* lies in the *discovery*': 'Love Unknown' and Reading Herbert." *ELH* 39:560–84.

Reprinted in *Essential Articles for the Study of George Herbert's Poetry*, edited by John R. Roberts (entry 1216), 473–93.

Revised and expanded as " 'Lord, in thee The *beauty* lies in the *discovery*': 'Love Unknown' as George Herbert's Neotypological Lyric Paradigm," in *Christ Revealed: The History of the Neotypological Lyric in the English Renaissance* (entry 1337).

Maintains that Herbert is "a radically typological lyricist, whose poems are structured on personal neotypology" (p. 560). Argues that in many of the poems of *The Church* Herbert creates a persona "who in contention against or in search of God discovers that he himself is a contemporary neotype of Christ akin to Old Testament types of Christ" (p. 560), that during the dramatic lyric the persona "discovers the beauty of God through situations Herbert has devised out of Christian recovery of types," and that thus the reader "reads through Herbert's persona and typological settings to discover the beauty of God" (p. 561). Presents a detailed reading of "Love unknown" to demonstrate this technique and shows how Herbert typically "teaches us to read typological situations, emblems, and diction; his symbolic matrices in *The Church*; his local poetic structure" (p. 583). Sees "Love unknown" as Herbert's version of Psalm 51.

**899. Daly, Peter M.** "Trends and Problems in the Study of Emblematic Literature." *Mosaic* 5:53–68.

Detailed discussion of the present state of scholarship in the study of emblematic literature, its major trends, and some of the remaining problems. Challenges certain assumptions in Rosemary Freeman's *English Emblem Books* (entry 337), especially her notion that "there is 'no necessary likeness' between an emblem image and its meaning" (pp. 56, 59). Brief references to Herbert.

**900. Dessner, Lawrence J.** "A Reading of George Herbert's 'Man.'" *CP* 5, no. 1:61–63.

Disagrees with those critics who see "Man" as one of Herbert's "expository and declaratory poems of praise" and argues that the poem is, in fact, "a dramatic monologue whose speaker's praise of God is criticized by the verbal actions of the poet" (p. 61). Maintains that the speaker's "faulty logic and the poem's diction expose him as one who has lost sight of *his* duty to that other 'world' which awaits *for* him, in exclusive contemplation of the world of Nature which waits *on* him" (p. 63). Comments on how the rhyme scheme and other technical features reinforce the meaning of the poem.

**901. Dundas, Judith.** "Levity and Grace: The Poetry of Sacred Wit." *YES* 2:93–102.

Discusses the inherent oppositions between wit and faith, attempts to identify those qualities "which distinguish poems that successfully marry wit and faith from those that merely yoke them together," and discusses the "form that sacred wit may take in poetry today" (p. 93). Argues that the tension between wit and faith "can be the very source of power in a poem by polarizing these opposites and then voluntarily sacrificing the cleverness of wit to the divine simplicity" (p. 96). Contrasts Christopher Harvey and Herbert in order to distinguish between true and false sacred wit. Comments specifically on "Prayer (I)" and sees the poem as "a good example of sacred wit in its incongruities, its far-fetched metaphors, both conventional and novel, which are nevertheless controlled both formally and emotionally" (p. 97).

**902. El-Gabalawy, Saad.** "George Herbert's Christian Sensibility: A Resumé by El-Gabalawy." *Cithara* 11:16–22.

Shows how completely Herbert's literary insights and art are informed by Christian doctrine and his sensibility permeated by Christian values and awareness. Maintains that to understand the subtlety and uniqueness of Herbert's art it is essential "to see his deeply-rooted affinities with the Christian tradition" (p. 21). Argues that, although Herbert's ideas are not original, he has the "enormous ability to 'make new' the traditional material which is common to all" and to reshape "the shared and known so that it acquires the uniqueness and freshness of a new revelation never known before" (p. 21).

**903. Ellrodt, Robert.** "De Platon à Traherne: L'intuition de l'instant chez les poètes métaphysiques anglais du dix-septième siècle," in *Mouvements premiers: Études critiques offertes à George Poulet*, 9–25. Paris: Librairie José Corti.

Relates the views of the metaphysical poets toward the "instant" or "moment" to those of Plato, Plotinus, Aristotle, and Kierkegaard and notes that an evolution of human spirit toward interiority and subjectivity can be observed. Maintains that Herbert is a poet of "the present," even though he often employs a narrative mode. Notes, however, that "l'instant n'a pas la même plénitude pour un poète qui le plus souvent évoque l'instant de joie extatique comme un instant déjà enfui, mais encore présent par le prolongement d'une vibration" (p. 19).

**904. Ende, Frederick von.** "George Herbert's 'The Sonne': In Defense of the English Language." *SEL* 12:173–82.

Reprinted in *Essential Articles for the Study of George Herbert's Poetry*, edited by John R. Roberts (entry 1216), 494–502.

Argues that, although "The Sonne" may be seen as a celebration of Christ's resurrection, it "is more than just another religious lyric honoring Christ: it is an assertion and a demonstration, in a concentrated classical oration form, of the capacity and the adequacy of the English tongue for glorifying the Son of God" and, by extension, is in fact "a defense of the English language" (p. 173). Shows that Herbert's proof of the adequacy of the English language rests primarily on the *sun-son* homonym in the poem, a traditional Christian image and a conventional pun in English Renaissance poetry. Maintains that lines 1–3 closely approximate the *exordium* and *narratio* of classical oration; line 4 is the *propositio*; lines 5–6 are the *partito;* lines 7–10 are the *confirmatio* and explain the many meanings of the *sun-son* homonym; and lines 11–14 approximate the *peroratio*, "applying the combined meanings of the *sun-son* to the Son of God and in so doing suggesting that any language which could say so much about both the humility and the glory of Christ in a single word could hardly be judged inadequate" (p. 173).

**905. Fish, Stanley E.** "Letting Go: The Dialectic of the Self in Herbert's Poetry," in *Self-Consuming Artifacts: The Experience of Seventeenth-Century Literature,* 156–223. Berkeley, Los Angeles, London: University of California Press.

Paperback ed., 1974.

Much expanded version of "Letting Go: The Reader in Herbert's Poetry" (entry 824). Maintains that Herbert's is "a poetics of tension, reflecting a continuing dialectic between an egocentric vision which believes in, and is sustained by, the distinctions it creates, and the relentless pressure of a resolving and dissolving insight" (p. 157). Argues that Herbert actually writes himself out of his poems and thus makes his poems a gift from God, not a gift to God. Contends that Herbert's poems "perform what they require of us, for as they undermine our reliance on discursive forms of thought, and urge us to rest in the immediate apprehension of God's all-effective omnipresence, they become the vehicles of their own abandonment" (p. 158). Notes that to read Herbert is thus "to experience the dissolution of the distinctions by which all other things are" (p. 158). Illustrates this concept by commenting on many more poems than in the earlier version. Discusses in detail "The Temper (I)," "Even-song," "Church-monuments," "Sepulchre," "The Holdfast," "The Pearl," "Miserie," "The Thanksgiving," "The Crosse," "The Elixir," "Love (I) and (II)," "Jordan (I) and (II)," "A true Hymne," "Coloss.iii.3," "The Altar," "The Forerunners," and the two sonnets written to Herbert's mother.

**906. Fisher, William N.** "*Occupatio* in Sixteenth- and Seventeenth-Century Verse." *TSLL* 14:203–22.

Discusses the rhetorical figure of *occupatio* (affirmation through denial) in various sixteenth- and seventeenth-century poems, "attempting to discover the essence of the figure, its thrust and its effects, the way it acts out a particular kind of felt experiential truth" (p. 207). Notes Herbert's use of *occupatio* in "Jordan (I)," "a poem that denies poetry the ability to say effectively what the poetry wishes to say: '*My God, My King*'" (p. 216). Maintains that by denying that poetry is adequate, "the poet affirms, along with his extralogical, extraverbal meaning, the poem itself, for he weaves his compact phrase into the poetic structure even as he denies its poetic efficacy" (p. 216). Comments also on Herbert's subtle uses of *occupatio* in "A Wreath," in which the poet denies that his poem, "the poore wreathe," can succeed in praising God, yet the poem does praise God "because, while the wreath contains and restricts and the word 'wreath' is contained and restricted within the poem, the poem and its poet do not presume to be more than they can be"; thus "it is possible that the poet may, with grace, someday be able 'to give thee a crown of praise': and with this awareness of the contingencies on that possibility, the poet can already bestow praise, as poor as it is" (p. 219).

**907. Freer, Coburn.** *Music for a King: George Herbert's Style and the Metrical Psalms.* Baltimore and London: Johns Hopkins University Press. xiv, 252p.

Discusses the affinities in both form and matter between Herbert's lyrics and the versified translations of the psalms. Chapter 1, "Introduction" (pp. 1–49), argues that the metrical psalms "offer helpful guides for reading a poet like Herbert who is concerned with religious praise and lament, expressed simultaneously through technical brilliance and homeliness" (p. 8); that by studying Herbert's relation to the versified psalms one can better understand "the role of humility in Herbert's religious thought and poetic" (p. 5); and that Herbert is inclined to "use the low style and offer (often by means of the high style) a critique of its poetic and its defense of poetic crudity in the translation of spiritual impulse" (p. 46). Presents a brief history of the development of the versified English translations of the psalms. Chapter 2, "Some Metrical Psalm Styles" (pp. 50–115), surveys and comments on various metrical psalm styles in Wyatt, the old version of the psalms (Sternhold and Hopkins, et al.), Sidney and the Countess of Pembroke, and George Wither. Chapter 3, "Orchestral Form" (pp. 116–93), discusses how Herbert's metrical structures, stanza forms, and patterns of sound and syntax "become integral parts of his poetic meaning" (p. 116), claiming that there is "an especially articulate orchestration in the way Herbert uses themes and conventions of the metrical psalm" (p. 116). Chapter 4, "Tentative Form" (pp. 194–241), argues that by studying Herbert's use of metrical psalm techniques one can see that "there is sometimes a discrepancy between the way a Herbert poem behaves and the way it says it behaves" (p. 194). Notes, for instance, that the literal sense of a poem "may be assertive while the form is hesitant; or the sense may be uncertain and the form suggest an answer" (p. 194). Illustrates this concept by a detailed discussion of a number of individual poems, especially "The Collar," "Praise (II)," "Justice (II)," "Longing," "The Banquet," "Affliction (I)," "The Flower," "The Familie," "Vertue," "The Quidditie," and the two Jordan poems. Chapter 5, "Epilogue" (pp. 242–45), reemphasizes the notion that the psalm style "is not an ornamental trim with Herbert, much less a glue or adhesive; it is part of his character, his 'real' character and his poetic character" (p. 243). Index.
Reviews:
Anon., *TLS*, 22 September 1972, p. 1099
Amy Charles, *Choice* 9 (1972): 1128
Paul Chossonnery, *EA* 26 (1973): 364–66
J. S. Lawry, *QQ* 80 (1973): 302–4
Rolf P. Lessenich, *SN* 45 (1973): 449–52
Mary Elizabeth Mason, *SCN* 31 (1973): 46–47
S. R. Maveety, *WCR* 7 (1973): 69–71
J. C. A. Rathmell, *RQ* 26 (1973): 532–34
H. Sergeant, *English* 22 (1973): 28–29
K. M. Lea, *N&Q* 22 (1975): 571–72
Maren-Sofie Røstvig, *English Studies* (Amsterdam) 56 (1975): 162–63
Louise Schleiner, *Archiv* 213, no. 1 (1976): 186–89

**908. [Gysi, Lydia. (Mother Maria)].** *George Herbert: Aspects of His Theology.* (Library of Orthodox Thinking.) Filgrave, Newport Pagnell, Buckinghamshire, Eng.: Greek Orthodox Monastery of the Assumption. 43p.
Reprinted in *George Herbert: Idea and Image* (entry 1003), 279–305.
Argues, through an examination of his verse and the theology that it reflects, that Herbert was able to surpass the rift inherent in the theology of his day. Maintains that the one theme that pervades all of Herbert's work is "the consciousness that this world stands in opposition to the world of grace, that the will of man stands opposed to the Will of God" (p. 1) and that with this consciousness comes his striving after

unity, the desire for harmony with the world of God. Characterizes Herbert's poetry as "a progression from conflict to conflict between his soul and God, until, in the end, in the submission of his will, he attained to perfect freedom" (p. 2) and claims that the poetry "discloses the day-to-day work of building the via media between imputed righteousness on the one side, and in-dwelling grace on the other" (p. 5). Contends that Herbert felt the inadequacy of any scheme of mystical ascent, favoring prayer above all else as a means of achieving heavenly and earthly harmony. Locates Herbert's theology and religious practices within an Anglican framework and concludes that Herbert's poetry exemplifies not only Anglican doctrines but also its practical spirituality and that a knowledge of Herbert's theology and spirit helps one locate Anglicanism more clearly within the Christian tradition.

**909. Hill, D. M.** "Allusion and Meaning in Herbert's *Jordan I*." *Neophil* 56:344–52.

Argues that an informed response to "Jordan (I)" consists of two states: (1) initially the reader is encouraged to see the apparent simplicity and affirmative nature of the poem's argument, and (2) as the reader becomes progressively more aware of the many complex ambiguities, ambivalences, paradoxes, and allusions in the poem, he is asked to reevaluate and qualify his initial response. Maintains that these two states "exist together, in a manner which seems to represent a condition of mind recurring whenever Herbert meditated upon his art and its relationship to his religion, the simple surface argument representing a wished-for clarity and confidence of response, the unfolding intricacies and ambiguities then gradually vying with one another for more and more attention" (p. 351). Presents a detailed reading of the poem to demonstrate this theory and comments in detail on the subtle allusions to Plato's *Republic* contained in the poem. Concludes that "Jordan (I)" "is much more a portrayal of mind than an argument," a poem in which Herbert through his art reveals "all the contradictory detail of his inner being" (p. 351).

**910. Hollander, John.** "The Poem in the Eye." *Shenandoah* 23, no. 3:3–32.

Appears in an expanded form in *Vision and Resonance: Two Senses of Poetic Form* (entry 1025), 245–87.

Discusses the importance and intricacies of the visual aspects of poetry and comments on the picture-like properties of much poetry. Discusses briefly the *technopaignia* (shaped verse) of Alexandrine poetry and comments on Renaissance imitators and critics of the practice. Calls Herbert's "Easter-wings" "the most remarkable instance of sophisticated shaping in the seventeenth century," a poem that, even more than "The Altar," "seems to create the pattern of its picture, rather than being forced into shape by it" (p. 9). Comments briefly also on certain modern poets who employ shaped verse, notably Apollinaire, Dylan Thomas, Gregory Corso, and May Swenson.

**911. Ishii, Shōnosuke.** "George Herbert no 'Kenshin'-ko (II)" [On George Herbert's "The Sacrifice (II)"]. *Shirayuri Joshi Daigaku Kenkyu Kiyo* [The Fleur-de-lis Review, Bulletin of the Shiruyuri Women's College] no. 8 (December): 22–35.

Part 2 of a two-part series of articles. Considers the meaning of "The Sacrifice" from various critical viewpoints and tries to clarify its significance in *The Temple*. For part 1, see entry 876.

**912. Jaeger, Henry-Evrard.** *Zeugnis für die Einheit: Geistliche Texte aus den Kirchen der Reformation*, band 3, *Anglikanismus*. Herausgegeben, eingeleitet und kommentiert von Henry-Evrard Jaeger, unter Mitarbeit von A. M. Allchin,

C. Hope, L. Gysi, J. I. Packer und L. Bouyer. Mainz: Matthias Grünewald Verlag. 288p.

Presents a general introduction to Herbert's life and poetry (pp. 113–15), followed by German translations of "The Collar," "Aaron," "Home," "The Temper (II)," "The Jews," "Sion," "Prayer (I)," "Love (III)," and "Josephs coat" (pp. 116–24). Contrasts Herbert's religious sensibility and his poetical techniques with those of Donne. Discusses Herbert's Anglicanism and how his religious attitudes are reflected in his poetry. Comments on the theological content of "The Collar." Notes that even modern nonbelievers often find Herbert's poetry attractive. Includes a bibliography of editions of Herbert's works, followed by a selected bibliography of critical studies (pp. 261–65).

**913. Jurak, Mirko, ed.** "George Herbert," in *English Poetry: An Anthology with a Critical and Historical Introduction for Foreign Students*, 77–79. Ljubljana, Yugoslavia: Drzovna Zalozba Slovenije.

Anthologizes "Life" and "Love (III)," with explanatory notes and questions. Maintains that in "Life" "the *carpe diem* theme is dealt with using a moral approach, showing the place of sensual perception in the poet's religious views" (p. 77) and that in "Love (III)" "the emotions are well conveyed with simple sentences composed of monosyllabic words, much more effective than an impassioned rhetoric might have been" (p. 79).

**914. Kawata, Akira.** "George Herbert no 'Prayer' (I) Kanken—Aristotle no Ju no Hanchu ni motozuite" [On George Herbert's "Prayer (I)" in relation to the Ten Aristotelian Categories]. *Fukushima Daigaku Kyoiku Gakubu Ronshu* (Bulletin of the Faculty of Education, Fukushima University) no. 24, part 2 (November): 27–39.

Argues that "Prayer (I)" summarizes all that is contained in *The Temple*. Discusses this poem in relation to logic and the Aristotelian categories in order to show what qualities of prayer Herbert meant to define.

**915. Leach, Elsie.** "T. S. Eliot and the School of Donne." *Costerus* 3:163–80.

Summarizes the shifts in Eliot's critical position toward the metaphysical poets and argues that "the changing emphases of Eliot's criticism parallel developments in his own verse" (p. 163). Maintains that "in nearly everything Eliot writes about Herbert he explains the poetry by reference to the personality of the poet" (p. 164). Shows how Eliot evidences an increasing enthusiasm for Herbert as his interest in Donne, Marvell, and Crashaw decreases: from 1931 on, Eliot's "evaluation of Donne is much less enthusiastic than earlier, and his evaluation of Herbert is more favorable" (p. 177). Summarizes Eliot's critical comments on Herbert and notes that his study of Herbert for the British Council's Writers and Their Works Series (entry 577) is the longest essay he wrote on a single metaphysical poet.

**916. Leitch, Vincent B.** "Herbert's Influence in Dylan Thomas's 'I See the Boys of Summer.'" *N&Q* 217:341.

Points out a number of parallels between Herbert's "The Search" and Dylan Thomas's "I See the Boys of Summer," especially the image of the "kissing poles."

**917. Low, Anthony.** "Herbert's 'Jordan (I)' and the Court Masque." *Criticism* 14:109–18.

Argues that "Jordan (I)" "is directed against court poetry (which would include much love poetry), and especially against the court masques of the Stuarts, those who wrote them, and the way of life that they represent" (p. 109). Presents a detailed reading of the poem to show that many of its difficulties, especially the ending, can be solved if it is read as an anti-court poem. Maintains that Herbert parodies or imitates the court masque in the poem and writes, in effect, "in miniature, a divine masque, designed as a compliment to God the King as the court masque compliments His human shadow" and that at the same time the poem is "a reduction of the courtly compliment from an elaborate masque and from fulsome flattery to a simple and direct statement of loyalty to God and to King" (p. 118).

**918. Martin, F. David.** "Literature and Immanent Recall," in *Art and the Religious Experience: The "Language" of the Sacred*, 183–227. Lewisburg, Pa.: Bucknell University Press.

Briefly comments on "The Altar" and maintains that, although shaped verse has now fallen into general disuse, there is a revival of sorts in "concrete poetry."

**919. Molesworth, Charles.** "Herbert's 'The Elixir': Revision Towards Action." *CP* 5, no. 2:12–20.

Compares the two versions of "The Elixir" and discusses Herbert's changes in order to show that he "was more than a careful craftsman, or, rather that his care in craftmanship was matched by a deepened sense of the mystery of the Incarnation" (p. 19). Argues that, through the rearrangement of stanzas, the development of thought, the subtle shifts in tone and figurative language, certain verbal substitutions, and so forth, Herbert fundamentally changes the whole emphasis and meaning of the poem: "The first states that man by adopting God's 'Light' dignifies his actions, but they still remain, in the context of the poem, fundamentally human actions" and "the later version speaks of a *transformation* (the stone 'turneth all to gold') and the actions themselves partake of the divine nature" (p. 13).

**920. Mollenkott, Virginia R.** "George Herbert's Epithet-Sonnets." *Genre* 5:131–37.

Categorizes various kinds of sonnets on the basis of their mode of presentation or their controlling technique and comments in particular on the epithet-sonnet, "which defines and clarifies its subject by means of a series of brief descriptive phrases" (pp. 131–32). Presents a close reading of "The H. Scriptures (I)" and "Prayer (I)" as sacred parodies of the Elizabethan epithet-sonnets, especially those of such poets as Sidney, Constable, Daniel, and Bartholomew Griffin.

**921. Morita, Katsumi.** "Imagery and Themes in George Herbert's Poems: 'Prayer (I)' and *The Temple* (3)." *Helicon* [Bulletin of the English Literary Society of Ehime University] no. 24 (March): 15–23.

Part 3 of a three-part series of articles. Deals with the development of the imagery and themes in "Prayer (I)." Comments on "Easter," "Deniall," "The Windows," and "The Priesthood." See also entries 710 and 733.

**922. Muraoka, Isamu.** "Shakespeare and George Herbert." *ShStud* 11 (1972–1973): 37–59.

Argues that Herbert borrowed a number of images, especially simple and homely images of everyday and domestic life, from Shakespeare and attempts to account for this influence. Maintains that, in part, Herbert was consciously trying to displace the profane with the sacred and comments briefly on the influence of Dionysius the Areopagite on Herbert's attitude toward imagery and symbolism. Cites a number of possible specific borrowings.

**923. Nagasawa, Kunihiro.** "*The Temple* ni okeru Chitsujo no Gainen ni tsuite" [On the Idea of Order in *The Temple*]. *Ibaraki Daigaku Kyoiku Gakubu Kiyo* [Bulletin of the Faculty of Education, Ibaraki University] no. 4 (March): 77–108.

Considers the meaning of the threefold division of *The Temple* into "The Church-porch," "The Church," and "The Church Militant" and discusses the idea of order revealed in Herbert's arrangement of the poems in *The Temple*.

**924. Okuda, Hiroko.** "Pruning to Perfection—An Essay on G. Herbert." *Shimane Daigaku Bunri Gakubu Kiyo* [Memoirs of the Faculty of Literature and Science, Shimane University] no. 6 (December): 97–110.

Japanese version of this article, partly revised, was published in *Bungaku ni tsuite* (entry 997).

Argues that as Herbert sought simplicity in his spiritual life, so he sought "neat-ness" in his poetry. Maintains that, for Herbert, *brevis* was closely related to *bonus*.

**925. Parfitt, George A. E.** "Donne, Herbert and the Matter of Schools." *EIC* 22:381–95.

Recognizes the influence of Donne on Herbert, especially on certain of Herbert's best poems, but distrusts the label *School of Donne* and argues that it "conceals more than it reveals" (p. 395). Contrasts Herbert and Donne as religious poets and sees Donne primarily as "the great religious poet of self-dramatization" (p. 382), who objectifies his experience in order to come to a personal understanding of his relation-ship to God and who projects in his poetry a great lack of confidence and sense of uncertainty in his belief. States that "Donne is better as a poet of individual faith and doubt than as a celebrator of the communion of Christian belief and of the great occasions of the life of the Church" (p. 386). Argues that Herbert, on the other hand, has a much stronger sense of the public function of his poetry and works diligently to communicate with his audience. Concludes that Herbert's poems are less egocentric than Donne's, less imbued with doubt and rebellion, and that Herbert sees his own experience as analogous to that of all Christians.

**926. Parks, Edna D.** *Early English Hymns: An Index*. Metuchen, N.J.: Scarecrow Press. viii, 168p.

Presents an index of early English hymns, in part to challenge the assumption that English hymn writing dates from Isaac Watts (1674–1748). Includes much religious poetry of the seventeenth century, since "much which was suitable was soon adapted and joined with a tune" (p. iv), even though it was not originally designed for congregational singing. Also includes poems that were never set to music if they conform to the definition of the hymn. Arranges the hymns in alphabetical order by first line and also presents (1) the meter, (2) the number of lines or stanzas in the earliest publication of the poem, (3) the name of the author, (4) date of publication and page or line numbers where the hymn can be found, and, when possible, (5) information about the tune and composer. Lists sixty-eight items for Herbert. Includes a bibliography (pp. 143–54), author index (pp. 155–62), composer index (pp. 163–65), and tune index (pp. 166–68).

**927. Patrides, C. A.** *The Grand Design of God: The Literary Form of the Chris-tian View of History*. (Ideas and Forms in English Literature, edited by John Lawlor.) London: Routledge & Kegan Paul; Toronto and Buffalo: University of Toronto Press. xvii, 157p.

Much amplified version of the author's earlier study, *The Phoenix and the Ladder: The Rise and Decline of the Christian View of History* (Berkeley, Los Angeles, London: University of California Press, 1964). Comments briefly on the influence that the Christian view of history had on the structure of Herbert's "The Collar," claiming that the poem "compresses within its thirty-six lines the broad circumference of the traditional vision of history" (p. 82).

**928. Sandler, Florence.** "'Solomon vbique regnet': Herbert's Use of the Images of the New Covenant." *PLL* 8:147–58.

Reprinted in *Essential Articles for the Study of George Herbert's Poetry*, edited by John R. Roberts (entry 1216), 258–67.

Maintains that, although most critics recognize the importance in *The Temple* of the New Testament notion that the functions of the Temple on Mount Sion have been replaced by the human heart, it has not been generally recognized that Herbert's images of the New Covenant fall consistently into three major categories—the temple, the altar, and the tablets of the Law—and that these categories correspond to the three traditional offices or roles of Christ—king, priest, and prophet. Argues that in the first category Christ is seen as taking up his abode in the temple or the palace of the human heart and conquering his enemies; in the second, the heart is seen as the altar upon which Christ exercises his priestly sacrifice; and in the third, the heart is seen as the tablet upon which Christ as prophet inscribes the New Law. Maintains that Herbert's uses of New Testament typology are precise and consistent, that his typology is particularly Pauline, and that his concepts are consistent with Reformation teaching and reflect his own comments in *Briefe Notes on Valdesso's "Considerations."*

**929. Schlüter, Kurt.** "Die Lyrik der englischen Renaissance," in *Renaissance und Barock*, vol. 10, edited by August Buck et al., 216–56. (Neues Handbuch der Literaturwissenschaft, Vol. 9 and 10, ed. Klaus von See.) Frankfurt am Main: Akademische Verlagsgesellschaft Athenaion.

Reprinted in *Englishe Dichtung des 16. und 17. Jahrhunderts*, by Horst Oppel und Kurt Schlüter, Athenaion Essays, 3; Studienausgaben zum "Neues Handbuch der Literaturwissenschaft," ed. Klaus von See (Frankfurt am Main: Akademische Verlagsgesellschaft, 1973), 54–94.

General historical and critical survey of English lyric poetry of the Renaissance, from Wyatt to Milton. Briefly evaluates Herbert's poetry (p. 246) and praises in particular his poetic craftmanship, calling him a master inventor of strophic forms. Notes with approval Herbert's use of elevated colloquial speech in his poems and his restraint of emotion. Sees Herbert as the most important link between Donne and the later metaphysicals.

**930. Steadman, John M.** "Herbert's Platonic Lapidary: A Note on 'The Foil.'" *SCN* 30:59–62.

Maintains that "The Foil" is an intricate and complex poem that "combines Platonic and Christian allusions into a lapidary meditation on a variety of traditional themes: the contrast between visible and invisible beauty and sensuous and intellectual vision, the dignity and misery of man, the antithesis between the splendor of virtue and the foulness of sin, and perhaps . . . on the contrast between the church and the world and the problem of the priest in persuading men to virtue by concrete examples or similitudes that they can see and understand" (p. 59). Presents a detailed reading of the poem, commenting particularly on its rhetorical aspects, its Platonic and Christian allusions, and its central conceit of the jeweler's foil.

**931. Strzetelski, Jerzy.** "The Art of George Herbert as Shown in Two Poems." *Zeszyty Naukowe Uniwersytetu Jagiellonskiego* 24:35–44.

Presents detailed structural analyses of "Redemption" and "Prayer (I)," maintaining that in both poems Herbert shows himself "a great master of syntax" (p. 37). Argues that the characteristic features of the two poems are fourfold: (1) "either sonnet is a unique self-dependent composition of syntactical elements"; (2) "the nonfinite verb structure makes for the richness of the poems, often replacing the main verb and even helping to hold the poem together"; (3) "the poems are characterized by speedy yet graceful transition from one structure to another"; and (4) "there is a constant subtle variation of otherwise repetitive structure in these poems, especially of the structure of simple modification" (p. 43). Concludes that the analyses point out that "some part of the overall perfection of the poet's art stems from the ingenious use he makes of syntax" (p. 43).

**932. Warnke, Frank J.** *Versions of Baroque: European Literature in the Seventeenth Century.* New Haven and London: Yale University Press. xi, 229p.

Uses the term *baroque* "to denote not a precisely definable style but a period complex made up of a whole cluster of more or less related styles—a complex which in its earlier phases (approximately 1580–1610), contains significant survivals of the preceding complex, or period style (i.e. the Renaissance), and, in its later phase (approximately 1650–90), anticipations of the subsequent complex (i.e. Neoclassicism)" (pp. 1–2). Maintains that a "literary period cannot be conceived of as a time span populated by authors expressing themselves in virtually identical styles, style itself being too individual a phenomenon to allow for such a conception" (p. 9). Rather defines a literary period as "a time span in which underlying shared spiritual preoccupations find expression in a variety of stylistic and thematic emphases" (p. 9). Isolates a number of emphases, preoccupations, and topoi of baroque literature and mentions the baroque characteristics of Herbert's art and sensibility throughout. Chapter 5, "Art as Play" (pp. 90–129), discusses the playful spirit of much baroque literature. Specifically cites *The Temple* as a prime example of the play-aesthetic and maintains that many modern critics fail "to recognize just how funny much of the poetry is, and just how necessary an appreciation of its funniness is to an appreciation of its profound, personality-transforming seriousness" (p. 94). Specifically comments on the play-element in "The Collar," "Deniall," "Trinitie Sunday," "The Forerunners," and the shaped or pattern poems. Praises Herbert's wit and "his tricks with language": "his volume becomes, from one point of view, an offering like that of the jongleur of Notre Dame" (p. 96). Chapter 6, "Metaphysical and Meditative Devotion" (pp. 130–57), deals with the baroque religious and devotional lyric, both English and Continental. Outlines major characteristics of the baroque devotional lyric, such as its private versus its public voice; its blend of levity and seriousness; its uses of sacred parody; its complex uses of paradox; its highly dramatic elements; its uses of a persona, specific setting, and implied audience; its capacity simultaneously to express individual emotion and complex thought; etc. Relates many of these characteristics to the art of discursive meditation and suggests reasons for the decline of baroque sensibility during the last half of the seventeenth century.

**933. Waswo, Richard.** "The True Believer," in *The Fatal Mirror: Themes and Techniques in the Poetry of Fulke Greville,* 109–54. Charlottesville: University of Virginia Press.

Contrasts Herbert and Greville. Analyzes "Love (III)" to illustrate Herbert's religious sensibility and poetic technique and contrasts the poem with Greville's sonnet

99, suggesting that the main difference between the two is Herbert's superior control and discipline, "the limitations of the possible connotation of the vehicle as such, the refusal to allow it to run away with the poem" (p. 140). Comments on Herbert's uses of dramatic narrative structure, simple diction, concrete and homely dialogue and metaphors, intimate tone, and extension of metaphors, all of which serve a precise theological function. Briefly contrasts Herbert's "Sinne (II)" with Greville's sonnet 100.

**934. Yoder, R. A.** "Toward the 'Titmouse Dimension': The Development of Emerson's Poetic Style." *PMLA* 87:255–70.

Comments on Herbert's influence on Emerson's poetic development, pointing out that Herbert provided Emerson with a model "not merely for simplicity of speech and imagery, but for combining simplicity with architectonic skill, with the concentrated and integrated organization that distinguishes the seventeenth-century meditative style" (p. 256). Maintains that from Herbert and his contemporaries Emerson also learned "the art of 'neatness': the way to structure a poem on a single metaphor or situation . . . ; the smoothness of tone and rhythm, conventional but always melodic, never jagged but sufficiently pointed and varied to gain the quality of speech" (p. 257). Points out Emerson's borrowings from "Sinne (I)" in "Grace," and from "The Elixir" in "Art," as well as noting the influence of "Man" on *Nature*.

# *1973*

**935. Allison, A. F.** *Four Metaphysical Poets: George Herbert, Richard Crashaw, Henry Vaughan, Andrew Marvell: A Bibliographical Catalogue of the Early Editions of their Poetry and Prose (To the end of the 17th Century).* (Pall Mall Bibliographies, no. 3.) Folkestone and London: Dawsons of Pall Mall. 134p.

Biographical sketch of Herbert and a chronological listing of the publication of Herbert's works to 1700 (pp. 13–14). Presents a bibliographical description of separate editions and issues of Herbert's poetry and prose to 1700 (pp. 14–23). Reproduces facsimiles of each title page, which are keyed to the entries (pp. 61–85). Includes an index of printers and publishers, also keyed to the entries (pp. 133–34).

**936. Asals, Heather.** "The Tetragrammaton in *The Temple*." *SCN* 31:48–50.

Comments on the various forms of, and explicit references to, the Name of God in *The Temple*. Maintains that, from Old Testament times onward, the Name of God was seen as a symbol and as an expression of God's very essence, not simply as a referent. Discusses how Herbert was aware of these subtleties in his precise use of God's name in *The Church*, defining and redefining his relationship with God by using various traditional forms of God's name.

**937. Bateson, F. W.** "As We Read the Living? An Argument. II. Editorial Reply." *EIC* 23:175–78.

Reply to Roma Gill (entry 947). Argues that great poetry must communicate some matter of essential human interest and questions if a poem can be read separately as "art" and as "life." Maintains that "the answer must surely be that a properly literary response combines both attitudes" (pp. 177–78). Briefly disagrees with Gill's evaluation of "Vertue" and "Jordan (I)," suggesting that the first poem is deficient in human content and that the second, a better poem, "reaches its 'plain' Christian conclusion by a series of laconic pagan obscurities, which in fact give the poem all its poetry" (p. 177).

**938. Chossonnery, Paul.** "Les 'poèmes figurés' de George Herbert et ses préten-dues fantaisies poétiques." *EA* 26:1–11.

Defends Herbert's shaped poems and uses of verbal ingenuity and reviews selected negative criticism of Herbert's practice by Hobbes, Dryden, Addison, Cowper, Coleridge, Palmer, and Margaret Bottrall. Maintains that such displays of ingenuity and play are not fantastic or mere virtuosity but are closely related to meaning: "Il y a une irréductible incompatibilité entre l'idée de fantaisie débridée et ce que nous savons du poète, de son caractère et de sa conception de la poésie" (p. 4). Challenges Joseph H. Summers's use of the term *hieroglyph* in describing Herbert's poetry and faults Summers for not noting important distinctions between much contemporary practice and Herbert's uses of shaped verse and verbal wit. Maintains that Herbert's uses of these devices reflect a theory of knowledge that was current at that time and held that man learns through the senses: "Ce que les critiques, depuis le milieu du XVIIe siècle, ont pris pour un exemple du mauvais goût chez un poète de la Renaissance, pour une simple ingéniosité ou une recherche de la difficulté à seule fin de la surmonter, n'était donc, dans son esprit, que le moyen d'expression le plus direct qu'il avait pu trouver, puisqu'il appliquait tout bonnement la théorie de la connaissance de son temps" (p. 8).

**939. Clements, A. L.** "Theme, Tone, and Tradition in George Herbert's Poetry." *ELR* 3:264–83

Reprinted in *Essential Articles for the Study of George Herbert's Poetry*, edited by John R. Roberts (entry 1216), 33–51.

Reexamines, in the light of disagreement among critics concerning Herbert's mysticism, the meditative and contemplative elements and traditions that inform his poetry. Presents a detailed reading of "Artillerie" and then relates "this and other Herbert poems to the curiously well integrated and great speculative tradition of late medieval Christian mysticism" (p. 265). Recognizes the influence of Scupoli's *Spiritual Combat* in "Artillerie" but maintains that the radical difference in tone between Herbert's poem and Scupoli's treatise "signalizes the spiritual distance or progress between the early or meditative stages of the religious life and Herbert's own attainment of more advanced or contemplative stages" (p. 273). Accounts for the difference in tone by considering the late medieval contemplative concept of man's twofold self, of "the phenomenal or finite ego, of which he is mainly conscious and which he tends mistakenly to reward as his true self, and an infinite and hence not wholly definable self, the inward man or image of divinity in him" (p. 275). Argues that *The Temple* "may very well be regarded as a various record of many spiritual conflicts, griefs, and joys, coordinated and made more coherent by the central theme of submission to God's will, particularly if this submission is understood as the major means for effecting the glorious changing of the fallen Adam into the Son of God" (p. 275). Discusses this theme in such poems as "The Altar," "Love (III)," "Clasping of hands," "The Quip," "The Temper (I) and (II)," "Love (II)," "The Search," "Grief," "The Crosse," and "The Flower."

**940. Coleridge, S. T.** *The Notebooks of Samuel Taylor Coleridge*, vol. 3, *Text and Notes*, edited by Kathleen Coburn. Princeton: Princeton University Press. xxii, 692; xxxv, 960p.

Includes four notebook entries (3532, 3533, 3580, 3735) in which Coleridge copies out lines from Herbert's poems. Notes that Coleridge used the 1674 edition of Herbert's poems, now in the Berg Collection of the New York Public Library.

**941. Colie, Rosalie L.** "Small Forms: *Multo in Parvo*," in *The Resources of Kind: Genre-Theory in the Renaissance*, edited by Barbara K. Lewalski, 32–75. Berkeley, Los Angeles, London: University of California Press.

Comments on the influence of emblem literature and the emblematic technique on Herbert's poetry. Argues that, in spite of certain recognizable groups of poems in *The Temple*, the book as a whole "resists schemes to organize it into a consistent structure, although scholars have tried to fit it to one or another Procrustean bed" (pp. 51–52). Maintains, however, that as a whole *The Temple* has a major emblematic subtheme: "The collection is, among other things, a 'school of the heart' much like continental devotional emblem books" (pp. 53–57). Comments on the various heart images and concludes that "the true temple of God is not a temple, but the human heart—for all its architectural poems, Herbert's book *The Temple* is written out of and for that metaphor: it is a school for the heart, teaching it to become a temple fit for God's dwelling" (p. 67).

**942. Costa, Francisque.** *L'oeuvre d'Izaak Walton (1593–1683)*. (Etudes Anglaises, 48.) Paris: Didier. 527p.

Comments in detail on Walton's *Life of Herbert* (1670), stressing how the biography was intended to be an Anglican saint's life and was built on the model of one who renounces the world for the life of the pastor and priest. Points out that Herbert appears in the first edition of *The Compleat Angler* (1653) and shows up again in the 1658 edition of *The Life of Donne*, in which Walton praises *The Temple*. Maintains that Herbert appealed to Walton as a subject primarily because he represented the pietistic and quietistic spirituality that characterized seventeenth-century Anglicanism. Contrasts Herbert and Donne, especially as priests, and notes that Walton "fut toute sa vie attiré et fasciné par la fonction sacerdotale" and that "Donne lui offrait le modèle du prédicateur" and "Herbert, celui du prêtre qui officie et dispense les sacrements" (pp. 104–5). Suggests that the biography "prend ainsi place dans la campagne que mène depuis longtemps l'Eglise anglicane pour améliorer le recrutement et élever le niveau de son clergé" (p. 106) and maintains that Walton's presentation of Herbert as a Laudian would have appealed to the adherents of the post-Restoration High Church movement. Scattered references to Herbert throughout.

**943. Croft, P[eter] J[ohn].** "George Herbert," in *Autograph Poetry in the English Language: Facsimiles of original manuscripts from the Fourteenth to the Twentieth Century*, 1:34. New York, St. Louis, San Francisco: McGraw-Hill Book Co.; Oxford: Oxford University Press.

Limited to 1,500 copies.

Reproduces a facsimile of the two pages from the Williams manuscript that contain "The Elixir" (first entitled "Perfection"). Notes that, although the poem was transcribed by an amanuensis, the corrections in the manuscript are in Herbert's own hand. Points out that Herbert's revisions here "are more extensive than in any other poem." Notes that the Williams manuscript "contains the only extant text of Herbert's poetry that he himself certainly handled" and presents a brief history of its transmission. Comments on features of Herbert's Italic hand.

**944. Eaker, J. Gordon.** "The Spirit of Seventeenth-Century Anglicanism." *South Central Bulletin* 33:194–96.

Comments on some of the beliefs and on the emerging spirit of seventeenth-century Anglicanism as they are reflected in the literature of the period and maintains that the "literary divines illustrate how the Anglican Church of the seventeenth century, by its 'gentle authority,' cultivated spiritual freedom in its adherents, never compelling, always persuading" (p. 196). Calls Herbert "the finest poet of the Church of England" (p. 195) and surveys some of his major ethical and moral beliefs as they appear in *A Priest to the Temple* and in *The Temple*, especially in *The Church-Porch*.

**945. Editors.** Editors' note. *N&Q* n.s. 20:165.
Points out two examples from the seventeenth century that quote lines 5–6 of *The Church-Porch*, in which Herbert asserts that the aims of poetry and preaching are the same: John Flavell's *Husbandry Spiritualized* (1669) and Edward Sparke's *Scintilla Altaris*, 2d ed. (1660). The editors thank K. J. Höltgen for the information. See also entry 946.

**946. El-Gabalawy, Saad.** "George Herbert: The Preacher Poet." *N&Q* 218:165.
Points out that lines 5–6 of *The Church-Porch*, in which Herbert asserts that the aims of poetry and preaching are the same, were frequently quoted in the seventeenth century by various writers of commendatory and devotional verse. Notes in particular Benlowes's *Theophila* (1652), Thomas Washbourne's *Divine Poems* (1654), John Rawlet's *Poetick Miscellanies* (1687), Samuel Speed's *Prison Pietie: Or, Meditations Divine and Moral* (1677), and Henry Delaune's *Patrikon doron. Or, a legacy to his sons* (1651). Concludes that all of these writers, like Herbert, see a basic relationship between the didactic function of poetry and preaching and that they "apparently regard Herbert as a great model of the poet preacher using his art as a means of persuasion and 'delightful instruction.'" See also entry 945.

**947. Gill, Roma.** "As We Read the Living?: An Argument." *EIC* 23:167–75.
Questions F. R. Leavis's premise that poets of the past should be read as if they were living and expresses concern for those undergraduate students who demand "sincerity" in poetry, who insist on biographical interpretations of poems, and who have no sense of tradition in poetry. Observes that students are less likely to read Herbert "as we read the living" than they are to read Donne in this manner. Points out that most undergraduates praise Herbert's simplicity but fail to recognize the immense effort and artistry that have gone into achieving it, citing the complexity of Herbert's uses of several traditions in "Jordan (I)." Maintains that because Herbert, like Donne, often consciously rejects literary traditions, "he is even more dependent upon them" (p. 173) and demonstrates this notion by commenting on his use of the *carpe diem* tradition in "Life" and "Vertue." For replies, see F. W. Bateson (entry 937) and S. W. Dawson, Harriet Hawkins, and Roger Elliott, *EIC* 24 (1974): 94–104.

**948. Hedges, James L.** "Thomas Adams, Robert Burton, and Herbert's 'Rope of Sand.'" *SCN* 31:47–48.
Comments on the proverbial nature of Herbert's phrase *rope of sands* in "The Collar." Points out that Tilley, in his *Dictionary of Proverbs* (Ann Arbor: University of Michigan Press, 1950; entry R174), traces it back through Jacobean drama and Bacon's commentaries to Erasmus's *Adagia*. Points out two other contemporary references: (1) Burton uses it in the 1624 edition of *The Anatomy of Melancholy* to describe a kind of melancholy arising from vain curiosity and to suggest needless industry about unprofitable things, and (2) Thomas Adams in 1625 refers to "a rope of sand" in his gloss on Jer. 5:22, stating that sand binds the sea (described as a "roaring monster"). Maintains that, although Adams's comment was not published

until 1633 in his *Commentary on Second Peter*, Herbert "may well have known the verse in Jeremiah as possible gloss on the proverb" (p. 48).

**949. Herbert, George.** *George Herbert: Selected by W. H. Auden.* (Poet to Poet Series.) Harmondsworth, Eng., and Baltimore: Penguin Books. 134p.

Pages 10–13 reprinted in *George Herbert and the Seventeenth-Century Religious Poets: Authoritative Texts/Criticism*, edited by Mario Di Cesare (entry 1140), 233–36.

Brief biographical and critical introduction to Herbert (pp. 7–13) by W. H. Auden. Confesses that the two poets he would most like to have known are William Barnes and George Herbert. Maintains that "since all of Herbert's poems are concerned with religious life, they cannot be judged by aesthetic standards alone" (p. 9). Calls Herbert's poetry "the counterpart of Jeremy Taylor's prose: together they are the finest expression we have of Anglican piety at its best" (p. 10). Comments on Herbert's religious sensibility and praises his poetry for its clever uses of antithesis and wit, its directness and ingenuity, and its technical excellence in securing musical effects. Maintains that "Prayer (I)" "seems to foreshadow Mallarmé" (p. 12). Selections from *The Temple* (pp. 15–126), from *A Priest to the Temple* (pp. 127–31), and from a letter to Mrs. Herbert (29 May 1622) from Walton's *Life*.

**950. Hollander, John, and Frank Kermode, eds.** "George Herbert," in *The Oxford Anthology of English Literature*, vol. 1, *The Middle Ages through the Eighteenth Century*, 1165–78. New York: Oxford University Press.

Reissued as *The Literature of Renaissance England: The Oxford Anthology of English Literature*, vol. 2. (New York: Oxford University Press, 1973).

Brief introduction to Herbert's life and poetry (pp. 1165–66). Maintains that Herbert's "greatness as a religious poet came in some measure from his struggle with the temptations of poetry itself" (p. 1165). Calls *The Temple* "an astonishing work, reflecting at once a discontent with the fashions of complex, post-Petrarchan amatory verse which we loosely call the Metaphysical tradition, and a brilliant and subtle use of all those arts of image-making and rhetoric practiced by Donne and used by Herbert to cast doubt on the purity of any discourse which would employ them" (p. 1166). Maintains that *The Temple* is "in one sense, a constant attempt, in poem after poem, to make poetry do the work of prayer and devotion" and that the individual poems "present a spectrum of almost celestial variety: not only is the range of versification and stanza form amazing" but "the centers of meditative attention in them vary widely as well" (p. 1166). Anthologizes twenty poems, with notes (pp. 1166–78).

**951. Jones, Roger Stephens.** "Herbert's 'Vertue.'" *AWR* 22:116–23.

Reviews various critics on "Vertue" and concludes that the poem is "far more complex than any of the critics have imagined" (p. 121). Presents a detailed reading of the poem and calls it an "extremely ascetic statement of Christian truth" (p. 122). Argues that those critics "who view the first three stanzas as a wistful and beautiful lament for the passing of earthly glory are grossly mistaken and have fallen victim to Herbert's deliberate deception of the reader" (p. 122). Maintains that Herbert's uses of the lyric form, the refrain, and conventional carpe diem images "are all literary devices which lure the reader into a sensuous and sentimental attitude towards the mutability of earthly beauty" (p. 122), but because of the puns and the various kinds of wordplay the reader comes to recognize this aesthetic deception.

**952. Kawata, Akira.** "George Herbert no Catholicism—Seibo Maria, Seijin Suhai to Seitai no Hiseki wo chushin ni" [On George Herbert's Catholicism—With

Special reference to the Devotion to St. Mary and the Saints, and the Holy Eucharist]. *Fukushima Daigaku Kyoiku Gakubu Ronshu* [Bulletin of the Faculty of Education, Fukushima University] no. 25, part 2 (November): 55–56.

Discusses Herbert's Roman Catholic attitudes in *The Temple*. Argues that, though Herbert's attitudes toward the veneration of Mary and the saints and toward the Holy Eucharist are subtle and delicate, his view is almost the same as that of the Roman Catholic Church.

**953. Kranz, Gisbert.** "Beziehungen zwischen Malerei und Dichtung," in *Das Bildgedicht in Europa: Zur Theorie und Geschichte einer literarischen Gattung,* 19–41. Paderborn, West Germany: Schöningh.

Historical and critical survey of the shaped poem with a brief discussion of Herbert's "Easter-wings" (with a German translation of the poem).

**954. Lawler, Thomas M. C.** "Fruitful Business: Medieval and Renaissance Elements in the Devotional Method of St. John Fisher." *M&H* 4:145–59.

Analyzes the structure and religious sensibility of St. John Fisher's meditations and comments on "some possible sources which illustrate the continuity between medieval and Renaissance elements in his devotional method" (p. 145). Points out various parallels between the devotional method of Fisher and Herbert's *The Temple* and maintains that "Bitter-sweet" "distills the Cistercian tradition that inspired Fisher" (p. 156).

**955. Lewalski, Barbara, and Andrew Sabol, eds.** *Major Poets of the Earlier Seventeenth Century: Donne, Herbert, Vaughan, Crashaw, Jonson, Herrick, Marvell.* Indianapolis and New York: Odyssey Press, a Division of Bobbs Merrill Co. xxxv, 1330p.

Includes a general introduction to earlier seventeenth-century lyric poetry (pp. xix-xxxi); a selected bibliography of studies of seventeenth-century poetry and its backgrounds (pp. xxxiii-xxxv); an introduction to Herbert's life and poetry (pp. 173–83); a selected bibliography of editions and studies on Herbert's life and poetry (pp. 183–84); poems from *The Temple*, with explanatory notes (pp. 185–389); an introduction to musical settings of seventeenth-century lyrics (pp. 1209–12), including a musical setting of "The Starre" by John Jenkins entitled "Bright spark" (pp. 1224–30); textual notes on Herbert's poems included in the anthology (pp. 1279–86); and an index of titles and first lines (pp. 1301–30). In the general introduction Lewalski outlines major critical trends in the study of early seventeenth-century poetry; notes the modern tendency to break down the rigid dichotomy between metaphysical and neo-classical poetry as well as to relate English poetry to Continental poetry of the period; comments on the trend to divert "attention away from broad generalizations about common features of style and toward the unique poetic experience which each of these poets can offer" (p. xxvii); and discusses the relationship between the lyric and music. In the introduction to Herbert briefly outlines his life and comments on major characteristics of his poetry, praising in particular his artistic control, his exactness of diction, his ease and simplicity, and his stanzaic experimentation. Maintains that the main concern in *The Temple* is "the maintenance and development of a personal, intimate relationship with Christ, a relationship grounded in social love" (p. 175). Comments on how the poems reflect Herbert's "complex and profound religious sensibility" (p. 174) but stresses that Herbert projects a persona who becomes "a species of Christian Everyman, finding in himself a restatement of the common conflicts and experiences of the Christian life" (p. 175). Discusses Herbert's use of biblical typology, Petrarchism, and the emblem. Comments in detail on the architectonics of *The Temple*.

**956. McCann, Garth A.** "Dryden and Poetic Continuity: A Comparative Study." *SAQ* 72:311–21.

Contrasts and compares Herbert with Donne and Dryden: "His images are midway between Donne's puzzling and Dryden's plain ones," but "he is more careful than they to link the imagery with the ethical ideas they are intended to develop" (p. 313). Comments briefly on "Man" and concludes that "like Donne, he uses concrete images; like Jonson, he makes moral mandates; like Dryden, he writes clearly" (p. 314). Compares Herbert's didacticism with that of Donne, Jonson, and Dryden and maintains that Herbert is more clearly didactic, his purpose being to teach men religion. Sees a link also between Dryden and his predecessors in that he attempts to couple generalizations with particular examples, as Herbert does, for instance, in "Vanitie (I)" and "Man."

**957. Mollenkott, Virginia R.** "George Herbert's 'Redemption.'" *ELN* 10:262–67.

Reprinted in *Essential Articles for the Study of George Herbert's Poetry*, edited by John R. Roberts (entry 1216), 503–7.

Presents a close examination of "Redemption." Argues that the speaker of the poem is not a mean-spirited materialist, as John R. Mulder suggests (entry 803), nor a dim-witted petitioner, as Arnold Stein suggests (entry 773), but is "the spiritual nature of Everyman, not thriving under the Old Testament covenant and finally seeking a New Testament one, with the smaller rent of grace taking the place of the old lease of the law" (p. 263). Sees the narrator as "that part of everyman's soul which desires peace with God, crystallized at the historical moment of Christ's incarnation and crucifixion" (p. 266). Finds the legalistic and business imagery appropriate to the allegory of the poem and well established in Christian tradition: it "is intended to point us to the real drama of God's relationship to man: He had 'dearly bought' the world long ago, by the act of creation, and because of the Fall must now 'take possession' by paying back—redeeming it—on the cross" (pp. 264–65). Views the poem as "an allegorical narrative in the first-person point of view" (p. 266) and comments on its dramatic elements.

**958. Morita, Katsumi.** "Love and Hope in George Herbert's *The Temple*." *Ehime Daigaku Kyoyobu Kiyo* [Bulletin of the Faculty of General Education, Ehime University] no. 5 (January): 52–65.

Considers the prevenient love of God in Herbert's poems in relation to the working of God's spirit and Herbert's belief in final salvation.

**959. Mulder, John R.** "George Herbert's *The Temple*: Design and Methodology." *SCN* 31:37–45.

In part a reply to John M. Steadman (entry 930). Argues that *The Temple* is a consciously structured sequence, since the persona, or speaker, goes through a dramatic series of spiritual changes and emotions in his struggle to understand God and human experience. Maintains that at first the speaker is faulty in thinking that he can himself be an effective instrument in giving God glory and is actually sinful in assuming that the Bible, nature, and human experience can be understood from a more or less anthropocentric point of view, but then, as God tempers the speaker's pride by leading him through a series of spiritual fluctuations and trials, he gradually comes to recognize that his earlier perceptions were wrong and that the presence of Christ is central to everything. Points out that once the persona sees Christ in a theologically correct way, his conflicts cease and his soul is filled with joy and peace. Argues that by using capital letters and italics for design, Herbert has actually created two authors for the poems in *The Temple*: the poet who, though limited, can order and reorder his perceptions of God and human experience; and God, who constantly orders the poet's perceptions and thus offers him lessons in the great mystery of His dealings with His people.

**960. Patrick, J. Max.** "Critical Problems in Editing George Herbert's *The Temple*," in *The Editor as Critic and the Critic as Editor*, with an introduction by Murray Krieger, 3–40. Los Angeles: William Andrews Clark Memorial Library.

Argues in the first part of the essay that the textual editor must make careful use of criticism and attacks Hutchinson's edition of Herbert (entry 266), claiming that much of Hutchinson's trouble results from his having been taken in by Walton's fictional account of how Nicholas Ferrar received the manuscript of Herbert's poems. Maintains that the first edition of *The Temple* (1633) was set up from Herbert's own fair copy, perhaps as early as 1632, and that thus the first edition is the authoritative source, rather than the Bodleian MS, which Hutchinson trusted in preparing his eclectic edition. Comments in the second part of the essay on the problems facing the editor of Herbert in making available to the reader the numerous subtleties of the patterned poems and the significant stanza shapes of Herbert's poetry. Points out, for example, that "The Agonie" is shaped to resemble not only a printing press and a winepress but also a well-known instrument of torture. Maintains that the modern editor must make sure that these significant forms are adequately reproduced.

**961. Paynter, Mary.** "'Sinne and Love': Thematic Patterns in George Herbert's Lyrics." *YES* 3:85–93.

Maintains that Herbert's religious consciousness and also the thematic structure of *The Temple* are dominated by the notion of "the constructive force of God's love set in dynamic opposition to the destructive power of sin" (p. 93). Points out that throughout *The Church* Herbert's primary image of love is that of the feast, the *sacrum convivium*, with its eucharistic suggestions, while the primary images of sin are the stony heart and the box. Shows that from "The Agonie" to "Love (III)" "the Christian experience of divine love, seen in the image of the feast, and the sense of personal sin, revealed in images of the stony heart and the closed box, are portrayed in vital counterpoint" (p. 93).

**962. Pollock, John J.** "George Herbert's Enclosure Imagery." *SCN* 31:55.

Points out that Herbert employs the concept of enclosure as a structural basis for a number of his poems (for example, "The Pilgrimage") and that he uses images of enclosure to render his notion of the Eucharist (in, for example, "The Priesthood").

**963. Quennell, Peter, and Hamish Johnson.** "The Seventeenth Century," in *A History of English Literature*, 93–201. London: Weidenfeld and Nicolson; Springfield, Mass.: G. C. Merriman Co. (Hamish Johnson does not appear on the title page of the American edition.)

Reprinted, London: Ferndale Editions, 1981.

Brief introduction to Herbert's life and poetry (pp. 127–29), stressing the urbanity and courtliness of his poetry and its "grave and gentle" (p. 128) music. Maintains that Herbert's images "are usually simple but exquisitely effective" (p. 128) and reproduces "The Collar" and "Love (III)" as examples of Herbert's art.

**964. Ramsaran, John A.** "Divine Infatuation: Crashaw and Mīram Baī; Herbert and Mīram Baī," in *English and Hindi Religious Poetry: An Analogical Study*, 89–108. (Studies in the History of Religions, 23.) Leiden: E. J. Brill.

Compares and contrasts Herbert's poetry with that of Mīram Baī, a late fifteenth- and early sixteenth-century Indian poetess. Maintains that, although Herbert's poetry is more personal in tone and diction, more intellectual and analytical, and more full of conflict and tension than that of Mīram Baī, the two poets were alike in many ways, especially their yearning for union with God. Compares several individual poems, especially "Home," "The Search," "The Flower," "Love (III)," and "Longing," with several of Mīram Baī's poems and concludes that those poems that reveal the more intimate and personal experiences of Herbert the man, rather than those that announce the general spirit of Christian worship, show the most affinities with the Indian poetess.

**965. Richmond, H. M.** *Renaissance Landscapes: English Lyrics in a European Tradition.* (De proprietatibus litterarum, Series Practica, edited by C. H. Van Schooneveld, 52.) The Hague: Mouton. 156p.

Discusses the evolution of the landscape lyric and briefly comments on Herbert's debt to *The Greek Anthology*, pointing out, however, that, unlike the Greeks, Herbert presents a "doctrinaire accommodation of landscape allusions to an exposition of Christian concepts" (p. 141). Briefly compares and contrasts Herbert with Alcman, Goethe, and Wordsworth.

**966. Rogers, Robert.** "A Gathering of Roses: An Essay on the Limits of Context." *HSL* 5:61–76.

Surveys the metaphorical uses of the rose and assesses "the potential range of thought and feeling of metaphoric beds of roses by glancing at a number of more or less unrelated contexts to discover what associations such images may have in common" (p. 62). Comments briefly on Herbert's use of the rose in stanza 3 of "Vertue" and discusses the wide-ranging symbolic value of the rose in "The Rose," concluding that the poem "produces endopsychic tension commensurate with the gravity of its subject by setting up a series of oppositions between conscious, conventional meanings and unconscious, psychosexual 'affective correlations' of the imagery" (p. 73)

**967. Røstvig, Maren-Sofie.** "Idehistorie og litteraer tekstanalyse." *Nordisk Tidsskrift For Litteraturforskning* 53:41–52.

Discusses the importance of cooperation between the history of ideas and close textual analysis, especially for an understanding of Renaissance poetry. Outlines certain trends in literary criticism since the First World War, evaluates their strengths and weaknesses, and insists that the history of ideas and a knowledge of tradition are necessary correctives to the excesses of "new" criticism and of psychological criticism. Specifically mentions William Empson's study of Herbert (entry 131) and sees Rosemond Tuve's *A Reading of George Herbert* (entry 409) as proof of the need to combine close reading with a knowledge of tradition. Presents a brief structural analysis of "Content" and "Deniall" to show that in order to understand the poems one must support textual analysis with the history of ideas and with a good grasp of informing traditions.

**968. ———.** "Structural Images in Cowley and Herbert: A Comparison." *ES* 54:121–29.

Shows through a close structural analysis of Herbert's "Deniall" and "Content" and Cowley's "The Resurrection," "Hymn to the Light," and "The Ecstasie" that

"Cowley's structural manipulations, although sufficiently impressive as a *tour de force*, fail to move; they seem static rather than dynamic" and that "in Herbert alone is the poetic impact perceptively increased and the meaning substantially enriched, by observing the import of the structure" (p. 129). Argues, therefore, that poetic structure is just as useful as poetic images in determining poetic excellence and should be studied and classified as carefully as images.

**969. Schwartz, Helen J.** "Herbert's 'Grief.'" *Expl* 31:item 43.
Maintains that "Grief" is an example of Herbert's technique of expressing the theme of a poem hieroglyphically: "The overflowing, immeasurable quality of the speaker's grief is the poem's subject; the overflowing of the sonnet form shows this idea in action."

**970. Stanwood, P. G.** "The Liveliness of Flesh and Blood: Herbert's 'Prayer I' and 'Love III.'" *SCN* 31:52–53.
Comments on "Prayer (I)" and "Love (III)" as poems that, when read together, illustrate each other: "'Love' demonstrates that prayer is possible, but Herbert's 'Prayer' is a poem of love" (p. 53). Maintains that the two poems represent in small a major pattern in *The Temple*: "They both characterize the external movement of the flesh and portray the sensitive and . . . wholly responsive answer of the spirit" (p. 52). Comments on the reciprocal movement between the poet and his desire in each poem: "a going forth in order to receive, and an offering that requires an acceptance" (p. 53).

**971. Treglown, Jeremy.** "The Satirical Inversions of Some English Sources in Rochester's Poetry." *RES* 24:42–48.
Points out that the opening of Rochester's poem "Woman's Honour" ("Love bade me hope, and I obeyed") inverts the sense of Herbert's opening line of "Love (III)" ("Love bade me welcome: yet my soul drew back"). Maintains that the speaker in Rochester's poem presents a sexual version of Herbert's submission to Love ("You must sit down, sayes Love, and taste my meat: / So I did sit and eat").

**972. Ward, David.** "'The Fire and the Rose': *Four Quartets*," in *T. S. Eliot: Between Two Worlds*, 223–88. London and Boston: Routledge & Kegan Paul.
Contrasts Eliot with Herbert and maintains that the major difference between the two poets is that Herbert is confident in his poetry whereas Eliot is racked with anguish and doubt. Briefly discusses how this fundamental attitude is reflected in the poetry of each.

**973. Wilkinson, Jean.** "Three Sets of Religious Poems." *HLQ* 36:203–26.
Compares and contrasts the religious and aesthetic sensibilities, the biases, and the views of experience of three Anglican poets—Herbert, Christopher Smart, and John Keble—who wrote series of poems dealing with the liturgical feasts of the Church and with certain doctrinal beliefs. Specifically contrasts the rhetorical elements, the uses of language, and attitudes toward art in Herbert's "Christmas," Smart's "Epiphany," and Keble's "Christmas Day." Argues that both Herbert and Smart are superior to Keble, who tends to sentimentalize, while Smart is Herbert's equal.

# *1974*

**974. Blamires, Harry.** "Metaphysical and Cavalier Poetry," in *A Short History of English Literature*, 113–32. London: Methuen.

Brief introduction to Herbert's life and poetry (pp. 117–19). Praises Herbert's lack of histrionics, his use of bold imagery, and his technical variety and excellence. Contrasts Herbert and Donne, noting that in Herbert "there is no lashing and flailing of the intellectual tail" (p. 118).

**975. Broadbent, John, ed.** *Signet Classic Poets of the 17th Century*, vol. 1. (The Signet Classic Poetry Series, gen. ed. John Hollander.) New York and Scarborough, Ont.: New American Library; London: New English Library. xviii, 377p.

In the introduction maintains that Herbert was greatly influenced by Donne and that "the central issue of his religious poetry is dedication; the chief means, imitation of Christ, or a sanctified imitation of secular art" (p. 5). Brief introduction to Herbert's life and poetry (pp. 136–42), followed by a bibliographical note (pp. 142–43) and twenty-four selections from Herbert's poetry, with explanatory notes (pp. 143–66). Comments briefly on aspects of Herbert's art, such as his use of oral imagery, ambiguous words, sacred parody, and typology. Maintains that, after Rosemond Tuve (entry 409) and William Empson (entry 131), "there has been no great criticism on Herbert" (p. 143).

**976. Brooks, Cleanth.** "Religion and Literature." *SR* 82:93–107.

Argues that the functions of religion and literature must be distinguished, disagrees with those who hold that poetry can perform the same function in an age of disbelief that religion performed in an age of belief, and argues further that poetry, in order to perform its special function, needs religion. Maintains that the reader is not necessarily compelled to share Herbert's belief in God when he reads "Love (III)," whereas religious experience "*does* make some claim upon our belief" (p. 95).

**977. Campbell, Gordon.** "Words and Things: The Language of Metaphysical Poetry." *Language and Literature* (Copenhagen) 2, no. 3:3–15.

Translated into Spanish as "Palabras y objetos: El lenguaje de la poesia metafísica," by Virginia Zúñiga Tristán and Roger Wright, *Káñina* 3, no. 2 (1979): 63–72.

Challenges critics, such as Rosemond Tuve, who attempt "to experiment with the analytical tools of the Renaissance in an attempt to recreate the sixteenth- and seventeenth-century readers' understanding of poetry" and argues that "these methods, although historically justified, are ultimately destructive, and that an appreciation of Renaissance poetry, particularly metaphysical poetry, is predicated on a knowledge of the poets' ideas about the nature of poetry rather than an ability to implement the philosophers' ideas on how a poem should be analysed" (p. 3). Challenges the notion that Ramism accounts for metaphysical poetry and summarizes the long debate among poets and philosophers of the Renaissance about the primacy of words or things. Sees Herbert as a poet who clearly aligned himself "with those who thought words should take priority over things, that rime rather than reason should unify a poem" (p. 10). Concludes that metaphysical poetry "is primarily a poetry of words rather than things" and that "it is a glorification of the power of words as words, and we should be content to admire it at that level" (p. 11).

**978. Cannon, Philip.** *The Temple: A Triptych for Unaccompanied Choir.* London: Kronos Press. 40p.

Musical settings for "Discipline," "Vertue," and "Heaven." First performed at Gloucester Cathedral by the Gloucester Choir under the direction of John Sanders at the Three Choirs Festival in 1974.

**979. Charles, Amy M.** "Mrs. Herbert's Kitchin Booke." *ELR* 4:164–73.

Discusses Magdalene Herbert's household account book kept by her steward, John Gorse, and frequently signed by her (now in the collection of the Earl of Powis at Powis Castle). Covers twenty-one weeks, from the day before Easter until early June 1601, soon after the Herbert household moved to London from Oxford. Records interesting details about the daily life of the Herbert family, its many guests and visitors, and what the Herbert sons were reading and studying during this period. Includes a reproduction of a portrait of Magdalene Herbert (perhaps the work of Sir William Segar) and facsimiles of folios 56 and 57 of the book.

980. **Chinol, Elio.** "The Metaphysical Poets," in *English Literature: A Historical Survey*, vol. 1, *To the Romantic Revival*, 315–22. (Le lingue e le civiltà straniere moderne, under the direction of Elio Chinol.) Naples: Liguori Editore.

Calls Herbert the best of the religious poets of the period and states that the chief characteristics of his poetry are serenity of faith and lyric grace. Maintains that, strictly speaking, Herbert is not a metaphysical poet, although the influence of Donne "can be traced in his wit and conceits" (p. 315). Reproduces "Easter-wings" and "The Altar" with Italian notes (pp. 316–18).

981. **Craven, Elizabeth.** "The Caldron of Affliction in the Journey Through *The Temple*." *Graduate English Papers* (University of Arizona) 6, no. 1:2–5.

Maintains that *The Temple* "traces the journey of a soul from a blind acceptance of the letter of the Law to complete communion with the spirit of the Law," that from *The Church-Porch* to "Love (III)" "the soul is moving from what is essentially ignorance toward an intimate knowledge of the spirit of Christ," that the "journey between these two points is marked by a series of trials through which the soul eventually learns the way of Christ," and that the five "Affliction" poems "mark these trials with the lamentations and protestations of the soul" (p. 2). Analyzes the five "Affliction" poems to illustrate this progression and maintains that "what the five 'Affliction' poems suggest in subtle progression, 'Love Unknown' explains in allegory" (p. 4).

982. **Dodge, Carolyn June.** "Kinaesthetic Effect in the Poetry of George Herbert." *RUO* 44:202–17.

Discusses Herbert's use of kinesthetic effects in his poetry and defines these effects as "the muscular, behavioral response to the sounds and rhythms of metrical structures" (p. 202). Argues that the rhythms of Herbert's poetry effect "an imitation of movement away from or toward God" and that thus the reader experiences "the physical, muscular sense or feeling which accompanies each spiritual act that constitutes the meaning experienced in the poetry" (p. 202). Maintains that Herbert may have known such a theory through medical tracts and poetic treatises of the Renaissance. Through a discussion of a number of specific poems, argues that kinesthetic effect "is associated with metrically emblematic structures such as counterpoint, contrast, and enjambment to express man's creatural relationship to God; with hieroglyphic forms; and with interrelated uses of sense imagery" (p. 217). Notes, for example, that the reader kinesthetically experiences spiritual flight in "Easter-wings" and the sense of rebellion in "The Collar." Concludes that the kinesthetic effect is, in fact, "part of the unity of images and idea, form and substance, subject and style in *The Temple* where the act of creation by the poet and the re-creation by the reader is an act of worship" (p. 217).

983. **Fish, Stanley.** "Catechizing the Reader: Herbert's Socratean Rhetoric," in *The Rhetoric of Renaissance Poetry: From Wyatt to Milton*, edited by Thomas O.

Sloan and Raymond B. Waddington, 174–88. Berkeley, Los Angeles, London: University of California Press.

Reprinted in *Essential Articles for the Study of George Herbert's Poetry*, edited by John R. Roberts (entry 1216), 199–211.

Argues that Herbert's poetic strategy is closely related to the method of catechizing discussed in chapter 21 of *A Priest to the Temple*. Maintains that the poet assumes the role of the questioner or catechist and that the reader becomes the one catechized and argues that such an approach accounts for the elements of order and surprise in Herbert's poetry: "The order belongs to the Questionist-poet who knows from the beginning where he is going" and the "surprise belongs to the reader who is 'driven' by 'questions well ordered' to discover for himself 'that which he knows not'" (p. 176). Shows how, for instance, Herbert often "strikes deliberately naive poses that are calculated to draw a critical or corrective response from an interlocutor; that is, he makes assertions which *function* as questions because they invite the reader to supply either what is missing or what is deficient" (p. 177). Demonstrates how this strategy functions in "Love-joy," "Love unknown," "The Holdfast," and especially "The Bunch of Grapes." Comments also on how this rhetorical strategy is consistent with Herbert's views on the moral purposes of poetry.

**984. Grant, Patrick.** *The Transformation of Sin: Studies in Donne, Herbert, Vaughan, and Traherne.* Montreal and London: McGill-Queen's University Press; Amherst: University of Massachusetts Press. xiii, 240p.

Approaches Donne, Herbert, Vaughan, and Traherne "in terms of a hypothetical encounter between guilt culture and enlightenment" (p. 38), in other words, in terms of a conflict between traditional Augustinian theology and sensibility and a new ethical view of man. Argues that "the conflict of the old and the new in the seventeenth century is not simply between Protestantism and Catholicism, or between Renaissance and Reformation, but between two modes of regarding the ethical nature of man" (p. 38). Although Herbert is mentioned throughout this study, three chapters specifically discuss him. Chapter 3, "Augustinian Spirituality and George Herbert's *The Temple*" (pp. 73–99), contrasts Herbert and Donne, maintaining that, although both were Augustinian and medieval in the main, Herbert's fascination with Calvinist predestination affords his poems those qualities which most readily distinguish them from Donne's" (p. 76). Outlines the influence of Augustinian tradition on Herbert and finds many similarities between his religious poems and the medieval religious lyric, which in turn was informed by Franciscan spirituality. Discusses the *Biblia Pauperum* and the *Speculum humanae salvationis*, two medieval handbooks of popular devotion imbued with Franciscan spirituality and concludes that "the medieval tradition on which George Herbert's devotional poetry predominately draws" is "primarily Augustinian, mediated to the Renaissance through a devotional tradition, mainly Franciscan" (p. 92). Chapter 4, "George Herbert and Juan de Valdés: The Franciscan Mode and Protestant Manner" (pp. 100–133), discusses the theology and spirituality of Juan de Valdés, pointing out important analogues between the Spanish writer and Herbert. Argues that Herbert's spirituality "is Franciscan in the manner that the spirituality of Valdés is also Franciscan" but notes that "we find in Herbert a traditional Augustinian piety modified by doctrines of justification by faith, election, and predestination, but modified in such a way that the opposing tendencies are sustained momentarily in harmony" (p. 123). Chapter 5, "Henry Vaughan and the Hermetic Philosophy" (pp. 134–69), although devoted primarily to Vaughan, includes a comparison of Herbert and Vaughan and points out a number of significant differences between the master and the disciple: "In their poetry of the fall and original sin, Herbert's object is behavior, Vaughan's is cosmology" (p. 144).

**985. Hammond, Gerald, ed.** *The Metaphysical Poets: A Selection of Critical Essays.* (Casebook Series, edited by A. E. Dyson.) London and Basingstoke: Macmillan Press. 254p.

Contains an introduction to the metaphysical poets, including comments on Herbert (pp. 11–32) and selections from criticism from the seventeenth century to the modern period. Herbert is mentioned in the following: (1) Selections from Edward Phillip's *Theatrum Poetarum Anglicanorum* of 1674 (p. 37); (2) selection from *Select Hymns out of Mr Herbert's Temple* of 1697 (pp. 40–41); (3) selection from Joseph Addison, *The Spectator* of 1711 (pp. 42–46); (4) selections from Coleridge taken from *Coleridge on the Seventeenth Century*, edited by Roberta Florence Brinkley in 1955 (entry 443) (pp. 59–60); (5) selections from Emerson's *Notebooks* (1831–1845) (pp. 67–70); (6) selections from George Macdonald's *England's Antiphon* of 1868 (pp. 71–74); (7) selection from Rosemond Tuve's *Elizabethan and Metaphysical Imagery: Renaissance Poetic and Twentieth-Century Critics* of 1947 (entry 330) (pp. 91–115); (8) S. L. Bethell's "Gracián, Tesauro, and the Nature of Metaphysical Wit" of 1953 (entry 411) (pp. 129–56); (9) selection from Joseph H. Summers's *George Herbert: His Religion and Art* of 1954 (entry 435) (pp. 157–81); (10) selection from Josephine Miles and Hanan C. Selvin's "A Factor Analysis of the Vocabulary of Poetry in the Seventeenth Century" of 1966 (entry 707) (pp. 182–96); (11) selection from Earl Miner's *The Metaphysical Mode from Donne to Cowley* of 1969 (entry 802) (pp. 197–214). Selected bibliography (pp. 243–45).

**986. Herbert, George.** *The English Poems of George Herbert*, edited by C. A. Patrides. London: J. M. Dent & Sons. 247p.

1st American ed., Totowa, N.J.: Rowman and Littlefield, 1975.

"To the Reader" (pp. 1–3) contains a note on abbreviations, a note on the text (except for six poems from the Williams MS and two from Walton's *Lives*, the primary authority is the first edition of 1633), and acknowledgments. "An Outline of Herbert's Life Within the Context of Contemporary Events" (pp. 4–5). A general critical introduction to Herbert's poetry, entitled "A Crown of Praise: The Poetry of Herbert" (pp. 6–25), stresses the grace, complex simplicity, and self-conscious plainness of Herbert's art and outlines major themes, techniques, and general characteristics of his poetry. Comments on the pervasive influence of the Bible, emblem books, wisdom literature, the parables, and music and discusses the structure of *The Temple*, commenting particularly on the importance of the Eucharist and of the concept of grace in Herbert's religious sensibility as reflected in his poems. "A Note on Typology" (pp. 26–27). *The Temple* (pp. 29–200) with notes. Appendix 1: "Poems not included in *The Temple*" (pp. 201–6). Appendix 2, "Three versions of a poem by Herbert" (pp. 207–8), gives three versions of "The Elixir." Appendix 3: "Some secular poems parodied by Herbert" (pp. 209–13). Extensive bibliography (pp. 214–38), index of titles (pp. 239–43), and index of first lines (pp. 244–47).
Reviews:
Peter Howe, *CritQ* 17 (1975): 286–87
J. W. Blench, *DUJ*, 71 (1978): 130–31
Robert Ellrodt, *EA* 32 (1979): 84–85

**987. ——.** *Selections from The Temple: George Herbert.* Charlottesville: Graham-Johnston. 21p.

Limited to 500 copies, printed on Strathmore Artlaid paper, in twelve-point Garamond set by hand, and hand-bound by the publisher, 400 in French marbled paper and 100 in half cloth.

Reprints twenty-one poems from *The Temple*, without notes or commentary.

**988. Higbie, Robert.** "Images of Enclosure in George Herbert's *The Temple*." *TSLL* 15:627–38.

Reprinted in *Essential Articles for the Study of George Herbert's Poetry*, edited by John R. Roberts (entry 1216), 268–79.

Maintains that Herbert's extensive use of enclosure imagery (walls, locked doors, houses, boxes, cabinets) forms one of the major unifying elements in *The Temple*. Suggests several reasons for Herbert's choosing such images: "Accepting God for him seems to have meant accepting some sort of containment, some boundaries within which God would protect him" (p. 627). Notes that "a temple itself is a kind of enclosure, and Herbert seems to have chosen the enclosure image for its relation to his concept of the temple," which "represents for him God's perfect enclosure, the ideal of which his earlier enclosure images are imperfect reflections" (p. 627). Maintains that the imagery in *The Temple* progresses, though not directly, "from the earthly man-made enclosure, the house and the church, to the divine enclosure of the temple, the perfection that the church tries to embody on earth" (p. 627). Views the conflicts, the contradictions, and the sense of constraint and limitation in *The Church* as Herbert's means of giving the reader "a sense of the straitness of our earthly dwelling-place, to make us feel imprisoned in it, and by doing so to make us want to transcend the earthly and seek the divine" (p. 628). Suggests that through his use of enclosure imagery and strict forms Herbert also intends to suggest that poetry itself, since it is man-made, is inadequate to lead us to God. Sees "Love (III)" with its eucharistic overtones as the climax of *The Church*: "It is for this final 'entrance' (l. 4) into God's enclosure that the enclosure imagery has been constructed, and this ritual act representing union with God is what it is meant to enclose" (p. 635). Argues that "it is not merely a physical but a spiritual enclosure, the place within which the union can be consummated," and this enclosure "is the temple to which Herbert's title refers—not an earthly temple, any more than the Eucharist taken inside it is earthly food, but rather an ideal, a temple raised in the heart" (pp. 635–36).

**989. Holloway, John.** "Poetic Analysis and the Idea of Transformation-Rule: Some Examples from Herbert, Wordsworth, Pope, and Shakespeare," in *Miscellanea Anglo-Americana: Festschrift für Helmut Viebrock*, edited by Kuna Schuhmann, Wilhelm Hortmann, and Armin Paul Frank, 279–96. Munich: Karl Pressler.

Reprinted as Appendix 1 of *Narrative and Structure: Exploratory Essays* (Cambridge: Cambridge University Press, 1979), 118–36.

Generally distrusts the application of linguistic theory to poetry as practiced by many linguists and literary critics but suggests that the literary critic should "allow his mind to play freely over two general ideas, which indeed come from linguistics in the context of linguistic transformation-rules, as possible helps to poetic analysis in certain cases" (p. 283). Maintains that the two ideas are "first, simply the idea of a rule itself; and then, the idea that the kind of rule he may find is operative will be a rule whereby sentences of one form are transformed systematically into sentences of another" (p. 283). Comments on the inversion of normal word order in Herbert's "The Windows" and contrasts it with the inversions in Wordsworth's "Anecdote for Fathers." Comments also on structural features in "Mortification."

**990. Kelliher, W. Hilton.** "The Latin Poetry of George Herbert," in *The Latin Poetry of English Poets*, edited by J. W. Binns, 26–57. London and Boston: Routledge & Kegan Paul.

Reprinted in *Essential Articles for the Study of George Herbert's Poetry*, edited by John R. Roberts (entry 1216), 526–52.

Detailed historical and critical survey of Herbert's Latin verse. Calls *Memoriae Matris Sacrum* "the masterpiece of Herbert's Latin poetry" (p. 47) and maintains that it clearly "illustrates by its highly personal tone no less than by the Metaphysical spirit that is evident in individual poems how Herbert's mastery of classical idioms was made to serve his own immediate needs rather than merely to fulfill a literary ideal" (p. 54).

**991. Linden, Stanton J.** "The Breaking of the Alembic: Patterns in Alchemical Imagery in English Renaissance Poetry." *WascanaR* 9:105–13.

Contrasts two literary uses of alchemy during the Renaissance. Points out that from Chaucer onward to Donne and Jonson, alchemy was presented with a satirical intent; it became synonymous with greed, deceit, self-delusion, and all kinds of moral depravity. Notes, however, that before this satirical tradition died out, there also developed (between 1580 and 1630) a new and different pattern of alchemic usage, one in which alchemy was used metaphorically to suggest growth, change, and even regeneration. Maintains that the poetry of Donne and Herbert gives us the best examples of the way that alchemy was utilized during the transitional period, since they "tend to use alchemy with an awareness and understanding of its full range of denotations, connotations, and associational nuances" (p. 109). Cites Herbert's "The Elixir" as an example.

**992. McFarland, Ronald E.** "Thanksgiving in Seventeenth Century Poetry." *Albion* (Washington State University Press) 6:294–306.

Surveys the background and tradition of Christian poems of thanksgiving and comments on a number of representative thanksgiving poems written during the seventeenth century in England. Contrasts Herbert's "The Thanksgiving" with thanksgiving poems by Herrick and Marvell and points out that Herbert's emphasis is "upon the *response* to God's most important gift—the possibility of salvation through Christ" (p. 304). Analyzes the poem and shows how its positioning in *The Temple* informs its full meaning. Maintains that Herbert's poem is "not in fact a thankful response, but rather a consideration of possible responses; it is not a poem of thanksgiving so much as it is a poem *about* thanksgiving" (p. 305) and argues that other poems, such as "Gratefulnesse" and "Praise (II)," more closely resemble the typical thanksgiving poems of the age. Concludes that the issue of the proper response to redemption "is fittingly resolved" in "Love (III)" (p. 306).

**993. McGuire, Philip C.** "Private Prayer and English Poetry in the Early Seventeenth Century." *SEL* 14:63–77.

Discusses the influences of private prayer, as opposed to formal discursive meditation, on poetic practice in the early seventeenth century as reflected in six poems by Donne, Jonson, and Herbert. Outlines contemporary attitudes toward, and definitions of, prayer and points out that Renaissance devotionalists "divided private prayer into a preface (which could also be a conclusion) and three major components— confession, invocation, and thanksgiving—which were organized either to praise God or, more frequently, to persuade him" (p. 65). Analyzes Herbert's "The Altar" as "a prayer of praise and petition in which the speaker's act of framing his prayer as a poem heightens his praise and the persuasiveness of his petitions" (p. 75).

**994. Mambrino, Jean.** "Simone Weil et George Herbert." *Etudes* 340:247–56.

Argues that the poetry of Herbert was a decisive influence on Simone Weil, who was first introduced to his poetry in 1938. Reproduces Weil's comments on Herbert and points out that she especially liked "Discipline," "Bitter-sweet," and "Love (III)," which she called "le plus beau poème du monde" (p. 250). Outlines affinities between the life, faith, and death of Herbert and those of Weil and presents French translations of "The Collar," "Discipline," "Bitter-sweet," "Vertue," and "Love (III)."

**995. Morillo, Marvin.** "Herbert's Chairs: *The Temple.*" *ELN* 11:271–75.

Considers Herbert's references to chairs in *The Temple* and disagrees with Hutchinson's gloss on the chairs in "Mortification" and "The Pilgrimage." Points out that in "The Temper (II)," "Jordan (I)," and "Church-rents and schismes," Herbert uses *chair* primarily in its etymological sense as "a seat of authority" or "throne," but that in both "Mortification" and "The Pilgrimage" he is referring to portable chairs, "conveyances in a stage of the allegorical journey rather than stationary places of repose" and that, "though indeed emblematic of old age, [the chairs] point specifically to old age in progress, not in repose" (p. 273). Maintains that "since journeys provide the allegorical terms in both poems and since abundant evidence indicates that 'chair' in that context would be readily understood as designating a conveyance for royalty, the sick, wounded, or the feeble aged, Hutchinson's note summons an image of the hearthside chair that is inconsistent with the controlling conceit of both poems" (p. 275).

**996. Nakamura, Masakatsu.** "George Herbert and His Metaphysical Poetry." *Sagami Kogyo Daigaku Kiyo* [Memoirs of the Sagami Institute of Technology] 8, no.1 (March): 35–43.

Considers the reality of love in the three "Love" poems in *The Temple*. Points out that Herbert pays special consideration to the words *dust* and *eyes* in these poems.

**997. Okuda, Hiroko.** "Buntai Riso to shiteno Kanketsu—G. Herbert no Baai" [Simplicity as a Stylistic Ideal—The Case of G. Herbert]. *Bungaku ni tsuite* [On Literature] no. 3 (March): 7–17.

Partly revised Japanese version of "Pruning to Perfection—An Essay on G. Herbert" (entry 924).

**998. Osmond, Rosalie.** "Body and Soul Dialogues in the Seventeenth Century." *ELR* 4:364–403.

Discusses the revival of interest in body-soul dialogues in the first half of the seventeenth century and presents a number of reasons for "this apparently anachronistic literary form" making "a sudden and brief appearance between 1602 and 1651 only to die out completely after that date" (p. 364). Maintains that "careful examination of the characteristics of both the form and content of the medieval debates makes it clear that they have much more in common with at least certain aspects of early seventeenth century thought and literature than one might suppose" (p. 364). Briefly comments on Herbert's uses of personification in his presentation of the soul in his poetry and shows that, although Herbert and his contemporaries "did not consciously believe the soul to be visible, they just as certainly did imagine it to be so" (p. 379) in their poems. Concludes that, although poetic images "cannot be taken at face value as literal statements of belief" (p. 379), they do subtly help to form certain theological attitudes and influence the general understanding of certain theological concepts.

**999. Segel, Harold B.** *The Baroque Poem: A Comparative Survey.* New York: E. P. Dutton & Co. xx, 328p.

Announces that the purpose of this study is twofold: (1) "to present a comprehensive survey of the Baroque: the state of scholarship in the field, problems in the definition and use of Baroque as a term and concept, the relationship of mannerism to Baroque, the political, religious, scientific, and philosophical background of the age, the possible impact of nonliterary events on the evolution of the Baroque taste, art, and outlook, the various types of Baroque poetry and aspects of Baroque poetic style" (pp. xix-xx) and (2) "to illustrate points made in the first, or survey, part of the book by giving a broad selection of representative poems, mostly lyrics, in the original languages and accompanying English translations" (p. xx). Contains 150 poems from the following literatures: English, American, Dutch, German, French, Italian, Spanish, Mexican, Portuguese, Polish, Modern Latin, Czech, Croatian, and Russian. Mentions Herbert throughout and sees him as a baroque poet. Includes eleven poems by Herbert.

**1000. Sharp, Nicholas.** "Herbert's 'Love (III).'" *Expl* 33:item 26.

Points out that the word *host* refers not only to a person who gives a banquet but also to the communion wafer. Claims that "Love (III)" is "a prayerful interchange between the modest communicant (the guest) and Christ really present in the communion host." Maintains that on a literal level, "with allegorical or anagogical exegesis, the poem concerns the Communion banquet which, as the structural ambiguity insists, is truly a feast of love." Argues that to miss this literal level is to miss "the distinction between Herbert's metaphysical piety and the similar but distinct piety of medieval religious verse."

**1001. Summers, Joseph H.** "Stanley Fish's Reading of Seventeenth-Century Literature." *MLQ* 35:403–17.

Essentially a review-article of Stanley E. Fish's *Self-Consuming Artifacts: The Experience of Seventeenth-Century Literature* (entry 905). Maintains that "the chief virtues of Fish's book derive from his recognition that the basic data of any literary criticism are the *experiences* of an alert, intelligent, and sensitive reader as he reads the text within time" (p. 417) but distrusts Fish's assumption "that admirable literary designs on the reader should always be antagonistic, tricky, or evangelical; that the ultimate recognition the best seventeenth-century works provide is the distrust of any sort of reliance on the 'self' or human reason; and that what they bring the reader to, again and again, is the recognition both of their own and the readers' inadequacies before divine revelation and the inexplicable will of God" (p. 406). Argues that, although Fish "observes numbers of important happenings which we need to notice, he omits or misinterprets a good deal by attempting to stick so closely to one perspective on the reading process" (p. 405). Points out that "with Herbert's marvellously artful poems, the major limitations of Fish's principal metaphor are most evident" and rejects Fish's notion that Herbert is primarily a dialectician unconcerned with beauty: "Any reading of Herbert's poems which ignores *any* notions of the beautiful is likely to be at best partial, if not peculiar" (p. 411). Challenges a number of Fish's interpretations of Herbert, noting that, for example, "it is Fish rather than Herbert who assumes that poetry per se is 'presumptuous' or suspect" (p. 412).

**1002. Taylor, Mark.** *The Soul in Paraphrase: George Herbert's Poetics.* (De proprietatibus litterarum: Series Practica, 92.) The Hague and Paris: Mouton. 127p.

Argues that *The Temple* "demonstrates Herbert's total poetic and linguistic involvement in the Christian experience" (p. 2). Chapter 1, "Poetry and Silence: Herbert's Art of Poetry" (pp. 9–52), discusses Herbert's theory of poetry and shows that "it is a theory of words, deriving from a sense of the inability of traditional scholastic rhetoric or the language of secular poetry to express the truth" (p. 2). Chapter 2, "Poetry and Time: Herbert's Image of Time" (pp. 53–84), comments on "the way in which verse can enable the poet to transcend the limitations of temporal mortality and enter into eternity, a movement that Herbert presents metaphorically as the subservience of the human words of poetic composition to the poem's God-given truth" (pp. 2–3). Chapter 3, "Poetry and Light: Herbert's Synaesthetic Imagery" (pp. 85–115), argues that a study of Herbert's synesthetic imagery "will show that, as God is both the Word and the Light, so can human words reflect the revealed light in which they have their origin; there is a sense in which visual and verbal transmission and perception are one" (p. 3). Maintains that all of these informing notions are unified by Herbert's personal, yet totally orthodox Christian experience and by his imaginative uses of certain concepts derived from St. Augustine. Selected bibliography (pp. 118–22).

Reviews:
Amy Charles, *Choice* 12 (1975): 224
Joan Bennett, *RES* 27 (1976): 215–17
Zoran Kuzmanovic, *SCN* 38 (1980): 44

1003. **Thekla, Sister.** *George Herbert: Idea and Image.* Buckinghamshire, Eng.: Greek Orthodox Monastery of the Assumption, Filgrave, Newport Pagnell. 308p.

Detailed discussion of the theological and spiritual dimensions of Herbert's poetry. Sees a double, simultaneous movement in *The Temple* and maintains that, although on one level *The Temple* can be seen as an exposition of Anglican theology and dogma in verse, on another level it is a record of Herbert's own mystical thinking: "It is this double movement which I have tried to lean towards in my exploration of *The Temple*, that is, the reality of Herbert's allegiance to his Church, the Church of England, on earth, with all the consequences, and, then, the reality of the love which can not be contained in the Church on earth, or indeed within the confines of the created world" (p. 14). Part 1, "The Work of Faith" (pp. 19–116), is divided into four chapters. Chapter 1, "Priest of the Church of England" (pp. 21–39), comments on Herbert's attitudes on, and love of, the Church and his attitudes on the priesthood. Chapter 2, "World of Grace and World of Nature" (pp. 39–69), discusses Herbert's theology of redemption and comments on such matters as redemption, faith, grace, and the imputation of righteousness. Chapter 3, "Theology in Practice" (pp. 70–96), discusses Herbert's attitudes on the saints, the Bible, the Eucharist, and the meaning of suffering in the Christian life. Chapter 4, "The Angry God" (pp. 96–116), traces "how, in the uncertainty of any assurance of continued Grace, in the no-knowledge of success, and, with a seemingly inherent distaste for an absolute doctrine of the imputation of Righteousness, Herbert found his path by a creative submission of *the Angry God*" (p. 116). Part 2, "The Work of Love" (pp. 117–205), is divided into three chapters. Chapter 1, "The Person of Christ" (pp. 119–51), outlines Herbert's Christology. Chapter 2, "Participation in Christ" (pp. 152–77), discusses Herbert's attitudes on sin, repentance, mortality, and death. Chapter 3, "The Offering of Praise" (pp. 178–205), comments on how Herbert sees all his work as a form of praise and views his poetry primarily as a medium of devotion. Part 3, "Key Poems of the Mystery" (pp. 207–46), presents a discussion of poems in which Herbert "explicitly gives the hint of his conviction of the Mystery, which, within him, transcends all systems of theology" (p. 209): "Divinitie," "The Flower," "The Answer," "The Collar," "Miserie," "Jordan (II)," "Josephs coat," "Love unknown," "The Pulley,"

"Mans medley," "Home," "The Pilgrimage," and "Hope." Part 4, "Synopsis of the Imagery" (pp. 247–75), presents a detailed discussion of Herbert's imagery illustrated by diagrams of the complexity of the interrelationships of the imagery. Conclusion: "A Note on the Place of Literature in Understanding Between the Churches" (pp. 277–78). Appended is Lydia Gysi's essay "George Herbert: Aspects of His Theology" (pp. 279–305), first published in 1972 (entry 908). Index of poems (pp. 306–7). Reviews:
A. J. Smith, *AWR* 24, no. 54 (1975): 206–8
C. C. Brown, *RES* 27 (1976): 68–70

**1004. Thwaite, Anthony.** "George Herbert, in *The English Poets from Chaucer to Edward Thomas.*, edited by Peter Porter and Anthony Thwaite, 108–17. London: Secker and Warburg.

General introduction to Herbert's life and poetry. Argues that, although he valued simplicity and "his poems aren't difficult if one has a reasonable familiarity with the Bible," Herbert himself "was a complex, sophisticated man" (p. 108). Calls him "the chief ornament of the Anglican Church" (p. 112) and calls his poetry "a poetry of reconciliation" (p. 108) that reflects his attempts to resolve the tensions and conflicts in his own life. Comments briefly on "The Pearl," "The Collar," "Redemption," "Prayer (I)," "Man," "Jordan (II)," "The Flower," and "Love (III)" and praises Herbert's technical variety, his dramatic simplicity, and his rhythmic subtlety and delicacy.

**1005. Tsur, Rueven.** "Poem, Prayer & Meditation: An Exercise in Literary Semantics." *Style* 8:405–24.

Discusses the relationship between devotional and aesthetic value in religious poetry, focusing on Donne and the seventeenth-century religious poets. Distinguishes among a poem, a prayer, and a meditation and uses Roman Jakobson's model of linguistic function "to show how these three 'deep structures' *can* be conveyed by the same words" (p. 410). Briefly mentions Herbert. Notes, for instance, Herbert's conviction that all of one's poetic powers should be dedicated to religious verse and that, although he believed that poems should be as perfectly crafted as possible, since they were gifts to God, his ultimate criterion for religious verse was not aesthetic but rather was "a matter of the devotion of the heart revealed by the words" (p. 406).

# *1975*

**1006. Baker, Herschel.** "George Herbert," in *The Later Renaissance in England: Nondramatic Verse and Prose, 1600–1660*, 201–20. Boston: Houghton Mifflin.

Biographical sketch of Herbert and general introduction to his poetry and prose (pp. 201–3), followed by a bibliography (p. 203), selections from his poems, the preface to *The Temple* (pp. 204–20), and notes. Calls *The Temple* "one of the most successful (and influential) books of poetry of the century" (p. 203).

**1007. Barcus, James E.** "A Visit to Bemerton—excerpt from the journal of James E. Barcus." *SCN* 33:45–46.

Account of a visit to Bemerton. Describes St. Andrew's and the present-day rectory.

**1008. Chambers, A. B.** "Christmas: The Liturgy of the Church and the English Verse of the Renaissance," in *Literary Monographs*, vol. 6, edited by Eric Rothstein and Joseph Anthony Wittreich, Jr., 109–53. Madison and London: University of Wisconsin Press.

Discusses the history, theology, and symbolism of the liturgy of the Christmas cycle; comments on how seventeenth-century divines interpreted these materials; and shows how an understanding of the Christmas liturgy is useful in interpreting late sixteenth- and early seventeenth-century poems on the birth of Christ. Argues that "Deniall," "Christmas," and "Ungratefulnesse" form a brief poetic sequence on the Christmas cycle within *The Temple* and presents critical readings of the poems. Contends that in the sequence Herbert translates "narration into dramatic action and biblical history into personal experience" and "brings the past into the present and the makes old situations seem forever new" (p. 130). Briefly compares and contrasts Herbert to Donne, Crashaw, Vaughan, Jonson, George Wither, William Alabaster, Edward Taylor, and Milton.

**1009.** [**Charles, Amy M.,** ed.] *Cross-Bias: The Newsletter of the Friends of Bemerton Society* no. 1 (December). 3p.

Reports on recent developments in the parish of Bemerton; notes the death of the Right Honorable Edward Robert Henry Herbert, Lord Herbert of Chirbury and fifth Earl of Powis, and points out that he has been succeeded by Col. Christian Victor Charles Herbert; comments on the recent identification of the chalice and paten cover used in St. Andrew's in Herbert's time, as well as the discovery in Warminster of the gold ring bearing Donne's seal of Christ upon an anchor that Donne sent to Herbert; comments on drawings and portraits of Herbert; and lists some recent publications and forthcoming studies on Herbert.

**1010.** ———. "George Herbert, Deacon." *MP* 72:272–76.

Examines the details of Herbert's life from his departure from Cambridge in 1624 to his installation at Lincoln Cathedral as prebendary in 1626. Argues, on the basis of a newly discovered document in the Lincolnshire Archives Office, that Herbert was ordained a deacon by Bishop John Williams before the end of 1624 while he was on leave as university orator from Cambridge and that he was made comportioner of the rectory of Llandinam in Montgomeryshire on 6 December 1624, a preferment that he held to the end of his life. Maintains, therefore, that Walton is incorrect when he says that Herbert cherished "court-hopes" until the death of James I on 27 March 1625. Points out that Herbert's ordination would have removed him from any possibility of secular preferment. Notes that until he settled in Bemerton, in his mid-thirties, Herbert "was never head of his own house or of his own table, but rather a part of the establishments of his family and of their connections" (p. 275).

**1011. Cloud, Jesse.** "George Herbert's Black Lady: An Exploration of 'Aethiopissa Ambit Cestum.'" *SCN* 33:43–45.

Argues that, although love is Herbert's dominant metaphor, appearing 109 times in *The Temple*, he is usually highly critical of poets who sanctify profane love. Finds it ironic, therefore, that Herbert "at a crucial moment in his life should write a late Petrarchan poem in Latin which extols secular love through the voice of a speaker such as *Aethiopissa*" (p. 43). Contends that the witty and fashionable Latin poem, along with the English poem, "To the Right Hon. the L. Chancellor (Bacon)," was sent to Bacon as part of his attempt to obtain preferment at the English court. Analyzes the conceits of darkness and light, the structure, and the argument of the poem and suggests the influence of the Renaissance theme of the dark lady and, in particular, of Marino's "La bella schiava," in which familiar Petrarchan conceits are reversed. Argues that the poem is "sophisticated, complex and witty" and "more than a *jeu d'esprit*" (p. 45). Maintains that Herbert, like Donne and the other metaphysical poets, regarded sex as a fit subject for verse ("the crime in his view was not love but stale language" [p. 45]) and that he was not reluctant to use Petrarchan conceits for his own ends.

1012. ———. "The Quidditie." *Expl* 34:item 32.
Argues that "The Quidditie" "exemplifies the manner in which [Herbert] simultaneously laughs at himself and others, while underneath the grave comedy lies a declaration of faith about the purposes of art." Notes that in the poem Herbert "states in eighteen ways what his poetry is not," a comic echo perhaps of Nicholas of Cusa's concept of "enlightened ignorance," a form of *theologia negativa* popular among medieval theologians. Comments on the double and triple puns in the poem to show that, "while apparently denying the place of his poetry in the world of society and affairs, he affirms its divine intent in the same phrases." Explains the difficult final phrase, "*most take all*," by referring to the popular card game "l'ombre" and notes that Herbert uses the device of circularity "to illustrate how divine verse mirrors the perfection of God."

1013. **Davidson, Clifford.** "Herbert's «The Temple»: Conflicts, Submission, and Freedom." *EM* 25 (1975–1976): 163–81.
Rejects Walker's notion (entry 596) that the threefold structure of *The Temple* is analogous to the tripartite division of the Hebraic temple. Argues that the unifying themes of *The Temple* are conflict, submission, and freedom. Analyzes the inner conflict between God and man portrayed in Herbert's verse, especially in *The Church-Porch*. Discusses the pattern of rebellion and submission in *The Temple*, focusing on "The Collar." Defines Herbert's concept of freedom as not simply liberty to do as one wishes, but as freedom from the bondage to sin and death, and finds in the orderly pattern of his verse the resolution of his inner conflicts. Analyzes the theme of Christian freedom as portrayed in "Paradise," "The Search," "Death," "Dooms-day," "Judgement," "Heaven," "Love (III)," and "The H. Communion." Concludes that "any further attempt to force some formal criterion of «organic unity» upon *The Temple* would be superfluous" (p. 181).

1014. **Davies, Horton.** *Worship and Theology in England: From Andrewes to Baxter and Fox, 1603–1690.* (Worship and Theology in England, vol. 2.) Princeton: Princeton University Press. xxiii, 592p.
Mentions Herbert throughout, especially commenting on his religious discipline and spirituality and agreeing with Martz (entry 431) that Herbert shows greater affinity with Salesian rather than with Ignatian spirituality. Maintains that, although Herbert's attitudes toward parsons, preaching, prayer, and so forth, can be found in *The Country Parson*, it is in his poetry that his spirituality "soars" (p. 104). Cites "Prayer (I)" as a poem that "says more about devotion and its potentialities than many pedestrian treatises" (p. 104) and singles out "The Banquet" as characteristic of Herbert's simplicity and sincerity. Comments on the church at Leighton Bromswold that Herbert helped restore. Notes Herbert's metrical translations of the Psalms and his contribution to the development of the hymn. Bibliography (pp. 539–66).

1015. **Duffett, M. F.** "George Herbert and Gerard Manley Hopkins." *Hopkins Kenkyu* [Hopkins Research, Bulletin of the Hopkins Society of Japan, Tokyo Area] no. 4 (July): 17–22, 61–62.

Compares the poetry of Herbert and Hopkins and comments on the religious sensibility of both poets.

**1016. Dust, Ph[ilip] [Clarence].** "George Herbert's Two Altar Poems." *HumLov* 24:278–87.
Argues that Herbert's earlier Latin altar poem, number XXIX of *Lucus*, "sheds considerable light" on his "more devotional and better known" (p. 278) English altar poem. Maintains that from a close comparison of the two poems his position as "a seventeenth-century Christian humanist emerges in greater relief" (p. 278), showing "a poetic development in which Herbert moved away from the combination of the classical poetic tradition with forms of Aristotelian scholastic logic to the more meditative and deeper personal Augustinian perspective," a shift fundamentally "from the academic to the clerical point of view" and from "the formalism of the late middle ages to the more appealing humanism of a rediscovered tradition" (pp. 286–87). Comments on the theological argument of each poem and on Herbert's process of christianizing humanistic pagan sources. Calls the Latin poem "a blueprint for Herbert's later English altar poem" and maintains that many other poems in *The Temple* "can be compared profitably with the poet's earlier Latin work" (p. 286).

**1017. ———.** "The Sorrow of a Black Woman in a Seventeenth-Century Neo-Latin Poem." *CLAJ* 18, no. 4:516–20.
Translates into English "Aethiopissa ambit Cestum Diuersi Coloris Virum" and points out that the poem is exceptional in an age when black people were, for the most part, regarded as oddities. Notes that the speaker of the poem laments the prejudice against her race and attempts to fight it by arguing that (1) black is beautiful and that (2) love is able to overcome racial barriers. Maintains that the poem was sent to Bacon as a serious protest against slavery. Analyzes the imagery, structure, and argument of the poem. Observes that, although Herbert's poem began a fad in seventeenth-century poetry, those who followed him, such as Henry King, Henry Rainolds, and John Cleveland, failed to see the seriousness of his purpose.

**1018. Dust, Philip Clarence, ed.** *The* Carmen Gratulans Adventu Serenissimi Principis Frederici Comitis Palatini Ad Academiam Cantabrigiensem. (Salzburg Studies in English Literature, Elizabethan and Renaissance Studies, edited by James Hogg, No. 8.) Salzburg: Institut für englische Sprache und Literatur, Universität Salzburg. 2 vols. cxviii, 122p; 123–311p.
First edition of the Vatican manuscript entitled *Carmen Gratulans . . .* [A Congratulatory Anthology on the Most Serene Prince Frederick Count Palatine at Cambridge Academy], prepared from a microfilm in the University of Illinois library. Notes that the two Latin poems by Herbert contained in the manuscript, one of the visit of Frederick, the Elector Palatine, and Prince Charles to Cambridge University in 1613, and the other an epithalamium for Frederick and Princess Elizabeth, daughter of James I, who were married on 14 February 1613, were first published and translated in 1962 by Leicester Bradner (entry 575). In Volume 1 discusses the manuscript (pp. iii-xxii), its approximately sixty authors (pp. xxiii-xliii), the historical background of the poems (pp. xliv-lxiii), the educational background of the poems (pp. lxiv-lxxxviii), the poems themselves (pp. lxxxix-cxii), and the method of the present edition (pp. cxiii-cxviii), and presents the text with English prose translations (pp. 1–122). Volume 2 contains biographical, textual, and literary commentary on the poems (pp. 123–226); bibliography (pp. 227–242); five appendixes—(1) Diagram poem (pp. 243–48), (2) Authors of the *Carmen Gratulans* who contributed to other early

seventeenth century Cambridge anthologies (pp. 249–54), (3) Manuscripts in Cambridge College Libraries in 1600 (pp. 255–56), (4) Parallel references between the pages of the MS and the pages of this edition (pp. 257–58), (5) Greek poems in the MS (pp. 259–305); index of authors (pp. 306–7); index of first lines (pp. 308–310), and index of first lines in Greek poems (p. 311). For the Herbert poems, with textual notes and translations, see pages 35, 85–86. For explanatory notes on the two poems, see pages 155–56, 198–99.

**1019. Ferrari, Ferruccio.** *La poesia religiosa inglese del Seicento.* (Biblioteca di cultura contemporanea, 115.) Messina and Florence: D'Anna. 202p.

Consists of two major parts: (1) "Un secolo di poesia religiosa" (pp. 9–125), which contains a series of essays on English religious poetry of the seventeenth century, and (2) "Robert Herrick, poeta religioso" (pp. 127–79). Mentions Herbert throughout the first part and briefly contrast him with Herrick in the second. In "La poesia metafisica. John Donne e i suoi imitatori" (pp. 34–48) comments on Herbert's deep personal spirituality and his devotion to the Church of England and maintains that his poetry expresses, often dramatically, "le esperienze religiose, l'analisi delle sue emozioni, l'introspezione, l'ansiosa inquietudine per l'inadeguatezza delle risorse umane di fronte al grande debito che abbiamo contratto con Cristo che ha patito ed è morto per noi" (p. 43). Reproduces "Affliction (I)" to show how much Herbert chose to sacrifice in order to give himself only to things spiritual. Maintains that for Herbert "il suo ideale poetico quindi è un ideale di purezza d'intenti: occorre semplicità e spontaneità per esprimere la fede a la riconoscenza a Dio" and that "la sua vocazione sarà duplici: vivere la *unblamed life* del cristiano ed essere il poeta di Dio e della sua Chiesa" (pp. 46–47). Notes that for Herbert there was no conflict between religion and poetry but "tra verità e artificio poetico, tra fede e invenzione poetica" (p. 47). In "L'emblema religioso" (pp. 114–25) discusses the emblematic nature of Herbert's poetry and his use of shaped poems, commenting on "Easter-wings," "A Wreath," "The Church-floore," and "Love unknown." In other essays comments on Herbert's influence on Crashaw and Vaughan, contrasts him with Marvell, discusses Ignatian influences on his concept of prayer, and comments on his attitudes toward devotion to the Virgin Mary.

**1020. Galdon, Joseph A.** *Typology and Seventeenth-Century Literature.* (De proprietatibus litterarum, edited by C. H. Van Schooneveld, Series Maior 28.) The Hague, Paris: Mouton. 164p.

Explains biblical typology to those not trained in theology and comments on the pervasiveness of typological images and themes in seventeenth-century literature. Discusses the role that the typological tradition played in shaping Herbert's poetry and contends that, "of all the seventeenth-century poets, George Herbert perhaps makes the greatest use of the Exodus typological themes" (p. 126). Comments on typological images, symbols, and themes in "The Holdfast" (p. 81), "Sunday" (p. 93), "Decay" (p. 119), "Jordan (I and II)" (pp. 124–26), "Bunch of Grapes" (p. 126), "The Windows" (p. 139), "Sion" (p. 139), "Aaron" (pp. 139–40), and especially "The Sacrifice" (pp. 83, 127–31). Maintains that *The Temple* is the best expression of temple typology in seventeenth-century literature and points out how the basic structure of *The Temple* is typological.

**1021. Gibaldi, Joseph.** "Petrarch and the Baroque Magdalene Tradition." *HUSL* 3:1–19.

Maintains that Petrarch's poem on the Magdalene "served as the fountainhead for a major literary tradition that began about two hundred years after the composition of the lyric and was to last for over a century" (p. 18) and points out how many elements in Petrarch's poem were imitated and developed in baroque poems on the subject. Observes, however, that, although Petrarch barely mentions the tears of the saint, baroque poets often focus on them. Maintains that Herbert's "Marie Magdalene" belongs to a didactic Magdalene tradition, along with poems by Tesselschade Visscher and Fray Luis de León. Observes that Herbert's poem contains imagery "related to Petrarchism but used in a more subdued, more instructive manner," noting that, "when Herbert, for instance, presents his reader with a paradox, he usually follows it up with a predicatory explanation elucidating all its ramifications" (p. 15). Concludes that the Petrarchan Magdalene "offered the Baroque poet the opportunity to harmonize the esthetic of Renaissance poetry with the religious demands of his own age" and that "it is this synthesis which is probably the very essence of the sacred Baroque" (p. 19).

1022. **Gorbunov, Andrei Nikolaevich.** "George Herbert," in *Kratkaia literaturnaia entsiklopediia* [A Brief Literary Encyclopedia], edited by A. A. Surkov et al., 8:265–66. Moscow: Soviet Encyclopedia.
Brief account of Herbert's life and poetry. Maintains that in his poetry he fruitfully combined the Donne tradition and the emblematic tradition with the traditions of oral folk poetry and folk sermons. Argues that at the basis of a Herbertian lyric lies a disenchantment with the ideas of the Renaissance, a position characteristic of the baroque poet. Comments on Herbert's influence on Christina Rossetti, Gerard Manley Hopkins, T. S. Eliot, and Dylan Thomas.

1023. **Haug, Claudia Chadwick.** "'The Elixir' by George Herbert: The Making of a Poem." *Rackham Literary Studies* 6:75–83.
Compares the three versions of "The Elixir" and gives a close critical reading of each. Maintains that Herbert's poetry "faithfully reflects the growth of his thoughts and feelings about himself and his relationship to his God" and that thus his revisions were made, "not for public perusal, but in order to form more precisely what he was trying to say" (p. 75). Details the changes Herbert made in the poem and shows that what we see is "not so much a serial development of an idea" but rather a "careful structuring of a symbol which seeks its expression in poetry by pushing and using linguistic patterns, structures, and words in as many different ways at once as the poem can accommodate" and that what we have, therefore, is "a movement of the symbol from surface to texture, or, in the language of the poem, from perfection to elixir" (p. 81).

1024. **Hill, J[ohn] P[eter], and E. Caracciolo-Trajo, eds.** *Baroque Poetry.* Selected and translated, with an introduction by J. P. Hill and E. Caracciolo-Trajo. London: J. M. Dent; Totowa, N.J.: Rowman and Littlefield. xx, 276p.
In the introduction defines *baroque* as a literary term and explains the rationale and organization of this anthology of English, French, Spanish, Italian, and German baroque poems of the sixteenth and seventeenth centuries. Maintains that, although individual poets and national literatures differ, baroque poetry is characterized by its uses of the conceit; its manipulation of syntax to create ambiguity or drama; excess, exaggeration, and a relatively uncontrolled energy; individualism; and similar themes. Divides the anthology into five sections, each introduced by a brief critical essay: (1) "Vision of Nature," (2) "Artifice," (3) "Love," (4) "On Life, Time and Death," which includes Herbert's "Life" and "Death," and (5) "The Love of God," which includes

Herbert's "The Pearl," "Deniall," and "The Collar." Gives literal translations of poems in foreign languages with text of the original. Selected bibliography (p. xviii).

**1025. Hollander, John.** *Vision and Resonance: Two Senses of Poetic Form.* New York: Oxford University Press. 314p.

Discusses Herbert in two previously published essays and in two new ones. Brief comparisons of Herbert and Jonson, along with a comment on Herbert's inventiveness in verse forms, in "Ben Jonson and the Modality of Verse" (pp. 165–85), first appeared in the introduction to *Selected Poems of Ben Jonson* (New York: Dell Laurel Editions, 1961), and comments on Herbert in "The Poem in the Eye" (pp. 245–87) first appeared in a shorter form in *Shenandoah* (entry 910). In "Rhyme and the True Calling of Words" (pp. 117–34) briefly comments on the effects of rhyme in "Paradise" and "Deniall" (pp. 130–31). In "'Haddocks' Eyes': A Note on the Theory of Titles" (pp. 212–26) discusses "various species of titles and the different kinds of relations they bear to, and effects they exercise upon, certain literary texts" (p. 213), especially the short lyric. Maintains that all the titles in *The Temple* are Herbert's own and are "amazingly radical, in that their expressive character is in each case a part of the poem's fiction" (p. 223). Observes that Herbert's titles "supply a text, a topic, or an emblem" (p. 223) for his poems.

**1026. Ishii, Shōnosuke.** "Keijijoshijin to Shūkyō—yonin no Keishijōshijen—Donne, Herbert, Crashaw, Vaughan" [Metaphysical Poets and Religion—Four Metaphysical Poets—Donne, Herbert, Crashaw, Vaughan], in *Eikoku Renaissance to Shūkyō* [Renaissance and Religion in England], edited by Shōnosuke Ishii and Peter Milward, 113–58. Tokyo: Aratake.

Comments on Donne, Herbert, Crashaw, and Vaughan as religious poets and maintains that Herbert's faith was the support of his life.

**1027. Jacobs, Edward C.** "Herbert's 'The World': A Study of Grace." *CP* 8:71–74.

Explicates "The World" to show how the poet "examines the nature of man and man's relation to God and a Christian 'supranatural order' through the sustained metaphor of the 'stately house,'" arguing that in each of the stanzas "the 'stately house' is in conflict with certain forces which would weaken or destroy the house if God did not supply particular measures that strengthen and save the house" (p. 71). Analyzes the argument of the poem and comments in some detail on its allegorical features. Maintains that the final turn of the poem's argument stresses God's generosity toward man and argues that the whole poem is an allegorical study of God's grace.

**1028. Kawata, Akira.** "George Herbert to 'Shi'" [George Herbert on Death]. *Fukushima Daigaku Kyoiku Gakubu Ronshu* [Bulletin of the Faculty of Education, Fukushima University], no. 27, part 2 (November): 27–37.

Discusses Herbert's concept of and attitude toward death. Maintains that his concept of death is influenced by contemporary conventions but that it has its own quality and meaning. Concludes that in *The Temple*, as a result of Christ's overcoming of death, death is welcomed heartily as a symbol of rebirth.

**1029. Laurens, Pierre, in collaboration with Claudie Balavoine, eds. and trans.** "George Herbert," in *Musae Reduces: Anthologie de la poésie latine dans l'Europe de la Renaissance*, 2:485–91. Leiden: E. J. Brill.

Biographical sketch of Herbert, brief introduction to his Latin poetry, and bibliography (pp. 485–86), followed by selections from *Passio Discerpta* and from *Lucus* with Latin and French on facing pages. Comments on the emblematic character of the poems and on their "rhétorique de la sincérité" (p. 486).

**1030. Lerner, Laurence.** "The Bunch of Grapes," in *An Introduction to English Poetry: Fifteen Poems Discussed*, 52–61. London: Edward Arnold.

Close critical reading of "The Bunch of Grapes," showing how the speaker's comparison of his own difficult spiritual journey to the journey of the Old Testament Israelites from Egypt through the wilderness to Canaan is essential to the meaning of the poem because "the poem is as much about the Bible as it is about the poet, and above all it is about the special relationship between the two" (p. 56). Maintains that in the poem Herbert asserts that the Bible must be read allegorically and that the lives of individuals must be seen in biblical terms. Discusses in detail the complexity of this assertion and examines the tradition of scriptural interpretation behind it. Contrasts "The Bunch of Grapes" with "The Collar," showing how in the first the speaker's personal experience "is not rendered dramatically," as it is in the second, "but is explained and discussed, so that the poem has much of the quality of an intellectual exploration" (p. 55). Observes that "The Bunch of Grapes" begins with the personal but "takes us almost to the other extreme by saying that the merely personal has 'small renown,' that richness of significance only comes when the individual life is seen as part of a larger whole that is full of resonant interconnections" (p. 61). Concludes that the poem "can be described as a poem about the meaning of meaning" (pp. 60–61).

**1031. Lewalski, Barbara K.** "Typology and Poetry: A Consideration of Herbert, Vaughan, and Marvell," in *Illustrious Evidence: Approaches to English Literature of the Early Seventeenth Century*, edited, with an introduction by Earl Miner, 41–69. Berkeley, Los Angeles, London: University of California Press.

Explores the literary uses of typology in the poetry of Herbert, Vaughan, and Marvell. Analyzes "The Bunch of Grapes" and maintains that it "affords the most explicit statement of Herbert's conception of typology as God's own symbolism, inherent in the nature of things and in the providential history recorded in his Word" (p. 44). Argues that *The Temple* is informed by a pervasive and essentially Protestant use of typology that contributes significantly in making it a coherent volume of poetry. Maintains that the most important typological features of *The Temple* are (1) the translation of biblical types into their antitypical fulfillments in the heart of the speaker ("On their surface, the various lyrics suggest various aspects of the Christian man in the Church, but in fact the true subject of all these poems is the church in the heart of man" [p. 45]); (2) Herbert's concept of *The Church* as a contemporary recapitulation of the Book of Psalms in that it records "the full range of a Christian's spiritual experience" and incorporates "the various generic and rhetorical kinds commonly assumed to be contained in the Psalms" (p. 50); and (3) the unification of the whole volume in terms of a very individualistic adaptation of temple-church typology.

**1032. McCanles, Michael.** "The Dialectical Structure of the Metaphysical Lyric: Donne, Herbert, Marvell," in *Dialectical Criticism and Renaissance Literature*, 54–117. Berkeley, Los Angeles, London: University of California Press.

Discusses the dialectical structure of metaphysical poetry, arguing that poems of Donne, Herbert, and Marvell "exhibit paradox in their personae's attempts to exhaust a multi-faceted reality in a single intuition or proposition" (p. 54). In the section on Herbert (pp. 74–95), argues that, unlike Donne's verse, the paradoxes in Herbert's verse are not verbal, but situational. Maintains that *The Church* "traces the dialectic of the persona's spiritual life from the simplistic moral categories of 'The Church-Porche,' to its becoming a type of the history of the whole Church seen from a God's-eye viewpoint in 'The Church Militant'" and suggests that "Love (III)" epitomizes the spiritual struggle that informs the whole of *The Church*. Argues that the poems are arranged "according to a sine wave of heights and depths which many of the individual poems take as their subject" (p. 77). Maintains that *The Church-Porch* is a non-dialectical, ironically simplistic prelude to *The Church* that presents a moral vision that lacks depth, whereas *The Church*, using a more sophisticated rhetoric and complex dialectical argumentation, reveals the paradoxes, ambiguities, and uncertainties that the truly spiritual man encounters in his quest for God and salvation. Comments on a number of individual poems in *The Church*, especially "The Altar," "The Sacrifice," "The Thanksgiving," "The Reprisall," "The Agonie," "Dialogue," "The Flower," and "Providence," to illustrate the dialectic of the persona's spiritual journey. Concludes that Herbert "announces the ineffability of the divine salvific economy through his persona's manifestly inadequate attempts to reduce it to clear thought and speech" and that the dialectic in Herbert's verse "comments finally neither upon the realms of history and of the divine, nor upon the ineluctable structures of human thought, but upon the confrontation between the two" (p. 94).

**1033. McLaughlin, Elizabeth, and Gail Thomas.** "Communion in *The Temple*." *SEL* 15:111–24.

Argues that the three parts of *The Temple*, "emphasized by the final couplet blessing the triune God" (p. 111), reflect the tripartite structure of the Anglican communion service as it appears in the Tudor Prayerbook—preparation for communion (*The Church-Porch*), the eucharistic experience itself (*The Church*), and the consequences of the communion for the body of believers (*The Church Militant*). Notes that "feast and sacrifice, together with architectural symbolism grounded in the eucharistic conception of the church, provide a complex and consistent pattern of communion metaphors through which the poems of *The Temple* interanimate one another" (p. 111). Maintains that "Love (III)" is directly derived from the exhortation given by the priest to sinners preceding the reception of the Eucharist. Argues that *The Church-Porch* "may be associated with the Old Testament law of God the Father," *The Church* "with Christ's new covenant offering redemption to law breakers," and *The Church Militant* "with the Church of the later New Testament, carrying out its world mission and triumphing over evil through the inspiration of the Holy Ghost" (pp. 114–15).

**1034. Milward, Peter.** "Anglican and Catholic in the Religious Poetry of the XVIIth Century." *ELLS* 11:1–12.

Maintains that had the Civil War and the resultant triumph of Puritanism not occurred, the Anglican Church might have been reunited to the Catholic Church by the end of the seventeenth century. Sees the poetry of Herbert and Crashaw as representative of two successive and continuous stages in the development of Anglicanism. Recognizes Herbert's negative attitudes toward the Papacy and the fundamentally Protestant temper of much of his theology but maintains that in his poems he "expresses an ideal of the Church and Christian worship which is fundamentally at one with Catholic tradition" (p. 6). Maintains that the merits and defects in the poetry of both Herbert and Crashaw "correspond in varying degrees to the merits and defects of the Anglican and Catholic communions of their period" (p. 10). Views

Herbert as perhaps more parochial and more English than Crashaw, who was more open to the Continental, baroque expressions of Christianity.

1035. **Miner, Earl, ed.** *Illustrious Evidence: Approaches to English Literature of the Early Seventeenth Century.* Berkeley, Los Angeles, London: University of California Press. xxiii, 135p.

Collection of six original essays by various hands that were originally given as papers at UCLA in 1971–1972. In the introduction, the editor comments on each of the essays and concludes that, as a whole, the essays are "exemplary as to method, useful even beyond the authors considered and beyond the century in which they lived" (pp. xxiii). Each essay that discusses Herbert has been entered separately in this bibliography (entries 1031, 1048).

1036. **Muraoka, Isamu.** "Shakespeare and George Herbert." *Shakespeare Studies* (The Shakespeare Society of Japan) 11 (March): 37–59.

Japanese translation appears in *Keijijoshi Kenkyu* (entry 1082), 139–74.

Notes that Herbert's use of images from Shakespeare has not been stressed. Argues that Herbert used many images that were closely modeled on the simplest and homeliest images of Shakespeare drawn from what might be called everyday and domestic life. Concludes that Herbert was interested in the displacement of the profane by the sacred in Shakespeare.

1037. **Nestrick, William.** "George Herbert: The Giver and the Gift." *Ploughshares* 2, iv:187–205.

Examines "gift-giving" as both image and theme in Herbert's verse, arguing that, ultimately, Herbert's poetry is his gift to God. Shows how in "The Thanksgiving" the poet's attempts to reciprocate God's gifts must end in human impotence when he is awed by God's gift of the Passion and points out that gift-giving thus involves learning more about God. Maintains that "Humilitie," "Hope," and "The Pulley" "dramatize gift-giving in an allegorical or mythical action" and that in poems like "Gratefulnesse," "Employment (I)," "Ungratefulnesse," "Even-song," "Unkindnesse," "Submission," "Obedience," "Dulnesse," and "A Wreath," speech acts between an *I* and *thou*, "quickly become examinations of the psychological, internal, and egoistic aspects of gift-giving" (p. 190). Using "Gratefulnesse" as an example, shows how these poems change directions midcourse as the poet discovers new perceptions about his relationship to God. Discusses "A Wreath" as a self-reflexive poem in which the rhetorical technique imitates the "crooked winding wayes" of the poet that are in opposition to the straight lines of a true life that tends to God. Calls "Ungratefulnesse," "The Starre," "Obedience," "An Offering," "Unkindnesse," and "Gratefulnesse" Herbert's "most complicated engagements in gift exchanges" whose "property to be exchanged [is] the human heart" (p. 200). Discusses "Sighs and Grones" as an example of God's gift-giving of food that has been poorly stewarded by the poet, especially the Eucharist. Concludes that Herbert discovers in the process of his writing that, since God's ultimate gift is to give himself through the Eucharist, man's only appropriate gift is himself: "The fit gift in return for God is for the poet himself to be the poem, the poem to be the poet" (p. 201).

1038. **Pop-Cornis, Marcel.** "Early Seventeenth Century Poetry and the Traditions of Modern English Verse," in *Modern English Poetry: A Critical and Historical Reader*, vol. 1, *From John Donne to Alexandre [sic] Pope (1590–1730)*, 1–54. Timisoara, Rumania: Timisoara University Press.

Argues that any survey of modern English poetry must begin with a study of seventeenth-century poetry and comments briefly on a metaphysical tradition from Donne to T. S. Eliot and Edith Sitwell. Surveys the political, intellectual, and religious history of the seventeenth century and comments on how the temper of the times is reflected in the poetry. Outlines major features of metaphysical poetry and briefly surveys the history of the term, especially commenting on Dr. Johnson's criticism of metaphysical poetry. In "George Herbert" (pp. 30–32) comments on major characteristics of Herbert's poetry, such as his metaphysical wit, the urbanity of his language and the purity of his diction, his uses of varied and musical verse forms, his employment of domestic and homely conceits, and his uses of personification and dialogue. Reproduces "Love (III)" and "Vertue" with study questions and brief critical comments. Selected bibliography (pp. 51–54).

**1039. Primeau, Ronald.** "Reading George Herbert: Process vs. Rescue." *CollL* 2:50–60.
Analyzes how Herbert's poems shape the responses of his readers and discusses the complex simplicity of his poetic themes and techniques. Maintains that, for Herbert, "experiential difficulty merely heightens man's helplessness" and that "the only state of restoration possible is effected in the 'rescue' of divine intervention" (p. 50). Argues that, "just as many theologically conventional poets of the time counterbalance straightforward homiletic patterns with the distraction of metaphysical complexity, so Herbert offsets underlying dialectical complexity with the distraction of plain talk" (p. 51). Maintains that Herbert "constructs poetic homily chiefly through the fusion of various kinds of sharply drawn opposites" that "are fixed and await reconciliation only in a transcendent state" (p. 52). Shows that, just as Herbert's view of grace is one of passive receptivity, so "there is a sense in which his poems emphasize reflection upon, rather than ongoing involvement in, experience" (p. 52) and undermine discursive forms of thought. Comments that in many of Herbert's poems "the solution to man's problems is represented by something closely resembling escapism to the transcendental and the other-worldly" (p. 57). Maintains that "most of the seventeenth-century poets we read today *heighten direct statements and mask traditional theology on the educative qualities of experience with complex images* while Herbert *softens dialectical positions and complex theology with simple statements* and that "these seeming inverse relationships between theme and style continue to dislodge the sensibilities of Herbert's readers in ways that are at once effective and puzzling" and thus "his readers react alternately with equally inexplicable adulation and disappointment" (p. 51).

**1040. Richards, I. A.** "The Conduct of Verse." *TLS*, 28 November, p. 1417.
Critical essay occasioned by the publication of Vendler's *The Poetry of George Herbert* (entry 1050). Praises Vendler's approach, maintaining that she is "especially discerning as to Herbert's dealings with the unexpected, the reinvented character of so many of his poems, the reconceptions from which their dramatic actions spring" but warns that critics must be careful not to focus too narrowly on Herbert's poetics: "It is much easier to measure line-lengths than sprinklings of grace." Contends that Herbert's influence on later poets has been "stronger, more salutary, more instructive than that of poets much more famous and more widely read" and stresses that his influence has been significant on poets who do not share his religious beliefs, such as Swinburne and Walter de la Mare. Maintains that the debt poets owe to Herbert "is far more than for his addition to the stockpile of devices, prosodic, figurative, thematic and

dramatic," it is due especially to "his surpassing powers of design and his singular fidelity to what his poem at every stage of its growth needed."

**1041. Ruoff, James E.** "Herbert, George," in *Crowell's Handbook of Elizabethan & Stuart Literature*, 200–203. New York: Thomas Y. Crowell.

Published in England as *Macmillan's Handbook of Elizabethan & Stuart Literature* (London: Macmillan, 1975).

Biographical sketch of Herbert with critical commentary on major features of his poetry. Maintains that the principal theme of Herbert's poetry is the conflict between his desire for worldly success and a life of religious renunciation. Praises his use of plain diction and of metaphors drawn from everyday life, nature, the Bible, and the liturgy but stresses that the poems, "so apparently spontaneous, informal, and collo-quial, actually represent what can be described paradoxically as a simplicity of elabo-rate obliqueness—a homely, almost prosaic roughening of an underlying polish and sophistication" (p. 201). Briefly contrasts Herbert and Donne but maintains that Herbert's poems "are squarely in the metaphysical tradition for their incongruous and extended metaphors, violent transitions and shock effects, rigorous concentration and linear construction" (p. 202). Discusses Herbert's use of sounds and rhythms and notes his experimentation with forms. Gives a brief explication of "The Pearl" and comments on "The Collar" and "Love (III)" as typical of Herbert's art. Selected bibliography (p. 203).

**1042. Saito, Takeshi.** "George Herbert," in "Sonogo no Metaphysicals" [Meta-physicals after Donne], in *Saito Takeshi Chosaku-shu* [Collected Papers of Take-shi Saito], 4 (Essays on English Literature), 226–49. Tokyo: Kenkyusha, 1975.

Traces the development of Herbert's faith and his poetic genius, with appreciative comments on several poems in *The Temple*.

**1043. Scheick, William J.** "Typology and Allegory: A Comparative Study of George Herbert and Edward Taylor." *ELWIU* 2:76–86.

Compares and contrasts Herbert's and Edward Taylor's poetic treatments of Aaron, Noah's ark, and the Hebraic altar in order to show the difference between Taylor's "conservatively historical" and Herbert's "liberally allegorical" use of typol-ogy and to observe "the effects of these two approaches upon the poetic self" (p. 78). Argues that Herbert's Anglican tradition permitted and encouraged him "to express his poetic imagination even in those poems in which he treated such traditional matters as typology," whereas the orthodox New England Puritan culture of Taylor "resulted in a contraction of the poetic self in his work" (p. 85). Acknowledges, however, that, "like Herbert, Taylor intuitively sought to participate in the typological system, to express his creative imagination and open the closed system so that it would allegorically admit the saint" (p. 85).

**1044. Schleiner, Louise.** "The Composer as Reader: A Setting of George Her-bert's 'Altar.'" *Musical Quarterly* 61:422–32.

Presents a reading of "The Altar" based on an analysis of a seventeenth-century musical setting of the poem that was probably composed by John Playford and was included among six solo songs at the end of his 1671 psalter, *Psalms & Hymns in Solemn Musick of Foure Parts On the Common Tunes to the Psalms in Metre*. Maintains that Playford may have included Herbert's poem as a kind of commentary on his book, "which was his own offering intended to inspire stony hearts to sing worthy praises to God before the real altars of churches" (p. 424). Shows, for example, how the musical structure of the setting "reflects the rigidity of Herbert's pictogram structure" (p. 427), how the music reflects the major argument of the poem, and how the sensory aspects of the poem's images are represented musically. Notes that because declamatory-song composers of the period considered their songs to be "a kind of interpretative reading of their texts," "we can, to some extent, read the poem as one of its seventeenth-century readers did, and at the same time clarify some features of the setting's musical structure which are extramusical in origin" (pp. 422–23). Reproduces the setting (p. 426). See also Vincent Duckles (entry 576).

**1045. Shurbanov, Alexander.** "Some Functions of Herbert's Imagery." *Annuaire de Université de Sofia. Faculté des Lettres. Littératures romanes et germaniques* 69, no. 4:21–60.

Detailed study of Herbert's imagery, showing how it unifies not only individual poems but also *The Temple* as a whole. Discusses the thematic and imagistic patterns in "Divinitie," "Church-rents and schismes," "The H. Scriptures (I)," "The H. Scriptures (II)," "Employment (I)," "Employment (II)," "Christmas," "Man," "Decay," "The Temper (I)," "Dooms-day," "Even-song," "Businesse," "Church-monuments," "Easter-wings," and "The Call." Discusses the organic unity of *The Temple*, claiming that "the whole book is structured as a web of imagery that stretches its threads in many directions and yet constitutes a single network" (p. 42). Comments on twenty-seven series of poetic figures that recur most frequently in Herbert's poems. Concludes that Herbert's images, both in single poems and in *The Temple* as a whole, "are less conspicuous and independent than those of his predecessors: they are dissolved in the more neutral medium of the underlying themes" and "are widely used to organize the poetic structure and carry the complex logical argument to its close" (p. 60).

**1046. Smithson, Bill.** "Herbert's 'Affliction' Poems." *SEL* 15:125–40.

Discusses each of the five "Affliction" poems "to show why the order of these poems as given in *The Temple* does not reveal a progressive development of spiritual growth" (p. 125) and argues that the order to reflect such growth would be (1) "Affliction (I)," which depicts the poet's early rebellious religious experience when, as a novice in the spiritual life, he first encountered grief; (2) "Affliction (V)," which reveals the poet's more mature view of grief as he begins to realize that it is a result of man's sinfulness and is given purposefully by God; (3) "Affliction (IV)," in which the poet expresses total trust in God, recognizing that God is the important one in the God-man relationship; (4) "Affliction (II)," in which the poet meditates on Christ's crucifixion and death; and (5) "Affliction (III)," in which the poet comes to see that Christ participates eternally in man's grief. Maintains that, "unlike the first and fifth poems, the fourth, second, and third acknowledge only grief as the means to know God, and the stages of spiritual growth they reflect are more subtle" (p. 139) and that the second and third poems "move away from a concentration on Herbert himself to a focus on Christ" (p. 140). Concludes that, although "we cannot know whether this ordering and interpreting of these poems accurately reflects the real mental voyage which Herbert experienced," it presents "a probable, logical, and coherent pattern of spiritual growth, whereas the order in which the poems appear in *The Temple* does not" (p. 140).

**1047. Stroup, Thomas B.** "'A Reasonable, Holy, and Living Sacrifice': Herbert's 'The Altar.'" *ELWIU* 2:149–63.

Argues by means of "a fuller consideration of its liturgical background, an observation of its possible autobiographical origin, a suggestion of a contemporary iconographical source, and a clarification of its position in *The Temple*" that "The Altar" "cannot be restricted to serve a 'low' church religious function or to become a self-consuming artifact" but rather "is best understood as a liturgy for the dedication of the Church's altar; as the rite for the dedication of a communicant or the ordering of a priest or an induction into his parish; as the petition of the communicant or the priest-poet that he may be able to offer incessant praise to his Maker; and as an oblation of the communicant or priest" by which "he may become a living sacrifice and be made one body with Him, a very member incorporate in His Church" (p. 150). Argues that "The Altar" may have been written at the time of or in anticipation of Herbert's induction as rector at Bemerton or at the time of his ordination, "for it is a masterful statement of a priest's commitment" (p. 152). Maintains that the shape and imagery of the poem may owe something to the title page of John Cosin's well-known *A Collection of Private Devotions* (1627) and contends that Herbert's early Latin poem, Number XXIX of *Lucus*, helps illuminate the meaning of "The Altar." Maintains that the poem "reveals a vast knowledge of Catholic and Anglican liturgy and a conscious employment of liturgy as it is based upon biblical sources, especially the offices of penitence," and thus "provides for those who acquaint themselves with its background a high poetic experience both in its form and in its substance" (p. 159).

**1048. Thorpe, James.** "Reflections and Self-Reflections: *Outlandish Proverbs* as a Context for George Herbert's Other Writings," in *Illustrious Evidence: Approaches to English Literature of the Early Seventeenth Century*, edited, with an introduction, by Earl Miner, 23–37. Berkeley, Los Angeles, London: University of California Press.

Analyzes Herbert's *Outlandish Proverbs*, pointing out that "the largest common denominator of the majority of the proverbs is their relevance to the ordinary conduct of ordinary human beings on ordinary occasions" (p. 27) and noting that the imagery of the proverbs most often comes from country life, especially animals, and from the life of merchants and and tradesmen and that frequent topics treated are religion, good physical health, the importance of friends, concern for children, and dislike of too much talking. Notes that over half of Herbert's English letters resemble the proverbs in both substance and imagery; that many proverbs or passages in the general form of proverbs appear in *The Country Parson*, a work that relies on proverbs "as a mode of setting 'rules' or 'marks' or 'aims' for human behavior" (p. 34); and that a number of poems in *The Temple* embody proverbs from *Outlandish Proverbs* or include passages reminiscent of proverbs. Concludes that the context that the *Outlandish Proverbs* offers for Herbert's other writings clarifies "how essentially he was concerned with ordinary human behavior, how he longed to have marks and aims that would be useful for himself and for others, how his mind ran toward understandable imagery that could aid understanding" (p. 37).

**1049. Van Nuis, Hermine J.** "Herbert's 'Affliction' Poems: A Pilgrim's Progress." *CP* 8, no. 2:7–16.

Maintains that the five "Affliction" poems compose a self-contained five-act drama that reflects microcosmically the same personal and cosmic concerns that inform *The Temple* as a whole: "the reduction of man's—Herbert's and Everyman's—stubborn will to God's just will and ways" (p. 7). Shows by a poem-by-poem analysis how the five poems, like *The Temple* as a whole, "move from a lack of faith in and rebellion against God, to an urgent plea to God for help, to a profound faith in and communion with God" (p. 7). Maintains that, having worked through his rebellion step-by-step, the speaker grows to full spiritual maturity, "having exchanged his discontent for gratitude, his rebellion for submission, his restlessness for peace" (p. 16). Notes that the five poems contain five major image clusters—money, food, military, marine-storm, and artifice (trap-bait-entanglement)—and demonstrates how Herbert's subtle use of these clusters gives unity and progress to the spiritual drama that unfolds.

**1050. Vendler, Helen.** *The Poetry of George Herbert.* Cambridge and London: Harvard University Press. 303p.

Chapter 1 was first published in *ArielE* (entry 851); chapter 2 was first published in *Forms of Lyric*, edited by Reuben Brower (entry 852), 25–56.

In the introduction (pp. 1–8) explains that this study will focus on critical readings of nearly all of Herbert's poems, not on new generalizations about his art; will compare Herbert with certain of his imitators and adapters "in order to point out what he possesses above and beyond devotional feelings, metrical invention, and emblematic interests"; and will discuss those literary genres that Herbert "found most congenial, marking out his range within a given genre as well as his individual use of its conventions" (p. 3). Challenges the notion that Herbert's poetry appeals only to those who share his religious beliefs by "offering a reading of Herbert which sees as the primary subject of his poems the workings of his own mind and heart rather than the expression of certain religious beliefs" (p. 4). Announces that the major concern of this study is to show "the depth of poetic resource discovered by Herbert, his resolute unwillingness to take the world for granted, his fixed intention to plumb every appearance for its significant and original reality, his willingness, as he puts it, to thrust his mind into whatever nourished it in order to find out the ingredients of that nourishment" (p. 6). For a synopsis of chapter 1, "A Reading of *Vertue*" (pp. 9–24), and chapter 2, "Alternatives: The Reinvented Poem" (pp. 25–56), see entries 851 and 852. In chapter 3, "Beauty in Discovery: Emblems and Allegories" (pp. 57–99) comments on how Herbert uses emblematic and allegorical materials in such poems as "Redemption," "The Altar," "Hope," "The British Church," "Humilitie," "Jesu," "Love-joy," "The Agonie," "Justice (II)," "The Windows," "The Rose," "Love un-known," and "The Pilgrimage." Maintains that in Herbert's poems allegorical and emblematic form undergoes "a constant critique of its own possibilities comparable with, but not identical to, the continuing critique of his own feelings so pervasively conducted in the lyrics" (p. 99). In chapter 4, "Imitators and Adapters" (pp. 100–136), discusses some of Herbert's literary predecessors and concludes that few truly resemble him in voice, nuance, structure, or effect. Maintains, however, that his imitators and adapters, can "tell us a good deal about what they saw, both good and bad, and can reveal to us what qualities in Herbert they were unable to attain" (p. 101). Compares and contrasts Herbert's poems with those of Christopher Harvey, Samuel Speed, John Wesley, and the anonymous compiler of *Select Hymns Taken out of Mr. Herbert's Temple* (London, 1697) and maintains that these lesser poets, having "a less confident sense of Providence than he, more often opted for simpler solutions and simpler phrasings of problems" (p. 136). In chapter 5, "'My God, I Mean Myself': Liturgical and Homiletic Poems" (pp. 137–79), discusses Herbert's poems on the feasts and seasons of the Church to show that, before he perfected his art, some Christian topics could "prompt him to sterile versified theology" (p. 138). Argues that in the successful liturgical poems, such as "Easter," "Easter-wings," "The Dawning," and "Good Friday," and in successful homiletic poems, such as "Sunday," "Mortification," "Mans Medley," and "The Bag," Herbert entered "in a personal sense into the problems set by the poem" and "often resisted successfully the temptation to let the homiletic or liturgical form impose on him socially acceptable sentiments or religiously praiseworthy attitudes" (p. 178). Maintains that the public occasions of these poems provided an "outline of received belief to provoke him into asking how much of that received belief he could make his own, or what additions, suppressions, corrections, or enhancings the doctrine or feast would need to become part of his own religious experience" (pp. 178–79). In chapter 6, "Configurations and Constellations: Ethical, Discursive, and Speculative Lyrics" (pp. 180–201), discusses those poems in which "a concentration on intellectual enquiry or speculation takes precedence over purely devotional expression," poems such as "Avarice," "Vanitie (II)," "Divinitie," "An Offering," "Businesse," "Self-condemnation," "Ungratefulnesse," "Decay," "The Bunch of Grapes," "Faith," "Praise (III)," "Providence," "Man," and "Death" that "versify what they mean, sometimes unremarkably and sometimes well" but "rarely contain those crosscurrents of powerful feeling that vex and freshen Herbert's best poetry" (p. 180). In chapter 7, "Fruit and Order: Formal Patterns" (pp. 202–30), analyzes Herbert's use of formal verse patterns in such poems as "The Call," "Antiphon (II)," "Praise (II)," "Grace," "Paradise," and "Heaven" to show that the practice of strict form was "essential to his innermost sense of both himself and his poetry" (p. 203). Maintains that Herbert "was delighted by innumerable strict conditions, self-set, upon his work" and that "he responded with energetic ingenuity at worst, passion and invention at best to those challenges" (p. 230). In chapter 8, "Conflicts Pictured" (pp. 231–76), traces "some of the many ways in which Herbert's central subject, the picture of his many conflicts with God, achieved expression, complication, and resolution" (p. 231) in that group of poems consisting of "personal colloquies, mimetic retellings of religious experience, simple first-person prayers, complaints, and laments" (p. 234), such as "Conscience," "Affliction (II and III)," "Discipline," "Ephes.iv.30," "The Odour," "The Starre," "The Glance," "Deniall," "Longing," "Home," "The Crosse," "The Forerunners," "The Elixir," and "Love (III)." Notes (pp. 279–97), index of titles (pp. 299–300), and index of first lines (pp. 301–3). Reviews:

Amy Charles, *Choice* 12 (1975): 1172
Frank Kermode, *New York Times Book Review*, 6 July 1975, p. 13
I. A. Richards, *TLS*, 28 November 1975, p. 1417
James R. Zurek, Jr., *America* 133 (1975): 125, 27
Anon., *VQR* 52, no. 3 (1976): 92
D. W. Harding, *EIC* 26 (1976): 257–64
J. L. Lievsay, *SAQ* 75 (1976): 403–4
Richard Strier, *MP* 74 (1976): 78–88
E. Webb, *WCR* 10, no. 3 (1976): 44
Delia A. Burke, *C&L* 25, no. 4 (1977): 35–41
Daniel W. Doerksen, *SCN* 35 (1977): 8–10
Richard L. Harp, *CEA* 39, no. 4 (1977): 28–30
Bruce King, *JEGP* 75 (1977): 595–96
Bridget Lyons, *GHJ* 1, no. 1 (1977): 61–63
P. W. Parmer, *SoR* n.s. 13 (1977): 213–16
Richard D. Jordan, *MLR* 73 (1978): 881–83

**1051. Wanamaker, Melissa C.** *Discordia Concors: The Wit of Metaphysical Poetry.* (National University Publications: Literary Criticism Series, gen. ed. John E. Becker.) Port Washington, N.Y., and London: Kennikat Press. x, 166p.

Employs the philosophical concept of *discordia concors* to explain wit in the poetry of Donne, Herbert, Vaughan, Marvell, and Milton. Distinguishes between two types: (1) unity in multiplicity and (2) a violent yoking of opposites. Argues that the metaphysical poets "found the philosophical concept of *discordia concors* as a yoking of opposites expressive of their own disturbingly discordant world" (p. 13). Although Herbert is mentioned throughout, chapter 3, "George Herbert: Discovery of Occult Resemblances" (pp. 37–54), is devoted exclusively to his attempts to reconcile opposites, not by a kind of Donnean violent yoking, but rather by finding resemblances in things that are apparently unlike. Argues that "initially Herbert sets up an apparent dichotomy between two opposite complexities in *The Temple*: true ones, which God transforms and makes most plain, and false ones, produced by human artifice which the poet seems to equate with playing games" but that "finally the two are conflated as the falsity of human 'invention' is purified and the secular comes to reflect the sacred in both art and life" (p. 37). Illustrates the first kind of complexity by discussing "The Sinner" and "The H. Scriptures (II)" and the second by discussing "Jordan (I and II)" and "Love (I and II)." Finds that "the answer to contrariety in Herbert's verse invariably consists of surrender to God" and that Herbert's ability to surrender "depends upon Christ's validating the poet's secular metaphors and assuring him that they are indeed divine rather than false complexities sprung from a false wit" (p. 49) so that "by his discovering an answer in God, discord is dissolved rather than forcefully yoked" (p. 50). Concludes that Herbert's wit "is characterized by the realization" that "only God can mend the defects and discords of art and human nature" (p. 50). Discusses also Herbert's use of Scripture, his attitude toward Petrarchism, and his art of simplicity or "hidden plainness." Compares and/or contrasts Herbert to Donne, Vaughan, and Marvell and regards him as a transitional figure between Donne and the later metaphysicals.

**1052. Whittier, John Greenleaf.** Letter of 6 May 1847, in *The Letters of John Greenleaf Whittier*, edited by John B. Pickard, 2:89.
   Reproduces a letter from Whittier to Thomas Tracy in which he says that Elizabeth and he "have been delighted with 'Holy George Herbert'" but notes that some of Herbert's conceits are "not agreeable to our taste" and that they "cannot always sympathise with his Church eulogies." Adds that "there is enough beside to make us love him."

# *1976*

**1053. Ahmed, Aziza Taleb.** "George Herbert: A Study of 'Emotive' and 'Propositional' Poetry." *JEn* 2:9–18.
   General introduction to Herbert's life and poetry. Discusses his subtle and complex uses of images, his fundamental simplicity, and his basic attitudes toward the nature and purpose of his art. Divides the poems into two broad categories—personal, emotive poems that present the feelings of the poet, and propositional poems, in which thoughts exist "for their own sake rather than for giving shape to some feeling" (p. 17). Comments in some detail on "The Collar" as an example of the first and discusses *The Church-Porch* and "Constancie" as examples of the second. Maintains that many of Herbert's poems are "propositional" and claims that such poems "which are only about ideas and for ideas have not for us, apart from their religious and philosophical value, the same aesthetic appeal as his personal poems have" (p. 18).

1054. **Aizawa, Yoshihisa.** "Keijijo-shi to Nihon: Oboegaki" [Metaphysical Poets and Japan: A Note], in *Keijijoshi Kenkyu* [Studies in Metaphysical Poets], 243–49. (Japan Society of 17th Century English Literature.) Tokyo: Kenseido.

Briefly outlines the history of the critical reception of metaphysical poetry in Japan.

1055. ———. "Nihon ni okeru Keijijoshi Kenkyu Shoshi" [A Bibliography of Writings about Metaphysical Poetry in Japan], in *Keijijoshi Kenkyu* [Studies in Metaphysical Poets], 1–32. (Japan Society of 17th Century English Literature.) Tokyo: Kenseido.

Bibliography of studies on metaphysical poets and poetry written in Japan from 1927 to 1975, including studies of Donne, Herbert, Crashaw, Marvell, Vaughan, and Traherne. Lists 33 items specifically on Herbert, all of which are included in this bibliography.

1056. **Babula, William.** "The Shaped Sound of Faith: George Herbert's 'Easter Wings.'" *Oral English* 2:13–14.

Argues that the oral/aural pattern in "Easter-wings" is "at least as crucial to its meaning as the visual emblematic form of two pairs of wings" (p. 13). Points out, for example, how the movement from iambic pentameter to spondaic monometer in the first and third stanzas reinforces aurally the poem's description of the decay of man and how the sound pattern of the second and fourth stanzas "expands from active iamb when treating of God" (p. 13). Observes that the lack of metaphors in the first and third stanzas contrasts with the metaphor of flight in the second and fourth stanzas and argues that this abrupt shift in language illustrates that, without God, the poet can only deal with mundane things, but that when he depends on God "he can become a poet, a maker of metaphors" (p. 14). Concludes that "what we hear—or *find* in an oral reading that builds concretely upon the detail of critical analysis—is something very close to silence when Herbert is without God" but that "what we hear when Herbert rediscovers his God is the joyous surprise of poetry" (p. 14).

1057. **Brisman, Leslie.** "George Herbert and the Skewing of Origins." *Diacritics* 6, no. 2:22–30.

Primarily a very detailed, mostly favorable review of Helen Vendler's *The Poetry of George Herbert* (entry 1050). Maintains that "it is a special distinction of Helen Vendler that she writes better books than she knows, and that while appearing to be one of the most productive and eloquent continuers of the tradition of New (or 'intrinsic') Criticism she introduces us to practical applications of ideas that transcend the assumptions of the critical ancestry with which she has been associated" (p. 22). Presents detailed analyses of "The Flower" and "Aaron," arguing that these poems, with Vendler's help, "can be understood on the model of Harold Bloom's six-fold pattern for the Romantic crisis lyric" (p. 24).

1058. **[Charles, Amy M., ed.]** *Cross-Bias: The Newsletter of the Friends of Bemerton Society*, no. 2 (October). 4p.

Announces the publication of *George Herbert, Rector of Bemerton* (entry 1066), a booklet published to support Herbert's parish; notes recent developments in the parish at Bemerton; reprints a parody of "The Elixir" by A. M. A. Sayers in response to a competition advertised in the *New Statesman* (see entry 779) and a verse reply by the current rector at St. Andrew's; lists work on Herbert in press and forthcoming; and announces upcoming conferences that will feature papers on Herbert.

1059. **Cohen, Gideon.** "Providence." *Expl* 35, no. 2:2.

Argues that "baths" in line 72 of "Providence" ("Clouds cool by heat, baths by cooling boil") "stands for hot springs, which when forced above ground cool down and let off steam, that is, they 'boil.'" Adds that the line is "just perfect because of its terse parallelism accentuating the contrast."

**1060. Dyson, A. E., and Julian Lovelock.** "Herbert's 'Redemption,' in *Masterful Images: English Poetry from Metaphysicals to Romantics*, 29–35. London: Macmillan; New York: Barnes and Noble.

Detailed critical analysis of "Redemption" that discusses its metaphysical characteristics. Comments on the deceptive simplicity of the poem and on Herbert's mastery of homely diction and imagery, his manipulation of time, his use of a leisurely yet compressed syntax, and his control of tone. Maintains that the most interesting feature of this sonnet, and perhaps the most disconcerting for a modern reader, is its use of imagery, "rooted chiefly in money transactions and very basic capitalism" (p. 33). Argues that the poem is a precise dramatization of Pauline theology and that Herbert uses "the language of everyday monetary transactions in the essentially homely manner of Christ himself" (p. 35). Sees the poem as an attack not on capitalism but on the world and maintains that the "crowning subtlety" of the poem is that the narrator, though good, "remains blinded by a worldly scale of values, so that the full cost of the paradox of redemption remains hidden from him right to the last" (p. 35). Briefly compares the central paradox in the poem with that of Donne"s "Goodfriday, 1613. Riding Westward."

**1061. Elder, David.** "l'image de l'épine dans la poésie métaphysique anglaise: Exerque et analyse," in *Etudes anglo-americaines*, 21–35. (Annales de la faculté des lettres et sciences humaines de Nice, 27). Paris: Minard.

Discusses the use of the figure of the thorn in poetry and notes that is is not found with frequency in metaphysical poems. Contends that for the English metaphysicals the thorn most often has biblical associations: "La couronne des martyrs et les épines du péché sont les plus caractéristiques de ses multiples emplois" (p. 23). Briefly notes Herbert's use of the thorn in "The Rose," "Love unknown," "The Thanksgiving," "The Collar," and "Providence" as well as in the Latin poems "De Magicis rotatibus," "In Arund. Spin. Genuflex. Purpur.," and "In Coronam spineam."

**1062. Fleissner, Robert F.** "Herbert's Aethiopesa and the Dark Lady: A Mannerist Parallel." *CLAJ* 19:458–67.

Points out analogies between the black lady of Herbert's "Aethiopissa ambit Cestum Diuersi Coloris Virum" and the Dark Lady of Shakespeare's sonnets and argues that Herbert's dark lady "might have been a composite of a number of Shakespearian references in the sonnets and plays" (p. 466). Maintains that Herbert's poem "as a whole may profitably be taken as an ironic response to the *ménage à trois* deplored in the Shakespearian [sonnet] sequence" (p. 466).

**1063. Grayson, Janet.** "Bernardine Paranomasia in Herbert's 'The Pulley.'" *AN&Q* 15:52–53.

Points out a passage in the seventh chapter of St. Bernard of Clairvaux's *De diligendo Deo* that "in tone, language, and intent suggests itself as the source of the word play in Herbert's 'The Pulley'" (p. 52). Shows that in St. Bernard and in Herbert "the device of language play, sustained paranomasia, conveys the paradox of human life and weariness" (p. 52).

**1064. Harnack, H. Andrew.** "George Herbert's 'Aaron': The Aesthetics of Shaped Typology." *ELN* 14:25–32.

Presents a detailed analysis of "Aaron" to show that "in the fusion of its theme, verse form, figural expression, typography, sound patterns, numerological symbolism, and liturgical tone" the poem is "an outstanding example of a beautifully shaped lyric whose design precisely complements its imaginatively quiet thematic use of Christian typology" (p. 26). Concludes that the poem "embodies not only a distinctly Christian typological ethos, but is itself an exceptional lyric expression of theological conviction shaped into a notably attractive aesthetic form" (p. 32).

**1065. Herbert, George.** *George Herbert.* [Kettering, Eng.]: [J. L. Carr]. [16]p.
Biographical note and brief quotes from critics, followed by a selection of eleven poems, without notes or commentary.

**1066. ———.** *George Herbert: Rector of Bemerton. Poems from "The Temple."* With an introduction by Amy M. Charles. Sewanee: University of Sewanee Press for the Friends of Bemerton. xiv, 38p.
Comments on the seven-hundred-year-old church of St. Andrew at Bemerton—"one of the holiest spots in all of England" because "one of its rectors was also one of the greatest English devotional poets" (p. v)—and presents a biographical sketch of Herbert and a brief introduction to his poetry, followed by forty-six of Herbert's poems, without notes or additional commentary. Stresses Herbert's love of the Church of England, which "embodied both religious beliefs and attitudes toward the faith and practice of the Church that paralleled almost exactly his own attitudes toward fitness and order, beauty and proportion" (p. ix). Comments on Herbert's use of form, his diction, his wit, and his restraint and maintains that, "if we try to name a dominant theme in *The Temple*, that theme must surely be the love of God for man" (p. xii). Briefly discusses Herbert's reputation, noting the important role that Coleridge played in the revival of interest in Herbert, and maintains that Herbert "continues to be read today because he continues to speak to our spiritual needs and experiences" (p. xiv). Includes three pencil sketches (two by John Buckler and one by Elizabeth Jerome Holder) and a short list of editions and recommended readings.
Review:
James R. McAdams *SCN* 35 (1977): 12–13

**1067. Himuro, Misako.** "The Language of Secular Love Poetry in 'The Temple.'" *Studies in English Literature* (English Number): 19–42.
Comments on the importance of love poetry in *The Temple* and considers in some detail how Herbert transforms the language of profane love and uses it in his poems of sacred love.

**1068. Hunter, C. Stuart.** "Herbert's 'The Pulley.'" *Expl* 34:item 43.
Maintains that the effectiveness of "The Pulley" in presenting the loving relationship between man and God depends on (1) the mechanics of the pulley conceit and (2) the definition of the word *rest* in line 10. Observes that, in addition to meaning, "stasis," "cessation of labor," and "remainder," the word is used in the Bible to describe "the final spiritual rest of the believer drawn to the bosom of his God" and contends that this meaning further explains the central conceit in the poem: "When man's restlessness is satisfied, by his return to a final sabbath rest within the bosom of a loving God, then the motion ceases and the pulley reaches a point of stasis, or final rest."

**1069. Ichikawa, Shuji.** "George Herbert no *The Temple* ni okeru Ontologia Imago Symbolica, Cognitio sui ni tsuite." *Kagawa Daigaku Kyoiku Gakubu*

*Kenkyu Hokoku* [Annual Reports of the Faculty of Education, Kagawa University], part I, no. 40 (March): 21–53.

Argues that it is necessary to grasp Herbert's own way of thinking in relation to the spirit of the age in order to understand *The Temple*. Discusses the intellectual and theological background Herbert used and out of which he grew.

**1070. Ishii, Shōnosuke.** "George Herbert Studies in Japan—A Tentative Report." *Renaissance Bulletin* (Tokyo) 3:18–22.

Observes that interest in Herbert's poetry "has been increasing among Japanese scholars and readers of English poetry since 1951" (p. 18). Notes that it is not known exactly when or by whom Herbert was first introduced to the Japanese but suggests that the first may have been En Kashiwai (1870–1920), who, in a talk given to his students at the Tokyo Academy of Theology in 1913, expressed his admiration for Herbert. Presents a brief history of criticism on Herbert in Japan and lists seventeen essays on Herbert in Japanese published from 1971 to 1975, translating the titles into English. Each of the items mentioned has been entered separately in this bibliography.

**1071. ———.** "George Herbert to Eikoku Kyokai" [George Herbert and the Anglican Church], in *Keijijoshi to Mejioshi* [Metaphysical Poetry and Meditation], 83–123. Tokyo: Aratake Shuppan.

Deals with the process of Herbert's development in Anglicanism, illustrated by various poems in *The Temple*.

**1072. James, Max H.** "The Child Image and Attitude in the Poetry of George Herbert." *C&L* 26:9–19.

Observes that "throughout *The Temple* the child appears in image and attitude" and maintains that "a study of Herbert's use of the child image illuminates both the childlike characteristics of his poetry and his bitter spiritual struggle to achieve and maintain this attitude, and results in an increased aesthetic response to *The Temple* so that we conclude with Herbert: 'Childhood is Health'" (pp. 18–19). Analyzes "H. Baptisme (II)," because it "embodies the most sustained development of the child image" and it "sets forth certain concepts which infuse the *Temple* poems with their recognizably childlike characteristics" (p. 9). Maintains that the major struggle in the poet's life was between himself as a man and himself as a child, "his self-will against the governmental authority of his heavenly Father" (p. 12). Traces the development of Herbert's struggle, his emptying out of himself and final submission to God, in such poems as "The Crosse," "Dialogue," "Christmas," "Longing," and "The Forerunners." Argues that "the wistful, humble, 'childlike' yearning for approval and the incessant insistence upon loving and being loved which one finds in Herbert's poetry is the 'stance' of a child" (p. 17) but stresses that there is nothing childish in his poetry. Maintains that Herbert's concept of spiritual childhood is fully informed by the New Testament and reflects a maturity of spiritual vision.

**1073. Japan Society Of 17th Century English Literature.** *Keijijoshi Kenkyu* [Studies in Metaphysical Poets]. Tokyo: Kenseido. ii, 249, 32p.

Collection of original essays on metaphysical poetry in Japanese. Essays in which Herbert is discussed have been entered separately in this bibliography (entries 1054, 1055, 1082, 1083).

**1074. Jordan, Richard Douglas.** "Herbert's First Sermon." *RES* 27:178–79.

Challenges the veracity of Walton's account of Herbert's first sermon at Bemerton, claiming that "what Walton has in fact done is to create a dramatically effective justification of Herbert's simple style of sermonizing, a justification that presents that style as a conscious choice by a well-educated man who was capable of a higher style" (p. 179). Suggests that Walton may have gotten his idea from the fourth book of St. Augustine's *Christian Doctrine*, in which the saint comments on an atypically florid letter by St. Cyprian, "a letter which Augustine argues, was included to show that Cyprian wrote in the plain style by choice rather than necessity" (p. 179). Concludes that Walton likely transformed Augustine's comments on St. Cyprian into an event in Herbert's life.

**1075. Kermode, Frank, and A. J. Smith.** "The Metaphysical Poets," in *English Poetry*, edited by Alan Sinfield, 54–72. (Sussex Books.) London: Sussex Publications.

Reproduces a discussion of the metaphysical poets between Kermode and Smith taken from recordings of an unscripted talk, followed by a selected bibliography. The speakers attempt to define the nature of metaphysical poetry and discuss similarities and differences among the metaphysical poets. Smith sees a common mode of apprehension, a shared sensibility, as uniting the poets, while Kermode stresses the differences among Donne, Herbert, Vaughan, and Marvell. Discusses in some detail "Prayer (I)" and comments briefly on "Church-monuments," "Jesu," "Hope," "Affliction (I)," "Man," "The Flower," "Redemption," and "The Collar."

**1076. Lapidus, Lawrence A.** "'Lean Not Unto Thine Own Understanding': Grammar as Theme in George Herbert's 'Good Friday' and 'Prayer (I).'" *QJS* 62:167–78.

Maintains that for Herbert "the working of English produced a continual sirensong, exciting hopes only to dash them, enticing him delightfully to what he always knew would be certain failure" and that, "in grappling with his linguistic adversary, Herbert very often took it not merely as the medium of expression but as the subject of expression itself" (p. 167). Presents an analysis of "Good Friday" and "Prayer (I)" and, to a lesser extent, of "The Holdfast," to show how "looking through grammar is replaced by a looking at grammar" and how "this promotes a consciousness of the more general spiritual limitations of language, and leads to an intuition of the transcendence of those limitations" (p. 174). Concludes that "to read Herbert's verse as it asks to be read is to learn to distrust it, to feel as though we are being led elsewhere; always to the Bible, always inward, into ourselves" and that "only when Herbert's verse succeeds in lifting us out of itself can we feel the unity of God and man as 'something understood'" (p. 178).

**1077. Lea, Kathleen.** "George Herbert: The Country Parson," in *The Beauty of Holiness: An Introduction to Six Seventeenth-Century Anglican Writers*, 22–35. Fairacres, Oxford: SLG Press.

General introduction to Herbert's life and to *The Country Parson*. Maintains that, although many social habits have changed since 1632, Herbert's book still speaks to the conscience and the concerns of modern man. Observes that *The Country Parson* can be seen either as "a small manual of instruction, or as an extended form of the popular character-writing of the period" (p. 25) and maintains that it accurately reflects the spiritual experiences and convictions of the author. Characterizes Herbert's prose as "unafraid, but not ostentatious, of racy expressions" and as syntactically "uncomplicated but never dull," in short, "a seemly dress for the muscular good sense of the book's contents" (p. 33).

**1078. Lein, Clayton D.** "Art and Structure in Walton's *Life of Mr. George Herbert.*" *UTQ* 46, no. 2:162–76.

Maintains that Walton's *Life of Herbert* "has a subtlety of artistic manipulation far exceeding any of his earlier efforts" and that "the special quality of the biography springs from the deft interweaving of the life pattern of George Herbert with the personal vision of Izaak Walton on the nature of holy living" (p. 162). Discusses "the elaborate structural control" that Walton exercises "through extensive parallelism and antithesis" (p. 162). Observes, for example, that in contrast to Puritan destroyers, Walton presents Anglicans as "builders, creators, and preservers" and that "the seminal informing idea within the *Life of Herbert*, in fact, is a vision of the loveliness, creativity, and exalted sensuousness of Anglican piety, a state of being clarified by the onslaught of a wholly aggressive and rapacious Puritanism" (p. 163). Shows how Walton contrasts Herbert and Andrew Melville, the Scottish divine, as representatives of their respective faiths and discusses how the structure of the biography "rests upon a great number of carefully matched events, situations, and details between the two halves of the work" (p. 165). Maintains that "the movement from lower to higher, earthly to spiritual, between the two halves is expressed . . . most interestingly in his ingenious development of the common seventeenth-century trope of 'learning and virtue'" (p. 168). Finds Walton's personal response to Herbert to be "the feature of the biography which best reveals the integration of his art and belief" (pp. 170–71). Observes that, for Walton, "Herbert's life itself communicated profound beauty" and that "he responds to that beauty in his narrative by striving to suggest a sensuous sublimity within a holy life" (p. 171).

**1079. McFarland, Ronald E.** "George Herbert and Yeats's 'Sailing to Byzantium.'" *FDP (Four Decades of Poetry, 1890–1930)* 1:51–53.

Comments on the possible influence of Herbert on Yeats's poetry. Maintains, for example, that "the purging of self (or of self-love) in order to accept grace, which most readers would probably agree is at the thematic heart of Herbert's poetry, is clearly described in *A Vision*" (p. 51). Suggests, in particular, that Yeats may have had in mind "Love (III)" when he was writing stanzas three and four of "Sailing to Byzantium" and points out that the two poems have a number of similarities in imagery, phraseology, and use of persona, as well as in theme and development.

**1080. Merrill, Thomas.** *Christian Criticism: A Study of Literary God-Talk.* Amsterdam: Rodopi N. V. 201p.

Discusses Herbert primarily in three chapters. In chapter 2, "Devotion and 'The Flower'" (pp. 21–40), discusses "The Flower" as a "devotional model" to test the critic's notions about the nature of devotional poetry or "God-talk." Chooses this poem because it is "relatively free of personal idiosyncracy and, therefore, more apt to provide an instance of pure God-talk" and because it is "a poem whose very structure is organized about a central metaphor" and "concerns itself with a potentially numinal theme: the recurring awareness of the presence and absence of God" (p. 27). Argues that to analyze the poem only in terms of its literary qualities and merits is insufficient; rather, the reader must take into account the principles of God-talk or theology that inform it. In chapter 4, "Herbert's Poetic God-talk" (pp. 55–72), notes that "the structure of language discernible in Herbert's poetic devotions" is designed "not to inform and not primarily to please" but to display "a constant fidelity to its vocation which is to create verbal situations capable of evoking the experience of the presence of God" and maintains that "its real mission is to draw attention to the vertical heights and depths normally ignored by conventional language because they are pictorially inexpressible" (p. 72). Illustrates Herbert's use of God-talk by analyzing "Coloss.iii.3," "Jesu," "Anagram of the Virgin Marie," "Paradise," "Affliction (III)," "The Collar," and "The Odour." Chapter 5, "'The Sacrifice'" (pp. 73–85), is a reprint (in slightly different form) of "'The Sacrifice' and the Structure of Religious Language" (entry 801).

**1081. Mills, Jerry Leath.** "Recent Studies in Herbert." *ELR* 6:105–18.
    Evaluative bibliographical survey of Herbert studies from 1945 to 1973, divided into three sections: (1) biographical and general critical studies; (2) selected topics (religious and philosophical backgrounds, language and style, the unity of *The Temple*, and the state of criticism); and (3) the canon and texts. Three selective listings of items: (1) general (biographical and general critical studies), (2) studies of selected topics (religious and philosophical backgrounds, language and style, and Herbert and music), and (3) studies of individual poems. Singles out Joseph Summers's *George Herbert: His Religion and Art* (entry 435) as "the essential general work, surveying most of the areas on which subsequent Herbert scholarship has been concentrated" (p. 106). Concludes that Herbert's reputation "was never higher than today," that most of the recent studies "respond, in terms either of refinement, modification, or reaction, to ideas advanced by Summers, Tuve, and Martz," and that, because of the emphases of these scholars, "a major goal has been to deliver Herbert from the aegis of Donne, raised by influential critics in the first half of the century, into his own proper status as an artist of unique achievement" (p. 113).

**1082. Muraoka, Isamu.** "Shakespeare to George Herbert" [Shakespeare and George Herbert], in *Keijijoshi Kenkyu* [Studies in Metaphysical Poets], 139–74. (Japan Society of 17th Century English Literature.) Tokyo: Kenseido.
    Japanese version of article that first appeared in English in *Shakespeare Studies* (entry 1036).

**1083. Nagasawa, Kunihiro.** "The Structure of *The Temple*," in *Keijijoshi Kenkyu* [Studies in Metaphysical Poets], 175–91. (Japan Society of 17th Century English Literature.) Tokyo: Kenseido.
    Explains the structural design of *The Temple* by the fusion of Elizabeth Stambler's "the poet's ever changing feelings" ("The Unity of Herbert's 'Temple,'" entry 540) and Louis Martz's "the poets' developing spirit" (*The Poetry of Meditation*, entry 431).

**1084. Ruud, Jay.** "Herbert's 'Sinnes Round.'" *Expl* 34:item 35.
    Points out that stanza 2 of "Sinnes Round," "concerned chiefly with sinning in *word*, uses the central image of expulsion—sinful thoughts are discharged through the mouth as infection through an open sore or boil" and maintains that the important phrase in the stanza is "vent the wares" in line 9. Contends that Herbert is using a less known sense of the word *ware* meaning "pus, matter." Thus "the poet's mouth gives voice to his sinful thoughts, 'venting' them, spitting them forth, expelling their pus-like infection, as if he were a boil or festering wound." Maintains that such an interpretation is consistent with the rest of the poem, in particular with the preceding image of Mount Etna ("the Sicilian Hill," line 8), which is described as spitting forth fire into the world.

**1085. Smith, Hallett.** "The Permanence of Curled Metaphors." *SR* 84:684–95.
    Review article of several books that include discussions of Herbert: (1) Michael McCanles, *Dialectical Criticism and Renaissance Literature* (entry 1032), (2) Thomas

O. Sloan and Raymond B. Waddington, eds., *The Rhetoric of Renaissance Poetry: From Wyatt to Milton* (Berkeley, Los Angeles, London: University of California Press, 1974), (3) Earl Miner, ed. *Illustrious Evidence: Approaches to English Literature of the Early Seventeenth Century* (entry 1035), and (4) Helen Vendler, *The Poetry of George Herbert* (entry 1050). Discusses Herbert specifically only in the review of Vendler's study. Comments on Herbert's deceptive simplicity and underlying complexity, noting that he "sometimes wrote things which are serious but playful, extravagant in conception or form" (p. 693). Praises Herbert's imagery and metaphors, singling out "The Flower" as his best poem and "The Bag" as his worst. Maintains that Herbert is clearly in the line of descent from Sidney, citing "Jordan (II)" as evidence.

**1086. Stanford, Donald E.** "The Imagination of Death in the Poetry of Philip Pain, Edward Taylor, and George Herbert." *SLitI* 9, no. 2:53–67.
    Argues that Philip Pain is closer in doctrine and tone to Herbert than to any New England poet of the seventeenth century. Points out verbal echoes of Herbert in Pain's *Daily Meditations* and notes that both poets use such standard seventeenth-century symbols as the hour-glass, the fading flower of mutability, and the anchor of hope. Maintains, however, that "in range and intricacy of subject matter and in variety and competence of verse technique, Herbert is, of course, far superior" (p. 59) and illustrates the point by contrasting Pain's *Meditation* 9 ("Man's life is like a rose") to Herbert's "The Rose." Argues that both poets have a similar attitude toward death and the Judgment Day and contrasts their attitude with the more rigidly Calvinistic attitude of Edward Taylor. Maintains that in those poems on his own death Taylor is clearly superior to Pain and even superior to Herbert.

**1087. Strier, Richard.** "'Humanizing' Herbert." *MP* 74:78–88.
    Detailed review of Helen Vendler's *The Poetry of George Herbert* (entry 1050). Argues that, although Vendler raises important critical issues about the nature of Herbert's art, she relies too heavily on Romantic concepts of originality. Maintains that what is needed in Herbert criticism is "more studies in detail of individual poems, more studies of related groups of poems, and a firmer and more precise theological context in which to locate our particular insights" (p. 88). Notes the renaissance of interest in Herbert during the past decade or so, citing the work of Arnold Stein and Stanley Fish.

**1088. Tarlinskaja, Marina.** *English Verse: Theory and History.* (De proprietatibus litterarum, edited by C. H. Van Schooneveld, Series Practica, 117.) The Hague and Paris: Mouton. vii, 351p.
    Translated from Russian. Discusses through induction the theory and history of English verse form from the thirteenth to the nineteenth centuries. Provides "a quantitative definition of the evolving structural and typological features of the classical English meters: the iambic tetrameter, the trochaic tetrameter, the non-dramatic iambic pentameter, the dramatic pentameter, the four-ictus ternary meter with a variable anacrussis as well as several transitional forms" (p. 7). Mentions Herbert in chapter 6, "The Nondramatic Iambic Pentameter" (pp. 138–58), in which various aspects of the syllabic and accentual structure of verse are discussed. Several charts and figures; see in particular Appendix 4 (pp. 219–28), Table 41 (pp. 279–80), Table 42 (pp. 281–82), Table 45 (pp. 287–88), Table 68 (p. 312), and Table 69 (p. 313).

**1089. Wickenheiser, Robert J.** "Tracking down a Herbert." *PULC* 37:219–30.

Describes and discusses a seventeenth-century manuscript (now in the Robert H. Taylor Collection of Princeton University Library) that contains an epithalamium in honor of Dorothy Fairfax's marriage to Richard Hutton, attributed by a contemporary hand to a "Mr Herbert," thought possibly to be George Herbert. Argues that the poem was, in fact, written in 1635 and that its author is Sir Thomas Herbert, a distant relative of George Herbert. Reproduces a reduced facsimile of the manuscript with a transcription of the poem.

# *1977*

**1090. Bell, Ilona.** " 'Setting Foot into Divinity': George Herbert and the English Reformation." *MLQ* 38:219–41.

Reprinted in *Essential Articles for the Study of George Herbert's Poetry*, edited by John R. Roberts (entry 1216), 63–83.

Through a study of Herbert's poems about Christ's sacrifice, argues that "the meditation on Christ's sacrifice, conventional and successful in the Latin poems, becomes self-conscious, introspective, uncertain, and finally unproductive in *The Temple*, where we see Herbert maturing in his commitment to the doctrines of the English Reformation, trying out and turning away from a traditional Catholic vision to create a more Protestant poetic voice and style" (p. 222). Maintains that, as Herbert became more Protestant in his theology, he discovered that religious poetry is "more fruitful if it is fresh and unconventional" and that "old conventions can be an extremely useful base for a protesting poetry," claiming that "much as Sidney and Donne raided and exploded the Petrarchan conventions, Herbert used and doomed the familiar images, postures, and goals of Catholic meditation" (p. 222). Contrasts Herbert's poems on Christ's sacrifice and human suffering with those of William Alabaster to show that, while both poets were aware of the conflict between Catholic meditation and Reformation theology, Herbert turned to a poetry of personal experience suited to his maturing Protestantism, while Alabaster became a Catholic.

**1091. Brunner, Larry.** "Herbert's 'Affliction'(I) and 'The Flower': Studies in the Theme of Christian Refinement." *C&L* 26, no. 3:18–28.

Argues that in "Affliction (I)" and "The Flower" Herbert depicts a central fact of the Christian experience, "the process of divine refinement of the human will," and notes that "it is precisely because this experience of suffering is not unique, not even surprising, that the poet's affliction becomes something more than a mere case history" (p. 19). Points out biblical parallels for the theme of spiritual refinement and shows how the plant metaphors in both poems offer Herbert an excellent vehicle for expressing his main idea. Contrasts the two poems, arguing that "Affliction (I)" "moves from joy of innocence to intermediate pangs of affliction," whereas "The Flower" "proceeds from affliction to the joy of a strengthened and purified heart" (p. 26). Concludes that the poems "move us from rebellion to acceptance, from pride to humility, from pain to that peace which perceives the love behind the severity of Christian suffering" (pp. 26–27).

**1092. Byard, Margaret M.** "Poetic Response to the Copernican Revolution." *Scientific American* 236, no. 6:120–29.

Discusses the impact of the Copernican revolution on seventeenth-century poets, including Herbert. Maintains that, unlike Donne, Herbert "exults in the spacious universe he portrays, even as he retains the old sense of man's role in it and kinship with it" (p. 123) and that, like Crashaw, he is "much at home in an outer world of stars and planets" (p. 125). Briefly points out how the new view of the universe and the role of the scientist show up in such poems as "The Temper (I)," "Man," "Vanitie (I)," and "The Agonie."

**1093. Carrive, Lucien.** "Le sentiment de la nature au début du dix-septième siècle," in *Autour de l'idée de Nature: Histoire des idées et civilisation: Pédagogie et divers*, 15–32. (Etudes anglaises, 74.) Paris: Didier.

Discusses the complex attitudes toward nature and the beauty of the created world as they are reflected in the work of English poets during the first half of the seventeenth century, including Herbert. Comments on several of Herbert's images drawn from the natural world, such as the bee and the flint, and shows that, as a Christian poet, Herbert saw nature not as an end in itself but as a reflection of God's presence and power in the world. Maintains that, as a Protestant, Herbert saw nature as the second book of God's revelation. Notes that Herbert saw God not as the great clockmaker postulated by later thinkers but rather as "le maître de la montre et son réparateur, et la montre a un besoin constant de l'horloger" (p. 23). Comments in particular on how Herbert's concept of the Incarnation affected the way he viewed nature. Points out that, like most seventeenth-century Christian writers, Herbert in his uses of nature rejected both the pagan aestheticism of the Renaissance and also the monastic asceticism of the Middle Ages.

**1094. Charles, Amy.** *A Life of George Herbert.* Ithaca and London: Cornell University Press. 242p.

First full-length biography of Herbert since that of A. G. Hyde in 1906 (entry 11). Stresses that most biographical studies of Herbert have relied too heavily on Walton's account and argues that Walton "handed on a stereotype of Herbert neither accurate nor becoming" (p. 6). Proposes "to examine all the documents and records that in any way relate to a life of Herbert" (p. 6) in order to correct and clarify many details about Herbert's biography. Discusses also Herbert's literary works, his relationship with Nicholas Ferrar and the community at Little Gidding, and a number of biographical and critical questions not previously examined in detail. Following a preface (pp. 5–10), contents (p. 11), a list of illustrations (p. 12), abbreviations (pp. 13–14), and a detailed chronology of Herbert's life (pp. 15–18), this study is divided into six major chapters: (1) "Montgomery, Shropshire, and Oxford (1593–1601)" (pp. 21–35); (2) "Charing Cross, Westminster, and Chelsea (1601–1609)" (pp. 36–65); (3) "Cambridge (1609–1623)" (pp. 66–103); (4) "Westminster and Chelsea (1624–1628)" (pp. 104–35); (5) "Wiltshire: Dauntesey, Baynton, and Bemerton (1628–1633)" (pp. 136–76); and (6) "Little Gidding, Cambridge, and London (1633–1662)" (pp. 177–99). Includes five appendixes: (A) "Herbert's Lives" (pp. 201–9), a discussion of the developments in the writing of the biography of the poet from Walton to the present; (B) "Herbert's Handwriting" (pp. 210–16), a description of the materials from which a study of Herbert's hand is possible and of certain peculiarities of his handwriting; (C) "Herbert's Ring and His Picture" (pp. 217–23), description of the ring (depicting Christ crucified on an anchor) that Donne sent to Herbert (now in the Lloyd's Bank in Warminster) and a description of Robert White's pencil drawing (now in the Houghton Library, Harvard University), which is the source of all known likenesses of Herbert; (D) "George Herbert at Venice, 1618)" (pp. 224–27), a rejection of the theory that the George Herbert, a young ensign under the command of Sir Henry Peyton in Venice, is the poet; and (E) "Thomas Laurence, Herbert's Successor at

Bemerton" (pp. 228–33), a discussion of charges of delinquency against Herbert's successor at St. Andrew's and a consideration of what they tell us about Herbert's liturgical practices and his Laudianism. Index (pp. 235–42).
Reviews:
Jerome R. Zurek, Jr. *America* 137 (1977): 292
John Bienz, *C&L* 27, no. 4 (1978): 64–65
Coburn Freer, *JEGP* 77 (1978): 433–36
J. L. Idol, Jr., *SCR* 10, no. 2 (1978): 105–6
John R. Mulder, *RQ* 31 (1978): 676–78
David Novarr, *GHJ* 1, no. 2 (1978): 49–62
J. Max Patrick, *SCN* 36 (1978): 1–4
A. L. DeNeef, *SAQ* 78 (1979): 130–32
Daniel W. Doerksen, *Ren&R* 4, no. 1 (1979): 117–19
Mary Ellen Rickey, *MP* 77 (1979): 221–23
Anon. (signed Paidagogos), *Expository Times* 91 (1980): 160

**1095. [Charles, Amy M., ed.]** *Cross-Bias: The Newsletter of the Friends of Bemerton Society,* no. 3 (April). 4p.
Includes a shaped poem, "An Easter Egg," by J. D. K. Lloyd; announces the establishment of the *George Herbert Journal*; comments on recent developments in the parish of Bemerton and explains how to get to St. Andrew's; offers summaries, by Charles Kovich, of papers on Herbert read at the 1976 MLA Convention; presents Herbertiana, such as a pattern for a cross-stitch rendering of St. Andrew's and the collect (prayer) for the remembrance of Herbert; and lists several recent publications and forthcoming studies on Herbert.

**1096. Cruttwell, Patrick.** "The Metaphysical Poets and Their Readers." *Humanities Association Bulletin* (Canada) 28:2–42.
Notes that metaphysical poets intended their poems for a specific, limited, and, in a sense, elitist audience and proposes "to investigate outwards, from the poems themselves, and from them to deduce the nature of the chosen reader" (p. 22). Argues that the metaphysical poets imagined their readers to be like themselves, both in their general knowledge and education and in their willingness to accept traditional attitudes. Maintains, for example, that the metaphysical poets and their readers regarded each other as social equals and did not hold with certain heroic pretensions about poetry or about poets that can be observed in earlier Renaissance poetry. Notes that, although the metaphysical poets and their readers evince an interest in scientific discoveries and philosophical speculations of their time, they "never think them of primary importance" since the poetry itself characteristically "moves through a triangle formed by body, soul, and God" and since, "within that triangle, it really did not make any difference whether the sun goes down or the earth comes up" (p. 29). Contends, however, that the metaphysical poets did expect their readers to know and respect scholastic philosophy and its method: "Hence the well-know tendency of this poetry to organize its material in the tripartite structure of a syllogism even when the material is blatantly untheological" (p. 30). Also notes the characteristic embedding of allusions in metaphysical poetry. Focuses primarily on Donne but refers to Herbert throughout. Contrasts "Affliction (I)" with Gerard Manley Hopkins's "Thou art indeed just Lord" to show that, whereas Hopkins's sonnet "seems disturbed, muddy," Herbert's poem, like the devotional poems of almost all the metaphysical poets, has a "serenity in the midst of anguish" primarily "because the poet, and the people he is

writing for no less, assume without question the given bases, axioms, on which their structures rest" (p. 39).

**1097. Di Cesare, Mario A., and Rigo Mignani, eds.** *A Concordance to the Complete Writings of George Herbert.* Ithaca: Cornell University Press. xiv, 1319p.

In the preface (pp. vi-xiv), explains the purpose and governing principles of this concordance to all of Herbert's poetry and prose in English, Latin, and Greek, lists acknowledgments, and presents a key to abbreviations. Uses Hutchinson's text (entry 266) and the 1633 edition, supplemented by the text of the 1613 Latin gratulatory poems edited by Leicester Bradner (entry 575) and the text of "Inventa Bellica" edited by G. M. Story (entry 594). Divided into three parts: (1) concordance to writings in English (poetry and prose) (pp. 1–993); (2) concordance to writings in Latin and Greek (pp. 997–1277); and (3) frequency lists (English, in frequency order; English, in alphabetical order; Latin and Greek, in frequency order; and Latin and Greek in alphabetical order) (pp. 1281–1319). In both concordances, words in poems are listed before words in prose in an entry. Eliminates *a, and, in, it, of, that,* and *the*; *to* is eliminated only for the prose. Includes words from doubtful poems and from the second part of *Outlandish Proverbs* but marks them clearly with a *D*. Titles are concorded but not numerals, dates of letters, and similar kinds of rubrics; also the long quote from *Valdesso* is not concorded. Identifying information gives page number in Hutchinson (except for the Bradner and Story texts), title of the poem, and line number. Sample entry:

| BUNCH | PAGE | TITLE | LINE |
|---|---|---|---|
| Anneal'd on every bunch. One standing by ............116 | | Love-joy | 3 |
| The bunch of grapes ...............................128 | | Bunch Gr. | T |

Reviews:
Amy Charles, *Choice* 14 (1977): 1338
Amy Charles, *CHum* 12 (1978): 299
Roberts W. French, *GHJ* 1, no. 2 (1978): 63–65
Daniel W. Doerksen, *Ren&R* n.s. 4 (1979): 117–19
Sidney Gottlieb, *LRN* 4 (1979): 42–45
J. B. Bamborough, *RES* n.s. 31 (1980): 458–60
J. Max Patrick, *SCN* 40 (1982): 14

**1098. El-Gabalawy, Saad.** "George Herbert and the Emblem Books." *EM* 26:173–84.

Points out parallels between images in *The Temple* and emblems in Quarles's *Emblemes*, Phillippe de Mallery's pictures in *Typus Mundi*, Herman Hugo's *Pia Desideria Emblematis*, Geoffrey Whitney's *A Choice of Emblemes*, Alciati's *Emblematum flumen abundans; or, Alciat's Emblems in their Full Stream*, Benedictus van Haeften's *Regia Via Crucis* and *Schola Cordis*, Alonso de Ledesma's *Epigramas y hieroglificos a la vida Christo*, Antonius Wiericx's *Cor Iesu amanti sacrum*, Georgette de Montenay's *Emblèmes, ou devises chrestiennes*, Daniel Cramer's *Decades quatuor Emblematum Sacrorum*, Maurice Scève's *Delíe*, Theodor de Bry's *Emblemata Saecularia*, Daniel Heinsius's *Emblemata amatoria*, Guillaume de la Perrière's *Theatre des bons engins*. Concludes that such parallels suggest that Herbert very likely knew the popular emblem books of his time but warns that direct influence of specific emblems on Herbert's images cannot be proved since "the similarity might be caused by a common origin with which the writers were acquainted as part of their cultural background" and thus "it is safer to think of Herbert's affinities with the emblematic mode in terms of wide application and impact" (p. 184). Notes a similarity between the images in Southwell's "The Burning Babe" and those in Herbert's "Love unknown."

1099. ———. "Two Obscure Disciples of George Herbert." *N&Q* 24:541–42.
Comments on Herbert's influence on two minor seventeenth-century poets, Cardell Goodman and Ralph Knevet, who are said to be "among the most interesting of Herbert's avowed disciples" (p. 541). Notes several close borrowings in their poems from *The Temple* that serve "to underline Herbert's mastery of form and poetic expression" (p. 542).

1100. **Fish, Stanley.** "Doing Scholarship: The Mystery of *The Temple* Finally Explained." *GHJ* 1, no. 1:1–9.
Maintains that during the past forty years Herbert criticism has given us two Herberts and two different bodies of poetry: the first is a "calm and resolute craftsman who writes from a position of achieved stability" and the other is "restless, changeable, and uncertain" and his poetry is "tentative, provisional, and unfinished, a succession of vacillations, alternatives, and reinventions" (p. 1). Maintains that a reconciliation of these viewpoints can be found in chapter 21 of *A Priest to the Temple*, where Herbert describes how the catechist draws out answers from his pupil. Argues that "one need only replace the catechist and his pupil with the poet and his reader: to one belongs the stability of prior and controlling intention, and to the other belongs the realization of that intention, a realization which will be preceded by uncertainty and arrive in the form of a surprise" (p. 2). Maintains that the catechist "is engaged in what we might call *sincere role playing*, a category of action which justifies not only indirection, but even (momentary) deception, so long as it is in the service of driving the reader-Answerer to one of the 'dark and deep points of Religion'" (p. 3). Argues also that the organizational scheme of *The Temple* corresponds to the sequence of events recommended for catechumens in Reformation catechisms—from moral instruction to baptism to reception of the Eucharist to instruction in the deepest mysteries of the Church to full membership in the Church Militant. Contends that *The Church Militant* fully reflects the *narratio* of salvational history found in catechisms of the period and that its seemingly inconclusive ending "fulfills its function in the sequence, and becomes part of the structure—the Temple of God—that is at once firm, secure, and completed, and precarious, shifting, and unfinished" (p. 8). For an extended discussion of this subject, see *The Living Temple: George Herbert and Catechizing* (entry 1144).

1101. **Gallagher, Philip J.** "George Herbert's 'The Forerunners.'" *ELN* 15:14–18.
Argues that the tension in the conclusion of "The Forerunners" is "not between the alternatives 'to die' or 'not to die'" as Stanley Fish suggested (entry 905) by alluding to Exodus, but is "between the attitude of the regenerate, to whom harbingers mark *through* death and therefore to eternal life (the ultimate Christian paradox), and that of the unregenerate, to whom the harbingers mark merely *for* death and therefore dissolution (or eternal damnation)" (p. 16). Maintains that the concluding couplet of the poem ("Let a bleak paleness chalk the doore, / So all within be livelier than before") embodies tension through its syntax and its imagery and notes that chalk was used by the ancients for cleansing garments and hence tropologically was "capable of removing spiritual melancholy" (p. 17). Points out that the *cressa nota* (chalk marking) trope was used by Plautus, Horace, Persius, and Catullus and concludes that in "The Forerunners" Herbert "baptizes a pagan trope, washes it with his tears, and

more, brings it to church well dressed and clad" and that, for the reader who recognizes the significance of the trope, the poem ends "not in tension but in resolution" (p. 18).

**1102. Gottlieb, Sidney.** "How Shall We Read Herbert? A Look at 'Prayer (I).'" *GHJ* 1, no. 1:26–38.

Argues that "Prayer (I)" is "a good example of a poem that becomes clarified by its context," presents a critical reading of the sonnet before examining it with other poems with which it is placed in the Williams MS (W), and finally considers it as it is placed among different poems in *The Temple* in order to demonstrate "how radically Herbert can alter the meaning and impact of a poem by shifting not its text but its background" (p. 28). Maintains that, when read in isolation, "Prayer (I)" "presents the reader with certain facts, impressions of energy, of rapid motion, and of the intellectual and emotional vigor required of a man praying and of a man writing about prayer" but that "in itself the poem gives the reader no sure sign of what these impressions signify" (p. 30). Shows that, when the sonnet is read in the context of W, where it is preceded by two poems entitled "The Christian Temper," poems that treat the frustrating changeability of everything that man experiences, the reader is led to think that the same theme and tone will appear in "Prayer (I)," but, as the sonnet progresses, the reader recognizes that "prayer is 'something understood' by man but at the same time man himself is 'something understood' in that his needs are recognized and satisfied through prayer" (p. 33). Concludes by demonstrating that when "Prayer (I)" is read in the context of *The Temple*, where it is preceded by "Faith," it "becomes a somewhat unmodulated poem of celebration" and "an exuberant expression of man's place in God's bountiful universe" (p. 36).

**1103. Guralnick, Elissa S.** "Herbert's 'Church-Monuments.'" *Expl* 35, no. 4:12–14.

Elaborates on Joseph Summers's assertion in *George Herbert: His Religion and Art* (entry 435) that "Church-monuments" is a hieroglyph in part because "the dissolution of the body and the monuments is paralleled by the dissolution of the sentences" (p. 12, quoting Summers, pp. 133–34). Argues that sentence structure in the poem "does in fact dissolve under the pressure of ambiguous syntax and ambiguous pronominal reference" so that the sentences "take on rich, ambivalent meanings that amplify the poem's significance" (p. 13). Argues that "Church-monuments" is a hieroglyph "not only by virtue of the fact that it is, like the monuments it describes, in a state of dissolution" but also "by virtue of the fact that meaning emerges from its dissolution: as the poem's reader confronts Herbert's meaning in the decaying sentences of the poem" (p. 13). Illustrates the point by showing that ambiguous and unstable syntax in lines 10–11 permit one to make at least four different interpretations and that in line 12 at least two different interpretations are possible.

**1104. Harman, Barbara Leah.** "George Herbert's 'Affliction (I)': The Limits of Representation." *ELH* 44:267–85.

Reprinted in *Essential Articles for the Study of George Herbert's Poetry*, edited by John R. Roberts (entry 1216), 508–24.

Appears in revised form as chapter 3 (pp. 89–105) of *Costly Monuments: Representations of the Self in George Herbert's Poetry* (entry 1345).

Observes that modern critics have noted that a number of Herbert's poems "end in collapse, reversing the process that has occupied speaker and reader for all but the final few lines" (p. 267). Examines in detail instances of reversal and collapse in

"Affliction (I)" to show (1) that the persona in Herbert's poems often is "already in possession of its ending (or one of its endings)" and therefore "exerts significant control over experience"; (2) that the speaker's control is, however, often problematic since "it contradicts a deep wish that experience were not conclusive"; (3) that often there is "an appearance of mastery in a Herbert poem, an illusion which rarely survives the story's end, and which exists only as long as the end is suppressed," a suppression that "permits the feeling of free movement observed by critics"; (4) that "if genuine mastery is re-assumed when the narrative's end is acquired, then having mastery is a troublesome and dubious distinction" that signifies "not only conclusiveness, but relinquishment of the illusion of freedom, and acceptance of an often untenable end," a conclusion "achieved at great cost" and frequently is "a humiliation"; and (5) that there are many poems in *The Temple* that "resurrect themselves after an illusory 'ending'" and that "require that the speaker relinquish whatever safety closure has to offer," the greatest difficulty in these poems being "the obligation to survive *beyond the end*" (pp. 269–70).

**1105. Herbert, George.** *The Williams Manuscript of George Herbert's Poems.* A Facsimile Reproduction with an Introduction by Amy Charles. Delmar, N.Y.: Scholars' Facsimiles & Reprints, xxxvi, fols. 119.

Portions of the introduction first appeared in "The Williams Manuscript and *The Temple*" (entry 897).

Contains a preface (pp. vii-viii), a detailed introduction (pp. ix-xxxvi), and a fac-simile reproduction of the Williams manuscript (MS. Jones B 62) in the Dr. Williams's Library (fols. 119). In the introduction maintains that the Williams manuscript (W) "is probably more important as a measure of his [Herbert's] poetic development than the more famous Bodleian manuscript" and "antedates by some years the version that probably served as the basis of the first edition of *The Temple* in 1633" (p. ix). Presents a full bibliographical description of the manuscript, assisted by Margaret C. Crum of the Bodleian Library, and comments on its provenance and its probable date. Compares the order of the poems in W with the order in the Bodleian manuscript (Tanner MS. 307) and in the first edition and argues that the order of W provided "the ground upon which the later variations are played" (pp. xxviii). Maintains that a study of W reveals that "Herbert's technical skill had already matured at the time this volume was compiled" and that "he clearly had in mind the tri-partite form that *The Temple* would follow" (p. xxxi). Suggests that "the variety in form and in rhyme and the revisions that reflect a tightening of concept, strengthened diction, and greater sense of the poet's confidence in handling his materials demonstrate amply that at this stage Herbert was already an accomplished poet" (p. xxxi).
Review:
Daniel W. Doerksen, *RenR* n.s. 4 (1980): 117–19

**1106. Higgins, Dick (Richard Carter).** *George Herbert's Pattern Poems: In Their Tradition.* West Glover, Vt., and New York: Unpublished Editions. 79p.

Surveys the history of visual poetry and discusses its aesthetic appeal in order to demonstrate that Herbert's two principal pattern poems, "The Altar" and "Easter-wings," "belong to a far richer and more varied tradition than is generally supposed, and that to treat them in isolation as flukes of some kind, which many a critic has done, is to miss the significance both of them as poems and of their cultural frame of reference" (p. 20). Notes that visual poetry has existed from antiquity to the present in many languages and regards modern concrete poetry as part of the tradition. Con-trasts "The Altar" with Herrick's "The Pillar of Fame," noting that Herrick's poem lacks the fervor of "The Altar," "whose poetic prayer is lent impact by the religious frame of reference which the pattern establishes" (p. 16) and compares "Easter-wings" to wing-poems by George Puttenham and the Greek Simmias of Rhodes. Reproduces twenty-seven examples of pattern poems, with brief descriptions and comments on each. Selected bibliography.

**1107. Hovey, Kenneth Alan.** "George Herbert's Authorship of 'To the Queene of Bohemia.'" *RenQ* 30:43–50.
Argues that "To the Queene of Bohemia," signed G. H. and first printed by H. Huth in 1870, was likely written by Herbert about 1624. Admits that "though no amount of circumstantial evidence can prove the poem to be Herbert's, it nonetheless deserves to be read closely and carefully as a metaphysical work of considerable interest" (p. 44). Puts the poem in its context vis-à-vis Herbert's life and relationships, supplements internal evidence of Herbert's authorship first noted by Grosart and Hutchinson, and presents a critical evaluation of the poem. Points out that, if the poem is Herbert's, it is "his longest English poem not included in *The Temple* and also the most substantial of his various Latin and English complimentary verses" (p. 44). Finds a number of similarities between the poem and *The Church Militant*, *Outlandish Proverbs*, and Herbert's early poetry in general and suggests that the most convincing evidence of Herbert's authorship is "the poem's overall excellence" (p. 50).

**1108. Hunter, Jeanne Clayton.** "Herbert's *The Temple*." *Expl* 35, no. 3:14–16.
Comments on how "The Bag" employs "an Old Testament allusion illuminated by Reformational commentaries to present its central image" (p. 15). Argues that in the poem "the Old Testament bag is transformed in forty-two dramatic lines from its Old Testament type, container of sins, to its New Testament anti-type, Christ's wound which contains our sins and transforms them into grace" (p. 15). Concludes that the metaphor of the bag, like the best of the lyrics in *The Temple*, "presents man and Christ engaged in an intense and personal drama which sounds those 'two vast, spacious things . . . Sinne and Love'" (p. 15).

**1109. Ishii, Shōnosuke.** "Futari no 'gentle' na Bunjin—Herbert to Herrick" [Two Gentle Men of Letters—Herbert and Herrick]. *Gakuto* [Light of Learning] 74, no. 8 (August): 12–15.
General survey of the lives of Herbert and Herrick, based on Marchette Chute's *Two Gentle Men* (entry 510).

**1110. Kelliher, Hilton.** "A Latin Poem Possibly by George Herbert." *SCN* 35, nos. 1–2:12.
Argues that an anonymous Latin poem entitled "Ad Authorem Instaurationis" in Bodleian MS. Rawlinson Poetical 246 is by Herbert. Contends that it is part of a "separate homogenous group of verses" in the manuscript and points out that the other poems in this group have been ascribed to Herbert. Notes that the manuscript, a commonplace collection, was compiled by Henry Somes, Fellow of King's College, Cambridge, from 1649 to 1658. Suggests that the poem was written not long after the publication of Bacon's *Novum Organum* in 1620. Reproduces the Latin text of the poem and gives a literal translation into English.

**1111. Kessner, Carole.** "Entering 'The Church-porch': Herbert and Wisdom Poetry." *GHJ* 1, no. 1:10–25.
Discusses the relationship between *The Church-Porch* and *The Church* and argues that Herbert's moralistic, long poem recalls the pre-Christian tradition of wisdom

literature. Maintains that "Superliminare" is informed by passages from Exodus and Deuteronomy and that the title and the two quatrains create a hieroglyph of a lintel and two doorposts that represents the concepts of purification necessary before entering the church door and protection by God after entrance. Further explains that each quatrain echoes a specific psalm: the first, Psalm 34, one of the wisdom psalms; the second, Psalm 24, one of the entrance psalms, both of which deal with moral instruction. Argues that *The Church-Porch*, therefore, states the conditions one must meet before entrance into *The Church*, while the later presents devotional experience that qualifies one to be God's guest at the heavenly banquet, the theme of "Love (III)," the last poem in *The Church*. Noting differences between *The Church-Porch* and wisdom psalms, offers as the more likely immediate source the *Wisdom of Joshua Ben Sira*, known also as *Ecclesiasticus*. Compares passages from each on subjects such as swearing, lying, and temperance to show similarities and concludes that *Ecclesiasticus* is "the lineal inheritor of the wisdom poetry of Hebrew Scripture" and "the spiritual and poetic ancestor" (p. 24) of Herbert's poem.

1112. **Lewalski, Barbara K.** "Typological Symbolism and the 'Progress of the Soul,' in Seventeenth-Century Literature," in *Literary Uses of Typology from the Late Middle Ages to the Present*, 79–114. Princeton: Princeton University Press.

Examines historically and critically how typological symbolism informs several major English seventeenth-century literary works that deal with the progress of the soul, including *The Temple*. Argues that "typological criticism became in the earlier seventeenth century an important literary means to explore the personal spiritual life with profundity and psychological complexity, and that certain characteristic Protestant alterations in the traditional typological formulae facilitated this exploration" and shows how "these alterations, together with the prominence of the theme of the progress of the soul, arise from the same cause—the new Protestant emphasis upon the application of Scripture to the self, that is, the discovery of scriptural paradigms and of the workings of Divine Providence, in one's own life" (p. 81). Discusses Herbert's use of typology in such poems as "The Bunch of Grapes," "The Altar," "The Collar," "Aaron," and "Jordan (II)," maintains that *The Church-Porch* and *The Church* are unified by typological symbolism, and indicates how typology informs *The Church Militant*. Argues that, for Herbert, "the Old Testament temple, with its intimations of permanence, has its true antitype solely in that church which is in the hearts of the elect, who can progress toward, and at length achieve, individual salvation" (p. 95). Comments on how the speaker in many of Herbert's poems sees himself as similar to David the Psalmist, who as a poet underwent similar spiritual experiences and confronted many of the same artistic difficulties, and points out that there are borrowings from and allusions to the psalms in many of Herbert's lyrics. Compares and contrasts Herbert's use of typology with that of Donne and Vaughan as well as Herbert's use of David as a *figura* for himself as a Christian poet and Traherne's use of this figural relationship and his use of the psalms in *The Thanksgivings*.

1113. **Magee, Pat.** *George Herbert: Rector of Bemerton*. With a foreword by Sir Arthur Bryant. Salisbury: Printed by Moxham Printers for the Friends of Bemerton. iv, 31p.

Booklet written by the Rector of St. Andrew's Church, Bemerton, in response to the interest shown by the many visitors to the church and in order to raise funds to restore Herbert's church. Presents a general introduction to Herbert's life and works, divided into five chapters—"Success in the World" (pp. 1–7), "Problems and Frustrations" (pp. 8–15), "Fulfilment" (pp. 16–20), "His Thought," and "Last Days" (pp. 28–

30)—followed by a selected bibliography of suggested readings and an index of poems mentioned. Calls Herbert a saint and focuses on his spirituality as reflected in his poetry and in *A Priest to the Temple*. Four illustrations.

**1114. Mehta, Digish.** "Metaphoric Traditions in Religious Poetry: Christian and Advaitic." *Indian Journal of English Studies* 17:8–17.

Points out that Herbert, as a Christian poet, was as keenly aware of the insufficiency or limitations of language to convey an adequate notion of God or the Absolute as was Akho, the seventeenth-century devotional poet of Gujarati, who belonged to the Advaitic tradition of Indian poetry. Maintains that both poets recognized the problem of the self in the creative act but solved the tension created by the self in quite different ways: the Christian poet, aware of his fallen nature, "feels himself called upon to renounce his claim to the creative faculty itself as the ultimate test of his faith in God" (p. 8), while the Advaitic poet has "access to a wider range of metaphors with the help of which he can depict the Self as immanent as well as transcendent" (p. 10).

**1115. Morneau, Robert.** "The Divine Host and Hesitant Guest: A Commentary on George Herbert's Poem 'Love.'" *Contemplative Review* 10:19–26.

Presents a "personal commentary" (p. 19) on "Love (III)," searching out "the implicit theology and tangible joy of Herbert's poem" (p. 20). Comments on Herbert's concepts of God, love, sin, and religious experience as manifested in the poem and shows how "an educational process goes on throughout the entire poem" (p. 21).

**1116. Nagasawa, Kunihiro.** "George Herbert's Idea of Writing Poetry." *Ibaraki Daigaku Kyoiku Gakubu Kiyo* [Bulletin of the Faculty of Education, Ibaraki University], no. 26 (March): 213–19. Explains from a theological viewpoint the apparent conflict between Herbert's plain style and an elaborate style in his verse. Maintains that as priest, as mediator between God and men, Herbert believes he must use his best style to praise and glorify God, but that as man, not divine, he realizes that all of his verse is only a copy of the form of the *Logos*. Concludes that Herbert's aspiration for artlessness in poetry and his belief in plain style reflect his humiliated realization that God as *Logos* is the author of all verse.

**1117. Petti, Anthony G.** "George Herbert (1593–1633)," in *English Literary Hands from Chaucer to Dryden*, 114–15. Cambridge, Mass.: Harvard University Press.

Points out characteristics of Herbert's handwriting. Also notes that his punctuation is "fairly meticulous with liberal use of the colon, and includes a circumflex accent on *a*" and that his abbreviations have "some distinctive features, notably the brevigraph for *m* and *n* which is a hook on the end of a tall, wavy ascender above the preceding vowel" (p. 115). Reproduces a facsimile of "Easter-wings" in the Williams manuscript (MS. Jones B 62, ff. 27v, 28), in which the corrections alone are in Herbert's hand, and selections from *Lucus* (MS. Jones B 62 ff. 113v, 114).

**1118. Pollock, John J.** "Herbert's *The Temple* as a Self-consuming Artifact." *LangQ* 15, nos. 3–4:21–22, 24.

Argues that Stanley Fish's conclusions about Herbert's poetry in *Self-Consuming Artifacts* (entry 905), based primarily on his analysis of Herbert's diction and sentence structure, "can in fact be substantiated by a broader analysis of Herbert's use of imagery and metaphor" (p. 21). Maintains that an examination of *The Temple* reveals that (1) Herbert "generally defines things, not by what they 'are,' but by what they do"; (2) he "constantly speaks of God and man in terms of what they enclose or are enclosed by, so that enclosure itself becomes the predominant method of establishing the nature of God and of man"; and (3) "in describing the Eucharist, Herbert resorts to imagery of interenclosure in which God and man are said to enclose and consequently define each other" (p. 21). Maintains that Herbert's view of the Eucharist in particular "suggests that at the heart of his poetic vision Herbert apparently DOES see a kind of annihilation of self in man's union with the God-head" (p. 24) and that thus Fish is correct about *The Temple* being a "self-consuming artifact."

**1119. Rickey, Mary Ellen.** "Herbert's Fool for Christ's Sake: A Note on 'Joseph's Coat.'" *GHJ* 1, no. 1:57–60.

Points out that the four italicized words in the last line of "Josephs coat" ("My *joyes* to *weep*, and now my *griefs* to *sing*") mark a near-quotation from one of the Fool's songs in *King Lear*, 1.4.166–67 ("Then they for sudden joy did weep, / And I for sorrow sung"). Argues that the poem "denotes not only the parti-colored nature of life, and the Old Testament type of Christ's body torn to give joy, but also the motley of the fool enabled, through imitation of Christ, to change from weeping in joy to singing in grief" and "denotes even more specifically, the distinguishing mark of those who are fools for Christ's sake, the apostles which St. Paul describes as capable of glorifying all adversity" (p. 58). Maintains that the speaker of "Josephs coat" is like the apostles of Christ, one who "wounded, can sing and tormented, can write" (p. 58). Suggests that the speaker may even be a Franciscan fool or perhaps the Tommy of English folk festivals.

**1120. Schmerling, Hilda L.** "A Critical Analysis of George Herbert's 'Peace,' " in *Finger of God: Religious Thought and Themes in Literature from Chaucer to Kafka*, 69–76. (Religion in Literature Series.) New York: Gordon Press.

Explicates "Peace" stanza-by-stanza, pointing out how the poem is both "a work of moral instruction in allegorical form" and "an affirmation of Herbert's own faith" (p. 75). Shows that in stanza 1 the seeker of peace begins his search in a secret cave, later identified as the tomb of Jesus; in stanza 2 the "secret" of Jesus is revealed by his resurrection and ascension; in stanza 3 the seeker goes to a garden of delight, mistaken for the garden of the Church; in stanza 4, recovering from his mistake, the seeker encounters "a rev'rend good old man," identified as the Holy Trinity, who directs him to a Prince of old, who is Jesus, who dwelt at Salem, which is Jerusalem, the City of Peace, and who offers him the Eucharist, made from the grain grown in the garden of the Church—which finally brings the seeker the peace he desires. Concludes that, "just as the cave remains secret to those who do not understand the meaning of Jesus' life, so this vertue remains secret to those who do not have faith in the consequences of the events of the Crucifixion and the Resurrection" (p. 75).

**1121. Shafer, Ronald G.** "Herbert's Poetic Adaptation of St. Paul's Image of the Glass." *SCN* 35, nos. 1–2:10–11.

Discusses Herbert's imaginative adaptations of the Pauline image of the glass in "The Sacrifice" (lines 117–19), in "The H. Scriptures (I)" (lines 7–8), and especially in "The Windows." Argues that in "The Windows" Herbert "establishes the image of the glass through which the glory of God shines in verse-paragraph one; in verse-paragraph two, he emphasizes the fact that the 'life' of God is superimposed upon man; and in verse-paragraph three, he stresses the role of the Spirit." Concludes that in both form and content Herbert's poem coincides exactly with 2 Cor. 3:18 and that the poem is a reworking of 1 Cor. 13 (verses 1, 13), 2 Cor. 3:18 and 4:3, 4, 6, all of which contain the image of the glass.

1122. **Sobosan, Jeffrey G.** "Call and Response—The Vision of God in John Donne and George Herbert." *Religious Studies* 13:395–407.

Argues that in *The Temple* Herbert reflects a more personal and intimate relationship with God, and especially with the person of Jesus, than Donne does in his *Divine Poems* and observes that "his God speaks to Herbert whereas the Divine in Donne does not speak" (p. 395). Maintains that Donne's imagery in his religious poems is predominantly visual, whereas Herbert's is more auditory. Contrasts Herbert's concepts of God, Christ, redemption, the Church, death, and sin with Donne's views and maintains that their sacred poems reflect their very different theological perspectives and spiritual temperaments. Argues that Herbert's poems reflect his "closeness to his God, his awareness of the humanity of Jesus, his great trust which is neither simple nor naive, his sense of God's providence and indwelling in the world" (p. 406) and maintains that "other poets in Herbert's own age, as before and since, have probably done richer justice to such characteristics as the majesty and power of God, but of the God found and known here and now in the small circumstances of our daily life Herbert has as much to say as any poet, and perhaps, says it more profoundly than most" (p. 407). Concludes that Herbert's poetry, "enriched by the presence and voice of God, speaks of a more significant relationship than does Donne's more objective poetry" (p. 407).

1123. **Tadokoro, Haru.** "George Herbert and Hymn." *Gifu Joshi Daigaku Kiyo* [Bulletin of Gifu Women's College], no. 6:147–81.

Gives a historical survey of the hymn as a literary genre and maintains that Herbert's idea of the hymn was as a song of praise and thanksgiving to God, expressing joy and triumph. Argues that Herbert's attitude toward the hymn is connected with his theological questions about man's unworthiness and God's surpassing greatness and with his understanding of the concept of redemption. Concludes that, although Herbert inherited the tradition of the congregational hymn, sung within the church community, he used the genre to express his personal faith.

1124. **Van Nuis, Hermine.** "Sincerity of Being and Simplicity of Expression: George Herbert's Ethics and Aesthetics." *C&L* 27, no. 1:11–21.

Argues that for Herbert sincerity and simplicity of expression go hand in hand. Maintains that Herbert's simplicity "is not to be equated with sloppiness, or artlessness" and "does not preclude intricacy of underlying structure nor suggests lack of sophistication" but is "the effect of simplicity of spirit" (p. 14). Stresses that "to achieve that kind of simplicity of expression requires a very sophisticated understanding of how to control art, of how to conceal its underlying complexity, and also how to avoid in style what might destroy this simplicity" (p. 14). Praises Herbert's balance and measure, his subtlety and ingenuity, his unity of direction and concentration, and his lack of pretense and affectation. Concludes that Herbert's art can "best be characterized as elegant simplicity" (p. 20) and that stylistically he has much in common with the plain stylists.

1125. **Wardropper, Bruce W.** "The Religious Conversion of Profane Poetry," in *Studies in the Continental Background of Renaissance English Literature: Essays Presented to John L. Lievsay*, edited by Dale B. J. Randall and George Walton Williams, 203–21. Durham: Duke University Press.

Comments on Herbert's conversion of love poetry into sacred verse. Prefers to call such adaptations *contrafacta* rather than sacred parodies. Notes that T. S. Eliot (entry 577) suggested that the line "Busie enquiring heart, what wouldst thou know," from

"The Discharge," echoes the first line of Donne's "The Sunne Rising" and discusses briefly Herbert's adaptation in "A Parodie" of "Song: Soules joy, now I am gone," variously attributed to William Herbert, third earl of Pembroke, and to Donne. Points out that Herbert "abandons line-by-line imitation after the third line, thereafter following only the rhythmic pattern of his model" (p. 204). Points out that such explicit imitation is unusual in Herbert's corpus and suggests that his intention was not simply to protest against love poetry but rather "to glorify even more the glorious lyric poetry of his age by turning it into devout song in praise of God" (p. 204). Briefly contrasts Herbert and Southwell as sacred parodists.

**1126. Westgate, Sam.** "George Herbert: 'Wit's an Unruly Engine.'" *JHI* 38:281–96.

Discusses in some detail Herbert's complex attitude toward wit, especially as it is advanced in the first epigram of *The Church-Porch*, in which the poet explains how he wishes both to delight and instruct his reader and how he hopes his wit, once it has attracted the reader to good, will finally be consumed in the flame of a higher purpose than mere delight. Argues however, that "consumed it never is" and that his "conceits, paradoxes, puns, rhymes, figures, and elaborate verse forms are never quite negated even if Herbert would ultimately have them disappear into some simple motto or elegant lesson" (p. 281). Considers selected passages in which "wit's delight is produced and then clearly 'sacrificed' to some higher purpose"; comments on "more difficult instances" in which "wit is not clearly subsumed under some more serious concern"; and finally examines how in some cases Herbert's wit triumphs over didacticism and "tends to privacy and in extreme cases to secrecy with no sure object other than the author's own amusement" (p. 282). Examines these various kinds of wit in such poems as the sixteenth, seventeenth, and last epigrams in *The Church-Porch*, "Love (I and II)," "Decay," "The H. Scriptures (I)," "Prayer (II)," "Evensong," and "The Answer" and concludes that Herbert's wit "tends to dissolve any easily understood, fixed stances, to complicate them, and to make them individual" (p. 296).

**1127. Wickenheiser, Robert J.** "George Herbert and the Epigrammatic Tradition." *GHJ* 1, no.1:39–56.

Maintains that, taken as a whole, Herbert's Latin epigrams "tell us a great deal about Herbert's development as a poet" and reveal "an affinity between epigrammatic and lyric poetry in the seventeenth century which most of us have tended to ignore in responding appreciatively to this poetry" (p. 39). Argues that the lyric mode grew out of the epigrammatic mode, that seventeenth-century poets did not distinguish sharply between the two modes, and that what we most like about metaphysical poetry may be the result of the influence of the epigrammatic tradition. Comments on a number of Herbert's Latin epigrams to illustrate their range and artistic quality and how they contain themes and stylistic features that are admired in his English poems, such as puns, paradoxes, startling contrasts, and especially a "subtle underlying intellectuality" that informs his "intensely emotional utterances" (p. 50). Shows how the epigrammatic mode pervades Herbert's English poems and even *Outlandish Proverbs*. Compares "Poem VIII" in *Memoriae Matris Sacrum* with "The Agonie," "The Collar," "Redemption," and especially "Love (III)" to illustrate how Herbert uses dialogue "to provide the basis for a quiet, resolved, but nonetheless pointed conclusion which then drives home to the reader the fulfillment of the poem's profound meaning" (p. 54). Concludes that Herbert never lost his fondness for epigrammatic form and wit and that *The Temple* is a "sometimes subtle, sometimes overt continuation of his earlier epigrammatic style, rather than a break with it" (p. 55).

**1128. Wilson, Raymond J., III.** "George Herbert's 'A Parodie': Its Double Meanings." *AI* 34:154–57.

Argues that in "A Parodie" Herbert compares the intensely emotional union of sexual lovers with the emotional-spiritual union of Christ and the Church. Maintains that throughout the poem Herbert uses a feminine voice, sustains the metaphor of Christ as a male lover, and uses words with sexual overtones. Contends that the resolution in the poem is presented in terms that suggest the release of built-up tension during orgasm. Concludes that the double meanings do not detract from a theological interpretation of the poem but that "the secondary sexual meanings reinforce and carry forward the poem's central metaphor of Christ-as-lover" and that "the orgasmic interpretation of the conclusion accounts far better for our subjective sense of the poem's emotional power" (p. 157).

# 1978

**1129. Alpers, Paul.** "George Herbert Our Contemporary." *University Publishing,* no. 4 (Spring): 1–3.

Discusses the appeal that Herbert's poetry has for the modern reader and academic critic and claims that in the twentieth century there has been "more good modern criticism of Herbert than of any other seventeenth-century lyric poet" (p. 1). Maintains that the question at the heart of modern evaluation of Herbert's poetry is whether or not the contemporary reader can identify with a poet "who saw the meaning of his life entirely in Christian terms" (p. 2). Surveys some of the major developments in modern Herbert criticism and compares and contrasts Helen Vendler's *The Poetry of George Herbert* (entry 1050) and Stanley Fish's *The Living Temple* (entry 1144) to show that recent studies "revive the old question in rather new terms" and give the study of Herbert's poetry "new vitality and interest" (p. 2). Concludes that the two studies "prompt us to reflect on the reasons we value poetry, and show, by opening up such problems as well as by making numerous poems newly vital and interesting, why Herbert is a poet who still matters to us" (p. 3).

**1130. Anselment, Raymond A.** "'The Church Militant': George Herbert and the Metamorphoses of Christian History." *HLQ* 41:299–316.

Maintains that *The Church Militant* "reveals a mode, carefully conceived though less familiar, that complements the sensibility apparent in the other more readily accepted poems of *The Temple* (p. 300). Argues that in *The Church Militant* Herbert assumes the role of a "time-bound poet-prophet" who presents "a typological vision of time" by interpreting "the significant interrelationships inherent in the Christian promise of fulfillment that unifies past, present, and future" (p. 301). Maintains that Herbert "exuberantly celebrates the moments of religion's apparent progress and ironically exposes the folly of self-seeking error" and observes that, "although an intensity of feeling may at times reveal the speaker's own involvement, a prophetic irony always sees in the metamorphoses of history a larger meaning of a divine providence" (p. 303). Discusses how the concept of *Theatrum Mundi* "determines Herbert's own dramatization of God's historical omnipresence" and how the five main divisions of *The Church Militant* "represent acts in the pageant of time" (p. 309). Shows how Herbert's view of time is essentially Augustinian, in which the past both reflects the present moment and prophesizes about future events.

**1131. Asals, Heather.** "Magdalene Herbert: Towards a *Topos* for the Anglican Church." *GHJ* 1, no. 2:1–16.

Maintains that Magdalene Herbert's life, dress, and art of writing provided both Donne and Herbert with a topos for the *via media* of the Anglican Church and argues that, like the English Church and like Herbert's poetic language, she is a living echo of the eternal in the present. Argues that Mrs. Herbert's "method in language presents to Herbert an idea of the middle way of the condition of language itself, its paradoxical reconciliation of extremes" and that, "by providing us with a parallel set of images for the Anglican Church in the literature about her life, Magdalene Herbert presents to the literary critic a key to the ontology of Herbert's poetry itself, the poetry of 'The Church,' to the locus and nature of the 'being' of a Herbert poem" (p. 1). Focuses on "The British Church" (lines 4–6), seeing *place*, *letters*, and *face*—central words in the poem—as "topoi current in the literature about Magdalene Herbert" and topoi that are "the very substance of George Herbert's poetic" (p. 2). Maintains that "the function of Herbert's poetry is similar to role of his Church and his mother Magdalene (the apostle of the Church) in giving God a place" because his poetry "locates a face on the surface of language itself (the 'letter' of the word, the 'bodie' and the 'letters' of language) from which the Spirit of the body and the letters emanates" (p. 8).

**1132. Blau, Sheridan D.** "George Herbert's Homiletic Theory." *GHJ* 1, no. 2:17–29.

Laments that none of Herbert's sermons have survived. Finds Walton's account of Herbert's first sermon to be implausible and considers Herbert's verse and prose, especially his chapter on preaching in *A Priest to the Temple*, the most authoritative sources on his homiletic theory and pulpit oratory. Maintains that Herbert followed the plain manner of preaching he advocated in *A Priest to the Temple*. Notes that the chapter on preaching is divided into three parts: (1) the means by which a preacher can gain and keep the attention of his audience, (2) the holiness that should mark a sermon, and (3) the proper method for handling the text that is the subject of the sermon. Argues that sermons conforming to these principles would differ from the seventeenth century sermons with which we are most familiar, such as those of Donne. Maintains that Donne saw his role as preacher as that of the "visible ambassador of a great lord," while Herbert saw himself as a "nearly unobtrusive medium through which God's messages might pass" (p. 21). Notes that Herbert's plainness was not devoid of rhetorical skill since he regarded the sermon as a means of moving the affections of his congregation and reviews the rhetorical figures that Herbert recommends to the preacher in *A Priest to the Temple*. Contends that Herbert's homiletic theory resembles that of the Puritans in that he condemns wit, eloquence, and erudition and argues that the sermon should be as holy as the preacher's life and the biblical text are. Concludes that Herbert did not subscribe to any specific set of Puritan rhetorical principles but rather suited his sermons to his country congregation.

**1133. Bloch, Chana.** "George Herbert and the Bible: A Reading of 'Love (III).'" *ELR* 8:329–40.

Presents a detailed critical reading of "Love (III)" to demonstrate the pervasive influence of the Bible on Herbert's poetry. Argues that the poem is "typically Herbertian in its dramatization of theological issues, its deceptive simplicity, its colloquial ease, its candor and tact, and its knowledge of the human heart" (p. 330) and shows how the poem's "dramatic situation, the images, the tension of ideas, the very shape of the plot, all have their source in the Bible" (p. 331). Maintains that "Love (III)" is essentially a love poem between God and man that "contains the *Temple* in brief" and that "tells us that when man's sin and God's love are weighed in the balance—and indeed, the poem proceeds by a series of careful balancings, tipping first to the one side and then to the other—it will come to rest, as it does in the last line, emphatically on the side of God's love" (p. 336). Notes that allegorical interpretations of the Song of Solomon gave Herbert the precedent for seeing the relationship of man to God in somewhat erotic terms and that "in this respect the Bible has freed his imagination to more direct expression than he would otherwise have attempted" (p. 339). Concludes that it is only by understanding how Herbert creatively used tradition that one can appreciate his originality.

**1134. Britting, Georg, ed.** "George Herbert," in *Lyrik des Abendlandes*, 251–52, 704. Gemeinsam mit Hans Hennecke, Curt Hohoff und Karl Vossler; ausgewählt von Georg Britting. Munich: Hanser.
Translation into German of "Vertue" by Richard Flatter (pp. 251–52) and a biographical note (p. 704).

**1135. Carney, Frank.** "George Herbert the Musician: Integration of Music into Poetry." *EIRC* 4:17–31.
Discusses seventeenth-century musical theory and argues that "a knowledge of the musical background of the seventeenth century can sharpen an understanding of seventeenth-century poetry" (p. 19). Examines the relationship between music and love and between music and meditation or prayer and explains the Neo-Pythagorean and Neoplatonist attitudes toward music that were fused in the seventeenth century. Discusses Walton's comments about Herbert's knowledge of and appreciation of music. Argues that in Herbert's poetry "musical technique fused with literary experimentation into a poetic form" and that any study of Renaissance musical forms is "the study of the ancestral forms of the stanzaic patterns of George Herbert's poetry" (p. 30). Discusses how musical techniques shape Herbert's sound patterns, rhythms, stanzaic forms and structures, and syntax. Comments specifically on the uses of music in "Deniall" and "Mortification."

**1136. Charles, Amy.** "Touching David's Harp: George Herbert and Ralph Knevet." *GHJ* 2, no. 1:54–69.
Argues that for Ralph Knevet, one of Herbert's lesser-known disciples, *The Temple* "proved a catalyst rather than a mere model" (p. 55) when he wrote *A Gallery to the Temple*. Contrasts Herbert's "The Sacrifice" and Knevet's "The Incarnation" to show how the latter poet "turned Herbert's method into his own" (pp. 59–60). Argues that Knevet used *The Temple* "almost as a handbook of lyric form" (p. 60) but that, although he often uses Herbertian devices, stanzaic forms, and even some titles, he often adapts them to his own voice and purposes. Examines several of Knevet's poems to illustrate his achievement in poetry. Maintains that his poems are characterized by "a strong sense of rhetorical construction" (p. 60), "effective openings" (p. 63), less than effective conclusions that do not always avoid "flatness and occasional bathos" (p. 64), and sometimes a unity that is achieved when he concentrates "on a single figure or on a series of closely related figures" (p. 65). Contends that Knevet has "little of the sense of dialogue with God that we find in Herbert" (p. 66) and that his poems

often are much more didactic and zealous than Herbert's. Maintains that Knevet comes closest to Herbert in "The Feast."

**1137.** [**Charles, Amy M., ed.**] *Cross-Bias: The Newsletter of the Friends of Bemerton Society*, no. 4 (June). 4p.

Announces the publication of the first issue of the *George Herbert Journal*, the Herbert session at the 1978 MLA Convention, and the third Biennial Renaissance Conference at Dearborn, Michigan, devoted entirely to Herbert; gives summaries of papers, by Charles Kovich, that were presented at the special session on Herbert at the 1977 MLA Convention; reports on Herbertiana, such as an exhibit of watercolor paintings of Bemerton by Edwin Young of Salisbury and copies of two Bemerton plays, *Under Salisbury Spires* by H. M. Dimont and *Dear Jane* by Evelyn Hart, now in the Herbert collection at the University of North Carolina–Greensboro; comments on recent developments in the parish of Bemerton; and lists recent and forthcoming publications on Herbert.

**1138.** **Clawsey, Mary Crawford.** "Some Seventeenth-Century Poems on the 'Black Is Beautiful' Theme," in *Studies in English and American Literature*, edited by John L. Cutler and Lawrence S. Thompson, 115–17. (American Notes and Queries Supplement, vol. I). Troy, N.Y.: Whitston Publishing Co.

Discusses the positive treatment of black in the poetry of Lord Herbert of Cherbury and in George Herbert's "Aethiopissa ambit Cestum Diuersi Coloris Virum." Maintains that Herbert's Latin poem is reminiscent of his brother's *Diana Cecyll* series and that lines 3–4 echo the paradox in "Another Sonnet to Black Itself." Argues that, except for the simplicity of its language, the poem "might be one of Lord Herbert's poems mistakenly attributed to George" (p. 116). Notes that "Aethiopissa" is untypical of Herbert, not only because it is secular, but also because it is somewhat erotic.

**1139.** **Crossan, Greg.** "Herbert's 'Love (III).'" *Expl* 37, no. 1:40–41.

Points out possible sexual overtones in "Love (III)," in which the speaker, "though desirous of intimacy with his lover, draws back because of his feelings of guilt and shame" (pp. 40–41) until "his lover takes his hand seductively and assures him that he is not imposing on her, that she herself initiated their intimacy" (p. 41). Maintains that "taste my meat" (line 17) can be paraphrased as "enjoy my flesh" (p. 41). Concludes that "the point of the analogy is that both physical and spiritual love require a purgation of guilt-feelings before there can be consummation or atonement (at-one-ment)" and maintains that the poem is "one of the most striking and apposite of all metaphysical minglings of love human and and love divine" (p. 41).

**1140.** **Di Cesare, Mario A., ed.** *George Herbert and the Seventeenth-Century Religious Poets: Authoritative Texts/Criticism.* (A Norton Critical Edition.) New York: W. W. Norton. xiv, 401p.

Anthology of poems by Herbert, Crashaw, Marvell, Vaughan, and Traherne. Calls Herbert and Marvell "major poets" and Crashaw, Marvell, and Vaughan "poets of real distinction" (p. xiii). "George Herbert" (pp. 3–70) includes a biographical sketch and seventy-nine poems from *The Temple* along with two sonnets from Walton's *Lives*, with explanatory notes. Bibliographical introduction to Herbert's poems and textual notes (pp. 203–11). Includes an original essay by Anthony Low (entry 1163) and seven previously published letters, essays, or sections from books that deal specifically with Herbert: (1) Samuel Taylor Coleridge, "Letters," two selections from *Collected Letters. . .* , ed. Earl Leslie Griggs (Oxford, 1956–), letters no. 1159 and

1524; (2) Aldous Huxley, "The Inner Weather," from *Texts and Pretexts* (entry 149), p. 13; (3) W. H. Auden, "Anglican George Herbert," from *George Herbert: Selected by W. H. Auden* (entry 949), pp. 10–13; (4) T. S. Eliot, "George Herbert as Religious Poet," from *George Herbert* (entry 577), pp. 15–25; (5) L. C. Knights, "George Herbert: Resolution and Conflict," from *Scrutiny* (entry 293), pp. 171, 175–86; (6) E. B. Greenwood, "Herbert's 'Prayer (I)'," from "George Herbert's Sonnet 'Prayer': A Stylistic Study" (entry 655), pp. 27–45; and (7) Joseph H. Summers, "The Poem as Hieroglyph," from chapter 6 of *George Herbert: His Religion and Art* (entry 435), with slightly abridged notes. Partially annotated bibliography (pp. 387–401).
Review:
Roberts W. French, *GHJ* 3 (1979–1980): 64–68

**1141. Dust, Philip.** "Sources for the Titles of Vaughan's *Silex Scintillans* in Herbert's Neo-Latin Poetry," in *Studies in English and American Literature*, edited by John L. Cutler and Lawrence S. Thompson, 110–12. (American Notes and Queries Supplement, vol. 1.) Troy, N.Y.: Whitston Publishing Co.
    Argues that "Patria" and "In Stephanum lapidatum," the second and third of Herbert's neo-Latin poems in *Lucus*, may be the source of Vaughan's title *Silex Scintillans*. Notes that "analogies to the ideas in Herbert's two poems are found throughout Vaughan's hymns" (p. 111).

**1142. Ellrodt, Robert.** "La Fonction de l'image scientifique dans la poésie métaphysique anglaise," in *Hommage à Emile Gasquet (1920–1977)*, 43–55. (Annales de la faculté des lettres et sciences humaines de Nice, 34.) (Etudes-anglo-americaines, 3.) Paris: Belles Lettres.
    Briefly compares the use of scientific imagery in the poetry of Herbert with that of selected other metaphysical poets, especially Donne. Notes Herbert's use of the circle in "The Sinner" and scientific images in "The H. Communion," "Coloss.iii.3," "To the Queene of Bohemia," and "Prayer (I)."

**1143. Evans, Gillian.** *The Age of the Metaphysicals.* (Authors in Their Age, ed. Anthony Adams and Esmore Jones.) Glasgow and London: Blackie & Sons. 140p.
    Introduces students to the major metaphysical poets and briefly defines the nature of metaphysical poetry. Discusses the religious, political, and educational backgrounds of the poets and comments on their shared view of the nature and function of poetry. Outlines the history and development of criticism of metaphysical poetry, maintaining that "twentieth-century readers, perhaps for the first time since the age of the metaphysical poets themselves, are in a position to appreciate their work on two levels at least: that of the pleasure of problem-solving, and that of the more familiar pleasures of poetry, the sharing of someone else's experience, the recognition of common sensations and shared responses to the happenings of life" (p. 131). In "George Herbert" (pp. 37–42) presents a biographical sketch of the poet and comments on his personality and holiness. Mentions Herbert throughout, especially noting his effective use of conceits and rhetoric, his strong opposition to poetic excess and obscurity, his shaped poems, and his sacred themes. Briefly compares Herbert to Vaughan and contrasts him with Carew. Selected bibliography (pp. 132–35).

**1144. Fish, Stanley.** *The Living Temple: George Herbert and Catechizing.* Berkeley: University of California Press. ix, 201p.

Argues that the conventions of Reformation catechisms provide a key to understanding the title and the overall structure of *The Temple* as well as an explanation for the various vacillations and reinventions in individual poems and between poems in the collection. In chapter 1, "Catechizing the Reader" (pp. 1–53), summarizes the critical debate about whether Herbert's poetry is calm and resolute or "provisional" and anguished and argues that, "rather than swinging back and forth between the poet of order and stability and the poet of change and surprise, Herbert criticism should ask the question posed by its own shape and history: how is it that a poet and the poetry he writes can be restless and secure *at the same time?*" (p. 5). Reviews the answers of certain critics, such as Martz (states of memory) and Vendler (reinvented poems), and maintains that these polarized views affect the readings of individual poems as well as the sense of the structure of *The Temple*. Argues that the form, style, and structure of Herbert's poems can best be understood in the light of Reformation catechistical practices. Distinguishes between a rote catechism and a Socratic catechism, the latter offering a strategy to produce self-discovery by the reader, and contends that the Socratic formula accounts for "the simultaneous presence in Herbert's poetry of order and surprise" (p. 25). Discusses in particular "Love-joy," "Jesu," and "The Church-floore" to elucidate the strategy of catechizing the reader. Argues that, because something cannot be known by natural capacities, the reader is moved to acknowledge his dependency on Christ. In chapter 2, "Work To Be Done/Work Already Done: The Rhetoric Of Templehood" (pp. 54–89), sets out to prove that Herbert had definite catechistical models in mind when he wrote *The Temple*. Links the forms and concerns of the catechism with the rearing of the temple in the heart of man that goes on in *The Temple*, documenting the link by quoting from numerous Reformation catechisms. Discusses the metaphors of "building" and of "milk" used in the rhetoric of catechisms, noting the ambiguity between being the temple and becoming the temple, the same ambiguity that exists in Herbert's work. Discusses "The Church-floore" and "The Windows" to show that the strategies that Herbert employs are those of the catechism of his day. In chapter 3, "The Children Of The Precept: Catechizing And The Liturgy" (pp. 90–136), shows that catechistical instruction was a progression in three stages—liturgical, from pre-Baptism to the Church Militant; stational, from the church porch to the altar and beyond; and educational, in morality, law, and the mysteries of religion. Discusses the order of poems in *The Temple* as random but patterned, based on the steps a sinner must take to prepare himself to receive the sacraments. Discusses "Love (III)" as catechistical and sees the resolution as peremptory on Christ's part, denying the speaker any part in the disposition of his case: the speaker "has been killed with kindness" (p. 135). In chapter 4, "The Mystery of *The Temple* Explained" (pp. 137–69), claims that his theory is both simpler and more explanatory than others but allows that the others have a place. Maintains that the theory explains *The Church Militant* as the final stage in the construction of the temple in man, embodying the history of salvation, but not the perfection of man, for that must wait until the Church Triumphant. Claims that Herbert "stands to God as his readers stand to Herbert" (p. 167). Answers his earlier question about how poetry can be both restless and secure at the same time: "The order in the poetry can be explained by attributing to the poet a conscious aesthetic strategy (to drive the reader to a deep and dark point of religion), but since the strategy is one for which he finally cannot claim responsibility, the explanation dissolves into mystery (the driving behind the driving)" (p. 168). In "A Conclusion in Which It May Appear That Everything Is Taken Back" (pp. 170–73), asserts that the purpose of his study is a persuasion rather than a demonstration of evidence. Bibli-

ography of primary and secondary sources (pp. 174–95), followed by an index of authors (pp. 196–201). See also Fish's essay, "Doing Scholarship: The Mystery of *The Temple* Finally Explained" (entry 1100), where some of this material is covered in less detail.
Reviews:
Ilona Bell, *MLQ* 39 (1978): 408–11
Annabel Patterson, *GHJ* 2, no. 1 (1978): 70–72
C. H. Sisson, *TLS*, 29 September 1978, p. 1075
Chana Bloch, *SCN* 37 (1979): 1–5
Gerald Hammond, *Critical Quarterly* 21, no. 3 (1979): 83
Virginia Mollenkott, *JEGP* 78 (1979): 255–57
Claude J. Summers, *C&L* 28, no. 2 (1979): 53–54
W. G. Madsen, *Criticism* 22 (1980): 86–88
Louis Martz, *RQ* 33 (1980): 300–303
C. F. Williamson, *RES* n.s. 31 (1980): 464–66
Robert Ellrodt, *EA* 34 (1981): 219–20
Barbara Leah Harman, *CL* 33 (1981): 197–202
Inge Leimberg, *Anglia* 101 (1983): 263–69
A. J. Smith, *YES* 12 (1982): 266–68

**1145. Friedenreich, Kenneth.** *"Silex Scintillans* (1650;1655)," in *Henry Vaughan*, 120–58. (Twayne's English Author Series, 226, edited by Sylvia E. Bowman.) Boston: G. K. Hall.

Argues that, although Vaughan's debt in *Silex Scintillans* to Herbert is considerable, it should not be overestimated. Comments on the multifaceted nature of Vaughan's borrowings and points out that Vaughan often freely adapts a word, phrase, image, theme, or stanza pattern from Herbert for his own purposes and thus does not imitate Herbert slavishly. Illustrates the point by contrasting passages from Vaughan's "The Proffer" and Herbert's "The Size." Maintains that Vaughan's most important debt to Herbert is "to the general concept of a book of related religious lyrics" but that, unlike Herbert, Vaughan "does not move indoors but from place to place outside, close to nature" (p. 125). Claims that Herbert inspired Vaughan "to offer to a subsequent generation of readers another book to move them to piety and to a defense of their embattled faith" (p. 125) and influenced him to instruct his readers by pleasing them aesthetically.

**1146. Gilman, Ernest B.** "The Pauline Perspective in Donne, Herbert, and Greville," in *The Curious Perspective: Literary and Pictorial Wit in the Seventeenth Century*, 167–203. New York and London: Yale University Press.

Shows how manipulation of perspective in late Renaissance art parallels the uses of metaphysical wit in poetry. Observes that the Pauline metaphor of the mirror appears frequently in devotional literature "as an image of our imperfect understanding" and that "wherever it appears it carries a concern with the limits of language and a dynamics of the mind striving for illumination against its own darkness" (p. 172). Notes also that during the Renaissance the Pauline mirror "assumes richer metaphoric possibilities by association with the curious perspective: conical or cylindrical 'glasses' could deform images or clarify others distorted anamorphically, while the range of the word *glass* now extended to the marvels of the new optics, refracting lenses, prisms, and telescopes ('perspective glasses')" (pp. 175–76). Comments on Herbert's concern with the difficulties posed by St. Paul's observation that fallen man can perceive ultimate realities only through a glass darkly and notes how he uses wit as a vehicle to achieve insight into mysteries that ordinarily lie covered with imperfect language. Points out Herbert's search for "a language of transparent perception" (p. 188) and notes how he often "succeeds in discovering a divine perspective hidden in the darkness of earthly vision," in an "oblique language of the spirit" (p. 203). Comments particularly on "The Sacrifice," in which Herbert exercises wit "to redeem language 'obliquely' from the dark perspective of the flesh" (p. 191).

**1147. Gottlieb, Sidney.** "Linking Techniques in Herbert and Vaughan." *GHJ* 2, no. 1:38–53.

Notes that Vaughan in *Silex Scintillans* uses the same or similar types of linking techniques that Herbert uses in *The Temple*. Discusses how individual poems in both volumes are linked by titles that draw poems together; by repeated words, images, actions, and styles from one poem to another that tend to redefine and resonate meaning; by techniques of self-reference (for example, when a question is raised in one poem and answered in another) that tend to "trace out a life being lived" (p. 44) and ask for an active, involved reader; and by the grouping of poems thematically, which allows a subject to be emphasized or viewed from another angle. Concludes that, "far from being unique and idiosyncratic, Herbert and Vaughan seem to be a part of a large and important literary tradition when they write 'ecchoing songs,' a tradition well worth investigating further" (p. 51).

**1148. Gottlieb, Stephen A.** "Dual Vision in Herbert's 'The Sacrifice,'" in *Studies in English and American Literature*, edited by John L. Cutler and Lawrence S. Thompson, 104–9. (American Notes and Queries Supplement, vol. 1.) Troy, N.Y.: Whitston Publishing Co.

Discusses the significant positioning of "The Sacrifice" as the second of four poems ("The Altar," "The Sacrifice," "The Thanksgiving," and "The Reprisall") that form a "sacrificial introduction" to *The Temple*. Shows how in the poem Herbert "manipulates groups of symbols to develop the full potential of Christ's irony" and how ambiguity in the poem "functions not only by distinguishing but also by unifying different points of view—Christ's, man's (the tormentor's as well as that of the faithful)—within Christ's broader perspective," thereby identifying "man's grief with Christ's grief" (p. 105). Maintains that the "densely ironic texture" of "The Sacrifice" results, in part, from Christ's monologue, which "constantly fuses the narrative function with the symbolic" (p. 105). Notes that verbal ambiguity gives Herbert a method "for generating dramatic perspectives both in relation to the liturgical drama behind 'The Sacrifice' and in relation to the early sequence of poems within which 'The Sacrifice' is placed" (p. 107).

**1149. Greenblatt, Daniel L.** "The Effect of Genre on Metrical Style." *Lang&S* 11:18–29.

Uses statistical profiles based on the Halle-Keyser theory of iambic pentameter "to demonstrate that the genre of a poem has an appreciable effect on its metrical style, at least for several important seventeenth-century poets, and that the effect of certain genres on metrical style is to some extent predictable" (p. 18). Presents statistical profiles of selected poems by Herbert, Donne, Crashaw, Jonson, Carew, and Marvell and shows that, "for all the poets tested except Marvell, the data suggest strongly that genre can exert a powerful influence on the metrical stylistic feature of complexity" and that, "in many cases, not only do these poets adapt their styles to different genres, they deal with their common genres in approximately the same way" (p. 23).

**1150. Harman, Barbara Leah.** "The Fiction of Coherence: George Herbert's 'The Collar.'" *PMLA* 93:865–77.

Appears in a revised form as chapter 2 (pp. 64–88) of *Costly Monuments: Representations of the Self in George Herbert's Poetry* (entry 1345).

Discusses the "disturbed relationship between storyteller and story" that occurs when the speaker "doubles back upon an already complete report" (p. 866) and, in particular, this type of relationship as it occurs in "The Collar." Argues that in the first 32 lines of the poem, speech "becomes a vehicle for self manifestation" (p. 868) and a "declaration of discontinuity" (p. 869) with the past. Notes that the reintroduction of a retrospective narrative voice in line 33 reminds us that the interior story of the first 32 lines is a past event being retold. Maintains that, in retelling the story, the narrator purchases "a guarantee against surprise, change, instability, and vulnerability" and "safety from that unwieldy, untraveled, potentially chaotic time in which we always live when we live in the present" (p. 871). Argues, however, that the speaker finally distances himself from that past and "acknowledges his obligation to return to the present" (p. 875). In conclusion, argues against the position taken by past critics (Summers, Stein, Martz, Vendler) who maintain that the poem's conclusion places the speaker at rest on "safe ground" (p. 876). Finds, rather, that the conclusion "relinquishes . . . the fiction of safe territory" and establishes a relationship with God "not in a world where order is necessary but in a vulnerable present where images cannot be secured" (p. 877). For a reply, see entry 1190.

**1151. ———.** "Herbert, Coleridge and the Vexed Work of Narration." *MLN* 93:888–911.

Appears in a revised form as part of chapter 1 (pp. 59–63) of *Costly Monuments: Representations of the Self in George Herbert's Poetry* (entry 1345).

Argues that in Herbert's poetry "narration is what there is to do when there is nothing to do at all" and that, although "it provides the deprived speaker with an arena in which self-generation, or the development of a project, can occur, it is always displaced by God's utterance which reappropriates the space of priority to which narration lays claim" (p. 888). Discusses "The Reprisall" as an example of narration taking the place of the speaker's barrenness of thought in the face of Christ's passion. Maintains that this work of narration becomes identified not as invention but as opposition and that what begins as a means to repay Christ's sacrifice ends as a statement about the impossibility of repaying the debt. Claims that, at the end of the poem, the speaker takes on the task of overcoming the self, of unmaking the "narrator and narrative at once" (p. 891) and that the poem suggests that "the speaker who sings best is a speaker without a text, someone who has given up the fiction that he can generate appropriate discourse on his own" (p. 897), one whose text instead comes from God. Argues that in "The Altar" the speaker becomes "the ground upon which articulation proceeds" (p. 898), for he disappears entirely into the altar, "so that the idea of narration as opposition, as a piece of work capable of stationing itself between the vulnerable speaker and his God, is inconceivable" (p. 899). Observes that "The Altar" is unusual because it performs what other poems in *The Temple* recommend—the penetration of the speaker into his setting. Contrasts Herbert's and Coleridge's views on narration and concludes that "the power of the theological frame to overcome lyric speech in Herbert's poems gives way in Coleridge to a lyric discourse troubled, but not overcome, by its alternatives" (p. 907).

**1152. Häublein, Ernst.** *The Stanza.* (The Critical Idiom, no. 38, edited by John J. Jump). London: Methuen. viii, 125p.

Mentions Herbert throughout this study of the relationship between the stanza and poetic structure. Briefly comments on Herbert's use of "counterpoint," of repetition, and of various devices for poetic closure and poetic unity. Comments in some detail on the structure of "Vertue" (pp. 82–85) and of "Aaron" (pp. 104–5).

**1153. Hecht, Anthony.** *Poetry Pilot*, February, pp. 1–12.
Newsletter of the Academy of American Poets that includes six poems by Herbert scattered throughout the issue, chosen by the poetry editor, along with his explanation for his selection. Notes that Herbert is "the only Anglican saint who does not also appear in the Roman Catholic calendar" (p. 9). Urges support of the Friends of Bemerton.

**1154. Honda, Kin-ichiro.** "George Herbert no Sekai" [The World of George Herbert], in *Geijutsu no naka no Europe-so* [A Picture of Europe in Art], 77–84. Tokyo: Shinozaki Shorin.
Comments on some elements underlying the medieval European sense of beauty found in Herbert's poetry.

**1155. Ishii, Shōnosuke.** "Saikin no George Herbert Kenkyu" [Recent Studies of George Herbert]. *EigoS* 124, no. 7 (October): 426–29.
Introduction to Herbert in Japanese with a bibliographical survey of recent studies on him by English and American scholar-critics. Comments in particular on Herbert's current literary reputation.

**1156. Keizer, Garret.** "George Herbert and the Tradition of Jacob." *Cithara* 18:18–26.
Argues that Herbert's struggles with himself and God in *The Temple* recall Jacob's wrestling with God, a struggle regarded by Christians as a type of Christ's agony in Gethsemani. Maintains that there are at least two ways to view Herbert's conflicts: (1) "to see the combat as a genuine struggle to move God in directions toward which his absolute justice and righteousness make him somewhat reluctant to go" or (2) "to regard the combat as man's illusion" (p. 20), in which "man fights to gain the very things he resists—so that the struggle is really with himself" (p. 21). Contends that, through faith, Herbert was able to live with the contradictions of the divine-human relationship: "Herbert's God can be wrestled, even held, but never 'pinned down'" (p. 24). Notes also that Herbert's struggles, like Jacob's, end with a blessing that "is a 'mixed' one in that it involves a wounding" (p. 24). Illustrates his argument with numerous references to Herbert's poems.

**1157. Kinnamon, Noel J.** "A Note on Herbert's 'Easter.'" *GHJ* 1, no. 2:44–48.
Argues that, although evidence for Herbert's knowledge of the metrical psalms of Sir Philip Sidney and the Countess of Pembroke "is mainly circumstantial," it is nevertheless "persuasive" (p. 44). Calls attention to several unnoticed parallels between "Easter" (composed of two separate poems) and the Countess of Pembroke's early version of Psalm 108. Observes that, although there are no verbal parallels between the two poems, the most interesting structural parallels are that they both divide into "two metrically different sections" (p. 44) and that the second section in both poems is a "song of praise promised in part one" (p. 47). Maintains that Herbert may have seen a copy of the Countess's Psalm 108 and that her poem may have been the stimulus to combine his two original poems into one.

**1158. Köppl, Sebastian.** *Die Rezeption George Herberts im 17. und 18. Jahrhunderts mit besonderer Berücksichtigung von George Ryleys Kommentar zu Her-*

berts *"Temple" (MS. Bodl. Rawlinson D. 199).* (Anglistische Forschungen, 129.) Heidelburg: Carl Winter Universitätsverlag. 291p.

Surveys Herbert's critical reception during the seventeenth and eighteenth centuries with special consideration of George Ryley's commentary on *The Temple* in MS. Bodl. Rawlinson D. 199. Foreword (p. 5); table of contents (p. 7–8); and a brief introduction to Herbert's critical reception (pp. 9–11). In chapter 1, "Der Dichter George Herbert: 'Metaphysical Poet' und religiöser Lyriker" (pp. 13–22), introduces Herbert's life, challenges the notion that he was a member of the "School of Donne" or the "Metaphysical School," and argues that Herbert's poetry can be best understood in the light of a broader tradition of English religious verse that reflects certain theological and linguistic features. Outlines the basic aspects of Herbert's poetry that shaped his reputation and critical reception. In chapter 2, "James Leekes neolateinische Übertragung von Herberts 'The Church Militant' und 'Good Friday' (The Durham Chapter and Cathedral Library. MS. Hunter XXVII)" (pp. 23–34), presents a complete version of Leeke's 1634 translation of *The Church Militant* into neo-Latin verse. Observes that, from the eve of the Civil War, Herbert's poetry was regarded as reflecting specific theological and political viewpoints. In chapter 3, "Herberts Rezeption im englischen Puritanismus" (pp. 35–77), maintains that, for the most part, the Puritans had high regard for Herbert's poetry while at the same time rejecting its theological content. Illustrates this point by discussing Herbert's influence on Richard Baxter's poetry and on his preface to *Poetical Fragments* (1681). In chapter 4, "George Ryley: Mr Herbert's Temple & Church Militant Explained & Improved by a Discourse on Each Poem Critical & Practical (MS. Bodl. Rawlinson D. 199)" (pp. 79–153), discusses Ryley's sources, intention, and basic points in his commentary on *The Temple* (1714/15). Maintains that Ryley presents one of the best and most detailed theological interpretations of Herbert's poems, throws light upon the poet's early eighteenth-century reputation, and frequently offers an effective gloss on many of Herbert's images, as well as a key to understanding Herbert's diction and wit. In chapter 5, "Herberts Rezeption im Zeitalter der Aufklärung und des Neoklassizismus" (pp. 155–206), comments on Herbert's late seventeenth- and eighteenth-century reception, especially among hymn writers, such as John Gambold and Charles and John Wesley, and among anthologists, such as William Dillingham, Simon Patrick, and Thomas Haywood. Notes that the general attitude toward Herbert's poetry was mixed: readers often admired Herbert's piety but found his style rather quaint. Illustrates this point by showing how a number of poems were stylistically altered to suit the religious and aesthetic tastes of the time. Conclusion (pp. 207–8), followed by an appendix that lists poems discussed by Ryley and contained in this study (pp. 209–10), abbreviations (p. 211), notes (pp. 213–69), and an extensive primary and secondary bibliography (pp. 271–91).
Reviews:
Inge Leimberg, *Archiv* 217 (1980): 420–23
C. F. Williamson, *RES* 31 (1980): 461–66

**1159. Labriola, Albert C.** "Herbert, Crashaw, and the *Schola Cordis* Tradition." *GHJ* 2, no. 1:13–23.

Discusses the influence of the *schola cordis* tradition on the poetry of Herbert and Crashaw and maintains that their reliance on the tradition indicates that there are often more resemblances than differences between Catholic and Protestant devotional poetry of the seventeenth century. Comments specifically on how both poets use the tradition to create images that have "complex and profound meanings and insights far exceeding those of cardiomorphic icons" found in emblem books and maintains that "these meanings and insights are directly related to the perception of the speaker, the diversity of his attitudes, and the range of his tone" (p. 15). Points out five major characteristics of *schola cordis* poetry: (1) the quotation or paraphrasing of scriptural passages that refer to the human heart, (2) a reflection of a typological perspective into biblical history, (3) an emphasis on Christ's Paschal mystery, (4) allusion to the sacramental celebration of the Paschal mystery, and (5) an acknowledgment of the importance of liturgical and communal worship. Presents a detailed reading of Herbert's "The Bunch of Grapes," observing that the poem "demonstrates the interrelation of essential characteristics of *schola cordis* poetry: the human heart as *locus* in which man's changing relationship with the Lord is understood and experienced, typological relationships between Old and New Testaments, the paramount importance of the Paschal or redemptive mystery, and the efficacy of liturgical and sacramental celebration" (pp. 20–21).

**1160. Lewalski, Barbara K.** "Emblems and the Religious Lyric: George Herbert and Protestant Emblematics." *HUSL* 6:32–56.

Emphasizes that religious emblem books were not just a Jesuit enterprise, but a Protestant one as well, and argues that Herbert, more than his contemporaries, "made the most extensive, complex, profound, and creative use of sacred, and especially Protestant, emblematics" (p. 33). Distinguishes Protestant emblematics from others, claiming that they drew their mottoes and figures directly from scriptural metaphors and thus "base their emblems directly upon the true wit of God's emblematic Word" (p. 34). Identifies five kinds of emblem books, calling the "School of the Heart" books of greatest importance for Herbert. Distinguishes Roman Catholic sequences from Protestant ones on the basis that the latter "present God acting upon the heart, not within it" (p. 40). Discusses poems from *The Church* that seem to allude to specific emblems—"The Flower," "Hope," "The Church-floore," and "The Altar"—and argues that *The Church*, as a whole, is a kind of Protestant "School of the Heart" book, "both in its general conception and in regard to the imagery of particular poems and passages," noting that "the governing biblical metaphor" in *The Temple* is "the temple in the heart of man" (p. 44), most clearly developed in "Sion." Points out also that emblem plates of the Protestants Heyns and Haeftenus and especially Cramer and Mannich serve as analogues to "Sion," "The Familie," "Decay," "The Altar," "Jesu," "Redemption," "Longing," "Discipline," "An Offering," and "Love unknown." Concludes that *The Temple* "reflects certain emphases in Protestant emblem-making," namely, the "literal and pictorial rendering of prominent biblical metaphors," an organization based on the "New Testament Temple in the heart of man," and a "random arrangement of poems" that suggests that the Christian life is not "an ordered progress by set stages to spiritual perfection" (p. 48).

**1161. Linden, Stanton J.** "Herbert and the Unveiling of Diana: Stanza Three of 'Vanitie (I).'" *GHJ* 1, no. 2:30–37.

Maintains that the scattered references to alchemy in *The Temple*, "though precise and effective," are "usually uncomplex and obviously derived from commonplaces of alchemical thought" (p. 30). Argues, however, that the reference to the "subtil Chymick" in the third stanza of "Vanitie (I)" is probably derived from "a figure common in several species of seventeenth-century literature where it is employed to render vividly the enlightened investigator's search for knowledge which will result either in discovery of the philosopher's stone or enable him to assume authority and control over nature in the largest sense" but that, "in transferring this image to a religious poem on the theme of vanity, Herbert emphasizes only the destructiveness of the Chymick's quest" (p. 35). Maintains that the poet intends the reader "to perceive the arrogance and presumptuousness of his 'subtil' empiricist's penetration into a private sanctuary that is the domain of the chaste, modest, and divine Diana, the exploited 'creature,' nature, of stanza three" (p. 35).

1162. Low, Anthony. *Love's Architecture: Devotional Modes in Seventeenth-Century English Poetry.* (The Gotham Library Series.) New York: New York University Press. xix, 307p.

Discusses and classifies modes of devotion that influenced seventeenth-century poetry. Maintains that poems in *The Temple* are "mixtures of speech and song" and that, "devotionally, they are skillful blends of mental devotion and vocal prayer" (p. 31). Chapter 4, "George Herbert: Varieties of Devotion" (pp. 82–115), surveys the poetic and devotional techniques of Herbert. Comments on the pervasive influence of music on Herbert's poetic style and discusses the hymns on the Christian year, including "Christmas," "Lent," "Easter," "Whitsunday," and "Trinitie Sunday." Also notes the striking visual elements of these poems. Classifies some of lyrics as hymns and psalms, genres of both meditation and song, and notes that, although some contemporary musical settings have survived, none of Herbert's have. Comments on the variety of devotional and poetic forms in *The Temple*. Discusses in detail the opening sequence of *The Church*, composed of ten poems. Notes that, beginning with "The Altar," which reminds the reader of God's transformation of the speaker, the sequence moves to "The Sacrifice," "a ritual monologue, Christ's lament to sinful man" (p. 94); then, in "The Thanksgiving," the poet addresses Christ in response to His suffering but appears to fail, whereas in "The Reprisall" he succeeds in creating a song while admitting there is no way to deal adequately with Christ's passion. Observes that "The Agonie" becomes a formal meditation, first on the passion, then on communion, where "the private returns to the liturgical" (p. 97) and that "The Sinner" is an examination of conscience, moving from sin in general to the sinner in particular, but at the same time addressing Christ. Observes that in "Good Friday" the speaker returns to the liturgical and emblematic mode and shows how "Redemption," "Sepulchre," "Easter," and "Easter-wings" complete the sequence. Points out other sequences in *The Temple*. Argues that in "The Search," "Grief," "The Crosse," and "The Flower" Herbert "pierces deeper into the spiritual life than anywhere else in *The Temple*" (p. 103). Maintains that these poems suggest that he either underwent a mystical experience or, at least, borrowed the "traditional language and modes of devotion that mystics used to express themselves" (p. 104). Finds in the first three poems of this sequence a sense of desolation but in the last poem a sense of freshness and relief. Concludes by noting that in *The Temple* "the variety of mood, technique, genre, and devotional mode is extraordinary" and that Herbert was "equally adept at psalm or hymn, petition, celebration, or complaint, song or speech, meditation or contemplation" (p. 114). Compares and contrasts throughout the entire study Herbert's poetic techniques and devotional modes with those of Donne, Vaughan, Crashaw, Herrick, Marvell, and Traherne.

1163. ———. "Metaphysical Poets and Devotional Poets," in *George Herbert and the Seventeenth-Century Religious Poets: Authoritative Texts/Criticism*, edited by Mario Di Cesare, 221–32. (A Norton Critical Edition.) New York: W. W. Norton.

Discusses the major characteristics of metaphysical poetry, such as masculine expression, naturalness and familiarity of tone, the combination of intellect and feeling, orderly or logical development, sense of drama or process, an interest in the inner movements of thought and feeling, private versus public mode, and the uses of the conceit. Discusses also devotional practices in the seventeenth century, such as vocal prayer, discursive meditation, and contemplation, and comments on how these devotional modes shaped and informed the religious poetry of the age. Compares and contrasts Herbert with Donne, Crashaw, Vaughan, Marvell, and Traherne. Maintains that Herbert's poems "deal mainly with the private relationship of the individual soul to God" and that most of his lyrics "reflect the complex and subtle processes, changes of attitude, struggles, and surrenders of the inner spiritual life" (p. 224). Praises Herbert for his wit, his strength and directness, his sense of drama, his ability to use conventional elements in new and passionate ways, the homeliness of his images—his "inimitable style" (p. 229). Comments briefly on the artistic success of several individual poems or parts of poems, such as "The Agonie," "Redemption," "The Collar," "Vertue," "Affliction (I)," "Deniall," "Dooms-day," "Sunday," "The Pilgrimage," "Death," "Judgement," and "Love (III)."

**1164. Marcus, Leah Sinanoglou.** "The Poet as Child: Herbert, Herrick, and Crashaw," in *Childhood and Cultural Despair: A Theme and Variations in Seventeenth-Century Literature*, 94–152. Pittsburgh: University of Pittsburgh Press.

Argues that Herbert uses the persona of a child in his poetry in a very sophisticated fashion, presenting a devout Christian as one who moves from "pride and intellectual searching to an acceptance of the 'narrow path' of mute, childlike humility" (p. 94). Compares Herbert's child persona with those of Herrick and Crashaw and sees Herbert's child as a form of aesthetic release, while in Herrick and Crashaw the child is more a form of self-imprisonment. Reviews Herbert's biography to show that the saintly legend that arose about him was not totally accurate and contends that, when he chose to restrict his life to the house of God, he gave up worldly interests, such as learning, honor, science, and doctrinal dispute. Argues that, aware of spiritual pride, Herbert asked to be made a child in spirit. Maintains that "H. Baptisme (I)" and "H. Baptisme (II)" are poems of the sacrament that make men anew, or like children, and finds the latter poem to be a key one "because it establishes Herbert's *persona* of child" (p. 104). Contends that Herbert's lapse into pride is seen in "The Collar," in which his rebellious will is subdued by a call of "child" that returns him to a dependence on God. Observes that in "Dialogue" the speaker has a rebellious intellect and that again he resigns himself to being a child of God. Maintains that often Herbert's rebellion and pride take the form of excessive language and that he then realizes that he must learn to "pare down his language from gaudy excess to humble plainness" (p. 107), as seen in "The Quip," "The Quidditie," "Jordan (I and II)," and "The Posie." Argues that, although Herbert rejects stylistic artifice motivated by pride, he finds linguistic playfulness, when sanctified by grace, a form of praise, as in "The Altar" and "Easter-wings." Maintains that in "Love (III)" the childlike persona is exalted into the honored guest at the sacrament of the altar. Contends that "within individual poems and from one poem to another, Herbert fights against his chosen role, then reaccepts it and merges it almost imperceptibly with other roles, then forgets and struggles again" but that "overarching this daily battle is the serene confidence that the battle is already won" (pp. 117–18).

**1165. Onizuka, Keiichi.** "Ningen to Kami tono Kankei—*The Church* ni miru George Herbert no Baai" [On the Relationship between Man and God—In the Case of George Herbert in *The Church*]. *Kyushu Daigaku Eigo Eibungaku Ronso* [Studies in English Language and Literature, Kyushu University], no. 28:1–19.

Discusses the relationship between man and God in such poems as "The Thanksgiving," "The Reprisall," and "Love (III)" in which the speaker emulates God in the act of love. Concludes that Herbert ultimately found himself reconciled with God's will so as to have the full assurance that he would be received by God with love, as he describes in "Love (III)."

**1166. Pebworth, Ted-Larry, and Claude J. Summers.** "Recovering an Important Seventeenth-Century Poetical Miscellany: Cambridge Add. MS 4138." *TCBS* 7:156–69.

Describes Cambridge Add. MS. 4138, an early seventeenth-century poetical miscellany given to Cambridge University Library in 1894 by Samuel Sandars that includes the texts of several poems that antedate their first printings and that presents new evidence for the authorship of a number of poems of doubtful attribution. Points out that the compiler of the manuscript, a student or fellow at Cambridge between 1610 and 1631, was conservative in assigning attributions and argues that his attributing to Herbert "To the Queene of Bohemia" and its accompanying "L'Envoy" is "a more compelling reason than any so far offered for identifying George Herbert as author of these 80 lines" (p. 163). Also points out that, although Herbert was not personally acquainted with the Queen of Bohemia, he contributed two poems, one of which was an epithalamium, to a volume of Latin poetry that was compiled for her husband when he visited Cambridge in 1613 (see entry 575) and that Herbert's friend and immediate predecessor as Public Orator at Cambridge, Sir Francis Nethersole, was appointed English secretary to the Queen in 1619. Maintains that the two poems, likely written in late 1621 or early 1622 to console the Queen for the loss of Bohemia and the Palatinate, are "not masterpieces" but are "fine examples of political poetry" that are "not unworthy of George Herbert" (pp. 163–64). See also Ted-Larry Pebworth (entry 1211).

**1167. Ray, Robert H.** "Spatial and Aural Patterns in 'The Windows.'" *GHJ* 1, no. 2:38–43.

Argues that "The Windows" is the last in a logical grouping of three poems, preceded by "Church-lock and key" and "The Church-floore," and shows that in the poem the light of God that comes through the chancel windows symbolically "provides absolution for the sinner who has come through the door" (p. 39). Maintains that the three poems prepare the reader "to visualize the preacher, elevated in the chancel, facing the altar and the windows, and addressing God in the first line of 'The Windows'" (p. 39). Observes that each stanza of the poem divides into three parts and has a spatial movement—"from God (beyond the windows) to the preacher (in the chancel) to the congregation (in the nave)"—and that the increasingly emphatic use of nasal sounds counterpoints with the visual images until in the last stanza "the perfect fusion of vision and sound is reached, both in the poem and in the preacher" (p. 41).

**1168. Roberts, John R.** *George Herbert: An Annotated Bibliography of Modern Criticism, 1905–1974.* (University of Missouri Studies, 68.) Columbia & London: University of Missouri Press. xv, 280p.

Lists alphabetically by year and fully annotates eight hundred books, essays, monographs, and notes written on Herbert from 1905 (the date of Palmer's edition) through 1974. Includes extended discussions of Herbert that appear in books and essays not centrally concerned with him, editions that contain significant critical discussion, and numerous items in languages other than English. Excludes mentions of Herbert in books and articles, references in encyclopedias and literary histories, book reviews, and doctoral dissertations. In addition to a preface (p. ix-xii), abbreviations of titles of journals (pp. xiii-xv), contains three indexes—author, subject, and Herbert's works mentioned in the annotations. All items have been included in the present bibliography.

Reviews:

Albert C. Labriola, *Cithara* 18, no. 1 (1978): 84–85
Jerry Leath Mills, *AEB* (Winter 1979): 57–58
C. A. Patrides, *SCN* 37 (1979): 73
Ted-Larry Pebworth, *GHJ* 2, no. 2 (1979): 44–49
Joseph H. Summers *RQ* 32 (1979): 440–42
Gordon Williams, *Library* series 6, 1 (1979): 387
Fram Dinshaw, *RES* 31 (1980): 346–48
Daniel W. Doerksen, *Ren&R* n.s. 4 (1980): 117–19
Robert Ellrodt, *EA* 39 (1986): 94

**1169. Rogers, Robert.** *Metaphor: A Psychoanalytic View.* Berkeley, Los Angeles, and London: University of California Press. x, 148p.

Discusses "the coordinate operations of the primary and secondary processes characteristic of human responses to complex language in such a fashion as to develop an hypothesis about the way ambiguity helps to generate synergistic patterns of thought and emotion" (p. 55). Uses, as an example, "Vertue" (pp. 55–58) and comments on the possible unconscious responses of the reader to the sensual and/or erotic undercurrents in the poem, especially to the image of the rose in the second stanza. Discusses also the subtle and very indirect anal and sexual implications in "The Rose" (pp. 125–28) and maintains that the poem "produces endopsychic tension commensurate with the gravity of its subject by setting up a series of oppositions between conscious, conventional meanings and unconscious, psychosexual 'affective correlatives' of the imagery" (p. 127). Maintains that rose imagery "reveals a full spectrum of the range of meanings possible within the framework of modal ambiguity" (p. 128).

**1170. Schabert, Ina.** "Zur Ideologie der poetischen Sprachstrukturierung: George Herbert und Byron." *Anglia* 96:387–408.

Discusses the ideology of poetic-language structuring by contrasting Herbert and Byron. Argues that the difference between the two poets is a result of their quite different views of the world and human existence. Maintains that Herbert regards artistic creation as an imitation of the God-created cosmos and as a reactualization of the harmony of creation as intended by God and suggests that Herbert's major achievement is the integration, in an especially intensive way, of poetic form with his view of the universe. Maintains that Byron, on the other hand, strives to create an aesthetically structured work, which holds together formally, in opposition to a reality that he perceives as senseless and chaotic.

**1171. Simpson, David L.** "Herbert's 'Vertue.'" *Expl* 37, no. 1:46–47.

Suggests that the phrase "season'd timber" in "Vertue" (line 14) means "not merely 'aged' timber, but timber that has been carefully tempered, ripened, and hardened in order that it might fulfill a specific purpose"; thus "a virtuous soul is like seasoned timber not only in being 'sweet' and 'powerful' but also in being supremely fitted to achieve its proper end" (p. 47). Points out also that the phrase may allude to the biblical cedars of Lebanon that "were considered the only material fit for building a lasting temple to God" and "were renowned for their strength and durability but also for their fragrance" (p. 47). Suggests that Herbert borrowed the image from "The Song of Solomon" in which it appears several times. Notes that both the biblical song and "Vertue" contain the same prominent images—"a bridal, roses, night and day, music, various fragrances and spices, timber, and coal" (p. 47).

**1172. Strier, Richard.** "Changing the Object: Herbert and Excess." *GHJ* 2, no. 1:24–37.

Contrasts Herbert's and Crashaw's uses of the sensual, especially the sexual, in positive religious contexts and argues that Herbert "does not participate at all in the Counter-Reformation cultivation of ecstasy, in the campaign to 'change the object, not the passion'" (p. 28). Argues that Herbert's poems, unlike Crashaw's, tend to end in praise, not ecstasy, and they do not court pain for the purpose of self-immolation but rather plead for an end of pain or ask God to allow him to endure and derive some spiritual good from the undesired experience. Reads "Bitter-sweet" not as reflecting "Teresan yearning," as Malcolm Ross suggests (entry 434), but as "something understood." Notes that "The Invitation" is an exception, for it presents sinners who have all the right instincts but who seek satisfaction in the wrong places. Reads the five stanzas of the poem as an invitation to all sinners to receive the Eucharist, which "seems to fall into the characteristically Roman error of treating the Eucharist as a 'converting' rather than a confirming ordinance" (p. 32). Maintains that the poem seems to posit the poet's opinion about sinners rather than God's opinion. Explains this uncharacteristic stance of Herbert by seeing the poem as linked with "The Banquet," which presents the joy of the poet at God's feast. Sees "The Invitation" in relation to "The Banquet" as really a "celebration rather than statement" (p. 34) and thus not alien to Protestant theology and not at all reflecting Teresan ecstasy.

**1173. Sugimoto, Ryutaro.** "George Herbert no Shi—Dento to Kosei" [The Poetry of George Herbert—Tradition and Originality]. *Osaka Joshi Daigaku Joshi Dai Bungaku* [Women's College Literature, Osaka Women's College], no. 3 (March): 21–36.

Discusses the characteristics of Herbert's poetry in the light of its tradition and its place in the so-called metaphysical school of poets.

**1174. Summers, Joseph.** "From 'Joseph's Coat' to 'A true Hymne.'" *GHJ* 2, no. 1:1–12.

Argues that one of the best ways to understand and appreciate Herbert's poetry is "to consider a sequence of poems in the order in which Herbert finally arranged them," for "such a consideration suggests not only the variety of forms and moods and tones of Herbert's poems, but also the ways in which he relates them to each other and created from them a moving emblem of the fluctuations of mood and achievement in the spiritual life" (p. 1). Considers a sequence beginning with "Josephs coat" and ending with "A true Hymne" that includes "The Pulley," "The Priesthood," "The Search," "Grief," "The Crosse," "The Flower," "Dotage," and "The Sonne" and maintains that these poems, which are concerned with grief, disorder, and a sense of God's absence, are held together by an underlying paradox: "if the expression were absolute, poetry would be impossible" but "so long as the poet can create a poem, he remembers or imagines or believes in or anticipates or is inspired by an order and value which reflect the divine" (p. 4). Observes that Herbert's poems often contain a "sub-text" that "seems to say something quite different from the primary or surface text" (p. 6). Maintains, however, that these "sub-texts" "no more undercut or destroy the 'texts' than the Resurrection denies or casts doubt upon the reality of the Crucifixion" but rather put them "in a larger, more nearly complete context—as if we viewed an event simultaneously in the lights of both time and eternity" (p. 7).

1175. **Yoder, R. A.** "First Poetic Fruits," in *Emerson and the Orphic Poet in America*, 77–88. Berkeley, Los Angeles, and London: University of California Press.

Discusses Herbert's influence on Emerson's poetry and maintains that in his early poems Emerson "appears to have taken Herbert as a specific model for poetic form" (p. 87). Notes direct borrowings from "Sinne (I)" in Emerson's "Grace" and observes that "the drudge in dusty frock" in Emerson's "Art" reminds one of the servant in "The Elixir."

1176. **Yule, Christine.** "The Art of Praise: The Poetry of George Herbert," in *From Dante to Solzhenitsyn: Essays on Christianity and Literature*, edited by Robert M. Yule, 73–95. Wellington: Tertiary Christian Studies Programme.

Biographical sketch of Herbert and general introduction to his lyric poetry. Maintains that *The Church* is "a personal diary showing all the undulations of a Christian's mood and spiritual experience" (p. 78). Stresses that Herbert's poems, like everything else in his life, were intended to praise God: "His art is not for art's sake, but for God's sake in God's praise" (p. 85). Discusses "Church-monuments," "Vertue," "The Flower," and "A Wreath" as examples of Herbert's consummate artistry and profound religious sensibility.

# *1979*

1177. **Barker, Arthur E.** *The Seventeenth Century: Bacon Through Marvell.* (Goldentree Bibliographies in Language and Literature, ed. O. B. Hardison, Jr.) Arlington Heights, Ill.: AHM Publishing Co. xi, 132p.

Unannotated, selected bibliography of studies on seventeenth-century English poetry and prose to 1975 (excluding Milton, Dryden, the drama, and dissertations). In addition to entries for thirty-nine authors, includes aids to research, major anthologies, general studies of literary history and criticism, and studies in backgrounds. Lists 14 modern editions, 4 bibliographies, 1 concordance, and 112 items of criticism for Herbert (pp. 68–74), all of which appear in this bibliography.

1178. **Bienz, John.** "George Herbert and the Man of Sorrows." *HSL* 11:173–84.

Comments on the visual or pictorial tradition of the Man of Sorrows from the late thirteenth century to the early seventeenth. Observes that the suffering Christ was often portrayed as a miraculous vision, appearing on the altar in pictures and in woodcuts that depict the legend of the Mass of St. Gregory. Argues that knowledge and appreciation of these combined traditions contribute to an understanding of the positioning of "The Altar" and "The Sacrifice" at the opening of *The Church* and of the content of the long narrative poem. Maintains that the traditional depiction of the Man of Sorrows, the pictorial representation of him in pictures of the miracle of the Mass of St. Gregory, the *Improperia* from the Good Friday liturgy, and the traditional Complaint of Christ poem "form a context for the opening poems of *The Temple*" (p. 182).

1179. **Booty, John E.** "George Herbert: *The Temple* and *The Book of Common Prayer*." *Mosaic* 12, no. 2:75–90.

Discusses Herbert's experience of *The Book of Common Prayer* in his daily life— from his baptism to his death—and comments on its pervasive influence on his poems.

Maintains that it is useful to read Herbert's poems in relation to Richard Hooker's *Of the Lawes of Ecclesiasticall Politie: The fifth Booke* (1597), which is "a commentary on the Prayer Book, as well as a defense of it against Puritan objections" (p. 76). Notes that the structure of *The Temple* reflects the influence of the Prayer Book and Anglican spirituality: "The Prayer Book Eucharist is structured about the contrition-praise sequence, and *The Temple* has a similar structure, for it opens with a kind of self-examination, leading to contrition expressed in 'The Altar' and 'The Sacrifice,' and it closes in 'The Church' portion with the climactic 'Love (III)' and a *gloria*" (p. 81). Points out that *The Temple* also contains matin and evensong poems and poems about the daily offices of the Church, as well as poems on praise, prayer, and the Holy Scriptures—all of which contain "evidence of the Prayer Book rhythm of contrition and praise" with an "emphasis on the perpetual intercourse of heaven and earth" (p. 83). Notes that in "De S. Baptisimi Ritu" Herbert defends the Prayer Book rites and that in "De oratione Dominica" he defends the Prayer Book's use of the Lord's Prayer against Puritan criticism. Observes that, following the dictates of the Prayer Book, Herbert acknowledged only Baptism and Holy Communion as sacraments and wrote with theological precision about each. Concludes that the Prayer Book "reflects the fundamental human rhythm of contrition and praise, but it also inspires and feeds it" and that *The Temple* "represents the Christian's struggle with those human emotions, inspired and fed by the church's liturgy, and by so doing helps the Christian reader to perceive more fully the true nature of humanity and the transforming power of grace mediated by the Word and the Sacraments" (p. 89).

1180. **Breiner, Laurence A.** "Herbert's Cockatrice." *MP* 77:10–17.
Points out that George Ripley, the fifteenth-century pioneer of English alchemy, in his *Compound of Alchymie* adopted the term *cockatrice* "as a native synonym for the 'basilisk' of continental alchemy, where that word indicated the final stage in the procedure by which the Philosopher's Stone was achieved" (p. 11). Maintains that in line 4 of "Sinnes round" Herbert uses the word in its technical sense and argues that the term brings together the monstrous, fiery, and uroboric features of the poem in a way that the mythological cockatrice cannot. Points out that, together with the references to "the Sicilian hill" or Mount Etna (line 8) and Babel (line 15), the alchemical cockatrice represents "sinful passion issuing in action" (p. 16). Concludes that, although there is no concrete evidence that Herbert was familiar with the alchemical cockatrice, "the language of the stanza in which the word appears suggests alchemy" and the alchemical cockatrice "hatches from fire as the ordinary cockatrice does not" and that since the cockatrice of alchemy "was frequently envisioned as having its tail in its mouth, the creature reflects the circular form of the poem, and so reinforces the representation of its subject, the repetitious cycle of sin" (p. 17). Briefly comments on other poems in which Herbert shows an interest in alchemy, such as "Easter," "Vanitie (I)," "Providence," and "The Elixir."

1181. **Cameron, Sharon.** "*Et in Arcadia Ego*: Representation, Death, and the Problem of Boundary," in *Lyric Time: Dickinson and the Limits of Genre*, 91–135. Baltimore and London: Johns Hopkins University Press.
Discusses the fusions (such as that of past and present, earth and heaven, the speaker as an individual and as a spokesman for everyman) and boundary crossings (such as the speaker's journey to heaven even though he has not yet died, his search for Christ before he could possibly know Christ) in "Redemption" and argues that their effect is twofold: "first, to cast the problem of man's salvation in inescapably

personal terms that bring him into direct and literal relationship with Christ so that he finds himself both the explicit cause of the sacrifice and its only beneficiary; and second, to depict both the petition and its granting as unalterably present tense" (p. 127).

**1182. [Charles, Amy M., ed.]** *Cross-Bias: The Newsletter of the Friends of Bemerton Society*, no. 5 (August). 5p.

Comments on a medlar tree reputedly planted by Herbert in the garden of the rectory at Bemerton, several saplings of which are now planted on the grounds of the University of North Carolina at Greensboro; announces the death of Dr. J. D. K. Lloyd, well-known Montgomeryshire historian; comments on recent developments in the parish at Bemerton; announces papers on Herbert given at recent conferences and other items of Herbertiana; lists some recent and prospective publications on Herbert and gives a description of a Ph.D. thesis on Herbert's reputation in the seventeenth and eighteenth centuries by Helen Wilcox.

**1183. Daly, Peter M.** *Literature in the Light of the Emblem: Structural Parallels between the Emblem and Literature in the Sixteenth and Seventeenth Centuries.* Toronto, Buffalo, London: Toronto University Press. xiv, 245p.

Introduction to the study of emblematic structure in English and German literature of the sixteenth and seventeenth centuries. Chapter 1, "The Emblem" (pp. 3–53), discusses the origins and nature of emblem books, comments on forerunners of the emblem, and surveys recent critical developments in emblem theory, especially endorsing the work of Albrecht Schöne in *Emblematik und Drama im Zeitalter des Barock* (Stuttgart, 1964; 2d ed., 1968). Chapter 2, "The Word-Emblem" (pp. 54–102), discusses the forms and functions of emblematic imagery in English and German literature. Chapter 3, "Emblematic Poetry" (pp. 103–33), chapter 4, "Emblematic Drama" (pp. 134–67), and chapter 5, "Emblematic Prose Narrative" (pp. 168–84), comment on the structural affinities between the emblem and poetry, drama, and prose fiction. Brief conclusion (pp. 185–88), notes (pp. 189–223), and selected bibliography (pp. 224–33), followed by an index of names (pp. 235–39) and an index of emblematic motifs (pp. 241–45). Mentions Herbert's use of emblematic imagery and structures throughout, primarily endorsing and quoting from the work of Rosemary Freeman (entry 337). Discusses the close relationship between emblematic poetry and pattern poems and briefly comments on "Easter-wings," endorsing the critical comments of Cedric Brown and W. P. Ingoldsby (entry 893).

**1184. D'Amico, Jack.** *Petrarch in England: An Anthology of Parallel Texts from Wyatt to Milton.* (Speculum Artium 5, edited by Aldo Scaglione.) Ravenna: Longo Editore. 202p.

Anthologizes English Renaissance poems that bear either directly or indirectly some recognizable thematic relationship to specific poems by Petrarch (printed in Italian with literal translations into English). Parallels Herbert's "Josephs coat" and Petrarch's Sonnet 134 ("Pace non trovo e non ho da far guerra") and also "My God, where is that ancient heat towards thee" from Walton's *Lives* and Petrarch's Sonnet 153 ("Ite, caldi sospiri, al freddo cote").

**1185. Dickey, Harold A.** "Herbert's 'The Collar': Rope of Sands." *AN&Q* 17:157–58.

Argues that Herbert may be thinking of an obsolete meaning of the word *sand* ("ordinance" or "message" sent by God) in the phrase "rope of sands" in "The

Collar" (line 22). Maintains that the speaker, a rebellious priest, "finds he has built himself good cable out of a collection of church ordinances" (p. 157). Argues that, by using an obsolete meaning of *sands*, the speaker "could be suggesting the obsoleteness of the church ordinances themselves" (p. 157). Acknowledges, however, that throughout the poem "the real constraint is inward and unified in the love of God and not in a set of ordinances exerting merely external constraint" (p. 157). Concludes that "using the obsolete *sands* may very well be a crucial step in the rebellious priest's learning about himself" (p. 158).

**1186. Doerksen, Daniel W.** "Nicholas Ferrar, Arthur Woodnoth, and the Publication of George Herbert's *The Temple*, 1633." *GHJ* 3, nos. 1–2 (1979–1980): 22–44.

Argues that letters (now in the collection known as the Ferrar Papers at Magdalene College, Cambridge) exchanged in 1633 between Nicholas Ferrar and his cousin Arthur Woodnoth, who was the executor of Herbert's will, support Walton's claim in his *Lives* that Edmund Duncon was involved in the transmission of Herbert's poems to Ferrar. Maintains that the correspondence also establishes that *The Temple* first appeared "about early September, 1633"; that comments in Woodnoth's letters "affected the tone and contents of Ferrar's influential preface" to the poems; and that the transmission of the poems through Duncon to Ferrar "caused difficulties in the otherwise close and cordial relationship between Ferrar and Woodnoth" (p. 23).

**1187. El-Gabalawy, Saad.** "Personification and Fable in George Herbert's Allegories." *ESC* 5:24–35.

Explains Herbert's "creative use of personification and fable as means of illustration, persuasion and 'delightful instruction'" (p. 24). Defines and differentiates allegory, prosopopoeia, and personification, using "Sunday," "The Church-floore," and "The World" to emphasize the distinctions. Discusses the uses of personification in "The Quip" and contrasts Herbert's more realistic and concrete usage with that of Spenser. Discusses the allegory in "Confession" and observes that, "though Herbert's allegories emanate from the wide and indefinite realities of inner experience, he always has in view their moral or homiletical value" (p. 30). Discusses the variety of allegorical narratives in Herbert's poems, ranging from animal fable to fantasy. Comments on "Humilitie" as an example of the former and "Love unknown" as an example of the latter. Concludes that, "through personification and fable, Herbert gives expression to his vital beliefs and translates the timeless values of the Christian ideology into concrete, narrative terms" (p. 34).

**1188. Engel, Wilson F., III.** "Christ in the Winepress: Backgrounds of a Sacred Image." *GHJ* 3, nos. 1–2 (1979–1980): 45–63.

Surveys the variety of meanings and associations of the image or motif of Christ in the winepress. Maintains that the Bible "provides the links between the winepress image and four key moments in sacred history: the Passion, the Last Judgment, Christ's Resurrection, and the Salvation of Man" (p. 47) and cites as the most important biblical *loci* Rev. 14:19–20 and 19:15, Lam. 1:15, Psalms 8:1 and 80:1, and especially Isa. 63:2–3. Notes that the image was also reinforced by classical iconography in which Bacchus, the god of wine, was seen as a Christ figure. Discusses the many ways in which the image was used in Patristic and Reformation commentary, in English liturgy and sermons, and in religious poetry, noting that "the many aspects of Christ in the Winepress were so pervasively part of the vocabulary of the seventeenth century that clear examples of allusion to it can be found with great ease" (p. 54).

Discusses in particular Herbert's use of the image in "The Agonie," in which the winemaking process makes clear "the cost of human salvation in terms of Christ's suffering" and "the enormous burden of man's sins on Christ in stanza 2 reminds the readers of the dangerous complicity of man in the Passion's cruelty" (p. 56). Compares and contrasts Herbert's use of the image in "The Agonie" and its use by such poets as Robert Southwell, Henry Vaughan, and especially Milton.

**1189. Gillham, D. G.** "Five Studies in Metaphor." *ESA* 22:57–69.

Discusses the metaphor of the preacher as church windows in "The Windows" to show that it "is worked out in detail, but with a quietness of tone that makes it impossible to label it a conceit" and to demonstrate how it "unobtrusively carries the weight of an extensive and fairly complex comparison" (p. 57). Argues that in "The Windows" Herbert uses "a single metaphor, develops it, and never lets it go" and thus the poem "has a unity, not only of figurative development, but in completeness of understanding" (p. 59). Concludes that "The Windows" "is fully metaphorical because the comparison made is more than superficially apt" and has "an extensive effect in causing us to see new features in the object of study, or to reappraise those seen before" (p. 60).

**1190. Gordon, David J.** "Herbert's 'The Collar.'" *PMLA* 94:324–25.

In a letter to the editor calls Barbara Harman's essay "The Fiction of Coherence: George Herbert's 'The Collar'" (entry 1150) "willfully naïve" and "antipsychological with a vengeance" (p. 325). Maintains that her interpretation is like "knocking down a straw man to call one perspective within a poem a self and then show it to be illusory or incomplete" and points out that "surely the central effect of Herbert's 'The Collar' is not the incommensurability of the parts but the very *turn* from the wonderfully drawn-out raving to the sudden awe" (p. 325). Maintains that readers are not deceived by the change in attitude on the part of the speaker but expect it and draw pleasure from it. For a reply, see Barbara Harman (entry 1191).

**1191. Harman, Barbara Leah.** "Herbert's 'The Collar.'" *PMLA* 94:325–26.

A reply to David J. Gordon (entry 1190). Claims that Gordon wishes to have a single presence in control of the representation he pictures and to see the poem as dramatizations of issues long since resolved. Calls this point of view "psychological simplicity," that is, "the insistence that the self is a master of all situations, that it is able to subsume all representations, to neutralize opposition, to own all versions of experience" (p. 325). Claims that Herbert's poems "resist this ideology of the well-ordered self" and instead acknowledge "both the desire for mastery and ownership and their ultimate inaccessibility" (p. 325).

**1192. ———.** "Herbert's 'The Collar.'" *PMLA* 94:947–48.

A reply to David J. Leigh (entry 1201). Accepts Leigh's biblical citations but claims that they do not alter her reading of "The Collar." Maintains that the biblical implications enter the poem later, not when the interior story is being told: "The drama and pathos of this poem are products of the discrepancy the speaker feels between his limited vision and the larger vision—sacramental and biblical—that finally surrounds and claims him" (p. 948). Argues that, if the story of the Prodigal Son stands behind the poem, we need to question what "standing behind" really means: "If biblical stories determine the outcome of personal stories in progress, we need to explore the implications of that fact for poetic speakers" (p. 948). Rejects Leigh's notion that "The Collar" is a simple poem and claims that its difficulties will not be "neutralized by the discovery that everything is already there in Scripture" (p. 948).

**1193. Hayes, T. Wilson.** "The Darkening Cloud," in *Winstanley the Digger: A Literary Analysis of Radical Ideas in the English Revolution*, 46–87. Cambridge, Mass., and London: Harvard University Press.

Compares and contrasts Herbert to the seventeenth-century pamphleteer Gerrard Winstanley. Argues that, like Winstanley, Herbert "has a way of 'drawing out' his soul's affliction, intensifying and objectifying it until he wraps his reader in a cocoon of self-identifying misery" and then "bursts into a cathartic release centered on an acceptance of God's mercy" (pp. 61–62). Maintains that Winstanley would have approved of Herbert's rejection of poetic adornment and quaintness and finds that both men shared "a perception of how moral reformation is linked to the reformation of language" (p. 63). Maintains that some of Herbert's most successful poems "show his engagements with the harsh facts of social reality" (p. 62) and often have political overtones and implications.

**1194. Huntley, Frank L.** "What Happened to George Herbert's Poem 'Good Friday'?" *ELWIU* 6:161–66.

Reprinted in revised and expanded form in "What Happened to Two of Herbert's Poems?" in *Essays in Persuasion: On Seventeenth-Century English Literature* (entry 1292), 65–76.

On the basis of textual history, manuscript evidence, and a knowledge of both the development of *The Temple* and the religious and poetic sensibilities of its author, argues that "Good Friday" should be divided into two separate poems (as it is in the Williams manuscript); that the second part, consisting of the last three stanzas of the poem, should be entitled "The Passion" (as it is in the Williams manuscript); and that the three-stanza poem should be restored to its original position before "Redemption" and the first five stanzas of the present "Good Friday," not after it.

**1195. Huxley, Herbert H.** "The Latin Poems of George Herbert (1593–1633)," in *Acta Conventus Neo-Latini Amstelodamensis*, Proceedings of the Second International Congress of Neo-Latin Studies (Amsterdam, 19–24 August 1973), edited by P. Tuynman, G. C. Kuiper, and E. Kessler, 560–65. Munich: William Fink.

Maintains that Herbert was "in his day one of the ablest British classicists" (p. 560) and presents a general survey of his Greek and Latin poetry, noting that Herbert composed 1,427 lines of Latin verse and 65 lines of Greek. Maintains that Herbert's most famous Latin poem is "Aethiopissa ambit Cestum Diuersi Coloris Virum" and that his most celebrated is "In Honorem Illustr. D. D. Verulamij, Sti Albani," his eulogy of Francis Bacon. Observes that much of Herbert's Latin verse is "of a high standard of technical excellence, particularly the hexameters, elegiacs and Horatian metres" but that "the iambics, both in Greek and Latin, occasionally lack caesurae" (p. 565). Points out that Herbert's vocabulary, "while basically that of Augustan Latinity, introduces words from Vegetius, Tertullian, Apuleius, and others" (p. 565).

**1196. Ichikawa, Shuji.** "George Herbert no *The Temple* to Franciscan Christianity" [George Herbert's *The Temple* and Franciscan Christianity]. *Eibungaku Kenkyu* [Studies in English Literature] 56, no. 1 (September): 1–19.

Compares *The Temple* to the major teachings of St. Bonaventure on the theology of contrition, natural theology, the didactic theory of beauty and art, and the idea of man. Points out a strong resemblance between Herbert's view of the dual nature of man and Bonaventure's idea of man and finds parallels between the Franciscan concept of nature and Herbert's vision of the direct relation between ordinary things and divine order.

**1197. Joscelyne, T. A.** "George Herbert's 'Easter' and St. Victorinus' 'Commentary on the Apocalypse of the Blessed John.'" *N&Q* n.s. 26:410–11.

Points out that Herbert's depiction of Christ's body stretched on the cross to form a stringed instrument in "Easter" has a patristic source in the *Commentary on the Apocalypse of the Blessed John*, written by St. Victorinus, Bishop of Pettau and the earliest exegete of the Latin Church, a work that Herbert may have found in Margarinus de la Bigne's *Bibliothecae Veterum Patrum*, published in Paris in 1609 and reissued in 1618 in an enlarged version as the *Magna Bibliothecae Veterum Patrum*. Notes also that the passage from St. Victorinus helps explain the transformation of earthly perfumes that appears in Herbert's poem. Maintains that "what is important is that it is through these analogies between the human senses and the spiritual life, brought together in the image of Christ's body on the cross as a stringed instrument, that Herbert's poem demonstrates the poetic persona's integration with the music of the saints, who are the beneficiaries of Christ's act" (p. 410).

**1198. Kawata, Akira.** "Anglicanism—George Herbert no Baai" [Anglicanism in George Herbert's *The Temple*], in *Anglicanism and Puritanism*, 36–47. Tokyo: Kinseido.

Considers Herbert's Roman Catholic and Puritan attitudes in *The Temple*, in which the spirit of Anglicanism is said to show its perfection. Chiefly examines Herbert's attitude toward the doctrine of predestination and toward the devotion to Mary, the saints, and the Holy Eucharist.

**1199. Keizer, Garret.** "A Possible Source for Herbert's 'Anagram.'" *ELN* 16:281–83.

Suggests that Lancelot Andrewes's sixth Nativity Sermon, preached before King James on Christmas 1611 and published in his *XCVI Sermons* in 1629, may be the source of the tent conceit in "Anagram of the Virgin Marie." Points out that Andrewes's sermon establishes "a direct association between 'the tent' of Christ's dwelling on earth and the martial implications of Christ's mission on earth," which is "the very association upon which Herbert's poem is built and by which the poem holds its place in *The Temple*'s design" (p. 282). Concludes that Herbert's conceit is in no way outlandish.

**1200. Lawler, Justus George.** *Celestial Pantomime: Poetic Structures of Transcendence.* New Haven and London: Yale University Press. xi, 270p.

Discusses "Easter-wings" as "moving circularly from infinite to finite and then by a *reditus* from that finite back to the infinite" (p. 34). In a discussion of enjambment "as a structure that resonates this personal bond between infinite and finite" (p. 101) comments on "The Church-floore," particularly the fourth stanza, which "breaks the previously established pattern of the single 'natural' virtues, patience, humility, and confidence, all embodied in end-stopped structures; while the transcendent, 'supernatural' dual virtues of love and charity are embodied in the structure of enjambment" (p. 94). Also comments on the use of emjambment in "The Windows" and "Giddinesse" to represent transcendence but claims that Herbert wishes to retain his finitude in his transformation into the infinite. Maintains that in "Aaron" Herbert embraces both Catholic metaphor, or transformation, and Protestant simile, or imputation, but in other poems the *via media* of Herbert "swerves toward the Protestant side" (p. 125) of arbitrary or gratuitous redemption. Claims that this structure is demanded by Herbert's view of the nature of existence. Discusses "Vertue" as a structure of "culmination" and "Redemption" as a structure of "complementarity," of a "conjoining the broken and fragmented with the harmonious and unified" (p. 222). Sees "Confession" and "Sinnes round" as circular or envelope patterns.

**1201. Leigh, David J.** "Herbert's 'The Collar.'" *PMLA* 94:946–47.
In a letter to the editor concerning Barbara Harman's essay "The Fiction of Coherence: George Herbert's 'The Collar'" (entry 1150) objects to Harman's attempt to rationalize the tension between the interior and frame stories of "The Collar," claiming that she fails "to take into account the most obvious 'frame narrative' of all—the Bible" (p. 946). Finds three texts that shed light on the poem: Matt. 11:29–30; Luke 15:13–21; and John 20:16. Claims that the opening lines of the poem refer to the Prodigal Son demanding release from his father and "thus not only provide a traditional context for the beginning but also suggest a hopeful ending to the interior story" (p. 946). Argues that the reader who is conscious of scripture is aware of "the present tense of the speaker, his past experience of rebellion, the biblical time of Jesus (and the fictional timelessness of his parable of the Prodigal Son), and the future time of reunion, foreshadowed by the return of the Prodigal Son to his father" (pp. 946–47). Regards the brief call of "child" and the answer of "Lord" as bringing forth numerous biblical images and analogues with theological implications that deny Harman's contention that Herbert "destructs all fictions" and thus "remains in a vulnerable present where images cannot be secured" (p. 947). Concludes that Harman's interpretation fails "because she has not placed the two narratives of the poem within the larger narrative frames provided by the biblical allusions" (p. 947). For a reply, see Barbara Leah Harman (entry 1192).

**1202. Lewalski, Barbara Kiefer.** *Protestant Poetics and the Seventeenth-Century Religious Lyric.* Princeton: Princeton University Press. xiv, 536p.
Presents a revisionist theory of current views on the English religious lyric of the seventeenth century and argues that Protestant emphases on the centrality of the Bible and Protestant appreciation and understanding of scriptural language, biblical genres (especially Psalms and Canticles), biblical rhetoric, and typology fostered a theory of aesthetics that defines both the poetics of the religious lyric and its spiritual contents. Stresses that the major religious lyricists of the period—Donne, Herbert, Vaughan, Traherne, and Edward Taylor—are much more indebted to contemporary English Protestant meditation, emblems, and sermon theory than to medieval Catholic and Continental sources. Following an introductory chapter (pp. 3–27), the study divides into twelve chapters in three major parts: (1) "Biblical Poetics" (pp. 29–144), (2) "Ancillary Genres" (pp. 145–250), and (3) "The Flowering of the English Religious Lyric" (pp. 251–426), followed by an afterword (pp. 427–28), notes (pp. 429–505), and an index (pp. 507–36). Although Herbert is mentioned throughout the book, chapter 9, "George Herbert: Artful Psalms from the Temple of the Heart" (pp. 283–316), is devoted exclusively to his poetry. Argues that Herbert's poetry fully reflects the new Protestant aesthetic and is founded on "biblical genre theory, biblical tropes, Protestant ways with emblem, metaphor, and typology, and Protestant theory regarding the uses of art in religious subjects—and that this poetic affords a necessary corrective to approaches to Herbert through medieval iconography, Salesian meditation, the plain style, or the so-called Augustinian abrogation of art" (p. 283). Discusses how Herbert's conception of the Christian life as reflected in both his poetry and prose is in complete agreement with Calvinistic Protestant-Pauline theology and how the "Protestant formulations of the temple trope and the typology of the Old Testament Temple provide the terms for Herbert's unifying motif, the temple in the heart of man" (p. 287). Maintains that the conceptual plan for *The Temple* "in regard to the genres

employed and the stances of the speaker owes something also to the analogy some-times drawn between the three parts of the Old Testament Temple and the three books of Solomon" (p. 289). Argues that *The Church-Porch* is "a Christian revision and fusion of Proverbs and Ecclesiastes (teaching moral precepts pertaining to exter-nal behavior and preparing for entry into the Church)" (p. 290). Maintains that *The Church* is "in some respects a new version of the Song of Songs, understood in its Protestant signification as an allegorical treatment of the relationship between Christ and every elect soul" (p. 292) and argues that an even more important generic source is the Psalms, noting that Herbert "seems to have conceived his book of lyrics as a book of Christian psalms, and his speaker as a new David, a Christian psalmist" (p. 300). Maintains that *The Church Militant* is Herbert's "Book of Revelation, rendering his own all-encompassing account of the providential course laid down for the visible Church throughout history" (p. 305). Comments in detail on Herbert's use of biblical language and biblical metaphors (such as sin as sickness, God as chastiser or gardener, and the heart as a temple) in *The Temple* and illustrates how Herbert's uses specifi-cally Protestant typology and symbols to define his speaker and to explore the very nature of the spiritual life. Compares and contrasts Herbert with Donne, Vaughan, Crashaw, Christopher Harvey, Herrick, Samuel Speed, and Edward Taylor.

1203. Lord, John B. "Herbert's Poetic Voice." *GHJ* 2, no. 2:25–43.
Points out that "poets work with sound effects, not the juggling of letters of the alphabet," and maintains that from a phonological study of Herbert's poetry two conclusions may be drawn: (1) "typical means by which the sound structure supports the semantic function of many poems become evident, and especially clear is the climatic moment when a given conceit is brought to its resolution" and (2) "a 'voice' of the poet—that is, the regularly repeated selection of a particular combination of acoustic features to dominate the sound of his poems—becomes clearly evident in a phonological model" (p. 25). Presents detailed phonological analyses of "The Win-dows," "Church-monuments," "The Quip," and "The Forerunners"—with graphs—to show how sound serves as a powerful support of the sense in these poems and how they "carry a greater freight of information than ordinary speech can" (p. 39). Adds phonological information on "The Pulley," "A Wreath," and "The Sonne" to increase the size of the body of data and concludes that Herbert "works especially hard with the features of Low and Vocalic, nearly always expanding them at the expense of both High and Mid on the one hand, and both Sonorant and Consonantal on the other"; that "he varies Nasal and Tense in both possible directions, either keeping them very infrequent or very much more frequent than normal, though he tends to avoid nasality significantly more often than he uses it"; that he likes "Round and Voiced"; and that "he avoids both Anterior and Coronal sounds, though this fact is probably a reflex of his preference for vowels, which by their nature can be neither" (p. 40).

1204. McDonald, J. C. "Redemption in *The Temple*," in *Anglicanism and Puri-tanism*, 48–61. Tokyo: Kenseido.
Considers the theological scheme of sin and salvation in *The Temple*. Maintains that Herbert believed that the action of God's atonement is shown by the death of Christ and that Herbert's main concern is the Incarnation and redemption of man-kind.

1205. Mercer, Richard. "Heaven in Ordinarie: A Comparison of George Herbert and Caravaggio." *SHR* 13:313–25.

Argues that Herbert and Caravaggio, though "worlds apart in space and temperament," created works of art "that teach similar lessons, that employ similar techniques, and that are informed by the same intention" and maintains that both "used their art to mediate between man and God, to teach religious lessons by depicting religious experiences which were personal and profound and thus dramatically intense" (p. 325). Outlines three ways in which Herbert and Caravaggio are similar: (1) both self-consciously renounce artfulness and sophisticated adornment, (2) both emphasize a definite moment of divine revelation and have an innovative way of depicting religious events, and (3) both create "intensely dramatic scenes in which to couch significant yet intimate and personal religious statements" (p. 323). Compares "Redemption" and "Love (III)" to *Supper at Emmaus*; "The Collar" to *The Calling of Saint Matthew*; and "Jesu," "The Bag," and "Love-joy" to *The Incredulity of Saint Thomas* in order to point out similarities between the two artists.

**1206. Miller, Edmund.** *Drudgerie Divine: The Rhetoric of God and Man in George Herbert.* (Elizabethan & Renaissance Studies, edited by James Hogg, No. 84.) Salzburg: Institüt für Anglistik und Amerikanistik, Univerität Salzburg. x, 250p.

Part of chapter 5 (pp. 124–28) revised as "Thom. Buck, the Anagram, and the Editing of *The Temple*" (entry 1258).

Chapter 9 first appeared in slightly modified form as "Herbert's Baroque: The *Passio Discerpta*" (entry 1207).

Announces in the foreword (pp. ix-x) that "the chief objective in this book is to present a full and balanced picture of Herbert as a Christian writer," maintaining that many recent critics have paid too much attention "to the pyrotechnics of his lyric poetry at the expense of the Christian content" (p. ix). Argues that readers need to examine seriously the whole of Herbert's canon, not just the lyrics of *The Church*. In chapter 1, "The Persona of 'The Church'" (pp. 1–19), argues that the "devotional dramatizations" in *The Church* reflect "the spiritual conflicts of a single persona" (p. 1) who unifies the whole collection. Analyzes the five "Affliction" poems to show how the persona adopts different voices and attitudes. Maintains that "the wide range of mood we see the persona adopt" is "delimited by the closed circle, the divine unifying circle of Christian devotion," and that the world of *The Church* is "the world of the individual Christian as a member of the Mystical Body" (pp. 9–10). Observes that the persona has no idiosyncrasies but is "any good Christian—or better, all Christians, a Bunyanesque typical Christian, a Mr. All-Christian" (p. 16). Argues that "The Sacrifice" is the only poem that does not have a narrator that the reader "feels is acting for him" (p. 23) and that Herbert had to introduce Christ as the narrator at this point to show "that Christ and the Christian are the two poetic sides of the same thing" and that "the voice of man and the voice of God merge exactly where the Love of God unites man in God" (p. 26). In chapter 2, "The God of 'The Church'" (pp. 30–57), maintains that God is "a metaphorically various God" (p. 30) and notes that in *The Church* there are "poems about God and then poems by God" (p. 31). Analyzes "The Thanksgiving" and "The Water-course" to illustrate "how wide the range is in the views of God adopted by the persona in the poems of 'The Church'" (p. 38). Maintains, for example, that God is described as a Petrarchan lover in "Love (I and II)" and "Dulnesse"; as a feudal lord in "Redemption"; as a sovereign in "The Pearl"; as the explicator of allegories in "Love unknown" and "The Pilgrimage"; and even as Cupid in "Discipline." In chapter 3, "Friends" (pp. 58–83), maintains that Herbert chose the metaphor of friendship as the primary way to explore the constant relationship between God and man and that it "contains the theological basis for all

the various specific metaphors of the individual lyrics" (p. 59). Comments on the theme of friendship in St. Ignatius Loyola; Thomas à Kempis; John Preston, an English Protestant reformer; and especially in *The Spiritual Friendship* by St. Aelred (or Ethelred) of Rievaulx and maintains that Aelred's "enthusiastic endorsement of spiritual friendship is exactly the attitude that must have been in Herbert's mind" (p. 82). Briefly contrasts Herbert's idea of friendship with those of Calvin and the Puritan theologian William Ames, as well as with the notion in the poems of Herbert's imitator Ralph Knevet. In chapter 4, "God's Work" (pp. 84–116), argues that Herbert makes God the ultimate author of his poems and that Herbert's ingenious use of visual and/or typographical metaphors in his shaped poems ("Deniall," "The Agonie," "Church-monuments," "The Bag," "Good Friday"), the acrostic ("Coloss.iii.3."), the pruning poem ("Paradise"), and the pattern poems ("The Altar" and "Easterwings") is evidence that "it is God who does the significant writing" (p. 116). Describes in detail the tradition and techniques of the two pattern poems. In chapter 5, "This Verse Marks That" (pp. 117–42), discusses the architectonics of *The Temple* and shows how poems are interrelated and are central to the whole by detailed readings of "Anagram of the Virgin Marie," "Deniall," and "Love (III)." Claims that the whole of *The Temple* is not only "an aid to devotion after the model of the Bible" but that "the poems in it are individually sacramental analogues" (p. 141). Argues that the preface to the 1633 edition is the work of the press editor, Thomas Buck, not of Nicholas Ferrar, as often claimed. In chapter 6, "Liturgy and Prophecy" (pp. 143–55), surveys several explanations about how *The Church-Porch* and *The Church* are related and argues that the division between the liturgy of the Word and the liturgy of the Eucharist in the Anglican Communion Service provides an explanation. Finds the relationship of *The Church Militant* to the other two parts more tenuous, contends that it is "extra-liturgical, a pretended prophecy" (p. 150), and concludes that it is "not *necessarily* part of *The Temple*" (p. 152). In chapter 7, "Herbert's Silence in the Forum" (pp. 156–93), maintains that Herbert consciously avoided theological controversy, not only in his religious lyrics but also in his works of piety and even in documents addressing theological issues. Illustrates this point by contrasting "The H. Communion" with the communion poem in the Williams manuscript, by commenting on the poems in *Musae Responsoriae* and *Lucus* as well as in "Briefe Notes on Valdesso's *Considerations*." In chapter 8, "Herbert's Preaching Style" (pp. 194–206), argues that *The Church-Porch* is a "gnomic conduct book," that "Providence" is a "gnomic sermon," and that *The Church Militant* is a "gnomic prophecy" (p. 205). Maintains that these didactic poems share in the tradition out of which came the *Outlandish Proverbs*. For a detailed discussion of chapter 9, "The Baroque Voice of the *Passion*" (pp. 207–18), see entry 1207. Chapter 10, "The Problem of Pastoral Prose" (pp. 219–47), analyzes *A Priest to the Temple, or, The Country Parson* to show that it has very impersonal and businesslike tone, is written in a middle style, and bears many resemblances to the *Cura Pastoralis* of St. Gregory the Great. Index to Herbert citations (pp. 248–50).
Reviews:
Philip Dust, *Cithara* 21, no. 1 (1981): 75–77
Helen Wilcox, *N&Q* 29 (1982): 171–72
J. Max Patrick, *SCN* 41 (1983): 5, 7

1207. ———. "Herbert's Baroque: The *Passio Discerpta*." *Ren&R* n.s. 3, no.2:201–8.
    Revised as chapter 9 of *Drudgerie Divine: The Rhetoric of God and Man in George Herbert* (entry 1206).

Maintains that, although the baroque tendency to go beyond the visual and to engage all the senses is noticeably absent in Herbert's English lyrics, one finds in *Passio Discerpta* "just such an in-dwelling of sensuous Baroque artistry" (p. 202). Argues that the twenty-one sacred epigrams are "very explicitly based on Salesian meditative technique" (p. 205), which contributed significantly to their sensuous dimension. Warns, however, that, one must be careful not to confuse poetry with theology, noting that Protestants often read and imitated Roman Catholic works of devotion "precisely because their purpose was pious and not theological or controversial" (p. 206). Argues that the "baroque intensity" of the Latin poems on Christ's passion is achieved "not simply by more sensuous imagery than we find in 'The Church' but by a significant tendency to dwell on the imagery" (p. 203). Maintains that, although *The Temple* and *Passio Discerpta* are in some ways complementary, the Latin sequence differs from *The Temple* "in its stylistic sensibility" and its "devotionalism" (p. 205). Calls the Latin collection "a chapel of ease perhaps and not a great cathedral, but clearly a finished, an exquisite work" (p. 206). Concludes that in *Passio Discerpta* "the senses are invoked, but the unity of the form as a whole is obviously a higher value to Herbert than any particular sensuous evocation" (p. 208).

**1208. Nelson, T. G. A.** "Death, Dung, the Devil, and Worldly Delights: A Metaphysical Conceit in Harington, Donne, and Herbert." *SP* 76:272–87.

Comments on the use of scatological imagery in works ranging from the frivolous *The Metamorphosis of Ajax* by Sir John Harington to the serious, devotional poems and prose of Donne and Herbert, noting that "in the same period the imagery of death, dung, the devil, and worldly delights proves equally adaptable to works at opposite ends of the literary spectrum" (p. 287). Maintains that one common trait in all of these works is "the desire to explore the relationship between matter and spirit and the insidious way in which they can become entangled, or even confused, with one another" (p. 277). Contends that "the use of scatological imagery in inspired texts is what chiefly emboldens Renaissance writers to make use of it themselves" (p. 281). Discusses "The Forerunners" as a "remarkably subtle and sophisticated treatment of the way in which the good and the evil, the worldly and the spiritual, can become entangled" (p. 285). Suggests that the poem "may well owe something to simple, popular *exempla* like the story of the angel and the courtesan in the *Metamorphosis of Ajax*" (p. 285). Notes that "The Rose" also "exploits the idea of worldly beauty as a source of corruption and uses the metaphor of purgation by means of repentance" (p. 286).

**1209. Onizuka, Keiichi.** "George Herbert ni okeru kami e no Hoshi to Hataraki" [To Work and to Be of Service to God in George Herbert]. *Kyushu Daigaku Eigo Eibungaku Ronso* [Studies in English Language and Literature, The English Language and Literature Society, Kyushu University] 29 (February): 1–19.

Points out that Herbert often scolds idleness itself or exhorts idle people to look for their own "employment" or "business." Argues that what Herbert means by idleness is a man's neglect of his own efforts to make full use of his "talent" in this world. Discusses Herbert's desire for secular employment and his final decision of taking holy orders.

**1210. Ottenhoff, John H.** "Herbert's Sonnets." *GHJ* 2, no. 2:1–14.

Maintains that Herbert's sonnets are characterized by "great vitality and wide variety" and show "a balanced exploitation of the freedoms of a strict verse form just as they admirably express the freedom he found in religious devotion" (p. 1). Comments in some detail on how Herbert "exploits the conventions of the sonnet in diverse ways: by introducing unexpected groupings of the rhyme and syntax, by using enjambment freely and expressively, and by altering his essentially smooth iambic pentameter verse to emphasize these individual uses" (p. 3). Divides the fifteen sonnets into two groups and discusses the major features of each group: (1) five narrative sonnets, each "written as a monologue or implied dialogue that strongly suggests actual speech and personal expression" ("Redemption," "The Holdfast," "Christmas," "Josephs coat," and "The Answer"); and (2) meditative or contemplative sonnets, four of which "are similar in their cataloguing of religious phenomena" ("The H. Scriptures (I and II)," "Prayer (I)," and "Sinne (I)"), four of which "are similar and have a strong devotional tone" ("Love (I and II)," "H. Baptisme (I)," and "The Sinner"), and two of which are "more conventionally impersonal rather than devotional" (p. 3) ("The Sonne" and "Avarice"). Through a detailed analysis of four sonnets—two from each of the above groups ("Sinne (I)," "H. Baptisme (I)," "The Holdfast," and "Josephs coat")—demonstrates how Herbert's sonnets "are not sonnets that represent conservative backtracking, but are complex and interesting poems that certainly fulfill his goal of turning an old form to new service" (p. 12).

1211. **Pebworth, Ted-Larry.** "George Herbert's Poems to the Queen of Bohemia: A Rediscovered Text and a New Edition." *ELR* 9:108–20.
Announces the discovery of Henry Huth's copy text of Herbert's two poems to the Queen of Bohemia in the Cambridge University Library, compiled by a Cambridge student or fellow between 1610 and 1631 (Add. MS. 4138). Argues that the manuscript "provides stronger evidence than any heretofore offered that Herbert wrote the two poems in question" (p. 109) and that the texts are "superior to all the others" (p. 114). Details the textual history, historical context, and occasion of the poems and comments on their theme and style. Argues that the poems were written to console the Queen for the loss of Bohemia and the Palatinate. Admits that the poems "are not masterpieces, but they are fine examples of a certain kind of political poetry, that in which art transforms objective loss into subjective gain," and maintains that, "informed with topical reality, they incorporate the immediate circumstances of defeat into a larger vision of ultimate victory" (p. 111). Presents an edition of the poems with variants (pp. 117–20). Reproduces a portrait of Elizabeth Stuart, Queen of Bohemia, by Gerard Honthorst and photographs of the poems in Cambridge Add. MS. 4138. See also Ted-Larry Pebworth and Claude J. Summers (entry 1166).

1212. **Pointon, Marcia.** *William Dyce, 1806–1864: A Critical Biography.* With a foreword by Quentin Bell. (Oxford Studies in the History of Art and Architecture, gen. eds. Francis Haskell, Charles Mitchell, and John Shearman). Oxford: Clarendon Press. xxiii, 229p, 163 [plates].
Comments on Dyce's *George Herbert at Bemerton* (1861). Observes that the oil painting "glows with remarkably jewel-like colour" and that "solitude as real experience pervades the picture" (p. 175). Notes that Herbert was an attractive subject for Dyce because "not only was he an artist in the service of God, but he was also one of a group of seventeenth-century divines whose writings were favoured by the Tractarians" (p. 175). Notes that in 1860 Dyce's friend Cyril Page was rector at Bemerton and that the picture was painted during a visit there. Points out that Dyce used White's portrait of Herbert (1674). Questions a nineteenth-century account that says that Dyce at first also included Walton in the painting but, when it was pointed out to him that the two men lived at different times, agreed to remove Walton but kept Walton's basket.

**1213. Pollock, John J.** "Motion vs. Position in *The Temple.*" *LangQ* 17, no. 3–4:49, 53.

Maintains that, because the dramatic conflicts in Herbert's verse are understated, his poetry has "profound appeal" (p. 49). Discusses Herbert's opposition of the concepts of motion and position throughout *The Temple*, pointing out that "the struggle between good and evil often takes the form of a quiet juxtaposition of these apparently similar, but for Herbert essentially anithetical, ideas" (p. 49). Maintains that in Herbert's poetry linear movement is suspect, even if one is seeking God, and that learning to be still is seen as important. Argues that an understanding of Herbert's ideas about linear motion and position "emphasizes his commitment to the Anglican doctrine concerning free will and good works" (p. 49), which holds that a self-instigated attempt to move toward God is futile and presumptuous and that motion is only salutary when God becomes the mover. Notes that often the tension between motion and position also serves to release tension in many of Herbert's poems. Comments on "The Pilgrimage" as a poem in which the dramatic impact depends "upon the persona's shift in perspective in the final lines," a shift best explained "when one views the poem as a conflict between motion and position" (p. 53).

**1214. Rajnath.** "From Image to Idea: A re-examination of T. S. Eliot's dissociation of sensibility." *Indian Journal of English Studies* (Calcutta) 19:149–61.

Argues that T. S. Eliot's theory of the dissociation of sensibility "is not only one of his major contributions to literary criticism but his most solid critical concept" and demonstrates "how the theory undergoes a shift of emphasis from image to idea in course of the development Eliot's critical career" (p. 149). Observes that, as time passed, Eliot tended to play down the importance of Donne and to put a much higher value on Herbert. Notes that Eliot's "first relatively detailed account of Herbert came as late as 1930" and compares Eliot's criticism on Donne with his assessment of Herbert to show that "his depreciation of the former goes side by side with his exaltation of the latter" (p. 157).

**1215. Rivers, Isabel.** *Classical and Christian Ideas in English Renaissance Poetry: A Students' Guide.* London, Boston, Sydney: George Allen and Unwin. 231p.

Introduction to the intellectual contexts of Renaissance literature. Comments on "Redemption," calling it "a deceptively simple narrative based on commonplace experience yet containing a religious meaning" (p. 6). Argues that the imagery used both "recalls the parables of Christ" and "embodies the principles of covenant theology" (p. 6) and maintains that to understand it one must be familiar with Protestant theology. Contends that Herbert's emphasis on the Eucharist in *The Temple* can only be understood "in the light of Laudian sacramentalism" (p. 101). Briefly comments on Herbert's attitude toward predestination and his use of biblical typology.

**1216. Roberts, John R., ed.** *Essential Articles for the Study of George Herbert's Poetry.* Hamden, Conn.: Archon Books. xvii, 601p.

Contains a preface that explains the guiding principles behind the selection of essays and a survey of Herbert's critical reception in the twentieth century (pp. ix-xvii); thirty-four previously published essays (reprinted without editorial changes), divided into seven major categories—(1) General Studies, (2) Rhetoric, Style, Form, (3) Images and Allusions, (4) Prosody, (5) The Unity of *The Temple*, (6) Individual Poems, and (7) Latin Poetry (pp. 3–552); notes from the individual essays (pp. 554–94); and a selected bibliography of modern scholarship and criticism on Herbert's poetry (pp. 595–601). The essays, all included in the present bibliography, are: (1) Robert Ellrodt, "George

Herbert and the Religious Lyric," from *English Poetry and Prose, 1540–1674*, edited by Christopher Ricks (entry 820), 173–205; (2) A. L. Clements, "Theme, Tone, and Tradition in George Herbert's Poetry," from *ELR* (entry 939); (3) Richard E. Hughes, "George Herbert and the Incarnation," from *Cithara* (entry 634); (4) Ilona Bell, "'Setting Foot into Divinity': George Herbert and the English Reformation," from *MLQ* (entry 1090); (5) Joseph H. Summers, "Herbert's Form," from *PMLA*, (entry 387); (6) Richard E. Hughes, "George Herbert's Rhetorical World," from *Criticism* (entry 555); (7) Robert L. Montgomery, Jr., "The Province of Allegory in George Herbert's Verse," from *TSLL* (entry 537); (8) Rosemond Tuve, "Sacred 'Parody' of Love Poetry, and Herbert," from *SRen* (entry 566); (9) Arnold Stein, "George Herbert: The Art of Plainness," from *The Poetic Tradition: Essays on Greek, Latin, and English Poetry*, edited by D. C. Allen and Henry T. Rowell (entry 774), 99–122; (10) Helen Vendler, "The Reinvented Poem: George Herbert's Alternatives," from *Forms of Lyric: Selected Papers from the English Institute*, edited by Reuben Brower (entry 852), 19–45; (11) Stanley E. Fish, "Catechizing the Reader: Herbert's Socratean Rhetoric," from *The Rhetoric of Renaissance Poetry*, edited by Thomas O. Sloan and Raymond B. Waddington (entry 983), 74–88; (12) Rosemary Freeman, "George Herbert and the Emblem Books," from *RES* (entry 263); (13) Fredson Bowers, "Herbert's Sequential Imagery: 'The Temper,'" from *MP* (entry 574); (14) Amy M. Charles, "George Herbert: Priest, Poet, Musician," from *Journal of the Viola da Gamba Society of America* (entry 720); (15) Florence Sandler, "'Solomon vbique regnet': Herbert's Use of the Images of the New Covenant," from *PLL* (entry 928); (16) Robert Higbie, "Images of Enclosure in George Herbert's *The Temple*," from *TSLL* (entry 988); (17) Albert McHarg Hayes, "Counterpoint in Herbert," from *SP* (entry 228); (18) Alicia Ostriker, "Song and Speech in the Metrics of George Herbert," from *PMLA* (entry 672); (19) Mary Ellen Rickey, "Herbert's Technical Development," from *JEGP* (entry 615); (20) Elizabeth Stambler, "The Unity of Herbert's 'Temple,'" from *Cross Currents* (entry 540); (21) Annabel M. Endicott-Patterson, "The Structure of George Herbert's *Temple*: A Reconsideration," from *UTQ* (entry 653); (22) Stanley Stewart, "Time and *The Temple*," from *SEL* (entry 715); (23) Valerie Carnes, "The Unity of George Herbert's *The Temple*: A Reconsideration," from *ELH* (entry 752); (24) Heather Asals, "The Voice of George Herbert's 'The Church,'" from *ELH* (entry 782); (25) Sheridan D. Blau, "The Poet as Casuist: Herbert's 'Church-Porch,'" from *Genre* (entry 858); (26) Amy M. Charles, "The Williams Manuscript and *The Temple*," from *RenP* (entry 897); (27) Rosemond Tuve, "On Herbert's 'Sacrifice,'" from *KR* (entry 369); (28) Jeffrey Hart, "Herbert's *The Collar* Re-read," from *Boston University Studies in English* (entry 550); (29) C. C. Brown and W. P. Ingoldsby, "George Herbert's 'Easter-Wings,'" from *HLQ* (entry 893); (30) Ira Clark, "'Lord, in Thee the *beauty* lies in the *discovery*': 'Love Unknown' and Reading Herbert," from *ELH* (entry 898); (31) Frederick von Ende, "George Herbert's 'The Sonne': In Defense of the English Language," from *SEL* (entry 904); (32) Virginia R. Mollenkott, "George Herbert's 'Redemption,'" from *ELN* (entry 957); (33) Barbara Leah Harman, "George Herbert's 'Affliction (I)': The Limits of Representation," from *ELH* (entry 1104); and (34) W. Hilton Kelliher, "The Latin Poetry of George Herbert," from *The Latin Poetry of English Poets*, edited by J. W. Binns (entry 990), 26–57.
Reviews:
Mario A. Di Cesare, *GHJ* 4, no. 1 (1980): 51–53
Paulina Palmer, *MLR* 78 (1983): 141–43

**1217. Sakurai, Shoichiro.** "Donne to George Herbert no Kekku" [The Concluding Part of the Sonnets of Donne and George Herbert], in *Kekku Ujo—Eikoku*

*Renaissance ki sonnet ron* [The Sentence of the Concluding Part of the Sonnet—Essays in the Sonnets of the English Renaissance], 341–71. Kyoto: Yamaguchi Shoten.

Points out that Herbert makes use of the concluding part of the English sonnet form to express himself. Maintains that the brevity and plainness in the condensed conclusions of Herbert's sonnets reflect his modesty.

**1218. Schleiner, Louise.** "Jacobean Song and Herbert's Metrics." *SEL* 19:109–26.

Studies Herbert's poems in the light of music of his day and argues that "a number of his stanzas were shaped by tunes he had in mind for them, either of his own or of someone else's composing" (p. 109). Considers primarily three metrical structures. Discusses two uses of the first type of structure, the fourteener—as a concluding couplet to give a feeling of a penultimate motion followed by resolution and repose and, in longer passages, to contrast rhythmically with other passages—and examines "A Parodie" and "Sunday" as examples of the first use and "Dialogue" as an example of the second. Comments on "Christmas," "Affliction (I)," and "Miserie" as examples of the second type of metrical structure, poems using longer and shorter lines to create rhythmic patterns that are "much like those in many song texts" (p. 118). Considers "Vertue," "Easter," "Dooms-day," "The Method," "The Dawning," "Gratefulnesse," "The Pilgrimage," "The British Church," and especially "Affliction (IV)" and "Peace" as examples of the third type of metrical structure, the use of dimeter to create effects similar to those created by musical composers of the period. Concludes that "the discipline of writing for music provided Herbert with a repertoire of rhythmic skills which helped to define his mature poetic idiom" (p. 123). Appends four examples of Jacobean music to illustrate points in the argument.

**1219. Slights, Camille.** "Herbert's 'Trinitie Sunday.'" *Expl* 38, no. 1:13.

Explicates "Trinitie Sunday" to show that in the poem Herbert emphasizes "the reciprocity of divine and human action" and that the final three words, "rest with thee," are "a consequence of redeeming and renewing grace *and* of human activity and achievement." Maintains that, although Herbert recognizes that every action starts and ends with God, he also stresses that "human choice and effort are a necessary part of the divine plan." Concludes that "the first and final words of the poem, 'Lord' and 'thee,' indicate Herbert's origin and his destiny, but the central line, 'For I confesse my heavie score,' is the hub on which the wheel turns."

**1220. Steanson, Karen E., ed.** Introduction to and commentary on Henry Colman's *Divine Meditations (1640)*, 1–52, 163–97. New Haven and London: Yale University Press.

Comments on the pervasive influence of *The Temple* on the content and style of Henry Colman's *Divine Meditations* (1640). Points out how frequently Colman's poems verbally echo Herbert's poems, how often he writes acrostics and anagrams in imitation of Herbert, and how many individual poems have their counterparts in *The Temple*—"The Altar" ("The Altar"), "On Prayer" ("Easter-wings"), "On my enemies vniust malice" ("The Quip"), "Another [on Death]" ("Heaven"), "On Drunkenesse" ("A Parodie"), "The Invitation" and "On the Lord's Supper" ("The Invitation" and "The Banquet"). Compares and contrasts Herbert's "The Altar" and Colman's poem by the same name to show how much Colman imitated from Herbert and how at the same time he was also independent. In the commentary notes many instances of Herbert's influence.

**1221. Strier, Richard.** "Herbert and Tears." *ELH* 46:221–47.

Rejects the idea advanced by Louis Martz (entry 431), Malcolm Mackenzie Ross (entry 434), and others that there is a connection between Herbert's poetry and the Counter-Reformation tradition of the "literature of tears." Notes that the "literature of tears" focused primarily on St. Mary Magdalene and St. Peter, saints associated in the minds of Catholic theologians with the sacrament of penance. Examines in some detail the controversy between Roman Catholics and Reformation theologians over penance and analyzes the theology and the style of "Marie Magdalene" to show that Herbert clearly reflected a Protestant understanding of penance and implicitly rejected the Catholic position. Claims that, "ultimately, for Herbert, Mary Magdalene is not the 'weeper' but the 'washer,' the redeemed sinner in whose loving response to the experience of Christ's love the workings and the meaning of grace are revealed" (p. 239). Maintains that stylistically "Marie Magdalene" "is not a poem in which Herbert treats tears in an elaborate and 'Crashavian' manner" (p. 240). Examines the theology and style of "Grief" and "Praise (III)," poems sometimes cited as influenced by Counter-Reformation ideas and the "literature of tears," and rejects the notion that the two poems reflect, devotionally or rhetorically, Tridentine theology or sensibility. Contends that, if it is not quite accurate to say that Herbert uses the extravagant mode ironically in the two poems, "it is certainly true that he is using it in such a way as to change its direction and assimilate it to a habit of mind and a type of poetry consistently more interested in what rather than how things 'show'" (p. 245). Concludes that Herbert's relationship with the "literature of tears" is complex, that his theology of penance "is always strongly Protestant," and that "his use of baroque rhetoric is never straightforward" and thus "his poem on the Magdalen and his attitude toward tears do not in any way compromise his Protestantism" (p. 243).

**1222. ——.** "'To All Angels and Saints': Herbert's Puritan Poem." *MP* 77:132–45.

Argues that "To all Angels and Saints" does not give any evidence that Herbert was attracted to Catholicism but rather shows "some of the most historically characteristic and significant features of the Puritan mind" (p. 132). Sees the poem as composed of two halves, separated by a turn at line 16, with the first half defending the speaker's character and the second half defending his position. Claims that in the first fifteen lines the speaker explains that his refusal to pray to the saints and the Virgin Mary is not "out of envie or maliciousnesse" (line 6) and that in the second half the speaker explains that the reason is that God "Bids no such thing" (line 18). Argues that the idea that God forbids whatever He does not bid is "distinctly Puritan in its tone and position" (p. 136). Shows that the fifth stanza continues to emphasize God's sovereignty and that line 21, "All worship is prerogative," means "not only that God decrees how He is to be worshiped, but also that to be worshiped is God's 'prerogative' alone" (p. 139). Maintains that in the poem God is presented as an Old Testament God who is jealous over worship. Cites "The Priesthood" as an example of "daring not" to follow good intentions rather than God's intentions and maintains that for Herbert to worship the Virgin, angels, and saints would be following his own impulses rather than being obedient to God. Discusses the last lines of the poem as an image of the Good Steward, which makes God less fearful than the fifth stanza suggests, but also sees the poem as about God the Father, not Christ the mediator, noting that Puritanism moved away "from the conception of personal mediation" (p. 143). Concludes that, while most of Herbert's poetry does focus on Christ and not the Virgin, angels, and saints, Herbert does not argue from a direct Christocentric position but from an indirect one by references to the Mother of Christ and maintains that these references are apparent but not real Catholicism.

**1223. Summers, Claude J., and Ted-Larry Pebworth.** "Herbert, Vaughan, and Public Concerns in Private Modes." *GHJ* 3, nos. 1–2 (1979–1980): 1–21.

Argues that, although neither Herbert nor Vaughan were public or political poets in the ordinary sense of those terms, both *The Temple* and the two parts of *Silex Scintillans* contain poems that concern public and political issues. Maintains that "the modes of these poems are private—lyrical expressions of joy, alarm, sorrow, reflection, and prayer—but they are set within Biblical and historical contexts that transcend the private convictions and personal desires of their authors" (p. 1). Argues that Herbert "creates public poetry by recognizing and lamenting the dangers that threaten the visible church, both from within and from without, and by placing the temporal and localized institution within a broad context of Judeo-Christian history that prophesied the apocalyptic destruction of God's enemies and the establishment of a New Jerusalem" (p. 1). Comments on "Divinitie," "Church-rents and schismes," and "The British Church" to show how these poems "participate in the religious controversies they decry" (p. 2) and are "public poems in private modes" (pp. 8–9). Maintains that frequently "the sweet tone of his speakers' voices conceals a passionate engagement in the very issues he seems to avoid" and that, in those poems that deal with issues of ecclesiastical schism, "such a vision is fundamentally political" (p. 9). Concludes that Herbert's "rejection of the rhetoric of controversy in favor of a more subtle rhetoric of allusion is itself a political strategy" and "may be his most important legacy to Henry Vaughan" (p. 9).

**1224. Summers, Joseph H.** "George Herbert," in *Great Writers of the English Language: Poets*, edited by James Vinson and D. L. Kirkpatrick, 483–86. New York: St. Martin's Press.

Biographical note on Herbert, selected list of the editions of his poetry and prose, selected bibliography of modern critical studies, and general evaluation of his poetry. Maintains that, in many ways, Herbert has more in common with Sidney than with Donne: both experimented widely with rhyme, line-lengths, patterns of argument, repetition, and variation; both created a context for their short poems within a larger whole; both wrote intimate, personal "love" poems; both prized sincerity; both explored the language proper to courtesy and humility; both liked direct, straightforward language; both wrote poems in which the argument is revealed step-by-step in a dramatic way; and both circulated their poems in manuscript form. Comments on the religious sensibility of Herbert's poems, his use of common speech, and his experimentation with forms and genres. Notes that Herbert may be the first English poet who "provided a significant title for every poem" (p. 486). Concludes that, even though all of the poems in *The Temple* are religious, a reader's chief impression "is not of monotony but of richness and variety" and that Herbert's language "establishes (or discovers) relationships between the most disparate human experiences and voices" (p. 486).

**1225. Todd, Richard.** "The Passion Poems of George Herbert," in *From Caxton to Beckett: Essays Presented to W. H. Toppen on the Occasion of His Seventieth Birthday*, edited by Jacques B. H. Alblas and Richard Todd, with a foreword by A. J. Fry, 31–59. (Costerus: Essays in England and American Language and Literature, n.s. 23.) Amsterdam: Rodopi.

Observes that throughout *The Temple* Herbert refers to the medieval Augustinian notion that God's work of creation and redemption can be apprehended in the Book of Nature and in the Book of Scripture. Argues that his poems show that Herbert believed that, in order to read the scriptures properly, one needed to take into account the central movement in God's revealed truth, which is primarily a "transcendence of the law by love" (p. 31). Maintains that, for Herbert, "the point of transcendence is contained in the culminating events of the Incarnation of Christ; that is to say, in the events of the Passion and Resurrection" (p. 31). Discusses Herbert's theology and art in the sequence of poems on Christ's passion, beginning with "The Sacrifice" and ending with "Sepulchre," and shows the pervasive influence of biblical typology and language, the *schola cordis* emblem tradition, and medieval modes of meditation, best represented by the pseudo-Bonaventurine *Meditationes vitae Christi*. Maintains that in the sequence Herbert invites his reader "to observe him exploring in an allusive fashion the connections between events and 'images' or signs of the Passion, the idea of the work of restoration, his own heart, and the agency of Divine Grace" and considers Herbert's "response to these associations, which can be seen as deriving from his reading of the Book of Scripture" (p. 33). Maintains that Herbert's poetry is "overridingly a poetry of relationship" and that, for him, "relationships are not simply to be stated, but alluded to and bathed in, in ways the compelling consequences of which his reader cannot escape" (p. 59). Concludes that "what is implied in Herbert's visual, emblematic treatment of the particulars of Christ's Passion is what may be construed as a more general truth about the poetry of *The Temple*," which "reflects the experience of a poet who feels and knows the existence of a relationship with the Divine" and who enables his reader "to sense their writer discovering the extent to which the two actions—of calling to God and of interpretatively apprehending the response—are related" (p. 59).

**1226. Wilcox, Helen.** "Puritans, George Herbert and 'Nose-Twange.'" *N&Q* 26:152–53.

Points out that a poem in Bodleian MS. Eng. poet. f. 16, written by a Cornishman named John Polwhele and entitled "On Mr. Herberts Devine poeme the church," shows that the phrase "nose-twange," a disrespectful way of describing Puritans, was in common usage in the 1630s and that Anglicans of the period felt increasingly threatened by nonconformists. Notes that Polwhele's poem is perhaps the earliest and least known of the many poems inspired by Herbert and that it is further evidence of the wide and positive response to Herbert's poetry following the publication of *The Temple*. Describes how Polwhele imitates Herbert.

**1227. Wood, Chauncey.** "A Reading of Herbert's 'Coloss.3.3.'" *GHJ* 2, no. 2:15–24.

Observes that "Coloss.iii.3" has received little attention from critics "because its demands on the reader seem to be easily satisfied" (p. 15). Discusses the biblical and cosmological backgrounds of the poem and maintains that it "confounds worldly wisdom by its unexpected use of the sun's two motions and by its requirement that we reject what appears to be a downward movement to our earthbound eyes for a larger perspective," that by changing the biblical text the poet "creates a more dramatic— because personal—poetic situation," that the poet by italicizing the words perhaps wants the reader to consider the meaning of the words, "which is more 'hidden' than are the words themselves," that thus the italics "are inserted to lead us on, rather than to stop us at the literal level" (p. 21), and that the sun's two motions, daily and annual, "are subsumed at last in the figure of the Son/Sun who is both efficient and final cause of what the poet has been talking about" (pp. 22–23). Concludes that, when understood in its complexity, the poem "shows the Christian poet both using and using up his own words and thoughts as the poem moves from poetic treasures of earthly words and transcends them as it arrives at Christ the Word, the Treasure, the Alpha and Omega, the Son and Sun" (p. 23).

# *1980*

**1228. Argento, Dominick.** *Let all the world in every corner sing: A Festive Hymn for Chorus, Brass Quartet, Timpani, and Organ.* [Farmingdale, N.Y.]: Boosey & Hawkes. 12p.

Musical setting of "Antiphon (I)" for four-part mixed voices (SATB), two trumpets, two trombones, timpani, and organ.

**1229. Beal, Peter, comp.** "George Herbert," in *Index of English Literary Manuscripts*, vol. 1, *1450–1625*, part 2, *Douglas—Wyatt*, 185–213. London: Mansell; New York: R. R. Bowker.

Comments on two important manuscripts of Herbert's poems, the Williams MS (Dr. Williams Library, MS. Jones B. 62) and the Tanner MS (Bodleian, MS. Tanner 307). Notes that the Williams is the only manuscript known to have been handled by Herbert and that it contains corrections and revisions in his hand. Maintains that the Tanner was probably produced from Herbert's copy of the poems by the community at Little Gidding under the direction of Nicholas Ferrar. Points out a small number of Herbert autographs and maintains that several letters are the most notable examples. Lists copies of poems in miscellanies before 1701 and other transcripts and comments on manuscripts of Herbert's work that have been reported since his death but remain unlocated. Catalogs of surviving known manuscript copies of individual poems (arranged in three categories: English poems by Herbert, English poems of uncertain authorship, and Latin poems by Herbert) and individual prose pieces. Photocopy of the first page of a letter, written by Herbert to Sir Robert Harley, dated 26 December 1618 (p. 188).

**1230. Bell, Ilona.** "The Double Pleasures of Herbert's 'Collar,'" in *"Too Rich to Clothe the Sunne": Essays on George Herbert*, edited by Claude J. Summers and Ted-Larry Pebworth, 77–88. Pittsburgh: University of Pittsburgh Press.

Argues that "doubleness is the central strategy" of "The Collar" (p. 84). Reads the poem first as an inner dialogue, where the speaker debates with his conscience and struggles with the dichotomy between the will and the heart. Finds that the final solution comes through love, which "settles all the speaker's conflicting, chaotic feelings" (p. 80). Contends that we are pointed to a second reading of the poem, with the dialogue between man and Christ, by the final words of the poem: "As he grew more fierce and wild at every word, he also thought that he could hear a voice calling at every word" (pp. 80–81). Presents this second reading, where Christ's voice points to "an alternative, transcendent solution" (p. 82) to the the speaker's internal conflict. Concludes that "Christ's answer is hidden within the speaker's words because God's offer of grace is continually present, though man is not always willing or able to accept it" and that the reader must repeat "the speaker's experience of error, of divine revelation, and of inspired reassessment" (p. 85).

**1231. Bloch, Chana.** "Spelling the Word: Herbert's Reading of the Bible," in *"Too Rich to Clothe the Sunne": Essays on George Herbert*, edited by Claude J.

Summers and Ted-Larry Pebworth, 15–31. Pittsburgh: University of Pittsburgh Press.

Contends that, for Herbert, "the understanding of Scripture is inextricably bound up with self-understanding" (p. 16). Claims that "The H. Scriptures (I and II)" reflect the Protestant belief that the Bible has special authority and that the ordinary believer can discern its true meaning. Uses "The Quip" to show how Herbert dramatizes the authority of Scripture as the speaker turns to the Psalms to help him answer those who scoff at him. Argues that in "Jordan (I)," "The Posie," "Divinitie," and "The Forerunners" the Word of God protects and sustains man. Demonstrates that other poems dramatize the authority of man in reading the Word and shows how "reading the text in the right way means reading oneself into the text" (p. 21), using "Coloss.iii.3" as an example. Disagrees with Fish's interpretation of the poem (entry 905), arguing that the speaker is not suppressed but fulfilled as the vessel of God's Word. Discusses also "Ephes.iv.30," "The Odour," and "The Pearl" to show how Herbert's "I" is, "in Hooker's phrase, the 'key which openeth the door of entrance into the knowledge of the Scripture'" (p. 27). Claims that this view counteracts "excesses of recent Herbert criticism" (pp. 27–28) by Fish and Vendler. Examines "The Crosse" to show that God's words, admitted into the heart of man, "do not obliterate the self but rather free it to fulfill its high purpose—as God's own creature" (p. 29).

**1232. Boone, Colin C.** *Praxis der Interpretation: englische Lyrik.* Tübingen: Max Niemeyer Verlag. x, 109p.

Scattered references throughout to Herbert. Briefly comments on "Easter-wings" as a pattern poem whose printed configuration is united with its content. Maintains that "The Collar" lacks a *tertium comparationis* or a *tenor* and thus certain details of the poem cannot be understood by the uninitiated reader. Comments briefly on the uses of a kind of hyperbole in "Vertue" that is not a contradiction of reality but constitutes a common linguistic enhancement in the poem. Uses "Deniall" to illustrate the flexibility of iambic lines.

**1233. Brisman, Susan Hawk, and Leslie Brisman.** "Lies against Solitude: Symbolic, Imaginary, and Real," in *The Literary Freud: Mechanisms of Defense and the Poetic Will,* edited by Joseph H. Smith (Psychiatry and the Humanities, vol. 4), 29–65. New Haven and London: Yale University Press.

Comments briefly on "The Collar" as a poem that exhibits "the daemonic power of calling into being a deity the sudden recognition of whom comes like a new creation" (p. 57). Maintains that the poem "illustrates a tendency of the religious imagination to regard the conversational and daemonic as initially or superficially antagonistic but ultimately coextensive" and suggests that "the dialogue in which one is called *Child* and responds *My Lord* represents the archetypal religious conversation" (p. 58).

**1234. [Charles, Amy M., ed.]** *Cross-Bias: The Newsletter of the Friends of Bemerton Society,* no. 6 (Advent). 5p.

Announces the reorganization of the English branch of the Friends of Bemerton; notes the relocation of documents formerly housed in the Salisbury Diocesan Record Office in Wren Hall, Salisbury Close, and points out that records of the Dean and Chapter are now housed in the Registry and that all diocesan records have been moved to the Wiltshire Record Office in Trowbridge; mentions a number of scholarly papers recently presented on Herbert at various conferences and outlines the main argument of several; announces forthcoming publications and conferences; and encourages Herbert scholars to visit Montgomery Castle and Chirbury.

**1235. Daniels, Edgar F.** "Herbert's 'The Flower,' 44." *Expl* 39, no. 1:45–46.

Maintains that the word *glide* in line 44 of "The Flower" ("To make us see we are but flowers that glide") has the obsolete meaning of "to fall" and that Herbert is saying that the petals of the flower fall, implying that the flower "undergoes a cessation that shows the vanity of its pretensions to permanence" (p. 46). Finds a similar treatment of the image, using the same word, in Herrick's "To Blossoms."

**1236. Di Cesare, Mario A.** "Herbert's 'Prayer (I)' and the Gospel of John," in *"Too Rich to Clothe the Sunne": Essays on George Herbert*, edited by Claude J. Summers and Ted-Larry Pebworth, 101–12. Pittsburgh: University of Pittsburgh Press.

For an expanded version of this essay, see entry 1284.

Examines "Prayer (I)" for its Johannine images and allusions, not because John "provides *the* key to the mysteries of this poem" but because his Gospel seems "peculiarly appropriate" to it (p. 103). Shows similarities between the Gospel and Herbert's poem—elusiveness, vertical imagery, amphibious movement between the world of spirit and the world of sense, and a pattern of return. Notes that four phrases in the poem that have troubled critics are made meaningful by John's Gospel: (1) "Gods breath in man returning to his birth" (line 2); (2) "Christ-side-piercing spear" (line 6); (3) "The six-daies world-transposing in an houre" (line 7); and (4) "Exalted Manna" (line 10). Reads line 2 as a reference to "creation and rebirth and grace" (p. 104), line 6 as a "synecdoche of the whole Passion and Crucifixion" (p. 106), line 7 as a reference to "the created world and its redemption" (p. 106), and line 10 as a reference to the Incarnation. Concludes that "in prayer creation and redemption are united; the hour of prayer contains the two-way traffic between this world and that, the recurrent dualism of heaven and earth, God and man, type and fulfillment, the vertical imagery of ascent and descent, and the mysterious theme of return" and that all of these in turn "point to the fundamental reciprocity or mutuality that is the major theme of both Herbert's poem and John's Gospel" (pp. 108–9).

**1237. Duenãs Martínez, Antonio.** "La fama de Juan de Valdés en Inglaterra." *Arbor* no. 414:35–42.

Regrets that the metaphysical poets are not better known in the Spanish-speaking world. Points out that one connection between the English poets and the Spanish mystics is that Herbert read carefully *Las ciento diez consideraciones divinas* by Juan de Valdés, the unorthodox mystic that many regarded as one of the powerful forces in the Reformation. Notes that Valdés's book was first printed in Basel in 1550 and was brought to England by Nicholas Ferrar, who translated it into English in 1638. Comments on Herbert's letter to Ferrar about the translation and on his *Briefe Notes on Valdesso's "Considerations"*. Maintains that, although Herbert expresses some reservations about Valdés's theology, he regarded him as a true servant of God, as a spiritual friend, and as a courageous spokesman for God in the midst of Popery. Contends that Ferrar's and Herbert's interest in Valdés reveals the need of the Anglican Church in the seventeenth century to return to classics of thought in the preceding century.

**1238. Dust, Philip.** "George Herbert's Pacifist 'Triumphus Mortis' and the Evolution of War," in *Acta Conventus Neo-Latini Turonensis*, edited by Jean-Claude Margolin, 2:1011–18. Paris: Librairie philosophique J. Vrin.

Argues that "Inventa Bellica" or "Triumphus Mortis" is important "as an early attempt to trace the development of war anthropologically and sociologically, as a theory of the cause of war, and as a pacifist anti-war tract" and emphasizes Herbert's "anticipation of twentieth-century views of the subject, especially those gathered by Quincy Wright in his *A Study of War*" (p. 1011). Points out that Herbert's "outspoken criticism of war is especially important when we remember that the dominant tradition in books about war in England were, for the most part, strongly militaristic" (p. 1011). Discusses the argument of the poem to show how Herbert fits "squarely in the tradition of Christian humanist pacifism" (p. 1012). Points out classical, medieval, and Renaissance sources and maintains that Herbert attacks war "on the basis of Neo-Stoic and Christian principles" (p. 1017). Maintains that Herbert's primary method of illustrating the evil evolution of war is to show the advances in weapon usage and notes that he, like Milton, regards the cannon as the ultimate weapon and devotes the better part of his poem to a description of its origin, development, and use.

**1239. Edgecombe, Rodney.** *"Sweetnesse readie penn'd": Imagery, Syntax and Metrics in the Poetry of George Herbert.* (Salzburg Studies in English Literature, Elizabethan and Renaissance Studies, edited by James Hogg, 84:2.) Salzburg: Institut für Anglistik und Amerikanistik, Universität Salzburg. iii, 180p.

Discusses aspects of Herbert's poetry—its imagery, syntax, and metrics—that "encompass large areas of his poetic practice, ramifying as they do into questions of theme, tone and structure" (p. i). Maintains that an examination of traditions from which Herbert drew his images allows one "to judge his resourcefulness, especially in the composites of emblem and symbol," and shows "the structural significance of image patterns in representative poems" (p. i). Following a preface and acknowledgments (pp. i-iii) and a brief introduction (pp. 1–9) that presents a biographical sketch of Herbert and comments on his religious sensibility, the study divides into three chapters. Chapter 1, "Imagery" (pp. 10–71), is in three parts: (1) a survey of the emblematic and symbolic traditions in which Herbert participated; (2) a discussion of selected major images in *The Temple* drawn from the liturgy, church architecture and furnishings, and liturgical properties associated with priests; the Bible, nature and animals; scientific knowledge; music; and public life, noting in particular the many images of enclosure in Herbert's verse; and (3) critical analyses of "Grace," "Sinne," "Marie Magdalene," "The Bunch of Grapes," and "The Flower" to illustrate how the images in these poems function as structural and coordinating devices. In chapter 2, "Syntax" (pp. 72–118), discusses the structural, tonal, and thematic effects of syntax in Herbert's poetry and comments on the interrelationship of imagery and syntax in his poems. Presents a detailed reading of "Miserie" to show how Herbert "controls the development of his argument (and indeed his tone, feeling and themes) with a careful and strategic use of syntax" (p. 82). Comments on "Deniall" (and to a lesser extent on a number of other poems) to illustrate some of the syntactical features and ploys of Herbert's art. Offers a detailed critical analysis of "The Flower" to show "its grammatical strategies and the effect these have upon the poet's statement" (p. 108). In chapter 3, "Metrics and Stanza Forms" (pp. 119–63), surveys Herbert's metrical practice and his uses of rhyme and stanzaic design to show that "all his poems indeed testify to a high degree of metrical finesse" (p. 119). Discusses "Praise (I)," "The Temper (I)," "Complaining," "The Collar," and "The Flower" to illustrate that "the intricacies of Herbert's workmanship frequently reveal a thematic function" and "contribute in no small way to the fine gradations of meaning, the lyric control of emotion and the subtly differentiated tones that much of his poetry exemplifies" (p. 163). In an appendix, "Some Notes on the Sonnets" (pp. 164–75), maintains that the sonnet "seems not to have drawn from Herbert his very best poetry" and that he is "more himself in stanzas of his own highly-wrought, individual architecture than in the inherited structure of the sonnet" (p. 164). Surveys Herbert's use of and modification of the sonnet tradition and discusses "Love (I)," "The H. Scriptures (I)," "Sinne (I)," and "Redemption." Selected bibliography (pp. 176–80).

**1240. Ellrodt, Robert.** "Angels and the Poetic Imagination from Donne to Traherne," in *English Renaissance Studies Presented to Dame Helen Gardner in Honour of her Seventieth Birthday*, edited by John Carey, 164–79. Oxford: Clarendon Press.

Compares and/or contrasts Herbert's attitude toward angels in his poetry with the views of Donne and Vaughan. Argues that Herbert is "unexpectedly closer" to Donne and that, unlike Vaughan, he "does not seem to delight in the contemplation of angels or yearn for their presence on earth" (p. 175). Maintains that "the angelic world in *The Temple* is always a transcendent world of grace whence music may call to man or manna flow" and that Herbert "entertains no dream of angelic immanence in the world of nature, for his theme is God's immanence in the human heart" (p. 176).

**1241. Elsky, Martin.** "History, Liturgy, and Point of View in Protestant Meditative Poetry." *SP* 77:67–83.

Studies the connections between liturgical presentation of time and Protestant meditative poetry and argues that the traditional Catholic view of the importance of memory in making present the major events of sacred history, both in the Mass and in private devotion, is given a much different emphasis by Protestant theology, which insists that the "real presence" is an internal experience. Maintains that, although Catholic and Protestant meditative poetry often bear striking resemblances, their fundamental difference is that "the center of reformed meditative verse is not just Christ, but Christ as experienced by the meditator" (p. 72). Argues that, "for reformed poets, applying Christ to the self often involves a union of subject and object, or the making present of Christ the object in the heart and soul of the meditating subject in a way that clearly reflects the internalized sacrifice of the Protestant Lord's Supper" (p. 73). Contrasts Herbert's "Good Friday" with Robert Southwell's "The burning Babe" to show the influence of liturgical changes on poetry, pointing out that Herbert, unlike Southwell, "has rejected a contemplation of Christ as an external object and instead has incorporated the event into himself, becoming himself the measurement of Christ's griefs" (p. 74). Points out other examples of Herbert's internalizing the events of Christ's life so that "meditating on Christ results in the making present Christ in oneself" (p. 74). Argues, by contrast, that Crashaw, like Southwell, does not internalize sacred history.

**1242. Fowler, Anne C.** " 'With Care and Courage': Herbert's *'Affliction'* Poems," in *"Too Rich to Clothe the Sunne": Essays on George Herbert*, edited by Claude J. Summers and Ted-Larry Pebworth, 129–45. Pittsburgh: University of Pittsburgh Press.

Examines Herbert's use of fictional voices in the five "Affliction" poems, singling out "Affliction (I)" as the finest of the five. Notes that the speakers of "Affliction (I)" and "Affliction (IV)" are "less mature and more disordered" yet "their insights are penetrating and reveal profound understanding of the human psyche" (p. 130). Contends that the distance between poet and speaker in these poems produces an ironic interplay that the other three do not achieve. Argues that "Affliction (II)" "demonstrates a competent understanding of the theoretical implications of the Passion but no internalization of that perception" (p. 131); that "Affliction (III)" "uses the format of the emblem book, where problem and resolution are presented almost simultaneously" (p. 131) so that the speaker "has discovered nothing by the end of the poem that he did not know at the beginning" (p. 132); and that "Affliction (V)" presents the serene and confident voice of a scholar and exegete, which is abandoned for the voice of a "keen metaphysical speculator," noting that the adjustment is "not a happy one" (p. 134). Explicates "Affliction (I)" and "Affliction (IV)," concluding that "notwith-standing their immaturity, distorted perspectives, and adversary postures toward God," the speakers of each "share an ability to articulate feelings in a concrete and personal language that is fully convincing, unlike the empty rhetoric, abstractions of scholarship, or peripherally relevant generalizations of the other poems" (p. 144).

**1243. French, Roberts W.** "Herbert as Jeremiah: A Note on 'Affliction (I).'" *PLL* 16:201–3.

Argues that "Affliction (I)" "gains significant depth and resonance when it is seen how the Book of Jeremiah takes its place in the background of this bold and subtle work" (p. 201). Points out similarities between Jeremiah's personal laments and Herbert's view of himself in the poem. Maintains that both Herbert and Jeremiah "had occasion to regard themselves as the abused servants of an apparently ungrateful God" and that, "in each case, the pattern of protest and submission runs along similar lines" (p. 201). Notes that at times Herbert and Jeremiah are dissimilar in tone and attitude: "Jeremiah's cries to God for vengeance upon his enemies, for example, would be unthinkable for Herbert" (p. 202), but maintains that these differences do not discredit the notion that the Book of Jeremiah is part of "the intricate fabric that forms the background of this great poem" (p. 203).

**1244. ———.** "'My Stuffe is Flesh': An Allusion to Job in George Herbert's 'The Pearl.'" *N&Q* n.s. 27:329–31.

Points out that in the third stanza of "The Pearl" Herbert makes a witty allusion to Job 6:12. Argues that, when the speaker says, "My stuffe is flesh, not brasse" (line 27), he is echoing Job's question, "Is my strength of stones? or is my flesh of brass?" Claims that by setting his complaint beside that of Job, the speaker becomes "a mock-heroic figure of ridicule" since "he laments the restrictions on his pleasure" while Job "laments the depth of his suffering" (p. 330). Notes that Herbert revised the last five lines of the stanza from what they were in the Williams manuscript and argues that the revision improved the stanza. Concludes that by adding the allusion to Job, Herbert "undercuts and undermines the speaker's confident posturings" (p. 330) and shows that "his assertions of human knowledge are really assertions of human pride" (p. 331).

**1245. Gilman, Ernest B.** "Word and Image in Quarles's *Emblems*." *CritI* 6, no. 3:385–410.

Detailed discussion of the emblem book, especially the connection between the verbal and pictorial aspects of the genre, and a study of Quarles's *Emblemes* (1635). Maintains that seventeenth-century poets, including Herbert, had a "logocentric bias" and that "Vasari's notion of God as the primordial painter and architect is alien to Herbert's conception of writing as the challenge to copy the 'fair, though bloudie hand' of a divine author" (p. 389). Notes that, like Donne, Herbert "associates himself as a poet with music and preaching" and that, when the analogy between poetry and painting is made, his point "is always that art has been tainted by 'lewd intentions'" (p. 389)

**1246. Gottlieb, Sidney.** "George Herbert Today—A Survey of Contemporary Research." *CahiersE* 8:29–41.

Claims that there is "a new Renaissance in Herbert studies" and that modern critics are drawn to Herbert (1) because he is "remarkably attentive to psychological shifts, nuances in faith, and the precarious position of even an exemplary believer in troubled times" and is known for "subtle and intimate self-portraiture," (2) because of the unquestioned artistry of his poems and his challenging complexity, which often appeals to "a generation of critics trained in close reading," (3) because "the awareness that *The Temple* is structured as a coherent whole and as a continuous body of poems, each calculated to reflect on the others, has opened up many new interpretive possibilities for critics to exploit," and (4) because Herbert is "a major poet who is up for grabs" and "has not been and perhaps cannot be easily assimilated to one tradition or critical cubby-hole" (p. 29). Notes that one sign of the revival of interest in Herbert is the appearance of basic research tools such as Amy Charles's biography (entry 1094), John R. Roberts's annotated bibliography of modern Herbert criticism (entry 1168), Mario Di Cesare and Rigo Mignani's computer-generated concordance (entry 1097), the facsimile edition of the Williams manuscript, introduced and edited by Amy Charles (entry 1105), the forthcoming facsimile edition of the Bodleian manuscript, edited by Amy Charles and Mario Di Cesare (entry 1429), and the facsimile reprint of the first edition of *The Temple* (entry 759). Notes that another sign of the revival of interest in Herbert is the increasing number of critical studies that have appeared in the last several years and offers detailed evaluations of three recent studies that are "important contributions to Herbert studies" and also show "some of the variety and, in certain instances, some of the limitations of contemporary approaches to Herbert" (p. 32): Helen Vendler's *The Poetry of George Herbert* (entry 1050), Leah Sinanoglou Marcus's *Childhood and Cultural Despair* (entry 1164), and Stanley Fish's *The Living Temple: George Herbert and Catechizing* (entry 1144).

**1247. Hammond, Gerald.** "Herbert's 'Prayer (I).'" *Expl* 39, no. 1:41–43.

Argues that in "Prayer (I)" "the piling up of images forces the reader to develop a growing sense of the impossibility of the poet's attempt to define the undefinable, to find the one image which might be adequate to describe this mysterious communication between man and God" (p. 42). Explicates the poem based on its final phrase, "something understood," noting that Herbert typically uses a final word or phrase to sum up his meaning. Argues that "Prayer (I)" is "subtly different" because "while the final phrase provides the reader with a satisfying conclusion to the search for a definition, it increases his frustration by withholding to eternity the syntactical satisfaction that the poem requires" (p. 43). Concludes that from the very beginning the reader notes that the phrases lack a verb, a lack that remains through the poem, until the reader finally understands that "he never will come to the poem's verb," and thus the definition "will remain something 'understood,' just as prayer's substance lies in what is not spoken" (p. 43).

**1248. Hermann, John P.** "Herbert's 'Superliminare' and the Tradition of Warning in Mystical Literature." *GHJ* 4, no. 1:1–10.

Maintains that the warning to the reader in the second stanza of "Superliminare" comes not only from the classical tradition of *procul este profani* but also from the tradition of introductory warnings in Christian contemplative writings and that an understanding of the tradition "can help clarify the curious tonal variation" in the poem and "provide a vantage point from which to discuss several problems raised by this poem, which is so crucial to the interpretation of *The Temple*" (p. 2). Maintains that the closest analogue to Herbert's poem is Jacob Boehme's treatise, *Of True Repentance*, but acknowledges that the tradition is too broad to cite any one specific source. Discusses how the tone and content of Herbert's poem reflects the Christian mystical tradition and concludes that *The Temple* should be seen as "a kind of *lectio divina*, quasi-sacramental in nature" and that appropriately in "Superliminare" "the profane are warned away in a tone of urgency and by means of a device that has a long history in the writings of the Christian mystics as well as in classical religious ritual" (p. 8).

**1249. Hinman, Robert B.** "The 'Verser' at *The Temple* Door: Herbert's *The Church-porch*," in *"Too Rich to Clothe the Sunne"*: Essays on George Herbert*, edited by Claude J. Summers and Ted-Larry Pebworth, 55–75. Pittsburgh: University of Pittsburgh Press.

Argues that "we cannot come to 'The Church-porch' at any time without discovering that, just as the Verser has assured us we would be, we have been had" and that "we discover hitherto unentered deeper recesses in 'The Church' when we realize how the experience of *The Church-porch* has prepared us for them" (p. 56). Maintains that Herbert "plainly states his determination to use the pleasure of the game in order to trick the coney into surrendering every pleasure to God" (p. 57). Contends that Herbert's verse, his every act as parson in or out of church, is meant to lure his audience to God and, as Verser, Herbert beguiles his reader (coney) into reverence. Maintains that "the coney's joy is the joy of being drawn into the Verser's game" and "the Verser's joy, gladly offered to the coney, is being drawn into Love's game" (p. 63). Claims that *The Church-Porch* and *The Church* open different ways into the Real Presence and the mystery of Love. Observes that to Herbert "the experience of the porch is sacramental and can suggest the poetic counterpart of sacrament to readers" (p. 71) and that, "just as, for Herbert, the world simultaneously reveals and *is* God, so he seeks to make his 'Church-porch' both point toward and *be* his Church" (p. 72).

**1250. Idol, John L., Jr.** "George Herbert and John Ruskin." *GHJ* 4, no. 1:11–28.

Surveys John Ruskin's admiration for Herbert's poetry and maintains that it "was woven into the fabric of Ruskin's life and thought" (p. 11). Points out that on numerous occasions Ruskin quoted from Herbert's poetry, recommended it to his friends and acquaintances (such as John Millais), and favorably commented on it in his literary criticism. Notes that Ruskin often found guidance in Herbert's poetry, especially *The Church-Porch*, on subjects ranging from art to economics to religion and found Herbert "a stable model of religious and aesthetic discipline" (p. 26). Points out, for instance, that Ruskin saw Herbert's poems as "buttressing ideas which he was promoting about art and the belief of artists," finding in Herbert "the ideal union of art and ethics" (p. 15). Comments on Ruskin's criticism of Herbert's poetry and notes that his remarks "range from consideration of Herbert's prosody to sensitive and informed comparisons of Herbert's mind, thought, and art to those of other writers" (p. 21). Claims that "not since the early attempts of George Ryley and not until the commentary of George Herbert Palmer, Canon Hutchinson and other modern critics was Herbert to receive such expert and insightful explication, prepared for in this case by Ruskin's repeated readings of the Bible and his knowledge of how symbols worked in Christian art" (p. 23).

**1251. Ishii, Shōnosuke.** "George Herbert no 'Sonnets' ni tsuite (Cuuksi no Hitotsu no kikironi—1)" [On George Herbert's Sonnets: A Tentative Commentary (1)]. *Soka Daigaku Eigo Eibungaku Kenkyu* [Studies in English Language and Literature, Soka University] no. 7 (4, no. 2) (March): 1–15.

Part 1 of a three-part series. Translations of Herbert's sonnets into Japanese, along with a brief commentary. Considers the devotional mode in Herbert's poetry, expressed in a seemingly conventional and conservative frame. Specifically discusses the two sonnets in Walton's *Lives* and the first three in *The Temple*. See also entries 1294, 1295.

**1252. Keizer, Garret.** "Fragrance, 'Marie Magdalene,' and Herbert's *The Temple*." *GHJ* 4, no. 1:29–50.

Maintains that in Herbert's profoundly incarnational theology "God is not impersonal, the individual is not illusory, and the acts of worship are neither superficial nor futile" (p. 29). Discusses these implications in Herbert's poetry: (1) by commenting on what is called "'fragrance' after the imagery through which biblical writers, and Herbert, expressed mutuality in the divine-human relationship, and especially man's ability to please his maker" (p. 29); (2) by showing how "Marie Magdalene" embodies the fragrance theme; and (3) by applying the interpretation of that poem to other poems (especially "The Holdfast," "The Thanksgiving," and "Dialogue")—in particular "as regards the treatment of the possibility of Christian action and the nature of Christian identity in Herbert's work—with a view toward challenging the studies of critics who have ignored or denied Herbert's capacity for 'fragrance'" (p. 30), singling out the work of Stanley Fish and Helen Vendler.

**1253. Maber, R. G.** "Celtic Prosody in Late Cornish: the *englyn* 'An lavar kǫth yu lavar guįr.'" *Bulletin of the Board of Celtic Studies* 28:593–98.

Points out that the first proverb in a three-line Cornish verse of two juxtaposed proverbs, "An lavar kǫth yu lavar guįr," was first published in English in *Outlandish Proverbs*. Argues that the poem is not likely of ancient Celtic origin but was most likely composed in the second half of the seventeenth century, possibly by an antiquarian known only as Mr. Eustick of St. Just, and was derived either from *Outlandish Proverbs* or Howell's *Proverbs* of 1659. Points out that there is some speculation that others contributed to *Outlandish Proverbs* after Herbert's death and notes that Nicholas Ferrar, Junior, the nephew of Nicholas Ferrar, apparently knew Cornish but dismisses the idea that he actually added the proverb. Argues that the source of Herbert's proverb is almost certainly Spanish and is likely derived from Gonzalo Correas's *Vocabulario de refranes y frases proverbiales*, a collection of proverbs first published in 1627.

**1254. MacKenzie, Elizabeth.** "The Growth of Plants: A Seventeenth-Century Metaphor," in *English Renaissance Studies Presented to Dame Helen Gardner in Honour of her Seventieth Birthday*, edited by John Carey, 194–211. Oxford: Clarendon Press.

Discusses seventeenth-century understanding of the growth of plants and of exhalations or vapors that rise naturally from the earth and comments on how poets of the period used plant and moisture imagery and metaphors. Points out that the comparison of the life of a tree or plant to that of man was a Christian commonplace. Comments briefly on how Herbert's "The Flower" reflects contemporary views on plants and suggests that "Grace" provides a good gloss on the poem, as do Job and St. Gregory.

**1255. Malpezzi, Frances M.** "Thy Cross, My Bower: The Greening of the Heart," in *"Too Rich to Clothe the Sunne": Essays on George Herbert*, edited by Claude J. Summers and Ted-Larry Pebworth, 89–100. Pittsburgh: University of Pittsburgh Press.

Reads "The Flower" as a conversion poem in which the persona "comes to understand his own nature and his relationship to God" (p. 90). Underscores the context of the poem, which follows "The Crosse," where the persona, like a Petrarchan lover, sighs and laments that he has to suffer but finally submits to his afflictions as Christ did. Claims that the visual tradition that depicts the Crucifixion and the Deposition places "the flower" at the foot of "the cross," as Herbert's arrangement does. Notes that "tropologically this flower is the Eden raised in the waste wilderness of the persona's soul; it is the paradise within" (p. 94) and that there are "a number of significant symmetric parallels between the prelapsarian garden" of Adam, "the garden of the Recreation in which Christ hung as fruit on the tree to redeem the garden man lost," and tropologically "the recreated garden of the persona's soul" (pp. 94–95). Concludes that the tradition of visual representations of Christ's death also informs the poem so that "the flower comes to represent not only the effect of Christ's sacrifice on each soul, but the offering the individual is expected to make in propitiation for that sacrifice" (p. 99).

**1256. Marcus, Leah Sinanoglou.** "George Herbert and the Anglican Plain Style," in *"Too Rich to Clothe the Sunne": Essays on George Herbert,* edited by Claude J. Summers and Ted-Larry Pebworth, 179–93. Pittsburgh: University of Pittsburgh Press.

Maintains that Herbert used an Anglican plain style rather than a Puritan plain style and that he "saw language in much the same way that he saw the liturgy" (p. 180). Argues that Herbert used the plain style when he wanted to appeal to the largest possible audience and that this style was "more affective, more playful in tone than the Puritan, more austere and hortatory than the Catholic" (p. 180). Traces the history of the plain style, noting that it had been "standard for didactic and homiletic poetry" (p. 181) since the Middle Ages, that the Anglican plain style was used for audiences other than the uneducated, such as learned men so absorbed in religious issues that they had lost devotional fervor, and that is was used to increase devotion and submission to the Church. Points out examples of the plain style in such poems as "The Collar" and "H. Baptisme (I and II)." Maintains that Herbert was interested "in the process by which outward forms of the church are so welded with the human spirit that the two become indistinguishable" (p. 187). Concludes that Herbert believed that "his style, like the liturgy, must reflect an ideal of beauty and order yet not lose touch with the struggles and vicissitudes of the individual soul" (p. 191).

**1257. Mason, Kenneth.** *George Herbert: Priest and Poet.* (Fairacres Publications, no. 74.) Oxford: SLG Press. 27p.

Stresses the value of Herbert's poetry for contemporary Christians, especially priests: "He does not speak of things we have not encountered, he has no doctrine of his own, but through his poetry he purifies our knowledge of the things which as Christians we already know" (p. 1). Comments on "The Collar," "Decay," "The Priesthood," "Aaron," "The Flower," and "The Crosse" and shows "how the poet's way with words illuminates the ways of God with the human heart in its inmost relationship with him" (cover).
Review:
P. G. Stanwood, *GHJ,* 4, no. 2 (1981): 61–62

**1258. Miller, Edmund.** "Thom. Buck, the Anagram, and the Editing of *The Temple.*" *Library* series 6, 2:446–48.

Revised from a part of chapter 5 (pp. 124–28) of *Drudgerie Divine: The Rhetoric of God and Man in George Herbert* (entry 1206).
Points out that "Anagram of the Virgin Marie" is the only poem in a different place in the first edition of *The Temple* and in the Bodleian Manuscript and maintains that

its placement in the manuscript is preferable, "where its wider significance is unescapable" (p. 446). Argues that it is likely that the printers, Thomas Buck and Roger Daniel, moved the poem from its original position because they saw there was not enough room on the page to print it properly and, recognizing that the poems in *The Temple* do not make up a sonnet sequence or narrative, erroneously concluded that the poem could be moved without destroying the unity of the collection. Maintains that, although the first edition is "one of the best edited books of the seventeenth century," it may be, in this case, "less faithful to Herbert's intention than the Bodleian Manuscript" (p. 448). Questions the common assumption that Nicholas Ferrar played a significant role as editor of the first edition and argues that most of the work was most likely done by the two University printers. Points out that Thomas Buck was Herbert's classmate at Cambridge, had good literary tastes, and was "personally a great go-getter and just the sort to have pressured Herbert into releasing *The Temple* for publication" (p. 447). Argues that the preface to the 1633 edition was composed by the printers and notes that, when Buck retired and Daniel brought out the 1641 edition, he changed the plural "The Printers to the Readers" to the singular.

**1259.** Mulder, John R. "*The Temple* as Picture," in "*Too Rich to Clothe the Sunne*": *Essays on George Herbert*, edited by Claude J. Summers and Ted-Larry Pebworth, 3–14. Pittsburgh: University of Pittsburgh Press.

Reads *The Temple* as a portrait of the poet who is preoccupied with offering a sacrifice of praise to God but whose recurring grief leads him to search for "the conditions that will allow his groans to be part of a divine harmony" (p. 3). Discusses the sequence consisting of "Dulnesse," "Love-joy," and "Providence" as "an illustration in miniature of Herbert's angling for perspective" (p. 6), a perspective that is constantly corrected as the poet manipulates his language "so that the self-centered application of his poet-person resonates against a more profound and traditional christological content" (p. 9). Sees the poet-person as a "foil by which Herbert himself retains aristocratic reticence" (p. 12) and as a seeker of God's motive who, in the process, reveals his own. Contends that Herbert uses religious doctrine not to promulgate it but to "playfully and wittily alter and adapt" it for "his own peculiar artistic and instructive purposes" (p. 12).

**1260.** Nardo, Anna K. "Play, Literary Criticism, and the Poetry of George Herbert," in *Play and Culture*, edited by Helen B. Schwartsman, 30–38. West Point, N.Y.: Leisure Press.

Discusses how various perspectives on play can join with three kinds of literary criticism—close reading, contextual criticism, and reader-response theory—"to expand our understanding of what a text is, means, and does" (p. 31). Examines Herbert's pattern poems or verse pictures, such as "The Altar"; his use of punning titles, such as that of "The Collar"; his employment of bizarre images, such as the description of Christ's wounded side in "The Bag"; and his writing of poems that are elaborate games or puzzles, such as "A Wreath." Maintains that a psychoanalytical description of play helps interpret such phenomena and concludes that, in his playful poems, Herbert "takes a piece of the non-self (an object of veneration like an altar, a word like 'collar,' a Bible story like piercing of Christ's side, or a church decoration like a wreath) and plays with it" to bring about "a rapturous merger of self (Herbert's emotions, understanding, and will) with non-self (God's love)" (p. 33). Examines "Deniall," in which Herbert uses his own cleverness "to emphasize God's art, not his own" (p. 35), and maintains that a theological description of play helps the contextual critic understand how Herbert resolved the conflict between artfulness and simplicity.

Examines "The Quidditie" and "Love (III)" to show how Herbert makes his reader "agree to play a game just to comprehend the poem" (p. 36) and "offers him an opportunity to share with Herbert the experience of sacred play in which reintegration of self and not-self is possible" (p. 37).

**1261. Nestrick, William V.** " 'Mine and Thine' in *The Temple*," in *"Too Rich to Clothe the Sunne": Essays on George Herbert*, edited by Claude J. Summers and Ted-Larry Pebworth, 115–27. Pittsburgh: University of Pittsburgh Press.

Claims that "mine and thine" is "the central rhetorical *topos* of Herbert's poetry" (p. 115). Discusses "The Altar," "The Sacrifice," "The Thanksgiving," and "Clasping of hands" as instances of the use of the *topos* and maintains that Herbert places these words at a climactic moment in these poems. Analyzes "Artillerie" and argues that Herbert "finds in the conversion of linguistic elements, in verbal altering, a parallel not simply for divine creation but rather for divine metamorphosis, a radical transcendence of mortality" (p. 127). For a reply, see Jeanne Clayton Hunter (entry 1349).

**1262. Nuttall, A. D.** "The Temple," in *Overheard by God: Fiction and Prayer in Herbert, Milton, Dante, and St. John*, 1–81. London, New York: Methuen.

Expands reader-response theory by arguing that, in *The Temple*, Herbert, the Christian artist, assumes the presence of God as reader or, at least, as his special audience and explores the logical, theological, and aesthetic problems and tensions that this traditional concept poses for the poet. For example, notes that in "Dialogue," the poet not only addresses God but also "speaks for" God and thus "Herbert, the character *within* the poem, displays the inept incomprehension of mere humanity, but Herbert the author undertakes to supply on God's behalf the answers only God can give" (p. 3). Comments on a number of poems, especially "Dialogue," "Love (III)," "The Quip," "Jordan (I and II)," "The Dedication," "Redemption," "The Thanksgiving," "Affliction (I)," "Affliction (IV)," "The Storm," "Artillerie," "The Holdfast," and "The Pulley," to show how God's "overhearing" the poet shapes the theological content of the poems and influences the poet's strategies within them. Insists that Herbert, not Donne, is the most radical of the seventeenth-century devotional poets. At first posits the possibility that Herbert's fictionalizing of God in his poetry rests squarely upon the Calvinistic doctrine concerning the nature of God and the fallen and degenerate condition of man, then shows that Herbert's poetry "pragmatically refutes the theology of Calvin" because Calvin's stern and angry God "is subjected to love in the poetry of Herbert and is proved to be unloveable" (p. 51). Maintains that "the confession of total depravity lies, inescapably, at the heart of Herbert's poems" but that "he triumphs over it, not by expelling it from his mind but by applying to it the strange test of charitable belief" (pp. 53–54). Observes that Herbert's poetry is riddled with moral and theological contradictions but insists that "the frequency of the contradiction implies not that Herbert's poetry is theologically superficial but the reverse" (p. 75). Maintains that Herbert's poetry thus "pierces the contemporary theology of Protestantism to the half-Platonic Augustinian ontology which lies behind it" (p. 75).

**1263. Osmond, Rosalie E.** "George Herbert: Richness in Austerity." *ESC* 6:133–44.

Observes that in Herbert's poetry many seemingly contradictory elements unite "almost as a set of oppositions pulling in different directions: matter/words, plain style/ornate style, intention/execution, Puritanism/Catholicism" and thus "it exhibits a poise and balance that is similar, on the poetic level, to the austere yet rich pattern of life and worship found at Little Gidding" (p. 134). Maintains that Herbert's poetry is "not so much poetry that steers a safe, conventional, middle course, as poetry that exists at the point of tension between two different theories of religion and art and exhibits something of this tension in its content and style" (p. 134). Discusses four devices that Herbert uses "to achieve the end of a poetic that is at once simple and 'pure' insofar as it is God-directed, but persuasive and 'eloquent' in that it is also man-directed—an intention that is genuinely sincere combined with a poetic that gives the impression of sincerity, and is effective as well" (p. 134): (1) the combination of "plain speaking on the verbal level with a richness of metaphor and association of ideas that radiate multiple meanings to the initiated reader" (p. 134), illustrated by "Sepulchre"; (2) a union of simplicity and sophistication through the use of parable and fable, illustrated by "Love unknown" and "Redemption"; (3) the use of wit (a) in which "the claims of wit and sincerity are clearly at variance" and the poet uses a formula phrase "to ward off the temptation of the delightful but insincere reply" (p. 140), illustrated by "The Quip," (b) in which wit and sincerity are at variance but the poet "completes the poem, allowing it to stand, clothed in its ingenuity, as a statement of both man's aspiration and imperfection" (p. 140), illustrated by "A Wreath," or (c) in which the wit is employed "as an instrument to disclose meaning"—often a wit that "deflates at the same time that it delights" (p. 141), illustrated by "Heaven"; and (4) the use of wit in which "the body of the poem is particular, often ornate, but which, at the end, 'opens out' in a general, plain affirmation that supersedes and climaxes everything that precedes it" (p. 141), illustrated by "Prayer (I)" and "Easter." Concludes with a critical reading of "Love (III)," a poem "that uses and combines most of the poetic devices discussed above" (p. 142).

**1264. Ray, Robert H.** "Two Seventeenth-Century Adapters of George Herbert." *N&Q* n.s. 27:331–32.

Discusses Joshua Poole's extensive use of *The Temple* in his handbook for young scholars and would-be poets, *The English Parnassus: or, A helpe to English poesie* (1657), and comments on William Croune's adaptation of part of "Love (I)" in his "Ode. To his Honoured Friend Dr. Woodford. On his Excellent Paraphrase of Salomon's *Song*," published in Samuel Woodford's *A Paraphrase Upon the Canticles, and Some Select Hymnes of the New and Old Testament, With other occasional Compositions in English Verse* (1679). Maintains that both adaptations "tend to accommodate Herbert's work to the rise of science and to the increasing respect for scientists in the century" (p. 331). Notes that Poole, who was a student of Barnabas Oley at Cambridge, adapts or quotes Herbert thirteen times in eleven sections of his handbook and gives two examples to show how Poole changed Herbert's lines to accord with "the new climate of feeling associated with the rise of science" (p. 332). Argues that Croune, who was a physician, a professor of rhetoric in Gresham College (London), a member of the Royal Society, and later appointed anatomy lecturer by the Company of Surgeons, changes Herbert's lines in order to focus more on creation and less on the Creator.

**1265. Reeves, Troy D.** "Herbert's 'The Agonie.'" *Expl* 39, no. 1:2–3.

Argues that the blood referred to in the second stanza (lines 7–9) of "The Agonie" is Christ's blood in the Garden of Gethsemani, not on Calvary, and maintains that the image of judgment (the winepress) is appropriate, "for Christ is taking the judgment of sin upon Himself" (p. 2). Notes that "this blood Herbert identifies with Sin in the second stanza, while the blood of Calvary is identified with Love in the third stanza" (p. 2). Points out also that the word *vice* in lines 11–12 ("Sinne is that press and vice, which forceth pain / To hunt his cruell food through ev'ry vein") has two relevant meanings—"screwpress" and "fault," "defect," or "failing." Maintains that the lines say that "Sin, the winepress, has forced into Christ's bloodstream a viciousness (fault, corruption, taint) that causes the Lord excruciating pain" (p. 2) and that, if vice is personified and if the antecedent of "his" in line 12 refers to vice, not pain, "then vice is sending pain foraging throughout Christ's bloodstream in search of something to eat" (pp. 2–3). Points out that the word *assay* in line 14 ("assay / And taste that juice") means "to test," thus the reader "is invited to become, for the moment, a wine-taster and to judge the quality of the 'juice' that flowed from Christ's side when He was pierced on the cross" (p. 3). Notes that the title of the poem comes from the Greek word *agon*, meaning "trial" or "test," and that in the poem Christ "is being tested by torture" and the reader "is invited to test for himself the fruit of that act of love" (p. 3).

**1266. Rollin, Roger B.** "Self-Created Artifact: The Speaker and the Reader in *The Temple*," in *"Too Rich to Clothe the Sunne": Essays on George Herbert*, edited by Claude J. Summers and Ted-Larry Pebworth, 147–61. Pittsburgh: University of Pittsburgh Press.

Maintains that Herbert differs from Donne in that "he often takes as his subjects things other than his own subjectivity" (p. 147). Distinguishes between his Sacred Poems, which are "more public, more doctrinal, more didactic," and his Private Ejaculations, which are more "private or personal experiences" (p. 148). Argues that these two modes are combined in Mixed Poems and cites "The Bunch of Grapes" as blending "pronouncements upon religious themes with seemingly personal responses to those themes" (p. 148). Discusses each of the modes in terms of psychoanalysis, calling the Private Ejaculations "psychocatharsis," the Sacred Poems "ego-reinforce-ment," and the Mixed Poems mostly ego-reinforcement but observes that readers respond to more than just these three voices. Analyzes the intended audiences of *The Church-Porch*, *The Church Militant*, and "The Sacrifice" and points out the difficul-ties of modern readers in identifying with the speaker. Notes characteristics that distinguish Sacred Poems from the other two modes and discusses the psychological response a reader may generally have, using "The British Church" as an example. Discusses the psychodynamics of Private Ejaculations and comments on the persona of "Affliction (IV)" as showing symptoms of identity confusion. Observes that readers may identify with him because "the poem dramatizes a therapeutic process" (p. 154) that moves from crisis to resolution. Comments on the differing patterns of the four other "Affliction" poems. Concludes that "just as there is only one Herbert, there is only one reader" but that "in the transaction that constitutes the aesthetic experience they join forces to create 'something new, something human, something personal'—the reader's own temple, a self-created artifact" (p. 158). In an appendix (pp. 158–59) divides the poems in *The Temple* into the three modes.

**1267. Rubey, Daniel.** "The Poet and the Christian Community: Herbert's Afflic-tion Poems and the Structure of *The Temple*." *SEL* 20:105–23.

Argues that the five Affliction poems "constitute a coherent structure organized around movement from the individual and autobiographical in 'Affliction (I)' to the communal and typological in 'Affliction (V),' where Herbert's personal history is enclosed within the historical community of the Church and the history of the earth itself"; that "this movement parallels the larger organizational structure of *The Tem-ple* as a whole in its movement from 'The Church-Porch' to 'The Church' to 'The Church Militant'"; and that "the series develops a conscious poetics in which God acts as Herbert's muse by using affliction to wring from him the poems which prove the relationship is functioning, tempering the poet and mending his rhymes in the process" (p. 107). Presents a detailed reading of each of the five poems to show that they "work as a series by using the Christian conception of history to create a system for the rational understanding and acceptance of human suffering" (p. 119). Argues that "it is the process of affliction which makes the speaker a true poet in Herbert's terms" (p. 122); that the poems "become proof that affliction is part of God's plan"; and that the ability even to write shows Herbert's "resiliency and refinement by the tempering process and God's active presence in the relationship" (p. 123). Concludes that there is a "sense of order and coherence behind the seemingly chaotic alternation of joy and woe which organizes the series of the Affliction poems and *The Temple* itself by a process of movement from the individualistic and biographic to the communal and eternal" (p. 123).

**1268. Schleiner, Louise.** "Seventeenth-Century Settings of Herbert: Purcell's 'Longing,'" in *"Too Rich to Clothe the Sunne": Essays on George Herbert*, edited by Claude J. Summers and Ted-Larry Pebworth, 195–207. Pittsburgh: University of Pittsburgh Press.

Observes that seventeenth-century composers who set Herbert's poems to music most often selected his "speaking-voice lyrics" rather than his songs and hymns and argues that this can best be understood by "considering the courses of stylistic change in seventeenth-century English lyric and song setting" (p. 195). Distinguishes between song mode and speech mode lyrics, noting that Herbert was at ease in both. Explains that during the seventeenth century, as the dramatic lyric of the speaking voice became more popular, English song composers more often chose these lyrics for settings than the flowing lyrics of an earlier time and even regarded their music as special readings of the poems. Lists song settings of Herbert's speech-mode lyrics that have come to light and notes that, while they are of little interest to music historians, they have value for literary historians "as records of contemporary readings of the poems" (p. 199). Discusses in particular Henry Purcell's setting of "Longing" (1688), claiming that the composer "felt no obligation to retain its meter, pitch patterns, or longer syntactic units" but "imitated the aspect of the poem most striking to him, the posturing and gesturing that dramatize the speaker's sequence of emotions" (p. 205).

**1269. Schmidt, Michael.** "George Herbert 1593–1633," in *A Reader's Guide to Fifty British Poets 1300–1900*, 153–60. (Reader's Guide Series, gen. ed. Andrew Mylett.) London: Heinemann; Totowa, N.J.: Barnes & Noble.

Biographical sketch of Herbert and general introduction to his poetry. Comments on the use of figurative language, imagery, simple diction, colloquial tone, logic, and music in Herbert's lyrics and stresses the dramatic and didactic nature of his art. Calls Herbert "a master of form" (p. 157) and briefly comments on the form of "Mortification." Discusses the use of language in "Prayer (I)." Calls "Affliction (I)" Herbert's most directly biographical poem and comments on its artistic merits. Contends that "Redemption" is "unequalled in English poetry before or since" (p. 160). Maintains that "a catalogue of the verbs in any of the better poems proves Herbert to be a poet of moral action or enactment rather than gesture" (p. 160).

**1270. Sessions, William A.** "Bacon and Herbert and an Image of Chalk," in *"Too Rich to Clothe the Sunne": Essays on George Herbert*, edited by Claude J. Summers and Ted-Larry Pebworth, 165–78. Pittsburgh: University of Pittsburgh Press.

Comments on Bacon's respect for Herbert and notes that, in his 1625 dedication of *Certaine Psalms*, Bacon "gives the first public recognition of Herbert's poetry" (p. 166). Assesses the influence of Bacon on Herbert, noting the Latin letters and poems Herbert wrote to Bacon and pointing out borrowings from Bacon in *The Temple* and *A Priest to the Temple*. Notes comments in Herbert's letters showing his appreciation of Bacon's *Magna Instauratio*, claiming that two themes emerge: (1) that Bacon has power and elegance of language and (2) that his concepts of science and technology will shape the world. Discusses Herbert's poems in honor of Bacon, noting that "In Honorem Illustr. D. D. Verulamij" is generally considered his finest Latin piece. Maintains that the structure of this poem illustrates that Bacon offered Herbert "a living example of that supreme control of style and manners that could direct time—and therefore be able to redeem it—through choosing the proper style and the proper audience" (p. 172) and that, in the final style of *The Temple*, "the Baconian principle of the properly 'chalked up' language is most vividly realized" (p. 174). Discusses "The Forerunners," the opening and closing images of which "are of the dedicated being 'chalked up'" (p. 174) and relates this idea to references in Bacon's writings. Concludes that Herbert learned from Bacon that economy of language reflects the economy of the universe.

**1271. Severance, Sibyl Lutz.** "Numerological Structures in *The Temple*," in *"Too Rich to Clothe the Sunne"*: *Essays on George Herbert*, edited by Claude J. Summers and Ted-Larry Pebworth, 229–49. Pittsburgh: University of Pittsburgh Press.

Claims that the tripartite structure of *The Temple*, the manner in which individual poems are fashioned, the way in which the lyrics in *The Church* are linked, and even the basic structure of *The Church* reveal Herbert's careful use of numerology. Maintains that the overall structure of *The Temple* reflects the Trinity and notes that the seven-line stanzas in "Sunday," when multiplied by nine, the number of stanzas, produce sixty-three, "the number denoting physical and spiritual transformation" (p. 231). Explains the numerology of "Trinitie Sunday" and "The Sacrifice," arguing that Herbert's purpose is homiletic, and shows how numbers counterpoint the verbal expression of "Justice (I)." Demonstrates how the linking of certain poems has a numerological basis, citing the internal linking of poems, the structuring of sequences in *The Church* to mark relationships between biblical passages, and the linking of two groups of six poems, six signifying the building of the church. Argues that numerological evidence can decide questions concerning the total number of poems in *The Church* and suggests 160—60 as the number of the church construction and 100 as the number of a return to unity. Concludes that "to measure *The Temple* as a whole, we must read numbers as well as words" (p. 247).

**1272. Shawcross, John T.** "Herbert's Double Poems: A Problem in the Text of *The Temple*," in *"Too Rich to Clothe the Sunne"*: *Essays on George Herbert*, edited by Claude J. Summers and Ted-Larry Pebworth, 211–28. Pittsburgh: University of Pittsburgh Press.

Argues that "the stanzaic form, structure, and metrics of the individual poems in *The Temple* have major significance for meaning within each poem and within the sequence" (p. 211). Notes that a problem exists with the seven double poems that are treated as single poems. Claims that, "if one of these double poems is two distinct poems, then two subjects, two treatments, two structures, and two image patterns exist with distinct conclusions" (p. 212). Argues that the double poems "Good Friday," "The H. Communion," "The Church-floore," "Christmas," and "Vanitie (II)" are each really two distinct poems, but that "An Offering" is not, making the complete number 170, or 168 if *The Church Militant* and "L'Envoy" are excluded. Points out how this view changes critical readings of the poems, such as Tuve's reading of "Good Friday" (entry 409). Explicates the two poems of "The Church-floore." Concludes by emphasizing the importance of determining individual poems, for "studies of the structure of *The Temple*, of numerological concepts at work, of proportion, interpretation, and artistic achievement are dependent upon each individual poem" (p. 221).

**1273. Stanwood, P. G.** "Seventeenth-Century English Literature and Contemporary Criticism." *Anglican Theological Review* 62:395–410.
Argues that modern critics of English devotional literature of the earlier seventeenth century need to develop a more adequate historical sense that would allow them to participate imaginatively in the life of another time and place. Reviews unhistorical trends in the criticism of English devotional poetry of the period and offers "from an Anglican and devotional point of view a plot of the critical course which may in the future be most profitably followed" (p. 396). Distrusts literary genealogies or groupings of writers into "schools" and maintains that most writers of the period are better defined by their differences than by any similarities. Argues that, since most of the writers were Anglicans, critics must understand the Anglican temper, "with its distinctive ethos and its familiar threefold appeal to Scripture, to tradition, and to reason" (p. 403). Recommends Richard Hooker's *Of the Laws of Ecclesiastical Polity* as a work that gives an insight into the Anglican Church of the period. Singles out Rosemond Tuve's work on Herbert and Louis Martz's work on the poetry of meditation as examples of informed historical scholarship and mentions approvingly the work of Joseph Summers and Amy Charles. Comments on "the happy spirit of Anglicanism" that informs Herbert's life and poetry and maintains that his poetry "is best met on its own terms by readers who share, or who want to at least try to share, in his beliefs" (p. 406).

**1274. Strier, Richard.** "Ironic Humanism in *The Temple*," in *"Too Rich to Clothe the Sunne": Essays on George Herbert*, edited by Claude J. Summers and Ted-Larry Pebworth, 33–52. Pittsburgh: University of Pittsburgh Press.
Claims that in his poetry Herbert at times advances the humanist position that man is "a rational and potentially self-governing creature," a position that creates tension with the Reformation counterview that self-knowledge "leads to self-condemnation and distrust" (p. 33). Sees "Man" as "the most important humanist document in *The Temple*" (p. 34) and argues that it seems to contradict ideas in other poems in *The Church*. Maintains that the rhetorical intent of the poem is to praise God through praising his creation, man, and to conclude that man's proper role is to serve God. Nevertheless, sees the basic premise of the poem—that man is a "stately habitation" (line 2) for God—as contradicting the Reformation view that man is a "chaotic thing" (p. 39). Discusses "The Pulley" as an "ironic companion piece" (p. 40) to "Man" that begins with a humanistic depiction of man that is checked by God's withholding of the "jewell" (line 12) of rest, because God knows that man would inevitably misuse it to adore himself, not God. Discusses "Sinne (I)" and "Humilitie" as Herbert's "most considered statement on ethical humanism" (p. 46) and maintains that the argument of the latter suggests that, "because of the undermining power of pride, the humanist ideal of control over the passions is possible only through grace" yet, even after receiving grace, we feel "such remains of imperfection as afford us abundant cause for humility" [Calvin] (p. 50).

**1275. Summers, Claude J., and Ted-Larry Pebworth, eds.** *"Too Rich to Clothe the Sunne": Essays on George Herbert.* Pittsburgh: University of Pittsburgh Press. xvi, 260p.

In an introduction, entitled "'Too Rich to Clothe the Sunne': Celebrating George Herbert" (pp. ix-xvi), the editors view some of the complex features of Herbert's poetry and comment on his attitude toward his art. Maintains that "Herbert's status as a major poet is now assured" and suggests that this collection "both confirms his position and celebrates his achievement" (p. xii). Notes that the fifteen essays in this collection originated as submissions to the third biennial Renaissance conference held on 20–21 October 1978 at the University of Michigan–Dearborn and that nearly all the original versions were presented at the conference, "several in abbreviated form" (p. xii). Maintains that the essays "explore the richness of Herbert's poetry" and that "together they mirror their subject's complexity in the wide variety of critical and scholarly approaches that they use" (p. xii). Each of the essays has been separately entered in this bibliography. Divided into five parts: (1) "Frame and Fabric" (pp. 1–52), which includes John R. Mulder, "*The Temple* as Picture" (entry 1259); Chana Bloch, "Spelling the Word: Herbert's Reading of the Bible" (entry 1231); Richard Strier, "Ironic Humanism in *The Temple*" (entry 1274); (2) "Constellations of the Story" (pp. 53–112), which includes Robert B. Hinman, "The 'Verser' at *The Temple* Door: Herbert's *The Church-porch*" (entry 1249); Ilona Bell, "The Double Pleasures of Herbert's 'Collar'" (entry 1230); Frances M. Malpezzi, "Thy Cross, My Bower: The Greening of the Heart" (entry 1255); Mario A. Di Cesare, "Herbert's 'Prayer (I)' and the Gospel of John" (entry 1236); (3) "Many Gifts in One" (pp. 113–61), which includes William V. Nestrick, "'Mine and Thine' in *The Temple*" (entry 1261); Anne C. Fowler, "'With Care and Courage': Herbert's *Affliction* Poems" (entry 1242); Roger B. Rollin, "Self-Created Artifact: The Speaker and the Reader in *The Temple*" (entry 1266); (4) "In Another Make Me Understood" (pp. 163–207), which includes William A. Sessions, "Bacon and Herbert and an Image of Chalk" (entry 1270); Leah Sinanoglou Marcus, "George Herbert and the Anglican Plain Style" (entry 1256); Louise Schleiner, "Seventeenth-Century Settings of Herbert: Purcell's 'Longing'" (entry 1268); (5) "The Builder's Care" (pp. 209–49), which includes John T. Shawcross, "Herbert's Double Poems: A Problem in the Text of *The Temple*" (entry 1272); Sibyl Lutz Severance, "Numerological Structures in *The Temple*" (entry 1271). Notes on the Contributors (pp. 253–56) and Index to Herbert's Works Cited (pp. 257–60).
Reviews:
Amy M. Charles, *C&L* 31, no. 1 (1981): 51–54
Anthony Low, *GHJ* 4, no. 2 (1981): 47–52
Mary Ellen Rickey, *RQ* 35 (1982): 130–33
John R. Roberts, *SCN* 40 (1982): 66, 68–69
Clayton D. Lein, *MP* 80 (1983): 413–16
Sidney Gottlieb, *RES*, May 1984, p. 227

**1276. Wooden, Warren W.** "A Question of Influence: George Herbert and R. S. Thomas." *Little Review* 6:26–29.

Argues that Herbert clearly influenced R. S. Thomas but that the relationship between the two poets is "a very complex one spanning both Herbert's roles as poet and priest" (p. 28). Maintains that the influence was "not narrow or specific enough to call Herbert an important 'source' for Thomas, in the sense of borrowed phrases or poetic strategies," but that there does exist "a shared attitude toward form, structural and linguistic economy, the distinctive use of metaphor, parable, traditional symbols, and the accent of absolute sincerity" (p. 28). Concludes that "these similarities go beyond accident or coincidence, yet they may well point beyond the simple case of one poet having studied and assimilated the other's work" (p. 28).

**1277. Yoshida, Sachiko.** "Shi wa Kanmuri ni Aruzu—George Herbert to shi no Giko no Kakawari" [George Herbert's Technique]. *The Albion* 26:1–19.
   Traces the development of Herbert's views on the nature and function of poetry as reflected in *The Temple*.

# 1981

**1278. Anselment, Raymond A.** "Seventeenth-Century Adaptations of 'The Church-porch.'" *GHJ* 5, nos. 1–2 (1981–1982): 63–69.
   Points out that in the seventeenth century *The Church-Porch* was Herbert's most popular poem and comments on three hitherto unexamined adaptations that show that "a wide range of seventeenth-century readers valued the practical as well as the religious emphasis of the poem's epigrammatic verse" (p. 63). Maintains that John Bryan, in the fifth of eight sermons published in 1670 as *Dwelling with God*, "valued the moral precepts" in Herbert's poem but not its "wit and craftsmanship" (p. 64). Notes that almost 40 percent of the "Youth's Alphabet: Or, Herbert's Morals," appended to the British edition of Thomas White's *A Little Book for Little Children*, a practical guidebook for the conduct of daily life, is "predominantly moralistic rather than artful" (p. 64) and "accentuates the epigrammatic and moralistic nature of Herbert's poem" (p. 65). Points out that *The Way to be Rich: According to the Practice of the Great Audley*, written by the unidentified G. B. and published in 1662, shows that Herbert's observations on moral conduct were used to give pragmatic advice to those seeking worldly success. Concludes that *The Church-Porch* "offered seventeenth-century writers both a model and a source for the wealth of epigrammatic lore which appealed both to the practical and the ideal" and that its scope "can support the views of conduct in Bryan's moralistic sermon as well as those of G. B.'s pragmatic pamphlet, just as its aphoristic character can inspire an alphabet of truisms" (p. 68).

**1279. Asals, Heather A. R.** *Equivocal Predication: George Herbert's Way to God.* Toronto, Buffalo, London: University of Toronto Press. xii, 145p.
   Maintains that in seventeenth-century theology equivocation replaced Thomistic analogy as a way of predicating God and argues that the pun, the equivocal predication—where "one thing equals two" (p. xi)—is the key to understanding Herbert's poetic vision. In the "Preface" (pp. xi-xii) argues that this study should be considered as a sequel to Joseph Summers's *George Herbert: His Religion and Art* (entry 435). In "Introduction: Holy Equivocation" (pp. 3–17) outlines her critical agreements and disagreements with earlier critics and announces her intention "to restore Herbert as a specifically Anglican poet" (p. 5). Discusses the importance of the Eucharist in understanding Herbert's poetry and argues that the eucharistic sacrifice in *The Temple* "is the sacrifice of language itself: the poetry is eucharistic because it consecrates the 'creature' of language as the ontological bridge to the divine" (p. 6). Maintains that her view of Herbert's language is an extension of Stanley Fish's in *Self-Consuming Artifacts* (entry 905) and that "what has been best said about Herbert's idea of

language to date is very much in line with what has been remarked on as his concern with the Many and the One" (p. 8). Discusses Herbert's view of equivocation and provides a vocabulary for discussing the varieties of equivocacy in *The Temple*. In chapter 1, "The Chirograph: Liturgy and Ontology" (pp. 18–37), explains that, for Herbert, the physical act of writing "connects itself in the eternal scheme of things" (p. 18) and that his poems become "verbal icons" that serve "as an ontological bridge, re-spelling the universe, and re-integrating the individuating language (which defines things separately) into oneness which is the Being of God" (p. 29). In chapter 2, "The Sacramental Voice: Distance Related" (pp. 38–56), discusses Herbert's use of a sacramental persona in *The Temple* and shows how "the coat, the robe, the garment of Christ is in Herbert's poetry a metaphor for the poet's voice which a man *puts on* in speaking to God" (p. 39). Claims that, when speaking to God, man actually "speaks *in* God" and "the roles of the addressing and the addressed break down" and become "sacramental interaction" (p. 40). Maintains that Herbert's persona "identifies more directly with the prophetic personality of David as type of Christ in the Psalms" (p. 42). In chapter 3, "Augustinianism: The Use and Enjoyment of Poetry" (pp. 57–75), discusses Herbert's Augustinian use of poetry to draw men to God and points out that "injunctions, emblem-tags, proverbs, and parables appear throughout *The Temple*, bearing a warning to the poet himself that he is but a wanderer in this world travelling to God on a sea of words" (p. 59). Maintains that "one of the maturing processes that *The Temple* records is the persona's growth into philosophical-theological understanding of the validity of synecdoche, of the part standing for the whole" (p. 72). In chapter 4, "Wisdom: The Seam and the Wine" (pp. 76–93), points out that proverbs "play an important part in the development and meaning of *The Temple*, in the organization of its concept of Wisdom, and in the emergence of its own self-reflective poetic theory" (p. 76). Notes that, from the time of the Church Fathers through the Renaissance, the Solomonic books of the Bible (*Proverbs*, *Ecclesiastes*, and *Canticles*) "were interpreted as setting forth the progression of Wisdom, in three steps, toward the Truth which is to be found on earth" (p. 80) and shows that Herbert wrote poems in all three groups. Comments on the effects of Wisdom literature on *The Temple*. In chapter 5, "One-Both and the Face of Anglicanism" (pp. 94–110), maintains that an understanding of Mary Magdalene, Magdalene Herbert, and the "both-one trope of Anglicanism" (p. 99) is central to an understanding of Herbert's poetics and discusses how the Anglican Church "is the reconciling *place* of Herbert's both mortal and transcendent aesthetic" (p. 95). In "Afterword" (pp. 111–12) maintains that this study is "a mixed genre of theology-criticism" (p. 111) and urges similar studies of Herbert. Stresses the importance of Renaissance logic and contends that to understand Herbert's poetry "we must practise another form of the willing suspension of disbelief and enter a world where things mean differently" (p. 112). Notes (pp. 115–29), bibliography of exegetical and doctrinal materials (pp. 131–39), and index (pp. 141–45).

Reviews:

Virginia Ramey Mollenkott, *GHJ* 5 (1981–1982): 87–90
Diana Benet, *MiltonQ* 16 (1982): 23
Alan Rudrum, *UTQ* 51 (1982): 417–19
Raman Selden, *TLS*, 11 June 1982, p. 647
R. A. Kimbrough, *ClioI* 12 (1983): 206–7
Leah S. Marcus, *JEGP* 82 (1983): 556–60
Mary Ellen Rickey, *C&L* 32, no. 2 (1983): 52–54
Daniel W. Doerksen, *ESC* 10, no. 2 (March 1984): 98–106

Jonathan F. S. Post, *JDJ* 3, no. 2 (1984): 221–47

**1280. Bradbrook, M[uriel] C.** "Herbert's Ground." *E&S* 34:66–87.
Examines Herbert's poetry and faith in light of his family life and his years at Cambridge. Describes *The Temple* as "entirely about personal relationships, although other human beings than Jesus are not the subject of it" and calls it "intimate without being personal" and "sensuous without being erotic" (p. 73). Maintains that, for Herbert, the psalms "provided a powerful integrative force for his imagination" and "pervade his English poetry to an extent unmatched by any other English poet" (p. 74). Argues that the doctrines of the Trinity and the Incarnation permeate Herbert's thinking and writing but that his poetry is not doctrinal but rather "the most inclusive form of experience" and "a practice of the presence of God" (p. 81). Notes that, in both Latin and English poems, Herbert concentrates often on Christ's passion and that "about a third of the poems in *The Temple* are variations on spiritual pain" (p. 79). Shows how Herbert's poetry "is full of contradictory moods, sometimes emphasized by contradictory titles" (p. 79). Disagrees with A. D. Nuttall's evaluation of Herbert's theology and religious sensibility (entry 1262). Comments on a number of poems, both English and Latin, and gives a reading of "Vertue," which "seems to enclose past, present, and future so that time finally is transformed" (p. 85) and contains two of Herbert's favorite images, the rose and the box.

**1281. Cain, T[homas] G[rant] S[teven].** *Jacobean and Caroline Poetry: An Anthology.* London, New York: Methuen. xiii, 334p.
In the introduction (pp. 1–8) rejects the conventional labels assigned to Jacobean and Caroline poets, noting that the so-called metaphysical poets do not form a unified group, school, or movement. Recognizes the great influence that Donne had on other poets but finds the idea of a "School of Donne" unconvincing. Suggests that it might be more accurate to talk about a "School of Herbert." Notes, however, that many of the poets of the period were related by the political, religious, and intellectual problems of their day and, in some cases, by the strategies they used to cope with them. Includes a sketch of Herbert's life and a selected bibliography (pp. 102–3), noting that the "simplicity" in Herbert's poems is "the weapon of the sophisticated rhetorician" (p. 102). Includes twenty-four lyrics from *The Church* (pp. 103–24), followed by notes on individual poems (pp. 315–16).

**1282. [Charles, Amy M., ed.]** *Cross-Bias: The Newsletter of the Friends of Bemerton Society*, no. 7 (Winter 1981/1982). 6p.
Comments on the saplings from a medlar tree in Herbert's garden that have been imported to the University of North Carolina–Greensboro; announces a number of scholarly papers given recently on Herbert at conferences and includes summaries by Edmund Miller and Charles Kovich; prints Garret Keizer's account of his visit to Bemerton and Salisbury and points out inexpensive accommodations in the area; presents a description of the bell in St. Andrew's; offers an brief evaluation of Grosart's edition of Herbert; and presents other items of interest to the members of the society, such as an obituary of Henry Herbert Rogers, longtime church warden at Bemerton, and an account of popular uses of Herbert's Proverb 524 from *Outlandish Proverbs.*

**1283. Davie, Donald, ed.** *The New Oxford Book of Christian Verse.* Oxford: Oxford University Press. xxix, 320p.

In the introduction (pp. xvii-xxix) explains the basis for including or excluding a poem ("Does it deserve to appear between the same covers as Herbert's 'The Collar' or his 'Church-monuments'?") and discusses the nature of Christian verse. Points out that Herbert and Vaughan are "lavishly" represented in the anthology and recognizes both as seventeenth-century "masters of the sacred poem in English" (p. xxiv). Reproduces fifteen lyrics from *The Church*, without notes or commentary.

**1284. Di Cesare, Mario A.** "Image and Allusion in Herbert's 'Prayer (I).' " *ELR* 11:304-28.
Portions of this essay first appeared as "Herbert's 'Prayer (I)' and the Gospel of John," in *"Too Rich to Clothe the Sunne"*: *Essays on George Herbert*, edited by Claude Summers and Ted-Larry Pebworth (entry 1236), 101-12.
Argues that in "Prayer (I)" Herbert treats prayer the way that other poets deal with love: "intuitively, experientially, speculatively, in metaphors that express, but that also probe and explore" (p. 305). Maintains that the poem is "not a doctrinal or technical exposition of prayer," as many recent critics suggest, but is "an enactment of the process of prayer" (p. 309) and "a struggle towards definition which finally surrenders in the abandonment of the self to the inability to control or define prayer" (p. 310). Presents a detailed commentary on the metaphorical descriptions of prayer in the poem, explaining numerous allusions to the writings of the Church Fathers, the mystics, and the saints; to the liturgy; to Christian iconography; and especially to the Bible. Finds a number of Johannine images and allusions. Discusses recurring themes, metrical patterns, and rhythmical organization of major parts of the poem but maintains that it "refuses a single reading" because its "subject is elusive and unstable, as spiritual reality must be in a human context" (p. 325). Concludes that the "approaching silence" of the final phrase "epitomizes the rest of the poem—a 'raid on the inarticulate'" (p. 328).

**1285. Elsky, Martin.** "Polyphonic Settings and the Voice of George Herbert's *The Temple*." *MLQ* 42:227-46.
Argues that the deconstructionist view that Herbert's poems show only the failure and annihilation of both the poet and his poetic text is exaggerated and that a close comparison of the poems to part-music will "redress some of the imbalances of this view and describe a model for Herbert's use of dramatic voice that is more historically accurate" (p. 228). Maintains that, "aware of the deficiency of the unaided human voice, Herbert uses verbal equivalents of musical polyphony" in order to "represent the interplay between divine and human voices" (p. 228). Through a discussion of poems such as "Easter," "Affliction (III)," and "The Sacrifice," shows that "polyphony describes the ideal relationship between the poet's voice and God's" and that "polyphony, especially polyphonic psalmic praise, also becomes a metaphor for the self" (p. 245). Concludes that, for Herbert, "the self is in its proper state only when it imitates Christ, an act accomplished by a submission to the divine will, just as the poet can properly praise God only when he submits to the divine voice" (p. 246). Quotes numerous examples to show that his view is supported both by contemporary musical authorities, such as Henry Peacham, John Case, Thomas Morely, and William Byrd, and by theologians, such as St. Athanasius, St. Augustine, and John Calvin.

**1286. Fraser, G. S.** "The Seventeenth Century," in *A Short History of English Poetry*, 112-59. Skepton Mallet, Somerset: Open Books.
Presents a general introduction to Herbert's poetry (pp. 120-22). Maintains that, unlike Donne, Herbert "seeks to make us aware of his devotion and God, its object,

but not of himself except as an ordinary Christian striving to do his duty" (p. 121). Summarizes the argument of "Hope" and suggests that Herbert's parishioners would not have understood it.

**1287. Gillham, David.** "Herbert's Restlessnesse." *UCTSE* issue 11:1–12.

Argues that Herbert can describe the restlessness, frustration, and intellectual struggle that confront one attempting to live the spiritual life while "keeping a sense of proportion, even of humour" (p. 1), as in "Hope" and "The Pulley." Observes that in most of his poems dealing with the frustration of his religious calling Herbert "is aware of the negative aspects of the intellectual or academic side of the activity" (p. 3) but that he also realizes that "thought is the stuff of human life, and, even when thinking is distressful and futile, the faculty is God's especial gift" (p. 9). Discusses "The Collar," "Affliction (I)," "Affliction (IV)," and "The Windows" to demonstrate that Herbert "shows an increasing understanding of his position and indicates an increasing satisfaction in his calling" (p. 3). Maintains that in "The Windows" Herbert "can accept the pains of the internal polemic and the endless wrestle to comprehend the light because he accepts the meaning of what it is to be a man and because he is given the example and the support of the Creator who could also accept the limitations of the restless human condition" (p. 11).

**1288. Gottlieb, Sidney.** "Herbert's 'Coloss.3.3' and Thomas Jenner's *The Soules Solace.*" *ELN* 18:175–79.

Points out that several sections of George Hakewill's *The Vanity of the Eie* (1608) present useful information on Herbert's reference to the "one eye" in line 7 of "Coloss.iii.3.," noting that for both Herbert and Hakewill "earthly and heavenly vision are inversely proportional" (p. 177). Argues that a more convincing source for Herbert's figure is Thomas Jenner's *The Soules Solace, or Thirtie and one Spirituall Emblems* (1626, reprinted in 1631, 1639), which contains an emblem of an archer using one eye as he aims his arrow at God's Glory and an accompanying poem that elaborates on the archer's one eye, and notes that the theme and figures in "Coloss.iii.3." are "virtually the same as Jenner's" (p. 178). Acknowledges that there is no proof that Herbert read either book but maintains that, in the case of Jenner, there are several other similarities (such as Jenner's emblem 23 and the end of the second part of Herbert's "Good Friday") that make his connection with Herbert more plausible.

**1289. Hegnauer, Salomon.** *Systrophe: The Background of Herbert's Sonnet "Prayer."* (European University Studies. Series XIV: Anglo-Saxon Language and Literature, vol. 87.) Bern, Frankfurt, Las Vegas: Peter Lang. 241p.

Analyzes the rhetorical complexity of "Prayer (I)" using a structuralist approach. Following "A. Methodological Remarks" (pp. 9–22), the work is divided into three parts. In "B. Induction: Phenomenology of Systrophe" (pp. 23–65), defines systrophe "from as many angles as possible" and tries "to distill the quintessence of systrophe by isolating all its pertinent features" (p. 22); in "C. Deduction: Applied Systrophe" (pp. 67–176), brings together "the pure substance of systrophe and the live poetic matter" (p. 22) and discusses the results; and in "D. Applied Systrophe" (pp. 177–238), discusses examples of systrophe in the poetry of Vaughan, Crashaw, and Herbert and presents a detailed analysis of the rhetoric of "Prayer (I)" (pp. 191–236). Calls the poem "the most conspicuous example of systrophe" (p. 191) and "faultless" (p. 192). Shows how the sonnet form "successfully counteracts the systrophic expansion" and how "by being combined with the sonnet form the systrophe gains a rare stringency and concentration" and claims that the fact that Herbert "succeeds in combining the dialectical movement of the sonnet—tending towards finality—with the rhetorical pattern of the systrophe—implying infinite definition—is one of the wonders of this poem" (p. 193). Maintains that "in applying a systrophic technique to a definition of a basically systrophic activity as prayer is, Herbert achieves a rare congruency of form and subject" (p. 196). Comments on the poem's metaphorical code by presenting detailed explanations of the metaphorical descriptions of prayer and claims that "they basically are controlled by the dogmatic and emblematic conventions of Christian symbolism" (p. 233). Discusses the subtlety and effectiveness of the closing phrase, "something understood," calling it "one of Herbert's most memorable phrases, and at the same time one of the triumphs of his art and heart" (p. 233). Bibliography of primary and secondary sources (pp. 239–41).

**1290. Herbert, George.** *George Herbert: The Country Parson, The Temple,* edited, with an introduction by John N. Wall, Jr., preface by A. M. Allchin. (The Classics of Western Spirituality.) New York, Ramsey, Toronto: Paulist Press. xxii, 354p.

In the preface (pp. xi-xvii) Allchin considers Herbert as "a significant contributor to the development of the spiritual heritage of the English speaking world" (p. xi) and comments on his religious sensibility and how it reflects a crucial period in the history of Anglicanism. Maintains that Herbert had a "remarkable capacity to hold together things often believed to be separable or opposed to one another" (p. xii) and observes that in both his poetry and prose "Herbert discovers the sacramental quality of all life" (p. xv). Claims that Herbert's appeal today is that, "without evading the complexity of things, without glossing over the fragility and brokenness of man's experience with life in time, he managed to reaffirm the great unities of Christian faith and prayer" (p. xvi). In the foreword (pp. xix-xxii) Wall outlines the editorial principles governing the collection and gives a brief account of Herbert's life and works. Argues that the two works included "are best seen as complementary presentations of an argument for the Christian life, as George Herbert experienced it" (p. xx). In the introduction (pp. 1–51) Wall presents a detailed account of Herbert's life and works, stressing that his life was "a model of priestly devotion" (p. 47) and that his prose and poetry are expressions of "the essential spirit of seventeenth-century Anglicanism" (p. 6). Comments on Herbert's religious sensibility, his attitude toward the Church, his uses of the Bible, his concept of priesthood, and his ideals for living the spiritual life, maintaining that his spirituality was a synthesis of Evangelical and Catholic piety. Presents a detailed introduction to *A Priest to the Temple* and *The Temple* and to their texts and details the editorial principles that govern the edition. Presents annotated modern-spelling editions of *A Priest to the Temple* (pp. 53–115) and *The Temple,* along with the texts of two prayers and a few poems not included in the first edition of *The Temple* (pp. 117–333). Selected bibliography (pp. 335–39), index to the preface, introduction, and notes (pp. 341–44), index to texts and scripture references (pp. 345–51), and index to poems (pp. 352–54).
Reviews:
Sidney Gottlieb, *GHJ* 5 (1981–1982): 91–93
W. H. Halewood, *Ren&R* 20 (1984): 67–68

**1291. Hovey, Kenneth Alan.** " 'Inventa Bellica'/ 'Triumphus Mortis': Herbert's Parody of Human Progress and Dialogue of Divine Grace." *SP* 78:275–304.

Argues that Herbert wrote "Inventa Bellica" between 1618 and 1623 as a companion poem to and parody of Thomas Reid's "Inventa Adespota" (pre-1624), which glorifies human progress by celebrating the invention of paper and printing. Observes that Herbert's poem, which opposes war, presents an ironic view of human progress, a mock progress or "progress only in evil," with the invention of the cannon bringing about "the ultimate curse on man for his sins" (p. 284). Notes that Herbert's poem circulated both alone and with Reid's poem and that later both poets wrote new versions of their poems, changed the titles, and altered the poems in such a way that they were no longer companion poems. Observes that Herbert entitled his new poem "Triumphus Mortis," appended his own new companion poem entitled "Triumphus Christiani: in Mortem," and finally included both in *Lucus*. Argues that Herbert's first poem was clearly intended as a parody of Reid's first poem but that his second poem is a serious dramatic monologue spoken to men by Death and its companion poem "is not a parody this time, but the Christian's response to Death's boast presented in the main poem, which together form a very simple dialogue" (p. 277). Concludes that these Latin poems are valuable in showing Herbert's earliest attempts at parody and at dialogue and in revealing his pessimistic view of history and of human progress. Appends an edition of "Inventa Bellica" and "Inventa Adespota" and a line-by-line blank-verse translation of each poem. Adds in brackets translations of all substantially different readings in "Triumphus Mortis."

**1292. Huntley, Frank Livingstone.** "What Happened to Two of Herbert's Poems?" in *Essays in Persuasion: On Seventeenth-Century English Literature*, 65–76. Chicago and London: University of Chicago Press.

Reprints, in a slightly revised and expanded form, "What Happened to George Herbert's Poem 'Good Friday'?" from *ELWIU* (entry 1194) and "A Crux in George Herbert's *The Temple*" from *ELN* (entry 833).

**1293. Hussey, Maurice, ed.** "George Herbert," in *Poetry 1600 to 1660*, 110–21, 173–79. Harlow: Longmans.

Anthologizes eleven lyrics from *The Temple* (pp. 110–21) and presents an introduction to Herbert's life and poems, with critical introductions and notes on individual poems (pp. 173–79). Maintains that "the metrical variety, the extremely careful structure of the stanza form and argument, the clarity and beauty of the images and the use of biblical and familiar language all make Herbert's poems more medieval in spirit than at all Donne-like" (p. 173). Compares Herbert to Langland and Hopkins "for his use of language and his pursuit of spiritual self-cultivation" (p. 174).

**1294. Ishii, Shōnosuke.** "George Herbert no 'Sonnets' ni tsuite (Chukai no Hitotsu no kokoromi—2)" [On George Herbert's Sonnets: A Tentative Commentary (2)]. *Soka Daigaku Eigo Eibungaku Kenkyu* [Studies in English Language and Literature, Soka University] no. 9 (5, no. 2) (March): 1–10.

Part 2 of a three-part series of articles. Deals with "Sinne (I)" and "Prayer (I)." See also entries 1251 and 1295.

**1295. ——.** "George Herbert no 'Sonnets' ni tsuite (Chukai no Hitotsu no kokoromi—3)" [On George Herbert's Sonnets: A Tentative Commentary (3)]. *Soka Daigaku Eigo Eibungaku Kenkyu* [Studies in English Language and Literature, Soka University] no. 10 (vol. 6, no. 1) (December): 1–16.

Part 3 of a three-part series of articles. Deals with the ten sonnets not discussed in the first two articles. Concludes that Herbert's sonnets afford much consolation and pleasure when they are read with careful and hearty appreciation, not only to people of the same faith, but also to non-Christian readers. See also entries 1251 and 1294.

**1296. Johnson, Parker H.** "The Economy of Praise in George Herbert's 'The Church.'" *GHJ* 5, nos. 1–2 (1981–1982): 45–62.

Maintains that two important elements in Herbert's poetry are "the problem of an appropriate poetic response to Christ's suffering and the persistent turn toward economic imagery" (p. 45) and argues that "the unpredictable congruencies of language point to legal and mercantile imagery of exchange as a way to explore the difficulty of response to God and the problem of praise" (pp. 45–46). Comments briefly on the highly developed art of praise in the seventeenth century and observes that in most of Herbert's poems there is "a constant meditation on the possibilities and problems of praise, a struggle with the self, and a continual conflict with God over the terms of such praise" (p. 46). Examines in some detail "The Altar," which "establishes that Herbert's poems are intended as a sacrifice of praise"; "The Sacrifice," a dramatic monologue that "sets up the conditions under which Herbert strives to fulfill the obligation of praise"; and "The Thanksgiving," "Herbert's first attempt at resolving the dilemma of praise," which "develops the rhetoric of exchange as one response to this problem" (pp. 48–49). Points out that "the possibility of contractual exchange" shows up in such later poems as "Affliction (II)" and "Obedience" "in the form of economic, legal, and mercantile imagery" (p. 56) but maintains that the subtle shift in imagery of "Affliction (IV)" indicates Herbert's "shifting conception of the purposes of devotional poetry" and his recognition that praise in religious poetry "is a day by day labor, not an attempt to repay Christ's sacrifice" (p. 61).

**1297. Kinnamon, Noel.** "Notes on the Psalms in Herbert's *The Temple*." *GHJ* 4, no. 2:10–29.

Discusses Herbert's use of Psalm structure, his allusions to individual Psalm verses, and his adaptation of particular Psalms "as the basis of otherwise highly original poems" (p. 10). Outlines two major groups of Psalms—those of praise and those of lamentation—each having a distinctive form, and shows how "Antiphon (I)" and "Antiphon (II)" are examples of the first and how "Affliction (IV)," "Deniall," "A Parodie," and a number of other poems are examples of the second. Points out specific allusions to individual psalm verses in "The Altar," "Love unknown," and "Mattens" and notes allusions to whole psalm texts in "The 23d Psalme," "Providence," "Praise (II)," "Easter," "Constancie," "The Flower," and "The Collar." Suggests that Herbert is more closely related to the writers of metrical psalms than critics have realized. Maintains that a comparison of "The Collar" and Psalm 73 "will enrich our understanding of his originality, of the uniqueness of his achievement," because "it illuminates still more clearly the qualities we most admire in his verse: the personal intensity, the dramatic vividness, and the complex variety of recreated experience" (p. 26). Concludes that Herbert's art "was nurtured by a tradition which enslaved others" and that, "except for the Sidneys to a lesser degree, no 'psalmodist' was ever able to distill the essence of religious feeling from the Psalms as Herbert did time and again in *The Temple*" (p. 26).

**1298. Klause, John L.** "George Herbert, *Kenosis*, and the Whole Truth," in *Allegory, Myth, and Symbol*, edited by Morton W. Bloomfield, 209–25. (Harvard English Studies, 9.) Cambridge, Mass.: Harvard University Press.

Argues that in Herbert the major conflict is between the humanist in him, who believes that truth "is compatible with the aesthetic and moral good he seeks to promote," and the Christian in him, who would like to be a humanist insofar as he can but "must acknowledge that in this finite, fallen world, *bonum* and *verum* are often in competition, to the distress of the later" (p. 211). Maintains that a consideration of the biblical notion of *kenosis*, or "emptying," one of most important themes in *The Temple*, will reveal "how intense and how crucial this struggle may have been"

(p. 213). Defines *kenosis* as "a self-diminishment that involves a deliberate departure from the truth" and maintains that Herbert "could not practice self-denial without demurrals that he was too honest to conceal" (p. 214). Maintains that ultimately Herbert saw *kenosis* not as self-annihilation but as self-forgetfulness and thus was able to confront "the threat that *kenosis* poses to his instincts and values" with "a faith that the deprivations brought about by self-neglect are somehow illusory" (p. 221). Argues that in order to embody these religious paradoxes into his poetry Herbert used the symbols that his faith provided, such as the Eucharist, the altar, the temple, and stones. Maintains that the stones in *The Temple* are the individual poems, which "can themselves be considered symbolic of the filling that preempts *kenosis*" (p. 223). Concludes that one reason Herbert's poetry is "so compelling" is that "it records the travail of a soul who perceives an ideal to which his feelings must be made to accord, of a soul not content with what is given but struggling toward a truth beyond momentary facts and appearances" (p. 225).

**1299. Kronenfeld, Judy Z.** "Herbert's 'A Wreath' and Devotional Aesthetics: Imperfect Efforts Redeemed by Grace." *ELH* 48:290–309.

Traces the long tradition of "wreath" or "garland" poems from pre-Christian times to the seventeenth century. Analyzes "A Wreath" to show how Herbert subtly turns an imperfect, man-made wreath into a poem of genuine praise. Argues that the central quandary in the poem is "the desire to praise and the felt imperfections of the praiser" (p. 295) and that the poem becomes "a meditation on the question of how to reach God" (p. 296). Maintains that, as the poem unfolds, it changes from an emphasis on what the speaker can do for God "to an emphasis on what God must do for him" (p. 299). Contends that ultimately Herbert "deals with the negative implications of wreaths by weaving a wreath that allows God to also weave for His own purposes, by himself making a crown conceptually inferior to the crown God can make of him" and that finally the apparent artifice of the poem, the speaker's "imperfect saying" is "redeemed by grace" (p. 303).

**1300. Matar, N. I.** "A Note on George Herbert and Peter Sterry." *GHJ* 5, nos. 1–2 (1981–1982): 75–77.

Argues that, although *The Temple* influenced writers of very different political and religious convictions throughout the Restoration, Peter Sterry is "one of the few Restoration nonconformists who responded to both Herbert's devotional as well as poetic contribution" (p. 75). Points out that, in a letter to his son Peter in the 1660s, Sterry recommended the reading of Herbert, probably *The Church-Porch*, for moral direction and edification and that in an eschatological poem, written toward the end of his life, Sterry used a horticultural metaphor similar to metaphors in "The Flower" and "Paradise." Concludes that Sterry "could not emulate Herbert's poetic versatility" (p. 76) but that his "resilient imagination helped him to respond favorably to Herbert, and to discover in *The Temple* inspiration for his last poem" (p. 77).

**1301. Meilaender, Marion.** "Speakers and Hearers in *The Temple*." *GHJ* 5, nos. 1–2 (1981–1982): 31–44.

Argues that Herbert "responds to the potential problems of religious poetics by affirming the ideal of simplicity while mapping the complicated path that human beings must take to reach that fulfillment" and that he frequently "conveys this double-edged truth by the use of personae and interlocutors, pitting them against one another to dramatize God's pursuit of the soul in the face of the latter's resistance" (pp. 42–43). Points out that "from the voice of the Lord in the Garden of Eden to the voice of the Alpha and Omega commanding the exiled St. John to write his Book of Revelation, the Bible is filled with divine voices that reach down unbidden to admonish, to instruct, and save" and maintains that "these voices echo in *The Temple*'s devotional lyrics" (p. 38). Notes that "before his divine audience, the poet seeks to give adequate, honest expression to his spiritual hopes, fears, joys, and sorrows" but that Herbert is also aware of another audience, "the human audience, for whom he must find a convincing way to share his private communion with God" (p. 42). Concludes that, "through a style that transmits a sense of process rather than a set of conclusions, Herbert invites the reader to share the experience captured in the poems" and thus "private devotion is given a universal dimension" (p. 43).

**1302. Merrill, Thomas F.** "Sacred Parody and the Grammar of Devotion." *Criticism* 23:195–210.

Maintains that the ways in which Herbert's poems "disrupt their own order, critique their own clichés, reinvent themselves, and promote a spiritually-salutary humiliation of the 'self'" are "fundamental to the very structure of religious language itself" (p. 199). Compares and contrasts "Song: Soul's joy, now I am gone," attributed to William Herbert, third Earl of Pembroke, and "A Parodie" to show that Herbert's conversion of Pembroke's love poem into a religious lyric "proves to be considerably more than a mere substitution of proper names," for as soon as Herbert "establishes 'Soules joy' as a divine rather than a mortal vocative, he sets in motion a grammatical contest between the 'natural' and a redemptive ontology" (p. 205). Points out that, by letting these conflicting language games exist simultaneously throughout the poem, Herbert "maintains a kind of double vision which, like a stereopticon, provides a religious third dimension impossible to achieve through ordinary discourse" (p. 203). Outlines two kinds of devotional language: language that has "empirical anchorage" (p. 206) and "emphasizes a connection" (p. 208) between man's experiences of himself and his world and his experience of God, and language of "logical docetism" (p. 208) that emphasizes a separation between human and divine. Disagrees with Fish's reading of Herbert and argues that Herbert's verse is language of "empirical anchorage" and connectedness rather than that of "logical docetism" and self-destruction.

**1303. Mroczkowski, Przemysław.** "Pióropusz i Kadzielnica," in *Historia Literatury Angielskiej*, 213–224. Wrocław, Warszawa, Kraków, Gdańsk, Łódź: Zakład Narodowy Im. Ossolińskich Wydawnictwo.

Discusses the general features of Herbert's poetry, commenting on its religious heritage and on its baroque, metaphysical character. Says of "The Collar" that its author replicates the presence of God.

**1304. Nuttall, A. D.** "Gospel Truth," in *Ways of Reading the Bible*, edited by by Michael Wadsworth, 41–54. Brighton, Eng.: Harvester; Totowa, N.J.: Barnes and Noble.

Discusses the problem posed by the devotional lyrics of Herbert in which "the praying Herbert is answered by God," pointing out that "the lines of God were written by Herbert" (p. 41), thus calling into question whether the external voice of God was truly God speaking or Herbert's own conscience, grounded in the teachings of Scripture. Briefly discusses "Love (III)" as an example of Herbert's engagement with the problem of humility in which the speaker finally realizes that God's grace does not depend on his personal desert. Discusses a similar problem with the source of the voice of God in the Gospel of John.

**1305. Plett, Heinrich F.** "Topik und Memoria: Strukturen mnemonischer Bildlichkeit in der englischen Literatur des XVII. Jahrhunderts," in *Topik: Beiträge zur interdisziplinären Diskussion*, edited by Dieter Breuer and Helmut Schanze, 307–33. Munich: Wilhelm Fink Verlag.

Discusses the uses of memory and mnemonic techniques in Herbert's *The Temple* and Christopher Harvey's *The Synagogue*. Notes that both poets wrote a large number of poems that refer to significant places inside and outside churches or temples— the altar, the windows, the chancel, baptismal font—and observes that these objects often act as emblems that figure forth significant theological and spiritual content. Contrasts the ways in which the two poets employ the topoi of the church and claims that Herbert "geht eher von dem subjektiven Gedächtnis der bedrängten christlichen Seele, Harvey eher von dem objektiven Gedächtnis der christlichen Glaubenslehre aus" (p. 323).

**1306. Richmond, Hugh M.** "Ronsard and the English Poets," in *Puritans and Libertines: Anglo-French Literary Relations in the Reformation*, 223–96. Berkeley, Los Angeles, London: University of California Press.

Argues that equation of Pharaoh's Egypt with the affectations of a contemporary court in Ronsard's sonnet beginning "Laisse de Pharaon la terre Egyptienne" helps explain the allusions in "Jordan (I)." Maintains that Herbert "complicates and synthesizes the shared material" and that "the allusion to Pharaoh is no longer overt in Herbert's poem but is more tactfully implicit in its title" (p. 256). Notes that Herbert's poem is far more Christian than Ronsard's but that "the aesthetic freshness lies often in just this unexpected synthesis of profane materials and religious explicitness" (p. 256).

**1307. Rickey, Mary Ellen.** "Herbert's 'Affliction (V)' 1–3." *Expl* 40, no. 1:16.

Argues that a homily by St. Basil apostrophizing Noah's ark is the likely source for Herbert's comparison of ark and the Garden of Eden in lines 1–3 of "Affliction (V)." Concludes that "the poem, then, the most immediately affirmative of the Affliction group, the only one in which the persona grasps the true value of human trouble from the outset of his utterance, is initiated by a figure captivating and provocative of further meditation about God's use of storms, but also authoritative, traditional, and credible."

**1308. Seelig, Sharon Cadman.** "Between Two Worlds: Herbert," in *The Shadow of Eternity: Belief and Structure in Herbert, Vaughan, and Traherne*, 7–43. Lexington: University of Kentucky Press.

Reviews attempts of modern critics from Palmer to Fish to impose a definite arrangement on the poems in *The Temple* in order to show how each is finally partial and inadequate. Discusses the variety of themes, patterns, and voices in *The Temple* as well as Herbert's manipulation of personae, language, meter, moods, and attitudes. Argues that each poem is "one of a long series of challenges we must meet before we can attempt the next" (p. 11). Maintains that *The Temple* "is not only a picture of the poet's many conflicts" but "is a reenactment of those conflicts within the soul of the reader" (p. 11). Comments on the eleven poems on Christ's passion that begin *The Church* to demonstrate "in miniature the instruction of the persona and the illumination of the reader" found throughout *The Temple* and suggests that these poem reflect two didactic and poetic techniques that are central to an understanding of Herbert's poetry—"the transformation of the meaning of words and the establishment of a significant relation between poetic form and statement, between patterns of verse and patterns of life" (p. 15). Discusses how the form of a Herbert poem embodies meaning; how structure, sound, and metrics "are vital elements of his dramatic didacticism" (p. 19); and how Herbert consistently uses "the tension inherent in his verse patterns to suggest the state of the persona's soul" (p. 20). Presents detailed readings of numerous poems, especially "Praise (I)," "Dialogue," "Businesse," "The Agonie," "Deniall," "Christmas," "Sinne (I)," the Affliction poems, "Mortification," "Death," "Prayer (I)," "Bitter-sweet," "The Odour," "Jesu," and "Heaven," and maintains that *The Temple* is "in some sense a single poem" and that "one of its chief subjects is words, the meaning of words, the true apprehension of meaning" (p. 41). Argues that *The Temple* is not "a chaos but a maze" and that its unity and complexity "consist precisely in its presentation of a world in which the truth is perceivable but not always perceived, in which battles won in the first poem must be won again even in the last, in which themes are constant but comprehension and treatment of them are not" (p. 42). Concludes that *The Temple* presents two views of reality—the earthly and the heavenly—"sometimes one is dominant, sometimes the opposing view" and "sometimes they are set in deliberate contrast" but the main point is that "both are always present, even as *The Temple* as a whole moves from one to the other" (p. 42).

**1309. Shaw, Robert B.** *The Call of God: The Theme of Vocation in the Poetry of Donne and Herbert.* Cambridge, Mass.: Cowley Publications. xiii, 123p.

Three lectures given in March 1981 to the members of the American Congregation of the Society of St. John the Evangelist and to friends of the community. In the preface (pp. ix-xiii) announces his intention to focus on close readings of individual poems, noting that many of the poems considered "are not allusions to vocation so much as they are embodiments of it" (p. xii). In chapter 1, "'Many are called': The Shaping of an Idea in Theology and Poetry" (pp. 1–31), defines the Christian notion of vocation, noting two ways in which the concept is used: (1) the call of God to those He has chosen for eternal life, and (2) the occupation or place in society that God assigns to an individual. Maintains that, although alike in many ways, Donne and Herbert differ significantly in their emphasis and tone: Donne focuses on the first sense of vocation and fears that, although he has heard God's call, he "may lack the power to respond to it," but Herbert "shuns these extremes of tone and import" and focuses on the second sense, "on duty rather than destiny" (p. 2). Reviews the lives of both poets and argues that there was in both a "tension between humanist aspiration and Calvinist discipline, between self-will and the will of God" (p. 22). Contrasts Donne's "Death be not proud" and Herbert's "Death," maintaining that "the way each poet views his end is keenly suggestive of the way he views the journey toward it" (p. 26). In chapter 2, "John Donne" (pp. 33–69), surveys Donne's concept of vocation and maintains that Donne was "so absorbed in the idea of vocation as the soul's final destiny that he pays relatively little attention to the nature of particular earthly callings—even to that of the priest or poet" (p. 66). In chapter 3, "George Herbert" (pp. 71–107), contrasts Herbert's focus on duty with Donne's emphasis on destiny and notes "how little troubled Herbert is by the questions upon which Donne expends such anguished speculation" (p. 71). Maintains that in *The Temple* Herbert's treatment of election and the last things is free of anxiety and that these topics are "directly engaged in relatively few poems" (p. 71). Insists that, "if Donne is an explorer of what we may term the vertical axis of Calvin's concept of vocation, Herbert just assiduously explores the horizontal axis" (p. 72). Examines a number of poems that reveal Herbert's discovery of pain and joy in his vocation and discusses those poems in which he examines his attempt to fulfill his calling. Discusses Herbert's concept of the priesthood and his views on poetry, arguing that "poetry and priesthood harmonize precisely in their being sacramental activities, each a means of realizing the presence of God and imparting that presence to others" (p. 95). Notes (pp. 111–20) and an index of names (pp. 121–23).

1310. ———. "Farewells to Poetry." *YR* 70:187–205.
Examines a number of poems in which poets bid a final farewell to the art of writing poetry, including "The Forerunners." Asserts that in his poem Herbert "discovers that he is to be more than compensated for the loss he is bound to suffer" (pp. 202–3). Argues that the repeated declaration, "Thou art still my God," slightly altered from Psalm 31, "is a sufficient talisman to ward off any adversity" (p. 203). Calls the line "the essence of writing, a kind of *ur*-poetry, if you will, which lives within this poet when all his beloved verbal devices, his best friends, have deserted him, and when illness and age, his enemies, have disfigured his outer walls with their bleak graffiti" (p. 203). Comments on Herbert's metaphorical treatment of the "lodgers" to whom he bids farewell as his adopted children and suggests that, by assuming the role of adoptive rather than natural parent, Herbert refers to "one of the great achievements of his writing, which was to borrow, to adapt, to parody seriously or to transform sacramentally the devices of secular poetry" and that he "fears that without his guidance the lovely metaphors may stray back to adorn objects less worthy of their loveliness" (p. 204). Concludes that Herbert adopts the role because "the only true progenitor of any beauteous words, whether secular or divine, is the Divine Word" (p. 205).

1311. **Sledge, Linda Ching.** "The Seventeenth Century," in *Shivering Babe, Victorious Lord: The Nativity in Poetry and Art*, 75–120. Grand Rapids, Mich.: William B. Eerdmans Publishing.
Calls the seventeenth century "the era of the finest Nativity poems in the English tongue" (p. 75) and maintains that these poems "can be seen as virtual historical documents chronicling the revolutionary tenor of the times" (p. 76). Claims that Herbert's "Christmas" fits into a "Laudian mold" and that it offers the reader "an opportunity for self-examination within traditional poetic forms, using ancient liturgical symbols" (p. 78). Argues that the poem is "a meditation, a poetic devotion leading from the contemplation of characters and events in Scripture to a direct encounter with God" (p. 79) and that its meditative technique suggests the influence of St. Ignatius Loyola. Maintains that the poem "shows the difficult path that even seventeenth-century 'High Church' Anglicans were treading, a path meandering perilously between the ancient symbols and sacraments of an authoritarian church tradition and a more probing, personal brand of contemporary Protestantism" (p. 82). Reproduces "Christmas" (p. 83).

1312. **Slights, Camille Wells.** "Casuistry in *The Temple*," in *The Casuistical Tradition in Shakespeare, Donne, Herbert, and Milton*, 183–246. Princeton, N.J.; Guildford: Princeton University Press.
Discusses the pervasiveness of casuistry in *The Temple*. Excludes *The Church-Porch* because its style owes "more to the aphorism and proverb than to the models of ingenious problem solving provided by casuistry" (p. 186). Argues that the lyrics in *The Church* are "less obviously but more deeply permeated with the casuistical habit of mind" and that in them the poet "draws on the moral theology developed by such Protestant theologians as William Perkins" (p. 186). Claims that, "combining logical rigor with the concrete particularity of individual experience," Herbert's lyrics "embody the careful, constant self-examination taught by the casuists" and "move through

problems, puzzles, and fine distinctions to conclusions that are models of spiritual peace" (pp. 186–87). Contends that "the influence of casuistry is most evident in poems where Herbert's speaker experiences bewilderment and doubt" (p. 226). Examines more than sixty of the lyrics in *The Church* to show how the casuistical tradition operates "in a variety of ways in Herbert's poetry—in its concrete particularity and fine moral discriminations, in its balancing of individual moral responsibility with faith in divine omnipotence, in its emphasis on self-examination and on practical action, and in the problem-solving structure of many of the lyrics" (p. 239). Maintains that Herbert's greatest debt to casuistry can be seen in his "self-correcting poems" that "constantly redefine general truths in terms of growing understanding of his particular case" and claims that his style "is firmly related to the moral theology that applies general laws to specific circumstances" (p. 239).

**1313. Sloane, Mary Cole.** *The Visual in Metaphysical Poetry.* Atlantic Highlands, N.J.: Humanities Press. 110p.

Argues that "the impact of the simultaneous existence of emblem, meditation, and epistemological upheaval had a profound effect on the visualizations one finds in metaphysical poetry" and "accounts for much that is dissimilar, as well as similar, in the visual imagery of the metaphysical poets" (preface). Maintains that, "within metaphysical poetry itself, there is a progressive tendency away from the concept that knowledge is part of a universal system of analogies and toward an emphasis on knowledge gained directly from sensory experience" (preface). In chapter 1, "The Noblest Sense and the Book of Nature" (pp. 1–23), discusses the effects of the epistemological upheaval that occurred in the seventeenth century and comments on how each of the metaphysical poets regarded the visual world from which he got his metaphors. Argues that all the metaphysical poets recognized that "the visual image was no longer able to carry the full meaning it had carried for the poets of the sixteenth century" (p. 13). Comments on a number of poems that show Herbert's skepticism and epistemological concerns, his distrust of the senses, and his awareness of the inadequacy of language. In chapter 2, "'With Hyeroglyphicks quite dismembred'" (pp. 24–46), argues that in metaphysical poetry the emblem and discursive meditation meet, helping to "produce those elusive characteristics that distinguish metaphysical conceits from the conceits of the Elizabethans" (p. 24). Maintains that the way in which Donne and Herbert employ emblems "denies rather than affirms the world view that the emblem originally represented" (p. 24). Observes that the complexity of Herbert's imagery "bears a greater relationship to the *Hieroglyphica*, which was so popular during the Renaissance, than it does to the medieval use of imagery" (p. 34). In chapter 3, "'Cannot thy *Dove* Out-strip their *Cupid* easily in flight?'" (pp. 47–72), discusses the visual imagery of Donne and Herbert and its parallels in discursive meditation and in seventeenth-century emblem books. Finds in the poetry of both a "psychological involvement and an immediacy that is as different from the poetry of the past as it would be from the poetry of the future" (p. 48) and attributes these qualities, in part, to their specific uses of emblems and meditation. Comments on three visual characteristics that help explain some of the peculiarities of Donne's and Herbert's conceits: (1) "the visualization of the soul as participant in the religious drama," (2) "the interiorization of the meditative image," and (3) "the equation of the persona of the poem with the object of meditation" (p. 50). In chapter 4, "Real Crowns and Thrones and Diadems" (pp. 73–95), traces the decline of the emblematic in the visual imagery of Crashaw, Vaughan, and Traherne and maintains that by the time of Traherne "the remnants of the hieroglyphically occult that characterize the poetry of Donne and Herbert and that were consistent with their skepticism regarding the validity of sense experience have given way to something more akin to the wonder in nature itself" (p. 94). Notes (pp. 95–105), followed by reproductions of six emblems and an index (pp. 107–10).

**1314. Stanwood, P. G.** "Time and Liturgy in Herbert's Poetry." *GHJ* 5, nos. 1–2 (1981–1982): 19–30.

Describes the use of time and liturgy in *The Temple* and claims that Herbert's poems are liturgical because they not only present a single experience but also transcend time and include all experience. Maintains that in poems written in the liturgical mode moments are "made imaginatively present rather than merely remembered" and that "there is spatial and temporal collapse, where everything pivots on one point, past and future become single in the present, infinity is finite, and the sphere and the circle provide natural figures of description" (p. 20). Observes that in individual poems, in groups of poems, and in *The Temple* as a whole Herbert "celebrates circularity" (p. 21) and that his plan is "cumulative and reverberative" in that "no one poem can be fully known without our reading all the others" and yet "each poem speaks separately as well as contextually" (p. 22). Comments on the circularity in individual poems, such as "Clasping of hands," "Sinnes round," and "A Wreath," points out the liturgical features of "Aaron," and notes how the poems from "The Collar" through the "Clasping of hands," "closely related by theme and language, form a circle of meaning, though each poem lives also by itself" (p. 27). Discusses "The Bunch of Grapes" as a "notable example of an action, complete in itself and emblematic of the whole" (p. 27). Maintains that "the backward and forward movement of the poems in *The Temple* reflects the simultaneous Godward and manward movement of all worship" and that "the structural motif of *The Temple* is the circle or the sphere—the true liturgical design—where time is everywhere and nowhere" (p. 28).

**1315. Steele, Oliver.** "Crucifixion and the Imitation of Christ in Herbert's 'The Temper (I).'" *GHJ* 5, nos. 1–2 (1981–1982): 71–74.

Argues that in "The Temper (I)" Herbert "subtly but persistently emphasizes the theme of the Christian's imitation of Christ even to the imitation of Christ's agony on the cross" (p. 71). Maintains that the speaker's identification with the suffering Christ is evident in three Crucifixion images: (1) the Old Testament harp (lines 22–24), which was considered by St. Augustine, Cassiodorius, Notker of St. Gall and other patristic writers as a type of the Crucifixion; (2) the spanning of man's arms to match the spanning of Christ's arms on the cross (lines 13–16), an image of imitating the suffering Christ; and (3) the vertical stretching images (lines 5–8), which "are themselves an image of the speaker's imitation of Christ" (p. 73). Concludes that "through the entire poem, then, the speaker has been an imitator of Christ and his imitation has been a kind of crucifixion" (p. 74).

**1316. Strier, Richard.** "George Herbert and the World." *JMRS* 11:211–36.

Rejects the notion that Herbert is an exemplar and exponent of Christian humanism because he does not espouse two essential beliefs of the true Christian humanist: (1) that man is rational and potentially self-governing and (2) that man should have a positive and affirming attitude toward nature and society. Devotes the essay to the second concept, having dealt with the first in an earlier essay (entry 1274). Argues that in "Home" the poet firmly rejects this world and refuses to accept the dual nature of man and maintains that "The H. Communion" best expresses his attitude toward the physical—"a strong asceticism mitigated just enough to remain on the hither side of complete rejection" (p. 215). Offers detailed critical readings of "Mans medley" and "The Size" to illustrate how Herbert equivocates, qualifies, limits, and retracts his position on the reality and rightness of earthly joys. Observes that Herbert's attitude toward politics and social life "is more strongly and unambiguously negative than his attitude toward nature and physical existence" (p. 222). Discusses *A Priest to the Temple*, "The Elixir," and *The Church-Porch* as examples of Herbert's negative view of social and civic humanism. Contends that in the second two-thirds of *The Church Militant* both Christ and Christianity "are presented as radically anti-worldly" (p. 235), thus negating the world-affirming humanism of the first third of the poem.

1317. ———. "History, Criticism, and Herbert: A Polemical Note." *PLL* 17:347–52.
    Maintains that "presuppositions about Herbert's religious position have hobbled and distorted the criticism of his poetry," which "has not, for the most part, been examined as evidence for his religious position, but rather approached through a predetermined sense of what his position is" (p. 347). Challenges the notion that Herbert chose a middle way between Rome and Geneva in both doctrine and worship. Argues that only in worship and ecclesiastical government did Herbert espouse a *via media* and that "there is no evidence in either his poetry or his prose that Herbert ever departed from Calvinism in theology" (pp. 347–48). Discusses "The British Church" to show that there are "some interesting and highly significant contradictions between the 'middle way' rhetoric of the poem and its actual presentation of the opposing liturgical poles" (p. 349). Points out that Herbert portrays the Roman Church as totally corrupt and attacks it in very anti-Catholic language whereas his stanza on the Genevan Church is "comical in mode and mildly pitying in tone" (p. 350) and "is phrased in terms which refer only to the Genevan liturgy, not to doctrine" (p. 351). Finds that Herbert's negative view of "naked spirituality" in "The British Church" is belied in other poems in *The Temple* and suggests that even his attraction to a spirituality free from externals is "not Genevan but antinomian or spiritualist, and its pull leads not to Geneva but beyond—to Amsterdam" (p. 351).

1318. **Summers, Joseph H.** "*George Herbert: His Religion and Art*: Its Making and Early Reception." *GHJ* 5, nos. 1–2 (1981–1982): 1–18.
    To commemorate the reissuing (in cloth and paperback) of *George Herbert: His Religion and Art* (entry 435) by Medieval & Renaissance Texts & Studies, presents a brief history of his personal and intellectual background, commenting especially on persons and events that shaped his interest in Herbert's poetry. Describes the various stages in the development of the book and comments on the difficulties in finding a publisher, the stages of re-writing and revision, and the final acceptance of the manuscript by Chatto and Windus and by Harvard University Press. Discusses briefly the favorable reception that the book received on both sides of the Atlantic. Concludes by noting that, "although there never was any risk of its appearing on any best seller list, the book did a good deal better than Chatto and Windus had predicted" (p. 18).

1319. **Suzuki, Akira.** "George Herbert no 'Juku'" [George Herbert's "Agony"]. *Reading* [Bulletin of the Graduate Student Literary Society, Tokyo University] no. 1 (February): 14–24.
    Argues that there is a rising and falling movement in Herbert's "The Agonie" and relates it to the emotion being expressed.

1320. ———. "'Juku' no Hanpuku—Herbert no *The Temple* wo megutte" [The Repetition of "Agony"—Centering on Herbert's *The Temple*]. *Reading* [Bulletin of the Graduate Student Literary Society, Tokyo University] no. 2 (December): 59–72.

Argues that Herbert composed his poetry as a model reader and a faithful recorder of God's word.

**1321. Tennyson, G. B.** *Victorian Devotional Poetry: The Tractarian Mode.* Cambridge, Mass., and London: Harvard University Press. xiv, 268.

Mentions Herbert throughout. Argues that "seventeenth-century poetry is paradigmatic for understanding the idea of devotional poetry" (p. 6) in English and contends that Anglican devotional poetry at its best is represented by Herbert's *The Temple* and John Keble's *The Christian Year.* Acknowledges that, although in his own day Keble's poetry was often compared to Herbert's and although Keble knew Herbert's poetry and admired it, *The Temple* cannot be considered a model for *The Christian Year.* Notes the influence of Herbert on Keble, Isaac Williams, and Christina Rossetti and briefly compares and contrasts Christopher Harvey's *The Synagogue* and *The Temple.*

**1322. Toliver, Harold E.** "Questers in an Icy Elysée: Moderns without Ancestry," in *The Past that Poets Make*, 160–93. Cambridge, Mass., and London: Harvard University Press.

Discusses Herbert and Donne as spokesmen for the traditionalist attitude toward objects and Wallace Stevens, William Carlos Williams, and Richard Wilbur as spokesmen for the modernist attitude. Argues that Herbert "is perhaps foremost among those who made objects into recurrent exemplars and hieroglyphs under the auspices of Christian dogma and Renaissance commonplaces" and that, "on the nature of history, the way the poet serves as a secondary creator, and the infiltration of the present by types and archetypes, he agrees basically with Milton" (p. 163). Sees *The Temple* as "the spiritual itinerary of the poet and of Everyman among personal and historical phases" where "the soul does not invent its destiny but inherits it" (p. 163). Claims that Herbert "concedes the inevitable scattering of the material world in historical time" but also "has some confidence in the tested and reaffirmed beliefs that guide one's journey" (p. 164). Finds that Herbert shares with other Renaissance poets "a combined sense of classical heritage and beginnings and endings" and "a certain hierarchy of natural and social forms and the hegemony of some concepts over others" (p. 166).

**1323. Tučapský, Antonín.** *The Sacrifice: A Cantata for Four-Part Chorus of Mixed Voices, Baritone Solo and Organ.* Toronto: E. C. Kerby. 76p.

Musical score, with lyrics from Herbert's "The Sacrifice."

**1324. Walker, Keith.** "Marking the Work of George Herbert, Priest and Poet." *The Times* (London), 28 February, p. 16.

Notes that on 27 February Herbert is commemorated in the Anglican liturgy. Offers a general and appreciative introduction to *The Temple*, stressing that, although a master of poetic technique in the construction of the short poem, Herbert wrote primarily "to enable the reader to worship God better." Maintains that what holds *The Temple* together and gives it "a final splendour" is Herbert's "celebration of Christian doctrine, ritual and man's development in God."

**1325. Weibly, P. S.** "George Herbert's 'Heaven': The Eloquence of Silence." *GHJ* 4, no. 2:1–9.

Points out that in "Heaven," the penultimate poem in *The Church*, Herbert presents the speaker as one who, having reached the final stage of his growth, is prepared "to contemplate directly 'those delights on high' (l. 1) in preparation for his ultimate union with Christ figured forth in 'Love (III)'" (p. 4). Maintains that the speaker's stance "requires Herbert to convey that perfect simplicity attained when a soul relinquishes itself to God and enters heaven, an experience demanding true words and, finally, the poet's personal silence" (p. 4). Points out that Herbert achieves these ends by artfully converting classical rhetoric and the classical echo poem into Christian art. Discusses how "reflected sound thereby fulfills the demands of the poet's conception of devotional poetry, providing him with a means to manifest God's Word through a human medium" (p. 7).

**1326. Wengen-Shute, Rosemary Margaret Van.** *George Herbert and the Liturgy of the Church of England.* Oegstgeest: Drukkerij de Kempenaer. 183p.
    Introduction (pp. 9–14); "Liturgical Sources" (pp. 15–72); "The Influence of the Liturgy" (pp. 73–144); conclusion (pp. 145–53); notes (pp. 155–66); bibliography (pp. 167–74); and index (pp. 175–83). Announces that the primary aim of the first part is to identify the sources in *The Book of Common Prayer* "to which certain phrases and images to Herbert's poetry can be traced" and "to show that recognition of their liturgical context deepens and enriches the reader's understanding of the poetry" (p. 11). Discusses Herbert's devotion to the Anglican liturgy, maintaining that it "forms an integral part of his intellectual and emotional make-up, and permeates his whole view of life" (p. 21). Describes how the Prayer Book illuminates the imagery of such poems as "The Sacrifice" and "Discipline." Stresses the centrality of the Eucharist and the Anglican communion service in Herbert's own theology and devotional practice and in *The Temple* and comments on the liturgical aspects of the influence of the Psalms on individual poems as well as on Herbert's thought as a whole. In the second part stresses that Herbert's debt to the Anglican liturgy "is not simply a matter of verbal echoes or chance connections" but "reflects on the part of the poet a liturgical mode of thought" (p. 75). Maintains that the liturgy "forms a stable and unchanging background against which the changing emotions of an individual are brought into their right perspective" and argues that "it is the very existence of this constant element in the spiritual life that makes it possible for Herbert to express his doubts and his dissatisfaction with such outspoken candour" (p. 85). Discusses how the liturgy both "transcends historical time" and yet "focuses on certain specific events of the past and transposes them into the present" (p. 90) and observes that "it is striking to find that among all the interwoven strands which may be traced in the richly complex patterns of Herbert's poetry, the two which stand out as being of prime importance, the Eucharist and the Psalms, both prove to be inseparably connected with Herbert's attitude to time" (p. 118). Acknowledges that the ordering of the poems in *The Temple* does not appear to have been governed by any one principle that might account for the position of each individual poem but contends that the Church calendar "did exert a strong influence on the poems themselves and on the shape of the work as a whole" (p. 135). Maintains that one can detect in *The Temple* "a gradual movement away from the formal treatment of the Church's seasons and services" that suggests a progression "to a state where he recognizes the Church itself to be temporal and transitory," a position he reached "through his devotion to the Church on earth and its liturgy, and through his profound understanding of its nature as a sacramental channel of God's grace" (p. 137).
Review:
Amy Charles, *GHJ* 6, no. 1 (1982): 37–41

**1327. Woods, Susanne.** "The 'Unhewn Stones' of Herbert's Verse." *GHJ* 4, No. 2:30–46.

Argues that Herbert's complex versification can be better understood if we consider "each of Herbert's poems to be an altar, centered by the poet's God-hewn hard heart, on which the sacrifice of his priestly poetic is performed or through which it is made manifest" (p. 31). Maintains that, "like the variously dimensioned stones used uncut by the Israelites to construct their altars, Herbert's various line lengths, stanzaic constructions, and rhyme schemes are fitted together so that the disproportionate is made more proportionate and the simple elements are put together to form a decorous whole" (p. 31). Notes that, "despite the characteristic variety of Herbert's verse forms, their basic elements are with rare exception limited and conventional" (p. 31). Claims that Herbert believed that "poetic form, like the poet himself, must not weave itself into the sense" but rather "must mirror and illustrate the sense, making possible the sacrifice of poetic teaching" (p. 32). Analyzes the technical features of the sequence of poems from "The Altar" to "H. Baptisme (II)" to illustrate Herbert's doctrine of sacrifice and its implications for his approach to versification. Argues that the elements of the biblical poetic described as "unhewn stones" are "a versification apparently natural, with coincidence between phrase and line the common and principal means of achieving that effect; form that supports and even imitates statement; uneven strophic construction," the last of which "is particularly characteristic of Herbert's versification and has an obvious Biblical analogue in the Psalms" (p. 43). Maintains that Herbert's "counterpoint" stanzas are "also analogous to altars of unhewn stones, which are equally a harmony of apparently uneven edges" and that "the unhewn stones of Herbert's verse, therefore, are simply the phrases of God-given speech, which are built up into lines, stanzas, and whole poems that reflect the abundant variety of God's creation" (p. 43). Concludes that Herbert's verse "is both simple and complex at the same time, both natural and artful"; that "its elements, like unhewn stones, are natural and various"; and that "its construction, like the Old Testament altars, turns artistry into dutiful and obedient worship" (p. 44).

# *1982*

**1328. Adler, Jeremy.** "*Technopaigneia, carmina figurata* and *Bilder-Reime*: Seventeenth-century figured poetry in historical perspective." *CCrit* 4:107–47.

Discusses the development of the shaped or patterned poem from the Greek *technopaigneia* by Simmias of Rhodes (4th century B.C.) to the modern era. Outlines five main styles of shaped poems in the sixteenth and seventeenth centuries: (1) imitations of the Greek *technopaigneia* in which lines vary in length to form the outline of an object, (2) Neo-Latin imitations of medieval *carmina figurata*, (3) combinations of the two main kinds in which an outline shape is combined with internal acrostics, (4) various geometrical shapes, such as that described by Puttenham in *Arte of Englishe Poesie*, and (5) cubic shaped poems, sometimes associated with the Cabala. Discusses how these poems "testify to an extraordinarily fertile and manifold interaction between the literary and graphic arts" (p. 127). Maintains that, in emblematic terms, the patterned poem "conflates *pictura* and *subscriptio* into a single word-image, thereby to become a kind of telescoped emblem, a modern equivalent of the hieroglyph" (p. 128) and that the shaped poem often "hinges on the belief that language is non-arbitrary, pictorial and essentially like that which it represents, yet different in form" (p. 129). Finds that patterned poems "can mediate directly between man and God" and contends that, by drawing together "eye, heart and intellect" and by "exploiting the inevitable associations of a significant shape," they "concentrate the mind in meditation on a Christian symbol" (p. 133). Comments on "The Collar," "A Wreath," "Clasping of hands," "The Church-floore," and especially "Easter-wings" to show how visual features are an integral part of many of Herbert's poems.

**1329. Bache, William B.** "A Note on Herbert's 'Coloss. 3.3.'" *GHJ* 6, no, 1:27–30.

Argues that the italicized biblical diagonal line in "Coloss.iii.3" "is not just a vain trick or a clever stunt" (p. 27) but forms "the core or the heart of the poem" and that "successful readings branch out from, and evolve out of, the italicized words" (p. 28).

**1330. Bell, Ilona.** "Circular Strategies and Structures in Jonson and Herbert," in *Classic and Cavalier: Essays on Jonson and the Sons of Ben*, edited by Claude J. Summers and Ted-Larry Pebworth. 157–70. Pittsburgh: University of Pittsburgh Press.

Argues that Herbert's poems may be more indebted to Jonson than to Donne, noting that Herbert "shares Jonson's concern for the book, for the poem as written and constructed rather than spoken, for poetic form and meaning joined as one through creation of the poem itself" (p. 157). Maintains that it is the "combination of simplicity and difficulty that makes the structure and language of *The Temple* resemble Jonson perhaps even more than Donne" (p. 160). Focuses on one aspect of the work of both poets, "a characteristic, circular strategy and structure" (p. 157), whereby the reader is included in the poetic process of discovery. Notes that Herbert's "self-corrections" in his poems, like Jonson's "overarching judgments," frequently "circle back on themselves, enabling us to discover in retrospect an ultimate, more trustworthy point of view" (p. 158). Compares Jonson's "To the Reader" and Herbert's "Dedication" of *The Temple*, in which Herbert warns us that the following poems "should be read as they unfold, then be reread from the perspective that can be attained after the poems are completed" (p. 160). Discusses how a number of Herbert's more subtle poems, such as "Affliction (I)," "The Collar," "and 'The Flower" have "circular structures which juxtapose earlier, more naive points of view against subsequent critiques and more valid discoveries" (p. 165).

**1331. Bennett, J. A. W.** "Donne, Herbert, Herrick," in *Poetry of the Passion: Studies in Twelve Centuries of English Verse*, 145–67. Oxford: Clarendon Press.

Discusses Herbert's passion poetry and its "medieval ancestry" (p. 153). Maintains that in "The Sacrifice" one can find "all the figural features that from the time of Prudentius till the printings of the so-called *Biblia Pauperum* in the fifteenth century had come to cluster around the theme of the Passion" and claims that the poem "is the summation of all the poetry that the Easter *Improperia* had generated" and that "its position at the forefront of *The Temple*, as well as its length, testifies to the prominence in Herbert's mind of Christ as the Man of Sorrows" (p. 153). Points out medieval analogues to the poem, in particular Friar William Herbert's fourteenth-century refrain poem "Quis est iste qui venit de Edom?," and notes how Herbert's poem differs from medieval examples of the theme. Discusses medieval affinities in "The Agonie," "Good Friday," "Easter," and "Redemption," claiming that the sonnet is "Herbert at his finest: dense in suggestion, and mounting quickly in the sestet to a pregnant climax" (p. 161). Considers Herbert's formal treatment of the Passion in *Passio Discerpta*, maintaining that "these epigrams are of a distinctly late Renaissance, almost baroque cast" and yet "their themes are precisely those of late-medieval devotion" (p. 166). Concludes that Herbert's treatment of the Passion testifies to his Christocentric theology.

**1332. Boenig, Robert.** "George Herbert & Mysticism." *SMy* 5, no. 2:64–72.
Surveys Herbert scholarship concerning the controversy over whether or not he was a mystic. Finds one group of scholars arguing for Herbert's mysticism, based on proofs that he was indebted to medieval and Counter-Reformation mystical theology, while another group denies that Herbert was a mystic, based on his "Protestant doctrine, earthly imagery, and Anglican sanity" (p. 65). Finds flaws in both positions, and, through close readings of "Love (III)" and "Prayer (I)," argues for a third definition of Herbert's mysticism: "the speaker's development of an effective rhetoric which is, at the end of a given poem, answered by an anti-rhetoric in which God communicates directly to the speaker's soul" (p. 69). Finds this technique operative in "Redemption," "Jordan (I and II)," "Deniall," "Vertue," "Jesu," "The Collar," and "The Answer."

**1333. ———.** "Vaughan Williams and Herbert." *SMy* 5, no. 4:28–38.
Argues that in *Five Mystical Songs* (entry 39), musical settings for "Easter" (divided into two separate settings), "Love (III)," "The Call," and "Antiphon (I)," the English composer Ralph Vaughan Williams "understood Herbert better than many literary critics, giving his listeners a work that is both pure Herbert and pure Vaughan Williams, underscoring a mysticism inherent in the poems themselves" (p. 28). Maintains that, when considered in Herbert's order, the mysticism of the poems is eschatological but when seen in Vaughan Williams's order, the mysticism is eucharistic. Analyzes the musical setting for "Love (III)" to show how the Eucharist is the controlling theme. Argues that Vaughan Williams's favorite method of expressing mysticism is the use of melisma, in which "a word, by being divided into many notes, loses its identity as a word and partakes of the inexpressible, as the soul joins God in a mystical union that transcends words" (pp. 31–32). Notes that Vaughan Williams also uses triplets to vary the tempo of the orchestral accompaniment and that in "Easter" this technique underscores the mysticism of Herbert's poetry.

**1334. Booty, John E.** "Contrition in Anglican Spirituality: Hooker, Donne, and Herbert," in *Anglican Spirituality*, edited by William J. Wolf, 25–48. Wilton, Conn.: Morehouse-Barlow.
Argues that Hooker, Donne, and Herbert share a common understanding of contrition for sin and that "they can help us to understand the importance of contrition in Anglican spirituality and in humanity at large" (p. 45). Maintains that, "above all, they affirm that true praise, joy and thanksgiving proceed out of that contrition which is the gift of divine love" (p. 45). Discusses how *The Temple* "moves from contrition to praise and is imbued with contrition in all its parts" (p. 36). Comments specifically on the sequence of poems from "The Altar" through "The Agonie" to show that it introduces *The Temple* as a whole and that "the predominant note is that of praise, although with contrition evident as an element of that praise" (p. 39). Points out how "Good Friday" yields to "Easter" and "Easter-wings" and how "Repentance" and "Love (III)" reflect Herbert's theology of contrition. Maintains that Herbert, like all of us, is tempted to take control of his own life and destiny and "to do that which merits the divine love, indeed coerces God to forgive us" but that finally he realizes that "the contrite, forgiven sinner is powerless to do anything but receive the Love which has cleansed and renewed him" (p. 42).

**1335. Brown, Cedric C., and Maureen Boyd.** "The Homely Sense of Herbert's 'Jordan.'" *SP* 79:147–61.

Maintains that the titles of the two Jordan poems refer to the biblical story of how Naaman, the powerful and rich Syrian, obeyed Elisha's advice to wash himself seven times in the Jordan, thereby curing his leprosy by his simple act of faith. Analyzes both poems, showing that they are a "celebration of the efficacy of doing simple things in words, against inclinations to vainglorious ostentation or difficulty" (p. 153). Maintains that in "Jordan (I)" Herbert "adopts the stance of the model poet, one of the despised few," whereas in "Jordan (II)" he "dramatizes the process of realization in the past, how prompted by Grace, he finally came to an understanding of what is best to write, or best in writing" (p. 153). Points out uses of the Naaman story by Herbert's contemporaries. Concludes that "the Jordan of Naaman, explored in the one poem and re-examined in the rewriting of the other, engages the paradoxes of both the religious and the literary" and that Herbert adopted the Jordan "as an emblem for his consciousness of the new, perhaps impossible, constraints on his poetic during those last few years of his life when he was the 'shepherd' who sang, the poet and the priest together" (p. 161).

**1336. Charles, Amy M.** "Sir Henry Herbert: The Master of the Revels as Man of Letters." *MP* 80:1–12.

Presents a biographical sketch of Henry Herbert, the younger brother of George Herbert, and surveys his public and private writings to show the range of his interests. Comments on the relationship between the brothers, noting, for instance, that Henry was quite important in raising funds to rebuild the church at Leighton Bromswold, Huntingdonshire, for which George was prebendary at Lincoln Cathedral and noting that possibly both brothers contributed to *Outlandish Proverbs*. Claims that Edward, George, and Henry Herbert "reflect their common heritage, the devotion in which they were trained as children, their shared concern for the knowledge and interpretation of history in the affairs of England and of Europe in their time" (p. 12). Concludes that, although Henry's reputation as a writer will not compete with that of his more famous brothers, "he *was* a man of letters, with serious intellectual and religious interests, whose studies and concerns influenced his judgments in both public and private matters" (p. 12).

**1337. Clark, Ira.** "'Lord, in thee The *beauty* lies in the *discovery*': 'Love Unknown' as George Herbert's Neotypological Lyric Paradigm," in *Christ Revealed: The History of the Neotypological Lyric in the English Renaissance*, 80–106. (University of Florida Monographs. Humanities, no. 51.) Gainesville: University Presses of Florida.

Revised and expanded version of "'Lord, in thee The *beauty* lies in the *discovery*': 'Love Unknown' and Reading Herbert" (entry 898).

**1338. Doerksen, Daniel W.** "'Growing and Groning': Herbert's 'Affliction (I).'" *ESC* 8:1–8.

Maintains that "Affliction (I)" should be seen as "a (Christian) paradigm of human experience in the form of a dramatic monologue, with considerable irony directed at its speaker, whose outward groans ultimately give way to inward growth" and shows that it is "a poem of spiritual conflict whose protagonist must learn that neither grudging resignation nor rebellion is the right way to cope with adverse circumstances" (p. 1). Argues that, seen in its literary and religious context, the poem reveals that the speaker's struggles are "internal, involving self-conquest in a process of maturing and growth" (p. 1). Contends that the poem "can be seen as a dramatization of the progressive man-to-God relationship that Reformation writers find expressed in Scriptures" (pp. 2–3), noting resemblances between ideas expressed in the poem and Calvin's theology. Concludes that readers should value in the poem "not only its compelling picture of a real person's life, but also its hard-won recognition that there is more to life than wanting and getting one's own way, and that that process of maturing may involve some awkward as well as difficult times" (p. 7).

**1339. Fowler, Alastair.** *Kinds of Literature: An Introduction to the Theory of Genres and Modes.* Cambridge, Mass.: Harvard University Press. vii, 357p.

Mentions Herbert throughout. Notes that Herbert was the first English poet to make full use of witty titles and that his highly expressive titles "anticipate a modernist form—the title so communicative as to be part of the poem, or at least an independent route to its meaning" (p. 96). Comments on the "modal extension of elements of emblem form" (p. 109) in Herbert's devotional lyrics. Discusses the conversion or transformation of the Petrarchan love sonnet into the religious or spiritual sonnet and notes that "even some of the best works in the divine poetry tradition, such as Herbert's *Parody*, altered the functions of a secular genre so directly as to amount to spiritual parodies" (p. 174). Claims that influential anthologies have reflected and shaped taste and have contributed to a poet's standing and notes that in the twentieth century Herbert has achieved major status.

**1340. Getz, Thomas H.** "Herbert's 'Confession.'" *Expl* 41, no. 1:21–22.

Stanza-by-stanza explication of "Confession" to show that, as in many of Herbert's poems, the speaker's final understanding of his relationship to God "is not artifactual, not something cut off from the dark swirlings of passion, grief, struggle," but rather that Herbert's speaker, like Jacob when God struggled with him, "must accept the struggle as the only way to the lucid simplicities of faith, peace, and understanding" (p. 22). Observes how Herbert subtly manipulates the images, the tense of verbs, sounds, rhymes, and voice to reinforce the theme of the poem. Argues that the speaker's "epiphany occurs in the silence between stanzas three and four" and that in the last stanza he is able to cry out in joy and confidence, thereby "balancing the pain of stanzas one, two, and three" (p. 22).

**1341. Ginkawa, Keisuku.** "George Herbert no *A Priest to the Temple* ni tsuite no ichi kisatsu—Augustine no *On Christian Doctrine* wo Haikei to shite" [A Study of George Herbert's *A Priest to the Temple*—with special reference to Augustine's *On Christian Doctrine*]. *Soka Daigaku Eigo Eibungaku Kenkyu* [Studies in English Language and Literature, Soka University] no. 11 (vol. 6, no. 2) (March): 49–67.

Examines the influence of Augustine on Herbert's works and comments on Herbert's treatment and application of Augustinian thinking. Deals more specifically with the concept of *caritas*.

**1342. Glaser, Joseph A.** "George Herbert's *The Temple*: Learning to Read the Book of Nature." *CLAJ* 25:322–30.

Notes that *The Temple* is rich in nature imagery and argues that Herbert "makes such images an integral part of his whole design by having his speaker dramatically uncover the significance of the natural world as the sequence of poems progresses" (p. 323). Shows how the poems present "an evolving attitude toward the external world as the speaker grapples with the problem of making nature part of his Christian frame of reference" and how Herbert's idea of nature "grows with the book, moving in general from states of simplicity to ones of greater and greater complexity until a moment of sudden illumination is obtained in 'The Flower,' one of the central achievements of Herbert's poetic imagination" (p. 323). Maintains that in the poem "'The Lord of Power' is transformed into a 'Lord of Love'" and "the contradictory world of appearances drops away, is seen as only a imperfect perception of a universe filled with supernatural but subtle beneficence" (p. 330). Concludes that "the very changes and uncertainties into which we are led by our search for the meaning of things is God's rhetoric, teaching us our limits" (p. 330).

**1343. Gottlieb, Sidney.** "George Herbert," in *Critical Survey of Poetry: English Language Series*, edited by Frank N. Magill, 3:1294–1305. Englewood Cliffs, N.J.: Salem Press.

Lists Herbert's principal collections of poetry (Latin and English) and comments briefly on his prose works (p. 1294), outlines his achievement, stressing his appeal to a wide range of readers and practicing poets (pp. 1294–95), presents a biographical sketch (pp. 1295–96), and offers a critical analysis of *The Temple* (pp. 1296–1304). Argues that, although *The Temple* is "one of the most inventive and varied collections of poems in the seventeenth century," Herbert's purpose "may be missed if his technical virtuosity is seen as an end in itself" (p. 1296). Stresses that "poetic creativity and devotion are welded together in *The Temple*" (p. 1297) and discusses its overall design, pointing out major features of the individual poems—an often playful sense of poetic structure, forms that reenforce content, language that is simple and direct but also rich and allusive, wordplay, and dramatic technique. Surveys major themes of Herbert's poems and insists that they "continue to strike readers as honest, perceptive, and compelling statements about his day-to-day affairs of the spirit, and perhaps about their own as well" (p. 1304).

**1344. Hachiya, Akio.** "Coleridge ni okeru Ai no Shokyo—'Work without Hope' Oboegaku" [Elimination of Love in Coleridge—A Note on "Work without Hope"] *Konan Joshi Daigaku Kenkyu Kiyo* [Bulletin of the Konan Women's College] no. 18 (March): 1–20.

Comments on Coleridge's praise of Herbert, especially "Employment."

**1345. Harman, Barbara Leah.** *Costly Monuments: Representations of the Self in George Herbert's Poetry*. Cambridge, Mass., and London: Harvard University Press. x, 225p.

A portion of the argument of chapter 1 (pp. 59–63) first appeared in "Herbert, Coleridge and the Vexed Work of Narration" (entry 1151).

The argument of chapter 2 first appeared in "The Fiction of Coherence: George Herbert's 'The Collar'" (entry 1150).

The argument of chapter 3 first appeared in "George Herbert's 'Affliction (I)': The Limits of Representation" (entry 1104).

In the "Preface" (pp. vii-viii) indicates that the aim of this study is to demonstrate that "the impulse toward self-representation is a powerful one in Herbert's work, and that it is also an impulse thwarted, and redesigned to suit what thwarts it, in enormously complex ways" (p. viii). In "Introduction: The Critical Controversy" (pp. 1–38) surveys modern critical controversy about Herbert's poems. Notes that such critics as Joseph Summers, Rosemond Tuve, Stanley Fish, and Barbara Lewalski assume that "culture determines the possibilities for selfhood and textuality" (p. 25), whereas such critics as William Empson and Helen Vendler hold that people "have the capacity to separate themselves from the culture—that they have value apart from it, and power over it" (p. 21). Announces that her approach to Herbert's poems "mediates between the opposing views of its predecessors" (p. 36), will emphasize the ways by which the self is "formed, deformed, shaped, [and] 'fashioned,'" and will show that in his poems "self-representation is a central, and also a vexed, enterprise" (p. 35). Part one, "Fictions of Coherence" (pp. 39–105), consists of three chapters. In chapter 1, "'So Did I Weave My Self into the Sense'" (pp. 41–63), maintains that, although speech in Herbert's poems "becomes a vehicle for self-manifestation in a world otherwise inhospitable to self-manifestation," the speakers of the poems often "make use of a language they also reject—so that the importance of speaking, and the difficulties associated with it, are analyzed and explored at once" (p. 43), as in "Jordan (I and II)." Through analyses of "Frailtie," "The Holdfast," "Good Friday," and "The Reprisall" illustrates the conflict "between self-representation and self-relinquishment, between personal and divine inscription, between the idea of self as an agent of writing and a vision of him as writing's object" (p. 59). Calls such poems "collapsing poems." In chapter 2, "Collapsing Personal Stories" (pp. 64–88), argues that "one of the most interesting versions of the disturbed relationship between storyteller and story characteristic of collapsing poems occurs with the appearance of a poetic speaker who doubles back upon an already complete report" (p. 64). Presents a detailed analysis of "The Collar" (and less detailed readings of "Miserie" and "Redemption") as collapsing poems and shows that in all these poems "Christian knowledge breaks in upon the speaker only as the poems end, and because this is the case, that knowledge, and the self who comes to bear it, have no real manifestation" (p. 86). Contends that in collapsing poems "the idea that it is possible to represent the self in ways either coherent or safe is reduced to the status of a cherished fiction and is, at last, relinquished" (p. 83). In chapter 3, "Autobiography and Beyond" (pp. 89–105), continues the discussion of collapsing poems by analyzing "Affliction (I)" as an autobiographical poem that "gives testimony to the power and importance of telling stories about the self and to the power and importance of relinquishing them" (p. 89). Argues that the speaker who "arrives at the end of his autobiographical account does not arrive at the moment of his life's greatest coherence, but at the moment of its most complete collapse" (p. 96) and learns reluctantly that "one is required to live on the other side of coherence: beyond representation, beyond the devastation endings impose, beyond the safety closure provides" (p. 101). Part two, "Chronicles of Dissolution" (pp. 107–69), consists of two chapters. In chapter 4, "'No Continuing City'" (pp. 109–37), discusses "dissolving poems" in which "speakers do not first appear and then disappear, as they do in collapsing poems," but rather "practice the lessons of dissolution *from the start*—learning them as the poems begin, absorbing and practicing them as the poems proceed" (p. 112). Maintains out that in dissolving poems the speakers "do not fend off the dissolution that surrounds them: they acknowledge it, make peace with it, sometimes, even, embrace it" (p. 112). Analyzes "Church-monuments" and "Mortification" to show that "being present to the Lord has nothing at all to do with being present to oneself in any of the ways practiced by the speakers of collapsing poems" (p. 129) and that "to *chronicle* one's own dissolution is not to lose but to *gain access* to representation, albeit to a new kind of representation" (p. 135). In chapter 5, "The Dissolution of Bodies and Stories" (pp. 138–69), continues the discussion of dissolving poems by analyzing "The Pilgrimage," which "provides an allegory of the relationship between self-representation and death" (p. 137). Discusses also "The Temper (I)," "Artillerie," and "The Flower," in which the speakers "learn to accept, to explore, and to elaborate upon the

instability of stories and selves, and as they do their understanding of what it means to be a self and to have a story undergoes transformation as well" (p. 151). In "Conclusion: The Bible as Countertext" (pp. 170–96) describes those typological poems in which the speakers "begin by telling idiosyncratic, independent stories, but end by rewriting them as biblical accounts" (p. 171). Maintains that this "alignment of the personal with biblical stories offers, in other words, a solution to the problem of self-representation" (p. 171). Analyzes "The Bunch of Grapes," "The H. Scriptures (I)," "Aaron," and "The Altar" and argues that a typological reading of these poems "establishes the relationship of person to Scripture by transforming entirely—not by conversing or valorizing—the idea of individual space" (p. 189). Concludes that, "if collapsing poems makes representation possible only by making it subject to recall, and chronicles of dissolution make it possible by dismantling coherent images of the self, typological poems make representation possible by making the speaker's enduring account the story of others rather than the story of the self" (p. 196). Notes (pp. 197–221) and index (pp. 223–25).
Reviews:
Ilona Bell, *MLQ* 44 (1983): 95–99
A. D. Nuttall, *TLS*, 22 July 1983, p. 787
John H. Ottenhoff, *SCN* 41 (1983): 65–67
Sidney Gottlieb, *RenQ* 37 (1984): 144–48
Bruce King, *SR* 92 (1984): 284–89
Jonathan F. S. Post, *JDJ*, 3, no. 2 (1984): 221–47
John T. Shawcross, *GHJ* 8, no. 1 (1984): 57–63
Richard Strier, *Criticism* 26 (1984): 86–91

**1346. Herbert, George.** *George Herbert's Book of English Proverbs*. Lincoln [Eng.]: Asgill Press, [1982]. [32]p.
    Reproduces a selection of Herbert's "outlandish proverbs" and points out in a brief introductory note that Herbert's poetry "shows his high regard for their pithy plainness, far-fetched ingenuity, and the force of feeling that has turned them, by the mouthings of generations, into true English idioms" [p. 5]. Notes that this selection of the proverbs is "merely a sampler of some that the English tongue is poorer for no longer using" [p. 5].

**1347. Himuro, Misako.** "*The Temple* to *Astrophel and Stella*" [The Affinity of *The Temple* and *Astrophel and Stella*]. *Waseda Daigaku Dagakuin Bungaku Kenkaka Kiyo* [Bulletin of the Faculty of Literature, Graduate School of Waseda University] no. 28:37–52.
    Compares and contrasts *The Temple* and Sidney's *Astrophel and Stella*, especially in terms of their plain style, conversational tone, introspective attitude and metrics, and treatment of love.

**1348. Hovey, Kenneth Alan.** "Church History in 'The Church.'" *GHJ* 6, no. 1:1–14.
    Argues that "in a small number of lyrics scattered apparently at random throughout Herbert's collection, the Church and its history occupy the position usually occupied by the Christian and his life" (p. 1). Comments on "Affliction (V)," "Decay," "Whitsunday," "Church-rents and schisms," "The World," and "Sion," as well as parts of other poems, to show that "the individual moments fit an overall pattern" that is "congruent with the pattern Herbert finds in the life of the Christian" and that "the history of the Church from its inception to its demise displays the same double motion

that the Christian reveals in his course from birth to death" (p. 12). Stresses that, considered together, these poems give "a coherent and well-balanced portrait of the Church in history" (p. 11). Points out that in *The Church Militant*, as well as in *The Temple*, Herbert holds that the Church "has been outwardly in radical decline, geographically depicted as a westward motion," but that it "has been inwardly progressing toward judgment, depicted as the east" (pp. 12–13). Concludes that, "as the personal judgment of each individual Christian, God will finally temper the woes of the corporate Church with full joy" so that "the Church so long militant and afflicted will finally rise triumphant" (p. 13).

**1349. Hunter, Jeanne Clayton.** "*Mine-Thine* in Herbert's *The Temple* and St. John's Gospel." *N&Q* n.s. 29:492–93.
In part a reply to William Nestrick (entry 1261). Notes the biblical use of *mine-thine* and *me-thee* and points to passages in the Gospel of John in which Christ "plainly speaks in *mine-thine, me-thee* terms of His uniquely personal relationship with God, with man, and man's relationship to God in Him" (p. 493). Argues that Herbert's use of these terms in his poetry "makes effective the deliberate simplicity of Christ's language," language which is a "simple yet profound expression of perfect communion" (p. 493). Notes the use of such language in "Clasping of hands."

**1350. ———.** "'Silk Twist': Line of Grace in Herbert's *The Pearl*. Matth. XIII. 45." *N&Q* n.s. 29:19–20.
Argues that Herbert's terminology in the last stanza of "The Pearl" is expressive of the Covenant of Grace, "a doctrine of salvation emphasized in seventeenth-century Puritan theology and figured in business and legal terms" that "express the binding relationship between God and man made possible through the sacrifice of Christ" (p. 19). Observes that in the poem Herbert "recounts God's transaction at Calvary" and maintains that "silk twist," in the context of the last stanza, is a metaphor "figuring God's relationship to man through His Grace in Christ" (p. 20). Points out the use of similar images to express the covenanted promises of God in a sermon by John Preston, a Puritan preacher at the court of James I, and in John Calvin's *Commentaries*.

**1351. ———.** "'With Winges of Faith': Herbert's Communion Poems." *Journal of Religion* 62:57–71.
Argues, through a reading of "The H. Communion," "The Banquet," and "Love (III)," that "what emerges from these poems—and their echo throughout *The Temple* —is a participatory pattern, a eucharistic blueprint" (p. 57). Maintains that, together, the poems "narrate the full eucharistic experience" and that "the interpretation of that sacrament which they figure forth is closely allied to the eucharistic teachings of John Calvin" (p. 57). Surveys the positions of Luther, Calvin, and Zwingli on the eucharist, acknowledging that Herbert's poetry "is not a precise espositon of anyone's doctrine" but insisting that "an understanding of Calvin's position on the Eucharist can lead to a fuller appreciation" of *The Temple* (p. 57). Argues that in "The H. Communion" Herbert is "closest to the Anglican position of indifference to the manner of Christ's presence in the Eucharist" (p. 68). Contends that, in the eucharistic poems of *The Church*, Herbert finally "drops argument for experience" and in "Love (III)," "with seemingly effortless art, he takes the moment of union and makes of it a dialogic reality" (p. 69). Concludes that "ascension, substantial sign, Real Presence, all figured in Herbert's eucharistic experience" and that he views the Eucharist "as an act of love raising the faithful heart to heavenly presence" (p. 71).

**1352. Jones, Nicholas R.** "Texts and Contexts: Two Languages in George Herbert's Poetry." *SP* 79:162–76.

Argues that, in order to achieve a poetic of humility, Herbert's poems contain a text (a word, phrase, or sentence that often has biblical overtones) that both interacts with, yet is separated from, the context (the rest of the poem without the text). Maintains that texts "bring to our attention a plain, undistorted, honest, and efficacious speech that potentially conveys a direct, unmistakable knowledge of God" and that "we attend to these purest moments because we have also become engaged in an obviously impure language—willful, witty, complex, and even on occasion perverse" (p. 164). Argues that this "text-context structure reflects the major subject of the poems themselves, the action of God in human life" (p. 164). Maintains that the text "has a numinous effect on the language of the rest of the poem" and the context "is needed for support, qualification, or explanation" but "inevitably the text will be the most powerful single instrument in the poem" (p. 165). Demonstrates this notion by analyzing "Jordan (II)," "Antiphon (I)," "Vertue," "The Forerunners," "The Quip," and "A true Hymne." Maintains that since "the text is in fact in a lower style than the rest of the poem," it "corroborates the importance of humility" and notes that "its presence allows its use—in most of the poem—of higher, more elaborate style than might be consonant with strict humility" and thus "the distinctness of the break between text and context creates the sense of liberation and expansion that is not present in poems of a uniformly plain style" (pp. 175–76). Contends that "the language of the context nonetheless remains the major vehicle of Herbert's poems" and, "though criticized by Herbert himself for its elaborate artificiality and falseness, the metaphysical poetic continues to provide the structure and most of the material for the poem" while the text "gives the poem a new frame—a controlling point of view" (p. 176).

**1353. Joscelyne, T. A.** "George Herbert's 'The Windows': A Parallel in Barbaro's *Vitruvius*." *N&Q* n.s. 29:493–94.

Maintains that the basic analogy that informs "The Windows" is that "as natural light reveals the artistic complexity of stained glass, so the passage of God's light through man illuminates his whole being," and observes that man is depicted "both as an individual body and as part of the communion" (p. 494). Points out that the image of the window in the poem is reminiscent of a passage from the introduction of book 3 of Daniele Barbaro's edition of Vitruvius's *De Architectura* (1556). Concludes that Herbert directs the application of the poem not only to the ordained priesthood but to "the priesthood of all believers" and that he maintains that actions are more potent than words "because they are realized not through the activity of man's will but through the illumination of the sun/Son" (p. 494).

**1354. Kennedy, Richard F.** "John Swan's Adaptation of George Herbert's 'Man.'" *GHJ* 6, no. 1:31–33.

Points out that John Swan borrowed, adapted, and published ten lines or so from "Man" in his *Speculum Mundi* (1635). Notes that Swan selected lines from the last six stanzas of Herbert's poem and put them together in a twelve-line poem written in couplets. Concludes that, by borrowing from Herbert, Swan "paid high tribute to the sacred poet, just as the transcendental philosopher Emerson was to do several centuries later when he quoted five stanzas of the same poem in the crucial final chapter of *Nature*" (p. 32).

**1355. King, Bruce.** *Seventeenth-Century English Literature.* (Macmillan History of Literature, gen. ed. A. Norman Jeffares.) London and Basingstoke: Macmillan Press. xiv, 295p.

General introduction to Herbert's life and poetry (pp. 100–103). Compares and/or contrasts him throughout to other seventeenth-century poets, especially Donne, Crashaw, Vaughan, Mildmay Fane (Earl of Westmoreland), Marvell, Patrick Cary, John Collop, Christopher Harvey, and Milton. Maintains that Herbert "showed how church symbols, hymns, Christian paradoxes and theological doctrines could form the basis of poetry treating of spiritual anguish, faith, hope and love" and "brought to the century's religious verse the introspective, implied personal narrative of the Petrarchan sonnet sequence" (p. 99). Discusses the organization of *The Temple* and Herbert's expression of "the doubts and anxieties which accompany spiritual progress through repentance, faith and perseverance, to grace" (p. 101). Comments on Herbert's mastery of poetic technique and maintains that each of the poems in *The Church* is "an ingenious, daring experiment in the religious lyric" (p. 102). Maintains that, even though Herbert's poetry has "the drama, introspection, intellectual vigour, colloquial language, unexpected metaphors and sometimes obscure learning associated with Donne, it is different from the strong-lined metaphysical manner of the preceding decades" (p. 103). Concludes that the poems are "varied in order and level of complexity so that there is sufficient intellectual difficulty to sustain interest despite the many pieces that are easy, didactic or playfully ingenious" (p. 103).

**1356. Klawitter, George.** "The Problem of Circularity in Herbert's Wreath." *GHJ* 6, no. 1:15–20.

Argues that in "A Wreath" Herbert "uses word convolutions in such an intensely musical setting to tease readers around a circle toward a finality repetitive of the poem's opening idea" (p. 15). Shows (with the help of a diagram) that the wreath is not simply a tightly circular crown but a "double wreath" that structurally and thematically doubles back on itself "exactly midway through the poem, at the use of the words 'to thee,' the repetition of which stands out in a bed of single end-word repetitions" (p. 19). Concludes that Herbert keeps the readers' attention "by his highly convoluted lines and rhetorical devices which highlight his mastery of form as well as his playfulness with it" (p. 19).

**1357. Law, Joe K.** "William Dyce's *George Herbert at Bemerton*: Its Background and Meaning." *The Journal of Pre-Raphaelite Studies* 3, no. 1:45–55.

Maintains that William Dyce's *George Herbert at Bemerton* (Royal Academy, 1861) can best be understood in the light of early nineteenth-century religious controversies and Dyce's personal involvement in them. Argues that, viewed thus, the painting "becomes much less a curiosity and much more clearly a part of the artist's own response to the ritualist controversies of the day" (p. 45). Discusses why Herbert appealed to Dyce and other High Anglicans of the first half of the nineteenth century. Maintains that Dyce's "own interests support an old-fashioned allegorical reading" (p. 50) of the painting. Comments in detail on the depiction of Herbert in the painting, the various objects in it (lute, Salisbury Cathedral, fishing rod, basket), and the landscape (river, earth, thistle, ivy, flowers, trees) to show that the painting forms a coherent statement about Dyce's attitude toward the religious controversies of his day.

**1358. Malpezzi, Frances M.** "Herbert's 'The Thanksgiving' in Context." *Renascence* 34:185–95.

Examines the poems from "The Thanksgiving" through "Easter-wings" to show that they, as a group, reveal Herbert's persona learning to give proper thanks to God.

Maintains that this sequence of poems "mirrors the overall movement within *The Church* as the speaker begins in pride and spiritual darkness and painfully makes his way toward humility and enlightenment" and that they "focus not only on the passion, death, and resurrection of Christ but on the concomitant agony of the speaker who finds there is no rejecting grief if one is to accept Christ" (p. 186). Finds that as the speaker progresses through *The Church*, "he is chastised by the rod of affliction and suffers medicinal corrections" but that "the rod that God administers is also one of direction, one meant to guide him on his pilgrimage as he follows Christ's footsteps on this *via purgativa*" (p. 194). Concludes that each cluster of poems in *The Church* "moves toward the culmination of spiritual perfection until the persona is fully tempered as a Christian in 'The Flower,' as the Christian priest in 'Aaron,' and as the Christian poet in 'The Forerunners'" and that "the climax of such spiritual perfection comes in 'Love' III where the betrothed Soul and her Spouse are finally united in the great feast that was promised, the final wonder of Love" (p. 194).

1359. **Manley, Frank.** "Toward a Definition of Plain Style in the Poetry of George Herbert," in *Poetic Traditions of the English Renaissance*, edited by Maynard Mack and George deForest Lord, 203–17. New Haven and London: Yale University Press.

Argues that throughout *The Temple* Herbert wrestled with the problem of how to be simple, plainspoken, direct, and authentic in poetry and at the same time remain truthful to himself. Maintains that one way Herbert confronted his dilemma was to develop a plain style in which he made the language of a poem mirror the complex way in which his mind worked. Contends that many of the poems in *The Temple* "proceed not according to a fixed, predetermined form like a pair of wings, an altar, a circle, or any of the other 'hieroglyphs' Herbert wrestled into language, but according to the mind's own patterning" and that "the result is a kind of poem that is not neat—not in essentials, anyway—not orderly or highly polished but jagged, with great logical gaps the reader must bridge himself if he is to follow the surge and rapidity of the thought" (p. 210). Maintains that Herbert was "not so concerned with the effect the poem will have on the reader or the reader's ability to follow the various turns and involutions of the overall movement" as he was "in the direct, authentic expression of his own thoughts and emotions" (p. 210). Discusses "The Crosse," "The Collar," "The Bag," "The Forerunners," "Decay," "Church-lock and key," and "Love (III)" as examples of Herbert's paradoxical plain style. Concludes that "the poetry that he came to write is not the simple, pietistic verse one would expect to be written by the country parson Herbert sometimes wished to become but expresses the man as he actually was" (p. 215).

1360. **Martz, Louis L.** "Meditation as Poetic Strategy." *MP* 80:168–74.

Essentially a review of Barbara Lewalski's *Protestant Poetics and the Seventeenth-Century Religious Lyric* (entry 1202) and an explanation or defense of his own position in *The Poetry of Meditation* (entry 431) and in several later essays. Concludes that Lewalski's book is learned but that her thesis "is overstated" and adds that "probably the truth lies somewhere in between the two positions—closer to my own" (p. 174). Mentions Herbert throughout. Argues that Herbert's view of the Eucharist "is essential to an understanding of George Herbert, whose constant use of eucharistic images is consistently underplayed by Lewalski, even to the point of ignoring the proven allusion to the *Improperia*, the reproaches spoken from the cross in 'The Sacrifice'" (p. 172). Points out that, "like Savonarola, whose treatise on *The Simplicity of the Christian Life* we know to have been one of his favorite books, Herbert's view of the Christian life demands both Scripture and Eucharist" (p. 172). Maintains that Herbert's notion of the Eucharist can be found in the printed version of "The H. Communion" in which he indicated his belief that "the physical elements of the sacrament possess a certain efficacy" but that this efficacy "is limited" and that "only the spiritual presence of Christ can reach the soul" (p. 173).

**1361. Müller, Wolfgang G.** "The Lyric Soliloquy as an Interior Dialogue with Special Reference to English Religious Poetry from Herbert to Hopkins." *Sprachkunst: Beiträge zur Literaturwissenschaft* 13:282–96.

Argues that "the identification and evaluation of elements of self-address and self-colloquy can be indispensable for the proper understanding of a poem's form and meaning and of its place in the history of the lyric genre" (p. 285). Discusses the "dialogization of lyric utterance" (p. 285) in "The Collar," finding that "the passionate nature of the controversy that takes place within the self manifests itself in the expressive syntax of the poem with its ellipses, excited questions, imperatives, and defiant self-affirmations and in its highly eccentric metrical structure" (p. 286). Maintains that the poem has its roots in the medieval body-and-soul debates but notes that "the conflict explicitly takes place within a single individual consciousness, i.e. a lyric self which is the carrier of two conflicting voices with their corresponding antithetical attitudes" (p. 286). Points out examples in which Herbert's "interior dialogue is a sign of spiritual unrest, of alienation from God" (p. 287). Observes that, when the poet wishes to suggest peace and union with God, he uses regular rhythmic patterns and harmonious rhymes. Defines two closely related types of self-colloquy in Herbert's poetry—"self-exhortation" and "self-catechization." Argues that, because of the prevalence of self-address in the poems, Stanley Fish's notion of the catechized reader in *The Living Temple* (entry 1144) is unacceptable.

**1362. Post, Jonathan F. S.** *Henry Vaughan: The Unfolding Vision.* Princeton: Princeton University Press. xxii, 243p.

Places Vaughan's relationship to Herbert "at the very center" of his study, "since that experience was at the center of the Welsh poet's life" (p. xviii), yet points out that his "overall strategy is nonetheless geared to freeing the younger poet from the shadow of his master" (p. xx). Maintains that Herbert "might have been a catalyst in Vaughan's poetic career, but as a pivotal force, he shaped rather than overwhelmed or displaced the Welsh poet's creative energies" (p. xx). Points out how in themes, attitudes, and poetic techniques Herbert influenced Vaughan and cites numerous examples of Vaughan's imitations of and direct borrowings from poems in *The Temple*.

**1363. Ray, Robert H.** "Henshaw, Venning, and Bates: Quotes of the Bible or of Herbert?" *GHJ* 6, no. 1:34–36.

Points out that Joseph Henshaw in *Horae Succisivae, Or Spare-Houres Of Meditations; Upon Our Duty to God, Others, Our Selves* (1635), Ralph Venning in *Things Worth thinking on; Or, Helps to Piety, Being Remains of some Meditations, Experiences, and Sentences* (1664), and William Bates in *Spiritual Perfection, Unfolded and Enforced* (1699) quote, without acknowledgment, from lines 3–4 ("*Lesse then the least / Of all thy mercies*") and/or lines 11–12 ("*Lesse then the least / Of all Gods mercies*") of "The Posie" in such as way as to suggest that the quotation is from Scripture, not from Herbert. Notes that Herbert's phrase is a scriptural adaptation of Gen. 32:10 and Eph. 3:8 and that, at the end of his preface to *The Temple*, Nicholas Ferrar maintains that the quotation was Herbert's motto. Observes that the phrase gained further currency by being quoted by Barnabas Oley and Izaak Walton. Mentions other unacknowledged borrowings from *The Temple* by Henshaw, Venning, and Bates.

**1364. Reimer, A. P.** "The Poetry of Religious Paradox—T. S. Eliot and the Metaphysicals." *SSEng* 8 (1982–1983): 80–88.

Argues that T. S. Eliot's "The Journey of the Magi" can be seen as his "homage to the metaphysicals, an attempt to replicate within the possibilities available to the modern poet some of those effects which made their poetry so richly imaginative and satisfying" (p. 88). Notes general similarities in subject matter, style, structure, and tone and points out specific likenesses between Eliot's poem and the poetry of Donne and Herbert. Notes, for example, that the mention of "vine-leaves" in Eliot's poem reminds one of Herbert's "The Bunch of Grapes" and compares and contrasts the emblematic features of Herbert's poetry and Eliot's poem.

**1365. Routh, Michael.** "A Crux of 'The Pulley.'" *SCN* 40, no. 3:44–45.

Discusses each of the five occurrences of the word *rest* in "The Pulley" to show that the meaning of the poem depends on Herbert's "conundrum-like word-play that informs his art" (p. 45). Concludes that Herbert's "linguistic acrobatics" reveal his view that "the poet can only express his comprehension of the ways of God in language that seems to contradict itself, emphasizing that God's ways must always remain at least partially inscrutable to man and therefore are not describable in unambiguous terms" (p. 45).

**1366. Sharratt, Bernard.** "Optional Extra, Seminar Contributions: Voices Reading George Herbert's Dedication," in *Reading Relations: Structures of Literary Productions: A Dialectical Text/Book*, 93–168. Atlantic Heights, N.J.: Humanities Press.

Critical discussion of "The Dedication" presented in the form of a seminar discussion among students, a teacher, Herbert, and an implied God. Focuses on what reading a poem means and comments on the relationship among religion, belief, and poetry. Maintains that, if one reads "The Dedication" seriously, he is "implicated in, drawn into, a whole set of basic philosophical-theological positions," or, "put another way, to probe the process of reading this text is to disclose some of the underlying premises of a certain religious 'ideology'" (p. 103).

**1367. Sherwood, Terry G.** "Tasting and Telling Sweetness in George Herbert's Poetry." *ELR* 12:319–40.

Discusses Herbert's spirituality of sweetness as it is reflected in *The Temple* and points out that the works of St. Francis de Sales, Richard Sibbes, and St. Bernard of Clairvaux shed light on Herbert's religious sensibility. Argues that the relationships among the sweetness of love, the taste and consumption of God, and fulfillment through language determine many of the distinctive qualities of Herbert's devotional lyrics. Maintains that throughout the *The Temple* "the varying experience of sweetness and bitterness is one essential way that Herbert expresses the struggle to achieve fruition in God" (p. 329). Discusses the spirituality of sweetness in such poems as "Jordan (II)," "The Odour," "The H. Scriptures (I and II)," "Virtue," "The Invitation," "The Banquet," and especially "Love (III)" and argues that, although the smell and sound of sweetness are important in Herbert's poems, taste is most important because "tasting, consuming, and assimilating configure much more closely the intimate relationship with the loving God, who enters, inhabits, nourishes, and conforms the believer to Himself" (p. 323). Discusses how this concept relates both to Scripture and to the Eucharist and maintains that "the depth of this physiological reality is most compellingly expressed in the Eucharistic conclusion of 'Love (III)'" (p. 340).

**1368. Steinmann, Theo.** "Antinomy as a Psychopoetic Technique in George Herbert's 'The Collar.'" *ArAA* 7:3–11.

Analyzes antinomy in "The Collar" as a deliberate technique that (1) "reveals the persona's subconscious struggle through the self-contradictory use of words and images" and (2) "induces a kind of double-think in the reader" in that "he understands simultaneously two mutually exclusive, yet equally plausible meanings" (p. 3). Maintains that the conflict in the speaker between obedience and rebellion produces "the continual ambiguity on the level of language which mirrors the fundamental dualism of the human predicament" (p. 4). Argues that in "The Collar" the mind of the speaker "selects images and particularly meaningful words to express and justify its rebellion against God," while, at the same time, the soul "manages to influence the choice and the actual wording in such a way that these images and key words convey their own negation together with the *prima facie* meaning" (p. 3). Observes that "thus the speaker's antinomical attitude is condensed into self-defeating images" and that "similarly the rhetorical and the prosodic structures reflect the coexistence of chaos and order, of disruption and continuity" (p. 3). Points out that the poem divides into "three proportionate parts (16 + 16 + 4), representing an equally systematic psychological progression" and that "the spiritual progress from the first word to the last which seems to end in the peace of God is only one movement between the anthropological opposites" (p. 11).

**1369. Stull, William L.** "Sacred Sonnets in Three Styles." *SP* 79:78–99.

Discusses the rhetorical traditions that informed the religious sonnet from Henry Constable to Milton. Points out that Petrarchan love poets of the Renaissance "confined themselves to the middle style aimed at pleasing a courtly mistress with flowered praise" but that "the religious sonneteers of the same period embraced a full rhetoric, one that encompassed all three *officia* and their corresponding styles" (p. 78). Discusses the "passionate plainness" in the sonnets of Fulke Greville, Donne, and Jonson; the "flowered middle style" in the sonnets of William Drummond, a style that poets like Henry Constable and Herbert deliberately converted to the service of God; and the grand, Italianate style of Milton's sonnets. Points out that in "Josephs coat," "Love (I and II)," and "The H. Scriptures (I and II)" Herbert "put conventionally Petrarchan conceits and hyperboles to use in the praise of divine love and Holy Scripture" and claims that "The H. Scriptures (II)" is one of the "most 'sugared' sonnets in English" (p. 85).

**1370. ———.** "'Why Are Not *Sonnets* Made of Thee?': A New Context for the 'Holy Sonnets' of Donne, Herbert, and Milton." *MP* 80:129–35.

Revised and expanded as "Sonnets Courtly and Christian," *HSL* 15–16 (1983–1984): 1–15.

Traces the development of the religious sonnet in England during the Renaissance, noting that it flourished "even as the Petrarchan vogue waxed and waned" (p. 129). Points out that, by the beginning of the seventeenth century, sacred sonnets "were legion in England, as they had long been in Italy and France" (p. 135). Calls Donne, Herbert, and Milton "great Christian sonneteers" and points out that they, "while far excelling their Tudor predecessors, write in the same literary tradition as Constable, Barnes, Lok, and Alabaster—as well as a host of minor religious sonneteers, such as

Nicholas Breton, John Davies of Hereford, and William Drummond of Hawthornden" (p. 135).

**1371. Swaim, Kathleen M.** "The 'Season'd Timber' of Herbert's 'Vertue.'" *GHJ* 6, no. 1:21–25.

Discusses the metaphysics and artistry of "Vertue," especially the conceit in the last stanza of the poem. Comments on the double significance of the word *coal* (line 15)—cinders and charcoal. Maintains that in the concluding conceit the poet says that, although the world will turn to cinders or ashes at the final conflagration, the soul, like "season'd timber" (line 14), will turn to charcoal, thus "purified by fire, the soul's sweetness and virtue not merely survive the destruction of earthly matter, but are intensified to the point of transcendence" (p. 24).

**1372. Thota, Anand Rao.** *Emily Dickinson: The Metaphysical Tradition.* New Delhi: Arnold-Heinemann; Atlantic Heights, N.J.: Humanities Press. 197, 4p.

Argues that the poetry of Emily Dickinson shows a profound similarity in both themes and technique to the poetry of the seventeenth-century British poets. Sees Dickinson as "intellectually less aggressive than Donne, as intricate in technique as Herbert, and as sensuously articulate as Marvell" (p. 139). Maintains that Dickinson "became a major metaphysical poet of the nineteenth century, without even being very conscious of the leading metaphysical poets of the seventeenth century" and that she is "a crucial aesthetic link between the seventeenth century metaphysicals and the twentieth century neo-metaphysicals" (p. 161). Mentions Herbert throughout and finds numerous echoes of and parallels to Herbert in Dickinson's poetry. Frequently compares and/or contrasts the attitudes, themes, and techniques of the two poets. Finds "a surprising parallel between Dickinson and Herbert in the mode of treating different types of human emotions in their verse" (p. 141) and maintains that both poets reveal a unified sensibility.

**1373. Williams, J. David.** "Metaphysical Poets," in *Questions That Count: British Literature to 1750,* 53–65. Washington, D.C.: University Press of America.

Presents a list of six general questions about metaphysical poetry that students might ask themselves (p. 53) as well as a list of twenty questions specifically on Herbert's poetry (pp. 55, 57).

# *1983*

**1374. Anders, Isabel.** "George Herbert—The Country Parson." *The Living Church,* 27 February, p. 2.

Briefly comments on the spiritual wisdom, especially the "practicality of true spirituality," that informs *The Country Parson,* claiming that the work reflects the best of the Anglican tradition.

**1375. Anselment, Raymond A.** "George Herbert's 'The Collar.'" *NM* 84:372–75.

Discusses the ironic and emblematic dimensions of the speaker's rebellion in lines 17–26 of "The Collar." Maintains that the speaker ironically fails to recognize the rest and security guaranteed by Christ to those who accept his yoke in the gospel of

Matthew and in the epistles of Paul. Observes that "emblematically the cage, which sometimes visualizes for the seventeenth century the plight of man yearning for spiritual liberation, paradoxically signifies true freedom" (p. 373). Notes that Jacob Cats in his emblem book, *Sive Protevus. Pars. Tertia* (Middleburgh, 1618), makes it clear that rebellion is foolish and that servitude is wise, and that Georgette de Montenay in his emblem book, *Monvmentva Emblematvm Christianorvm Virtvtvm* (Frankfurt, 1619), "with striking similarity to major images in Herbert's poem" presents an emblem to show "the contrast between the easy, mild fetters of the yoke and the new collar ensnaring the prideful, rebellious man" (p. 374). Concludes that, although the speaker "will wear no collar" and "scorns all who foolishly bow their heads under a selfless burden," he cannot in his heart "deny the knowledge tacitly and ironically present in the mounting biblical and emblematic associations" (p. 375).

**1376. Barber, Charles.** "Themes and Topics: Religious Poetry," in *Poetry in English: An Introduction*, 178–94. New York: St. Martin's Press.
Brief introduction to Herbert's life and poetry (pp. 181–83). Argues that Herbert's poetry is an extension of his pastoral work, "aiming at the edification of others rather than concentrating (like Donne's) on his own experience" (p. 182). Maintains that in his poems of spiritual conflict "we seem to be directly following the movement of the mind and feelings of a man who is supremely honest about his doubts and motives" (p. 183). Concludes that "perhaps spiritual assurance is a more characteristic mood of Herbert's" (p. 183).

**1377. Borsch, Frederick H.** "Love Bade Me Welcome." *The Living Church*, 9 October, pp. 12–13.
Gives a biographical sketch of Herbert and maintains that Herbert's poetry "reveals faith, but also ongoing uncertainties" (p. 12). Argues that, for Herbert, "music and poetry were ways of arranging and composing life's disorder—of giving it a shape, probing it for significance," and that "into his poetry he poured all he was and had been—rhetorician, musician, courtier, statesman, scholar, lover, pastor" (p. 12). Comments on Herbert's colloquial speech, concrete imagery, dialetic argumentation, inventive and original metrical patterns and rhyme schemes, complex simplicity, and gentle humor and irony. Contends that the major theme of *The Temple* is "the love of God for man and of man for God" (p. 13). Explicates "Love (III)" and agrees that it is "one of the finest poems in the English language" (p. 13).

**1378. Briggs, Julia.** "Religion," in *This Stage-Play World: English Literature and Its Backgrounds, 1580–1625*, 66–94. Oxford, New York: Oxford University Press.
Briefly contrasts Herbert and Donne as religious poets and as sermon writers. Argues that, although Herbert says his poems reflect his "many spiritual conflicts," the reader may find them more tranquil than Herbert's phrase suggests, "partly because the courteous and graceful manner in which the poet dresses his discontents can be deceptive" (p. 89). Maintains that the differences between Herbert and Donne in their preaching manner are a result of the different expectations of their congregations. Comments briefly on "The British Church" as representing the *via media* of seventeenth-century Anglicanism.

**1379. Brugaletta, John J.** "'Something Understood': The Making of Christian Poetry in Our Time." *Anglican Theological Review* 65:273–85.
Comments on the nature and function of Christian poetry. Briefly compares and contrasts Herbert's "The Sacrifice" with W. H. Auden's "Musée des Beaux Arts" and

Isaac Watts's "When I survey the wondrous cross." Praises the *via media* of Herbert's verse, maintaining that "The Sacrifice," "with all of the intellectual force that has gone into it," is not "accessible only to intellectuals" (p. 282).

**1380. Burden, Dennis H.** "George Herbert's 'Redemption.'" *RES* 34:446–51.
Offers an explication of "Redemption." Comments on the use of legal language in the sonnet and notes that the description of the covenant as the leasing of land has important Old Testament associations. Maintains that the poem "is liturgical in its origin and reference" and that it "looks to the state of mind in which the sacrament of Holy Communion should be approached" (pp. 448–49). Shows that the "apparent accidental sequence of the narrative is in essence tautly logical" (p. 450) and observes that Herbert's speaker "shows the right combination of humility and boldness" (pp. 449). Concludes that, although Herbert's approach is "poker faced and low-key" with "the fictions apparently flat and frustrating," the narrative "is in fact put together in a peculiar and ingenious way" so that "one comes away from it with increased estimate of Herbert's wit and also, and more importantly, with a deep understanding of what redemption really means in the life of the believer" (p. 451).

**1381. Charles, Amy M.** "George Herbert: Poet, Musician, Priest." *The Living Church,* 9 October, pp. 10–11.
General introduction to Herbert's life and poetry for the nonspecialist, Christian reader. Describes the organization of *The Temple* and maintains that, in many ways, it is "a record of God's loving pursuit of man, offering him the benefits of his love, and man's persistent delay in accepting the gifts proffered" (p. 11). Briefly comments on general features of the poems—intellectual wit, word play, subtle form, disciplined diction, images drawn from everyday life, use of various voices, and joy and playfulness in composition.

**1382.** ———. "The Original of Mr George Herbert's Temple." *GHJ* 6, no. 2:1–14.
Reprinted, in expanded form, in the introduction to the facsimile edition of the Bodleian manuscript (entry 1429).
Discusses the provenance and date (mid-summer 1633) of the Bodleian manuscript (Tanner MS. 307) of Herbert's poems. Comments on Herbert's friendship with Nicholas Ferrar and his connection with Little Gidding. Compares the Bodleian and Williams manuscripts to show that "all the changes Herbert made demonstrate in various ways his growth in both poetry and religion, his more mature literary judgment" (p. 11).

**1383. [Charles, Amy M., ed.]** *Cross-Bias: The Newsletter of the Friends of Bemerton Society,* no. 8 (September). 11p.
Comments on events held throughout the year in both the United Kingdom and the United States to mark the 350th anniversary of Herbert's death and also of the publication of the first edition of *The Temple*; reprints the shaped verse entitled "An Easter Egg" by J. D. K. Lloyd that first appeared in no. 3 of *Cross-Bias* (entry 1095); calls attention to recent and forthcoming studies of Herbert; presents summaries by Edmund Miller of papers on Herbert given at the 1982 MLA meeting; reports on the discovery of woodworms in the church at Little Gidding; and comments on matters of interest to members of the society, such as the loss of the cartoon of the stained-glass window at the west end of St. Andrew's, several obituaries of scholars and friends, and the latest parish news from Bemerton.

**1384. Cramer, Carmen.** "Herbert's 'Ungratefulness.'" *Expl* 41, no. 4:17–19.

Argues that enclosure is "the motivating image" of "Ungratefulnesse" and that it is appropriate "not only because the entire *Temple* sequence is theoretically occurring within an enclosed building, but also because the Christian paradoxes, to die (implying the prison or enclosure of death) that one might live, and to become a servant (implying the state of bondage) so that one may be free, are a center of Herbert's religious concern" (pp. 17–18). Discusses each of the enclosure images in the poem— the grave, cabinets, treasure chests, circles, the heart. Maintains that the first stanza is a composition of place by memory; that the second, third, and fourth stanzas are an analysis by the understanding of God's gifts; and that the last stanza is a colloquy, "an exhortation of humankind's ungratefulness for those gifts" (p. 19). Concludes that "this ungratefulness creates the enclosure of mortality, the theme of Herbert's poem" (p. 19).

**1385. Di Cesare, Mario A.** "The Bodleian Manuscript and the Text of Herbert's Poems." *GHJ* 6, no. 2:15–35.

Reprinted, in expanded form, in the introduction to the facsimile edition of the Bodleian manuscript (entry 1429).

Argues (1) that the Bodleian manuscript (Tanner MS. 307) "deserves careful attention" and that "the tendencies of some editors to give primary or unique authority to *1633* are not solidly based and must at the very least be viewed with skepticism" and (2) that Hutchinson's edition (entry 266) "remains the most substantial one" although the Bodleian manuscript "must clearly influence future editorial practice" (p. 17). Compares the Bodleian manuscript with the first edition of 1633 to show that Thomas Buck, the Cambridge printer, and the editors who followed his edition "have been misled into errors of orthography, punctuation, and format which often lead to interpretations far removed from Herbert's original intentions" (p. 32). Concludes that "it is essential to investigate *all* the textual questions that arise—words, punctuation, incidental elements, as well as problems of the pattern poems, the sonnets, the contextual relationships of individual poems to each other" and that these matters "can be studied properly only with reference to the *B* manuscript" (pp. 32–33).

**1386. Dinshaw, Fram.** "A Lost MS. of George Herbert's Occasional Verse and the Authorship of 'To The L. Chancellor.'" *N&Q* n.s. 30:423–25.

Discusses a group of poems ascribed to Herbert and addressed to Bacon that are commonly grouped together in seventeenth-century manuscripts. Maintains that on the authority of James Duport in *Ecclesiastes Solomonis* (Cambridge, 1662) "we can confidently ascribe four to Herbert" but "about the others we cannot be so sure" (p. 424). Argues that the first printing of "To the Right Hon. L. Chancellor (Bacon)" by John Fry in 1816 "provides stronger grounds for reinstating the poem" in Herbert's canon and "also suggests that the canon of Herbert's occasional verse may yet be enlarged" (p. 424).

**1387. Du Priest, Travis.** "George Herbert, Priest, 1633." *The Living Church*, 9 October, p. 11.

Nine-line original poem on Herbert.

**1388. Elsky, Martin.** "George Herbert's Pattern Poems and the Materiality of Language: A New Approach to Renaissance Hieroglyphics." *ELH* 50:245–60.

Argues that the importance of Renaissance ideas for Herbert's poetry is evident "in the Renaissance view of words as material things that belong to the same network of resemblances that endows natural objects with allegorical meaning—a view that underlies the Renaissance interest in hieroglyphs and emblem literature" (p. 245). Maintains that the words and letters that make up "the typographical pictograms of Herbert's hieroglyphic pattern poems" are "also the written marks of the poet's utterance—his prayer, his plea, his spoken word" and that "in this regard Herbert's hieroglyphs depend on the confluence of two strands of Renaissance linguistic thought: the Humanist interest in language as uttered speech transcribed in written letters, and the cabalist Neoplatonic interest in words and letters as physical things with symbolic significance" (pp. 245–46). Discusses "The Altar" and "Easter-wings," as well as poems such as "Jesu," "Love-joy," "The Sonne," and "Anagram of the Virgin Marie," to show that Herbert "sees meaning as divinely ordained in the sensible elements of language" (p. 252). Concludes that Herbert "holds that language is a thing in the world like other things" and that "its physical properties—visibility and audibility—are tied to the spiritual significance of its referents and even possess an ontological status similar to that of other material things" (p. 258).

**1389. Harnack, Andrew.** "Deconstructions and George Herbert." *KPAB* no. 10:33–51.

Presents a deconstructive reading of "Prayer (I)." Maintains that it is "an elegant testimony to what it is not" and that it "is neither prayer nor a definition of prayer and artfully says so" (p. 44). Claims that, "by refusing to be or become a stable and determinate text," the poem "enters, not simply a plurality of meanings, but a rich and ample plenitude measured—or more properly, implied—in each reading of the poem" (p. 45). Maintains that "we do not experience a loss in the deconstructive loosening up of its text" but rather "by decentering the poem and freeing it from determinancy, we play it toward a fullness that saves it from exhaustion, from the fatigue of mere repetition" (p. 46). Predicts that Herbert "will be particularly attractive to deconstructionists because in his own way he committedly distrusts his own poetry" and, "sensitive to the illusionary power of words, Herbert resists the temptation to use words for ends they cannot realize" (p. 46).

**1390. Houston, John Porter.** "Devotional Poetry: A Confluence of Styles," in *The Rhetoric of Poetry in the Renaissance and Seventeenth Century*, 160–201. Baton Rouge and London: Louisiana State University Press.

Comments on stylistic features of "The Collar," "Aaron," "The Sacrifice," and "Prayer (I)" to show that Herbert "frequently exploited the resources of low style, in the manner peculiar to English poets" (p. 186). Observes that Herbert's poetry "has been shown to be even richer in liturgical and biblical references than it appears on the surface" and points out that, "while there are passages of distinct visual interest in Herbert's poetry, the effects of sound and prosodic structure generally draw our attention first" (p. 186). Comments on Herbert's "subdued language," the "low-keyed intricacy" of his poems, the "exceptional features" of his syntax, and his "remarkable capacity for making complex figures like those of 'Prayer' subdued and fitting to low style" (pp. 187–89). Briefly contrasts Herbert's style to that of Donne and Jean de La Ceppède. Calls Herbert a baroque poet, "though one so heavily influenced by the English low-style lyric tradition that his range of style is variously slim or subtly florid" (p. 189).

**1391. Idol, John L., Jr.** "The 1894 Sale of a First Edition of *The Temple* in New York." *GHJ* 6, no. 2:47–48.

Points out that someone at Dodd, Mead & Co., perhaps Robert Dodd, who ran a rare-book store in New York, paid $1,050 for a first edition of *The Temple* in the autumn of 1894, a sum that, if difference in buying power is considered, exceeds the amount paid for first editions at two more recent sales—$13,000 on 15 November 1978 at Sotheby's and £7,000 on 14 June 1979 at Christie's.

**1392. Johnson, Wendell Stacy.** "Halfway to a New Land: Herbert, Tennyson, and the Early Hopkins." *HQ* 10:115–24.

Notes that, throughout his life, Hopkins saw Herbert as representing "the most attractive aspects of English religious art and life" (p. 116). Examines several of Hopkins's earlier poems, especially "Barnfloor and Winepress," "Soliloquy of One of the Spies left in the Wilderness," "Heaven-Haven," and "New Readings," to show that there are similarities between his use of biblical typology and imagery and that of Herbert. Observes that in his later poems Hopkins's use of biblical typology becomes much less prevalent.

**1393. Kawata, Akira.** "George Herbert to Shi—Shinko tono kanren de" [George Herbert's Poems—in Relation to his Faith], in *Eibungaku Shiron* [Essays in Honor of the 77th Anniversary of the Birth of Professor Isamu Muraoka], 135–46. Tokyo: Kinseido.

Discusses the evolution of Herbert's poetics. Argues that his use of plain style is related to his choice of symbolism, that the use of dissimilar and incongruous images is appropriate for expressing the nature of God, and that it fits his attitude as a country parson and his belief in the simplicity of grace. Concludes that when he tries to write poetry to celebrate truly spiritual sincerity, Herbert solves the dilemma of poetry and faith.

**1394. Kronenfeld, Judy Z.** "Probing the Relation between Poetry and Ideology: Herbert's 'The Windows.'" *JDJ* 2, no. 1:55–80.

Recognizes two general tendencies in modern Herbert criticism: "the one defines a Herbert confident in the meaningfulness of ritual, sacrament and image" whose poems "are little incarnations" in which "tenor and vehicle are by definition of equal weight," a Herbert "confident in the presence of the divine in the earthly," and the other defines a Herbert "so wracked by the division between nature and grace, often categorized as a 'Calvinist' or 'Puritan' dilemma, that he contrives to make his poems undo themselves in order to avoid claiming anything for the natural man or the artificer" (p. 57). Using "The Windows" as an example, argues that "differing notions of Herbert's religious position shape our interpretations of his poems" (p. 58). Presents a detailed reading of the poem that "pursues the *particular* oppositions or versions of available oppositions at issue that it is the critic's task to elucidate in a work, the *particular* nature of Herbert's view of the relation of 'the inward worship of the heart' and the 'external worship of God in His Church'" (p. 64). In this pursuit of "an appropriately complex and tonally appropriate interpretation," allows the poem "to reverberate fully with Biblical allusions" (pp. 64–65). Argues that in the poem "it is the life of the minister in a double sense—his actions and the internalization, the pathos or coloration of his words, that show he feels what he says—that wins souls to salvation" (p. 74). Maintains that Herbert "uses the inner glow of stained glass as a metaphor for the dynamic, living image of Christ in the preacher" and yet, "insofar as stained glass contained actual images and was attacked by the iconoclasts, it emblematized what was often diametrically opposed to such an internal dynamic image" and thus the poem "almost redefines windows as it implicitly redefines 'image'" (p. 76). Concludes that "the shining light" in "The Windows" "is a remarkably inward phenomenon" and that the poem "is finally 'about' that inner faith very much more that it is 'about' or justifies the 'sacramentals' of the church" (p. 77).

**1395. Moreland, Kim.** "The Rooted Flower and the Flower that Glides: An Interpretation of Herbert's 'The Flower.'" *GHJ* 6, no. 2:37–45.

Argues that "The Flower" not only "functions as the spiritual climax of the smaller pattern that exists within the larger pattern of *The Temple*" but also "recapitulates the systolic and diastolic rhythm of *The Temple* as a whole," embodying "several conflicts, each of which is followed by a spiritual triumph" (p. 37). Maintains that even the structure of the poem underscores "this alternating movement" (p. 38) and shows that there is a "whole series of conflicts and triumphs presented in the poem, the last of these triumphs being the most intense and the most elevated" (p. 39). Contends that the speaker's "willful attempts to regain Eden are doomed to failure" and that "only when he abandons such attempts can he gain the new paradise available to post-lapsarian man" (p. 44). Concludes that, in the final lines of the poem, the poet "mulls over his experiences, reflecting on what he has learned about the nature of paradise as well as the natures of God and man, because of the conflicts and triumphs experienced in the process of the poem" (p. 44).

**1396. Ottenhoff, John H.** "The Shadow and the Real: Typology and the Religious Sonnet." *HSL* 15–16 (1983–1984): 43–59.

Examines the religious sonnets of Barnabe Barnes, Henry Lok, and William Alabaster to show that "their various shapings of typological symbolism, an important element in religious literature through the ages, reveal different theological emphases but a common development of the sonnet's devotional possibilities" (p. 43). Argues that in these sonnets we see "not simply sanctification of form but the development of rich—and different—modes of devotion and biblically derived aesthetics" (p. 56). Maintains that, rather than belonging to "a meditative tradition that ostensibly proceeds from Southwell," Herbert "is more aptly placed in a Protestant poetic to which significant contributions were made by the sonnets of Barnes and Lok" (p. 55). Discusses examples of typological symbolism in devotional sonnets of the 1590s, such as the high priest Melchizedek and the bunch of grapes, to show how they are aesthetic antecedents to the more mature sacred poems of Herbert.

**1397. Passarella, Lee.** "The Meaning of the Tent in George Herbert's 'Anagram.'" *ELN* 21, no. 2: 10–13.

Surveys the critical views of Rosemond Tuve (entry 409), Louis Leiter (entry 666), and Robert Reiter (entry 712) on the "tent" (line 2) in the "Anagram of the Virgin Marie" and argues that the image is connected to both the Old and the New Testament, stressing the "temporary nature of the tabernacle" (p. 11). Maintains that the "tent" refers to the first temporary repository of the Ark of the Covenant in the Old Testament but also that the tent or tabernacle "as temporary shelter has everything to do with the Incarnation" because Mary's womb was "only a temporary dwelling of Christ" (p. 12). Notes parallels between the Ark of the Covenant and Christ, the Law of the Old Testament and the New Covenant, and the Temple of Solomon and the Church. Concludes that until the day comes "when the tabernacle will be put off at last," "the Church lives in merely temporary quarters" (p. 13).

**1398. Patrides, C. A.** *George Herbert: The Critical Heritage.* (The Critical Heritage Series, gen. ed. B. C. Southam.) London, Boston, Melbourne and Henley: Routledge & Kegan Paul. xix, 390p.

Presents seventy-four selections or excerpts of critical commentary on Herbert and his poetry from the second decade of the seventeenth century (Donne's "To Mr George Herbert, with one of my Seal[s], of the Anchor and Christ") to 1936 (an

extract from Austin Warren's "George Herbert" in *American Review*, entry 206). In the introduction (pp. 1–53) surveys Herbert's fluctuating critical reputation. Observes that seventeenth-century remarks focused primarily on Herbert the saintly man and writer of hymns, not the lyric poet, although "the intrinsic merits of Herbert's poetic practice were recognised by some of the numerous poets who strove to imitate him" (p. 1), especially Vaughan and Edward Taylor. Points out that Addison in 1711 was the first critic to condemn Herbert and notes "the stony silence of both Pope and Johnson" (p. 14). Comments on adaptations of the poems by Wesley and others for congregational singing and notes the eighteenth-century attempts to "improve" Herbert's poems by bringing them into line with the literary tastes of the time. Notes the favorable reception extended to Herbert's poetry by Coleridge, Emerson, Ruskin, James Russell Lowell, Oliver Wendell Holmes, and Alice Meynell in the nineteenth century and maintains that, notwithstanding some adverse criticism, Herbert's reputation "remained steadily high ever since the early 1800's" and that throughout the nineteenth century Herbert "enjoyed a popularity not even remotely matched by Donne or Crashaw or Vaughan or Cowley" (p. 28). Observes that in the first three decades of the twentieth century critical opinion on Herbert was divided. Comments on Palmer's edition (entry 2) and notes that, "the unwarranted rearrangement of the poems apart," the edition "is a major achievement because of his infectious enthusiasm for the poetry, his manifest conviction that Herbert is a conscious artist, and his expansive commentary on the general as on the particular" (p. 31). Notes also the importance of the criticism of T. S. Eliot and H. J. C. Grierson in the modern revival of interest in Herbert and calls the 1930s "the most crucial in Herbert's critical heritage, the turning point in his recognition as a poet" (p. 33). The main text is divided into four major sections: "Herbert in the Seventeenth Century" (pp. 55–148), thirty-five entries; "Herbert in the Eighteenth Century" (pp. 149–65), six entries; "Herbert in the Nineteenth Century" (pp. 166–277), nineteen entries; and "Herbert in the Twentieth Century" (pp. 278–356), fourteen entries. Each entry is accompanied by notes and commentary by the editor. "Appendix I: Seventeenth-Century Musical Settings of Lyrics by Herbert" (pp. 357–73) contains John Jenkins's setting of the first four stanzas of "The Starre," John Wilson's setting of four stanzas from "Content," John Playford's setting of "The Altar," John Blow's setting of "Ephes.iv.30," and Henry Purcell's setting of seven stanzas of "Longing." "Appendix II: Eighteenth-Century Versions of Herbert's 'Vertue'" (pp. 374–77) contains adaptations of Herbert's poem by John and Charles Wesley, an anonymous adapter in *Universal Harmony or, the Gentleman & Ladie's Social Companion* (1745), the anonymous adapter in *The Charmer: A Choice Collection of Songs, Scots and English* (1749), W. H. Reid, and George Horne. Index of Herbert's works (pp. 378–81) and index of names (pp. 381–90).
Reviews:
C. H. Sisson, *TLS*, 8 April 1983, p. 358
Helen Wilcox, *GHJ* 6, no. 2 (1983): 51–54

**1399.** Pearlman, E. "George Herbert's God." *ELR* 13:88–112.
    Discusses the poems in *Memoriae Matris Sacrum* and argues that they "offer with little disguise or dissimulation a new perspective on Herbert's inner life" (p. 97). Maintains that three important insights about Herbert's complex psychological makeup are revealed in these Latin poems: (1) that Herbert "thought himself to be uniquely the child of his mother and presumed that in writing poetry he fulfilled her expectations or instructions," (2) that his "sense of the sacred cannot be divorced from his relationship with his mother, for both Lady Danvers and his God are

celebrated in similar terms and in similar language," to which "is related the confusion of gender, perhaps arising out of the incomplete differentiation of his own identity from that of his mother," and (3) that he suggests "by the building and enclosing of defined spaces (gardens, houses, temples), maternally modeled security both profane and religious can be recaptured and expressed" (p. 97). Explores each of these psychological themes in Herbert's life and poetry.

**1400. Pollard, David L.** "The Organs of the Eye and Ear: Complementary Modes of Perception: George Herbert's *The Temple*." *Cithara* 22, no. 2:62–72.
    Discusses Renaissance debates on the hierarchy of the senses and points out that most Protestant writers tended to agree with Aristotle rather than with Plato that hearing, not sight, is the highest and most trustworthy of man's senses. Maintains that "the problem of right and accurate perception furnishes Herbert with some of his most characteristic themes as well as opportunities to display his immense poetical virtuosity" (p. 64). Comments on Herbert's symbolic uses of seeing and hearing in *The Temple*. Maintains that Herbert's visual imagery "is by no means worked out in painterly detail" but typically "steers the eye to some spiritual referent behind or beyond it" (p. 69). Observes that Herbert "balances the attention given to sight with an ample attention to sound" and that, "while the eye is forever getting into spiritual difficulty" in his poems, "the ear is to be trusted" (p. 70). Maintains that *The Temple* has "no larger unifying thematic preoccupation than simply that of hearing and being heard by God" (p. 70).

**1401. [Porter, H. Boone.]** "George Herbert." *The Living Church*, 9 October, p. 14.
    Notes that 1983 marks the 350th anniversary of the death of Herbert. Calls Herbert "the virtual founder of Anglican pastoral theology" and suggests that his poetry and prose "remain an imperishable part of the Anglican literary patrimony." Maintains that Herbert "has never been more popular among serious readers than in the present century."

**1402. Rogers, William Elford.** "Gestures Toward a Literary History of Lyric," in *The Three Genres and the Interpretation of Lyric*, 176–270. Princeton: Princeton University Press.
    Argues that, although Herbert's "The British Church" and Donne's "Show me deare Christ" deal with the same subject matter, draw on the same Christian tradition for their images and symbols, and have many verbal similarities, the two poems have quite different meanings and attitudes. Maintains that the differences arise primarily "in the way the poets use the figures generated by the main symbols" (p. 204). Distinguishes between natural wit and verbal wit and suggests that this distinction "is a means of articulating how these Metaphysical poems are like each other and thus distinctive of their literary movement" and that this distinction "can be grounded, if at all, in the genre-theory that associates lyric with reciprocal relations" (p. 212). Maintains that the likenesses between Herbert's poem and Donne's are more important than the differences, "even though the differences are probably more striking" (pp. 212–13). Argues that, although both poems use verbal wit, their differences arise because Herbert uses "scholastic wit" and Donne uses "paradoxical wit." Maintains that, "in discovering the words that can be applied both to the Mother and the Church," Herbert "reaffirms the value of the traditional symbol" and that whereas Donne "questions the adequacy of any linguistic means of expressing religious truth, Herbert emphasizes the adequacy of the symbol he has chosen" (p. 218).

**1403. Rygiel, Mary Ann.** "Hopkins and Herbert: Two Meditative Poets." *HQ* 10:45–54.

Studies Hopkins's "Carrion Comfort" and "the way in which a reading of it is informed by and made more satisfying through a knowledge of Herbert's 'The Collar'" and mentions other poems by both poets that "bear on this focus" (p. 45). Discusses similarities and differences in the structure, use of speaker, occasion, imagery, language, rhetoric, and tone of both poems. Maintains that what is interesting in the two poems is "the imaginative way in which the poets prove anew what for them is already known" (p. 52).

**1404. Schoenfeldt, Michael C.** "Submission and Assertion: The 'Double Motion' of Herbert's 'Dedication.'" *JDJ* 2, no. 2:39–49.

Explicates "Dedication" to show that, in spite of its "initial gesture of surrender," the poem reveals "a self which is demanding, assertive, even aggressive toward the God to Whom it attempts to submit" and argues that "this 'double-motion' of self-abnegation and self-assertion" in the poem "depicts both the goal of Herbert's poetic project—submission of the self and its creations to God—and the inherent difficulties of achieving that goal through an act of human creation" (p. 39). Maintains that "Dedication" "emerges as a paradigm of Herbert's recurring concern with the problems of making art of his intercourse with God" (p. 39). Argues that Herbert's "extended use of the metaphor of a poet addressing his patron in his dedication of his poems to God provides him with a supple language able to register the extremes of self-assertion and self-abnegation, aggression and submission" and that the poem "directs our attention as readers not only to Herbert's faith, but also to his faithfulness to the difficulty of human submission to God" (p. 47).

**1405. Severance, Sibyl Lutz.** "Self-Persistence in *The Temple*: George Herbert's 'Artillerie.'" *HSL* 15–16 (1983–1984): 108–17.

Maintains that Herbert's poetry "recurringly details the experiences of the 'I'—the God seekers and self-examiners" and that "their conflicting activities and longings shape the poetry" (p. 108). Discusses Herbert's concept of the self and his uses of multiple poetic voices, stressing that "any classifying of what happens to the self in *The Temple* can be challenged with exceptions" since "systems are, finally, inadequate because of the priest's paradoxical beliefs and the poet's purposeful making all new" (p. 109). Analyzes "Artillerie" to show "the moving mind and the contraries that press self and reason throughout *The Temple*" and argues that to understand the poem "we must understand the genesis of Herbert's self-consciousness in his work" (p. 109). Maintains that "perhaps no other poem in the Herbert canon so vividly illustrates thought and devotion united—and the fragility of such a union, the plight of the mind that refuses to slight its mission as God's instrument" (p. 112).

**1406. Shawcross, John T.** "An Allusion to 'The Church Militant' in Howell's *An Institution of General History*." *GHJ* 6, no. 2:49.

Points out that in *An Institution of General History, From the beginning of the World to the Monarchy of Constantine the Great* (London: Printed for Henry Herringman, 1661) William Howell, an important historian in the later half of the seventeenth century, quotes lines 47–100 from *The Church Militant*. Observes that Howell used a later edition of Herbert, "since line 54 reads not 'Christ-Crosse' but 'Christs-Crosse,' found in editions between 1641–1809 except for 1674."

**1407. Sinfield, Alan.** *Literature in Protestant England 1560–1660.* London and Canberra: Croom Helm; Totowa, N.J.: Barnes and Noble. viii, 160p.

In this survey of English Renaissance literature in relation to Protestantism mentions Herbert several times and uses examples from his poetry and prose to illustrate Protestant concepts and attitudes. Observes, for instance, that in "The Glance" and in "Love (III)" Herbert reflects an "assurance of election" (p. 15) that was usual for Protestants of his day. Maintains that Herbert rejected secular poetry entirely and consciously converted his talents to the service and praise of God. Briefly comments on Herbert's idea of God's providence, noting that "he subscribed to the protestant conviction that providence determines everything, and was happy to attribute specific human disasters to God's direct wish" (p. 107).

**1408. Stephens, John.** "*B. C. P.*, with apologies to George Herbert." *The Living Church*, 9 October, p. 12.

Twelve-line original poem on *The Book of Common Prayer* that imitates Herbert's style.

**1409. Strier, Richard.** *Love Known: Theology and Experience in George Herbert's Poetry.* Chicago and London: University of Chicago Press. xxi, 277p.

In the "Introduction" (pp. xi-xxi) announces that the purpose of this study is to argue for the centrality of the doctrine of justification by faith in Herbert's theology and poetry. Maintains that, although not a Lutheran, Herbert "understood and experienced the doctrine of justification by faith in much the way Luther did" (p. xiii); points out the pervasiveness of the theology of both Luther and Calvin in the seventeenth-century English Church; and argues that, although always loyal to the established church, Herbert's devotional and theological temper was closer to that of John Cotton, John Downame, and Richard Sibbes than that of Richard Hooker, Archbishop Laud, and Lancelot Andrewes. In chapter 1, "Dust and Sin: The Denial of Merit" (pp. 1–28), argues that Herbert was fully committed to the most fundamental position of Reformation theology, "the denial that man can in any way merit salvation" (p. 1), and illustrates Herbert's concept of man's sinful condition by discussing a number of poems, especially "Giddinesse," "Sepulchre," "Unkindnesse," and "Ungratefulnesse." Argues that Herbert's concept of God is one of power and love and that "the effort of Herbert's poetry is almost always to collapse the two terms into one, to see power as love" and maintains that Herbert's concept of man as weak and malicious or selfish emerges "dialectically from this conception of God" (p. 6). In chapter 2, "The Attack on Reason" (p. 29–60), argues that Herbert, like Luther, tends to think of sin in psychological and intellectual rather than in sensual terms. Comments on the pervasiveness of his attack on reason by discussing "Confession," "Sighs and Grones," "The World," "Sinnes round," and "Jordan (II)." Points out that in these poems the attack is primarily through allusion and imagery, whereas in "The Agonie," "Vanitie (I)," and "Divinitie" it is more direct and leads the reader more explicitly "toward the theological core of Herbert's attack on reason" (p. 40). Shows that in "The Thanksgiving," "The Reprisall," "Good Friday," and "Redemption" Herbert dramatizes the strangeness of grace and reveals that Christianity affronts natural reason and common sense. In chapter 3, "Interlude: Theology or Philosophy?" (pp. 61–83), discusses Herbert's attack on reason and challenges Stanley Fish's understanding of the attack. Shows that in "The Holdfast" Herbert "dramatizes and celebrates the full implications of the Reformation doctrine of grace" (p. 66). Calls "Love (III)" its companion piece and argues that Herbert "dramatizes his awareness that the doctrine of faith alone can be undermined not merely by assertions of merit and cooperation, but by assertions of unworthiness as well" (pp. 73–74). Maintains that "Dialogue" clarifies the attack on rationalism in "Love (III)" by pointing out that humility is often a kind of arrogance. In chapter 4, "*Vindiciae Gratiae*: The Rejecting of Bargaining" (pp. 84–113), locates Herbert's anti-rationalism in its historical context and through readings of "The Pearl," "Obedience," "Miserie," and "Artillerie" shows that Herbert criticizes and rejects the underlying rationalistic tendency of covenant theology. Presents a detailed reading of "Assurance," which "manifests and explains the joy Herbert normally found in the rejection of the covenant idea" (p. 105). Discusses Herbert's relationship with the Puritans and claims that "he is close to them when they sound the major note of the Reformation" but "departs from them when they depart from it" (p. xx). In chapter 5, "The New Life: Conversion" (pp. 114–42), focuses on Herbert's understanding of the phenomenology of conversion and regeneration. Maintains that "nothing more strongly links Herbert to the initial impulses of the Reformation more than his insistence on assurance as the essential Christian experience and his conception of assurance as dependent wholly upon God's nature and Word, and not, in any respect, upon man's actions" (pp. 114). Analyzes "Conscience" and "The Discharge" as poems directly related to the concept of assurance and comments on "Justice (II)" and "Aaron" as poems in which Herbert most clearly and powerfully expresses his views on and joy in the doctrine of alien righteousness. Concludes by examining "The Glance" as a poem in which Herbert presents conversion as a felt as well as an understood experience. In chapter 6, "The Heart Alone: Inwardness and Individualism" (pp. 143–73), discusses the inwardness, individualism, and functionalism in Herbert's theology as reflected in such poems as "The Church-floore," "The H. Scriptures (II)," "The Altar," "Christmas," "The Bunch of Grapes," "Love unknown," "Praise (III)," "Bitter-sweet," and "Longing." Comments that Herbert replaces the traditional Great Chain of Being concept "by a functionalist framework" (p. 173). In chapter 7, "The Heart's Privileges: Emotion" (pp. 174–217), discusses the central position Herbert gives to the emotions and maintains that his stress on the emotional is his strongest connection with the radicals of the English Revolution. Presents a reading of "Sion," arguing that it shows the heart "as the locus of the emotions" (p. 179), and an analysis of "The Storm," maintaining that it "provides the clearest vision in Herbert of the way in which God can be affected by human emotional need" (p. 185). Supplies the theological context for Herbert's insights on the emotions and relates them to his attitude toward art. Comments especially on "The Altar," "Jordan (II)," "A true Hymne," and "The Forerunners" to elucidate Herbert's view on art. In chapter 8, "The Limits of Experience" (pp. 218–52), examines a number of Herbert's most complex poems, such as "The Collar," "The Temper (I)," "The Search," "A Parodie," and especially "The Flower," to show how they express and dramatize Herbert's double attitude about "the unreliability as well as the integrity of immediate emotional experience" (p. xxi). Points out that "the simultaneous respect for and criticism of experience which Eliot called wit, Herbert would have called faith, the Christian temper" (p. 252). In the "Afterword" (pp. 253–54) suggests aspects of Herbert's poetry that remain to be studied. Bibliography (pp. 255–69), index of Herbert's poems (pp. 271–72), and general index (pp. 273–77). Reviews:

Jonathan F. S. Post, *JDJ* 3, no. 2 (1984): 221–47
Barbara K. Lewalski *GHJ* 8, no. 2 (1985): 45–48
John N. Wall, Jr., *Anglica Theological Review* 67, no. 2 (1985): 192–94

**1410. Wadman, Karen L.** "'Private Ejaculations': Politeness Strategies in George Herbert's Poems Directed to God." *Lang&S* 16:87–106.

Examines "Sighs and Grones," "Ephes.iv.30," "Longing," "Discipline," "Affliction (I)," "The Temper (I)," "Submission," and "Bitter-sweet" in the light of a sociolinguistic theory of politeness strategies developed by Penelope Brown and Stephen Levinson to show that not only is the speaker's relationship to God in Herbert's poems defined in terms of his "face-saving" acts and his politeness strategies but that the relationship also often changes in the course of many of Herbert's poems and the "change can be defined by politeness strategies Herbert employs as a means to an end" (p. 87).

**1411. Wood, Chauncey.** "George and Henry Herbert on Redemption." *HLQ* 46:298–309.

Discusses the problems of chronology in "Redemption" and argues that the reader "must reconcile Herbert's first-person story with the prior historical date of the crucifixion, and must also account for the disparity between the Lord's taking possession of his 'land' only at the time of the crucifixion, even though he had 'dearly bought' it 'long since'" (p. 298). Observes that God's first covenant was made with the Israelites after he freed them from Egyptian bondage and points out that "this Sinaitic covenant, with its idea of a treasure, or valuable possession, along with the sense of the Lord's acquisition of the people of Israel, has widely been understood as a 'redemption' not only in the sense of deliverance or liberation, but also in the sense of a purchase—the idea that is particularly important for drawing parallels between the old and new testaments" (p. 299). Notes that the idea of two covenants appears in Jer. 31:31, "in which the Lord acknowledges the Sinaitic covenant and promises another" (p. 299), and in Paul's epistle to the Hebrews (Heb. 9:8). Argues that the concept of the two covenants resolves the chronological problems in "Redemption": "God may properly be described as buying the world long before the time of Christ and taking possession of it only at the moment of the Crucifixion, while the poem's speaker can simultaneously be Herbert and any other Christian or even would-be Christian" (p. 301). Points out that Herbert's brother Henry in his prose piece, *Herbert's Golden Harpe*, first describes himself metaphorically as a Gentile without a covenant and later as a Jew who is under the law but not in grace. Notes that, like his brother, Herbert adopts different personae in *The Temple*.

**1412. Yates, Keith.** "Christ: 'my onely musick': The Spirituality of George Herbert." *The Way: A Quarterly Review of Contemporary Christian Spirituality* (London) 23:312–23.

Comments on Herbert's spirituality, primarily as it is reflected in *The Country Parson* and *The Temple*, and challenges the notion that Herbert's piety merely reflected the mild and tepid spirituality of seventeenth-century Anglicanism. Points out that, although Herbert's was "an active spirituality, a priestly ministry both practical and exemplary," it was also "something more—a personal discipline of rigour and depth within which he faces, without evasion, his failures and frustrations, his anger with God and himself, his despair no less than the joy and peace of the life of faith" (p. 313). Maintains that Herbert's poetry "is the key to the disciplined life of prayer which informed the active, public ministry"; that poetry, for Herbert, was "essentially prayer, a practice of the presence of God"; and that poetic structure, therefore, was "an expression of faith in a divine order within which the disorder of human experience could be contained" (p. 313). Argues that Herbert's "unselfconscious apprehension of life and experience in metaphorical and symbolic terms" (p. 314) links him with medieval Catholicism. Notes that "the sacrifice of Calvary, personally conceived, is at the heart of the spirituality" of Herbert (p. 315) and suggests that he combines late-medieval Franciscan devotion, Calvinism, and counter-reformation spirituality, especially the devout humanism of the Salesian tradition. Comments on Herbert's view of Scripture, the Sacraments, and especially the Eucharist, noting that "Eucharistic imagery pervades *The Temple*" (p. 318). Suggests that Herbert saw both of his vocations, that of priest and that of poet, as sacramental and maintains that his poetic mastery "was achieved as the realization, the articulation of the profundity of his spirituality" (p. 320).

**1413. Yearwood, Stephanie.** "The Rhetoric of Form in *The Temple*." *SEL* 23:131–44.

Maintains that *The Temple* "is constructed as it is because the primary intent is rhetorical" (p. 144) and that "to do Herbert justice, we must read him with a constant awareness of his religious and literary purpose—to change lives" (p. 131). Maintains that *The Church-Porch* "posits a classical, not Christian, value system in which human conscientiousness and exertion in ethical matters are all that is necessary to be rewarded" and that the "limited perspective" of the poem "must be corrected and expanded" in *The Church*, "where the gradual learning process will prove it to have been partially wrong" (pp. 135–36). Observes that "not only is there a growing understanding of the persona in the volume, but there is also an increasing attempt to engage us, as readers, in that persona's change as he comes to understand the relationship of self and God, and words to Word" (p. 136). Shows that "the rhetorical modes of *The Temple* change and expand to include the reader more and more as he progresses through the volume" (p. 136) and stresses that in *The Church* "the individual poems move so gracefully between individual and communal expression and establish so explicitly the communality of man that we come, finally, to identify ourselves with the persona," who "becomes everyman" (p. 140). Notes that *The Church* ends with "Gloria," not "Love (III)," and calls this the "last communal word of praise and thanksgiving which we must all speak together" (p. 142). Sees *The Church Militant* as asserting equally "that sin will 'win' on earth, and that it does so by virtue of a divine plan which deems that rewards shall be given only in heaven" (p. 142) and maintains that in the poem Herbert "asserts the inter-connection of the everyday (to which the reader must return) and the eternal" (p. 143).

# *1984*

**1414. Ashe, A[nthony] H[amilton].** *George Herbert: Selected Poems.* (York Notes, gen. eds. A. N. Jeffares and Suheil Bushrui, 233.) Beirut: York Press; Harlow: Longman Group. 96p.

Handbook for students. Part 1 (pp. 5–13) contains a biographical sketch of Herbert, a general introduction to seventeenth-century poetry, and a note on the text. Part 2 (pp. 14–77) presents brief summaries of 105 poems, along with notes and glosses. Part 3 (pp. 78–84) offers a general commentary on *The Temple*, calling the poems "a series of linked meditations and prayers without any distinct organisational principle" and maintaining that, although "there are certainly some appropriate sequences," the poems "are unified only in that they record aspects of Herbert's spiritual life as a devout Christian" (p. 78). Comments on general features of the poems—dramatic qualities, use of argument, piety, unique uses of language, and adaptation of form to meaning—and on the rudiments of Christian belief and practices in general—the Bible, the liturgical year, and the rituals of the Church. Part 4 (pp. 85–93) gives "hints for study," suggestions for preparing for examination questions, and a few sample examination questions and answers. Part 5 (p. 94) gives a short list of works for further reading.

**1415. Aycock, Roy E.** "George Herbert: The Soul in Verse." *IR* 41:21–26.
Notes that throughout *The Temple* there are numerous comments about poetry in general and Herbert's concept of poetry in particular, pointing out that nineteen poems "make mention of the actual physical process of writing verse" while many others "make oblique but unmistakable reference to poetry" (p. 22). Briefly comments on Herbert's views on poetry in the two sonnets to his mother, "Jordan (I and II)," "The Temper (I)," "Praise (I)," "The Quidditie," "Deniall," "Obedience," "Home," "Dulnesse," "Providence," "Assurance," "Grief," "The Flower," "A true Hymne," "The Forerunners," and "The Banquet." Maintains that *The Temple* is "a veritable textbook on prosody" (p. 25) and comments briefly on Herbert's plain and simple diction, the regularity of his rhythms, his fondness for the iambic foot, his manipulation of stanzaic form, and his love of word play and other displays of wit.

**1416. Bawcutt, N. W.** "New Revels Documents of Sir George Buc and Sir Henry Herbert, 1619–1662." *RES* n.s. 35:316–31.
Points out that for many years scholars have tried to locate the missing revel documents of Sir Henry Herbert, the brother of George Herbert. Notes that in the missing materials were at least four letters by George Herbert to his brother Henry, which were published in Rebecca Warner's *Epistolary Curiosities, Series the First* (1818). Observes that the present head of the family that possessed the original documents has an indenture dated 14 July 1628 and signed by George Herbert. Points out that if George Herbert is the poet, then this document provides a new example of his signature.

**1417. Bell, Ilona.** "Revision and Revelation in Herbert's 'Affliction (I).'" *JDJ* 3, no. 1:73–96.
Maintains that Herbert's poetry "appeals more powerfully today than ever since the Restoration, largely because Herbert's beliefs, like ours, are inherently provisional" (p. 75). Presents a critical reading of "Affliction (I)" in the "controversial context of early seventeenth-century Protestantism" (p. 76) and shows that some of the reverberations between the high Anglicans and the Calvinists are present in Herbert's poetry—"natural reason vs. divine revelation; general providence vs. special providence; formal church ceremony, with all its effort of will and visible stability, vs. inward and spiritual grace, with all its ensuing helplessness and unpredictability" (p. 78). Maintains that the poem shows that "Herbert's sympathies turned away from Hooker and high Anglicans toward Calvin and the reformers," reflecting "significant changes in Herbert's own attitude toward the Church" (p. 78). Comments on the disjointed narrative structure of the poem—"the movement from balanced reassessment to remembrance of things past to dramatic immediacy"—and shows how it "makes the poem a revelation—for us, for the speaker, and perhaps for Herbert himself, as he discovers the complex, inspired truth of his own poetic formulation" (p. 91). Concludes that "Affliction (I)" is "a coherent reassessment clinched by a dramatic revelation—a crucial transition in the spiritual vision of *The Temple*, and that the poem clearly reflects Herbert's "Calvinistic ontology" (p. 92).

**1418. Benet, Diana.** *Secretary of Praise: The Poetic Vocation of George Herbert.* Columbia: University of Missouri Press. 207p.

Discusses "from a biographical perspective Herbert's own concept of his vocation as a poet and the implications that concept had for his art" (jacket). In chapter 1, "The Poet and His Religion" (pp. 1–30), maintains that the doctrines of grace and charity "lay the foundation for an understanding of Herbert's poetic vocation, his typical didactic strategies, the dramatic and emotional situation on which his book builds, and his spiritual autobiography" (p. 2). Presents a biographical sketch of Herbert and a summary of his theology to establish the background for the following chapters. Examines possible reasons for Herbert's delay in being ordained a priest: "Initially, he intended to go into orders, but he came to aspire to an eminent position as a religious statesman" and then, "when attainment of that goal seemed improbable and unpalatable, he reverted to his original plan" (p. 14). Describes basic attitudes of the English Church toward sin, grace, faith, good works, justification, charity, and predestination. In chapter 2, "'The Temple' and the Typical Christian" (pp. 31–63), maintains that, although *The Temple* is "the symbolic record of the life of a Christian engaged in an intimate and personal relationship with God," the Christian concept of community "is fundamental to our understanding of Herbert's approach to poetry, of the speaker's perspective on the world and his fellow man, and of the modes of grace, of God's active participation in the Christian life" (p. 32). Argues that Herbert's poetry is not private but is intended to praise God and to instruct all Christians by revealing the inner workings of one typical Christian's experience in the spiritual life. Presents readings of such poems as "Sepulchre," "Ungratefulnesse," "Christmas," "Assurance," "Longing," "The Bag," "The Storm," and "The Sinner" to show that, for Herbert, "the Christian life is a unity of the personal and the communal, the particular and the typical, the immediate and the timeless" (p. 63). In chapter 3, "Self-Observation and Constant Creation" (pp. 64–100), argues that the two major characters in *The Temple* are the Christian speaker and God and that, "since dramatic interaction between God and man characterizes Herbert's poetry, the theological concepts most emphasized in *The Temple* are grace and charity" (pp. 64–65). Analyzes these two concepts "with special emphasis on the character of the divine and human lovers and their relationship" and "in the context of poems that enable us, at the same time, to observe two of Herbert's heuristic strategies: title-linked poems and the dispersed poetic sequence" (p. 65). Observes that, since most of the "action" in *The Temple* occurs within the speaker's mind and heart, self-analysis is crucial; illustrates this notion by commenting on "Christmas" and "The Size." Discusses "Mans medley," "Josephs coat," "The Glimpse," and "The Glance," poems that "highlight the Christian's helpless and dependent condition" (p. 81), and shows that these poems "complement one another, that the explication of one poem often depends on the reading of another, and that one poem may function as a corrective to another" (p. 70). Discusses "Nature," "The Temper (II)," "Mattens," "Man," "Giddinesse," "The Pulley," and "The Priesthood" as "a dispersed poetic sequence" that achieves unity "by the image of God as Creator or artist" and by the theme of "constant creation," a sequence that is about "man's unworthy nature, its perfectibility, and the divine role in the process" (p. 83). In chapter 4, "'All Things Are Busie'" (pp. 101–32), as well as in the next two chapters, focuses on the speaker's search for vocation. Maintains that a sequence of twenty-three dispersed poems "begins with the Christian struggling to find an active mode of expressing his love" and "ends with the Christian, who has identified himself as a poet and finally becomes a priest" (pp. 101–2). Discusses "The Sacrifice," a poem about prevenient grace and God's unqualified love for man,

as a necessary preface to the employment sequence and analyzes "The Thanksgiving,"
"Affliction (I)," "Employment (I)," "Grace," "Praise (I)," and "Even-song" as poems
in which the speaker defines and refines himself "according to a growing understanding of God and divine love" (p. 131), even though seeking fit employment "can be
disheartening and frustrating, even for a willing Christian as eager to do his duty as
Herbert must have been" (p. 132). In chapter 5, "The 'Blest Order'" (pp. 133–73),
discusses how Herbert "dramatizes the Christian's recognition of divine love's requirements and their effects" and how both the Christian and the reader "learn of
Christ's right to command imitation" as well as "the difficulties of obedience" (p.
157) through analyses of "Content," "The Starre," "Man," "Life," "Submission,"
"Obedience," and "Dialogue." Illustrates the speaker's progress in "Providence,"
"The Method," "Praise (III)," and "The Priesthood," poems in which, "instead of
continuing to stumble over his difficulties, he pauses to find his own way around
them" and then moves forward "with unaccustomed speed and good spirits" (p. 158).
In chapter 6, "The Priest and the Poetry" (pp. 174–99), considers the relation of the
poems to Herbert's own struggles to find his proper vocation. Through a discussion of
"The Crosse," "The Answer," "Aaron," "The Windows," "The Invitation," "The
Elixir," and "Love (III)," traces the last stage of the speaker's journey to the priest-
hood. Argues that, although the sequence is not "the kind of information that is
essential to sound biographical interpretation," it is "probably a fairly reliable gloss
on some of the considerations and problems pertaining to vocation that Herbert
confronted" (p. 196). Selected bibliography (pp. 200–203) and index (pp. 204–7).
Reviews:
Charles Guenther, *St. Louis Post-Dispatch*, 4 August 1984
A. C. Labriola, *Choice* 22 (1984): 265
Jonathan F. S. Post, *JDJ* 3, no. 2 (1984): 221–47
Robert B. Shaw *GHJ* 8, no. 1 (1984): 64–68
Ilona Bell, *RQ* 38, no. 3 (1985): 585–88
Claude J. Summers *C&L* 34 (1985): 72–74
John N. Wall, Jr. *Anglican Theological Review* 67 (1985): 192–94
Michael Piret, *C&L* 35 (1986): 58–60

**1419. Boenig, Robert.** "Listening to Herbert's Lute." *Ren&R* 20, no. 4:298–311.
   Maintains that, although Herbert left no musical settings, he may have composed
some of his lyrics as lute songs. Observes that the most important characteristics of
lute songs were (1) "their subtle stanzaic form, in which the nuances of given line or
half-line often would repeat throughout the entire piece—the type of structuring at
which Herbert excels" (p. 299) and (2) word painting, that is, "the connection between setting and words that causes close correspondences" (p. 301), noting that
Herbert is well known for an analogous technique in his poems—"causing metre and
stanza structure to participate in the poem's meaning" (p. 306). Discusses "Deniall,"
"The Thanksgiving," "Sunday," and "Vertue" as poems possibly written for lute
accompaniment. Maintains that Herbert is "one of our most musical poets" and that
"the numerous settings of his poetry—from John Wilson through John Wesley and
Ralph Vaughan Williams—are proof enough of that" (p. 310).

**1420. ———.** "The Raising of Herbert's Broken Consort: A Note on 'Dooms-
day,' 29–30." *N&Q* n.s. 31:239–41.
   Argues that the phrase *broken consort* in "Dooms-day" (line 29) means not only a
group of instrumentalists playing on various musical instruments but also suggests the
number and kind of instruments—the tenor viol (or violin), bass viol, lute, cittern,

bandora, and flute (or recorder) and that Herbert has "the set ensemble, associated with decidedly secular—not sacred—music, in mind" (p. 240). Maintains that the word *raise* in the same line is "a specific reference to pitch as well as to the salvation of God's royal consort who is broken in sin" (p. 240). Notes that at the time several of the instruments in the broken consort were pitched higher for sacred music and maintains that Herbert's line should be taken literally in its musical sense: "God should raise the pitch of the instruments in the broken consort so that they may participate not in secular music of the theatre and court but in the sacred music of Heaven" (p. 240). Concludes that "the complexity of the musical component of the double-entendre in the last two lines of 'Doomsday' matches that of the theological, with the instruments' rise in pitch functioning as a metaphor for the Christian's change in life leading to salvation" (p. 241).

**1421. Booty, John.** "Joseph Hall, *The Arte of Divine Meditation*, and Anglican Spirituality," in *The Roots of the Modern Christian Tradition*, edited by E. Rozanne Elder, with an introduction by Jean Leclercq, 200–228. (The Spirituality of Western Christendom, II.) Kalamazoo, Mich.: Cistercian Publications.

Discusses Joseph Hall's *The Arte of Divine Meditation* (1606) as illustrative of seventeenth-century Anglican spirituality. Maintains that *The Temple*, if seen as a kind of catechism, as Stanley Fish would suggest, "involves in important ways the Hallsian process of meditation" (p. 224). Contends that *The Temple* is "as a whole a lengthy meditation" and that in it "there is such material for meditation as the ordinary Christian may be expected to be able to engage in without being overtaxed, but also with being able to escape the inevitable realization that God's love requires our submission in the participation whereby we and the earth are renewed" (p. 225).

**1422. Clifton, Michael.** "Staking his Heart: Herbert's Use of Gambling Imagery in *The Temple*." *GHJ* 8, no. 1:43–55.

Points out that throughout *The Temple* Herbert employs images of gambling or gaming that are "expressed largely in terms of the card game primero, though also in those of an unknown dicing game," and maintains that this imagery "not only illuminates a fresh dimension of the poems' sacred parody" but also "unifies their playful spirit under the single concept of play" (p. 43). Comments on "An Offering," *The Church-Porch*, "The Quidditie," "Love (I)," "Jordan (I)," "The Reprisall," "Affliction (I)," "Mattens," "The H. Communion," "The Forerunners," "Sunday," and "The Windows" to show that Herbert's use of gaming imagery is "far more systematic than has to this point been suspected" (p. 53). Points out that the speaker's "ups and downs, his wins and losses," become lessons and Herbert's "chief means of rhyming his readers to good" and passing on to them "that secret of surrender that is the key to success when one 'gambles' with God" (p. 54).

**1423. Doerksen, Daniel W.** "Recharting the Via Media of Spenser and Herbert." *Ren&R* 20, no. 4:215–25.

Maintains that nineteenth-century Tractarians and others incorrectly claimed that the *via media* in the Elizabethan and Stuart Church was simply "a middle course between Rome and Geneva, steering just as far away from protestantism as from papistry" (p. 215). Argues that the English Church from the accession of Elizabeth in 1558 to the death of Herbert in 1633 "sought to avoid papistry" but "was itself theologically protestant" (p. 216). Argues that Anglicans of the time did not regard Puritanism or Calvinism as doctrinally dangerous but rather considered Catholicism and Separatism or Anabaptism as the two extremes that had to be avoided and that it was only in matters of ritual and ceremony that Anglicans wished to steer a course between Rome and Geneva. Maintains that in "The British Church" Herbert writes of a golden mean, appropriately using images of clothing and grooming that concern primarily externals, and that in his Latin poem in reply to Melville he uses the language of the *via media* only after announcing that his disagreement with the Scotsman is only about ritual and ceremony. Observes that "beyond these early writings, and specifically in his mature poetry, Herbert says virtually nothing about church polity, and not very much about ceremony as such" (p. 217). Maintains that "the concept of a doctrinal *via media* is much more important and helpful for understanding Herbert's English poems than is that applying to ritual only" and suggests that "The British Church," "far from being representative of *The Temple*, is an isolated exception," noting that the presence of "smugness and exclusiveness (though not the loyalty) of the closing lines is most unusual in the mature Herbert" (p. 217). Maintains that few of Herbert's poems would have been unacceptable to a Nonconformist.

**1424. Elsky, Martin.** "The Sacramental Frame of George Herbert's 'The Church' and the Shape of Spiritual Autobiography." *JEGP* 83:313–29.

Argues that *The Church* reflects a Protestant understanding of biblical typology and chronicles the spiritual and emotional life of the poet between the Passion ("The Sacrifice") and the end time ("Dooms-day"). Maintains that the same two references frame the boundaries of the Church on earth and the Anglican eucharistic liturgy. Argues that the pattern of the poet's life presented in *The Church* also imitates the scheme of redemptive history and that his poetic mode is both autobiographical and liturgical. Acknowledges that the poet's "achievement of coherent selfhood is usually momentary and transitory" and that those moments of integrating the Scripture and liturgical patterns into his life "are separated by long periods of spiritual degeneration and a painful sense of incompleteness that ultimately results from the Protestant emphasis on the incomplete nature of typology in the age of the Church itself" (p. 317). Finds these "discontinuities" "central to the design of Herbert's symbolic Protestant autobiography" and that "the spiritual and poetic resolution and irresolution are both characteristic of the experience recorded in the poems" (p. 329).

**1425. Ford, Brewster.** "George Herbert and Liturgies of Time and Space." *SoAR* 49, no. 4:19–29.

Argues that the structure of *The Temple* is partially shaped by the liturgy of time and the liturgy of space, but acknowledges that individual poems are fitted into this structure "with a considerable amount of flexibility" (p. 19). Describes the liturgy of time as (1) the calendar of Christian feasts, defined for Anglicans by *The Book of Common Prayer*, and (2) the liturgical pattern of the Christian life, defined by the sacramental services of baptism, confirmation, marriage, and burial. Maintains that the number and order of poems in *The Church* constitute the most convincing evidence of how the ritual passage of time shapes the volume. Defines the liturgy of space as (1) the rituals and ceremonies enacted within the church building itself and (2) the objects that occupy space within that building, such as monuments, choirs, the floor, and so forth. Concludes that, "in the space and context of the church itself, each of these objects, each of these acts, each of these liturgical manifestations becomes a buttress to the faith of the Christian seeker" and that "as he becomes accustomed to them, learning to love the times of the year through which he lives and the space of the church which encloses him, he is led to love God himself in ways that could never be accomplished by 'speech alone'" (pp. 27–28).

**1426. Garrett, John.** "Sin and Shame in George Herbert's Poetry." *RCEI* 8:139–47.

Maintains that in many of his poems Herbert expresses "the agony of one who failed to come to terms with his own sexuality or to establish a satisfactory heterosexual relationship" (p. 141) and argues that by examining his poems in the light of Freud "we may attain new insight into the personal anguish and torment that underlies the creation of ecclesiastical poetry" (p. 146). Comments on manifestations of Herbert's arrested sexuality, examining in particular the role of his mother in his development. Discusses "Sinnes round" as "poignantly expressive of the *Angst* of the auto-eroticist" (p. 141) and considers "Sighs and Grones" as a poem in which Herbert experiences self-disgust at his sexual inadequacy and indicates his fears of the punitive consequences of his offenses—blindness, castration, and perhaps even death. Maintains that on a subliminal level Christ appears in "Love (III)" as a "*femme du monde* about to initiate a young man into the rites of love" and that the speaker "displays the guilt-feelings and impotence of the habitual masturbator" (p. 144) and argues that the poem "points not only to a resolution of the speaker's spiritual conflict, but also to a remission of the guilt-feelings caused by masturbation and sexual inadequacy" (p. 145).

**1427. Halli, Robert W., Jr.** "The Double Hieroglyph in George Herbert's 'Easter Wings.'" *PQ* 63:265–72.

Argues that in "Easter-wings" Herbert creates a double visual hieroglyph in that "the lines that look like wings when the poem is held sideways look like hourglasses when it is held in normal reading position" (p. 266). Maintains that, as the wing hieroglyph "relates most directly to the second half of each stanza," so the hourglass "relates to the first" and contends that the poem "is largely concerned with the passage of time and with its transformation or annihilation by Christ's 'victories' over Sin and Death," noting that "the first half of each stanza is anchored in the past tense, while each second half flies into the future, or into eternity" (p. 266). Observes that, during the Renaissance, both wings and hourglasses were used to depict mortality and immortality. Shows that "the thought pattern of each stanza is analogous to the symbol of the contrasting wings" and that "both because of the hourglass emblem and because of its insistence on a complete union of man and God" the poem "passes from concern with events in Time to exultation over the possibility of timeless eternity" (p. 267). Argues that the first stanza deals with the history of mankind, while the second is concerned with the personal history of the poet. Notes that the hourglass shape is "two triangles joined at their apexes" (p. 268) with the first stanza pointing down to "death, hell, and oblivion" and the second "up to God, heaven, and eternal life" (p. 269). Maintains that the hourglass hieroglyph "supports the poem's insistence on a temporal contraction to the least point from which man expands into the timeless" (p. 270) and ends the poem "with the mixed tone of personal humbleness and Christian exultation found in many of his best poems" (p. 271).

**1428. Hatakeyama, Etsuro.** "*The Temple* ni okeru 'Stone' Imagery" ["Stone" Imagery in *The Temple*]. *Tohoku Gakuin Daigaku Ronshu—Eigo Eibun Gaku* [Tohoku Gakuin University Review—Essays and Studies in English Language and Literature] 75:39–58.

Discusses three variations that Herbert plays on the motif of the human heart as stone. Notes that in such poems as "The Sacrifice," "Grace," and "Church-lock and key" stone is used as the image of the hard and sinful heart; that in such poems as "Sepulchre," "The Altar," and "The Windows" stone is used as the image of the sacred place for praise to God as well as the hard and sinful heart; and that in such poems as "Man," "Christmas," "The Church-floore," "The World," and "The Fam-ilie" stone is used as the image of man's strong faith. Examines stone imagery in "Sion" and briefly discusses Herbert's concept of redemption: only those human beings who are agonized and afflicted with the sense of sin can be redeemed.

**1429. Herbert, George.** *The Bodleian Manuscript of George Herbert's Poems: A Facsimile of Tanner 307.* Introduction by Amy M. Charles and Mario A. Di Cesare. (Scholars' Facsimiles and Reprints Series, no. 373.) Delmar, N.Y.: Schol-ars' Facsimiles and Reprints. xli, 303, [6]p.
   Facsimile of the Bodleian manuscript (Tanner MS. 307). Contains a table of con-tents (p. v), a preface by the two editors (p. vii), and a list of abbreviations (p. viii), followed by a two-part introduction: "Part One: The Bodleian Manuscript" consists of an expanded version of Amy M. Charles's "The Original of Mᵣ George Herbert's Temple" (entry 1382), with a bibliographical description of the manuscript by Mar-garet C. Crum and illustrations of the watermarks (pp. ix-xix); "Part Two: The Manuscript and the Text" consists of an expanded version of Mario Di Cesare's "The Bodleian Manuscript and the Text of Herbert's Poems" (entry 1385), with a collated table of contents (the manuscripts, the 1633 edition, and Hutchinson's edition) (pp. xix-xli). Facsimile of the manuscript (pp. 10–303) followed by table of contents on six unnumbered pages.

**1430. ———.** *George Herbert.* Foreword and introduction by Mary Hobbs. (Masters of Prayer.) London: CIO Publishing. 43p.
   Intended as a manual of meditation for modern readers. Presents a biographical sketch of Herbert and a brief introduction to his spirituality (pp. 4–7). Maintains that "because his poems show that he was so clearly a good, humble, lovable man, even those to whom Christianity means nothing find themselves attracted by them, with their penetrating picture of the human condition" (p. 4). Anthologizes twenty-four poems (or parts of poems), with explanatory notes. Includes six contemporary photo-graphs.

**1431. Hunter, William B., Jr.** "Herbert and Milton." *SCRev* 1, no. 1:22–37.
   Maintains that in many ways Milton's early life and career parallel Herbert's and that as young men they even shared many of the same political and religious attitudes. Notes, however, that as youthful Latin poets, Milton "typically is expansive," while Herbert is "compressive" (p. 24). Argues that, although Milton probably never met Herbert, he probably knew *The Temple*, although "no convincing evidence has ever been cited for its influence upon his work" (p. 25). Acknowledges that the relationship between Herbert's and Milton's poetry is "at most tenuous" (p. 36). Compares and contrasts them as sonneteers, suggesting that Milton may be indebted to Herbert's development of the form. Claims that Herbert's most important innovation was "his ability to sustain a long sentence through the complex vagaries of a sonnet's rhyme" (p. 31), as seen in "The Answer." Discusses "Prayer (I)" as Herbert's "most successful achievement of tension between meaning and form" (p. 33), maintaining that Milton "never went so far" (p. 35). Adds, however, that Milton never wrote anything "quite so pedestrian" (p. 35) as "The Holdfast."

**1432. Huntley, Frank L.** "George Herbert and the Image of Violent Contain-ment." *GHJ* 8, no. 1:17–27.
   Examines Herbert's images of containment, beginning with such things as boxes, cases, chests, cabinets, cupboards, vessels, urns, glasses, bottles, cups, and hourglasses,

proceeding though drops of tears and such parts of the body as the head and heart, and ending with the Passion of Christ, which, for Herbert, "contains in one Person, in a very short interval of time, in one tiny geographical spot, all the sacrifice, all the love, all the tears, all the drama, all the cruelty, all the forgiveness that millions of human beings all over the world have experienced for two thousand years" (p. 26). Sees in such images a kind of violence, "first as straining our credulity in the capacity of the container to contain, and then as challenging our faith in the power that is released" and maintains that the violence "increases as we pass from the concrete, through the metaphorical, into, finally, the mystical" (p. 18). Maintains that Herbert's art "is one of creating compendiums" (p. 24) and discusses "Anagram of the Virgin Marie" as a short poem that contains much. Concludes that the sometimes "harrowing tension" in Herbert's art "arises from his art of epitome, of cramming—literally, meta-phorically, and religiously—so much in so small a space as to induce in the reader the kinaesthetic sensation of strain" (p. 27).

**1433. Jeffreys, George.** *Rise, heart, thy Lord is risen: Verse anthem for Easter day*: for STB soli, SSATB chorus and organ, words by George Herbert, music by George Jeffreys (d. 1685), transcribed and edited by Peter Aston. Sevenoaks, Kent: Novello. 16p.
   Musical setting of the first eighteen lines of "Easter." Presents a biographical sketch of George Jeffreys (circa 1610–1685), organist to Charles I, and comments on his musical works. Includes editorial notes on the anthem.

**1434. Kinnamon, Noel J.** "The Psalmic and Classical Contexts of Herbert's 'Constancie' and Vaughan's 'Righteousness.'" *GHJ* 8, no. 1:29–42.
   Discusses the complex relationship between "Constancie" and Vaughan's "Right-eousness" to demonstrate that, although Vaughan's poem clearly is indebted to Her-bert's, it is "more conspicuously based on Psalm 15 than on Herbert's poem" and that Vaughan's poem is "more closely related to the psalm" than is Herbert's, which "seems to be indebted to Psalm 112 as well" (p. 29). Argues that both poets were influenced not only by the so-called Wisdom psalm but also by the *beatus ille* (or *beatus vir*) tradition developed by Renaissance poets, primarily from praises of coun-try life in Homer and Virgil, and later turned into a Christian motif by Casimire Sarbiewski. Maintains that, although "Constancie" appears more classical in tone, less dependent on biblical sources, less explicitly Christian than Vaughan's poem, and perhaps even more ethical than religious, it becomes, when considered in the context of *The Temple*, "more religious or spiritual" and that Herbert's speaker "knows he is not self-sufficient and that he must depend on more than human reason to become the inerrant, honest man" (p. 38). Concludes that a comparison of the two poems shows "the wider literary context" (p. 38) in which both poets wrote and also demonstrates Vaughan's independence from Herbert "even when he is to some extent indebted to him" (p. 39).

**1435. Linden, Stanton J.** "Alchemy and Eschatology in Seventeenth-Century Po-etry." *Ambix* 31, part 3:102–24.
   Argues that during the late sixteenth and early seventeenth centuries the literary functions of alchemy underwent an important change: the satirical tradition, reaching back to Chaucer and extending through Jonson, waned and a new pattern of alchemi-cal imagery emerged that placed "primary emphasis on positive change, purification, moral transformation and spirituality" (p. 103). Notes that an interesting part of the later tradition is a poetic imagery that "represents the fusion of alchemy and eschatol-

ogy, and of alchemy and millenarinism" (p. 103). Observes that only six or seven of Herbert's poems contain alchemical images and that they "seldom invoke the art to bear a substantial part of the verse's intellectual or emotional weight" (p. 111). Maintains that Herbert's use of alchemy is "simple and not showy, always subordinate to the larger requirements of plainness and clarity" (p. 111). Notes that, except in "Vanitie (I)," all of Herbert's references are "of the non-satiric sort and clearly belong in the tradition of spiritualized alchemy" (p. 111). Briefly comments on the alchemical references in "To all Angels and Saints," "The Elixir," and "Easter." See also Linden's earlier essay on alchemy (entry 991).

**1436. Lindley, David.** "A Dowland Allusion in Herbert's 'Grief.'" *N&Q* n.s. 31:238–39.
    Argues that there is a specific parallel between the beginning of John Dowland's twentieth song in his *First Booke of Songes or Ayres* (1597) ("Come beauty sleepe, the Image of true death: / And close vp these weary weeping eyes") and the ninth line of Herbert's "Grief" ("My weary weeping eyes too drie for me"). Maintains that the last lines of the poem suggest that Herbert "conceives the first part of his poem specifically as a parody of song" and that "this dimension of the poem is wittily confirmed by the allusion to the musician whose most popular song began with the words 'Flow my tears,' and who composed a set of lute pieces entitled *Lacrimae*" (p. 239).

**1437. Mathis, Gilles.** "Vaughan, Herbert et la rhétorique de répétition." *BSEAA* 18:9–44.
    Catalogs and discusses the uses of the rhetoric of repetition in the poetry of Herbert and Vaughan. Maintains that Herbert engages in much more linguistic and prosodic experimentation than Vaughan does and that Herbert "semble plus disposé à sacrifier à la rhétorique que son disciple" (p. 14). Identifies and discusses six different kinds of refrains in Herbert's poetry—(1) "retour parfait," (2) "rupture d'un refrain parfait dans la dernière strophe," (3) "variation interne du 'refrain' mais les derniers mots ne changent pas à la fin des strophes," (4) "refrain discontinu," (5) "double refrain," and (6) "refrain en libre répétition" (pp. 14–15) and comments on his uses of anaphorically structured stanzas, framing figures, epizeuxis, and anadiplosis. Discusses "The Dawning" and Vaughan's "Easter-Day," "Praise (III)" and Vaughan's "Praise," "A Wreath" and Vaughan's "Love-sick" to show the differences between Herbert's use of repetition and Vaughan's. Concludes that Herbert's poems are more rhetorically elaborate than Vaughan's and that Vaughan's most highly structured poems are almost always the result of imitation and seem to be stylistic exercises.

**1438. Morrison, Peter.** "Taking the H out of Shame: The Blemished Mirror in La Tour's *Magdalen* and Herbert's 'Easter Wings.'" *NOR* 11, nos. 3–4:54–68.
    Analyzes George de La Tour's *The Repentant Magdalen* (Fabius, circa 1635) and "Easter-wings" and points out that both are "formally and thematically organized by overt reduplication" and have an "'intimate minimalism,' a formal reduction whereby terms such as *stillness, immediacy, presence,* and *grace* begin to fill up our interpretative lexicon" (p. 54). Argues that "it is just at this intersection of *presence* and yet *reduplication,* of *intimacy* and yet *refraction,* of *immediacy* and yet *saying again,* that criticism and the attempt at determining meaning must lie, though such a structural intersection may be needlessly, or even hopelessly dialectical" (p. 55). Notes that over one-fifth of the poems in the Bodleian manuscript "belong to sets of doubles, including twelve pairs, two triplets, and one title ('Affliction') which produces five poems" and that "Anagram of the Virgin Marie" is "exactly reduplicated after a thirteen-

poem intermission, a doubling too bewildering even to the editors of the first edition (1633), who elected to print only the second of the two (as have subsequent editors)" (p. 60). Observes that the reduplication gives the reader a feeling of being "perpetually retold something and that this retelling is somehow very important" (p. 61). Shows that the Williams manuscript "demonstrates rather convincingly that at least at some point Herbert was writing poetry as if virtually every other poem required retelling, as if there were something alternative in the poetic idiom *itself*, or something fundamental to his conceptualization of the order and significance of the poems in *The Temple*, that recurrently fostered reiteration and redoubling" (p. 61). Shows that a number of poems in the 1633 edition can be recognized as originally double poems and argues that perhaps *The Temple* should be seen as "a linguistic activity captured at a particular state of evolution rather than as a finished anthology possessed of a compelling structure and deep governing logic of organization" (pp. 62–63). Maintains that "Easter-wings" is "one of the more curious of the reduplicating poems" (p. 64) in *The Temple* and that in fact it is two poems, not one. Argues that in pattern, prosody, rhetoric, syntax, and diction the poems "carefully mimic each other" and that the first poem is "emblematic of the poet's longing and desire, the other of the risen Christ's angelic wings" (p. 66). Shows that the "braided pattern of the rhymes provides for the imping of one poem upon the other" (p. 67) and that both poems "long for the eradication of language by language, manifest in the complex doubling and blemishing, in the way language is articulated and then re-articulated in the poems" (p. 68).

**1439. Post, Jonathan F. S.** "Reforming *The Temple*: Recent Criticism of George Herbert." *JDJ* 3, no. 2:221–47.

Review article of Heather A. R. Asals's *Equivocal Predication: George Herbert's Way to God* (entry 1279), Barbara Leah Harman's *Costly Monuments: Representations of the Self in George Herbert's Poetry* (entry 1345), Richard Strier's *Love Known: Theology and Experience in George Herbert's Poetry* (entry 1409), Diana Benet's *Secretary of Praise: The Poetic Vocation of George Herbert* (entry 1418), and Chana Bloch's *Spelling the Word: George Herbert and the Bible* (Berkeley: University of California Press, 1985). Comments on the revival of scholarly and critical interest in Herbert in the United States that is now in its fourth decade and points out three phases of this renewed interest: (1) the work of such scholars as Rosemond Tuve, Louis L. Martz, and Joseph Summers that "refined and expanded upon Coleridge's perception" and "sought to establish the religious region in which Herbert's poetry moved"; (2) the work of such critics as Mary Ellen Rickey, Arnold Stein, Coburn Freer, Stanley Fish, and Helen Vendler that "coincided with the triumph of New Criticism" and "largely eschewed doctrinal and religious questions in favor of analyzing textual complexities and rhetorical strategies"; and (3) the work of such authors as the five reviewed here, a third generation of readers who "seeks to stake out his or her particular territory" (pp. 222–23). Observes that, with this last group, *The Temple* "seems more like the hall of Appleton House, changing shape with the separate entrance of each reader" (p. 233). Examines each of the five books and discusses the allegiances each has with the work of past and present critics.

**1440. Quinn, William A.** "'The Windhover' as *Carmen Figuratum*." *HQ* 10:127–44.

Points out three allusions to poems by Herbert in Gerard Manley Hopkins's "The Windhover": "ah my dear" (line 13) is an explicit echo of "Love (III)" (line 9); line 10 of Hopkins's poem suggests the fire imagery in the first five lines of "Love (II)," and the marginal indentations in "The Windhover" perhaps are a nonverbal allusion to

"Easter-wings." Maintains that the patterning devices that Hopkins employed in his sonnet place him "in the tradition of George Herbert, and, more generally, in the tradition of emblematic composition" (p. 127).

**1441. Quitslund, Jon A.** "Sidney's Presence in Lyric Verse of the Later English Renaissance," in *Sir Philip Sidney and the Interpretation of Renaissance Culture: The Poet in His Time and in Ours: A Collection of Critical and Scholarly Essays*, edited by Gary F. Waller and Michael Moore, 110–23. London: Croom Helm; Totowa, N.J.: Barnes & Noble.
Argues that Herbert was deeply indebted to Sidney, especially for his "refined colloquialism, his playfulness, the intertwining of narrative and discourse, surprising twists in his trains of thought, and carefully controlled ironies—self-directed ironies rather than the counter-factual hyperboles of Donne" (p. 121). Maintains that "some of Herbert's urbanity was mediated through Jonson and other poets with classical tastes" but that "it stemmed ultimately from Sidney" (p. 121). Argues that "Jordan (II)" is patterned on the first and third sonnets of *Astrophel and Stella*.

**1442. Randall, Dale B. J.** "The Ironing of George Herbert's 'Collar.'" *SP* 81:473–95.
Comments on past interpretations of the "collar" in the title of Herbert's poem, such as "to slip" the clerical collar or animal collar of restraint; the rope about the main masthead of a ship; and puns on "choler" and "caller." Adds to these readings the possible puns on the word *calor* or *heat* and on *colour*. Argues that the "collar" may also refer to the iron collar that was sometimes used to confine animals, slaves, sinners, and madmen and "especially favored in Scotland for disciplining those who strayed from the straight and narrow" (p. 495).

**1443. Schleiner, Louise.** "Herbert's 'Divine and Moral Songs,'" in *The Living Lyre in English Verse from Elizabeth through the Restoration*, 46–71. Columbia: University of Missouri Press.
Divides the chapter into two parts: (1) "Herbert's Song-Mode Prosody and Lute Songs" (pp. 46–63) and (2) "Herbert's Speech Mode and Declamatory Song" (pp. 63–71). In the first part discusses Herbert as a Jacobean lute-song lyricist and maintains that many of his poems "depend more on figures of sound than on figures of sense for their primary effects" (p. 46). Shows how song-mode metrics influenced Herbert's prosody and comments on Herbert's use of fourteeners or common meter lines, similar structures consisting of a longer and a shorter line, and dimeters "to create rhythmic patterns like those in many song texts" (p. 58). Maintains that Herbert's use of song mode "contributes significantly to that often-noted impression of richness in simplicity left by his poems" and that "the discipline of writing for music provided Herbert with a repertoire of rhythmic skills that helped to define his mature poetic idiom" (p. 63). In the second part discusses Herbert's mastery of speech mode and shows that many of his poems proved "especially suitable for declamatory setting in the midcentury decades" (p. 64). Contends that declamatory song composers saw themselves as presenting a particular "reading" of the text and that they often "point up features of the poems that might not be noticed without the musical perspective" (p. 64). Comments on John Wilson's setting of "Content" to show how the composer, "with his careful stanza selection, pictorialism, following of the poem's syntax, effective distribution of accents, and coordination of his harmonic climax with the climax of the text's argument, has read the poem well and structured his text and music in accordance with its prominent features" (p. 69). Concludes that midcentury

composers found Herbert appealing "because they could recognize the thorough and consistent song-relatedness of his prosody, reminding them of the recent glories of the lute-song era, and because at the same time they could find in his speech-mode verse, with its dominant 'affetuoso' tone of intensity, suitable texts for the new style of their small-scale declamatory or monodic songs" (p. 71).

**1444. Shaw, Robert B.** "George Herbert: The Word of God and the Words of Man," in *Ineffability: Naming the Unnamable from Dante to Beckett,* edited by Peter S. Hawkins and Anne Howland Schotter, 81–93. (AMS Ars Poetica, no. 2.) New York: AMS Press.

Comments on Herbert's recognition of the limits of language in expressing divinity and sacred mysteries. Points out several poems in which Herbert uses adynaton, "the admission on the part of the speaker that what he has to say is beyond the power of words to convey" (p. 82). Argues that the deliberately plain style of Herbert's poems "gives the effect of language coming as close to silence as words can come" and that his "persistent care as a stylist is to narrow the unavoidable gap which exists not merely between human words and holy mysteries but also and just as definitely between words and the visible creation" (p. 83). Sees "Frailtie" as "one extreme of Herbert's thinking about language" (p. 84). Discusses "Prayer (I)" as an example of Herbert's piling metaphor upon metaphor in an attempt to define prayer until, in the last phrase, he recognizes the inability of words to express the inexpressible. Maintains that Herbert solved his problem with language by recognizing God as a co-author of his poems and realizing that "he need not rely on his own artistry but that of God" who enables the poem "to speak truly by 'rhyming' the motions of the heart with the words which alone would be inadequate praise" (p. 87). Shows that Herbert regards language as sacramental and concludes that "fallen language may be redeemed through the willingness of the Word to assume the burden of human utterance" (p. 90).

**1445. Smith, Nigel.** "George Herbert in Defence of Antinomianism." *N&Q* n.s. 31:334–35.

Points out lines from several of Herbert's poems that are quoted in *Nil Novi. This Years F[r]uit, From the last Years Root* (1654) by Henry Pinnell, the Antinomian preacher and sometime New Model Army chaplain, in support of his claim to the living of Christian Malford in Wiltshire. Contends that the appropriation is noteworthy "not merely as an instance of *The Temple* being used in an ecclesiastical controversy, and therefore as an example of the way in which the poems were read in the 1650s" but because "it also throws light upon the resources of the radical religious imagination during the Interregnum" (p. 334).

**1446. Stewart, Stanley.** "Herbert and the 'Harmonies' of Little Gidding." *Cithara* 24:3–26.

Argues that the literary works produced at Little Gidding, especially the "Harmonies of the Four Evangelists," provide valuable evidence about the audience for which Herbert wrote his poems. Details the personal and literary relationship between Nicholas Ferrar and Herbert and shows that there are striking resemblances between Herbert's poetry and the devotional spirit and method found in the "Harmonies." Maintains that this evidence "indicates that liturgical, meditative, and iconographic traditions" cited by Rosemond Tuve (entry 409) and Louis L. Martz (entry 431) are "neither medieval or irrelevant" but rather were "the received contexts of expression at Little Gidding" (p. 22). Shows that, in particular, the "Harmonies" throw light on

"The H. Scriptures (I and II)," poems that deal with "the way in which God organized his message to mankind" and that "obliquely reflect the way in which *The Temple* is organized as well" (p. 11). Observes that, "just as a verse from various parts of Scripture interrelate, so figures set out in one Herbert poem are developed in others" (p. 13). Argues that Herbert's attitude toward Mary and the saints in "Anagram of the Virgin Marie" and "To all Angels and Saints" would be in agreement with the "Harmonies" and with the High Anglican spirit of Little Gidding. Contends that the "Harmonies" indicate that Herbert's audience at Little Gidding would have found many of the symbols that Barbara K. Lewalski (entry 1202) thinks "excessively medieval and Catholic" (p. 21) as quite topical and Anglican and that, although Richard Strier (entry 1222) may consider "To all Angels and Saints" a Puritan poem, "it would not have been so construed by Nicholas Ferrar" (p. 21). Maintains that "the pendulum in recent Herbert criticism has swung too far toward a Protestant reading of the poet's work" and suggests that critics "deemphasize ideology, in particular, the polarity between Catholic and Protestant poetic norms" (p. 21). Concludes that, if we want to find a Protestant Herbert, we should examine Wesley's adaptations of Herbert's poems rather than the edition that Ferrar presented to the reading audience in 1633.

**1447. Summers, Claude J., and Ted-Larry Pebworth.** "The Politics of *The Temple*: 'The British Church' and 'The Familie.'" *GHJ* 8, no. 1:1–15.

Observes that, for all his "apparent self-absorption and mild latitudinarianism," Herbert actively "engages in sectarian controversy, consistently rebuking Puritan attacks on the Established Church" and, though no Laudian, he "defends the Church's authority and deplores its fragmentation by Puritan 'wranglers'" (p. 1). Challenges Richard Strier's presentation of Herbert (entry 1317) as less than a normative Anglican of his time. Offers readings of "The British Church" and "The Familie" to show that "failure to recognize Herbert's anti-Puritanism is both to distort his religious position and to neglect a significant dimension of the poetry" (p. 13). Argues that Strier's reading of the first poem "seriously underestimates the crucial importance Herbert attached to liturgy and utterly ignores the network of biblical allusions that condemn Geneva and Rome equally and establish the British Church as simultaneously a temporal institution and the New Jerusalem of the apocalyptic future" (p. 3). Maintains that "The Familie" is a public poem, as well as a private devotion, in which Herbert protests vehemently against "the disorderliness and noise of the Puritan wranglers who defile God's Church" (p. 5) and that dramatizes the need for uniformity "on grounds of familial discipline" (p. 8). Argues that in *Musae Responsoriae (XXX)*, in "Church-rents and schismes," and in other poems, as well as in *The Country Parson*, Herbert celebrates the *via media* of the English Church.

**1448. Toliver, Harold.** "Herbert's Interim and Final Places." *SEL* 24:105–20.

Observes that in *The Temple* Herbert often depicts God as dwelling "in the heart, in frames, in arks, cabinets and cupboards, altars, houses, and windows" and "in scripture and sacrament" and notes that in order to situate God in a definite, fixed locale Herbert "comes recurrently to the lowly preposition 'in' among other words that signify an in-dwelling presence as opposed to a transcendent law giver" (pp. 105–6). Maintains that in his poetry Herbert "thinks in terms of interpenetration, filled places, and mutual habitations of body and spirit" (p. 106). Argues that, although the temple is the major place of presence, it "opens onto external realms and transplants the plenary world into its own enclosed space, where the poet can establish relations between man and creator" and notes that "rites, charms, rituals, word games, and festivities assist in its sacramental manipulation of presence" (p. 106). Acknowledges that "all means of bringing God into localities are imperfect" and that ultimately "no placement less than paradise can be fully satisfactory" (p. 106). Through a detailed discussion of "Affliction (I)" shows that Herbert's "quest for a fixed accord and a defined career is inseparable from such matters of placement" (p. 106) and illustrates how Herbert casts "a longing eye on the advantages of rootedness and the still more attractive prospect of rising into God's place directly" (p. 112). Comments on placement in such poems as "The Temper (I)," "Employment (I and II)," "The Flower," "Vertue," "Anagram of the Virgin Marie," "The H. Scriptures (II)," "Peace," and "Heaven" and contends that "Love (III)" "implicitly provides the chair of grace the poet has asked for earlier and resolves the discrepancy between the rootedness of the mortal poet and the desire for transcendence" (p. 119).

**1449. Westerweel, Bart.** *Patterns and Patterning: A Study of Four Poems by George Herbert.* (Costerus, n.s. 41.) Amsterdam: Rodopi. 273p.

Contextual and comparative study of "The Altar," "Easter-wings," "The Pilgrimage," and "Love (III)" that interprets the poems primarily in the light of the Renaissance traditions of pattern poems and emblematics. In chapter 1, "The Introduction" (pp. 1–24), declares that the aim of the study is "to establish the intended meaning of certain poems" and describes the approach as "applied scholarship" (p. 23). Maintains that "the best result that one can hope for in pursuing applied scholarship is that it will help to turn readers into informed readers and random guesses at meanings into guess-work that is at least as educated as possible" (p. 24). In chapter 2, "A Study of Herbert's Pattern Poems, Part One: What Herbert Knew" (pp. 25–52), argues that, for Herbert and his contemporary audience, the pattern poem was an acceptable and effective vehicle for expressing the most profound religious ideas and feelings. Contends that "the basic *rationale* of the visual element in Herbert's verse, of which the pattern poems are but special instances, is the hieroglyphic view of the universe" and points out that, "within the context of this special way of looking at reality the visual pattern of these poems reflects something of the order and beauty of God's universe as a whole" (p. 52). Maintains that the "moral and didactic corollary of the hieroglyphic view of the universe is the notion of *utile dulce*," argues that emblems and pattern poems are a specific manifestation of the doctrine of *ut pictura poesis*, and claims that *opsis* "provides a rhetorical justification for Herbert's use of the pattern poem" (p. 52). In chapter 3, "A Study of Herbert's Pattern Poems, Part Two: Analysis" (pp. 53–139), discusses the structural relationship between "The Altar" and "Easter-wings" and *The Church* as a whole. Examines the emblematic aspects of the two poems and comments on their classical and contemporary sources. Points out that "The Altar" has "several elements in common with the altar-poems of Vestinus and Porfirius, notably the emphasis on the relationship between workmanship and the non-human origin of the altar," and that "Easter-wings" "shares, among other aspects, the intricate relations between shape and sense with Simmias' 'Wings'" (p. 76). Maintains that Herbert's contemporaries would have appreciated his sacred parodying of pagan poems. Asserts that, in addition to knowing the pattern poems in the *Greek Anthology*, Herbert was familiar with numerous contemporary examples. Discusses altar-poems by Richard Willis, Joshua Sylvester, Francis Dawson, and others and wing-shaped poems by Richard Willis, Stephen Hawes, Christopher Harvey, and Patrick Cary to show that Herbert's poems are part of a long tradition and to emphasize that no other poet of the time was more successful than Herbert in converting pagan shapes for Christian

purposes. Discusses the two pattern poems in the light of the sacred emblem tradition, especially the Amor/Anima emblem books and the Schola Cordis emblem books. Argues that "it is a sign of Herbert's power and control as a poet that he managed to transcend and transform his sources" (p. 138). In chapter 4, "A Study of 'The Pilgrimage'" (pp. 140–210), argues that "The Pilgrimage," a more complex poem than most critics have thought, "both merits and requires as close an analysis as some of the better known Herbert poems" (p. 141). Maintains that the poem "reflects the main concern of the central section of *The Church*: the trials and errors of the itinerant Christian" (p. 141). Claims that its two-part structure "is based on the allegorical pilgrimage that is its subject" and that "the stages of the journey are demarcated by fundamental changes in tone and vocabulary" (p. 146). Comments in detail on Herbert's metaphor of the "two hills" and claims that it "determines the allegorical structure, the dramatic progression and the dénouement of the poem" (p. 151). Cites numerous possible sources for and analogues to the metaphorical use of the "two hills," especially those found in emblem books. Discusses line 35 of the poem ("After so foul a journey death is fair") and links it to the *ars moriendi* tradition as well as to the traditional themes of *dulce amarum* and *desiderans dissolvi*. Suggests that the "chair" in line 36 "could be regarded as a chariot that serves to convey the soul to Heaven after the death of the body" (p. 204) and points out references to and depictions of the chariot. Concludes that, although the sources and analogues for "The Pilgrimage" are "mainly of a verbal nature," visual materials help "to elucidate at least two crucial aspects of the poem: the two hills and death's chair" (p. 210). In chapter 5, "A Study of 'Love (III)'" (pp. 211–50), surveys and evaluates criticism of "Love (III)." Disagrees with Stanley Fish's interpretation (entry 1144), arguing that the Exhortation of the Service of Holy Communion from *The Book of Common Prayer* is more relevant to an understanding of the poem than is the Catechism. Maintains that the most profitable way of studying the poem is to investigate its use of sense images, especially images of sight, and argues that Herbert's understanding of the senses can be best explained by the Bible, the liturgy of the Anglican Church, and the emblem tradition. Argues that, although "Love (III)" is filled with allusions, "its origins cannot be traced back to one exclusive source" and emphasizes that the poem "is a coherent, self-contained whole in which the conventional and the transformational aspects of Herbert's art are perfectly balanced" (p. 239). Maintains that Herbert's poems are "closer in spirit to the Platonism of the humanists than to the moralizing mythography of the Middle Ages in which blind Cupid came into being" (p. 250). In "A Final Word" (pp. 251–53) summarizes the emphases of the study and defends his methodology. Bibliography (pp. 254–63), an index (pp. 264–68), and a summary in Dutch (pp. 269–73. Forty-five illustrations.
Review:
Michael Piret *GHJ* 8, no. 2 (1985): 54–57

1450. **Wilcox, Helen.** "'Heaven's Lidger Here': Herbert's *Temple* and Seventeenth-Century Devotion," in *Images of Belief in Literature*, edited by David Jasper, 153–68. New York: St. Martin's Press.
    Argues that the reactions of seventeenth-century readers of Herbert's poetry make it clear that his admirers "came to rely upon his example and his work in a way closely resembling Herbert's own attitude toward the Bible" and observes that, although *The Temple* is praised by modern critics as "a triumph of the literary imagination," in its own day it was viewed primarily as "a source of religious inspiration and a model for practical devotion," becoming "no ordinary devotional text but, it seems, a kind of seventeenth-century Scripture" (p. 153). Maintains that the punning phrase "Heav'ns Lidger here" reflects Herbert's attitude toward the Bible: "Lidger" means "an ambas-

sador," and thus, the Bible is "God's envoy on earth, actively combating the 'states' of 'death and hell,'" and it also means "ledger," and thus is "the book in which are recorded God's transactions with man" (p. 155). Maintains that, "just as Herbert discerned a dual function in Scripture," his readers responded to him as "an ambassador of God, combating evil in his verse and in his life," and regarded his poems as a record of his experience with God "from which others might gain instruction and joy" (p. 155). Maintains that for many of his early readers Herbert's life and works reflected the good old days of Anglicanism before the Civil War, while others, such as the Puritans, also found their devotional needs met in his poetry. Notes that in the seventeenth century Herbert was often compared to David and praised for having restored poetry to its sacred purpose.

**1451. Williams, Anne.** "Gracious Accommodations: George Herbert's 'Love (III).'" *MP* 82:13–22.

Maintains that "Love (III)" "yields its complexities (and dramatic simplicities) most clearly in the context of Herbert's theology" (p. 13) and that the most important theological concept informing the poem is the notion of "accommodation," a familiar term in Reformation theology that "denotes the variety of ways in which God has manifested himself to man since the Fall" (p. 14). Through a detailed reading of the poem shows that, faced with the artistic and theological difficulties of portraying the soul's meeting with God, Herbert turned to the concept of "accommodation" and "created a poem that embodies the term 'accommodation' itself in seemingly innumerable ways" (p. 16). Argues that "Love (III)" is not an allegory, strictly speaking, but rather is a "lyrical parable" (p. 20), in which Herbert adapts a biblical narrative genre "to the perspective of the lyric; that is, to private, imagined experience" (p. 22).

**1452. Woods, Susanne.** "The Mimetic Achievement of Shakespeare, Donne, and Herbert," in *Natural Emphasis: English Versification from Chaucer to Dryden*, 237–71. San Marino, Calif.: Huntington Library Press.

Maintains that Herbert is "a master of mimetic strophic constructions, of mimetic rhythms within and across a series of lines, and, in a summary and extension of these skills, he makes his verse mimetic of an entire Biblical poetic" (p. 261). Illustrates Herbert's mimetic strophic constructions by calling attention to "The Altar" and "Easter-wings"; to the concluding quatrain of "The Collar," which resolves all the disorder of the poem; and to the mending of the rhyme in "Deniall." Illustrates Herbert's mimetic skills by commenting primarily on "The Sacrifice," which "offers excellent testimony to Herbert's facility with lineation, enjambment, phrasing, and metrical substitution" (p. 262). Maintains that Herbert's poems "reflect the asymmetries of the Psalms" (p. 266), especially the Sidney-Pembroke versions. Concludes that Herbert's poetry is "both simple and complex at the same time, both natural and artful" and his poetic "is a deliberate sanctification of the mimetic artistry available through English Renaissance versification" (p. 267).

**1453. Young, R. V.** "Christopher Dawson and Baroque Culture: An Approach to Seventeenth-Century Religious Poetry," in *The Dynamic Character of Christian Culture: Essays on Dawsonian Themes*, edited by Peter J. Cataldo, 127–58. Lanham, Md., and London: University Press of America.

Maintains that Christopher Dawson regarded the baroque as "the last truly Christian culture" and discusses how seventeenth-century England "provides an attractive territory to the cultural historian interested in exploring the concept" (p. 128). Examines facets of the religious poetry of the period as a way of assessing Dawson's ideas concerning baroque culture in a specific setting. Maintains that many of the great Protestant artists of the baroque period "were truly Protestant, but they were not truly part of the bourgeois culture which came to flourish in the wake of the Reformation and the disintegration of Christendom" (p. 132). Argues that, although "To all Angels and Saints" is a "thoroughly Protestant poem" in that it repudiates Catholic poetry, Herbert writes in "a mood quietly but thoroughly baroque" (p. 143). Maintains that "Mattens" recalls the spirit of hope in Lope de Vega's *Rimas sacras* and finds in Herbert confidence that "the *vestigia dei* in the creation, the order and beauty of the natural world, can lead man to God if he will but regard the 'workman' as well as the 'work'" (p. 144). Sees this as a repeated theme in *The Temple* that shows up explicitly in "Providence" and "The Flower." Contrasts Herbert's conviction in the validity of the contemplation of creation with Anne Bradstreet's Puritan view in "Contemplation," which "affirms the gulf between nature and grace in Calvinistic theology" (p. 144). Comments on the sacramental character of Herbert's poetry as reflected in "Love (III)," a poem again reminiscent of Lope de Vega. Concludes that, although Herbert's poetry is "not so replete with striking and extravagant conceits as the poetry of Donne, its tone and characteristic themes are in some ways closer to the mood of the continental baroque" (p. 146).

# Index of Authors, Editors, Translators, Composers, and Illustrators

# Subject Index

(The following is an index of subjects mentioned in the annotations of this bibliography. The reader is advised to check all general studies related to a specific topic.)

# Index of Herbert's Works Mentioned in Annotations